Fred Thomas · Fundamentals of Sailplane Design

Fundamentals of Sailplane Design

Grundlagen für den Entwurf von Segelflugzeugen

Fred Thomas

Professor of Aerodynamics,
Technical University of Braunschweig

Former Director, DLR
Braunschweig Research Center

Judah Milgram, translator and contributor

College Park Press

Photos: Akaflieg Braunschweig (6); George Betz (page 117); DG Flugzeugbau (4); Fa. Glasflügel (1); Grob Luft- und Raumfahrt (2); Bernd Junker (2); J. Milgram (8); A. Schleicher Segelflugzeugbau (2); Schweizer Aircraft Corp. (page 117); Peter Selinger (15); Hans Zacher (4); Martin Zikesch (1)

"eta" graphics courtesy Dr. Reiner Kickert, Flugtechnik & Leichtbau, Braunschweig

ISBN 0-9669553-0-7

Library of Congress Catalog Card Number: 99-61150

Thomas, Fred and Milgram, Judah (contributor), "Fundamentals of Sailplane Design", College Park Press, College Park Maryland, USA, 1999. Includes bibliographic references and index.

Contents

Foreword

L. M. M. Boermans

President, OSTIV

Germany's long history in sailplane design began 100 years ago with the famous pioneer Otto Lilienthal, and to this day many talented designers have applied their knowledge and creativity to new sailplane designs. An improved understanding of theoretical and applied aerodynamics and the development of composite materials have led to today's safe, high-performance sailplanes. Production sailplanes with glide ratios of around 60 are now available.

This success would never have been possible without the continuous efforts of numerous students of the Akafliegs, working under the guidance of professors, scientists and engineers of the Technical Colleges, Universities, and the German Research Centre for Aerospace (DLR). Fred Thomas has performed the soaring world a great service by compiling a wealth of experience, methodology, and data on sailplane design and optimization in this excellent textbook.

At Delft University of Technology, all students in the Department of Aerospace Engineering are required to conduct a preliminary airplane design at the end of the first three years of study. This exercise is intended to enable the student to synthesize knowledge obtained in separate courses in aerodynamics, aircraft performance, stability and control, materials, structures etc. Some students have elected to design a high-performance sailplane under my guidance, and, for these students, Prof. Thomas' book, in its original German, has been the most valuable basic tool.

Recently it was decided that this successful synthesis/design exercise should be performed by groups of ten students in order to provide experience working as part of an interdisciplinary team. It was also decided to internationalize the curriculum, presenting all engineering courses in the English language. Thus, this new English edition of the book comes at the right time for Delft, but more importantly, the translation is a most valuable asset for all those throughout the world who, in the course of their professional training or career, are interested in the science and art of high-performance sailplane design.

As President of OSTIV, the International Scientific and Technical Gliding Organisation, I am very pleased with the publication of this standard work on high-performance sailplane design. It will satisfy the interested reader and enable future designers to create ever better sailplanes.

Loek M. M. Boermans

Delft, May 1999

Vorwort

Die Fortschritte in der Entwicklung der Segelflugzeuge sind von Beginn an in starkem Maße den akademischen Fliegergruppen der deutschen Technischen Hochschulen und Universitäten, kurz «Akafliegs» genannt, zu verdanken. Immer wieder bis in die jüngste Zeit hinein wurden durch zum Teil bahnbrechende Entwürfe der Studenten der Akafliegs neue Grenzen gesetzt. Dabei werden immer höhere Anforderungen an das Fachwissen der Konstrukteure gestellt. Da andererseits durch die Straffung des Studiums immer weniger Zeit für die Arbeit in den akademischen Fliegergruppen übrig bleibt, gerät deren Tradition, den Fortschritt im Segelflugzeugbau voranzutreiben, mehr und mehr in Gefahr.

Sinn und Zweck des vorliegenden Buches ist es, durch eine zusammenfassende Darstellung des für einen optimalen Segelflugzeugentwurf erforderlichen Fachwissens dem angehenden Segelflugzeugkonstrukteur eine Hilfe an die Hand zu geben, die es ihm gestattet, sich schnell das nötige Grundlagenwissen anzueignen. Auf diese Weise erlangt der junge Akaflieger sehr viel schneller die Fähigkeit, an einem neuen Entwurf aktiv mitzuarbeiten.

Der Segelflug ist ein Sport, der ein verhältnismaßig hohes Wissen um die physikalischen Zusammenhänge des Fluges und die Technik des Segelflugzeugs verlangt. Bereits die Auswahl eines geeigneten Segelflugzeugs, vor allem aber sein optimaler Einsatz im Überlandflug und insbesondere im Wettbewerb, stellt den Segelflieger vor erhebliche Probleme, wenn er sich nicht nur auf das Urteil sachverständiger Kollegen verlassen will. So wendet sich das Buch ebenfalls an alle Segelflieger, die sich etwas genauer mit ihrem Sportgerät befassen wollen.

Um auch dem technisch weniger Vorgebildeten die Lektüre dieses Buches zu ermöglichen, ist bewußt auf eine mathematische Darstellung der physikalischen Zusammenhänge verzichtet worden. Es wurde statt dessen auf eine möglichst anschauliche Beschreibung der Tatbestände Wert gelegt, was durch die große Zahl von Diagrammen zum Ausdruck kommt.

In allen Diagrammen und Tabellen wird das vorgeschriebene internationale Maßsystem mit den Einheiten [kg] für die Masse, [m] für die Länge und [s] für die Zeit benutzt. Für die Kraft wird die Einheit «Newton» verwendet. Um die gewohnten Zahlengrößen für die Kraft, die bisher in [kp] angegeben wurde, beibehalten zu können, wird hier das Deka-Newton benutzt (1 daN = 10 N). Da 1 N = 1 kg · 1 m/s^2 und 1 kp = 1 kg · 9,81 m/s^2 sind, weichen das daN und das kp nur um 2% voneinander ab.

Der Inhalt dieses Buches ist zusammengestellt aus einer Vorlesung, die der Verfasser seit Jahren an der Technischen Universität Braunschweig hält, aus Ergebnissen einer Serie von Studien- und Diplomarbeiten, die während der vergangenen Jahre von Studenten der Akaflieg Braunschweig nach Aufgabenstellungen des Verfassers angefertigt worden sind, aus Arbeiten der ehemaligen Abteilung Segelflug und Leichtflugzeuge (Leiter: H. Zacher), die zum Verantwortungsbereich des Verfassers in der Deutschen Forschungs- und Versuchsanstalt für Luft- und Raumfahrt e.V. (DLR[1]) gehörte, sowie aus einzelnen jeweils zitierten Arbeiten, insbesondere den Publikationen der Organisation Scientifique et Technique Internationale du Vol à Voile (OSTIV). Im Text ist stets Bezug genommen auf die im Literaturverzeichnis angegebenen Originalarbeiten.

Ich möchte an dieser Stelle allen danken, die mir bei der Erstellung des Buches geholfen haben. Darüber hinaus habe ich denen zu danken, die mir die Fotos zur Verfügung gestellt haben, besonders Herrn M. Zikesch für das Titelfoto und Herrn P. F. Selinger, dessen reichhaltiges Archiv ich nutzen durfte und dessen Rat mir sehr geholfen hat. Mein besonderer Dank gilt meinen Mitarbeitern K. H. Horstmann, A. Quast und G. Stich, die mit zahlreichen wertvollen Hin-

[1] DLR, since 1997, the "Deutsches Zentrum für Luft- und Raumfahrt" (German Aerospace Center) and from 1989–97 "Deutsche Forschungsanstalt für Luft- und Raumfahrt" (German Aerospace Research Establishment). Earlier, from 1968–89, the DFVLR, "Deutsche Forschungs- und Versuchsanstalt für Luft- und Raumfahrt" (German Aerospace Research and Test Establishment)

weisen bei der Entstehung dieses Buches Hilfe geleistet haben.

Braunschweig, im Mai 1979

Since the beginning of the sport of soaring, progress in sailplane development has been due in large part to the Akafliegs of the German technical schools and universities. The pioneering designs of the Akafliegs have repeatedly set new standards for sailplane performance. While this progress has increased the demands placed on the designer's expertise, the rigors of academic life make it increasingly difficult for the average student to devote time to Akaflieg projects, with the result that the Akafliegs' traditional role in the advancement of sailplane technology is gradually becoming endangered.

This book is intended as an aid to the fledgling sailplane designer, permitting him to rapidly acquire a basic level of expertise through a comprehensive presentation of the fundamentals of sailplane design optimization. This will hopefully reduce the training period required before the young Akaflieger can productively participate in the development of new designs.

As a sport, soaring demands a high degree of understanding of sailplane technology and the physics of flight. Even the choice of an appropriate sailplane — to say nothing of its proper utilization in cross country and contest flying — can pose serious problems for the sailplane pilot who does not wish to rely entirely on the opinions of better informed colleagues. So this book is intended as well for all soaring pilots who wish to develop a better understanding of their aircraft.

Mathematics has been kept to a minimum in order to keep the book accessible to those with little technical background. Instead, emphasis is placed on a clear presentation of the basic physical relationships, supported wherever possible with illustrations.

The metric system is used in all diagrams and tables. The fundamental units are [kg] for mass, [m] for length, and [s] for time. The formerly used unit of force, [kp], has been replaced with the "Newton." In order to retain a "feel" for the numerical values of the force, in this book forces are expressed in Deca-Newtons (1daN= 10N). Since $1\,\mathrm{N} = 1\,\mathrm{kg} \cdot 1\,m/s^2$ *and* $1\,\mathrm{kp} = 1\,\mathrm{kg} \cdot 9.81\,m/s^2$*, the daN and the kp deviate from each other by less than 2%.*

The book is based on a course that the author has given for many years at the Technical University of Braunschweig; on results from a series of theses and research projects completed over many years by students of the Akaflieg Braunschweig under supervision of the author; on the work of the former Sailplane and Light Aircraft Division of the German Aerospace Research and Test Establishment (DLR, formerly DFVLR), headed by H. Zacher under the direction of the author; and individually cited works, in particular publications of the Organisation Scientifique et Technique Internationale du Vol à Voile (OSTIV). The original sources are listed in the Bibliography.

At this point I would like to thank all those who helped with the preparation of the book. I am further indebted to those who made the photographs available, especially Martin Zikesch for the cover photo and Peter F. Selinger, who made his extensive archive available and who provided helpful advice. My special thanks go to my colleagues Karl Heinz Horstmann, Armin Quast, and Gerd Stich, who provided numerous helpful suggestions as the book was being prepared.

Vorwort zur 2. Auflage

Der zügige Verkauf der 1. Auflage des Buches macht bereits nach 5 Jahren eine weitere Auflage erforderlich. Um die Kosten und damit den Verkaufspreis niedrig zu halten, wurde beschlossen, einen Nachdruck mit nur den allernötigsten Änderungen vorzunehmen. So ist das Buch in der 2. Auflage nahezu unverändert geblieben. Es wurden lediglich die Neuentwicklungen im Profilentwurf von Horstmann und Quast berücksichtigt und das Literaturverzeichnis um die Zitate 3a, 23a, 53a und 69a ergänzt. Die Lufttüchtigkeitsforderungen für Segelflugzeuge und Motorsegler liegen inzwischen in einer europäisch abgestimmten Form vor [49]. Die Abb. 165 und 166 wurden durch neu gestaltete Bilder ersetzt. Völlig überarbeitet und aktualisiert wurden die Datentabellen der Flugzeugparameter im Anhang.

Braunschweig, May 1984

The rapid selling out of the first edition of the book makes another edition necessary after only five years. To keep the costs and purchase price low, it was decided to prepare a reprint with only the most necessary revisions. In its second edition therefore the book is nearly unchanged. Only the latest developments in airfoil design by Horstmann and Quast have been included and the Bibliography was expanded to include References 3a, 23a, 53a, and 69a[2]*. The airworthiness requirements now exist in a form accepted throughout Europe (Ref. [49]). Figures 165 and 166 were replaced. The table of aircraft design data in the Appendix was fully reworked and brought up to date.*

Foreword to the Third Edition

Following the sale of about 5000 copies of the 1st and 2nd editions, requests from all over the world made it obvious that there was demand for another edition. Many inquiries came from English-speaking countries and countries

[2] References 164, 9, 78, and 184 in the 1999 edition

where English is in common use as a technical language. With an offer from Judah Milgram to do the translation, the decision was made to produce this third edition in English.

Although the fundamentals of sailplane design have not themselves changed significantly, considerable progress has been made since the appearance of the first edition 20 years ago. We have seen the evolution of new sailplane classes such as the FAI World Class and the 18m class. The frontiers of sailplane design have been pushed both towards higher performance ("eta") and lower cost (PW 5), Flying wings with laminar flow airfoils have been developed, and winglets — though the subject of occasional controversy — have become popular. Higher speeds and very high water ballast loads have made aeroelasticity an increasingly important issue. A new set of certification regulations, JAR-22, has been accepted world-wide, and a large number of new sailplanes have been designed and manufactured. The rapid advances in avionics, including GPS and flight computers, have exerted considerable influence in flight operations, flight test, and design. Solar energy and boundary layer control are being discussed as possible further steps for the future.

In many areas the text of this edition has been adapted to the latest development. The list of sailplane data in the appendix was extended considerably with the inclusion of a large number of modern sailplanes and additional sailplanes from countries outside Germany. The bibliography was also enlarged by many new entries. Most of the sources are OSTIV publications, to which every design engineer has easy access.

As with the previous editions, the international measurement system is used exclusively with the basic units mass (kg), length (m) and time (s). In accordance with JAR 22 the unit for force and weight is the Deca-Newton (1 daN=10 $kg{\cdot}m/s^2$).

Again I would like to thank everyone who has contributed to the production of this book, above all my old companions Karl-Heinz Horstmann, Armin Quast and Gerd Stich, but also to the many others who have assisted by providing the many data in the appendices or contributing to the text (F. Kießling, D. Schmerwitz) and the cooperative people from the LBA (H. Friess and H. Fendt). Thanks are due as well to Gordon Leishman, Joe Parrish, Michael Steckner, and, especially, Loek Boermans and Mark Maughmer for carefully reviewing the draft and offering valuable suggestions.

More than to anybody else I have to thank Judah Milgram, who has done such a tremendous job not only by performing an excellent translation and layout but also by contributing his own ideas to the text (e.g. the sections on aeroelasticity, winglets, and the World Class), the figures, and the appendices. Without him it would have been impossible to produce this book.

Of course, as we plan an updated edition in a few years, we would appreciate all suggestions or corrections from our readers (postal and e-mail addresses below).

Fred Thomas Braunschweig, August, 1999

College Park Press
P.O. Box 143
College Park, MD 20741
USA

sailplanes@cgpp.com

Basics of Aerodynamics and Flight Mechanics

Fluid Dynamics and the Sailplane

Inviscid Incompressible Flow

Physical properties of the atmosphere

The flow of air around a sailplane in flight is determined by the laws of fluid mechanics. The state of the air is defined by a number of physical properties such as pressure, density, temperature, compressibility, kinematic viscosity, and relative humidity. Due to gravity, the properties of the atmosphere vary with altitude. Pressure, density, and temperature all decrease with altitude. Solar radiation and topography also play a role, causing considerable variation in the atmospheric properties. This effect is especially pronounced at low altitudes.

Several standard atmospheric models are used to compare aircraft data (*e.g.* sailplane performance measurements) at different altitudes. Table 1 and Fig. 1 summarize some data of interest from the 1964 ICAO (International Civil Aviation Organization) Standard Atmosphere [12], a commonly used standard that represents an atmosphere free from meteorological influences. Other idealized models have been defined, including the 1962 US Standard Atmosphere (identical to the 1964 ICAO model up to 65,000 ft; revised in 1976), the 1959 ARDC (U.S. Air Force) atmosphere [17], and MIL-STD-210A, which reflects the extreme ambient temperatures encountered in polar or tropical climates. The results presented in this book are based on the 1964 ICAO model [12].

It should be emphasized that these standard atmospheric models are idealizations based on empirical data and/or simplified mathematical models. The pressure, p, density, ρ, and absolute temperature T of an ideal gas are related to one another through the *ideal gas law*:

$$p = \rho R T \tag{1}$$

where R is the specific gas constant for the gas or mixture of gases. For example, an increase in pressure results in an increase in density and/or air temperature. The process of thermal formation, familiar to all sailplane pilots, is also governed by these physical laws. Solar radiation increases the temperature near the ground, leading to a local reduction in air density. The affected parcel of air becomes buoyant and climbs skyward as a thermal.

Table 1: ICAO 1964 Standard Atmosphere [12]

Altitude h m	Pressure p [hPa]	Density ρ [kg/m³]	Temp. T °K	Kinematic Viscosity ν 10^{-5}[m²/s]	Speed of Sound a [m/s]
0	1013.3	1.225	288.2	1.46	340.3
500	954.6	1.167	284.9	1.52	338.4
1000	898.7	1.112	281.7	1.58	336.4
1500	845.6	1.058	278.4	1.65	334.5
2000	795.0	1.007	275.2	1.71	332.5
2500	746.8	0.957	271.9	1.79	330.6
3000	701.1	0.909	268.7	1.86	328.6
4000	616.4	0.819	262.2	2.03	324.6
5000	540.2	0.736	255.7	2.21	320.5
8000	356.0	0.525	236.2	2.91	308.1
11000	226.3	0.364	216.7	3.91	295.1
15000	120.4	0.194	216.7	7.34	295.1
20000	54.7	0.088	216.7	16.15	295.1
30000	11.7	0.018	226.7	81.95	301.8

Fig. 1: Atmospheric properties per 1964 ICAO Standard Atmosphere [12]

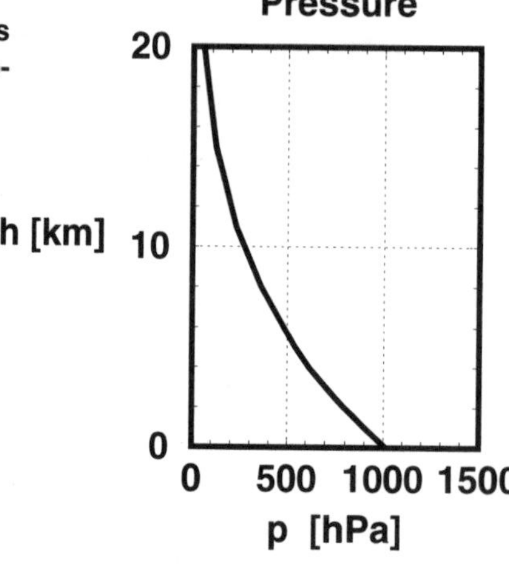

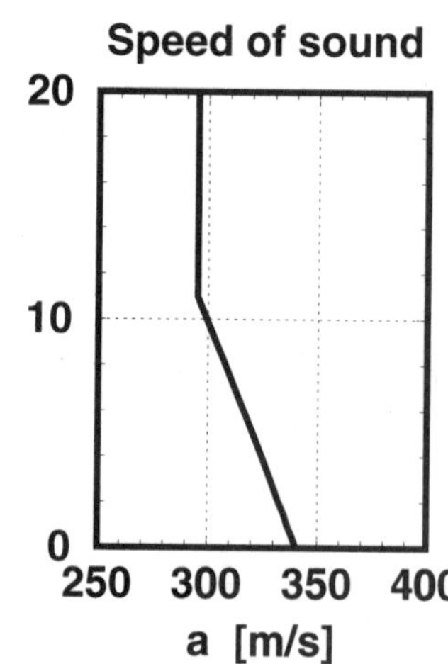

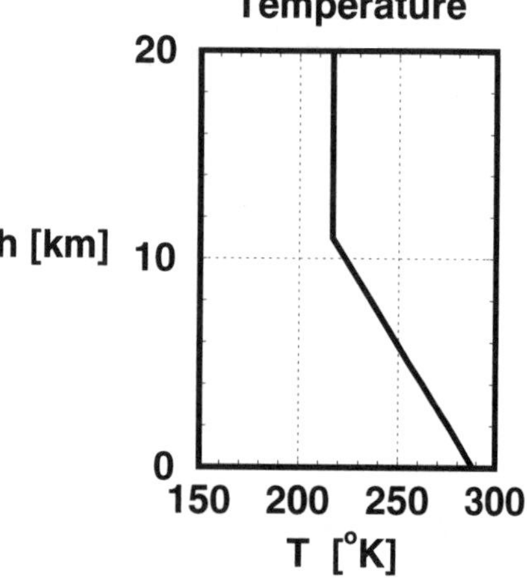

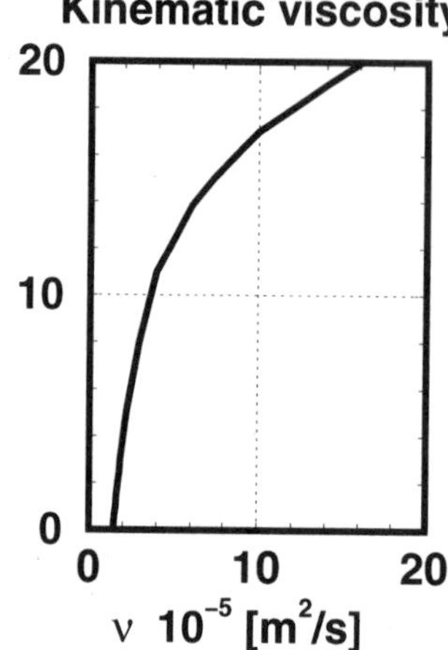

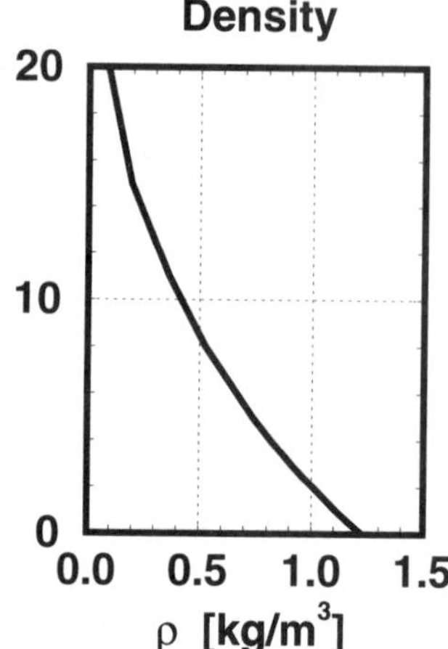

Often, the data in Table 1 are presented in nondimensional terms:

$$\delta = p/p_0 \quad \text{Pressure ratio} \tag{2}$$

$$\sigma = \rho/\rho_0 \quad \text{Density ratio} \tag{3}$$

$$\theta = T/T_0 \quad \text{Temperature ratio} \tag{4}$$

where p_0, ρ_0, and T_0 are the sea level values of pressure, density, and absolute temperature. In nondimensional units, the universal gas law (Eq. 1) becomes simply:

$$\delta = \sigma\theta \tag{5}$$

Standard atmospheric models permit the pressure and density to be expressed indirectly as altitudes. *Pressure altitude*, (h_p) for example, is the altitude in the standard model corresponding to the ambient pressure. *Density altitude*, h_d is defined in a similar manner. Note that while h_p and h_d are expressed as altitudes [m], they actually serve to define a pressure [Pa] and density [kg/m^3].

Basics of fluid mechanics

Equation 1 is the equation of state for ideal gases at rest. The equations governing the flow about an aircraft are considerably more complicated. Air particles flowing past an aircraft are accelerated, compressed, and sheared against one another. Acceleration leads to inertial forces, com-

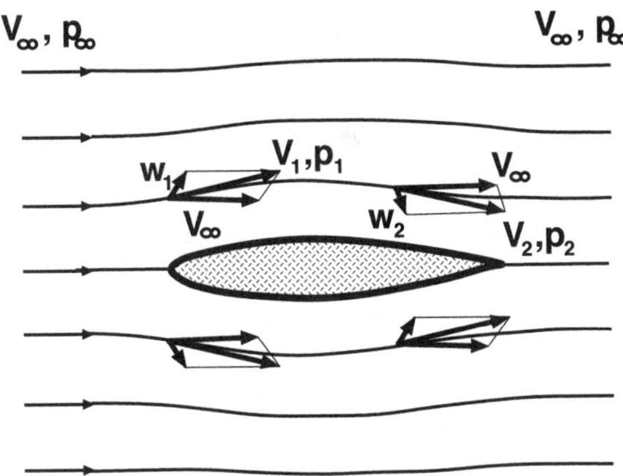

Fig. 2: Flow field near an object in steady flow.

V_∞	freestream velocity
$V_{1,2}$	local velocities
$w_{1,2}$	local perturbation velocities
$p_{1,2}$	local pressures
p_∞	freestream pressure

pression to elastic forces, and shearing to viscous forces. The relationship between these forces and the geometric form of the aircraft is defined by the *Navier-Stokes equations*, the fundamental equations of fluid mechanics. Given the geometric shape of a body, for example an airfoil, the Navier-Stokes equations may be used to calculate the velocity and pressure distributions in the resulting flow.

The flow field is defined by the local velocity (speed and direction) and pressure at each point in the field. As will be discussed, the pressure and velocity at a given point are directly related to one another. The local velocity is the sum of the freestream velocity V_∞ (the velocity of the undisturbed flow far upstream of the object) and local perturbations due to the presence of the body. The latter decrease in magnitude as the distance from the object increases (Fig. 2).

Incidently, it does not matter whether a body is placed in a stream of flowing air — *e.g.* in a wind tunnel — or moves with constant velocity through a mass of still air. In both cases the flow field is identical.

The flow fields considered here are *steady*, that is, they do not vary with time. The path along which an individual air particle travels is a *streamline*. According to this definition, air particles do not move perpendicular to a streamline. Consequently, the surface of a body in a flow field must be a streamline (two dimensional flow, for example around an airfoil section) or defined by a set of streamlines (three dimensional flow, for example a wing or fuselage). In all the cases examined here the law of conservation of mass applies — in fluid mechanics this principle is expressed through the *continuity equation*.

Reynolds number and boundary layer

Due to their complexity, the Navier-Stokes equations do not lend themselves to closed-form solutions suitable for use in calculating the aerodynamic characteristics of sailplanes. Fortunately, the nature of sailplane aerodynamics allows these equations to be simplified considerably. The primary simplification results from the fact that, throughout most of the flow field, the inertial forces are considerably more significant than the viscous forces. For a given flow field, the relationship between these forces is characterized by the *Reynolds number*, defined as follows:

$$Re = \frac{V_\infty l}{\nu} = \frac{\text{Inertial Forces}}{\text{Viscous Forces}} \qquad (6)$$

Here V_∞ is the freestream velocity [m/s], l a characteristic length [m] of the body (for example the airfoil chord or the fuselage length), and ν the kinematic viscosity of the air [m^2/s]. The Reynolds number itself is dimensionless.

Table 2: Typical sailplane Reynolds numbers. Based on kinematic viscosity $\nu = 1.5 \cdot 10^{-5} m^2/s$ and a range of wing chords, c.

Freestream Velocity V_∞	Chord c [m]	Reynolds Number Re [-]
20 m/s (72 km/h)	1.00	$1.33 \cdot 10^6$
	0.75	$1.00 \cdot 10^6$
	0.50	$0.67 \cdot 10^6$
	0.30	$0.40 \cdot 10^6$
50 m/s (180 km/h)	1.00	$3.33 \cdot 10^6$
	0.75	$2.50 \cdot 10^6$
	0.50	$1.67 \cdot 10^6$
	0.30	$1.00 \cdot 10^6$

Typical Reynolds numbers for sailplane airfoils are shown in Table 2. The data indicate that the inertial forces in the flow field about a sailplane are around a million times larger than the viscous forces. For this reason the viscous forces can be neglected throughout most of the field, allowing use of the simpler inviscid flow equations. Viscous forces become significant only in a relatively thin layer near the surface of the aircraft, the *boundary layer*. The higher the Reynolds number, the thinner the boundary layer becomes relative to the characteristic length of the body. The boundary layer near the leading edge of a sailplane wing is typically around a few millimeters thick, growing steadily to a centimeter or more near the trailing edge.

The idea of splitting the fluid flow problem into an inviscid, potential theory part and a viscous part, the boundary layer, originated with L. Prandtl in 1904 and is the cornerstone of modern fluid mechanics and aerodynamics. Boundary-layer theory plays a crucial role in determining the aerodynamic properties of an aircraft and has become a science of its own (see H. Schlichting [22]). Airfoil drag and maximum lift coefficients are strongly affected by boundary-layer phenomena. On the other hand, the effect on pressure distribution and lift is relatively insignificant. An underlying assumption in boundary-layer theory is that the static pressure at a given point on the surface of an aircraft remains constant throughout the thickness of the boundary layer. In other words: the pressure at the edge of the boundary layer is identical to the pressure at the corresponding location on the aircraft surface (Fig. 3).

$$p(x,z^*) = p(x,0) \tag{7}$$

When determining the pressure distribution and lift (with the exception of the maximum lift) one may assume inviscid flow without introducing significant errors. Improved results are obtained by correcting the pressure distribution to account for the thickness of the boundary layer.

The assumption of inviscid flow reduces the Navier-Stokes equations to the considerably simpler *Euler equations*. It can be shown that all solutions to the *potential equation*, a well known equation in mathematical physics (electromagnetic theory, in particular), are also solutions to the Euler equations. Inviscid flow around an airfoil or a three-dimensional body is therefore referred to as *potential flow*.

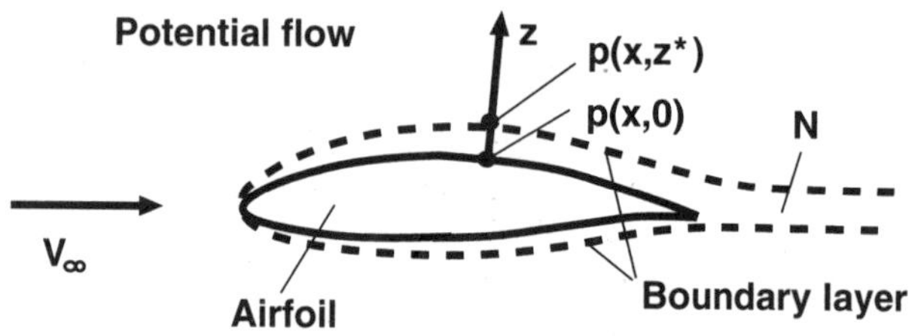

Fig. 3: Potential (inviscid) and viscous flow.

N airfoil wake
p static pressure

Mach number and incompressible flow

A further simplification results from the fact that sailplane airspeeds are small compared to the speed of sound (a = 340m/s at sea level). The ratio of the airspeed to the speed of sound is the *Mach number*.

$$M = \frac{V_\infty}{a} = \text{Mach number} \tag{8}$$

At low Mach numbers (M less than around 0.3), the elastic forces in the air flow can be neglected, *i.e.* the air can be considered incompressible without significant error. In this case the density ρ becomes a constant, no longer dependent on the pressure. Since, for the most part, sailplanes fly with $M < 0.3$, this book assumes incompressible flow throughout.

This assumption is not warranted in the case of modern transport and military aircraft. Unlike sailplanes, these aircraft require swept wings to perform well at high subsonic Mach numbers.

Some elementary solutions to the potential equation

For incompressible flow, the potential equation is linear and thus particularly easy to solve. The property of linearity permits solution of complex flow fields by superimposing elementary solutions of the potential equation. Airfoil and wing theory employs *linear superposition* to build up complex solutions from the following basic solutions to the potential equation (Fig. 4):

- uniform translational flow
- point vortex
- sources and sinks

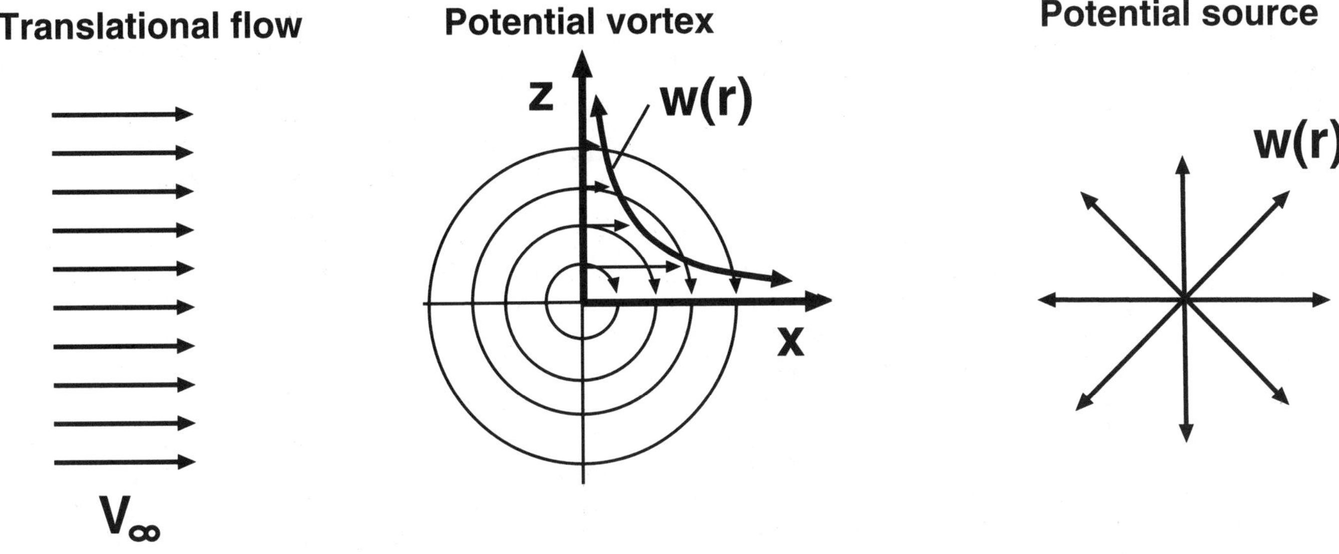

Fig. 4: Elementary solutions to the potential flow equation.

w local velocity
r distance from center

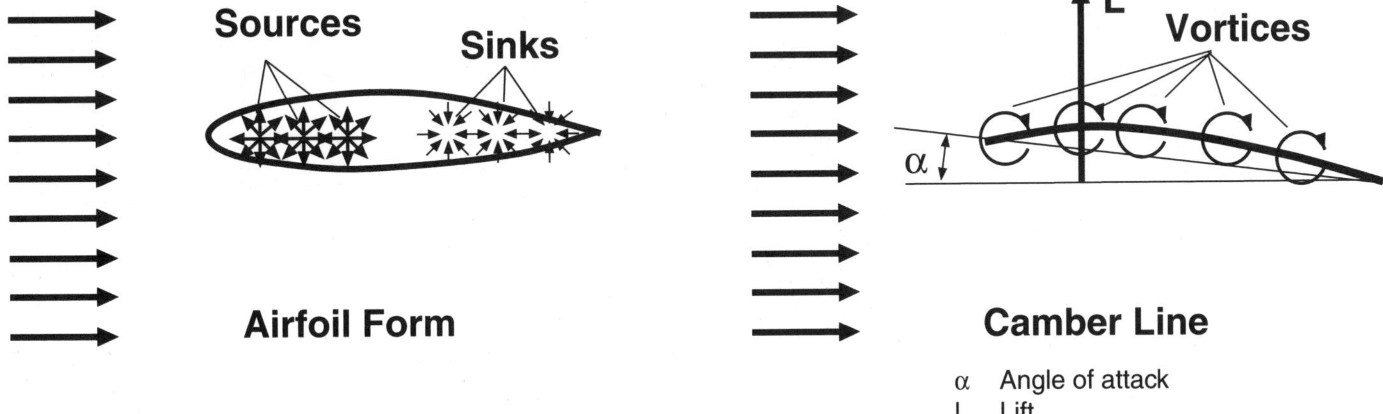

α Angle of attack
L Lift

Fig. 5: Thickness form and camber line formed by superposition of sources, sinks, and vortices in uniform translational flow.

For example, linear superposition can be used to calculate the flow field around a symmetric airfoil at zero angle of attack by combining the solutions of a system of sources. An airfoil at a non-zero angle of attack and/or with camber can be formed by adding a system of point vortices (Fig. 5).

The mathematics involved in developing solutions to the potential equation need not be discussed here in great detail. However, it should be mentioned that there is a direct relationship between vorticity and lift that plays an important role in determining the flow about a complete three-dimensional wing. This will be discussed in a following section — but first another important result must be introduced.

Bernoulli's equation

Integrating the Euler equations leads to a relationship known as *Bernoulli's equation* (Eq. 9), which states that in steady, incompressible, inviscid flow, the total pressure p_T, *i.e.* the sum of the static pressure p and the dynamic pressure q, remains constant along a streamline. If the flow is irrotational, the result applies to the entire flow field. This means, for example, that the sum of the static and dynamic pressures far upstream of the aircraft (p_∞ and q_∞, respectively) is equal to the sum of the local static and dynamic pressure p_1 and q_1 at any arbitrary point on the aircraft (Fig. 6):

$$\begin{aligned} p_T &= p_\infty + q_\infty \\ &= p_1 + q_1 \end{aligned} \qquad \underline{\text{Bernoulli's Equation.}} \quad (9)$$

The dynamic pressure is a measure of the kinetic energy of the air particles in the flow field and is defined as follows:

$$q_\infty = \frac{\rho}{2} V_\infty^2 \qquad \underline{\text{Dynamic Pressure.}} \quad (10)$$

The static pressure is a measure of the potential ("pressure") energy of the air particles. In this interpretation, Bernoulli's equation is an expression of the law of conservation of energy. An increase in the local kinetic energy (*i.e.* local velocity) is accompanied by a corresponding reduction in potential energy (static pressure). As will be discussed, this exchange between pressure and velocity is of particular significance to the production of lift.

Airspeed measurement

Total pressure, static pressure, and dynamic pressure can be measured using static ports and/or probes positioned within the air flow (Fig. 7).

The total pressure is measured with a *Pitot tube*, a tube with an opening on the forward end into which the freestream enters and is decelerated to zero velocity. The total pressure and static pressure measurements are often combined in a single *Prandtl tube* (Pitot-static tube, Fig. 7).

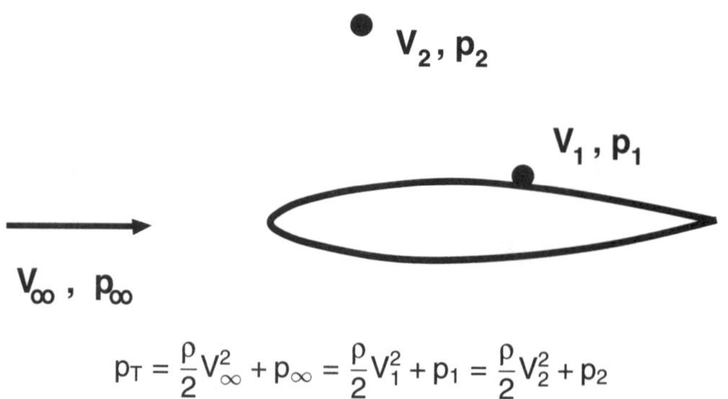

$$p_T = \frac{\rho}{2} V_\infty^2 + p_\infty = \frac{\rho}{2} V_1^2 + p_1 = \frac{\rho}{2} V_2^2 + p_2$$

Fig. 6: Relationship between velocity and static pressure (Bernoulli's equation)

Instead of a combined Pitot-static tube, a simple Pitot tube may be used together with static ports positioned at points on the aircraft surface where the local static pressure is approximately equal to the freestream static pressure. However, the ideal position varies with angle of attack (*i.e.* airspeed), giving rise to a *position error* in the airspeed measurement. Static pressure may also be measured using a simple tube, closed at the front, with holes drilled on its sides some distance from the forward end.

Dynamic pressure is the difference between the measured freestream static pressure p and total (Pitot) pressure p_T. The airspeed indicator is essentially a pressure gauge that measures the difference between the static and total pressure. From Eqs. 9 and 10:

$$V_\infty = V_{TAS} = \sqrt{(2/\rho)(p_T - p)} \qquad (11)$$

Since the air density ρ varies with ambient conditions (in particular, altitude), the airspeed indicator is calibrated to sea level standard conditions:

$$V_{EAS} = \sqrt{(2/\rho_0)(p_T - p)} \qquad (12)$$

V_{EAS}, the *equivalent airspeed*, is equal to the true airspeed only at sea level standard conditions. V_{EAS} is the primary quantity of interest when considering the forces acting on a sailplane. In JAR-22 [49] the airspeeds at which the maneuver loads, gust loads, and flutter characteristics must be investigated are equivalent airspeeds, V_{EAS}.

A simple relationship between equivalent and true airspeeds can be derived from Eq. 3 and the definition of dynamic pressure, q_∞ (Eq. 10):

$$V_{EAS} = \sqrt{\sigma} V_{TAS} \qquad (13)$$

Fig. 7: **Pressure measurement for airspeed systems**

(a) Pitot probe (total pressure)
(b) Static probe (static pressure)
(c) Pitot-static (Prandtl) tube (dynamic pressure)

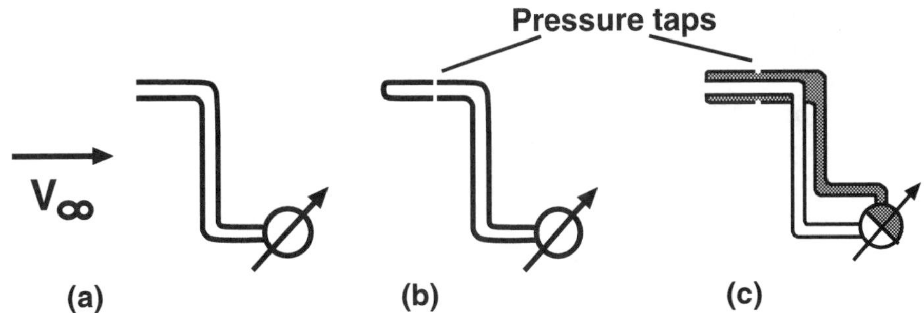

Fig. 8: Relationship between Mach number (M), equivalent airspeed (V_{EAS}), true airspeed (V_{TAS}), calibrated airspeed (V_{CAS}), indicated airspeed (V_{IAS}), and dynamic pressure q.
In sea level standard conditions, $V_{EAS} = V_{TAS} = V_{CAS} = a_0M$.

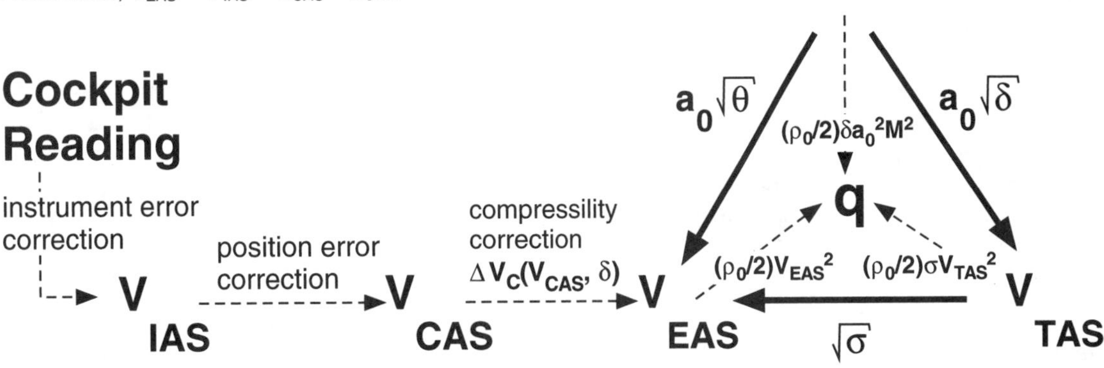

Both equivalent and true airspeed are directly related to Mach number. The speed of sound in dry air varies only with ambient temperature:

$$a = \sqrt{\gamma RT} \tag{14}$$

where γ is the *specific heat ratio* (γ = 1.4 in air). This relationship, together with the definition of Mach number (Eq. 8), the universal gas law (Eq. 5), and Eq. 13, lead to the following simple relationships:

$$V_{EAS} = a_0M\sqrt{\delta} \tag{15}$$

$$V_{TAS} = a_0M\sqrt{\theta} \tag{16}$$

The relationship between true airspeed, equivalent airspeed, Mach number, and dynamic pressure is shown schematically in Fig. 8.

Due to the effects of compressibility, the total pressure in the Pitot tube is slightly higher than that predicted by Bernoulli's equation. Thus, even assuming zero static position error and a perfectly calibrated instrument, the airspeed indicator may indicate an airspeed that is slightly higher than V_{EAS}. This is the *calibrated airspeed*, V_{CAS}. Since the compressibility correction varies with pressure ratio, δ, it is not possible to calibrate an airspeed indicator to indicate equivalent airspeed at all altitudes. In practice, airspeed indicators are calibrated so that compressibility correction ΔV_C is zero at sea level (*i.e.* $V_{CAS}=V_{EAS}$). Sailplanes typically operate at airspeeds and altitudes for which the compressibility correction is negligible — at h_p = 10,000 m and V_{CAS}=300 km/h, the correction ΔV_C is only approximately 3 km/h. The details of the calculation of the compressibility correction may be found in texts on aircraft performance, for example S. K. Ojha [19].

Another parameter of interest is the *indicated airspeed*, V_{IAS}. This is what the pilot reads on the airspeed indicator, and reflects all sources of error (compressibility, position error, instrument calibration, etc.). Unlike the structural requirements, which are defined with respect to equivalent airspeeds, JAR-22 requires that operating airspeed limitations be provided to the pilot in terms of *indicated* airspeed [49].

In this book, where not otherwise specified, airspeeds are assumed to be V_{TAS}.

Lift and Potential Flow

Circulation and lift

The primary purpose of the wing is to provide lift. Central to the production of lift is the relationship between the wing geometry (airfoil, planform, and twist) and the distribution of lift over its surface. This relationship is calculated using point vortices and a derived quantity, *circulation*.

An individual vortex is associated with a radially symmetric velocity field having circular streamlines centered around the vortex location (Fig. 9). The velocity w is constant along a given streamline, but decreases with the distance from the vortex center. Multiplying the velocity w at a distance r with the length of the streamline (that is, the circumference of a circle with radius r) yields the circulation:

$$\Gamma = 2\pi r w(r) \tag{17}$$

The flow about a vortex has the property that the circulation measured along any path enclosing the vortex is the same, regardless of the shape or size of the path. This result is generalized to a system of vortices: the circulation measured about any closed path enclosing a system of vortices is equal to the sum of the circulation due to each individual vortex (Fig. 10):

$$\Gamma = \oint w \cos \varphi ds \tag{18}$$

$$\Gamma = \Gamma_1 + \Gamma_2 + \Gamma_3 + \Gamma_4 + \Gamma_5$$

Fig. 11 shows the velocity field due to a system of vortices superimposed on a uniform translational flow field. Above

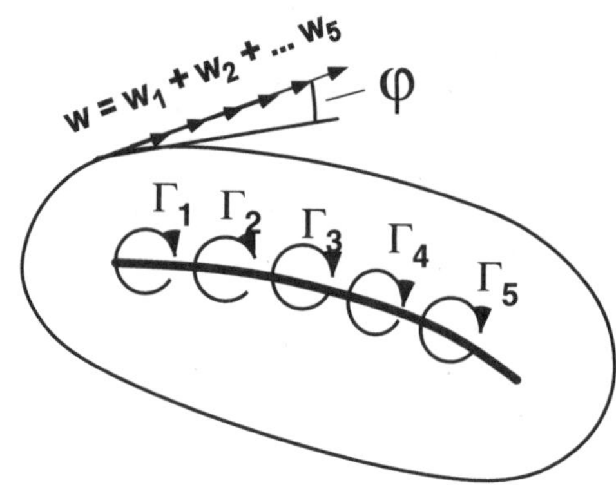

Fig. 10: Circulation around a system of two-dimensional vortices. $\Gamma = \Gamma_1 + \Gamma_2 + \Gamma_3 + \Gamma_4 + \Gamma_5$

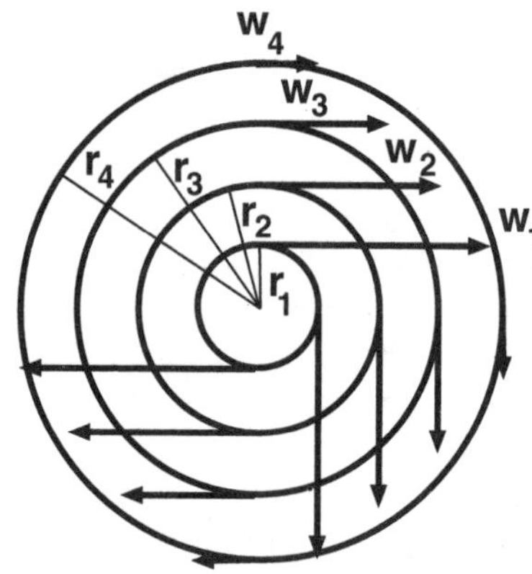

Fig. 9: Velocity field induced by a two-dimensional vortex of strength Γ.
$\Gamma = 2\pi r_1 w_1 = 2\pi r_2 w_2 = 2\pi r_3 w_3 = 2\pi r_4 w_4$

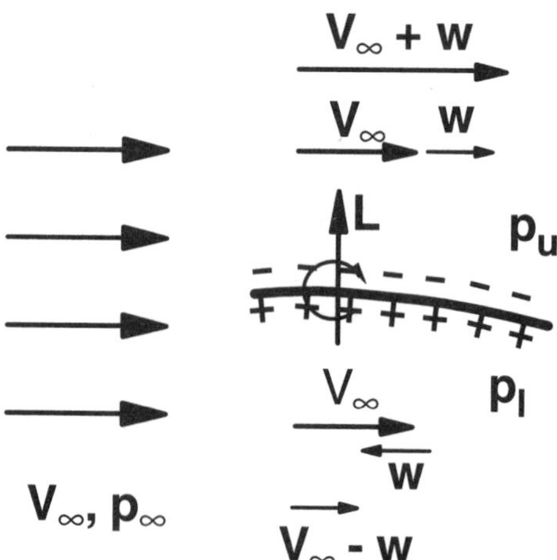

Fig. 11: Lift produced by superposition of a system of vortices in uniform translational flow.
w perturbation velocity induced by vortex system

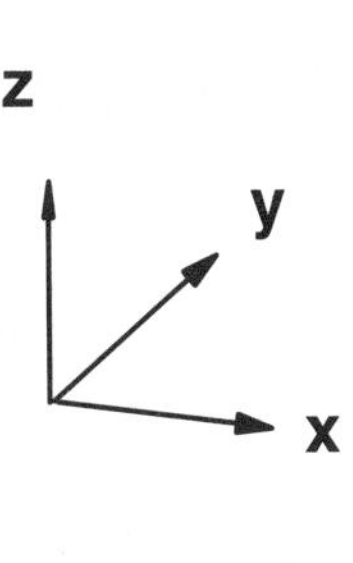

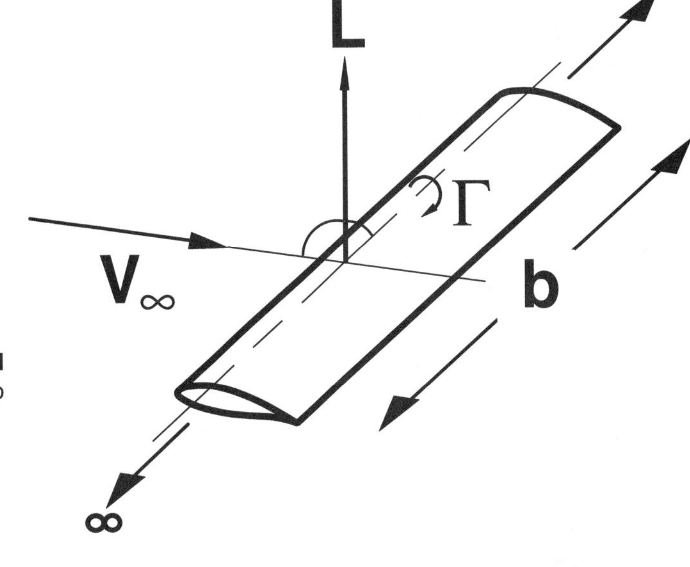

Fig. 12: Lift L due to bound vortex of strength Γ in potential flow. According to the Kutta-Joukowsky theorem, lift L = ρVΓb and is perpendicular to both velocity vector and bound vortex.

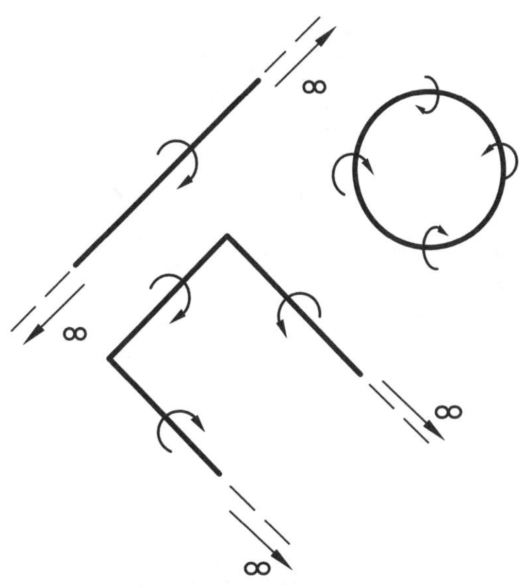

Fig. 13: Vortex models in Helmholtz vortex theorem.

- infinitely long vortex
- ring vortex
- horseshoe vortex

the vortex system, the translational velocity V_∞ is added to the velocity due the vortex system, resulting in an increased velocity $V_\infty + w$. On the other hand, below the vortex system the velocity contribution from the vortices opposes the freestream velocity, resulting in a reduced total velocity of $V_\infty - w$. Therefore, according to Bernoulli's equation, the static pressure above the vortex system p_u is lower than the freestream pressure, p_∞, and below the vortex system the static pressure p_l is higher. If the vortex system is located within an airfoil, this pressure difference results in an upwards force L perpendicular to the freestream velocity V_∞. By convention, the force acting perpendicular to the direction of flow is defined as lift, and the force along the direction of flow, drag.

The lift L is proportional to the total circulation Γ of the vortex system, the freestream velocity V_∞, the density ρ, and the span b (Fig. 12):

$$L = b\rho V_\infty \Gamma \tag{19}$$

This result is the *Kutta-Joukowsky* theorem.

Modeling wings with vortices

Before the Kutta-Joukowsky theorem is used to calculate the flow about a wing, a few special characteristics of vortices must be mentioned. According to the *Helmholtz vortex theorem* individual vortices in an inviscid three-dimensional flow field neither begin nor end in the fluid — they must either be infinitely long or form a closed path (Fig. 13). This property leads to a distinction between the

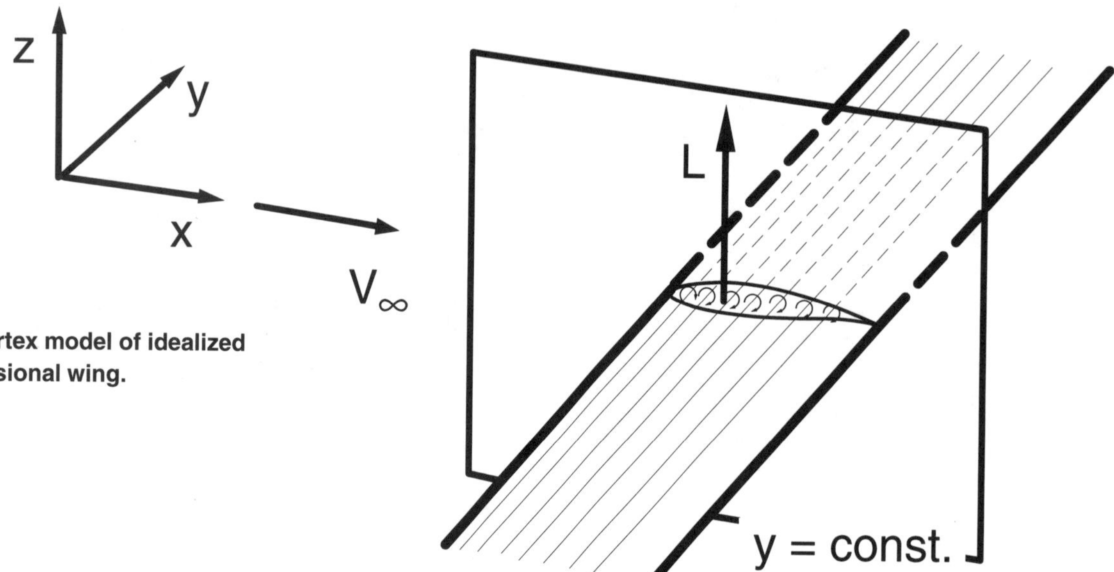

Fig. 14: Vortex model of idealized two-dimensional wing.

two-dimensional problem (airfoil theory) and the three dimensional problem (wing theory).

For a two-dimensional wing, the vortex model consists of a system of infinitely long vortex filaments distributed along the chord of the wing (Fig. 14). The two dimensional wing extends to infinity in the y-direction — that is, perpendicular to the freestream velocity and direction of lift. The flow field is thus identical in any plane defined by y=constant. Airfoil geometry and pressure distribution are functions of x and z only, hence the term "two-dimensional" wing.

The vortex model for a finite span wing is considerably more complicated. According to the Helmholtz vortex theorem, the vortex filaments cannot simply come to an end at the wingtips, but instead bend backwards, extending downstream to infinity. This forms a *horseshoe vortex*, consisting of a "bound" vortex within the wing and a pair of free vortices trailing aft from the wing tips (Fig. 15).

If a wing were modeled with a single horseshoe vortex, the lift would be evenly distributed along its span. In reality, the lift (in other words, the circulation) varies along the wing, tapering to zero at the tips. At a given point on the wing, a spanwise change in the bound circulation $\Delta\Gamma$ must be accompanied by a trailing vortex of the same strength. One can thus model the flow about a wing with a system of superimposed horseshoe vortices (Fig. 16). The trailing vortices are particularly strong near the tip, tending to "roll up" a short distance downstream of the wing to form a pronounced tip vortex. Tip vortices are easily visualized, for example, with a small windmill placed downstream of the wingtip of a wind-tunnel model.

Just as the lift on a wing can be determined by combining a system of vortices with a uniform flow field, the actual form of the aircraft, in particular the thickness distributions of the wing and fuselage, can be modeled by further superimposition of a system of sources. This need not be discussed in detail here; rather, the reader is referred to the aerodynamics texts listed at the end of this section.

Velocity induced by a vortex system

Uniform translational flow is characterized by constant velocity and pressure. Introducing a system of sources, sinks, and vortices produces an additional velocity field, inducing a perturbation velocity throughout the entire flow field. The local velocity at a given point in the field is the sum of the translational and perturbation velocities, with the local static pressure following from Bernoulli's equation.

Induced effects are of particular importance to aircraft design and analysis. For example, an analysis of the flow around a wing must consider the fact that the wing is operating in an induced flow field generated by its own vorticity. The fuselage and empennage are also affected by the velocity field induced by the wing, and in turn gener-

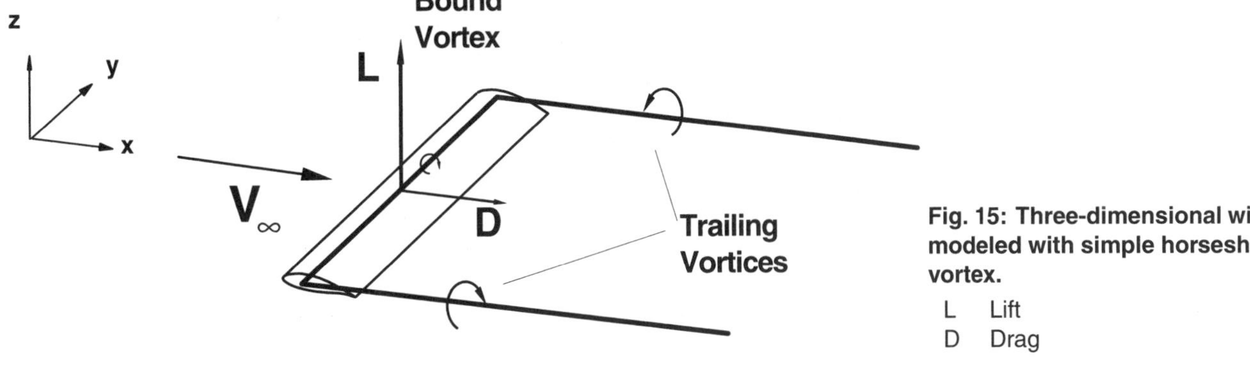

Fig. 15: Three-dimensional wing modeled with simple horseshoe vortex.

L Lift
D Drag

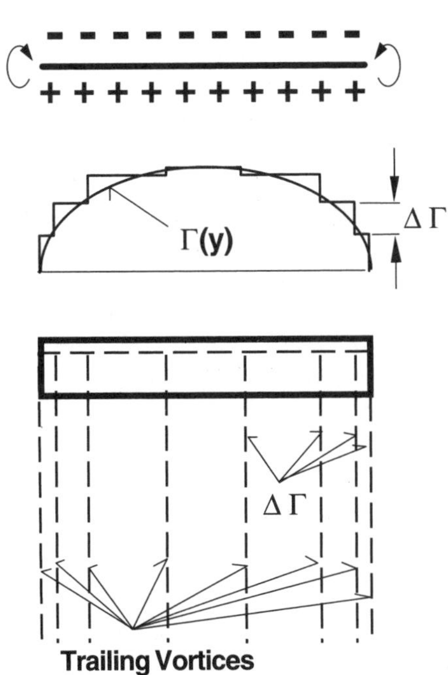

Fig. 16: Representation of a three-dimensional wing by a system of horseshoe vortices.

- pressure equalization at wingtips
- circulation distribution
- vortex system

ate an induced flow field affecting the wing. These latter effects are termed *wing-fuselage interference* and *wing-empennage interference*. The wing induces an upwash on the portion of the fuselage extending upstream of the wing, and a downwash on the aft portion of the fuselage and empennage. This variation in induced velocity along the longitudinal axis of the sailplane influences the design of the fuselage and horizontal stabilizer (Fig. 17).

The velocity field associated with a system of vortices and potential sources is calculated using the *Biot-Savart law*. For the general case of a vortex system of arbitrary geometry, the resulting expressions can be quite complex. Considerable simplification results, however, by assuming that the vortex filaments are straight and infinitely long. Fortunately, in the case of sailplane wings, this proves to be a valid assumption.

Computational methods in wing and airfoil aerodynamics

Analytic methods for wing and airfoil aerodynamics are directed at two problems. In the first, a pressure and velocity distribution over the airfoil and/or wing are specified, and the airfoil and wing planform required to generate these distributions are determined. This is the *design problem* (also called the *inverse problem*). In the second case, the airfoil and wing planform are prescribed, and the resulting pressure and velocity distributions are computed. This task is the *analysis problem*. Both problems arise frequently in the course of aircraft design.

Computational methods for sailplane aerodynamics are based on the vortex and potential source models described in the previous sections. Another class of methods, based on *conformal mapping*, are frequently used as well. Practical implementations of computational methods have been developed by Riegels, Weber, Eppler and Drela [1,23,24,173,177–180,191].

Typically, the problem is broken down into two parts, (1)

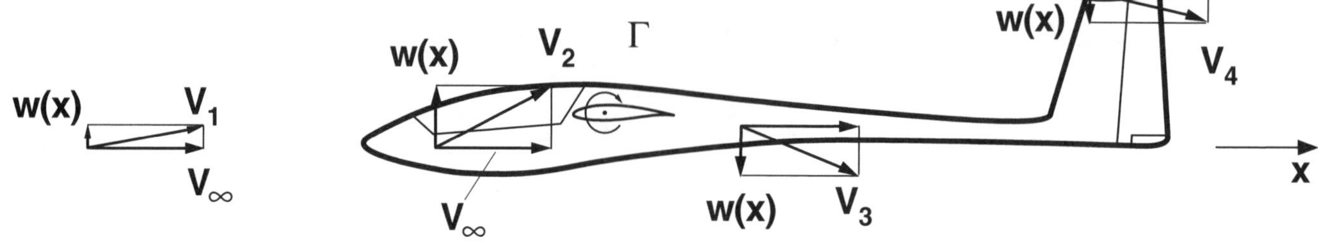

Fig. 17: Velocity perturbations induced by wing on fuselage and empennage

determination of the induced velocity over the wing using the Biot-Savart law and (2) application of a kinematic boundary condition to obtain the actual flow field about the wing. The boundary condition states that at every point on the wing the resultant velocity is parallel to the local surface (Fig. 18). This is equivalent to stating that no air flows through the surface of the wing.

The mathematical expression of the kinematic boundary condition can be quite complex and, depending on the method used, finding a solution to the governing equations that satisfies the boundary conditions can require considerable computational effort.

While the most powerful computational hardware is usually found at universities and research organizations, the advent of inexpensive personal computers has made it possible for almost anyone to make use of sophisticated computational tools for aerodynamic analysis. Several software packages are commercially available. A detailed understanding of the underlying theory is not absolutely necessary; it suffices to understand the preparation of the input data such as airfoil coordinates, analysis options, and so forth.

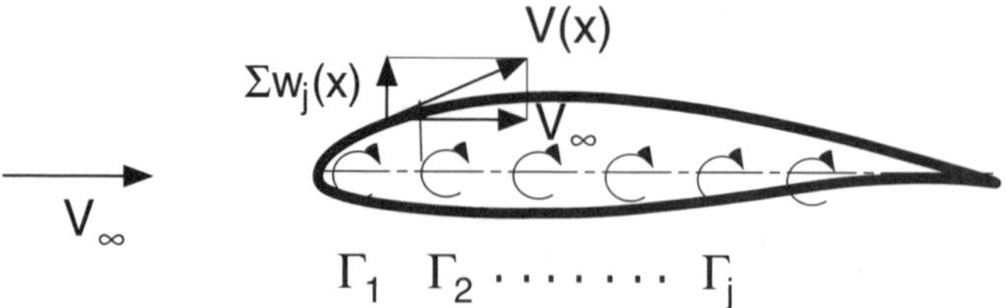

Fig. 18: Kinematic boundary condition. Local velocity is tangent to airfoil surface.

One important boundary condition is the *Kutta condition*, which plays a central role in determining the flow about an airfoil. The Kutta condition states that the flow departs the sharp trailing edge of an airfoil in a smooth fashion, or, said another way, that the rear stagnation point always lies at the airfoil trailing edge[1]. The Kutta condition establishes the circulation about an airfoil, and for this reason small modifications to the trailing edge can have a significant effect on its lift.

The aerodynamics of a finite span wing depend on the effects of the vorticity it trails downstream. Analyzing a wing of arbitrary planform requires considerable computational effort because the effects of the complete vortex system must be integrated over the entire wing. The well known *lifting-line theory* of L. Prandtl, the first method to allow calculation of the aerodynamic characteristics of a finite-span wing, is based on a number of simplifying assumptions (Fig. 19):

- The wing and its system of trailing vortices lie entirely in the $x - y$ plane.
- The wing is unswept and the trailing vortices are consequently of equal length.
- At any spanwise location y, the local downwash induced by the trailing vortex system does not vary over the chord of the wing.

The latter assumption implies that the wing chord is small compared to the wing span, *i.e.* the aspect ratio is large (a value of $\mathcal{R} = 5$ is considered the minimum for application

[1] for cusped trailing edges, the condition simply requires the upper and lower surface velocities to be identical at the trailing edge

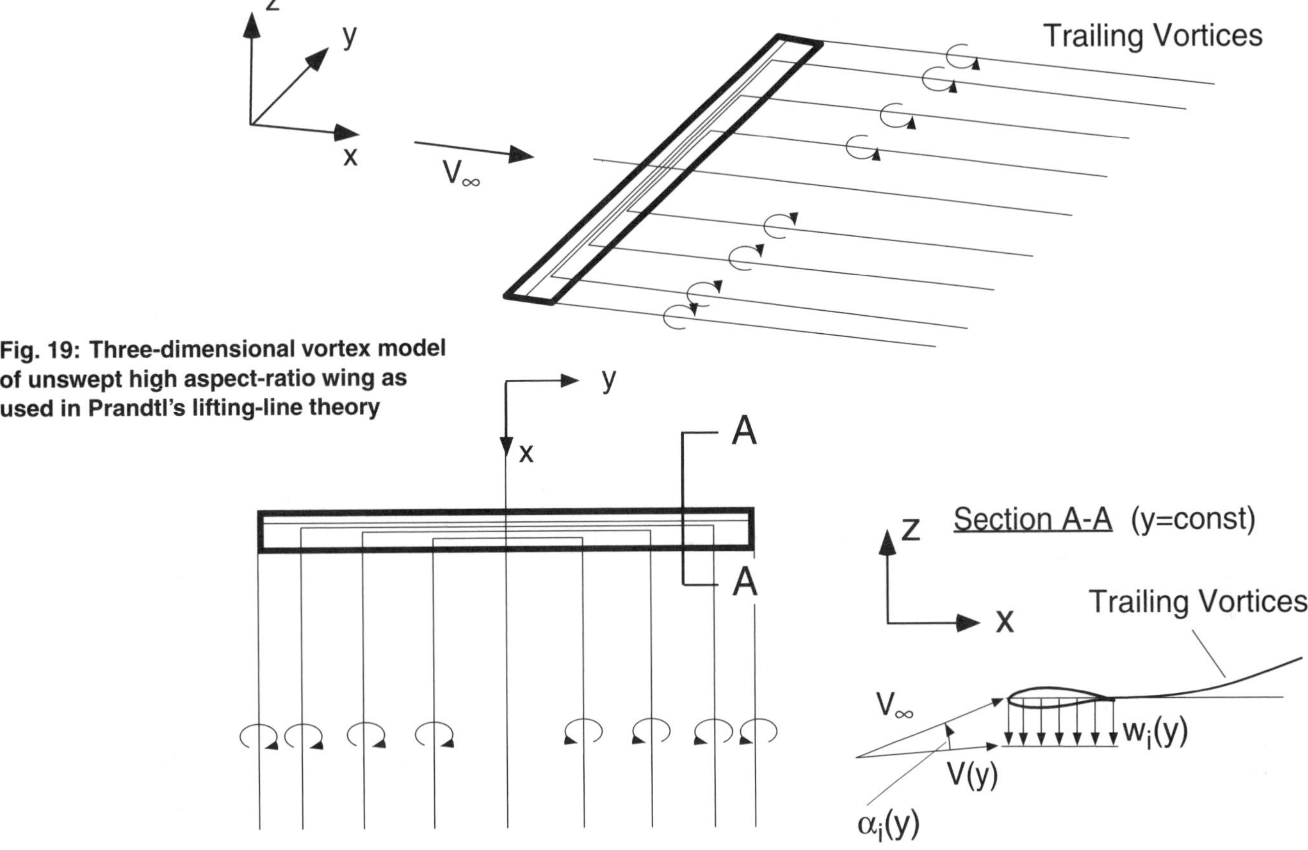

Fig. 19: Three-dimensional vortex model of unswept high aspect-ratio wing as used in Prandtl's lifting-line theory

of lifting-line theory), and allows the downwash w_i to be treated as a function of a single variable, the spanwise coordinate y.

The effect of superimposing the induced downwash w_i on the free stream velocity V_∞ can be approximated by rotating the free stream velocity V_∞ through an angle $\tan \alpha_i(y) = w_i(y)/V_\infty$. As with the downwash, this *induced angle of attack* varies along the wing span.

The wing has a geometric angle of attack α_g relative to the direction of flight, *i.e.* to the free stream velocity V_∞ far upstream of the sailplane. If the wing is built with twist, the geometric angle of attack will vary along the span of the wing, and is therefore a function of the spanwise coordinate y as well.

The induced downwash has the effect of reducing the geometric angle of attack at a given spanwise location by an amount equal to the induced angle of attack, resulting in an effective angle of attack (Fig. 20):

$$\alpha_e(y) = \alpha_g(y) - \alpha_i(y) \qquad (20)$$

This is an equation of considerable importance. It may be interpreted as follows: At each location along the span of an unswept, high aspect ratio wing subject to a steady free stream velocity at angle of attack α_g, the local aerodynamics may be represented by a two-dimensional section having an identical airfoil and operating at an effective angle of attack α_e.

This result allows the results of two-dimensional airfoil theory to be transfered to a finite span wing on a section-by-section basis. The pressure distribution over a cross section of a three-dimensional wing can therefore be determined from two dimensional results obtained for the same airfoil operating at the effective angle of attack, α_e.

Incidently, for a given lift (that is, for a sailplane of given weight), the greater the wing span, the smaller the downwash and induced angle of attack. As the span increases without limit, the downwash approaches zero and the flow about the wing becomes increasingly two-dimensional.

Prandtl's lifting-line theory allows us to calculate the induced angle of attack and sectional (local) lift along the wing span. However, despite the simplified vortex system that assumed by the theory, the mathematics remain somewhat complex (see also [23, 24]). It was only with the introduction of Multhopp's numerical method [96] that this theory became useful for practical applications. The Multhopp method can be easily implemented in a computer program (for example, see Redeker [103]) that takes the wing planform, twist distribution, and two-dimensional airfoil characteristics as inputs, and calculates the spanwise distributions of induced angle of attack, global lift and moment, and induced drag (the latter is discussed in a following section). The method is readily extended to allow analysis of wings with various flap and aileron deflections (see also Feifel [78]).

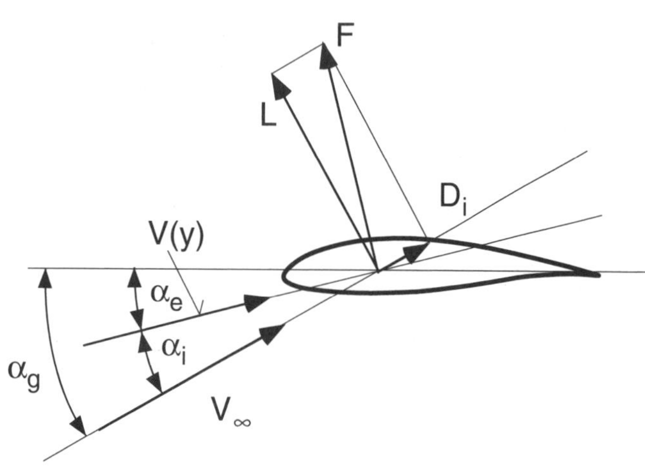

Fig. 20: Local velocity vector V(y) and resulting force vector F at cross section y of a three-dimensional wing (see also Fig. 19).

α_g	geometric angle of attack
α_e	effective angle of attack
α_i	induced angle of attack
D_i	induced drag
L	lift

Induced Drag

According to the Kutta-Joukowsky theorem, a vortex placed in a free stream is associated with a force perpendicular to both the local velocity and the vortex line. In the case of a finite-span wing, the direction of the freestream velocity V_∞ is modified by the induced angle of attack α_i. The lift is generated perpendicular to the *local* effective velocity, not the velocity far upstream of the wing. Since the lift and drag of the complete sailplane are defined as forces perpendicular and parallel to the direction of flight (*i.e.* velocity far upstream), the local sectional lift contributes to the drag as well as the lift (Fig. 20). This *induced drag* is an inevitable consequence of the production of lift on a finite-span wing and is present even in an inviscid fluid. According to Prandtl's lifting line theory, the coefficient of induced drag C_{D_i} is proportional to the square of the lift coefficient and inversely proportional to the aspect ratio.

The energy lost by the aircraft due to induced drag appears as kinetic energy in the trailing vortex system, particularly in the tip vortices. The tip vortices trail relatively far downstream, gradually dissipating due to viscous effects. All pilots are familiar with the dangers associated with these tip vortices and are trained to follow wake avoidance procedures when operating in the vicinity of large aircraft. An

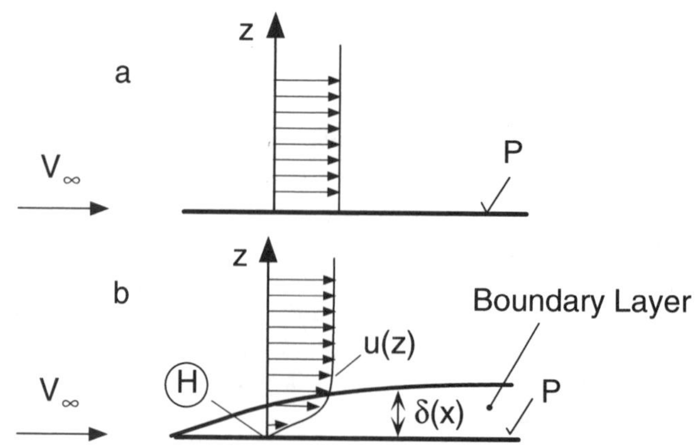

Fig. 21: Flow along a flat plate.

(a)	inviscid flow
(b)	viscous flow
(H)	no slip condition
$\delta(x)$	boundary-layer thickness
u(z)	velocity profile within boundary layer

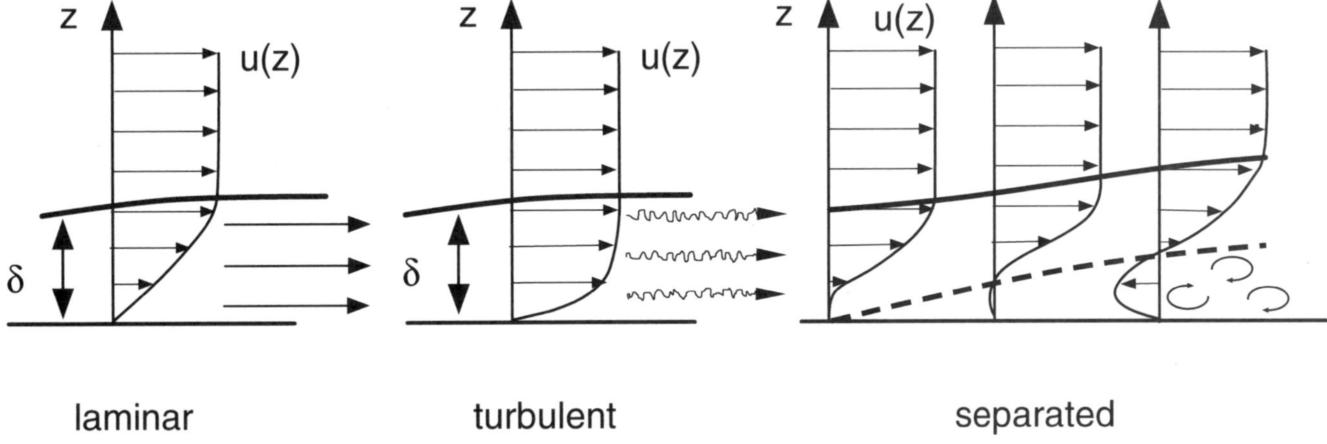

Fig. 22: Velocity profiles u(z) and particle motions for laminar, turbulent, and separated boundary layers.

encounter with the wake turbulence generated by a large transport aircraft can cause loss of control or structural failure [8].

Viscous Effects and Boundary Layers

Laminar and turbulent boundary layers

Although the boundary layer is very thin, extending over only a small portion of the flow field around the aircraft, it plays an important roll in determining a number of aerodynamic characteristics. Drag and separation-related phenomena such as maximum lift coefficient and pitching moment variation can be explained only with reference to boundary-layer theory.

Inviscid flow assumes that the flow field extends to the surface of the body, with no decrease in velocity as the surface is approached. In reality, a boundary layer exists adjacent to the body in which the velocity diminishes from the local potential flow velocity down to zero at the surface (Fig. 21). This so-called *no-slip condition* results from the fact that the air can interact with the surface at a molecular level, even when the surface is highly polished. Starting at zero velocity at the surface, within the boundary layer, the velocity gradually increases from zero at the surface to the velocity predicted by inviscid potential flow. The velocity distribution within the boundary layer is its *velocity profile*. The *boundary-layer thickness* is defined as the distance from the surface to the location at which the velocity reaches 99% of its local potential-flow value.

Boundary layers are classified as *laminar*, *turbulent*, and *separated*. In a laminar boundary layer, the air particles travel along smooth streamlines parallel to the surface. The velocity varies within the boundary layer, giving rise to shear stresses and loss of kinetic energy in the flow (Fig. 22).

In a turbulent boundary layer, the air particles undergo additional high-frequency velocity variations of a random nature. Although these variations are small compared to the average velocity, they contribute to the energy exchange between the boundary layer and the external flow, as well as within the boundary layer itself. The velocity profile in a turbulent boundary layer is thus "fuller" than that of a laminar boundary layer, exhibiting higher velocities near the surface and a steeper velocity gradient at the surface itself. With increased velocity gradients come increased shear stresses, so that in general, turbulent boundary layers produce higher skin friction than laminar boundary layers.

Separated flow

In the presence of an *adverse pressure gradient* (increasing static pressure), the boundary layer may separate from the surface of the body. The flow travels away from the surface at a *separation point* in a chaotic fashion. Separated flow is often characterized by large-scale unsteady turbulence

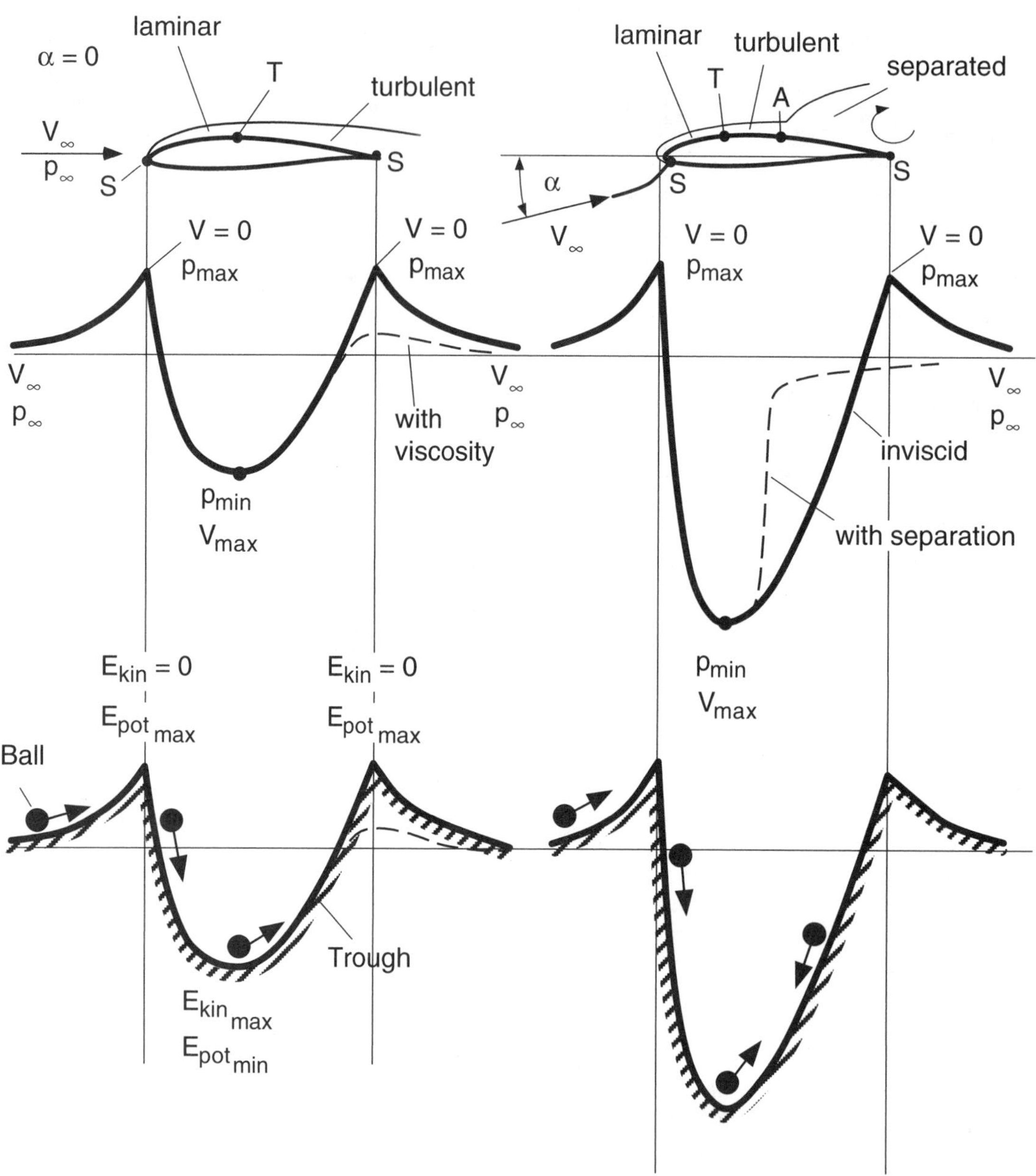

Fig. 23: Pressure distribution on an airfoil with boundary-layer transition and separation:

S Stagnation point
T Boundary-layer transition point
A Point of boundary-layer separation

and mechanical analogy:

E_{kin} kinetic energy
E_{pot} potential energy

with no clearly defined streamlines. The velocities near the surface may actually become negative. On the other hand, a laminar boundary layer may separate smoothly, often reattaching shortly downstream of the separation point.

In order to understand the process of separation, consider the path of an air particle near the upper surface of an airfoil (Fig. 23). The particle travels along a streamline that defines the airfoil surface. This streamline originates far upstream of the airfoil and leads to the stagnation point at the leading edge of the airfoil, at which point it splits and extends over the upper and lower surfaces of the airfoil. The streamlines join again at the trailing edge and from there extend downstream of the airfoil.

The pressure distribution along this streamline is a function of the airfoil geometry and angle of attack. Let us consider a typical airfoil (1) at zero angle of attack and (2) at a relatively high angle of attack. In the first case, a flat pressure distribution develops with little variation in pressure. In the second case, however, one observes a very strong pressure gradient and flow separation.

In both cases the flow decelerates from the freestream velocity V_∞ to zero velocity at the forward stagnation point. Subsequently, the flow accelerates and the static pressure decreases to a certain minimum value. In inviscid flow, aft of the point of minimum static pressure, the static pressure increases and the velocity decreases until the trailing edge, where the velocity is theoretically zero. The flow accelerates downstream of the airfoil until it reaches its original (freestream) velocity and static pressure. Thus, a continual exchange between kinetic energy (velocity) and potential energy (pressure) takes place along the streamline.

In viscous flow, however, there are energy losses in the boundary layer. Even when the pressure gradients are weak, the total pressure at the trailing edge will be considerably lower than the freestream total pressure; however, the effect on the overall flow field is minimal. On the other hand, if the adverse pressure gradients aft of the pressure minimum are sufficiently strong, the flow in the boundary layer may decelerate to a full stop and even begin to travel in the reverse direction. That is, the flow separates.

Separation may be visualized with the help of a simple physical analogy. A ball rolled with initial velocity V along a curved track with the same shape as the airfoil's pressure distribution will experience an exchange between kinetic and potential energy analogous to that experienced by the air particles. If the ball loses energy through friction, it may come to a halt before the second peak, failing to reach the top and rolling back towards the low point in the path. In the analogy, this corresponds to flow separation.

Separation occurs in sailplanes wherever sufficiently strong adverse pressure gradients are encountered. These are always present on wings at high angles of attack and limit the maximum attainable lift. At the same time, the airfoil drag increases due to changes in the static pressure distribution. Strong adverse pressure gradients are also found on the aft faces of blunt bodies such as landing gear and dive brakes, leading to local flow separation and substantial increases in drag.

Boundary-layer transition

The boundary layer over a sailplane wing begins as laminar and attached, and may progress in sequence to lam-

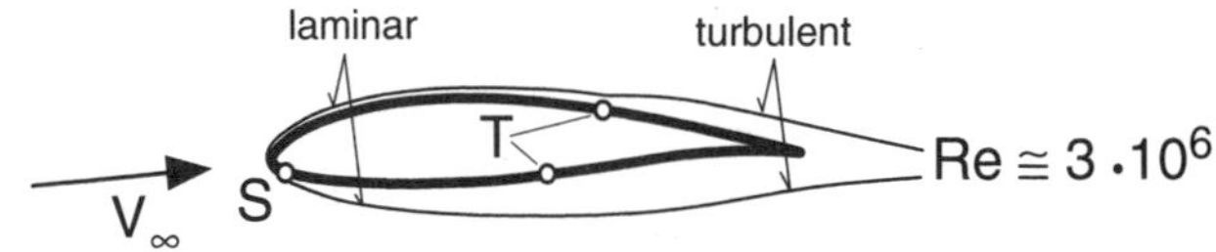

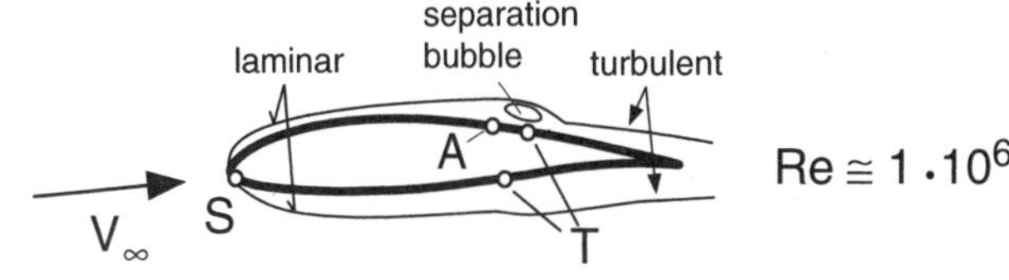

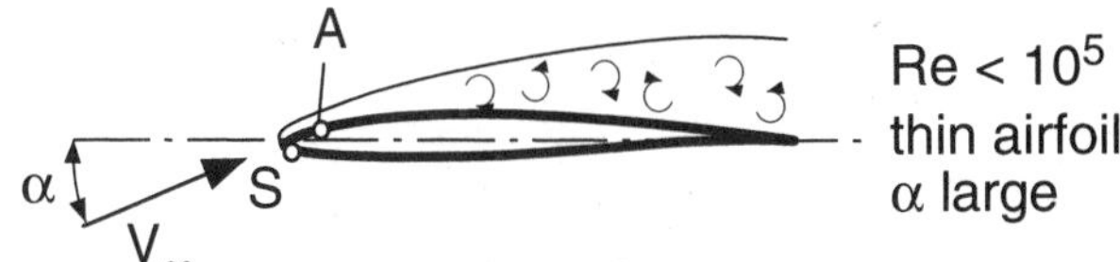

Fig. 24: Behavior of laminar boundary layer under various pressure distributions and Reynolds numbers:

- Transition
- Separation bubble
- Laminar separation

S Stagnation point
A Separation point
T Boundary-layer transition

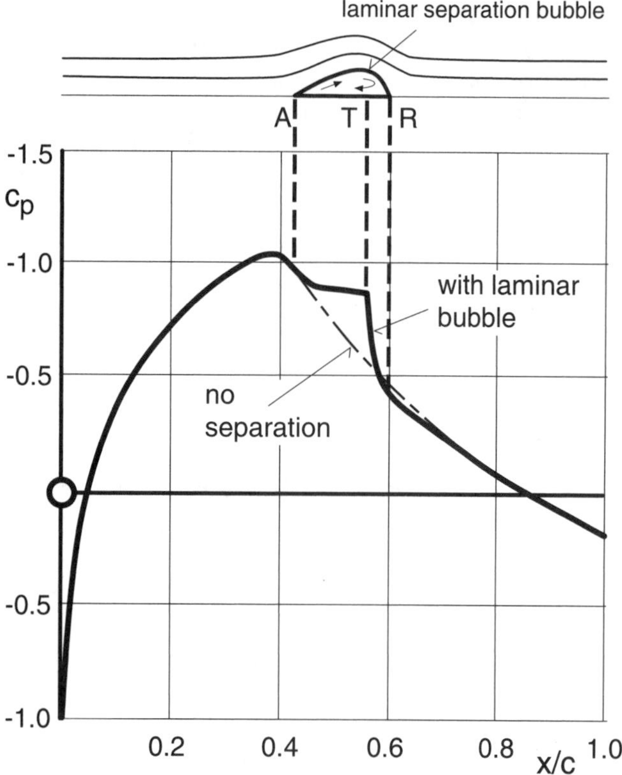

Fig. 25: Pressure distribution in the vicinity of a laminar separation bubble measured on an FX 66-S-196 V1 airfoil by J. H. M. Gooden [181]. Upper surface pressure distribution corresponding to $\alpha = -1.0°$ and $Re=0.49 \cdot 10^6$.

A	separation point
T	transition point
R	reattachment point

inar/separated, turbulent, and turbulent/separated. At the forward stagnation point, where the boundary layer forms, the flow is normally laminar. However, the laminar flow is only stable under certain conditions, so that in general the boundary layer will transition to a turbulent state after a certain distance. Both laminar and turbulent boundary layers may separate in the presence of an adverse pressure gradient along the direction of flow. However, since turbulent boundary layers are characterized by increased energy transfer with the flow outside the boundary layer, they are better able to overcome adverse pressure gradients without separation. Laminar boundary layers, on the other hand, may separate in the presence of relatively small adverse pressure gradients. Depending on the local flow conditions, a laminar boundary layer may separate permanently or become turbulent while separated and reattach. The latter case is accompanied by the formation of a so-called *laminar separation bubble* (Figs. 24,25).

Whether and where these phenomena occur depends on the following parameters:

- Pressure distribution (Airfoil geometry and angle of attack)
- Reynolds number
- Surface quality (smoothness, waviness, contamination by rain, snow, ice or insects)
- Level of turbulence in the oncoming flow

The following factors help maintain laminar flow:

- Favorable pressure gradients, for example in the area of the leading edge
- Low Reynolds numbers, for example as observed on model airplanes and birds
- High surface quality with no roughness, waviness, or contamination (as typical of modern fiberglass sailplanes)
- Low turbulence in the oncoming flow, for example in flight or in laminar wind tunnels.

While low frequency atmospheric turbulence presents no problem in this respect, the high frequency turbulence typical of many wind tunnels can have a significant effect on boundary-layer development.

A sound physical understanding of boundary-layer transition phenomena is a prerequisite to the design of high performance sailplane airfoils. Since skin-friction coefficients are so much lower when the boundary layer remains laminar, it is important to ensure that boundary-layer transition occurs as far back on the airfoil as possible. Separation, on the other hand, incurs large drag penalties, and for this reason care must be taken to ensure that the transition occurs before the boundary layer can separate. This is accomplished by tailoring the airfoil geometry, and, where required, by means of special devices such as "zig-zag tape" or pneumatic turbulators (Fig. 26; see also [72, 166, 168, 183–185, 192]). It is especially difficult to develop airfoil shapes with extensive laminar flow

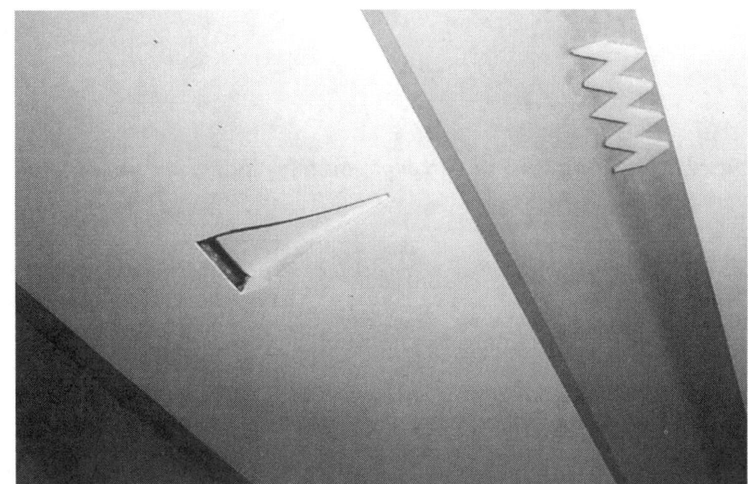

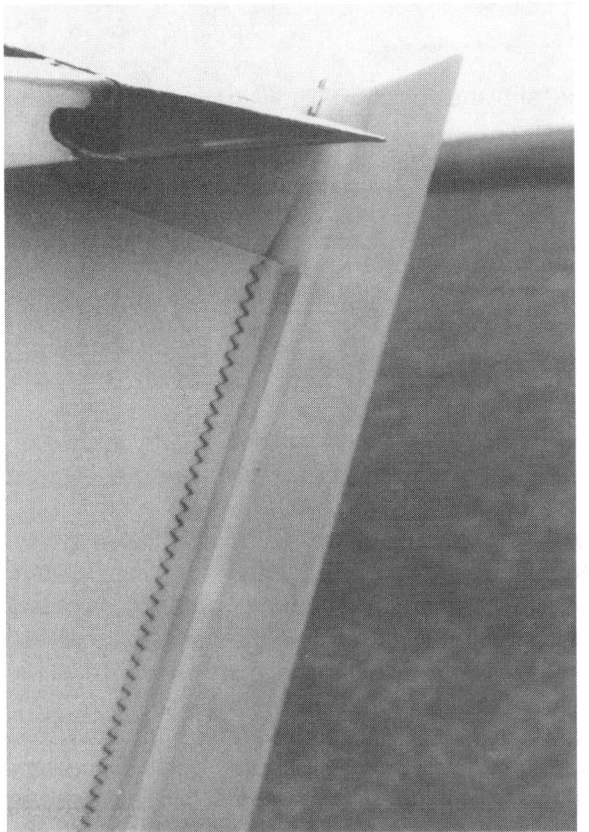

Fig. 26: Boundary-layer tripping devices (turbulators) have become a common sight on modern sailplanes. Above left, "zig-zag" tape bonded to the airfoil underside just ahead of the aileron (Nimbus 4 inner wing panel). The tape terminates just before the end of the wing panel to allow the gap to be properly taped during assembly. Left, zig-zag tape on vertical stabilizer, in this case integrated with the rudder hinge gap seal. Above right, ASW-27 outer wing section lower surface. Here, laminar flow extends onto the aileron itself. The boundary layer is tripped by means of a series of blow-holes arranged spanwise along the aileron lower surface. The holes communicate with a plenum that receives air either from a small Pitot tube or (in this case) a NACA-inlet. The short length of zig-zag tape upstream of the inlet improves inlet efficiency by energizing the boundary layer.

Fig. 27: Pressure drag due to separation (cylinder) and skin-friction drag due to boundary layer (flat plate)

at both low and high angles of attack (that is, both in high speed and thermaling flight). See also R. Eppler [176] for an empirical approach to the prediction of boundary layer transition.

Friction drag and pressure drag

The shear stresses associated with the boundary layer act in a direction parallel to the local surface; when integrated over the entire surface of an aircraft or an airfoil, they yield the *friction drag*. Similarly, the local static pressure also acts on the aircraft surface, albeit *perpendicular* to the local surface. The integrated effect of the static pressure includes a drag component termed the *pressure drag* (Fig. 27).

Separated flow, whether over a stalled airfoil or an unfaired strut, can be a significant source of pressure drag. Even if there is no flow separation, the shear forces within the boundary layer can have an adverse effect on the static pressure distribution, providing a further source of pressure drag. The induced drag of a finite-span wing may also be categorized as a form of pressure drag. Other significant sources of pressure drag include unfaired landing gear, antennas, exposed control linkage, extended dive brakes, localized areas of separation about the wing-fuselage junction, the empennage, and unsealed control surface hinge gaps.

Friction drag is present with both laminar and turbulent boundary layers. Consider a flat plate oriented parallel to the freestream. In the inviscid potential flow solution, the static pressure along the plate is constant, allowing the boundary layer to be examined free of influence from pressure gradients or flow separation. For this reason the flat plate is a popular model for both theoretical and experimental boundary-layer research. Of particular interest are the results relating the boundary layer thickness and

Table 3: Theoretical drag coefficients and boundary-layer thicknesses for flat plates. See also Schlichting [22], Chapters 7 and 21.

	laminar	turbulent
drag coefficient, c_d (both sides)	$2\frac{1.328}{\sqrt{Re}}$	$2\frac{0.074}{\sqrt[5]{Re}}$
boundary-layer thickness $\delta(x)$	$\frac{5x}{\sqrt{Re_x}}$	$\frac{0.37x}{\sqrt[5]{Re_x}}$

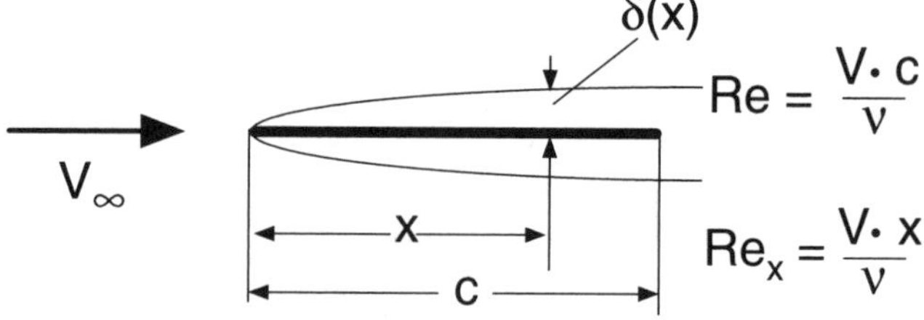

friction drag, both of which are functions of Reynolds number. Analytic results for these quantities are presented in Table 3.

For example, for a flat plate 1m long subject to a freestream velocity of 30m/s, these formulas yield a boundary-layer thickness of 3.5mm (laminar boundary layer) or 20mm (turbulent) at the trailing edge. The corresponding Reynolds number ($Re = 2 \cdot 10^6$) is typical of sailplane airfoils.

The friction drag as calculated by these formulas is presented graphically in Fig. 28. In order to facilitate comparison with data from actual airfoils, the results are presented for a two-sided flat plate. At low Reynolds numbers, the boundary layer remains laminar over the entire plate. Conversely, at very high Reynolds numbers the drag contribu-

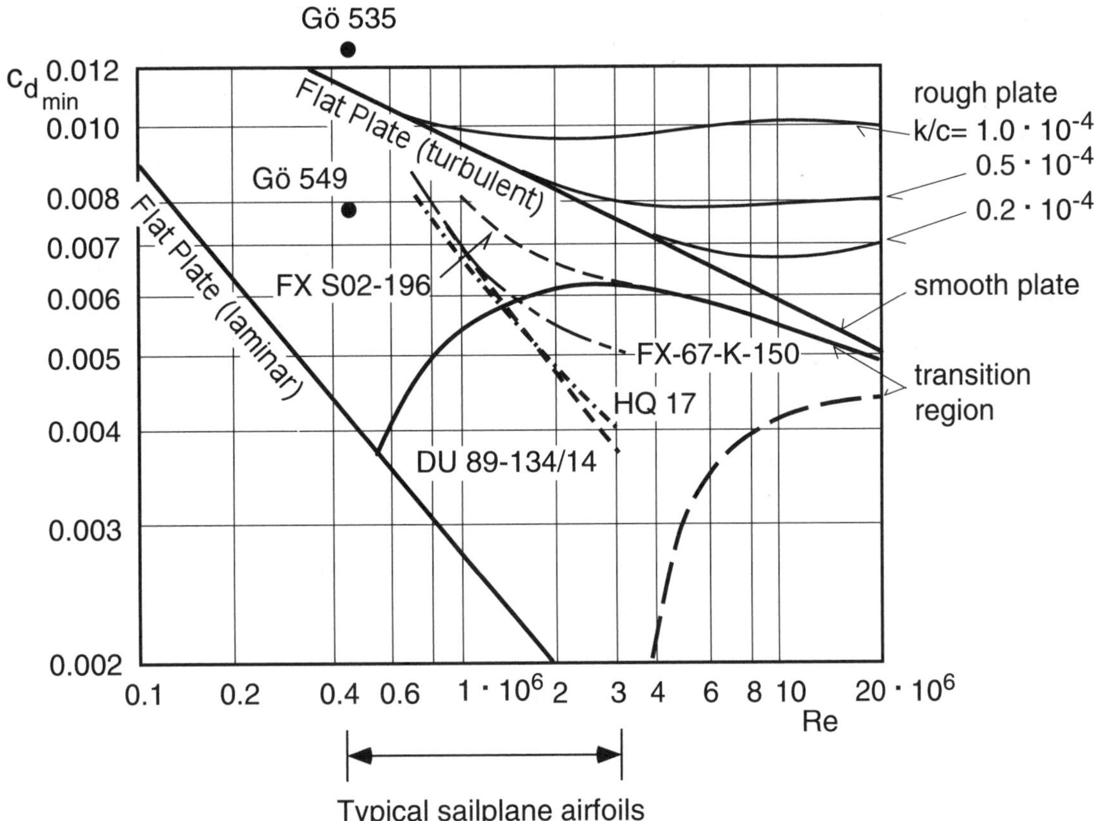

Fig. 28: Skin friction drag of two-sided flat plate as a function of Reynolds number, compared with minimum drag coefficients of some typical airfoils.

—— Transition region, high turbulence environment (typical wind tunnel)

– – – Transition region, low turbulence wind tunnel or free atmosphere

tion from the initial laminar portion of the boundary layer is negligible, and the drag approaches the value obtained by assuming a completely turbulent boundary layer. Sailplane airfoils typically operate in a transition region where both the laminar and turbulent portions of the boundary layer contribute significantly to the total drag. It is apparent that where the boundary layer is primarily turbulent, the drag is much higher than would be observed with a primarily laminar boundary layer. Low drag requires the boundary layer to remain laminar to the greatest extent possible.

Figure 28 includes data for a few sailplane airfoils for reference. The airfoil data differ considerably from the simple flat plate results because of the static pressure variations present along the airfoil surfaces. More detailed airfoil analysis may be performed using one of several modern software tools for the detailed design and analysis of airfoils. One well-known program by Eppler [177,180] is specifically intended for use in the design of airfoils for special applications ("airfoil tailoring"). This program computes the lift, drag, and pitching moment coefficients of prescribed airfoils as a function of Reynolds number and angle of attack. Boundary-layer effects are included. The program also solves the inverse problem (determining the airfoil shape required to achieve a prescribed velocity distribution). Another well-known program is XFOIL by M. Drela [173], an interactive, graphical design and analysis tool with similar capabilities, including viscous analysis of existing airfoils, prediction of boundary-layer transition, laminar separation bubbles, turbulent separation, solution of inverse problem, and rapid evaluation of airfoil modifications.

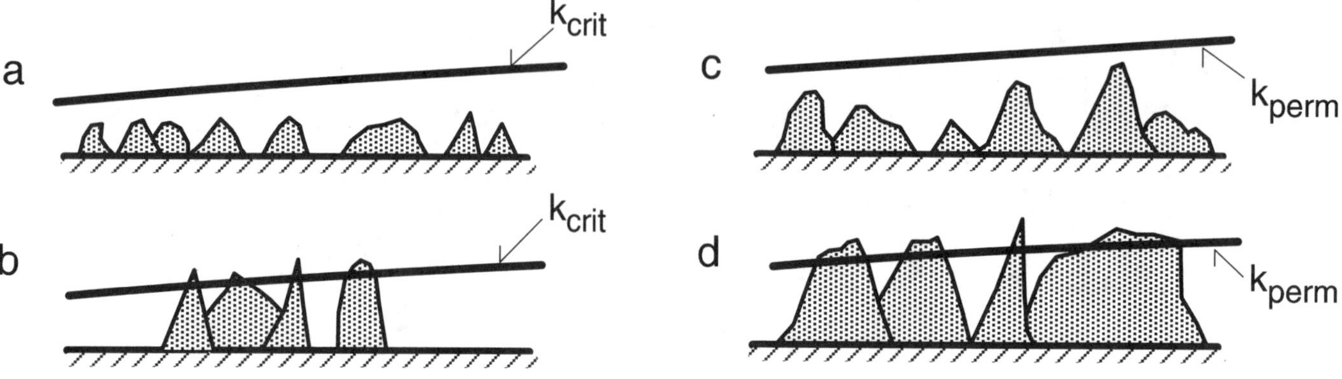

Fig. 29: Effect of surface roughness on laminar (a,b) and turbulent (c,d) boundary layer.

a) no effect
b) transition due to roughness
c) hydraulically smooth
d) increased drag due to roughness

Importance of surface quality

Irregularities on the surface of a flat plate or airfoil affect laminar and turbulent boundary layers in different ways.

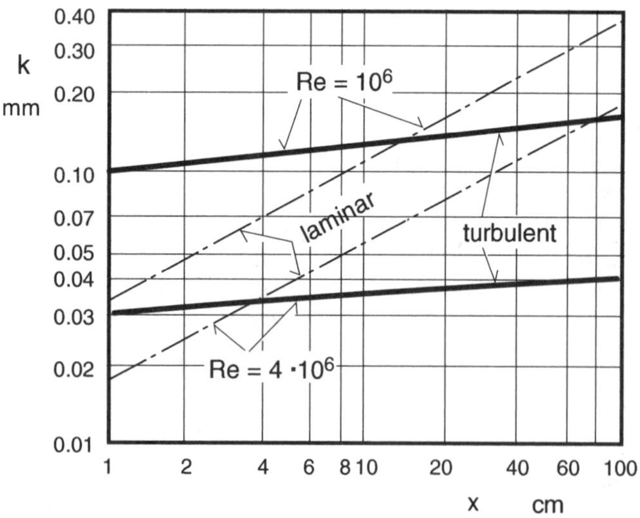

Fig. 30: Critical and permissible surface roughness as a function of boundary-layer length per F. X. Wortmann [115]. Reference length for Reynolds number is c = 1m.

Surface roughness is essentially a field of small amplitude irregularities. In a laminar boundary layer, if the irregularities exceed a certain maximum height, the flow may become turbulent. This maximum tolerable roughness is termed the *critical roughness* and is a function of the Reynolds number and pressure distribution. For a flat plate, the critical roughness k is given by the following formula:

$$\frac{k_{crit}}{\delta} = \frac{2.4}{\sqrt[4]{Re_x}} \qquad \text{Critical Roughness} \qquad (21)$$

This means that the roughness must not exceed a value of 1/10 to 1/15 the local boundary-layer thickness. If the roughness remains below this value, it has no influence on the laminar boundary layer or the drag (Fig. 29).

For turbulent boundary layers, the drag begins to increase as soon as the roughness exceeds a minimum significant value, known as the *permissible roughness.* The permissible surface roughness is also a function of Reynolds number:

$$\frac{k_{perm}}{x} = \frac{100}{Re_x} \qquad \text{Permissible Roughness} \qquad (22)$$

If the roughness is less than the permissible roughness, the surface is considered *hydraulically smooth.* If the roughness is greater than k_{perm}, the drag varies directly with the degree of roughness, as shown in Fig. 28. In the presence of pressure gradients, however, the surface friction coefficients may vary considerably from their flat plate values.

Figure 30 presents a simple surface roughness diagram developed by F. X. Wortmann [115] for use with sailplanes. The figure presents the critical surface roughness (laminar boundary layers) and permissible surface roughness (turbulent boundary layers) as a function of boundary-layer length and Reynolds number. It is evident that surface roughness as small as 1/100 to 1/10 mm may be detrimental. Surface waviness has a similar effect. Sailplane manufacturers and pilots therefore devote considerable effort to achieving and maintaining a high surface quality. Even raindrops or insects can lead to premature transition. Airfoils vary considerably, however, in their sensitivity to such surface contamination.

Concluding Remarks

The preceding sections reviewed the basics of fluid mechanics relevant to sailplane design. A mathematical presentation has been deliberately avoided; rather, emphasis has been placed developing a physical understanding of the most important phenomena such as the production of lift and drag. A sound understanding of the physics of the problem is essential, for only then can one take advantage of the full range of design possibilities.

This level of understanding is also valuable when interpreting wind-tunnel and flight-test data. These experimental results often reveal surprising and unexpected phenomena, and a good understanding of the basics helps in developing solutions to unforeseen aerodynamic problems.

The "big picture" is especially important when surveying the extensive technical literature in aerodynamics, as it allows ready identification of material having relevance to sailplane design. Table 4 presents a summary overview of the main topics in fluid mechanics, outlining the manner in which the complex fundamental equations are reduced to the simpler relationships used in sailplane design.

For more detailed presentations of aerodynamic theory, the reader is referred to texts such as H. Schlichting and E. Truckenbrodt [24], J. D. Anderson [3, 4], and M. Kuethe and C. Chow [15]. See also R. T. Jones [14] for a concise overview of wing theory.

Table 4: Overview of topics in fluid mechanics.

Fluid Mechanics, general case:

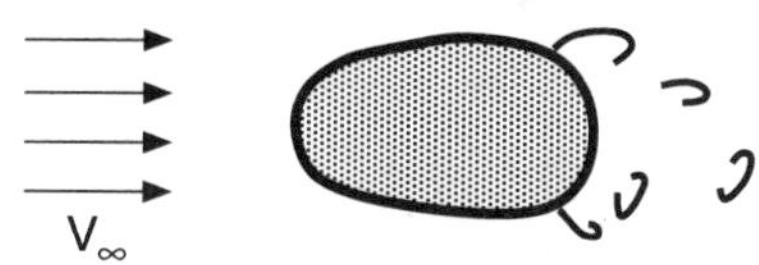

Compressible, viscous flow:
Navier-Stokes Equations
Gas laws
Continuity Equation

Flow at high Reynolds numbers (Re $> 10^5$) :

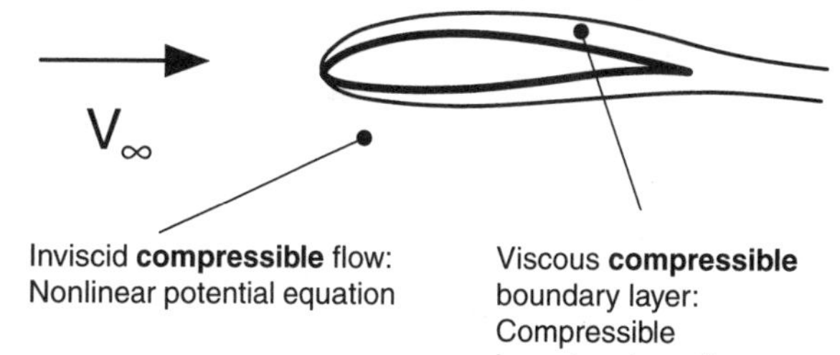

Inviscid **compressible** flow: Nonlinear potential equation	Viscous **compressible** boundary layer: Compressible boundary-layer theory

Low Mach numbers and High Reynolds numbers
($M < 0.3$, $Re > 10^5$) :

Inviscid **incompressible** flow:	Viscous **incompressible** boundary layer:
Linear potential equation: Elementary solutions: Potential vortices and sources, Superposition principle	**Boundary-layer theory:** Laminar, turbulent, and separated boundary layers
Airfoil theory: Pressure distribution, lift, moment	Transition, separation, influence of Reynolds number and surface quality
Wing theory: unswept wing with large aspect ratio, Prandtl lifting-line theory	Friction drag, pressure drag, maximum lift
Lift distribution Induced drag	

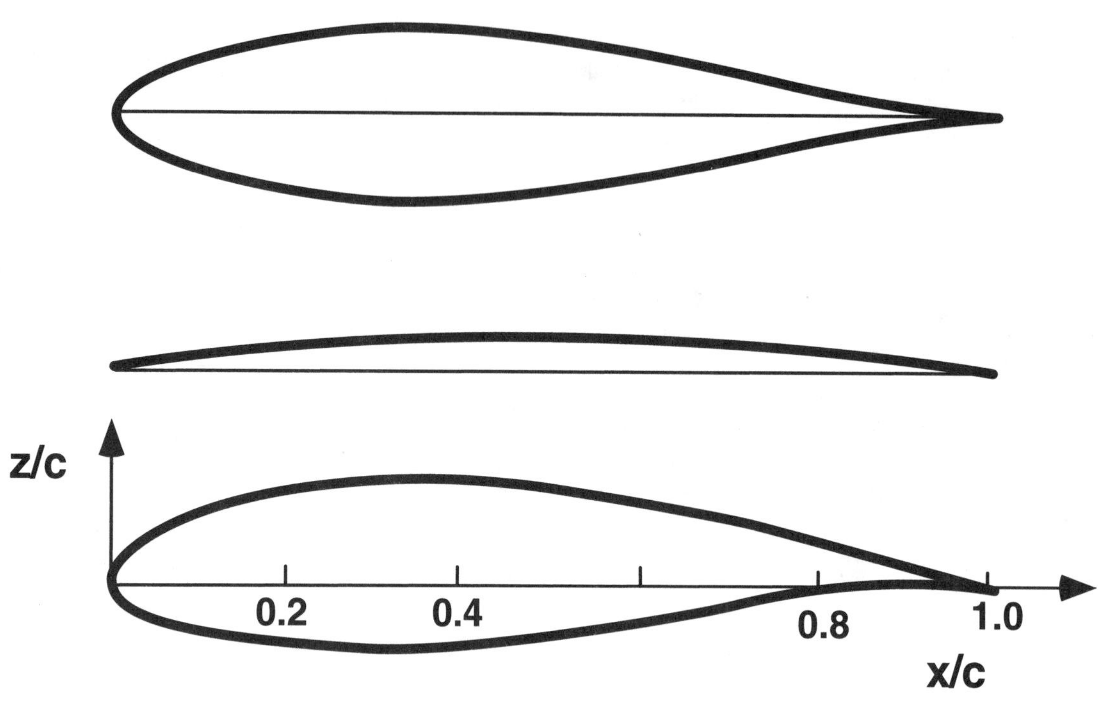

x/c	0.01	0.05	0.10	0.15	0.20	0.30	0.40	0.50	0.60	0.70	0.80	0.90	0.95	1.0
$100 \cdot z_u/c$	2.6	5.6	7.9	9.3	10.4	11.8	12.1	11.3	9.7	7.5	5.1	2.5	1.3	0
$100 \cdot z_l/c$	-1.3	-3.2	-4.3	-5.1	-5.6	-6.0	-5.6	-4.6	-3.2	-1.7	-0.3	0.6	0.6	0

Fig. 31: Form, camber line, and geometry for NACA $63_3 - 618$

Airfoil and Wing Theory

Wing/Airfoil Geometry and Aerodynamic Coefficients

Airfoil geometry

Since an airfoil is a cross section of a wing in the plane defined by y = constant, the airfoil geometry is defined only in terms of the coordinates x and z. The airfoil geometry is typically presented as a table of chordwise locations x and corresponding upper and lower coordinates z_u and z_l. In order to make this information independent of the size of the airfoil and the choice of dimensional units, the coordinates are normalized to the airfoil chord, c (Fig. 31). The coordinates are presented as x/c and z/c, the values of which range from zero to unity.

Every airfoil can be defined as a combination of a thickness distribution and a camber line (mean line). The chord is the distance between the endpoints of the camber line. The 1/4-chord point, the point on the chord line lying one quarter of the chord length aft of the leading edge, plays an important role as a reference point for the aerodynamic pitching moment. The angle of attack is the angle between the chord line and the direction of freestream flow.

Although a fairly large set of coordinates is required to specify the airfoil geometry to a sufficient degree of precision, to a certain extent airfoils can be characterized using just a few parameters. These are the maximum thickness, the location of the point of maximum thickness, the maximum camber, location of maximum camber, the leading-edge radius, and the trailing-edge angle (included angle at the trailing edge). These parameters are illustrated in

Fig. 32. Usually these are normalized to the airfoil chord in the same manner as the coordinates.

Wing geometry

A complete description of the wing includes not only the airfoil geometry, but the wing planform and the spanwise airfoil variation as well.

In most cases, the leading and trailing edges of sailplane wings consist of straight line segments. Thus, the basic sailplane wing planforms are rectangular, tapered, rectangular/tapered, and double or triple tapered (Fig. 33). Mention may also be made of the elliptical wing, which, although seldom used in modern sailplanes, is of great theoretical importance in wing theory. Most of the effects of wing planform can be expressed as a function of two geometric parameters: the *aspect ratio* and the *taper ratio*, defined as follows (Fig. 34):

$$\mathcal{R} = b^2/S \qquad \text{Aspect Ratio} \qquad (23)$$

$$\lambda = c_t/c_r \qquad \text{Taper Ratio} \qquad (24)$$

For a rectangular wing, the aspect ratio is simply the ratio of the span to the chord ($\mathcal{R}$ = b/c). In the case of the rectangular-tapered and double-tapered wing, the location of the taper break and the taper ratios of the inner and outer portion of the wing are required to complete the definition of the wing geometry.

Most sailplane wings are unswept or only slightly swept. It should be kept in mind that if the wing is both swept and tapered, the sweep angles of the leading edge and the 1/4-chord line (the locus of points located at x/c = 1/4) are different. The angle between the wing and the y axis is the *dihedral*.

Another important geometric parameter is the *twist*, the spanwise variation of the geometric angle of attack (Fig. 34). The angle about the y axis between a reference line in the wing (for example, the wing chord line on its plane of symmetry) and the reference axis of the fuselage is the wing *angle of incidence*.

The geometry of the tail surfaces is defined using similar parameters.

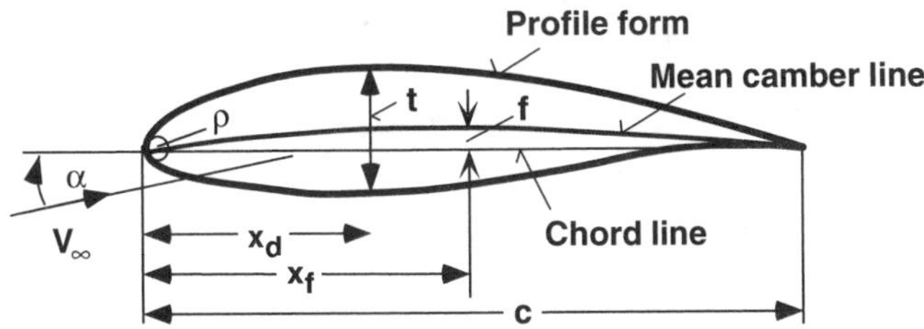

Fig. 32: Airfoil geometric parameters.

- **t** thickness
- x_d location of maximum thickness
- **f** camber
- x_f location of maximum camber
- ρ leading-edge radius
- **c** chord

Pressure coefficient

The pressure distribution over an airfoil and its importance to the development of the boundary layer has already been discussed. When considering the pressure distribution, it is useful to present the pressure as a nondimensional *pressure coefficient*. This is the differential pressure between the static pressure p at a particular location in the flow field and the static pressure p_∞ far upstream of the aircraft, normalized to the dynamic pressure q_∞:

$$c_p = \frac{p - p_\infty}{q_\infty} \qquad \text{Pressure coefficient} \qquad (25)$$

$$q_\infty = \frac{\rho}{2} V_\infty^2 \qquad \text{Dynamic pressure} \qquad (26)$$

Upon application of Bernoulli's equation to the local velocity u, the pressure coefficient can be expressed as

$$c_p = \frac{p - p_\infty}{q_\infty} = 1 - \left(\frac{u}{V_\infty}\right)^2 \qquad (27)$$

The pressure coefficient c_p is used primarily to present calculated or measured airfoil pressure distributions (Fig. 35). Conventionally, in figures such as Fig. 35, negative pressures are plotted in the positive direction of the vertical axis. In nondimensional terms, the pressure coefficient at the stagnation point in incompressible flow is exactly 1. The differential pressure Δc_p between the upper and lower sides of the airfoil is a function of the chordwise coordinate x.

Aerodynamic coefficients

The total aerodynamic force acting on a wing or airfoil may be resolved into components perpendicular and parallel to

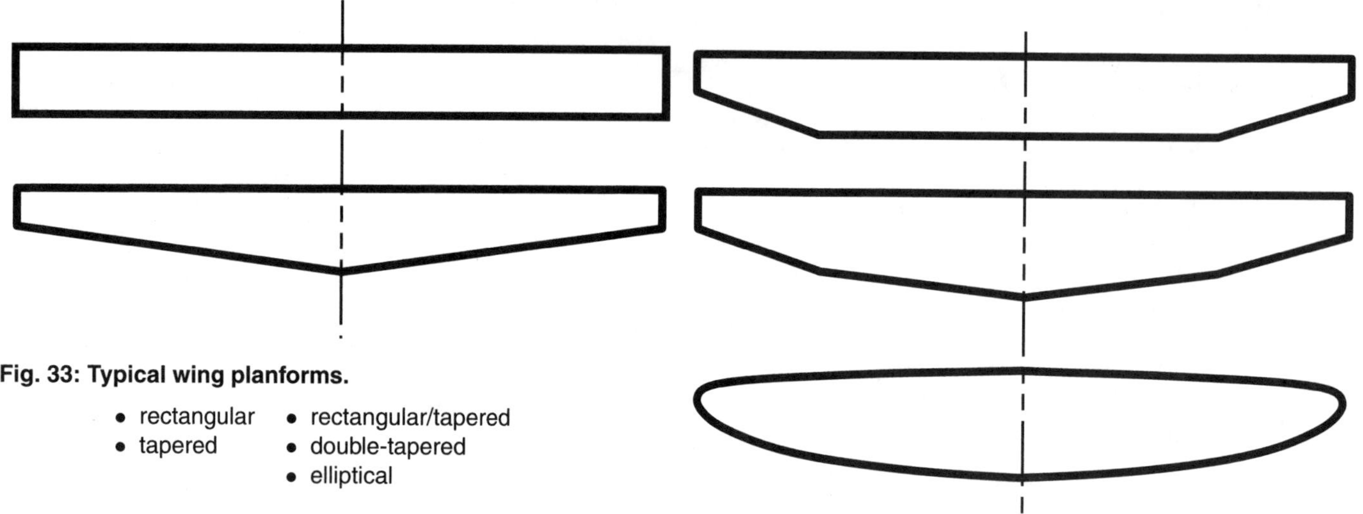

Fig. 33: Typical wing planforms.

- rectangular
- tapered
- rectangular/tapered
- double-tapered
- elliptical

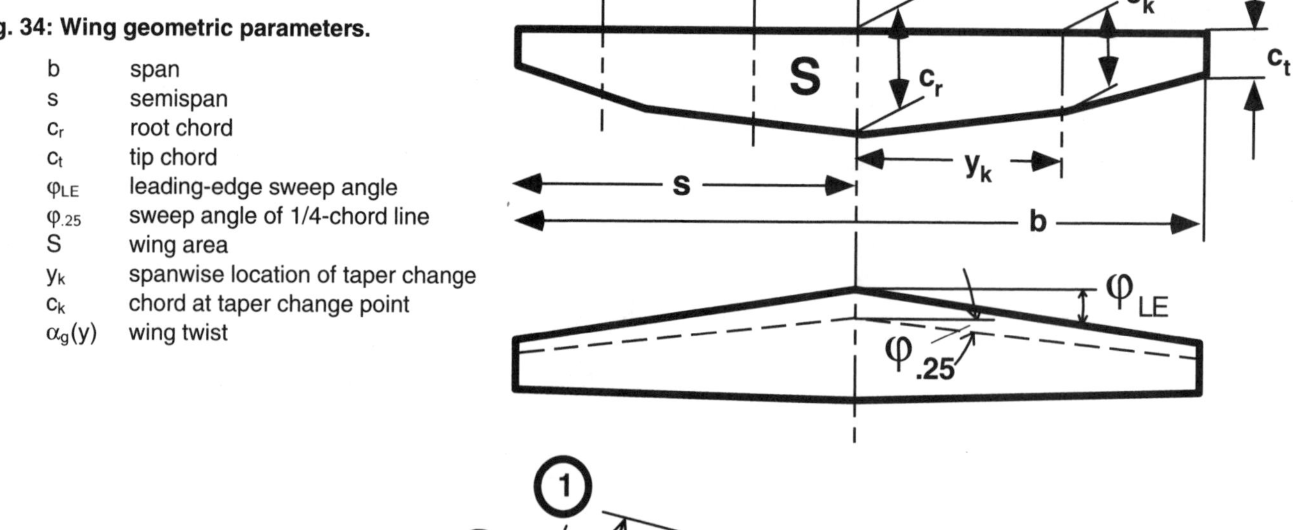

Fig. 34: Wing geometric parameters.

b	span
s	semispan
c_r	root chord
c_t	tip chord
φ_{LE}	leading-edge sweep angle
$\varphi_{.25}$	sweep angle of 1/4-chord line
S	wing area
y_k	spanwise location of taper change
c_k	chord at taper change point
$\alpha_g(y)$	wing twist

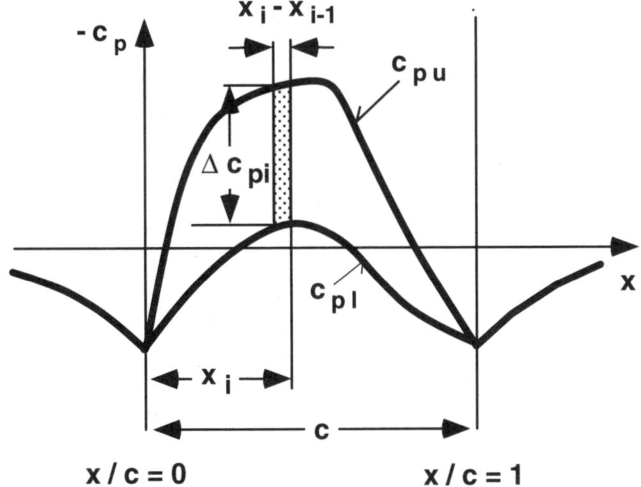

Fig. 35: Nondimensional pressure distribution over airfoil.

Δc_{p_i} pressure difference between upper and lower surface at x_i

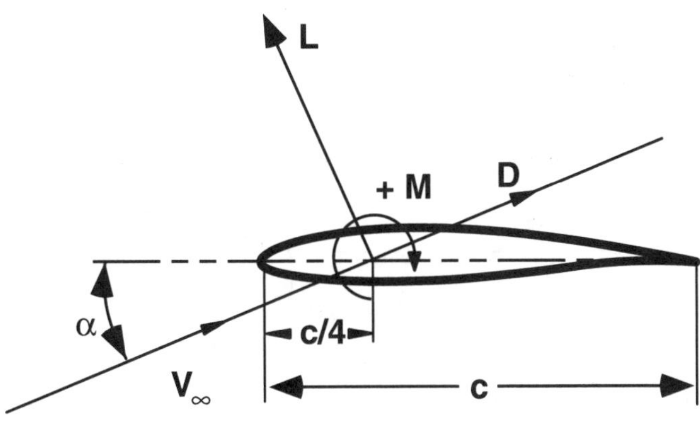

Fig. 36: Aerodynamic forces and moment on an airfoil.

L Lift D Drag M Pitching moment

the flow velocity together with a moment about a prescribed reference point. The three quantities are *lift*, *drag*, and *pitching moment*, respectively. The pitching moment is referenced to a specified point on the airfoil, usually at the 1/4-chord point, and the lift and drag may be thought of as being applied at this location (Fig. 36). If the pitching moment tends to increase the angle of attack of the wing, it is defined as positive, or "nose-up".

As with the pressure coefficients, the lift, drag, and pitching moment of a two-dimensional airfoil are expressed as nondimensional coefficients. The reference quantities are the free stream dynamic pressure, q_∞, and the chord c:

$c_l = l/q_\infty c$	Sectional Lift Coefficient	(28)
$c_d = d/q_\infty c$	Sectional Drag Coefficient	(29)
$c_m = m/q_\infty c^2$	Sectional Pitching Moment	(30)

These coefficients also define the local sectional loads, that is, the lift, drag, and pitching moment per unit span of the wing. For example, $c_l(y)$ denotes the lift distribution along the span of the wing.

Similar definitions apply to the global (total) forces acting on a wing:

$C_L = L/q_\infty S$	Lift Coefficient	(31)
$C_D = D/q_\infty S$	Drag Coefficient	(32)
$C_M = M/q_\infty Sc$	Pitching Moment	(33)

As will be discussed, a suitable reference chord c must be chosen for non-rectangular wings.

The sectional lift coefficient c_l is obtained by integrating the pressure difference between the upper and lower airfoil surfaces over the entire chord:

$$c_l = \int_0^1 \Delta c_p(x) d(x/c) \approx \sum_{i=1}^{n} \Delta c_{p_i}(x_i - x_{i-1})/c \qquad (34)$$

Experimental and theoretical aerodynamic characteristics are typically presented in a format such as that of Fig. 37 in order to highlight the variation of the aerodynamic coefficients with the angle of attack. Pitching moment data are presented as a function of lift coefficient in order to simplify stability analysis.

The figure shows that at moderate angles of attack, the lift and pitching moment coefficients exhibit a linear relationship with angle of attack. Above a certain value of angle of attack, these coefficients depart from their linear relationships due to flow separation. In the linear region, the lift and pitching moment coefficients are expressed as follows:

$$c_l = \frac{dc_l}{d\alpha}(\alpha - \alpha_0) \qquad (35)$$

$$c_m = \frac{dc_m}{dc_l} c_l + c_{m_0} \qquad (36)$$

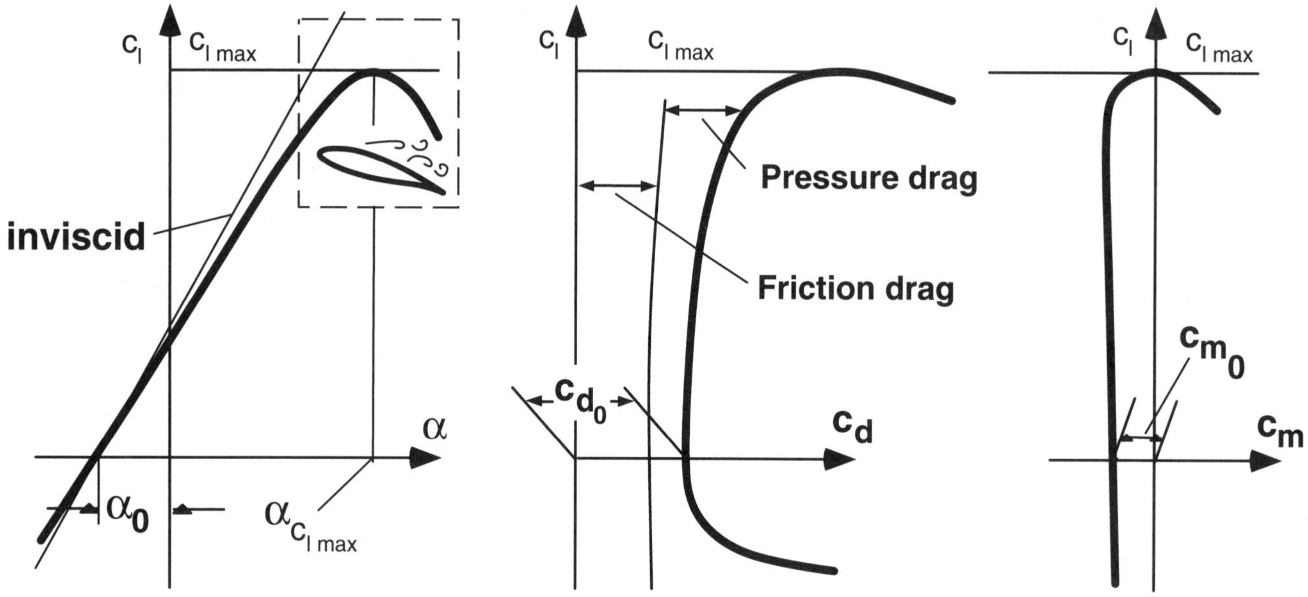

Fig. 37: Aerodynamic forces and moment on an airfoil as a function of angle of attack and lift coefficient

The linear representation of the lift and moment curves therefore depends on following four parameters:

$\frac{dc_l}{d\alpha}$	Lift-curve slope
$\frac{dc_m}{dc_l}$	Moment gradient
α_0	Zero-lift angle of attack
c_{m_0}	Zero-lift moment

The lift-curve slope determines how rapidly the lift coefficient increases with angle of attack. For this purpose the angle of attack is usually expressed in radians.

Zero-lift angle of attack and zero-lift moment are illustrated in Fig. 38. If the airfoil is symmetrical (and, in the case of a three-dimensional wing, if the wing is untwisted), both the zero-lift angle of attack and zero-lift moment are zero. If the airfoil is cambered (or the wing twisted), these parameters are generally non-zero (Fig. 38). An exception here would be a cambered airfoil with a reflexed mean line.

These four parameters in the linear airfoil model lend themselves to theoretical calculation since they are not strongly influenced by viscous effects. While the lift-curve slope and moment gradient are relatively independent of the actual airfoil shape, the zero-lift angle of attack and pitching moment are strong functions of the airfoil camber. As the camber increases, these quantities become increasingly negative in value.

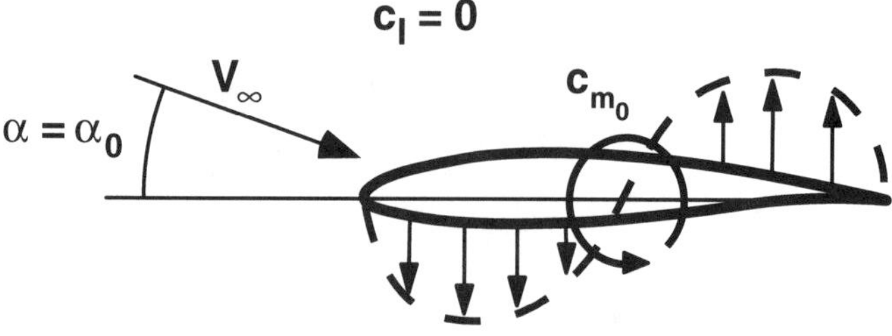

Fig. 38: Zero-lift moment on cambered airfoil.

Thin airfoils in inviscid flow have a theoretical lift-curve slope of 2π (6.28) per radian. In practice, viscous effects tend to reduce the lift-curve slope while thickness tends to increase it. For the relatively thick airfoils commonly used on sailplanes, the actual sectional value of the lift-curve slope is fairly close to this idealized value.

As will be shown, the lift-curve slope of a three-dimensional wing is also a function of its aspect ratio.

Due to the pronounced influence of turbulence, airfoil drag and maximum lift coefficient can only be measured in low-turbulence wind tunnels or in flight test.

Aerodynamic center and center of pressure

The pitching moment gradient dc_m/dc_l is affected by the choice of the moment reference point. This is evident in Fig. 39, which compares moment curves obtained using various reference points. The figure assumes that the lift acts at a fixed location (this is in fact the case for a symmetrical airfoil). If the airfoil leading edge is chosen as the moment reference point, a pitching moment will result, becoming increasingly negative (nose-down) as the lift increases. On the other hand, if the moment is calculated about the trailing edge, the pitching moment will become increasingly positive (nose-up) as the lift increases. Between the leading and trailing edges there exists a particular reference point about which the moment remains constant as the lift varies, that is, the moment gradient is zero. This reference point, the *aerodynamic center*, is of particular interest to the study of aircraft stability and control, and is defined by the following relationship:

$$\frac{dc_{m_{ac}}}{dc_l} = 0 \qquad (37)$$

Here the subscript "ac" indicates that the aerodynamic center is used as the reference point for the moments.

Since the pitching moment about the aerodynamic center does not vary with angle of attack, it is identical to the zero-lift moment. The aerodynamic forces on an airfoil may therefore be broken down into a constant pitching moment c_{m_0} about the aerodynamic center, and a lift applied at the aerodynamic center, varying with the angle of attack α (Fig. 40). This result applies only to the linear region of the lift and moment curves, that is, no flow separation. Slight variations may arise even in the linear operating range due to viscous effects.

Thin airfoil theory predicts that the aerodynamic center is located precisely at the airfoil 1/4-chord, that is,

$$\frac{x_{ac}}{c} = 0.25 \qquad (38)$$

$$c_{m_{ac}} = c_{m_{1/4}} \qquad (39)$$

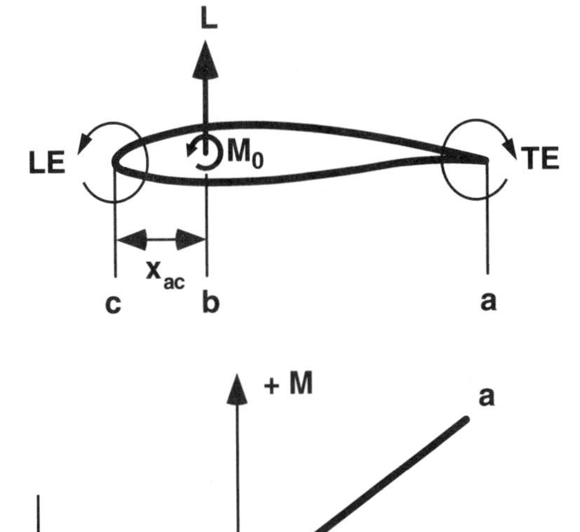

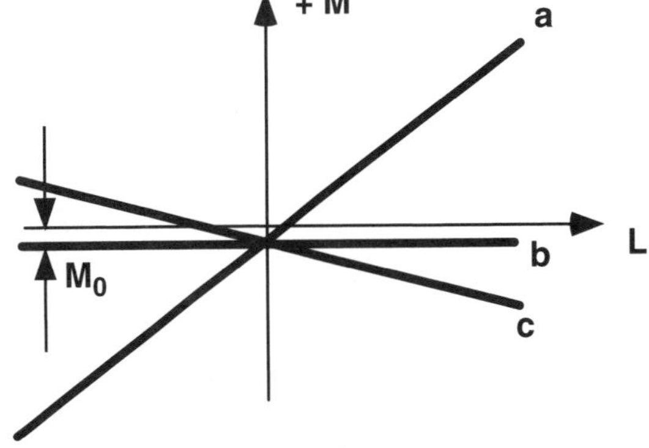

Fig. 39: Effect of moment reference point on pitching moment gradient.

Reference point at:
a) trailing edge (TE)
b) aerodynamic center
c) leading edge (LE)

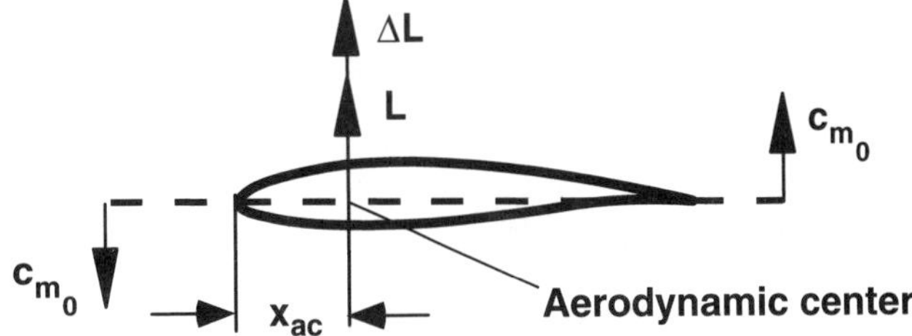

Fig. 40: Aerodynamic center and zero-lift moment.

Here the "1/4" subscript indicates that moments are measured about the airfoil 1/4-chord. In practice, the aerodynamic center may vary slightly from the 1/4-chord location, in which case the relationship becomes:

$$c_{m_{1/4}} = c_{m_0} + \left(\frac{1}{4} - \frac{x_{ac}}{c}\right) c_l \qquad (40)$$

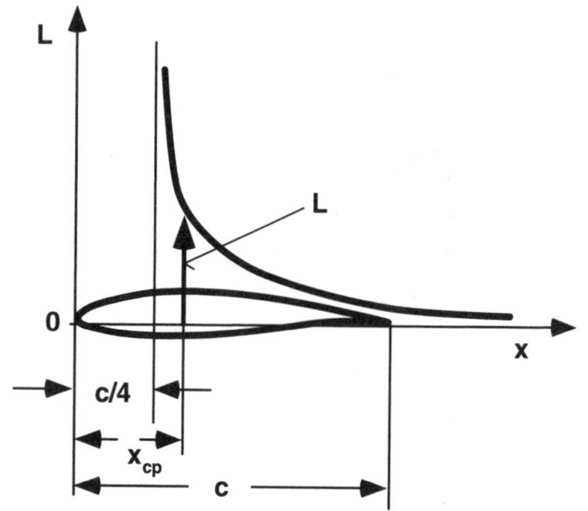

Fig. 41: Variation of center of pressure

Not to be confused with aerodynamic center is the *center of pressure*. This is the point on the airfoil at which the lift acts; that is, the reference point about which the pitching moment is zero. For symmetrical airfoils (c_{m_0} = 0), the center of pressure coincides with the aerodynamic center at the 1/4-chord. In the case of cambered airfoils ($c_{m_0} \neq 0$), the center of pressure varies with lift coefficient, migrating forward from infinity towards the 1/4-chord point as the lift coefficient is increased (Fig. 41). The center of pressure is rarely used in stability analyses; modern practice favors the aerodynamic center as a reference point for describing airfoil properties.

Geometric aerodynamic center and mean aerodynamic chord

Since the aerodynamic center is of great significance in stability analysis, it is useful to define an aerodynamic center for a three dimensional wing as well. In practice, viscous effects cause the aerodynamic center to vary from its theoretically determined position, and a distinction must be made between the geometric aerodynamic center and the experimentally measured aerodynamic center. The geometric aerodynamic center of a wing is analogous to the 1/4-chord point of an airfoil, and, accordingly, the geometric aerodynamic center of a rectangular wing lies along its 1/4-chord line.

If the wing is tapered or swept, an equivalent rectangular wing may be defined, having the same forces and moments of the original wing. The 1/4-chord line of the rectangular wing corresponds then to the aerodynamic center of the actual wing. The geometry of the equivalent wing is determined by imagining the 1/4-chord line of the original wing as a beam loaded with weights proportional to the local chord (Fig. 42). The geometric aerodynamic center is then the center of gravity of this structure. The chord of the equivalent rectangular wing, the *mean aerodynamic chord*, is based on the chord of the original wing:

$$\text{m.a.c.} = c_\mu = \frac{1}{S}\int_{-s}^{+s} c^2(y)dy \tag{41}$$

The mean aerodynamic chord is not to be confused with the average wing chord, defined as

$$c_{avg} = \frac{S}{b} \tag{42}$$

The lift on an individual wing half may be thought of as acting at a distance

$$y_s = \frac{2}{S}\int_0^s c(y)dy \tag{43}$$

from the plane of symmetry.

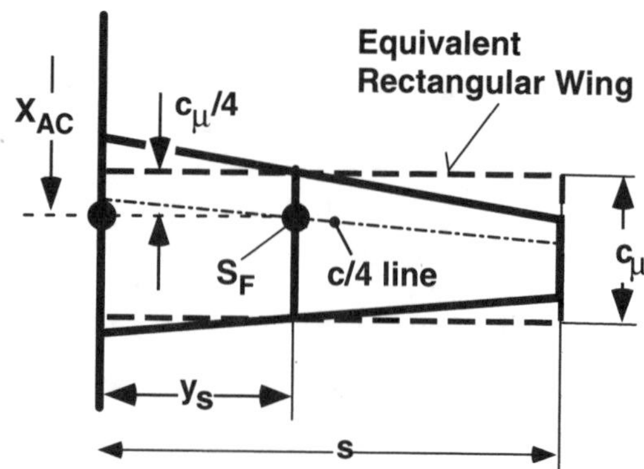

Fig. 42: Mean aerodynamic chord and equivalent rectangular wing.

c_μ	mean aerodynamic chord
x_{AC}	location of wing aerodynamic center
S_F	center of mass of c/4-line, assuming local mass loading proportional to local chord
s	wing semi-span

Airfoil Geometry and Aerodynamic Characteristics

Airfoil families and profile catalogs

The aerodynamic properties of an airfoil are functions of its geometry, angle of attack, Reynolds number, and surface quality. The large number of geometric parameters allows the definition of a virtually unlimited variety of airfoil shapes. Designers are often faced with the difficult task of selecting airfoils based on various operational requirements, and it is therefore useful to classify airfoils systematically according to certain characteristics. A number of *airfoil families* have been defined and their geometric and aerodynamic data tabulated in airfoil catalogs.

Over the years, several profile series have been of particular significance to sailplane designers. A few of these are now of only historical importance. After the cambered flat plate used by Lilienthal in his first glider, the first family of airfoils were the Joukowsky airfoils, defined and analyzed in closed form using conformal mapping. The Joukowsky airfoils are more of theoretical interest rather than practical significance. Relatively few were suitable for use in actual aircraft. The Göttingen series followed, of which the Gö 535 and Gö 549 were frequently used in early sailplanes.

The NACA four- and five-digit profile series are classified according to the parameters defining their geometry. Although seldom used in sailplanes, they find occasional application even today in powered aircraft. The NACA 6-series profiles are *laminar profiles*, designed specifically to allow the boundary layer to remain laminar over the forward part (30-60% chord) of the airfoil. These airfoils were quite well suited to the needs of sailplanes and found frequent application in early high-performance sailplanes. Experimental and theoretical aerodynamic data for these NACA profile series are found in a report by I. H. Abbott and A. E. von Doenhoff [1]. See also F. W. Riegels [191]. One of the earliest design methodologies for laminar flow airfoils was developed by W. Pfenninger [99].

Airfoils specifically intended for sailplanes were developed by R. Eppler [174, 175, 178–180] and F. X. Wortmann [163, 168, 196, 198–202]. These airfoils led to tremendous improvements in sailplane performance and quickly replaced virtually all earlier profiles. A large body of experimental data for these airfoils was obtained in the Stuttgart laminar wind tunnel [203] and published in the well-known Stuttgart Profile Catalog [168]. See also [164, 167].

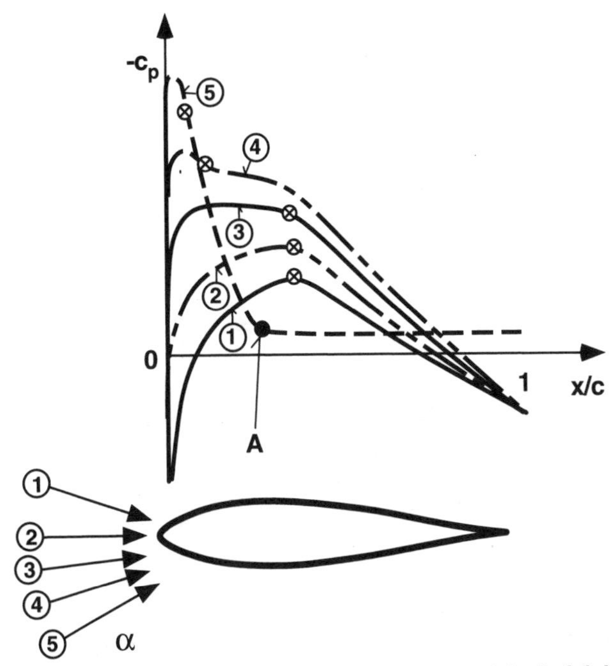

Fig. 43: Pressure distribution over a symmetrical airfoil at various angles of attack.

① - ⑤ upper surface pressure distribution at various angles of attack (see also Fig. 44)

② zero angle of attack, upper and lower surface pressure distribution

⊗ boundary-layer transition point

A separation point

Further laminar airfoils were developed by K. H. Horstmann and A. Quast [182, 193] at the German Aerospace Center (DLR, formerly DFVLR). The drag of these airfoils is minimized by inhibiting the formation of laminar separation bubbles either by use of pneumatic turbulators or application of a special flow-tripping "zig-zag" tape [72, 74, 170] or "bump tape" [165, 166, 183–185]. More recently, L. M. M. Boermans and his students at the Delft University of Technology have developed and tested several very low drag airfoils [74, 170–172]. Delft's low-turbulence wind tunnel proved a valuable asset in this research. Additional work by D. M. Somers and M. D. Maughmer in the USA include a profile specially developed for the World Class [169, 188, 195].

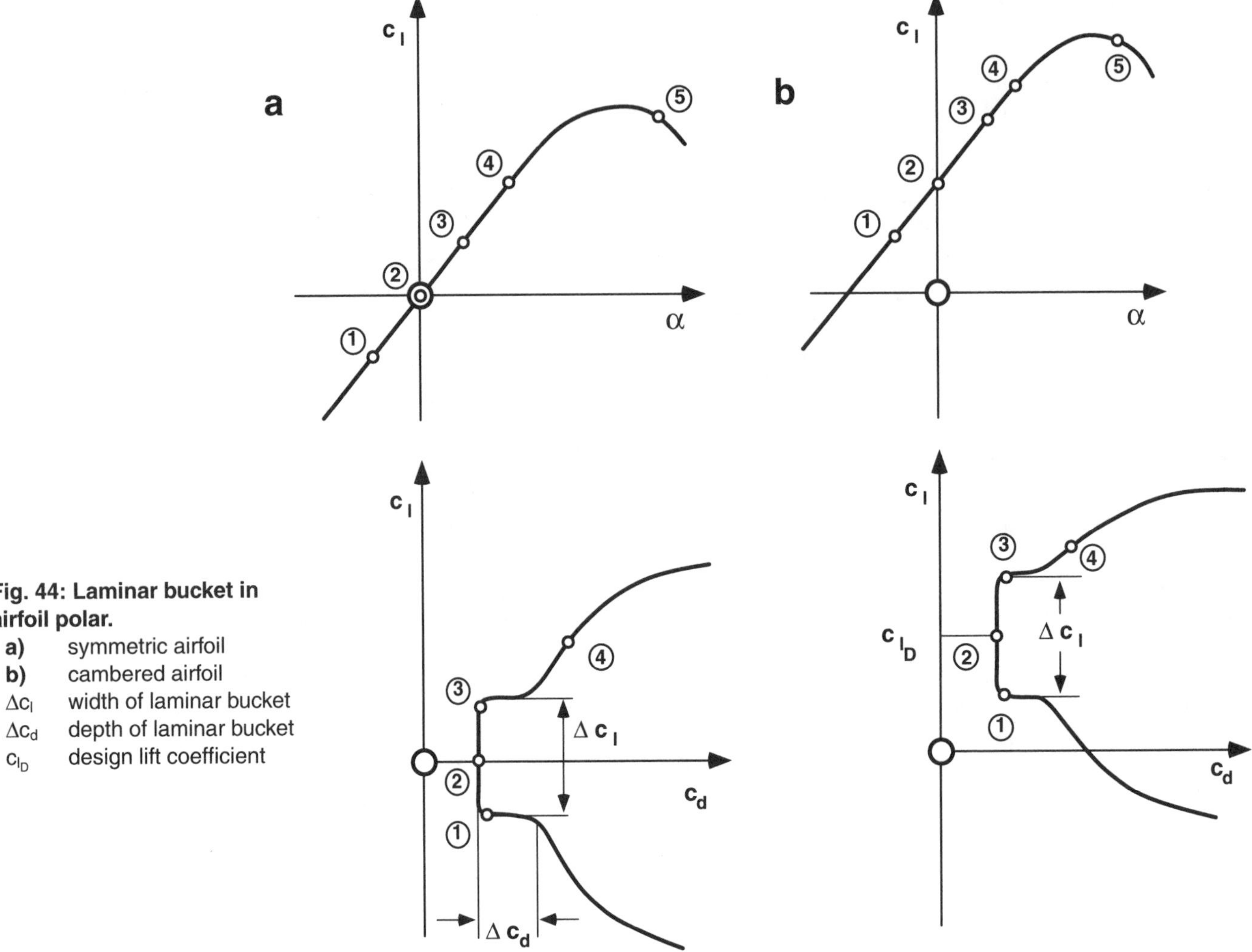

Fig. 44: Laminar bucket in airfoil polar.
a) symmetric airfoil
b) cambered airfoil
Δc_l width of laminar bucket
Δc_d depth of laminar bucket
c_{l_D} design lift coefficient

The laminar bucket

The boundary layer on an airfoil operating at typical sailplane Reynolds numbers remains laminar until slightly beyond the point of minimum static pressure. For small angles of attack, this minimum pressure point occurs near the location of maximum thickness. For this reason, laminar airfoils are characterized by a relatively aft location of the point of maximum thickness.

However, the pressure distribution also varies with the angle of attack. This may be examined in detail taking a symmetrical airfoil as an example. At $\alpha = 0$, a symmetrical airfoil generates identical pressure distributions over the upper and lower surface. If an angle of attack is introduced, additional pressure variations are superimposed on these basic $\alpha = 0$ distributions. The resultant force of this modified pressure distribution appears as lift at the 1/4-chord (aerodynamic center). This is related to the pressure distribution by observing that the pressure differential over the forward portion of the airfoil increases much more rapidly with angle of attack than the pressure differential on the aft portion of the airfoil. This distortion of the basic $\alpha = 0$ pressure distribution has an effect on the location of the point of minimum pressure and, in turn, the boundary-layer transition point.

This is made clearer by considering the effects of successive increases in angle of attack (Fig. 43). We consider only the upper surface as this is where the greatest pres-

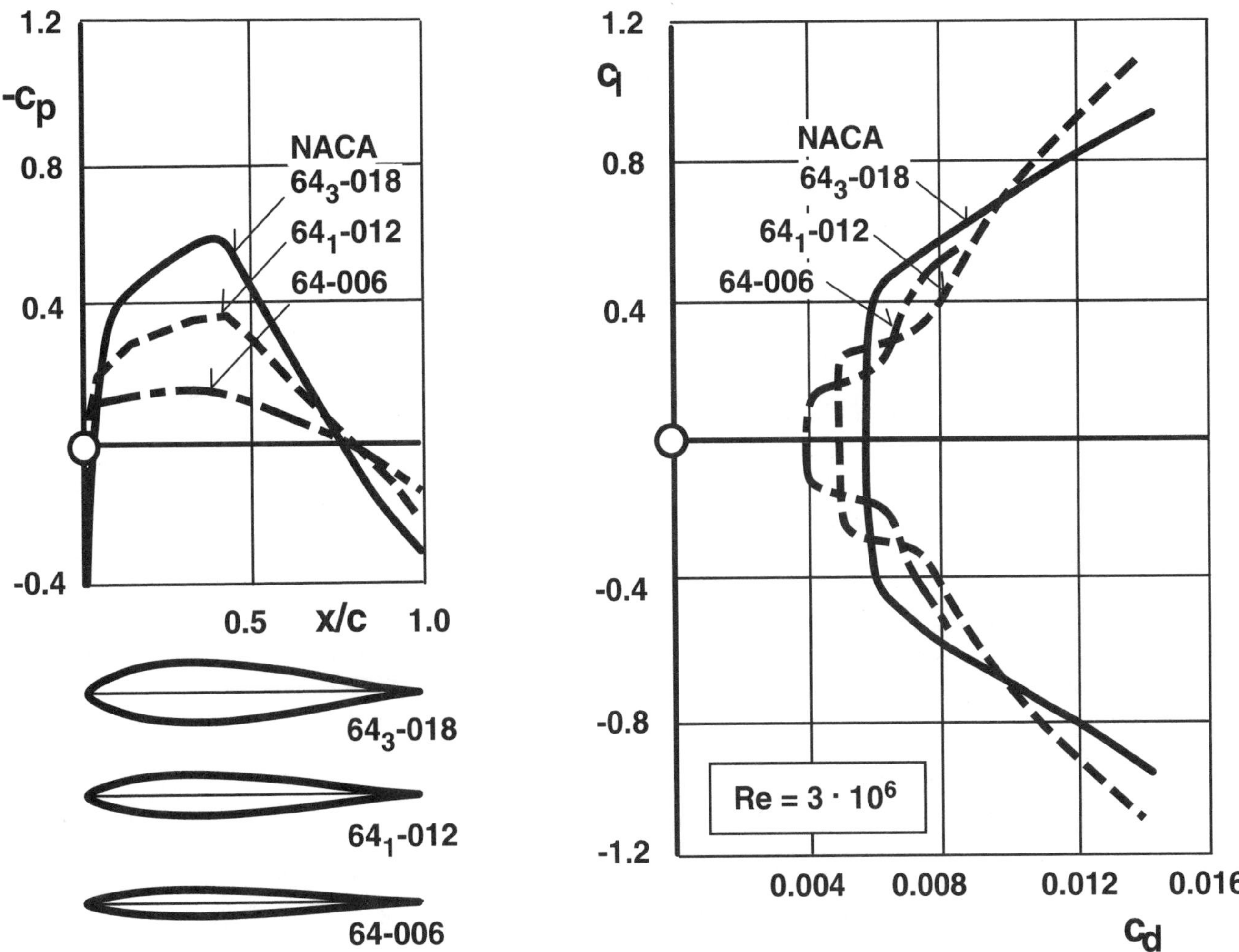

Fig. 45: Effect of airfoil thickness on pressure distribution and drag polar (from [1]).

sure variations due to angle of attack are expected. At negative angles of attack it is the lower surface that becomes critical.

Figure 43 shows the airfoil pressure distribution for four successively higher angles of attack. At small angles of attack the location of minimum pressure (and thus the boundary-layer transition point) is located relatively far aft on the airfoil. As the angle of attack is increased beyond a certain value, the minimum pressure and boundary-layer transition points shift relatively abruptly toward the airfoil leading edge. The portion of the boundary layer that remains laminar is shortened considerably, with a corresponding increase in drag. If the angle of attack is further increased, the pressure gradient becomes so steep that the flow separates, with a further increase in drag as well as a decrease in lift.

Both flow separation and the migration of the boundary-layer transition point are easily recognized in the airfoil drag polars (Fig. 44). While the drag at small angles of attack may be quite low, beyond a certain angle of attack a rapid increase may be observed due to the forward shift in the boundary-layer transition point. The region of reduced drag at low angles of attack is the *laminar drag bucket.* The width of the laminar bucket defines the c_l range over which

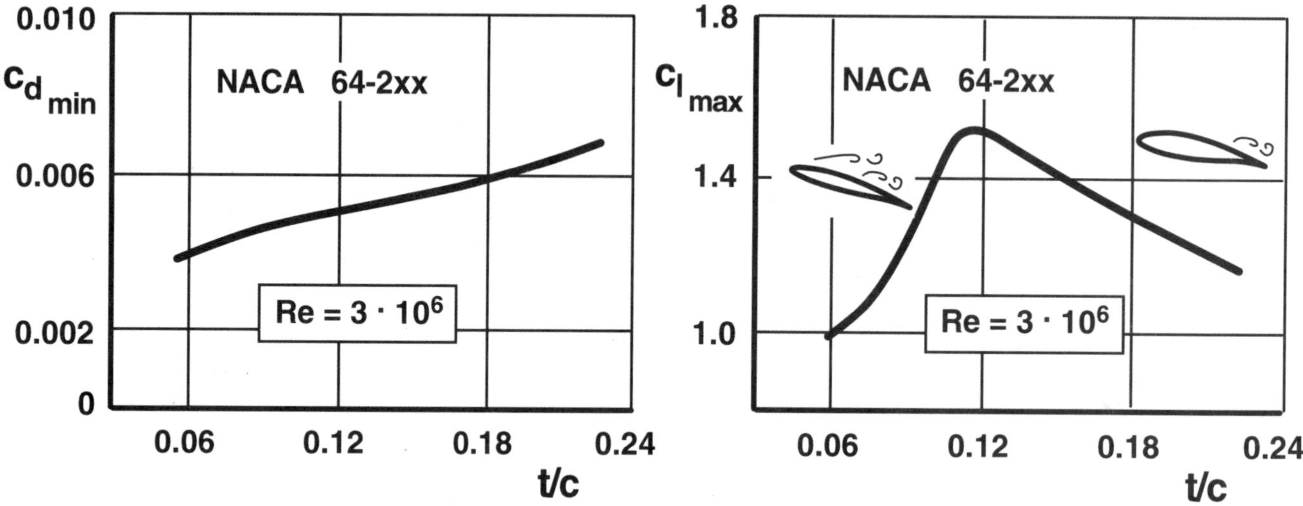

Fig. 46: Influence of airfoil thickness on minimum drag and maximum lift coefficient (from [1]).

reduced drag is present, and its depth is the drag reduction itself. Boundary-layer separation at high angles of attack occurs outside the laminar bucket and is recognizable as an additional increase in drag.

The same considerations apply to cambered airfoils. Here, however, the camber of the mean line generates an additional pressure variation that is superimposed over the basic pressure distribution. The laminar bucket shifts upward (that is, towards higher values c_l — Fig. 44). The value of c_l lying in the center of the laminar bucket is the *design lift coefficient*.

Influence of airfoil geometry

Airfoil selection is critical to sailplane design, and proper airfoil selection in turn necessitates a fundamental understanding of the effects of individual airfoil geometric parameters. These effects are illustrated with the example of the NACA 6-series airfoils, at one time frequently used in high performance sailplanes.

The designation numbers of the 6-series airfoils contain some useful information regarding their aerodynamic characteristics. Take for example the NACA 65_2-415. The first digit denotes the 6-series. The next digit indicates the location (in tenths of a chord) of the lowest static pressure for the basic symmetrical section at zero lift ($5 \rightarrow x_d = 0.50c$). This is usually near the point of maximum airfoil thickness. The subscript is half the width of the laminar bucket ($2 \rightarrow \Delta c_l = 0.4$). The first digit following the hyphen defines the design lift coefficient ($4 \rightarrow C_{l_d} = 0.4$) and the final two digits provide the airfoil thickness ($15 \rightarrow d = 0.15c$). This numbering scheme allows the effects of various airfoil design parameters to be examined using data from airfoil catalogs such as [1].

The effects of varying the airfoil thickness are most apparent in a symmetrical airfoil. The upper and lower surface pressure distributions on a symmetrical airfoil at zero angle of attack are identical. If the thickness is varied while holding the basic form constant, the pressure distribution varies in proportion to the thickness (Fig. 45). The location of the point of minimum pressure remains unchanged. The most important effect of varying the thickness is observed in the drag polar. Thick airfoils exhibit relatively wide, shallow laminar drag buckets. As the airfoil is made thinner, the minimum drag coefficient is reduced, while the range of c_l for reduced drag — that is, the laminar drag bucket — becomes narrower.

Figure 46 shows the variation in minimum drag and maximum lift coefficient directly as a function of airfoil thickness. Steep pressure gradients observed over the aft portions of the thicker airfoils increase the likelihood of boundary-layer separation, particularly at high angles of attack. This is why the maximum lift coefficient diminishes with increas-

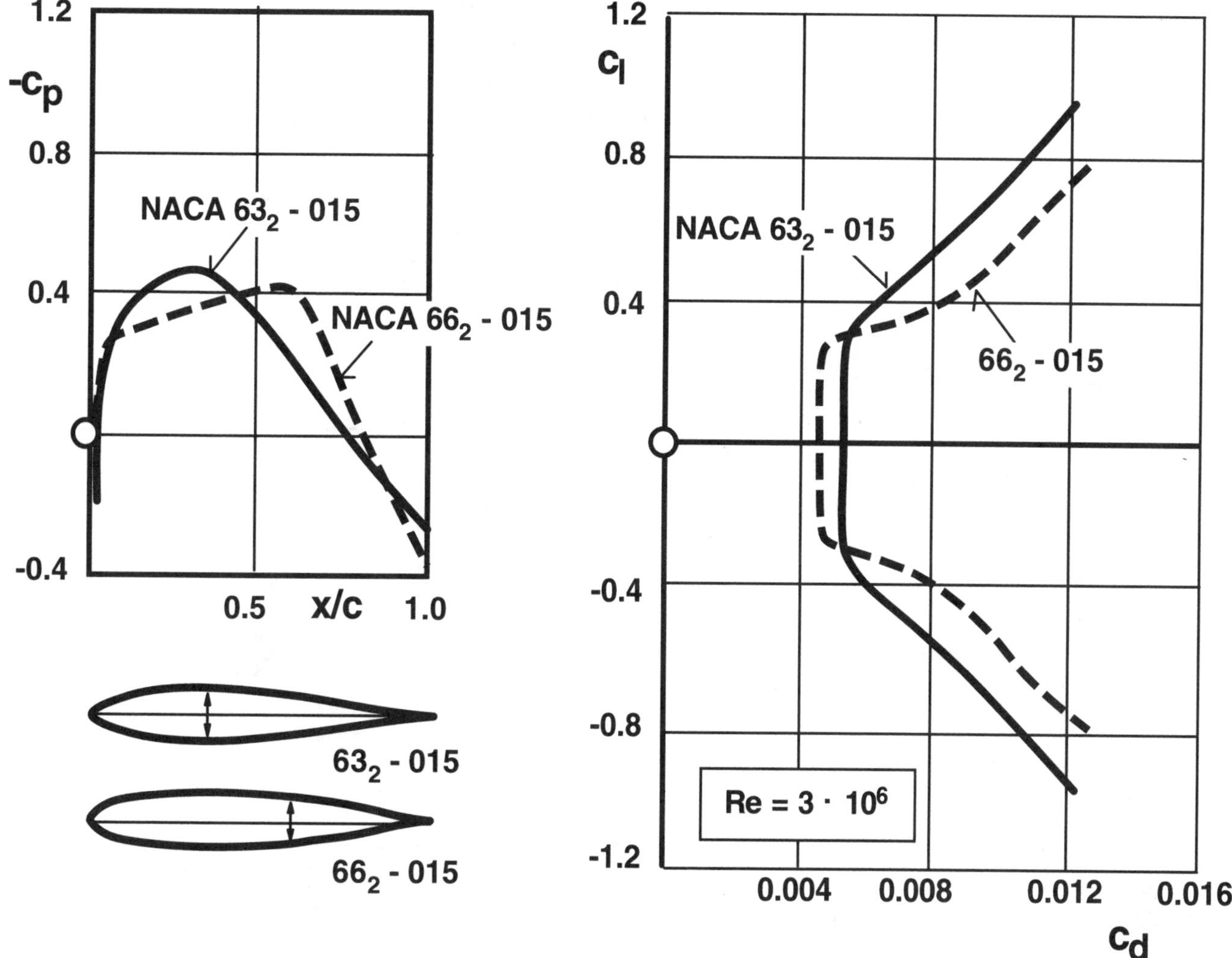

Fig. 47: Effect of location of point of maximum thickness on airfoil performance (from [1]).

ing airfoil thickness (Fig. 46). Below around 12% thickness the maximum lift coefficient also decreases since the leading edge becomes sharper and the flow tends to separate at this location. From a practical point of view, this phenomenon places a lower limit on the thickness of airfoils used in horizontal and vertical stabilizers.

As discussed, the chordwise location of the point of maximum thickness determines the location of the minimum static pressure, and in turn influences the boundary-layer transition point (Fig. 47). Typically, the point of maximum thickness lies between 30% and 50% of the airfoil chord (NACA 63, 64, and 65-series). If the point of maximum thickness is shifted further aft (as with, for example, the NACA 66-series), the adverse pressure gradient in the aft portion of the airfoil becomes too steep, leading to premature separation.

Although the position of maximum thickness has little influence on the width of the laminar bucket, it has a considerable effect on its depth. Shifting the position of maximum thickness aft may however have a detrimental effect outside the laminar bucket due to increased adverse pressure gradients and flow separation.

If the airfoil is cambered, the resulting asymmetry gives rise to differences in pressure distribution over the upper

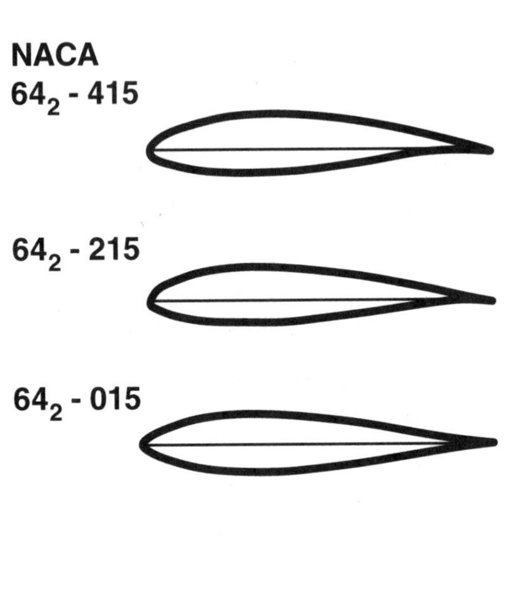

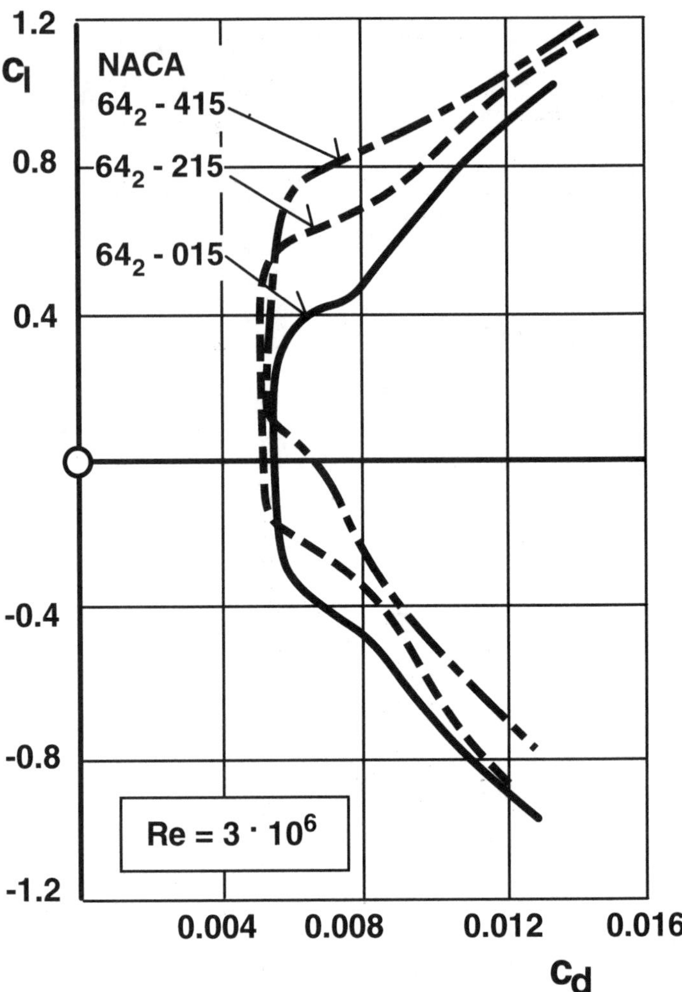

Fig. 48: Effect of camber on drag polar [1].

and lower surface, even at zero angle of attack. On the upper surface, the pressure shifts upward (in the $-c_p$ direction) and on the lower surface, downward (in the $+c_p$ direction). The effect is proportional to the maximum camber. Camber is usually introduced in the NACA 6-series airfoils using a mean line that produces a uniform increase in velocity distribution on the upper surface and a uniform decrease on the lower surface (the "a = 1.0" mean line). The velocity gradients, which are of primary importance to the development of the boundary layer, do not change. Consequently, although the center of the drag bucket shifts to a new design lift coefficient, the width and depth of the bucket remain essentially unchanged (Fig. 48). As the maximum camber increases, the laminar bucket shifts in the direction of increased lift coefficient. Unlike the airfoil thickness and position of maximum thickness, the degree of camber and the chordwise position of maximum camber have a very strong influence on the pitching moment. Figure 49 shows an example of the increase in zero-lift angle, zero-lift moment, and maximum lift coefficient with increasing camber.

As the name suggests, a camber-changing flap has an effect similar to that of airfoil camber (Fig. 49). Camber-changing flaps allow the aerodynamic characteristics of the airfoil to be changed in flight. Specifically, the laminar bucket may be shifted as required by repositioning the flaps. Since camber-changing flaps introduce camber at a relatively aft location on the airfoil, they have an especially

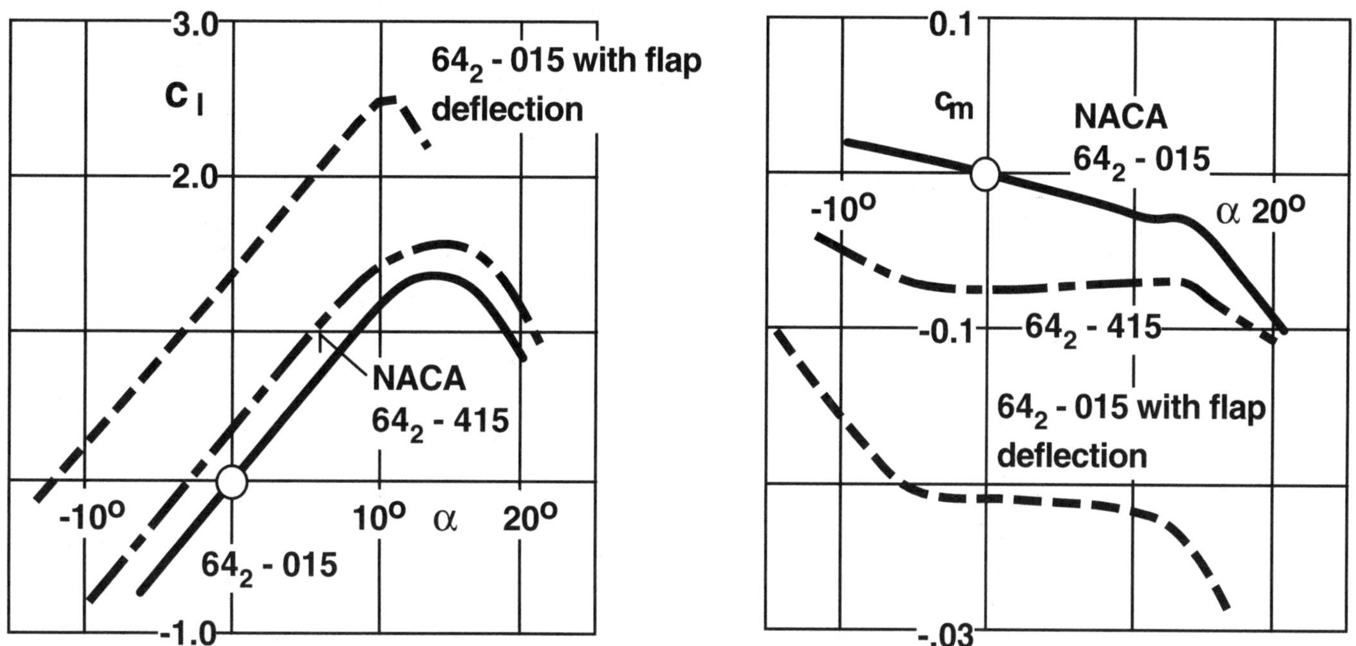

Fig. 49: Influence of camber and flap deflection on lift and pitching moment characteristics.

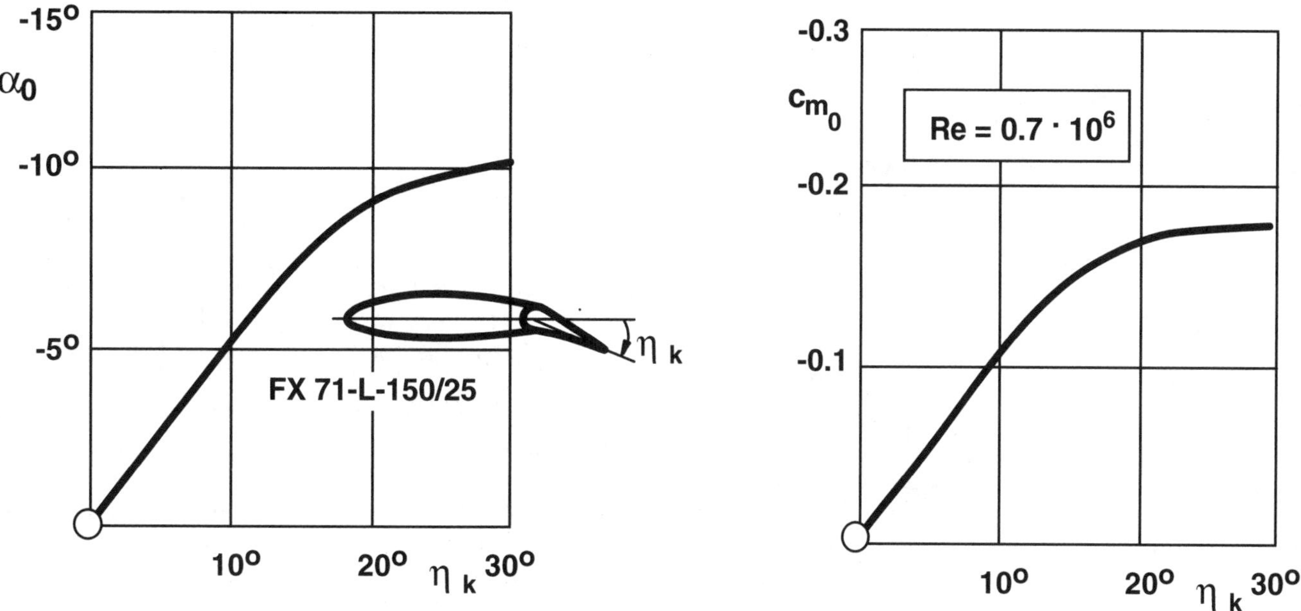

Fig. 50: Influence of flap deflection on zero-lift angle and zero-lift pitching moment.

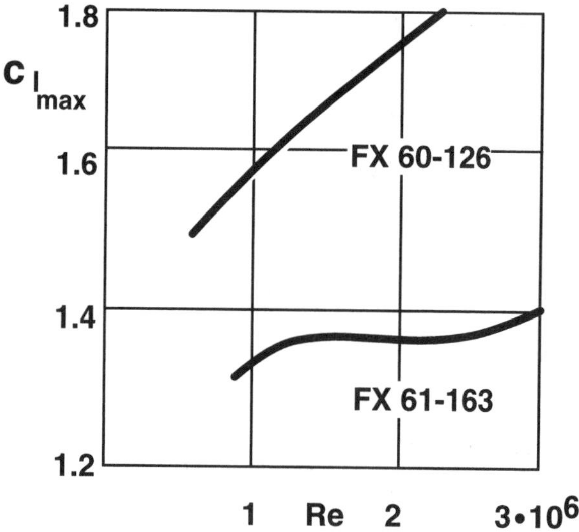

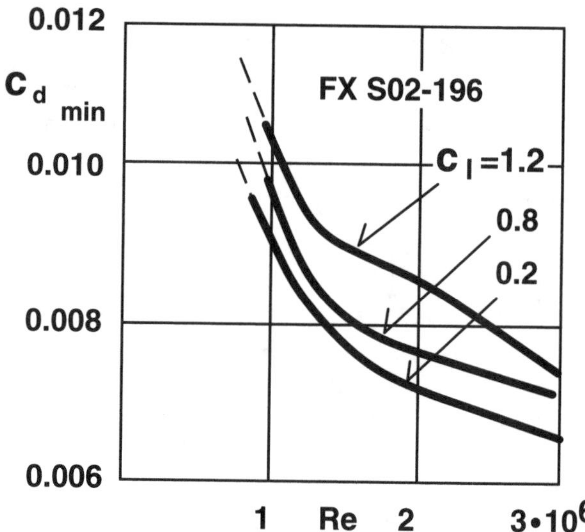

Fig. 51: Variation of maximum lift coefficient and minimum drag with Reynolds number.

strong effect on the zero-lift pitching moment (Fig. 50).

Reynolds number and surface quality

As discussed, Reynolds number and surface quality have a considerable effect on the development of the boundary layer. In practical terms, the effects are seen mainly in the lift-curve slope, minimum drag, and maximum lift coefficient. At Reynolds numbers typical of sailplanes, airfoil performance generally diminishes with decreasing Reynolds number. In particular, the increased tendency to form laminar separation bubbles and the overall increase in viscous losses leads to a reduction in the lift curve slope, the maximum lift coefficient, and an increase in minimum drag (Fig. 51).

The influence of surface quality is of particular interest in view of the high likelihood of insect impact during flight as well as the possibility of operating in rain [171, 197, 235]. In both cases the boundary layer becomes turbulent near the airfoil leading edge. In turn, the minimum drag coefficient increases, depending on airfoil thickness, to a value ranging from 0.008 to 0.012. At higher lift coefficients, additional drag penalties arise due to flow separation near the trailing edge. An increase in surface roughness leads to greater energy losses in the boundary layer, leaving it less able to overcome the adverse pressure gradients and remain attached in the aft portion of the airfoil.

Drag penalties due to insect contamination appear to be less severe for thin airfoils with sharp leading edges than for thick airfoils with large leading-edge radii.

Wing Planform and Lift Distribution

Elliptical wings

For the high aspect ratio wings typically found on sailplanes, the chordwise pressure distribution at each spanwise location depends only on the airfoil geometry at that location and the corresponding effective angle of attack. Planform and twist affect only the spanwise lift distribution. The lift distribution has an important effect on

- load assumptions for the structural analysis,
- induced drag,
- wing/fuselage and wing/empennage interference effects, and
- stall characteristics

A special case in wing theory is the untwisted elliptical planform wing. Prandtl's lifting-line theory predicts that this wing will generate an elliptical spanwise circulation and

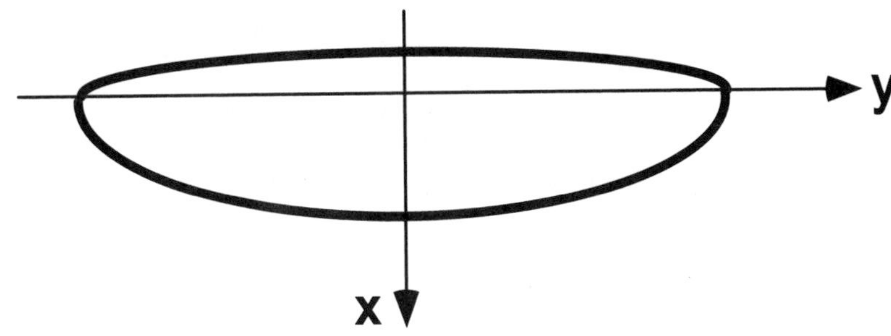

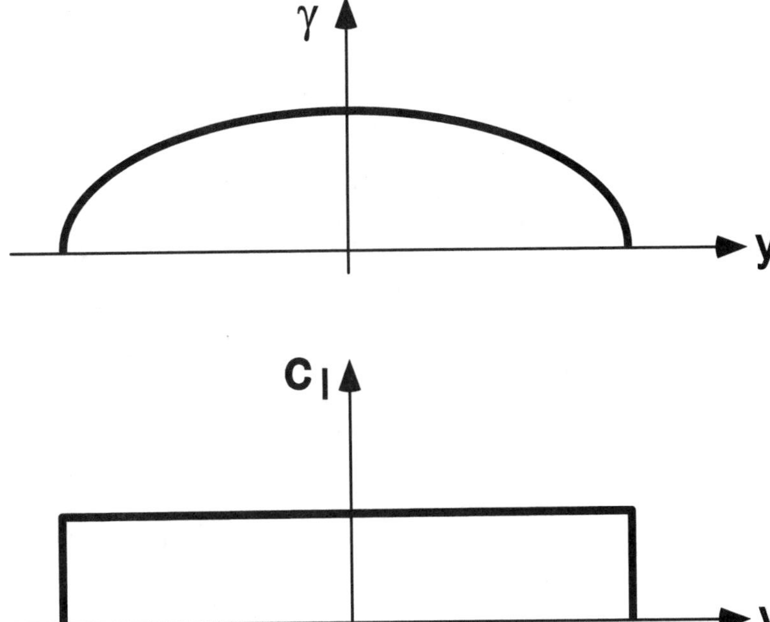

Fig. 52: Untwisted elliptical wing.

- planform
- nondimensional circulation distribution $\gamma(y) = \Gamma(y)/bV$
- sectional lift coefficient $c_l(y)$

lift distribution ($\Gamma(y)$,$L(y)$), regardless of angle attack. A central result of this theory is that the elliptical distribution is precisely the optimum distribution for minimum induced drag. Another interesting property of an untwisted elliptical wing is that the local induced angle of attack α_i and local lift coefficient c_l remain constant over the entire span of the wing (Fig. 52).

The total wing lift is obtained by summing the local products of the lift coefficient and chord:

$$C_L = A\!\!R \sum_{i=1}^{n} \frac{c_{l_i} c_i}{2b} \frac{\Delta y_i}{s} = A\!\!R \int_0^1 \frac{c_l(y)c(y)}{2b} d(\frac{y}{s}) \qquad (44)$$

According to lifting-line theory, the induced angle of attack and induced drag coefficient of an elliptical untwisted wing are functions of lift coefficient and aspect ratio:

$$\alpha_i = \frac{C_L}{\pi A\!\!R} \qquad (45)$$

$$C_{D_i} = \frac{{C_L}^2}{\pi A\!\!R} \qquad (46)$$

Fig. 53 presents the induced drag of elliptical wings as a function of aspect ratio. The induced drag of a wing with a non-elliptical lift distribution is greater than that of an elliptical wing by a factor k:

$$C_{D_i} = k\frac{{C_L}^2}{\pi A\!\!R} \qquad (47)$$

The factor k depends on lift coefficient and typically lies a few percent above 1.0.

The total aircraft drag reflects additional contributions (profile drag, parasite drag) having terms proportional the C_L^2. Sometimes these terms are combined with the induced drag and written as

$$\frac{C_L^2}{\pi \mathcal{R} e} \tag{48}$$

Here, e is the *Oswald span efficiency factor.* With the total aircraft drag written in its customary form

$$C_D = C_{D_0} + \frac{C_L^2}{\pi \mathcal{R} e} \tag{49}$$

the span efficiency factor e accounts for these additional C_L^2 terms. The factor k in Eq. 47, on the other hand, reflects induced drag only.

According to Prandtl's lifting-line theory, the lift-curve slope of an elliptical wing depends only on its aspect ratio (Fig. 54):

$$\frac{dC_L}{d\alpha_g} = \frac{2\pi \mathcal{R}}{\mathcal{R} + 2} \tag{50}$$

As the aspect ratio is increased, the lift-curve slope gradually approaches the value corresponding to a two-dimensional airfoil. The lift-curve slope falls off sharply at the lower aspect ratios. Lifting-line theory is based on the assumption that the wing span is large compared to its chord. Below an aspect ratio of approximately $\mathcal{R} = 5$, this condition is no longer satisfied and lifting-line theory loses its validity (Fig. 54).

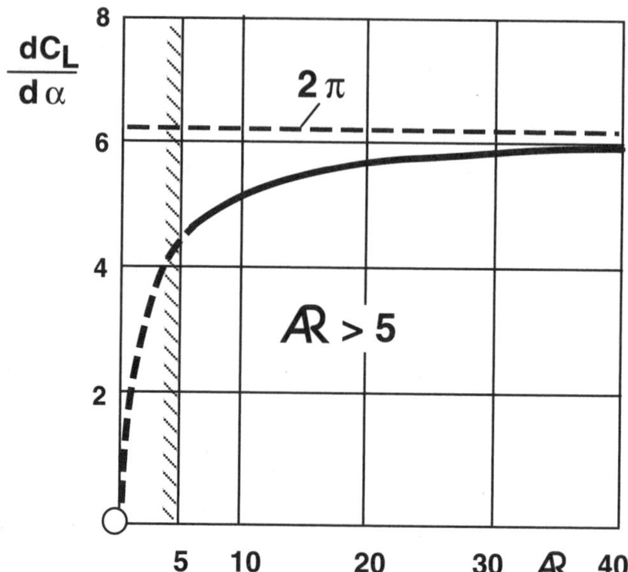

Fig. 54: Effect of aspect ratio on lift-curve slope of elliptical wing per Prandtl lifting-line theory for $\mathcal{R} > 5$.

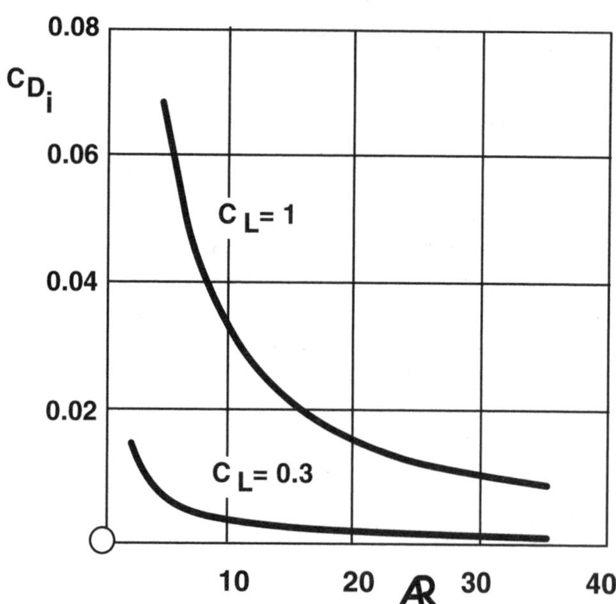

Fig. 53: Induced drag C_{D_i} of an elliptical wing as a function of aspect ratio.

Basic lift distribution and angle of attack

Even if the total wing lift is zero, a non-zero spanwise lift distribution may be present, particularly if the wing is twisted. In this case, regions of both positive and negative lift are present that, when integrated, yield zero net lift. This is the *basic lift distribution*, occurring at the zero-lift angle (Fig. 55). If the wing angle of attack α_g is varied, an *additional lift distribution* is superimposed over the basic lift distribution. The additional lift is proportional to the angle of attack $\alpha_g - \alpha_0$. Summing the basic and additional contributions yields the net lift distribution.

The additional lift is a function of the aspect ratio, the taper ratio, and wing planform. In addition to these basic parameters, the basic lift depends on the spanwise airfoil distribution, wing twist, and, if camber changing flaps are used, spanwise distribution of flap/airfoil deflections.

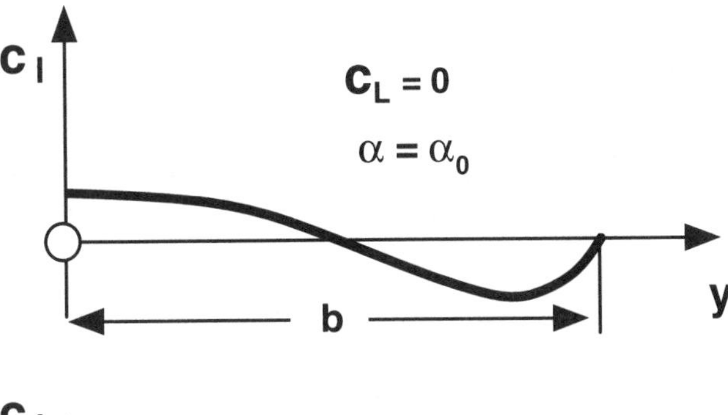

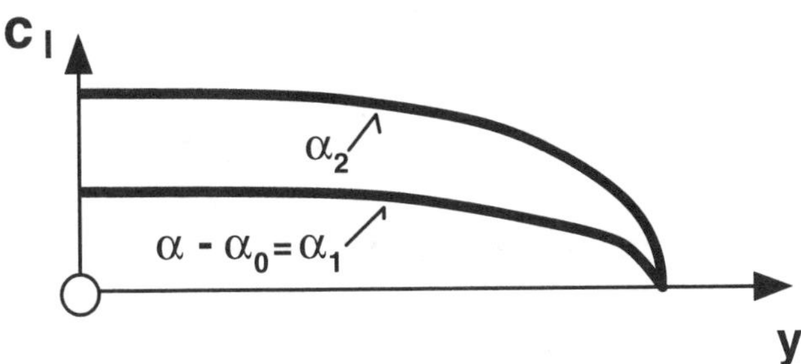

Fig. 55: Lift distribution on twisted wing.

- basic lift distribution for $\alpha = \alpha_0$
- additional lift due to angle of attack $\alpha - \alpha_0$

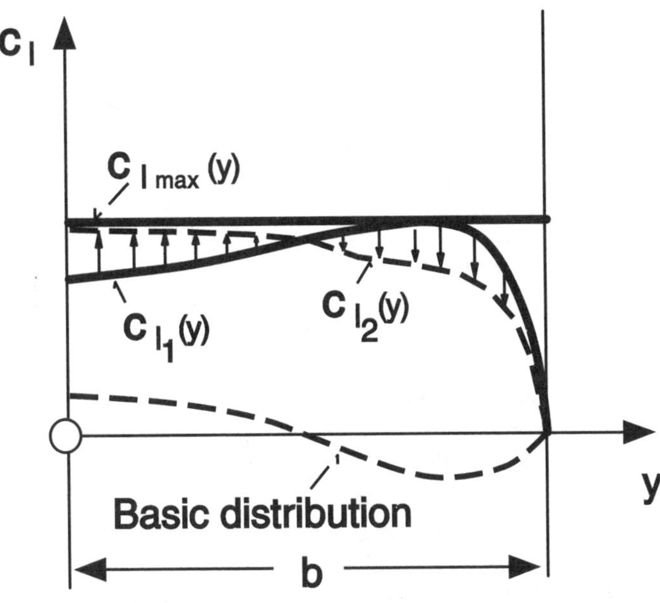

Fig. 56: Improved stall characteristics through superposition of an appropriate basic lift distribution.

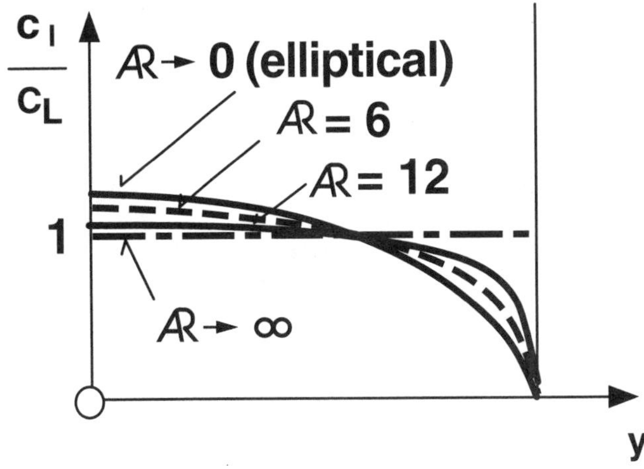

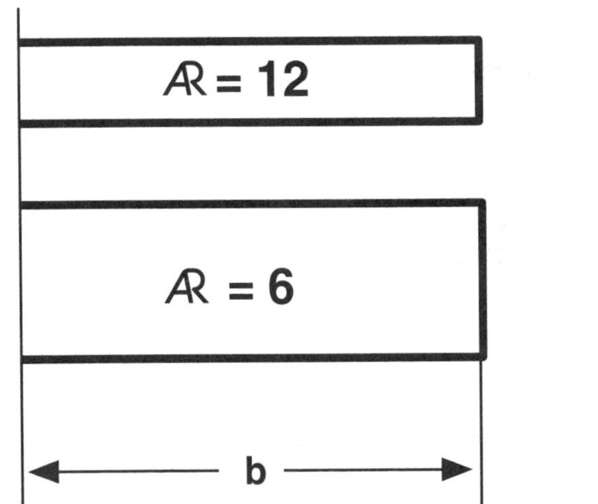

Fig. 57: Effect of aspect ratio on lift distribution of a rectangular wing.

It is almost always possible to tailor the lift distribution at a given lift coefficient through appropriate combination of these two contributions. For example, even if the planform is non-elliptical, wing twist may be used to achieve an elliptical lift distribution and thereby minimize the induced drag. This, however, is possible only at a single value of the lift coefficient C_L — at all other operating conditions the lift distribution will deviate from the elliptical.

The twist distribution also plays an important role in determining the stall characteristics. The spanwise location at which the stalling angle of attack is first exceeded can be determined by comparing the local lift coefficient $c_l(y)$

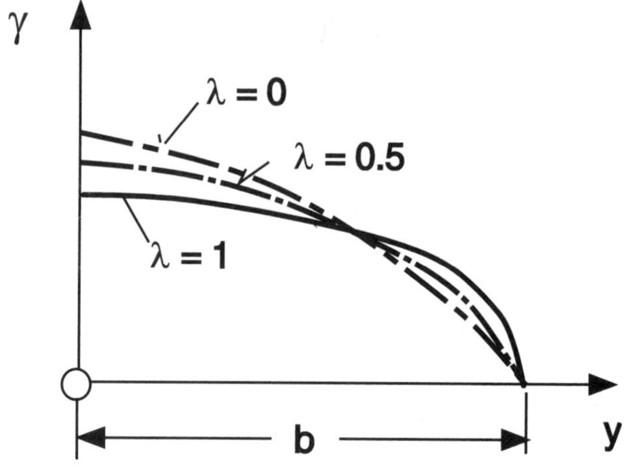

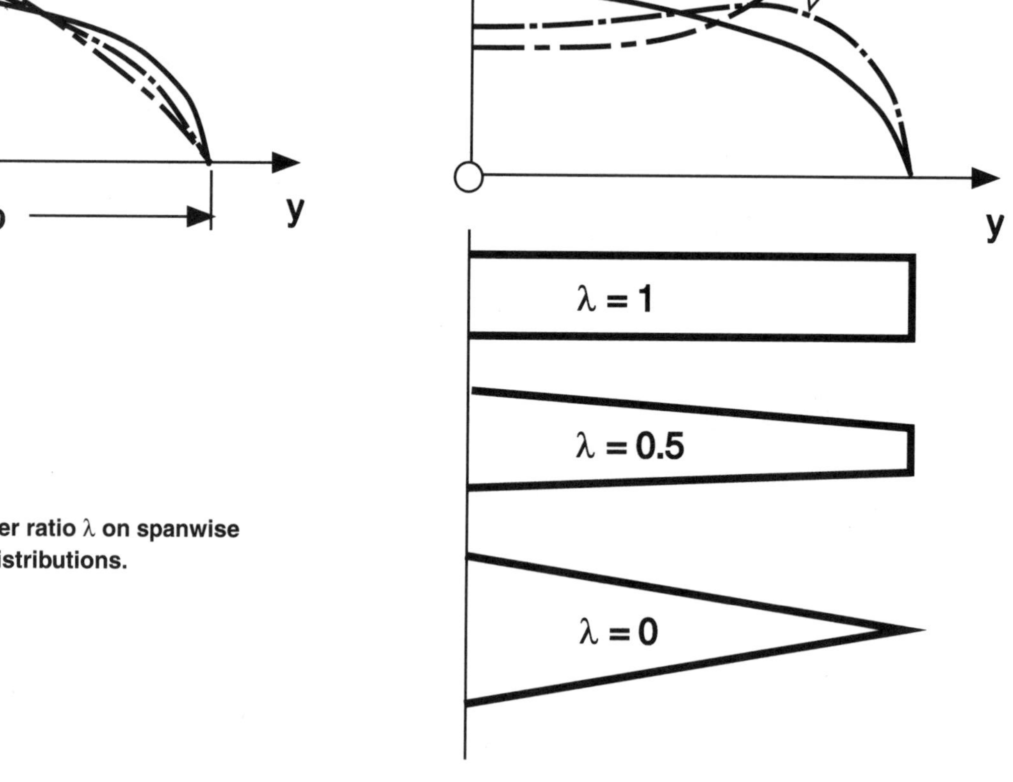

Fig. 58: Effect of taper ratio λ on spanwise circulation and lift distributions.

with the local maximum lift coefficient $c_{l_{max}}(y)$. For reasons that will be discussed in a later chapter, it is desirable for the stall to initiate near the wing root if possible, and in any event away from the tip. Unfavorable stall characteristics may often be improved by modifying the lift distribution using wing twist (Fig. 56).

Aspect ratio and wing taper

Aspect ratio and wing taper have a pronounced effect on circulation and lift distribution. Fig. 57 shows the effect of aspect ratio by comparing the lift distributions for rectangular wings of various aspect ratios. The limiting cases are $AR \rightarrow \infty$ (two-dimensional wing) and $AR \rightarrow 0$. In the first case, the circulation is constant along the wing, while in the latter case the lift distribution gradually becomes elliptical as the aspect ratio is reduced.

Figure 58 shows the influence of taper on lift distribution. The sharp increase in lift coefficient observed near the tip of the highly tapered wing indicates that the stall will develop first in this region. This is why highly tapered wings are often associated with poor stall characteristics. Rectangular and moderately tapered wings present less of a problem in this respect.

Fig. 59: Balance of forces in trimmed flight.

(a) airplane
(b) sailplane
L lift
D drag
W weight
T thrust
F resultant airload
V flight velocity
γ glide angle
V_S $= V \sin\gamma$

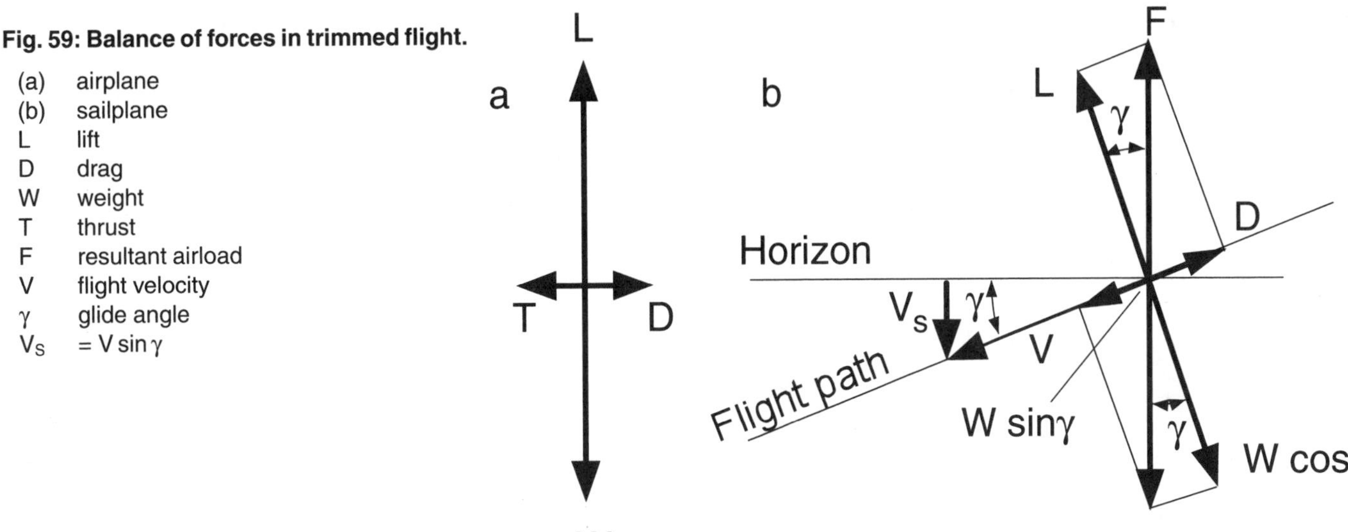

Performance and Flying Qualities

Performance

Airspeed and rate of sink

The aerodynamic forces acting on the sailplane may be resolved into components perpendicular to the path of flight (lift) and parallel to the path of flight (drag):

$$L = C_L \frac{\rho}{2} V^2 S \qquad (51)$$

$$D = C_D \frac{\rho}{2} V^2 S \qquad (52)$$

In order to maintain steady level flight in still air, the lift must equal the aircraft's weight, and a thrust T must be provided to balance out the drag. Since the sailplane is by definition unpowered, the thrust T = 0 and a steady trim condition is possible only in a descending glide. As with the aerodynamic forces, the weight of a gliding sailplane is resolved into components perpendicular and parallel to the path of flight. In a trimmed glide at constant airspeed, the flight path angle γ is the angle that provides equilibrium among the individual forces (Fig. 59):

$$L = W \cos\gamma \qquad (53)$$

$$D = W \sin\gamma \qquad (54)$$

The flight path angle in a steady state glide is the *glide angle*. From Fig. 59 it follows that the tangent of the glide angle is the ratio of the lift to the drag:

$$\tan\gamma = \frac{D}{L} = \frac{C_D}{C_L} \qquad (55)$$

The lift-to-drag ratio is also known as the *glide ratio*:

$$L/D = \frac{C_L}{C_D} = \frac{1}{\tan\gamma} \qquad (56)$$

Most sailplanes have maximum glide ratios between 20 and 50. The corresponding glide angles lie between approximately 3° and 1°.

The trim airspeed in a steady glide is obtained by introducing the expression for the lift L (Eq. 51) in the equilibrium equation, Eq. 53:

$$W \cos\gamma = C_L \frac{\rho}{2} V^2 S \qquad (57)$$

Sailplane glide ratios are usually so large, and the flight path angles γ so small, that one may assume $\cos\gamma = 1$ with

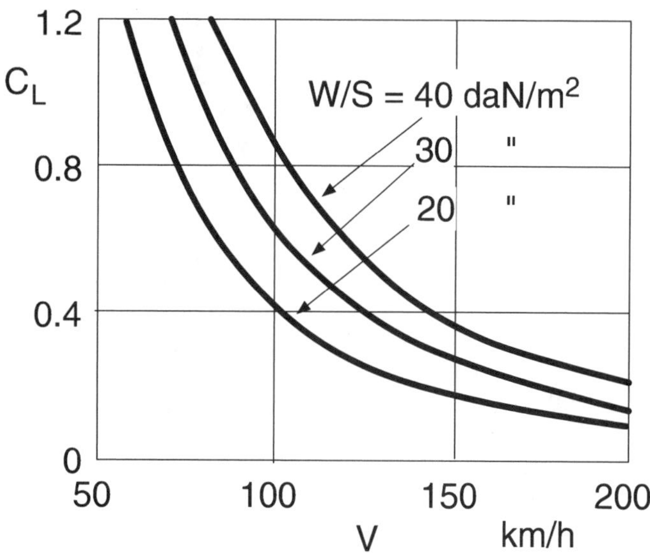

Fig. 60: Relationship between airspeed V and lift coefficient C_L for various wing loadings W/S.

negligible error. Introducing this small angle assumption into Eq. 57 leads to:

$$V = \sqrt{\frac{2}{\rho}\frac{W}{S}\frac{1}{C_L}} \tag{58}$$

This equation, which relates the airspeed to the wing loading W/S and the lift coefficient C_L, is of fundamental importance to sailplane performance analysis.

Figure 60 presents the relationship between airspeed and lift coefficient for a range of wing loadings. Low lift coefficients are associated with high airspeeds, and high lift coefficients with low airspeed. The figure also shows that:

1. at high speed, a small change in lift coefficient corresponds to a large change in airspeed, and
2. at low speed, a large change in lift coefficient corresponds to a small change in airspeed.

These relationships should be kept in mind when selecting a wing airfoil based on its $c_{l_{max}}$ and the characteristics of its laminar drag bucket.

Since the lift coefficient is limited due to boundary-layer separation, for a given wing loading there is a minimum flight velocity below which the sailplane will no longer be able to maintain steady gliding flight:

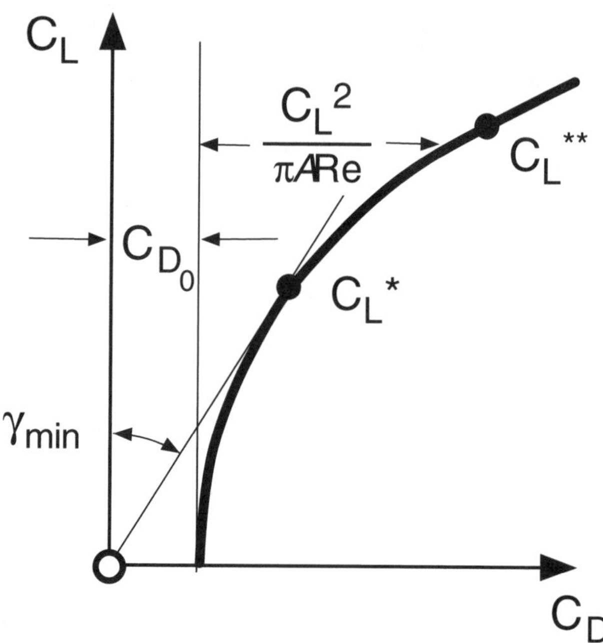

Fig. 61: Typical drag polar for complete aircraft.

C_{D_0} Drag coefficient at $C_L = 0$
C_L^* Lift coefficient for best glide angle
C_L^{**} Lift coefficient for minimum sink

$$V_{min} = \sqrt{\frac{2}{\rho}\frac{W}{S}\frac{1}{C_{L_{max}}}} \tag{59}$$

For a given $C_{L_{max}}$, this minimum speed increases with the wing loading.

The sink speed V_s is obtained from the glide angle and the flight velocity:

$$V_s = V \sin\gamma \tag{60}$$

Introducing the expression for V in this equation as well as the usual small angle assumptions $\sin\gamma = \tan\gamma = C_D/C_L$ leads to the sink speed in steady gliding flight:

$$V_s = \frac{C_D}{C_L}\sqrt{\frac{2}{\rho}\frac{W}{S}\frac{1}{C_L}} = \frac{C_D}{C_L^{3/2}}\sqrt{\frac{2}{\rho}\frac{W}{S}} \tag{61}$$

The term $C_D/C_L^{3/2}$ is a *climb index* indicating the sailplane's rate of sink. Equation 61 shows that the sink speed is directly affected by changes in the wing loading.

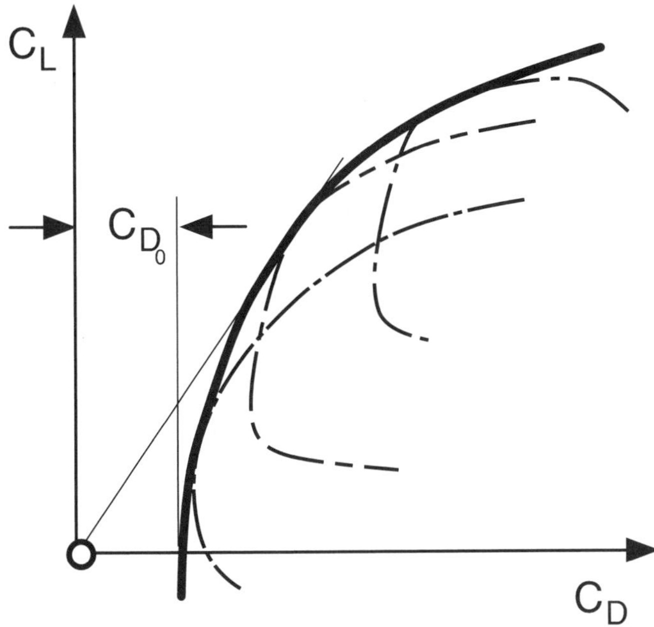

Fig. 62: Composite drag polar built up for polars of wings with various airfoils and flap settings.

Drag polars

The expressions for flight velocity and sink speed developed in the previous section underscore the importance of the relationship between the coefficients of lift and drag. Each sailplane has a unique *drag polar*, a diagram showing the functional relationship between the lift and drag coefficients.

As we have seen, there are three distinct contributions to the aircraft's drag — pressure, friction, and induced drag. At zero lift the drag consists only of friction and pressure drag (C_{D_0}). The total drag varies quadratically with the lift coefficient, with the second-order terms arising not only from the induced drag but also from friction and pressure drag. This is accounted for by the Oswald factor e (Fig. 61).

$$C_D = C_{D_0} + \frac{C_L^2}{\pi Ae} \qquad (62)$$

Each point on the polar is associated with a specific glide ratio and climb index. The best glide ratio is determined by constructing a line from the origin and tangent to the drag polar curve. The point where the line touches the polar curve defines the value of C_L at which the best glide ratio is achieved. The lift coefficient for best climb index is always 1.73 times ($\sqrt{3}$) greater than that for the best glide ratio.

The assumption that the friction and pressure drag have their minimum at zero lift is correct only for symmetrical airfoils. In reality, polar diagrams tend to depart from the idealized quadratic polar shown in Fig. 61 due to airfoil camber, wing twist, and flap deflections, and Reynolds number effects. This is especially true when laminar airfoils with high design lift coefficients are employed. However, the quadratic polar in Eq. 62 and Fig. 61 may be viewed as a limiting curve for all polars for a sailplane with the aspect ratio held constant (Fig. 62). Each of the individual polars match the idealized polar at a particular value of C_L, which may be a function of the airfoil geometry, wing twist, and flap setting. In many cases it is practical to work directly with the idealized limiting polar.

Of greater interest to the pilot is the *airspeed polar*, which may be obtained from the drag polar using the previously derived expressions for flight velocity and sink speed. A typical airspeed polar is shown in Fig. 63. By convention the sink speed is plotted positive down.

The relationship between the drag polar and the airspeed polar is governed by the wing loading, W/S. Since a given sailplane may operate at different gross weights depending on water ballast and occupant weights, it is customary to show polar curves for at least two different values of the wing loading. The airspeed polar in Fig. 63 is typical of most sailplanes in that increased wing loading is advantageous at higher airspeeds, and detrimental at low airspeeds. The airspeed at which the best glide ratio is achieved varies with wing loading. However, the best glide ratio is the same for all wing loadings (other than for small Reynolds number effects). Airspeed polars are often drawn to show the glide ratio $\gamma(V)$ in addition to the sink speed.

Dynamic Stability

Types of stability

A sailplane in steady level flight is in equilibrium — that is, the lift and drag exactly balance the components of weight, and all the moments about the center of gravity sum to zero. The sailplane's behavior following a disturbance in equilibrium is classified as stable, unstable, and neutrally stable.

Fig. 63: Effect of wing loading on airspeed polar. With water ballast: 45 daN/m²; without ballast: 30 daN/m²

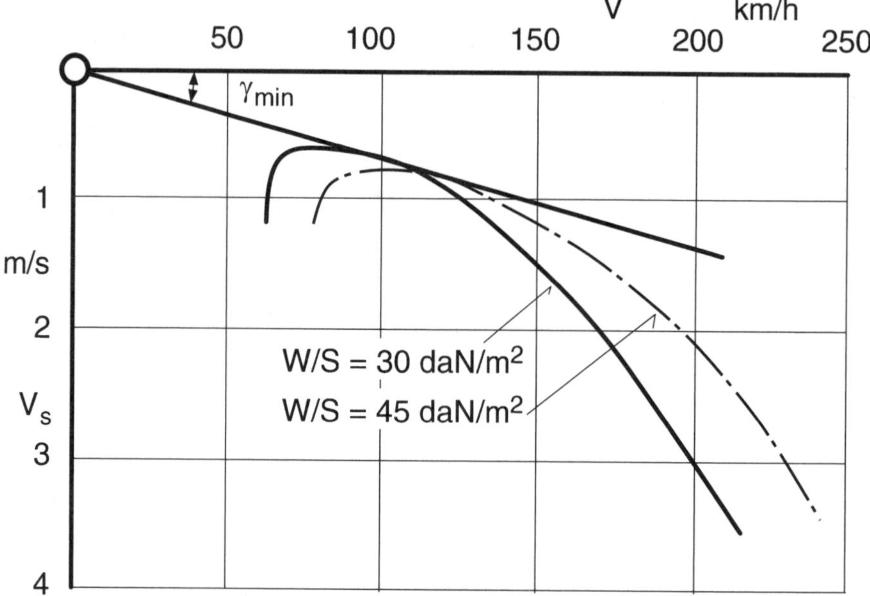

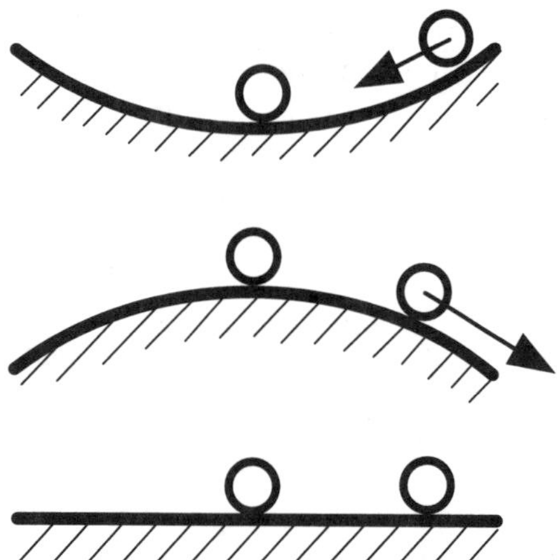

Fig. 64: Stable, unstable, and neutrally stable behavior.

If the forces arising as a result of the disturbance tend to bring the sailplane back into equilibrium, the resulting behavior is said to be statically stable. On the other hand, the sailplane is statically unstable if the resulting forces tend to further increase the disturbance. If the disturbance in equilibrium generates neither a restoring nor a destabilizing force, the system is said to be neutrally stable. These three cases may be visualized by considering the behavior of a ball on the three surfaces in Fig. 64.

This classification of the types of stability takes into account only the direction of the force developed following the disturbance. However, the nature of the resulting motion is of interest as well. The aircraft may undergo a series of oscillations, which may or may not gradually die out. Four typical cases are shown in Fig. 65 — critically damped or overdamped (stable); lightly damped (stable oscillations); statically unstable (divergent); and dynamically unstable (divergent oscillations).

If the damping is very light, the system will exhibit stable oscillations following a disturbance. As the damping is increased, the oscillations decay more rapidly. At a certain damping level, the response ceases to be oscillatory, exhibiting instead a simple exponential decay. This borderline case the system is said to be *critically damped*. Systems in which the damping exceeds the critical damping are termed *overdamped*.

Static stability is present if a disturbance in the equilibrium condition results in a restoring force, that is, a force that opposes the disturbance.

Dynamic stability requires, in addition, that the subsequent motion is stable.

An aircraft may exhibit dynamic instability even if it is statically stable.

Fig. 65: Types of transient response:

(a) critically damped/overdamped (stable)
(b) lightly damped (stable oscillations)
(c) statically unstable (divergent)
(d) dynamically unstable (divergent oscillations)
t time

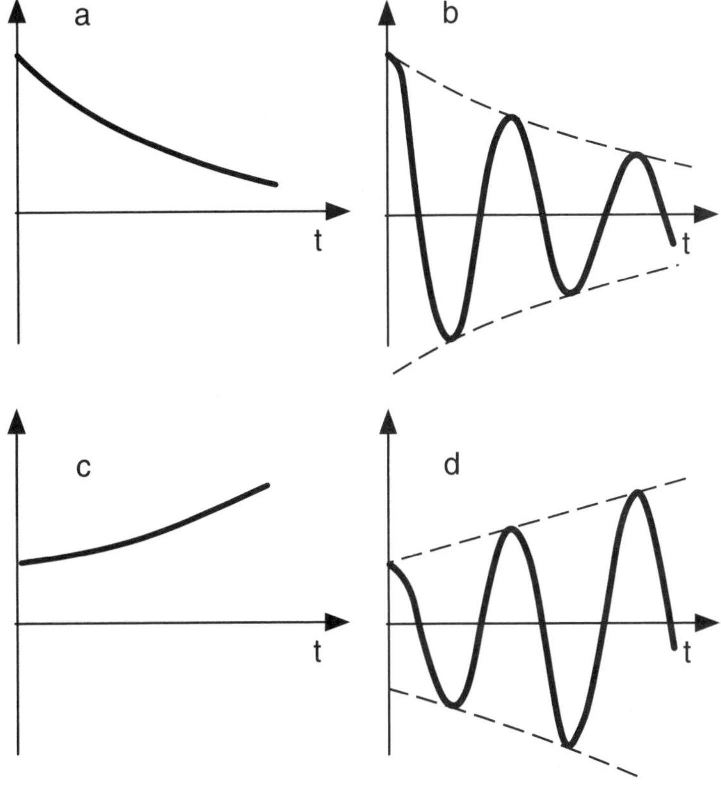

A complete stability analysis takes into account all six "rigid body" degrees of freedom of motion (Fig. 66). These include the three translational degrees of freedom (the longitudinal, lateral, and vertical components of velocity) and the three body angles (pitch, roll, and yaw). The vertical and lateral components of velocity are related to the angle of attack and sideslip angle, respectively. Control surface motions (in particular, those of the elevator) are also considered independent degrees of freedom. As will be discussed, elastic degrees of freedom of the structure and control system may also play an important roll.

Sailplanes invariably exhibit lateral symmetry, allowing the stability analysis to be divided into two independent problems. *Longitudinal stability* is the stability of motion in the sailplane's plane of symmetry, that is, forward velocity, pitch, and angle of attack. *Lateral stability* considers motions occurring out of the plane of symmetry — slipping, rolling, and yawing. This analytic simplification is not applicable to all aircraft types — for example, rotating components such as airplane propellers or helicopter rotors may generate strong gyroscopic forces and significant coupling between the longitudinal and lateral degrees of freedom.

In the following sections we will consider dynamic and static stability, in each case treating both the longitudinal and lateral cases.

Longitudinal dynamic stability

Dynamic longitudinal stability may be modeled mathematically as a set of linear differential equations in four independent variables: velocity, angle of attack, pitch angle, and elevator position. Of the four solutions to this system, two are of particular interest: the *phugoid mode*, and the *short-period mode*. In each case the behavior depends on specific aspects of the design.

The phugoid is an oscillation involving variations in airspeed V and pitch angle θ at constant angle of attack (Fig. 67). The problem is completely defined by these two degrees of freedom, so that although the altitude H varies as well, it is not counted as an independent state. For small amplitude oscillations about a nominal trim condition, it can

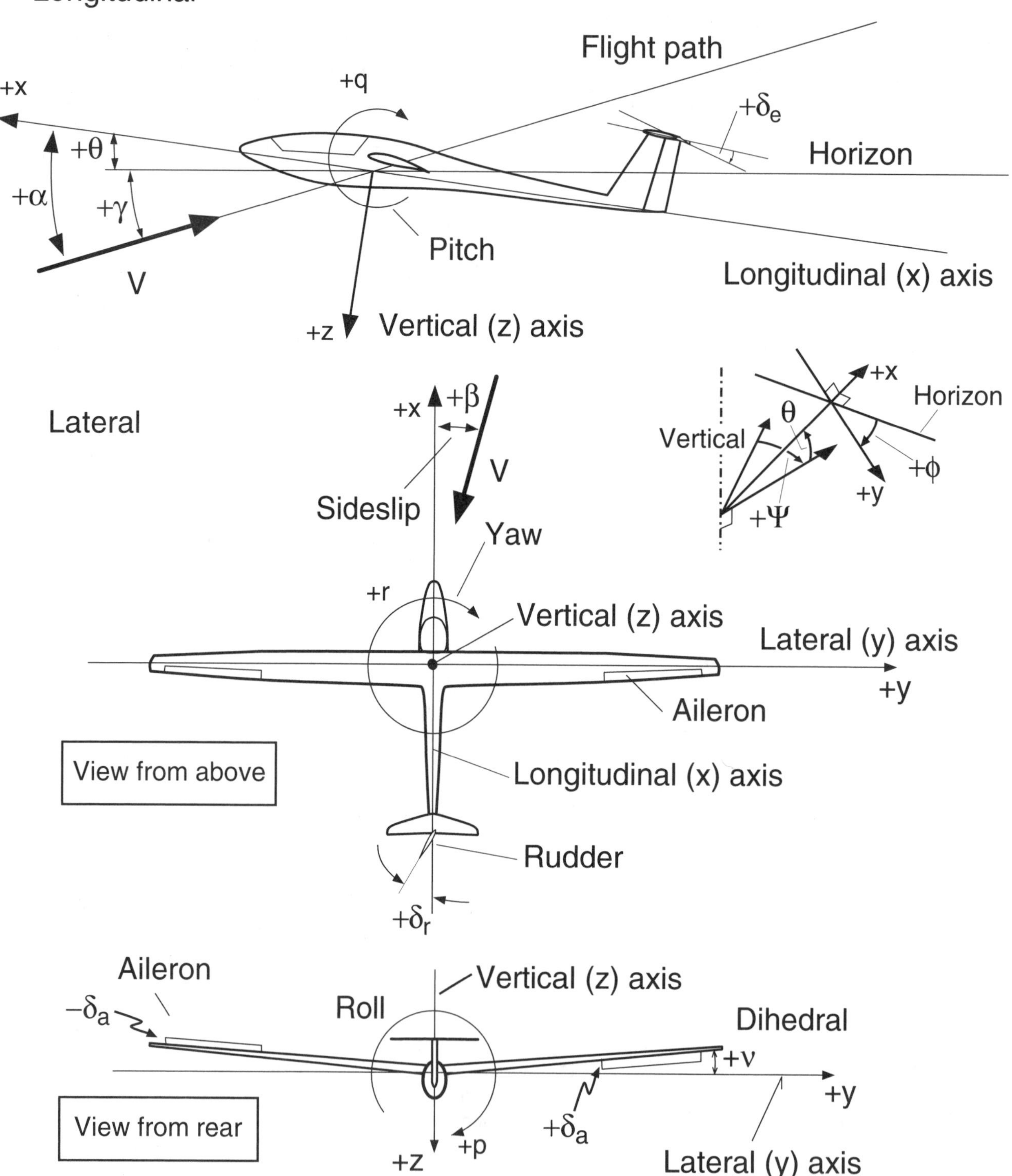
Longitudinal
Flight path
+x
+q
$+\delta_e$
+θ
Horizon
+α
+γ
Pitch
V
Longitudinal (x) axis
+z
Vertical (z) axis
Lateral
+x
+β
+x
Horizon
θ
Vertical
V
+ϕ
+y
Sideslip
+Ψ
Yaw
+r
Vertical (z) axis
Lateral (y) axis
+y
Aileron
View from above
Longitudinal (x) axis
Rudder
$+\delta_r$
Aileron
Vertical (z) axis
$-\delta_a$
Roll
Dihedral
+ν
+y
View from rear
$+\delta_a$
+z
+p
Lateral (y) axis

be shown that the period of oscillation is proportional to the trim airspeed, and the damping inversely proportional to the lift-drag ratio L/D. In modern sailplanes, the phugoid is therefore very lightly damped and may even be slightly unstable. However, due to the long period (typically around 15 seconds), the pilot can control it easily, with little conscious effort.

The other solution, the short-period mode (Fig. 67), is excited (for example) by flying through a sharp-edged vertical gust and is characterized primarily by variations in pitch angle θ and angle of attack α, with relatively little variation in altitude and airspeed. The damping depends considerably on the location of the center of gravity relative to the neutral point (see page 53) and aerodynamic damping about the pitch axis. In most sailplanes, the motion is well damped, dying out within a single period, so that the short period mode is generally of little importance to conventional sailplanes. Flying wing sailplanes feature inherently low aerodynamic pitch damping and may therefore exhibit marginal longitudinal dynamic stability. Wing elastic degrees of freedom may also participate in the short period motion of flying wing sailplanes [140, 145, 154].

Lateral dynamic stability

The differential equations of motion used to model lateral dynamic stability have as degrees of freedom sideslip, yaw angle, roll angle, and aileron and rudder position. Three solutions are of interest.

The first, the *spiral mode*, is lightly damped or divergent. If divergent, the motion gradually develops into a spiral dive, with steadily increasing airspeed and bank angle. However, in visual meteorological conditions, even a lightly unstable spiral mode is easily controlled by the pilot.

The *roll mode* is so strongly damped that it usually goes unnoticed by the pilot.

Finally, the *Dutch roll mode* is a short period mode involving sideslip, roll, and yaw motions. It is of little importance to most sailplanes. In contrast, many high speed aircraft exhibit severe Dutch roll tendencies and require automatic stabilization systems.

In summary, with the exception of flying wing sailplanes, the design requirements related to sailplane dynamic stability are not particularly challenging. For the two most important response modes, the phugoid and the spiral mode, acceptable flight characteristics may generally be achieved without great effort on the part of the designer.

Fig. 66: Axis and angle definitions for sailplane stability analysis. See also [6]

ψ	azimuth, measured *e.g.* from North
θ	pitch angle
ϕ	roll angle
V	flight velocity
p	roll rate
q	pitch rate
r	yaw rate
β	sideslip angle
α	angle of attack
γ	flight path angle, $\theta - \alpha$
δ_e	elevator deflection
δ_r	rudder deflection
δ_a	aileron deflection. For individual aileron, positive for trailing edge deflected down. As control input, positive for left aileron.
ν	dihedral

Static Stability

Definition

Although the analysis of dynamic stability is more challenging from a mathematical point of view, in the case of sailplanes it is static stability that tends to be the more important design issue. As with dynamic stability, longitudinal and lateral stability may be investigated as separate, uncoupled problems. The following definitions apply:

- An aircraft exhibits longitudinal static stability if a perturbation in angle of attack produces a pitching moment that tends to counteract the perturbation.
- Static lateral stability is present if the introduction of sideslip and roll angle leads to aerodynamic moments that tend to return these angles to zero.
- As a special case, if only sideslip is involved, the problem is referred to as *directional stability*.

Lateral static stability

Due to the strong coupling of roll, yaw, and sideslip, changes in one of these angles will lead directly to changes in the other two.

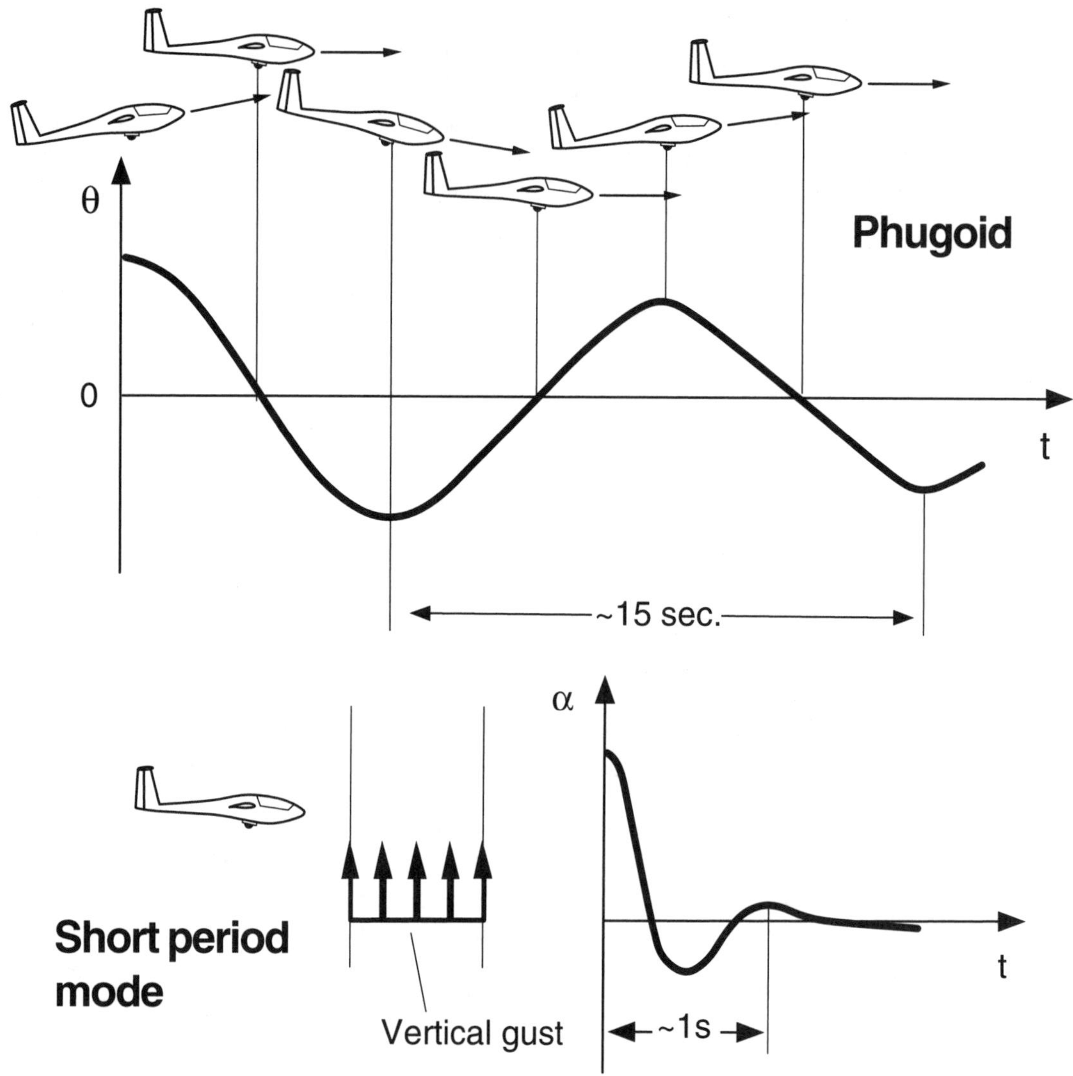

Fig. 67: Phugoid and short period modes.

For example, if the aircraft rolls slightly in response to a gust or other disturbance, the lift vector is directed away from the vertical, introducing a lateral force, in turn inducing a sideslip (Fig. 68).

Due to the asymmetric flow conditions due to sideslip, the lift on the two wings differs, giving rise to a roll moment, the strength and direction of which are determined by the dihedral. Raising the position of the wing on the fuselage has the same effect as increasing the dihedral (Fig. 69).

If the aircraft is directionally stable, a side load will develop on the vertical stabilizer tending to yaw the aircraft into the direction of the flow (Fig. 70).

Yawing motion induces small changes in airspeed over the span of the wing. For example, if the aircraft yaws to the right, the left (forward moving) wing is subjected to a slightly higher airspeed, and the right (aft moving) wing a slightly lower airspeed. The forward moving wing experiences increased lift and induced drag; while on the right wing these aerodynamic forces are reduced. These effects combine to produce yaw damping (an aerodynamic moment that tends to diminish the yaw motion) together with roll/yaw coupling (Fig. 71).

Similarly, when the aircraft rolls about its longitudinal axis, the downwards moving wing is subject to increased lift, resulting in roll damping. This also produces coupling between roll and yaw due to the spanwise variation in induced angle of attack (Fig. 72).

Additional aerodynamic coupling effects are observed when the ailerons are deflected to initiate a turn. The aileron opposite the direction of turn is deflected downwards, producing increased lift and induced drag. This is the source of *adverse yaw*, an undesirable aerodynamic moment that tends to yaw the aircraft away from the direction of the turn (Fig. 73). When entering a turn, the adverse yaw due to the initial aileron deflection is compensated via an appropriate rudder input.

A sailplane's success depends strongly on its handling in turns, so that a proper balance of the various coupling effects is essential. Here the main design challenges are establishing the proper dihedral effect (wing dihedral and placement) and minimizing the adverse yaw by avoiding any additional drag on the downward deflected aileron (for example, due to separation). Adverse yaw is also minimized by using differential aileron rigging or Frise ailerons (ailerons hinged to create additional drag when deflected upwards — see for example [21]). Small spoilers ("spoilerons") deflecting upward with the ailerons have also been employed.

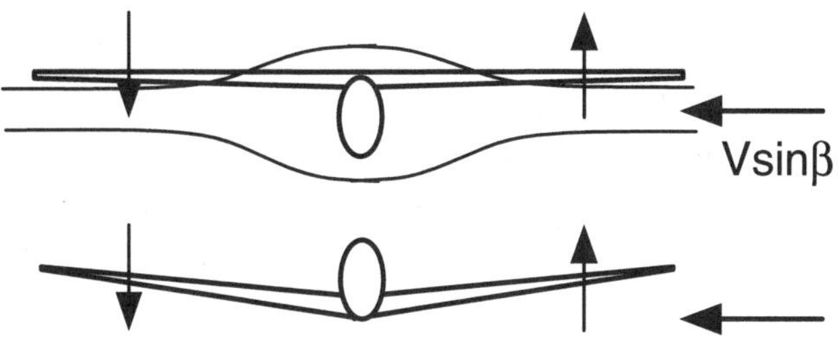

Fig. 69: Effect of wing placement on dihedral effect.

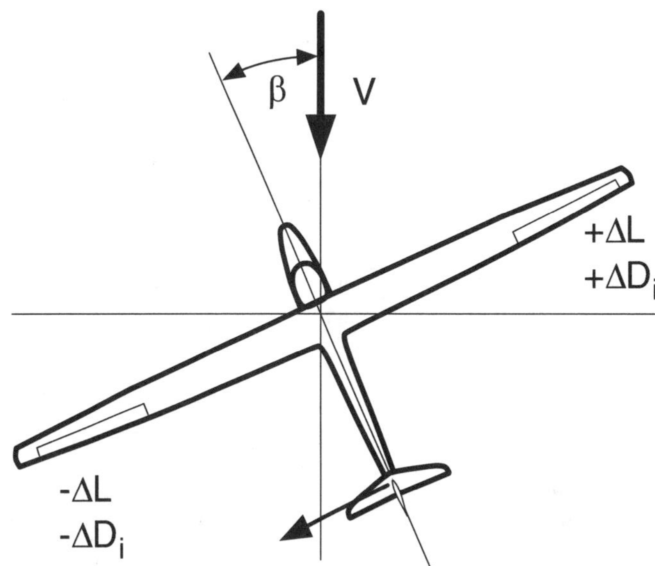

Fig. 70: Directional stability: the vertical stabilizer develops a lateral force, leading to a restoring moment about the yaw axis. **Dihedral effect:** The wing develops an asymmetric lift distribution due to dihedral and wing placement, leading to a roll moment away from the direction of slip

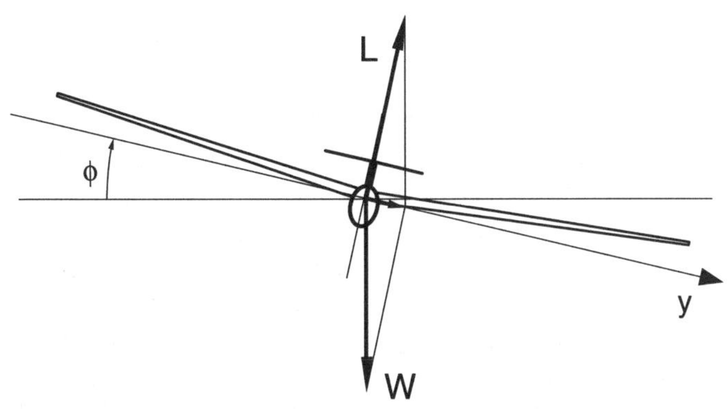

Fig. 68: Sideslip induced by roll displacement, ϕ.

Longitudinal static stability

Static equilibrium requires that (1) the aerodynamic forces balance the components of the weight, and (2) all aerodynamic pitching moments about the center of gravity sum to zero (Fig. 74).

Per Fig. 74:

$$L = W\cos\gamma$$
$$D = W\sin\gamma$$
$$\sum M = 0$$

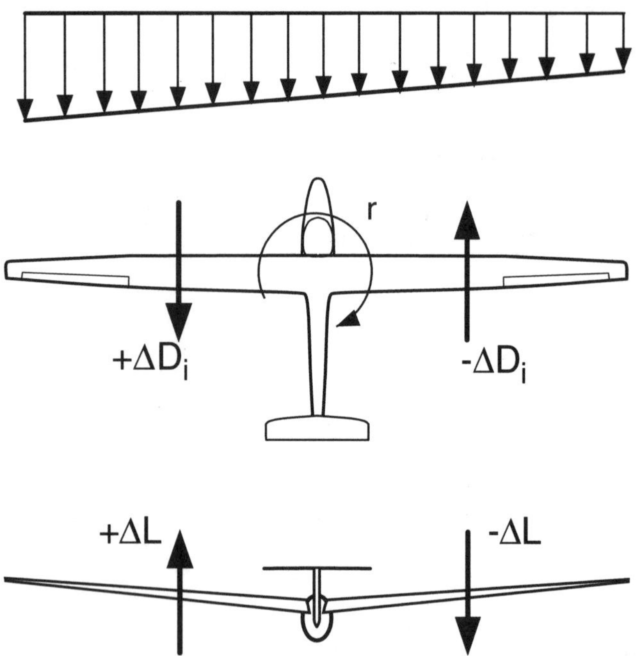

Fig. 71: Yaw damping:results from change in vertical stabilizer angle of attack and spanwise variations in induced drag. **Roll due to yaw:** asymmetric flow due to the yaw motion leads to spanwise variations in dynamic pressure, producing a roll moment in direction of yaw.

In the figure, the reference point for the pitching moments is the aircraft center of gravity. This is a common practice in stability analysis, as it allows the moment due to the weight to be ignored.

Following a disturbance in equilibrium, for example, due to a gust, the aircraft will develop an aerodynamic pitching moment that tends either to restore equilibrium (statically stable) or lead to a further departure from equilibrium (statically unstable). Stability is related to the pitching moment curve in Fig. 75. A positive gradient in the pitching moment curve ($dC_{M_{CG}}/d\alpha > 0$) indicates that, following a nose-up disturbance in equilibrium, the aerodynamic pitching moment will become more positive, that is, more nose up — a statically unstable situation. On the other hand, a negative pitching moment gradient indicates that a restoring force will be generated - that is, static stability.

The equilibrium condition is observed in Fig. 75 as the

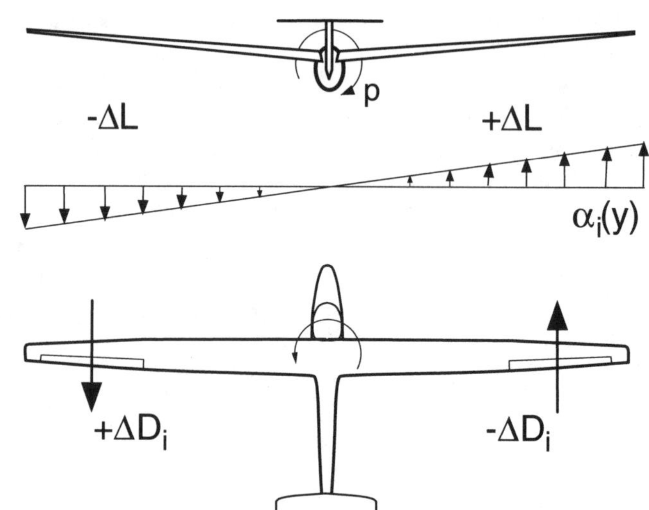

Fig. 72: Roll damping: roll rate induces a spanwise variation in angle of attack. The resulting roll moment resists the rolling motion. **Yaw due to roll:** the asymmetric lift distribution due to roll rate produces a spanwise variation in induced drag and, in turn, a yaw moment away from the direction of roll. See also Perkins and Hage [21] and Schlichting and Truckenbrodt [23, 24].

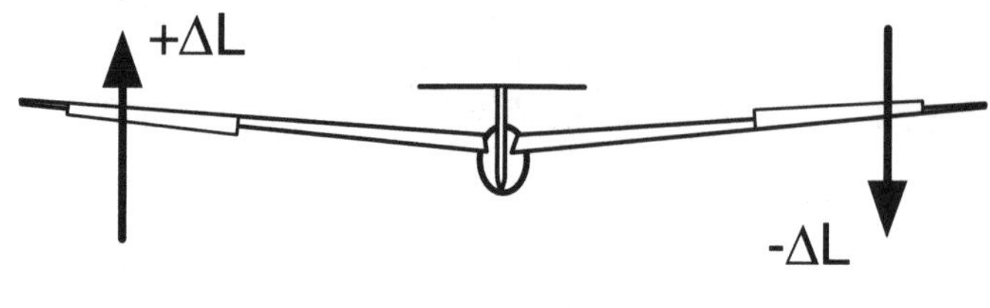

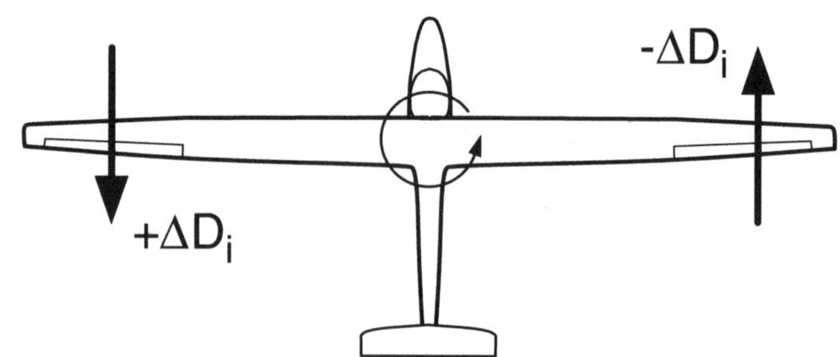

Fig. 73: Adverse yaw: the asymmetric lift distribution due to aileron deflection produces a spanwise variation in induced drag and, in turn, a yaw moment away from the direction of aileron input.

intersection of the pitching moment curve with the x-axis (*i.e.* $C_{M_{CG}} = 0$). Since the trim lift coefficient is always positive in normal flight, a negative pitching moment gradient implies that the zero-lift pitching moment must also be positive, *i.e.* nose up (Fig. 76). Consequently, longitudinal static stability is characterized by:

$$\frac{dC_{M_{CG}}}{d\alpha} < 0 \tag{63}$$

$$C_{M_0} > 0 \tag{64}$$

By themselves, wings typically have a negative pitching moment due to airfoil camber and are thus fundamentally unstable. Therefore, a horizontal stabilizer is required to fulfill the stability criterion in Eq. 64 (positive zero-lift moment). The zero-lift moment for the entire aircraft may be adjusted by varying the angle of incidence of the horizontal stabilizer relative to the wing (Fig. 76). Each zero-lift moment corresponds to a certain equilibrium value of C_L, in turn corresponding to a particular airspeed. The pilot establishes the desired trim airspeed by using the cockpit controls to vary the angle of incidence of the horizontal stabilizer (or equivalently, the elevator deflection).

Center of gravity and neutral point

Analogous to the aerodynamic center of an isolated wing, a *neutral point* is defined for the complete aircraft. This is the point about which the sum of the aerodynamic pitching moments is independent of lift coefficient. This definition allows the aerodynamic loads acting on the aircraft to be expressed as a combination of lift, acting at the neutral point and varying with angle of attack, and a constant pitching moment, controlled by the pilot via elevator inputs.

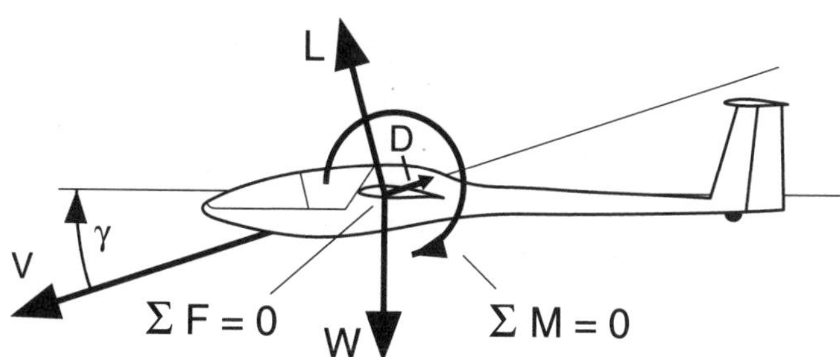

Fig. 74: Equilibrium condition in unaccelerated flight.

The location of the sailplane center of gravity relative to its neutral point provides a convenient measure of equilibrium and static stability. Consider first the two situations illustrated in Fig. 77. With the center of gravity ahead of the neutral point, the lift, acting at the neutral point, contributes to a nose-down pitching moment. Static equilibrium requires that the horizontal stabilizer generate a nose-up moment of equal magnitude. On the other hand, with the center of gravity positioned behind the neutral point, static equilibrium is achieved with the horizontal stabilizer providing a nose-down pitching moment.

These two cases exhibit entirely different stability characteristics. For example, with the center of gravity ahead of the neutral point, a slight increase in angle of attack leads to an increase in lift on both wing and horizontal stabilizer (Fig. 78a). By definition, these act in combination at the aircraft's neutral point, generating a nose-down pitching moment about the center of gravity. This stable behavior stands in contrast to the case where the center of gravity lies behind the neutral point (Fig. 78b). Here, the additional lift produces a nose-up pitching moment, and the aircraft is statically unstable (see also Fig. 75)[2].

Longitudinal static stability is thus present if and only if the center of gravity lies ahead of the neutral point:

$$x_N - x_{CG} > 0 \tag{65}$$

The neutral point may be determined directly from the gradient of the pitching moment curve. Moment equilibrium at the center of gravity requires:

$$C_{M_{CG}} = -C_L\left(\frac{x_N}{c_\mu} - \frac{x_{CG}}{c_\mu}\right) + C_{M_0} \tag{66}$$

Differentiating this with respect to C_L yields (Fig. 79):

$$\frac{dC_{M_{CG}}}{dC_L} = -\frac{(x_N - x_{CG})}{c_\mu} \tag{67}$$

Stability margin and controllability

Equation 67 provides a criterion for ensuring longitudinal static stability. It is also of interest to consider the *degree* of stability. Since the restoring moment following an angle

[2]This discussion and Figs. 77-78 notwithstanding, the static stability criteria do not preclude the possibility of a horizontal stabilizer producing positive (upward) lift in trimmed level flight.

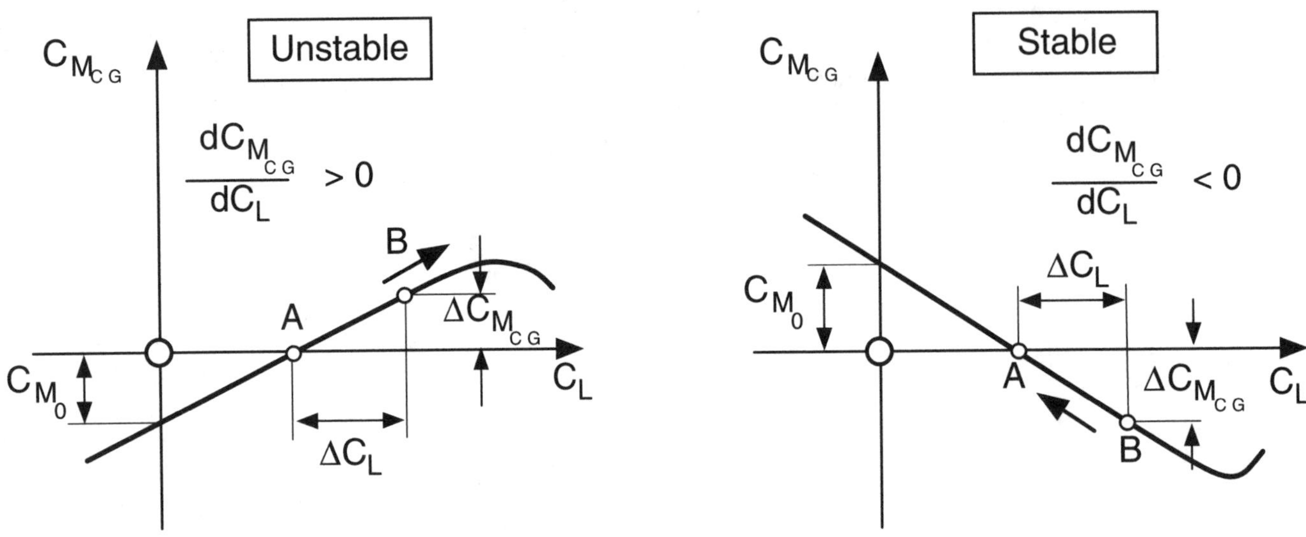

Fig. 75: Unstable and stable pitching moment gradients for the complete aircraft.

A equilibrium condition
B following a disturbance

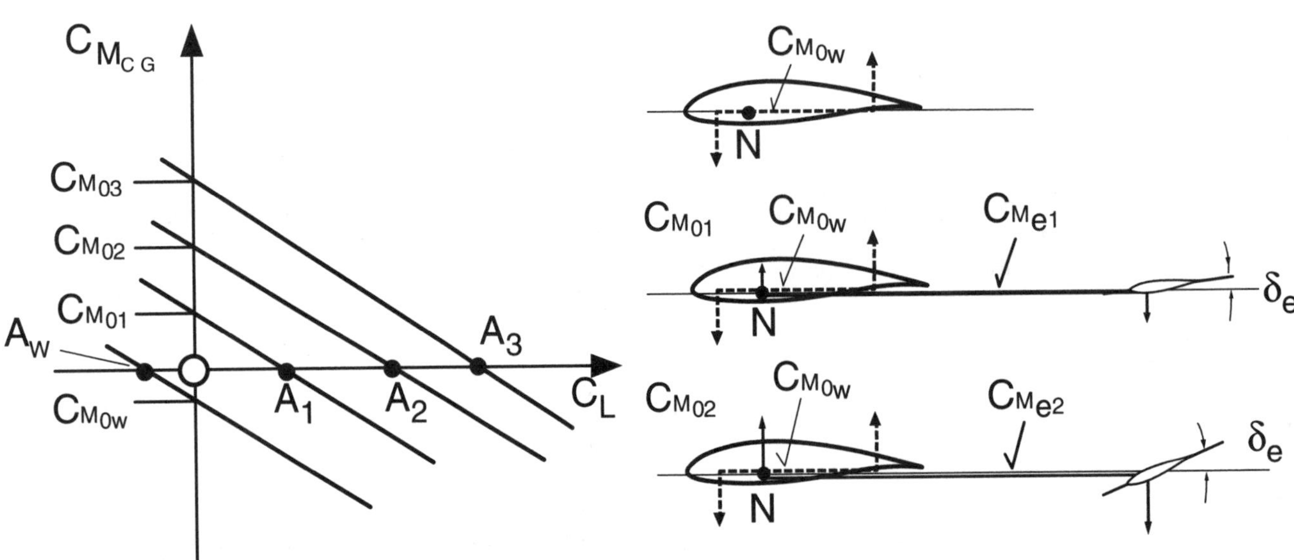

Fig. 76: Pitching moment curves for stable trim conditions A_F (wing only, with negative C_{M_0}) A_1, A_2, and A_3 (with horizontal stabilizer, producing positive C_{M_0}). $C_{M_0} = C_{M_{0_F}} + C_{M_{0_e}}$

Fig. 77: Pitching moment contribution $L_e l_e$ from horizontal stabilizer required to balance the pitching moment about CG due to the wing lift.
$(L + L_e)(x_N - x_{CG}) = L_e l_e$

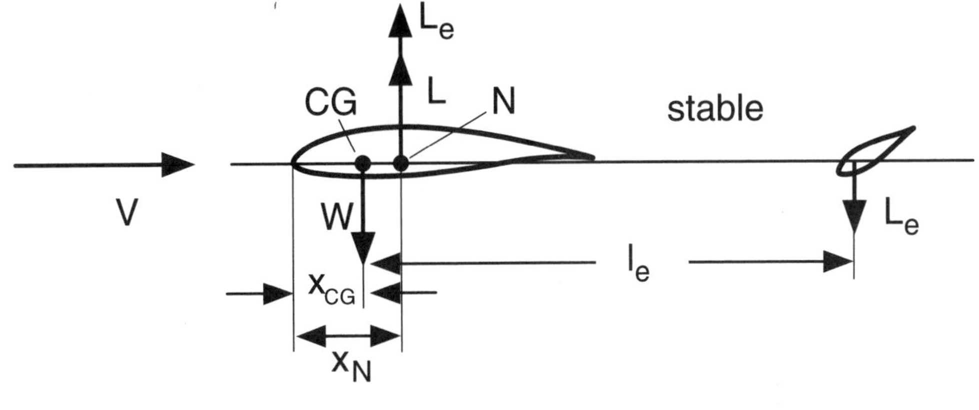

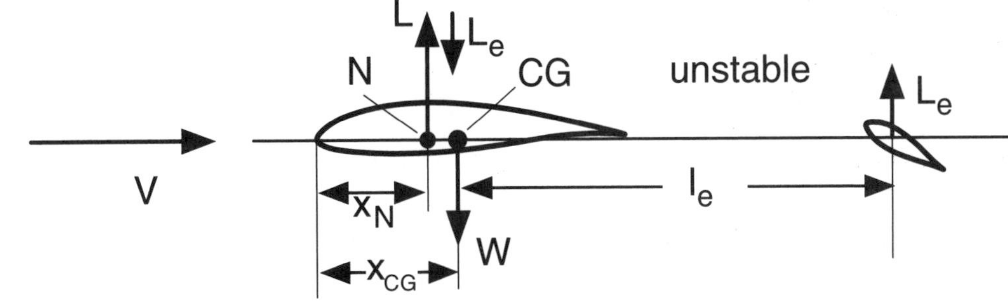

Fig. 78: Effect of disturbance in angle of attack on longitudinal equilibrium for two CG locations.

a) $x_N - x_{CG} > 0$: incremental force ΔL_α produces a restoring moment about the center of gravity (stable).

b) $x_N - x_{CG} < 0$: incremental force ΔL_α generates a pitching moment that further increases the angle of attack (unstable).

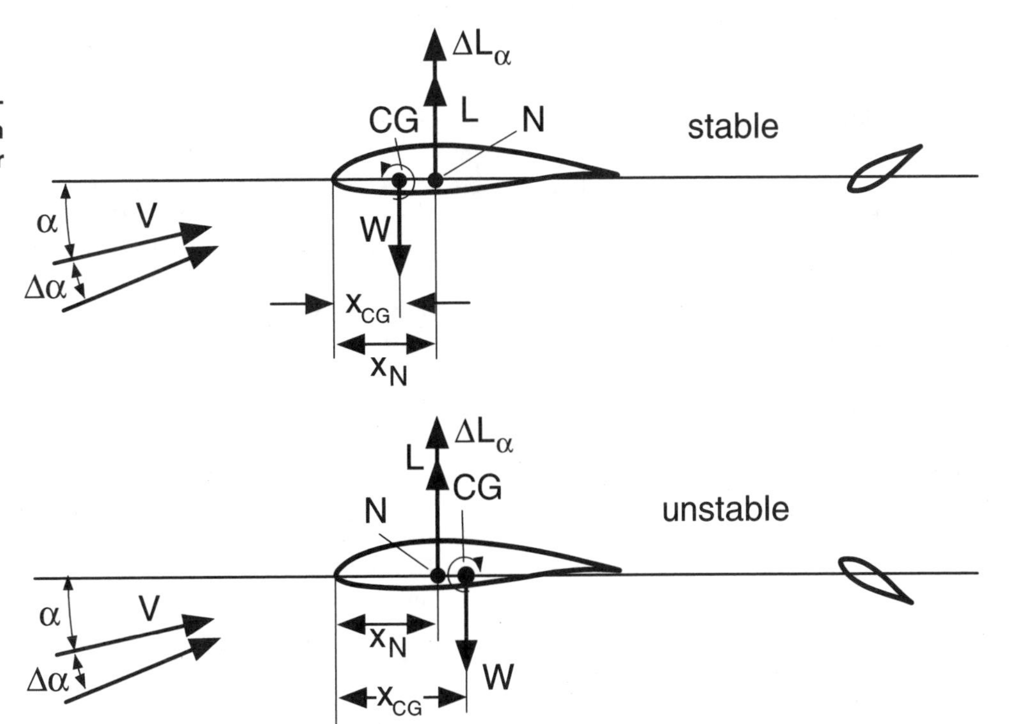

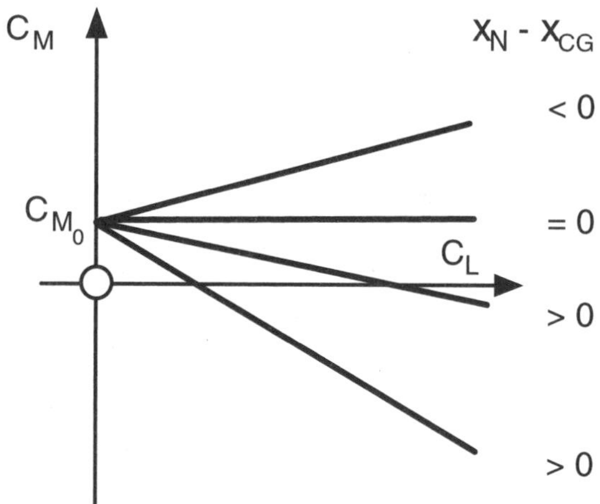

Fig. 79: Relationship between pitching moment gradient and location of center of gravity.

$x_N - x_{CG} > 0$ stable
$= 0$ neutrally stable
< 0 unstable

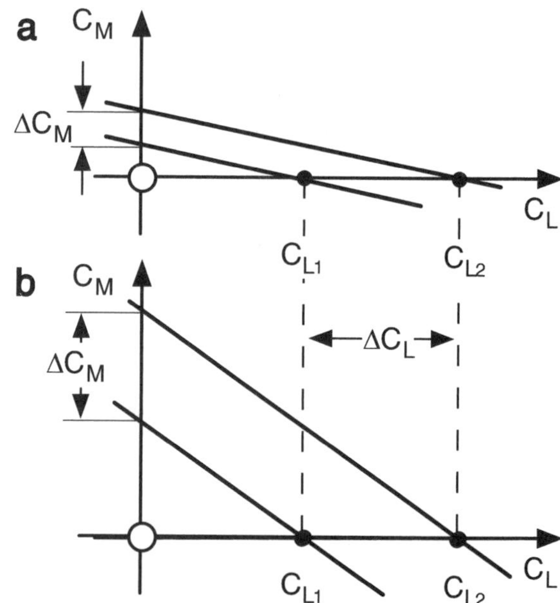

Fig. 80: Incremental pitching moment $\Delta C_M = l_e \Delta C_{L_H}$ required to change the trim lift coefficient by ΔC_L.

a) small stability margin $x_N - x_{CG}$
b) large stability margin $x_N - x_{CG}$

of attack change is proportional to $dC_{M_{CG}}/dC_L$, the quantity $(x_N - x_{CG})/c_\mu$ in Eq. 67 provides a measure of stability and is referred to as the *static margin*. The greater the static margin, the greater the tendency of the aircraft to return to its equilibrium condition following a perturbation in pitch.

For a given sailplane, the magnitude and direction of the stabilizer lift is largely a function of the CG location. At aft CG locations, where the stability margin is very low, very little stabilizer lift is required to change the equilibrium lift coefficient of the aircraft (Fig. 80). As the static margin is increased, higher stabilizer lift forces are required. Associated with this increased lift is an increase in the drag contribution from the horizontal stabilizer, the *trim drag*. This is one reason why an excessive static margin is undesirable. Sailplanes are typically designed with their aft CG limits very close to the neutral point, often within only 5–10% of mean aerodynamic chord. While an experienced pilot may be able to control the aircraft with the CG located further aft, perhaps even at or slightly behind the neutral point, this practice leaves no safety margin to cover uncertainties in the empty weight and CG, and pilot fatigue. F. Irving [56,86,87] has published results suggesting that, for typical production sailplanes, there is little performance to be gained by placing the CG at an extreme aft position. For further discussion of sailplane trim drag see E. E. Larrabee [91], I. Kroo [88], C. Vernon [114], and E. V. Laitone [89].

The stability analysis discussed in the preceding sections assumes that the elevator is held fixed by the pilot. In addition to stick-fixed stability, the case where the elevator is allowed to float freely is also of interest. Neither of these situations is completely realistic — in practice, even with the stick fixed, the control system may exhibit a degree of flexibility, while on the other hand a small amount of friction and inertia in the control linkage will be present even if the stick is completely released. Nevertheless, they are useful idealizations. Each is associated with its own stability criteria.

From a practical point of view, static stability is related to the stick positions and control forces required to trim the aircraft as a function of airspeed. The variation of stick position with airspeed provides a measure of the stick-fixed static stability, while the stick force trend indicates the degree of stick-free static stability.

If the stick positions in trimmed level flight always increase (move forward) as the trim airspeed is increased, the aircraft is statically stable for the stick-fixed case. The gradient of stick position with respect to airspeed is a function of the stick-fixed static stability margin

Similarly, stick-free static stability requires a positive gradient of stick force with airspeed, that is, flying at higher speeds should require more forward pressure on the stick (assuming the elevator trim control is not readjusted). The slope of the stick-force vs. airspeed curve provides a measure of the degree of stick-free static stability.

JAR-22 [49] (discussed in the next chapter) requires the stick force gradient to be positive, but the stick position gradient may be negative provided that the stick force gradient is adequate.

Stick free static stability is a particularly important topic for designs with all-flying tails.

To avoid any misunderstandings, it should be emphasized that the topic of static stability applies only to steady state flight conditions. Transient maneuvers such as the landing flare, pullups, turn entries, stalls, and spins require separate analytic treatment. This will be discussed in a subsequent chapter in connection with the discussion regarding layout of the empennage.

Numerous textbooks have been written on the subject of aircraft stability and control. The reader is referred to texts by B. W. McCormick [16], B. Etkin and L. D. Reid [7], C. D. Perkins and R. E. Hage [21], X. Hafer and G. Sachs [9], and F. G. Irving [13]. A recent work by M. J. Abzug and E. E. Larrabee [2] discusses airplane stability and control from a historical perspective, with numerous examples based on actual case histories. Further discussion may be found in [25, 26]. For a more detailed treatment of static stability and control specifically oriented to sailplane design, see P. Morelli [95].

Aeroelasticity

The preceding discussion of stability and control assumes the sailplane to be a rigid body. *Aeroelasticity*, on the other hand, considers the static and dynamic interactions between the elastic structure and the surrounding air flow. Although a detailed discussion of aeroelasticity is beyond the scope of this book, it is a topic of considerable importance and sailplane designers and pilots should be familiar with the basic concepts. For a more detailed treatment, the reader is referred to textbooks by R. L. Bisplinghoff, H. Ashley, and R. L. Halfman [155] and H. W. Försching [157]. The general problem of sailplane flutter is discussed by F. Kießling [158] and W. Stender and F. Kiessling [160], who provide useful design guidelines for minimizing the possibility of flutter. Interesting footage of a flutter encounter in the SB-8 is found in [153, 211]. See also M. J. Abzug and E. E. Larrabee [2] for aeroelastic effects on airplane stability and control.

As with flight mechanics, it is convenient to divide aeroelastic problems into static and dynamic phenomena.

Static Aeroelasticity

Structural divergence

For slender beam structures such as sailplane wings, elementary beam theory predicts the existence of a spanwise *elastic axis* along which a transverse load (lift) may be applied without inducing twist. An upward load applied ahead of the elastic axis will generate a nose-up twist. Thus, if the local aerodynamic center lies ahead of the elastic axis, any increase in lift will lead to an increase in the wing angle of attack, in turn leading to additional lift, and so forth. This destabilizing effect is proportional to dynamic pressure. At a sufficiently high airspeed, linear theory predicts that the wing will bend and twist without limit. In practical terms, the wing structure will fail. This phenomenon is termed *structural divergence*.

For the idealized case of a wing at zero angle of attack mounted to a rigid support, explosive divergence may occur without warning when the critical structural divergence speed is reached. In the case of a free-flying sailplane, the destabilizing effect may manifest itself well below the divergence speed as a degradation in longitudinal stability [159].

Factors affecting the divergence speed include the wing sweep, torsional stiffness, and location of the elastic axis. Forward sweep reduces the critical speed due to the kinematic coupling between wing bending and rotation of wing sections perpendicular to the flow. *Aeroelastic tailoring* using anisotropic composite materials can provide beneficial structural coupling between wing bending and twisting.

Aileron reversal

A downward deflected flap or control surface, in addition to increasing the local aerodynamic lift, generates a nose-down aerodynamic pitching moment (see Fig. 50). In the case of an aileron, this pitching moment induces a wing twist that reduces the roll moment produced by the aileron deflection. As with structural divergence, the effect is proportional to dynamic pressure and, as the airspeed is increased, the aileron effectiveness diminishes. Above a certain airspeed, the ailerons will actually induce a rolling moment opposite to that intended.

The aileron reversal speed decreases with aft wing sweep due to the kinematic coupling mentioned above. Sufficient aileron effectiveness is maintained by providing sufficient wing torsional stiffness and/or by aeroelastic tailoring.

Effects on performance

The aerodynamic performance of a sailplane wing is a strong function of twist distribution. Wings are manufactured with a certain built-in twist, and any elastic twist induced by aerodynamic loads that is not accounted for properly in the tooling may lead to (1) increased induced drag resulting from changes in the spanwise lift distribution, and (2) increased profile drag due to changes in local sectional lift coefficient shifting the operating point of the airfoil out of its laminar range. See for example G. Stich [162] for an experimental investigation into aeroelastic effects on performance.

Dynamic Aeroelastic Problems

The central dynamic aeroelastic problem is that of *flutter*, an unstable oscillation of the aircraft structure. The sailplane's dynamic characteristics are defined primarily by its *normal modes* (natural frequencies and mode shapes). Experience shows that it is usually sufficient to consider only those modes with frequencies below a certain limit [158, 160]. Although, in general, the modes define deformations of the entire sailplane, they are often associated primarily with specific structural components. Hence, the normal modes are frequently characterized as wing bending or torsion modes, stabilizer modes, fuselage bending or torsion modes, control surface deflection modes, etc. Because the system is symmetric, the modes may be further classified as symmetric or antisymmetric. The wing first symmetric bending mode, for example, is well known to any pilot who has gently shaken a wing by its wingtip during a preflight inspection. By shaking at higher frequencies it is possible to excite other wing modes such as the first antisymmetric bending mode.

In flight, the structural deformations associated with these modes produce aerodynamic loads that change the dynamic behavior of the sailplane and couple the modes observed on the ground to one another. The stability of the complete system depends on the degree and nature of the coupling effects.

For example, the first antisymmetric wing bending mode is aerodynamically coupled to aileron motion, in that aileron deflection generates a spanwise load that is properly distributed to excite the antisymmetric wing motion. In addition, if the aileron is not properly mass balanced, the two degrees of freedom will be inertially coupled, since wing movement will induce inertial aileron hinge moments directly affecting the aileron motion. Additional coupling effects may result from kinematics and mass properties of the aileron control linkage.

Aerodynamic coupling effects are a strong function of airspeed and a given mode or combination of modes will generally become unstable at a certain critical airspeed. Of course, the overall stability boundary is defined by the mode with the lowest critical airspeed. Above this critical airspeed, the combined inertial, elastic and aerodynamic effects may lead to an unstable situation in which the wing bending and aileron motion, for example, become properly phased to drive one another. The resulting unstable oscillation will then increase in amplitude until limited by nonlinear effects (such as the ailerons hitting their mechanical stops [153] or the wing airfoil reaching $c_{l_{max}}$) or structural failure.

Unfortunately, unlike static aeroelastic problems, flutter analysis is mathematically complex and is usually reserved for the specialist. Nevertheless, there are a few basics with which designers and pilots should be familiar.

- Aeroelastic instabilities are extremely dangerous. When flutter occurs, the pilot may not have time to reduce airspeed before the structure disintegrates.

- Flutter is *self excited*. That is, the forces required to produce the motion derive from the motion itself. In mathematical terms, it is a stability problem, rather than a forced response problem. Therefore, although it may initially be triggered by a gust, flutter also develops in perfectly still air.

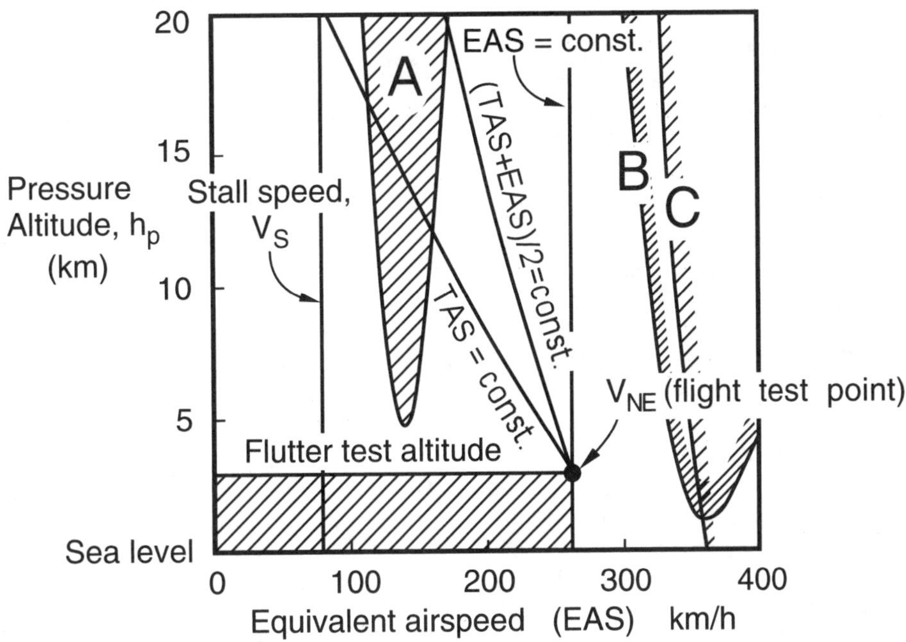

Fig. 81: Example of altitude effects on aeroelastic stability boundaries, from W. Stender, F. Kiessling, and J. Kuettner [161]. Note the small margin at high altitude between the constant TAS line and the stalling speed. The safety margin between the constant EAS line and flutter boundaries B and C also decreases with altitude.

- A Region of reduced aeroelastic stability of first antisymmetrical wing bending, coupled with aileron deflection. This mild flutter tendency can be eliminated by mass balancing the ailerons.
- B Second wing antisymmetrical mode coupled with aileron deflection. Mass balancing the ailerons would eliminate this unstable region as well.
- C Symmetrical wing torsion coupled with first symmetric wing bending. Treating this instability would require an expensive redesign of the wing structure.

- Flutter is distinguished from *buffeting*, a forced response phenomenon involving unsteady aerodynamic excitation, such as periodic vortex shedding from a wing strut, wing wake impingement on the empennage during stalls, or the flow around an extended dive brake.
- Increasing wing stiffness in torsion and decreasing the wing static moment with respect to the elastic axis tend to improve the aeroelastic stability with respect to classical wing bending/torsion flutter.
- Large masses located away from the fuselage centerline, in particular, horizontal stabilizers mounted in a T-tail arrangement, require increased stiffness to counteract the reduced modal frequencies and the increased mass coupling between the important modes.
- Mass balancing of control surfaces is generally favorable, and often necessary to a large degree. It should be noted that the location of the balance mass is also important. For example, in the case of the aileron/wing bending flutter discussed above, it is more effective to place the mass balance on the outboard end of the aileron, where the amplitudes of the antisymmetric wing bending mode are larger.
- In some cases, low-frequency aeroelastic phenomena may adversely affect longitudinal dynamic stability. See [154] for a discussion of a flying wing sailplane that experienced stability problems due to interaction of the rigid body short period mode and the wing first elastic symmetric wing mode (see also [2]).
- Unlike the case of static aeroelastic phenomena, the

aerodynamic effects of concern to flutter analysis are not a function of dynamic pressure alone, and critical flutter speeds cannot simply be stated in terms of fixed equivalent airspeeds. Typically, flutter speeds (as V_{EAS}) decrease somewhat with density altitude. The exact variation of the flutter boundary with altitude must be determined by repeating the aeroelastic analysis and/or flight test over a range of altitudes. The situation is quite complex because different flutter modes may become critical at different altitudes [156].

- JAR-22 requires freedom from flutter up to the design maximum speed V_D, by definition an equivalent airspeed. Also, the never-exceed speed V_{NE} is listed in the Flight Manual and cockpit placards as an indicated airspeed (in this case, nearly the same as equivalent airspeed). This has led to some confusion among pilots as to whether and how V_{NE} needs to be adjusted with altitude in cases where it is not explicitly stated in the aircraft Flight Manual. It is unclear whether there is a sound engineering basis for the well-known rule of thumb of adjusting V_{NE} to follow a constant true-airspeed line. W. Stender, F. Kießling, and J. P. Kuettner [161] have recently provided results suggesting that in some cases, adjusting V_{NE} along a constant $(V_{TAS} + V_{EAS})/2$ line may be more appropriate (see also Fig. 81). In any event, before applying any rule of thumb, pilots should first refer to their aircraft's Flight Manual or contact the manufacturer for guidance. Note that as of Change 5 to JAR-22, any altitude variation in V_{NE} must be indicated on or near the airspeed indicator [49].

Design Requirements

Certification Requirements

The first step in designing a sailplane is understanding what it will be expected to do. There are two aspects to the "mission definition." Obviously, pilot requirements and the type of use (competition, training, aerobatics, etc.) play a primary role. But first, numerous regulatory requirements must be satisfied before the aircraft is even placed in service.

Until the late 1970's, airworthiness requirements varied from country to country. An early international standard was promulgated in 1962 by OSTIV [51] (Organisation Scientifique et Technique Internationale du Vol à Voile, an arm of the Fédération Internationale Aéronautique, or FAI). Although lacking the force of law, the OSTIV Airworthiness Standards (OSTIVAS) provided a set of uniform guidelines which formed the basis for the official German requirements as well as those of most other countries. The OSTIV airworthiness requirements are revised periodically to keep them up-to-date with the official certification requirements.

In Germany, certification of sailplanes is the responsibility of the *Luftfahrt Bundesamt* (LBA) in Braunschweig, which, in the early 1970's, issued a set of airworthiness regulations for sailplanes known as the *LFSM* (Lufttüchtigkeitsforderungen für Segelflugzeuge und Motorsegler - Airworthiness Requirements for Sailplanes and Powered Sailplanes).

In 1979 the airworthiness authorities of several European countries established a common set of airworthiness requirements known as the *Joint Airworthiness Requirements*[1] (JAR). JAR-22 [49], which covers sailplanes and motorgliders, is based on the LFSM and OSTIVAS and accepted by all the JAR countries, including Germany, where JAR-22 has replaced the LFSM [50]. JAR-22 is also accepted in the United States and Australia. In the United States, the Basic Glider Criteria Handbook [47] is no longer accepted as a basis for certification but remains a useful source of information on design criteria and practices [48].

JAR-22 covers the following areas:

- General Requirements
- Flight: Takeoff and landing characteristics, flying qualities, control authority, trim, stability, stall and spin characteristics, high speed handling, aerobatics.
- Structure: Loads in flight, wing, empennage and control surface loads, control system loads, dive brakes and flaps, loads during aero tow, winch launch, landing, etc.
- Design and Construction: Materials, safety factors, flutter, control system, tow hook, landing gear, cockpit, etc.
- Equipment: Installation of equipment and instruments.
- Operational limitations and information: Airspeed limitations, weight and balance, markings and placards, flight and maintenance manuals.

These requirements are found in detail in the JAR [49] and need not be further discussed here.

Additional design considerations include manufacturing costs and the FAI class definitions. The FAI classes are:

- Open class (no limitations),
- 15 meter class (wingspan limited to 15 meters),
- Standard class (15 meter span; flaps prohibited),
- World class (easy to fly, low cost, single design),
- 18 meter Class, and
- Multiplace Class

Apart from the regulatory and class requirements, a primary design requirement for any sailplane is the ability to fly cross country with the highest possible average groundspeed.

[1] Also: "Joint Aviation Requirements"; see JAR-22 Change 5 [49]

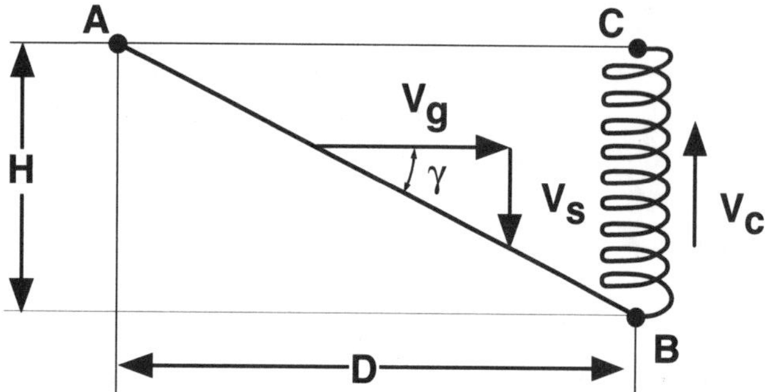

Fig. 82: Idealized segment of cross-country flight.

A – B	glide
B – C	climb
V_c	rate of climb
V_s	sink rate in glide
V_g	airspeed in glide
H	altitude gain in climb
D	distance covered in glide
γ	glide angle

Cross-Country Theory

Modeling Cross-Country Flight

The optimization process considers the effects of variations in individual design parameters on the sailplane's overall performance. To this end, cross-country flight must be expressed in a mathematical form incorporating the various design parameters of interest. Such models are, of necessity, only simplified representations of an actual cross-country flight and do not reflect the countless variations due to local geographic and meteorological conditions. Above all, the designer must keep in mind that these models are not intended to predict actual cross-country speeds. The goal is rather to provide a basis for comparison of different designs, allowing a quantitative determination of the influence of individual design parameters (aspect ratio, airfoil selection, etc.) on cross-country performance.

Average cross-country speed

In its simplest form, cross-country soaring involves a series of climbs and glides from thermal to thermal. Within a given thermal, the area of lift is limited and the climb must take place in a continual turn. The simplest possible cross-country model assumes that the strength of the thermals remains constant throughout the flight and does not vary with altitude. It is also assumed that the transition from glide to climb occurs without delay, *i.e.* the time spent searching for lift is not taken into account. A segment of such a cross-country flight is shown in Fig. 82.

The average cross-country speed, V_{avg}, is determined by the time t required to glide the distance D to the next thermal and to regain the altitude lost in the glide. This is the sum of the time spent climbing, t_c and the gliding time t_g:

$$V_{avg} = \frac{D}{t} = \frac{D}{t_c + t_g} \qquad (68)$$

These are expressed in terms of the average rate of climb V_c, the rate of descent V_s in the interthermal glide, and interthermal gliding speed, V_g:

$$t_c = \frac{H}{V_c} \qquad (69)$$

$$t_g = \frac{H}{V_s} \qquad (70)$$

$$D = \frac{V_g}{V_s}H \qquad (71)$$

$$\frac{V_{avg}}{V_g} = \frac{V_c}{V_c + V_s} \qquad (72)$$

The rate of climb V_c is a function of the thermal strength V_T (the rate of climb of the thermal itself) and V_{s_c}, the sink rate of the circling sailplane:

$$V_c = V_T - V_{s_c} \qquad (73)$$

The average cross-country speed is therefore optimized by designing the sailplane for:

- a low sink rate V_{s_c} while circling,
- a low sink rate V_s while gliding between thermals, and
- a high interthermal glide speed V_g.

Since $\gamma \approx \tan\gamma = V_s/V_g$, the glide angle γ may be used in lieu of the interthermal sink rate V_s. The goal then is to find an appropriate balance between V_{s_c}, γ, and V_g. The inherent difficulty in optimizing the design is immediately recognized in the contradictory requirements for a high glide speed V_g and a small glide angle γ. Further complications arise due to the need to make assumptions regarding weather conditions encountered during the flight.

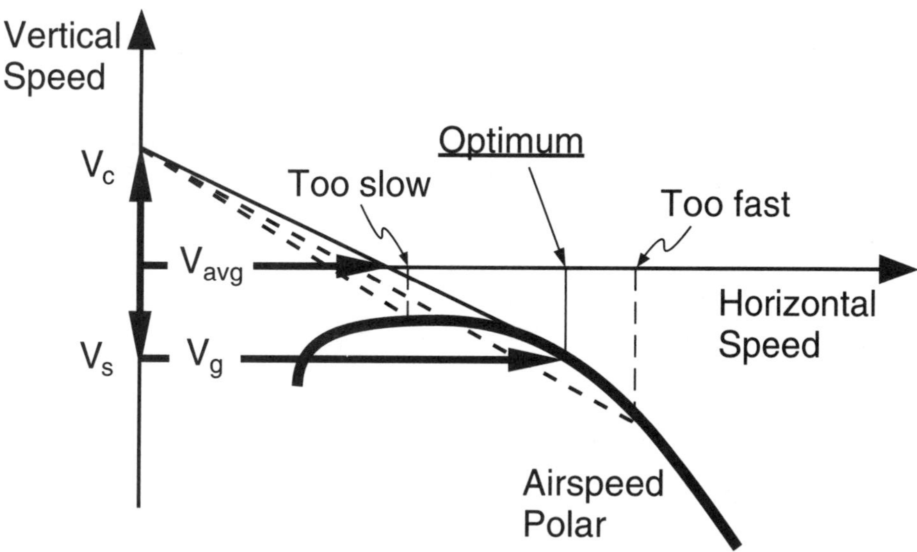

Fig. 83: Graphical solution to optimum interthermal glide speed V_g (Eq. 72).

Figure 83 presents a graphical solution to the average cross-country speed, Eq. 72. The figure shows the airspeed polar $V_s(V_g)$ together with a straight line constructed from the point $(0,V_c)$ on the vertical axis to the operating point $(V_g,V_s(V_g))$. For a given interthermal glide speed V_g, the two right triangles sharing the vertex $(0,V_c)$ are geometrically similar, so that

$$\frac{V_{avg}}{V_g} = \frac{V_c}{V_c + V_s} \qquad (74)$$

(compare with Eq. 72). Thus, the airspeed defined by the intersection of the straight line and the horizontal axis is the average cross-country speed, V_{avg}. It follows that V_{avg} is optimized when the line originating at $(0,V_c)$ is tangent to the airspeed polar. The figure is adjusted for winds and interthermal sink by shifting the airspeed polar as required. For further discussion see Reichmann [61].

Climb Performance in Thermals

Performance in turns

The rate of climb achieved in a thermal depends strongly on its performance and handling qualities in turning flight. An analysis of turn performance reflects *centrifugal force*, which results from writing Newton's second law, $F = m\mathbf{a}$, in a rotating frame of reference. For an object traveling in a circular path, the *centripetal acceleration* $\mathbf{a}_{cent}$ points towards the center of the circle. The centrifugal force $CF = -m\mathbf{a}_{cent}$, directed *away* from the center of the circle, is often termed a *fictitious force* because it is not a direct result of mechan-

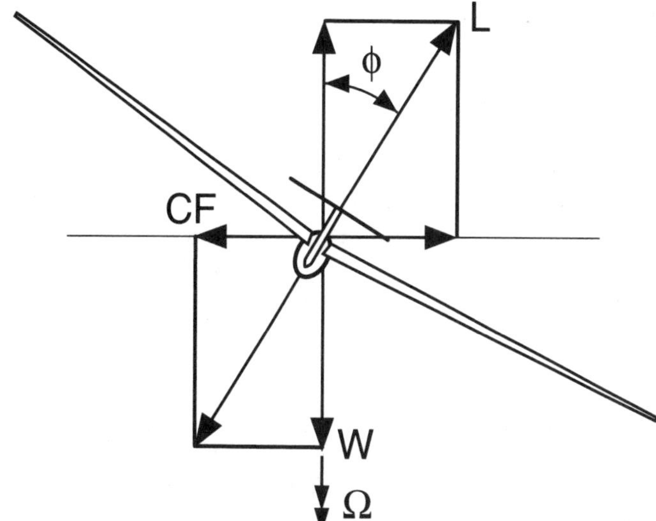

Fig. 84: Equilibrium of forces in turn.

L	lift
W	weight
CF	centrifugal force
ϕ	bank angle
Ω	turn rate

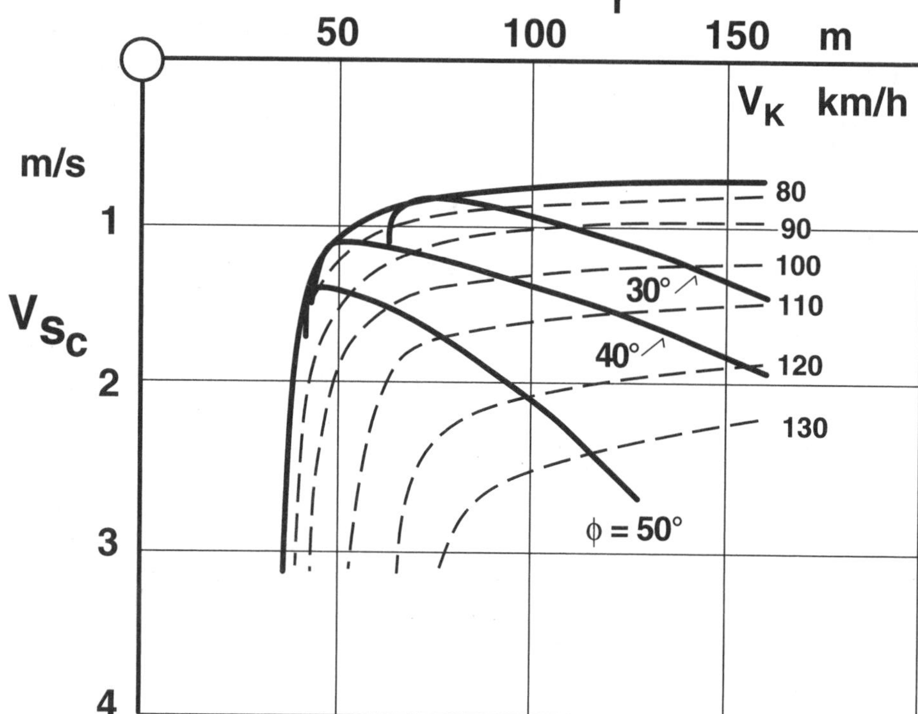

Fig. 85: Rate of sink V_{s_c} vs. turn radius r for various airspeeds V_K and bank angles ϕ

ical interactions between the body and its surroundings. Nevertheless, the force is real in the sense that it can be used to write a dynamic equilibrium equation (D'Alembert's principle).

Figure 84 presents a dynamic equilibrium diagram for a turn, with centrifugal force balanced by banking the sailplane so that a component of its lift lies in the horizontal plane. Weight, W, centrifugal force CF, and lift L are related to bank angle through the following relationships:

$$W = L\cos\phi \qquad (75)$$

$$CF = L\sin\phi \qquad (76)$$

The lift required in a turn is greater than that required in level flight because only a component of the lift is available to support the sailplane's weight. The expressions for airspeed and sink rate, (Eqs. 58 and 61) are modified accordingly:

$$V_K = \sqrt{\frac{2}{\rho}\frac{W}{S}\frac{1}{C_L\cos\phi}} \qquad (77)$$

$$V_{s_c} = \frac{C_D}{C_L^{3/2}\cos^{3/2}\phi}\sqrt{\frac{2}{\rho}\frac{W}{S}} \qquad (78)$$

Introducing the elementary relationships

$$CF = \frac{mV_K^2}{r} \qquad (79)$$

$$W = mg \qquad (80)$$

leads to

$$\tan\phi = \frac{CF}{W} = \frac{V_K^2}{rg} \qquad (81)$$

$$V_K = \sqrt{rg\tan\phi} \qquad (82)$$

$$r = \frac{V_K^2}{g\tan\phi} \qquad (83)$$

with the acceleration of gravity $g = 9.81\,m/s^2$. Given any two of the parameters ϕ, V_K, and r, Eqs. 81-83 determine the third. For example, a sailplane circling at V_K = 80 km/h = 22.2 m/s and a bank angle of 45° has a turn radius r = 50m. Although the bank angle ϕ and the circling speed V_K are the appropriate parameters for defining the trim state in the turn, it is the turn radius which relates the path of flight to the region of lift.

Note that according to Eqs. 61 and 78, the minimum sink rate in a turn will be higher than the minimum sink rate in level flight by a factor of $1/\cos^{3/2}\phi$.

The turn rate Ω resolves in components $\Omega\cos\phi$ and $\Omega\sin\phi$ about the sailplane vertical and lateral axes, respectively (Fig. 84). Therefore, a turning sailplane has angular velocities in both pitch and yaw, both of which contribute to the empennage angles of attack and affect the elevator and rudder inputs required to maintain the turn.

Figure 85 is a *turn diagram* relating the turn radius and bank angle to the sink rate. The figure shows, for example, that for a constant airspeed V_K, the turn radius can be reduced only by increasing the bank angle. Along with the increased bank angle comes an increased sink rate. If, on the other hand, the bank angle is held constant, the turn can be tightened only by reducing the airspeed.

Plotting the calculated sink rates for various bank angles on a single turn diagram leads to a limiting curve defining the lowest sink rate achieved by a particular sailplane flying a turn of given radius. Note that the minimum sink speed always increases as the turn radius is decreased. The limiting curve may be thought of as the sailplane's *circling polar*. Turn diagrams such as Fig. 85 also show the beneficial effect of reduced wing loading on climb performance.

The relationships developed previously may be used to express the sink rate while circling as a function of the various design parameters.

First, the airspeed from Eq. 77 is substituted into Eq. 82 and both sides are squared:

$$\frac{2}{\rho}\frac{W}{S}\frac{1}{C_L}\frac{1}{\cos\phi} = rg\frac{\sin\phi}{\cos\phi} \tag{84}$$

$$\sin\phi = \frac{2}{\rho}\frac{W}{S}\frac{1}{rgC_L} \tag{85}$$

Applying a trigonometric identity leads to

$$\cos\phi = \sqrt{1-\sin^2\phi} = \sqrt{1-\left(\frac{2}{\rho}\frac{W}{S}\frac{1}{rgC_L}\right)^2} \tag{86}$$

This result is substituted into the expression for sink rate (Eq. 78):

$$V_{S_c} = C_D C_L^{-3/2}\sqrt{\frac{2}{\rho}\frac{W}{S}}\left[1-\left(\frac{2}{\rho}\frac{W}{S}\frac{1}{rgC_L}\right)^2\right]^{-3/4} \tag{87}$$

Breaking down the drag into its main components - induced drag, profile drag C_{D_0}, and parasite drag C_{D_P} - results in the following expression:

$$V_{S_c} = \left(\frac{kC_L{}^2}{\pi AR} + C_{D_0}(C_L) + C_{D_P}(C_L)\right) \cdot C_L^{-3/2}\sqrt{\frac{2}{\rho}\frac{W}{S}}\left[1-\left(\frac{2}{\rho}\frac{W}{S}\frac{1}{rgC_L}\right)^2\right]^{-3/4} \tag{88}$$

The parasite drag includes the fuselage drag, empennage drag, and drag due to the various attachments (antenna, tip skids, etc). Since the empennage drag includes the trim drag, the parasite drag may be a function of C_L. Profile drag refers to the friction and pressure drag of the airfoil itself and is also a function of the lift coefficient, particularly if the airfoil polar features a pronounced laminar bucket.

In the final analysis it is not the sink rate, but the net rate of climb that is important. Hence, before discussing the implications of Eq. 88, we must first develop a model for the lift distribution within the thermal.

Modeling thermals

Nature provides a countless variety of thermals. Diverse geographic and climatic conditions as well as localized meteorological phenomena lead to the formation of thermals of varying strength, width, and structure. Fortunately, when evaluating sailplane designs, we do not require detailed models of every possible thermal - generic descriptions of a few typical thermal types suffice.

Limited data from inflight measurements of thermal lift distributions have been published (see, for example, D. A. Konovalov [57]). Nevertheless, there is no unanimity of opinion concerning the most appropriate mathematical model for thermals. Up to now, most analyses have been based on Carmichael's model [53], which categorizes thermals as narrow/strong, narrow/weak, and wide (Fig. 86).

Although useful results have been obtained with this model (see for example A. Quast [101]), starting in the early 1970's, many researchers began to recognize the need for a more refined approach. Based on systematic analyses and numerous in-flight investigations, K. H. Horstmann [55] proposed an improved set of standard thermals that has proven somewhat more realistic, particularly when modeling typical European weather conditions. This model is based on four typical thermals, varying in overall strength

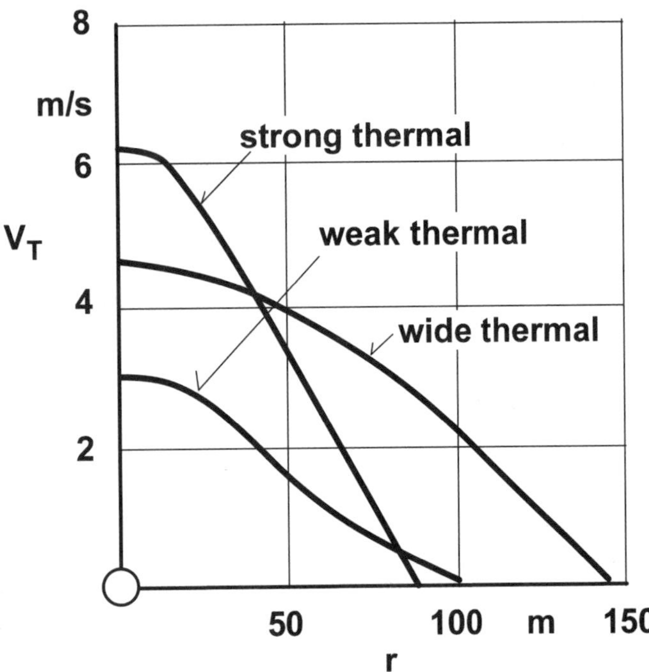

Fig. 86: Standard thermal profiles in Carmichael model [53].

V_T Thermal strength
r Distance from center of thermal

and width (Fig. 87). Each thermal type has a specific radial distribution of lift. See also E. E. Larrabee [90], L. Welch, A. Welch and F. Irving [69], and F. Irving [56] for further discussion on the subject of thermal models.

The remainder of the discussion will be based on the Horstmann model.

The rate of climb achieved while thermaling is determined by plotting the thermal strength distribution together with the circling polar in a single diagram as has been done in Fig. 88 for the example of an ASW-19. The best climb rate is achieved at a turn radius $r \approx 64$m. If the pilot tightens the turn by increasing the bank angle, the increased lift near the thermal's center will not make up for the higher sink rate associated with the increased centrifugal force. On the other hand, flying the aircraft with too great a turn radius will place it in the weak outer zone of the thermal. Figure 89 shows the climb rates achieved by a typical standard class sailplane in the four standard thermals. The figure shows that it makes little sense to circle at a bank angle of more than 45°, even in a narrow thermal. From here on it will be assumed that the aircraft is always flying at the bank angle that maximizes its climb rate in a given thermal. In practice, of course, this will not always be the case; nevertheless the assumption provides a consistent basis for evaluating parametric design variations.

Influence of various design parameters on rate of climb

Having derived an expression for the sink rate in a turn, selected a thermal model, and made the assumption that the pilot always flies at the optimum bank angle, we are ready to evaluate the effects of variations of individual design parameters on the rate of climb achieved in a thermal. Due to the complexity of the expression for the sink rate, only one parameter is varied at a time. The optimum bank

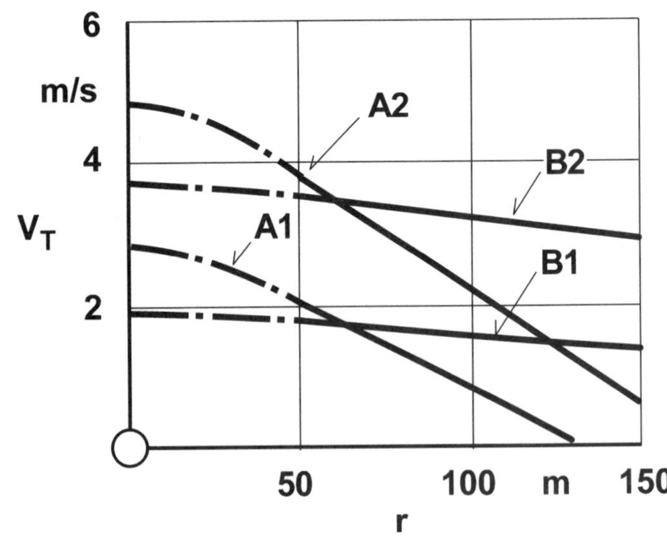

	A1	A2	B1	B2
V_T [m/s] at r = 60m	1.75	3.50	1.75	3.50
Gradient $\left[\frac{cm}{s}/m\right]$	2.5	3.20	0.45	0.60

Fig. 87: Standard thermal profiles in Horstmann model [55].

V_T Thermal strength
r Distance from center of thermal

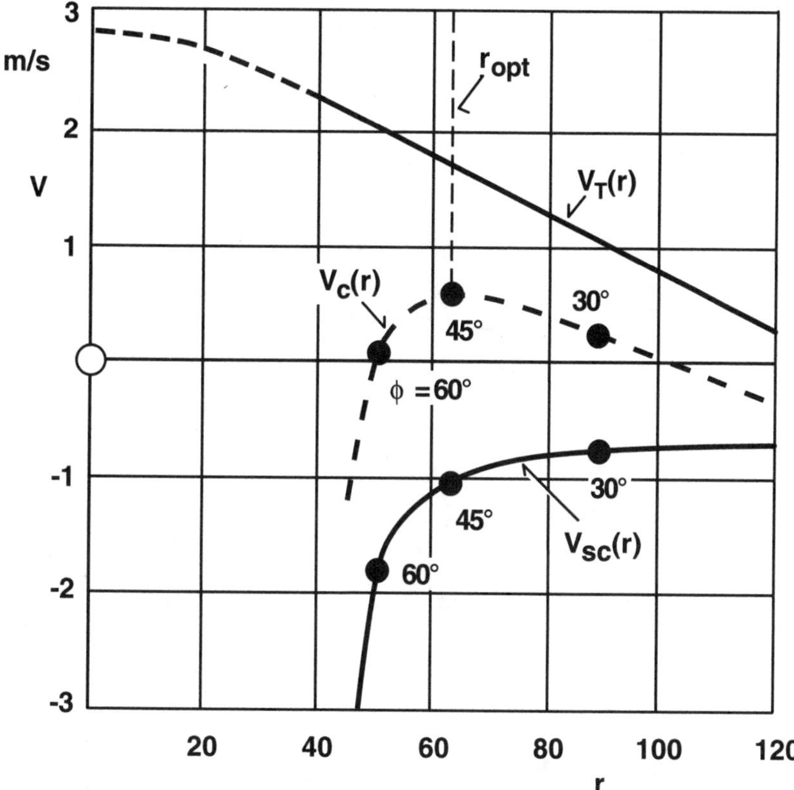

Fig. 88: Rate of climb vs. turn radius for ASW-19 in type A1 thermal.

V_T thermal strength
V_{sc} sink rate in turn
V_c net rate of climb
$V_c(r) = V_T(r) - V_{sc}(r)$

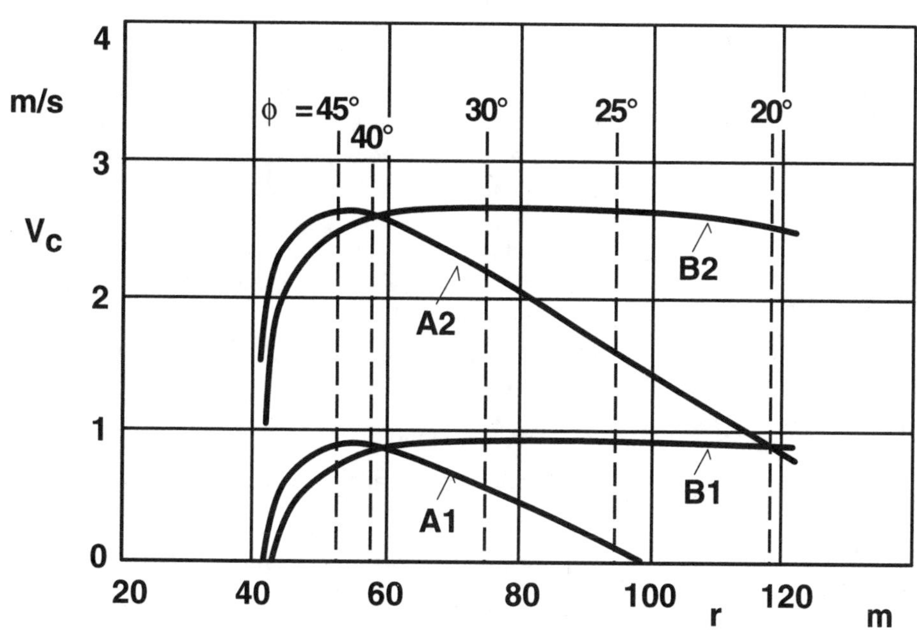

Fig. 89: Rate of climb vs. turn radius and bank angle for a typical Standard Class sailplane in various thermal types [55].
W/S = 28 daN/m^2

Fig. 90: Influence of airfoil performance on climb performance.

- airfoil optimized for high speed (NACA 64_2-415)
- airfoil optimized for low speed (NACA 63_3-618)
- airfoil with camber changing flaps (FX 62-K-131)

— · — · lines of constant achieved rate of climb

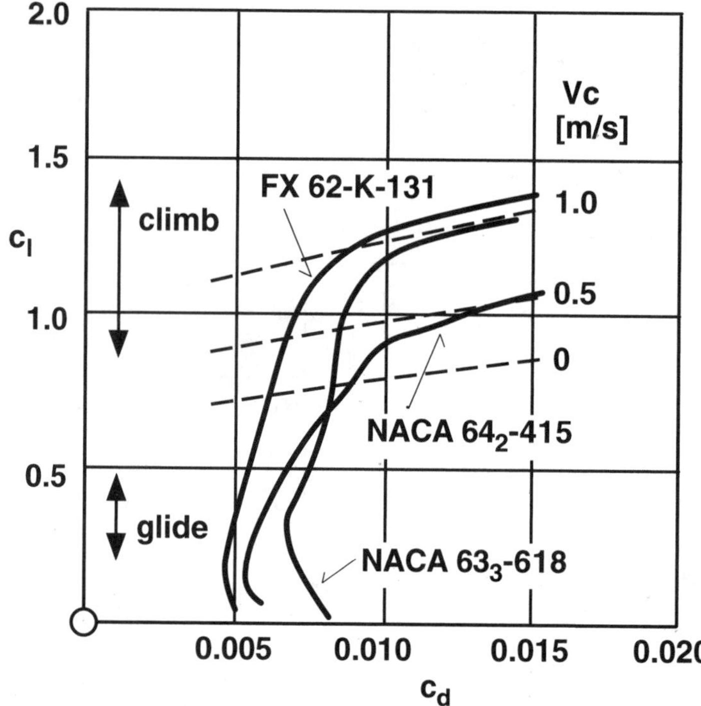

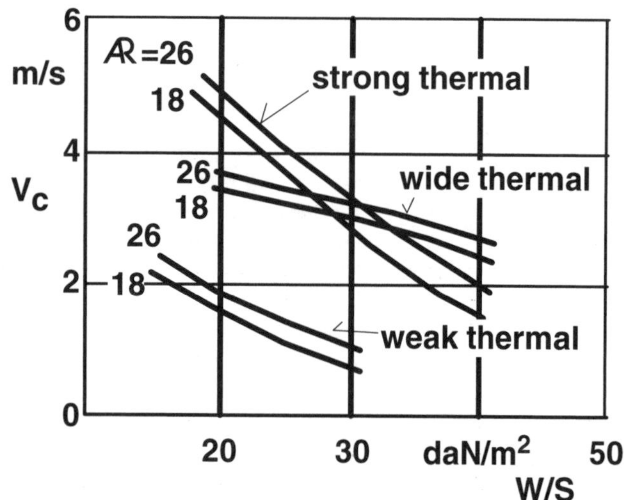

Fig. 91: Typical variation of best rate of climb V_c with wing loading, aspect ratio, and thermal strength [101]. Wing chord held fixed; Carmichael thermal model.

angle is determined by calculating sink rate diagrams such as Fig. 88.

Since airfoil polars generally do not lend themselves to representation with simple mathematical functions, it is difficult to incorporate specific airfoil characteristics in the climb model. One approach is to calculate the rate of climb for a matrix of combinations of c_l and c_d, presenting the results together with the actual airfoil polars (Fig. 90). Such diagrams confirm that the best climb rates are achieved with airfoils that produce high lift coefficients together with low drag coefficients. Design variations that shift the climb rate lines downwards will improve the best climb rate possible with a given airfoil.

With these factors in mind, it is evident that the best rate of climb is improved by:

- reducing wing loading,
- increasing aspect ratio,
- increasing Reynolds number,
- reducing profile and parasite drag, and
- ensuring that the lift distribution is as close to ideal (elliptical) as possible.

These conclusions are confirmed by diagrams such as Fig. 91, which shows the effects of wing loading, aspect ratio, and thermal type on the climb rate.

Interthermal Glide

Optimum speed for the interthermal glide

Having examined the influence of various design parameters on the climb rate, the interthermal gliding phase must be investigated in some more detail. Indeed, the goal is not to optimize the climb rate, but the average cross-country speed.

When exiting a thermal, the pilot must choose the airspeed to fly to reach the next thermal. This interthermal glide speed has a pronounced influence on the average cross-country speed, as depicted in Fig. 92. If, for example, the pilot flies at the airspeed (or rather, the lift coefficient) for the best glide angle, the sailplane will reach the next thermal with the least loss of altitude (case A). At a higher airspeed (cases B and C), the sailplane reaches the next thermal at a lower altitude, but also earlier than the best glide speed case (case A). The optimum airspeed depends on the anticipated rate of climb in the next thermal and the sailplane's airspeed polar. If the lift is strong enough, the extra altitude lost by flying faster to the next thermal may be regained before the slower flying aircraft even reaches the thermal. On the other hand, if the lift is weak or if the speed chosen is too fast for the conditions, the time saved in the glide will not suffice to compensate for the extra time spent climbing (case C). For a given sailplane at a given wing loading, the optimum interthermal glide speed V_g is a function of the strength of the lift.

An analytic expression for the optimum airspeed is developed starting with the expression for the average cross-country speed V_{avg} (Eq. 72). The glide speed V_g is replaced with the expression in Eq. 58 and V_s, the sink speed in the glide, is replaced with Eq. 61.

$$V_{avg} = \frac{V_c C_L^{-1/2}}{(C_{D_0} + C_{D_P})C_L^{-3/2} + \frac{k}{\pi AR} C_L^{1/2} + \frac{V_c}{\sqrt{\frac{2}{\rho}\frac{W}{S}}}} \qquad (89)$$

In this expression, the drag coefficient has been broken down into its induced, profile, and parasite drag components. Differentiating this expression with respect to C_L and setting the result to zero yields the lift coefficient at which the interthermal glide should be flown to maximize the average cross-country speed V_{avg}:

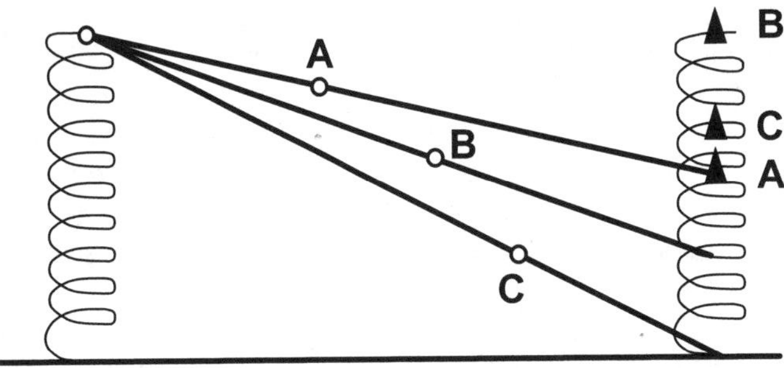

Fig. 92: Optimum interthermal glide speed.

A too slow
B optimum
C too fast

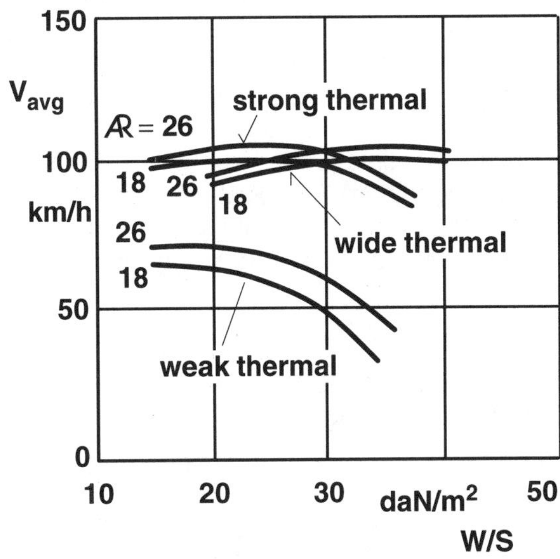

Fig. 93: Typical variation of average ground speed V_{avg} with wing loading, aspect ratio, and thermal strength [101]. Wing chord held fixed; Carmichael thermal model.

$$\frac{dV_{avg}}{dC_L} = 0 \qquad (90)$$

$$C_{D_P} + C_{D_0} - \frac{k\, C_{L_{opt}}^2}{\pi AR} - \frac{V_c\, C_{L_{opt}}^{3/2}}{2\sqrt{\frac{2}{\rho}\frac{W}{S}}} = 0 \qquad (91)$$

Equation 91 shows that the lift coefficient for the optimum interthermal glide speed depends on the parasite drag, profile drag, lift distribution, aspect ratio, air density (*i.e.* density altitude), wing loading, and achieved rate of climb while thermaling. The latter, as we have seen in the preceding section, itself depends on a considerable number of design parameters including, above all, the size and strength of the thermal.

What simple, useful results may be obtained from this relatively complex equation? Before answering, it must be observed that the pilot and the designer are interested in fundamentally different kinds of information.

To the pilot, the aircraft and its various design parameters are a known quantity, and the problem is one of tailoring the flying strategy to the actual weather conditions encountered. By observing the achieved rate of climb during a given flight, the pilot can make an assumption regarding the expected rate of climb in the next thermal and calculate the optimum interthermal glide speed directly from Eq. 91. Traditionally, the computations are made in advance for a typical range of climb rates and entered on a ring (the "MacCready speed ring", after P. MacCready, originator of speed-to-fly theory) mounted on the variometer, so that the pilot's work is reduced to adjusting the ring according to the expected climb rate. The variometer needle then indicates the "speed-to-fly" on the speed ring, properly reflecting the influence of variations in vertical air movement during the interthermal glide. Speed-to-fly theory is described in detail by F. Weinholtz [68] and H. Reichmann [61]; see also F. Irving [56].

Good cross-country strategy obviously involves more than simple speed-to-fly theory. Recent years have seen the development of onboard computers for sailplanes that combine GPS navigation together with performance computations that take into account a wide variety of factors - wind, thermal strength variation with altitude, performance degradations due to insect accumulation, water ballast, etc. Nevertheless, as far as the pilot is concerned, the basic problem remains the same: how to get the most out of a given sailplane design.

The designer, on the other hand, is interested in variations in the sailplane design itself and their impact on overall cross-country performance. By using a standard thermal model and assuming that the aircraft is flown in an optimum manner between thermals, the designer can evaluate the influence of the various design parameters in a consistent manner, identify optimum combinations for various weather conditions, and make basic design decisions.

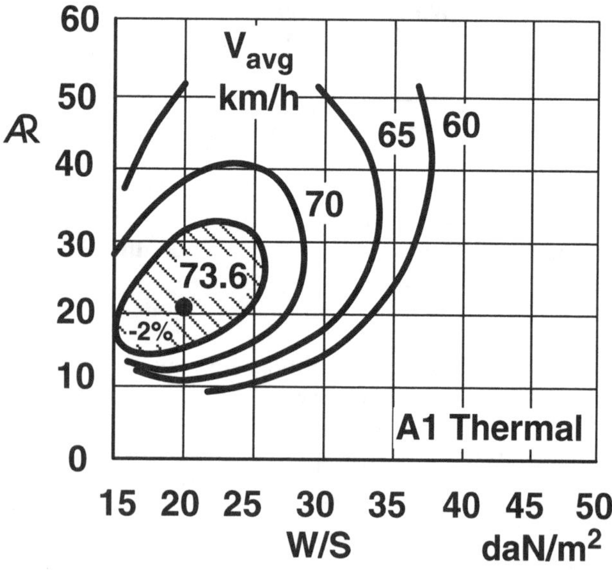

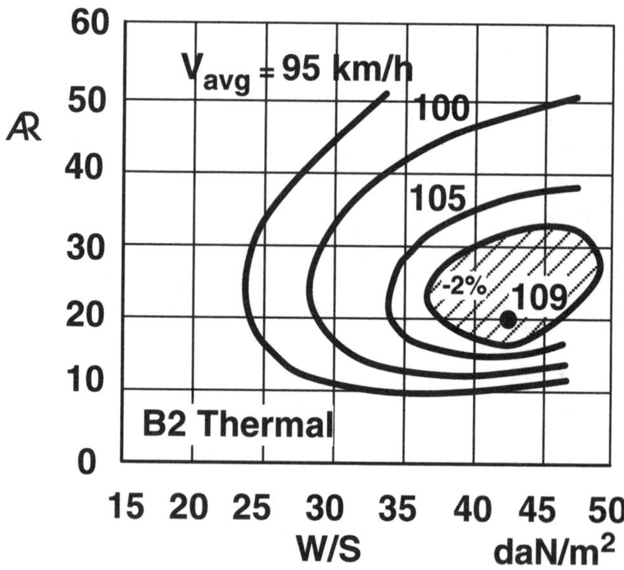

Fig. 94: Effect of aspect ratio and wing loading on average cross-country speed. Wingspan held fixed at b=20m; FX 67-K-150 airfoil; Reynolds number effects included.

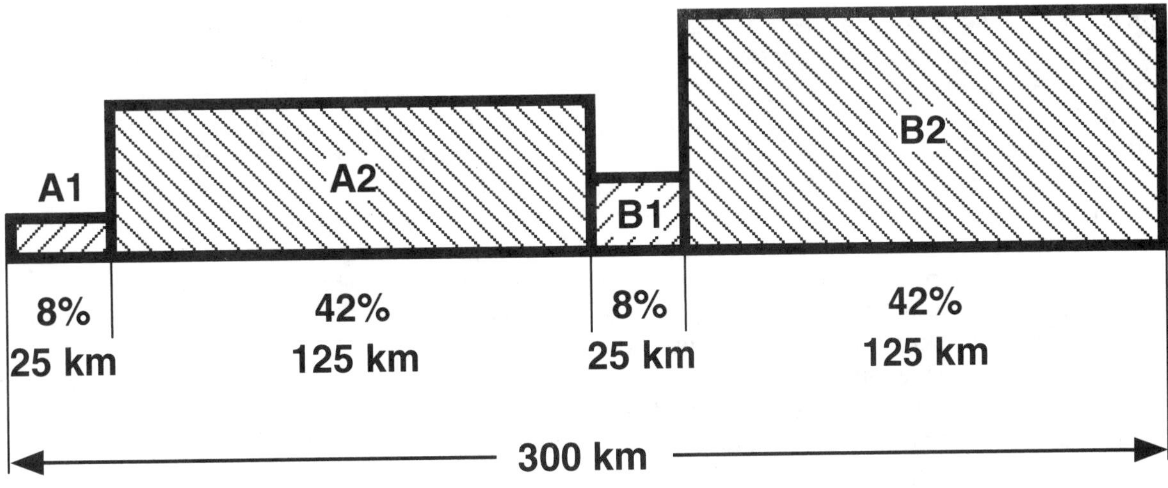

Fig. 95: Quast's weather model [60] applied to a typical 300km flight. Flight is modeled in four phases, each with different thermal model.

The question of the optimum speed to fly between thermals arose in the 1930's as the first long cross-country flights were made during the Rhön competitions. A number of pilots and scientists worked independently to solve this problem (see H. Reichmann [62]). One of the first was W. Späte [65], who applied his analysis to win the 1938 Rhön contest. The earliest literature on the subject was published in Poland by R. Szuklewicz and L. Szwarc and, later, by W. Kasprzyk, all in 1938. Published in Polish shortly before the war, these works remained unknown to the western world. Rigorous mathematical analysis was first applied to the problem in 1949 by K. Nickel [59] and P. MacCready [58]. These references are, however, relatively difficult to find. Independent of these investigators, E. Dewing had already written a short note on the topic in 1947. Speed-to-fly theory finally came into widespread use with the introduction of the MacCready ring in the 1950's. In 1982, G. Schänzer [63] analyzed the energy transfer due to vertical motion of the atmosphere in more detail and showed that continually varying the airspeed according to MacCready theory is useful only in large-scale vertical gust fields. When passing through smaller-sized gust fields as typically encountered in central Europe, it is more efficient to ignore local areas of lift and sink and hold the airspeed constant at the MacCready speed corresponding to the rate of climb expected in the next thermal. This result had already been anticipated by many pilots based on experience, without theoretical proof.

Design for cross-country performance

Numerical results from parametric design studies show that, for a given achieved rate of climb, the optimum interthermal glide speed increases with aspect ratio, wing loading, improved lift distribution, and reduced parasite and profile drag. The interthermal glide speed is usually much higher than the circling speed in thermals and the lift coefficients in the two flight conditions differ accordingly. Although, while thermaling, the wing is operating near its maximum lift coefficient, the glide is usually flown at a lift coefficient considerably smaller than the lift coefficient for best glide angle.

This leads to a number of conflicting design requirements:

- the wing loading should be high for the interthermal glide but low while thermaling,
- to ensure good performance in both climb and glide, the drag coefficients must be low over a wide range of lift coefficients,
- the circulation distribution should be as nearly elliptical as possible, whether thermaling or gliding between thermals.

Finding a compromise that satisfies these requirements to the greatest possible extent is one of the most difficult challenges facing the designer. One useful technique is to plot the calculated cross-country performance as a function of the individual parameters. Although a great number of parameters are of interest, only a few can be treated in any single diagram. Typical results are shown in Fig. 93. The diagram shows the effects of wing loading, aspect ratio, and thermal type with all other design parameters held constant. In this example, increased aspect ratio is always favorable. The study assumes that wing chord remains constant, so that increasing aspect ratio corresponds to increasing the wingspan. Note as well that the optimum wing loading varies with the thermal type.

Cross-country performance may also be presented as a function of two design parameters in one diagram (Fig. 94). The figure shows the optimum configuration as well as the penalty for deviating from the optimum. Since conflicting requirements - in particular, the need for good performance in a wide range of weather conditions - always necessitate design compromises, figures of this type are especially useful in design studies.

When optimizing a sailplane for the highest average cross-country speed, different assumptions regarding the strength and width of the thermals will lead to widely differing designs. In practice, however, the pilot will encounter a wide range of soaring conditions, even during the course of a single flight. A. Quast [60] has proposed a mixed weather model with the four Horstmann thermal models occurring in specified proportions (for example, Fig. 95). Results obtained with such weather models are relatively insensitive to changes in the proportions of the individual thermal types.

In the following chapter, Quast's weather model will be used to assess the influence of the various design parameters on cross-country performance.

Sailplane Design Optimization

Basic Considerations

The previous chapter discussed methods for evaluating the influence of primary aerodynamic design parameters on cross-country performance. These parameters - wing loading, aspect ratio, and airfoil selection - are subject to certain practical constraints. For example, despite the availability of carbon fiber and other advanced materials, structural weight cannot be reduced below a certain minimum, placing a lower limit on the wing loading. Similarly, span and aspect ratio tend to be limited by cost and handling considerations. Indeed, aerodynamic efficiency is only one of the many considerations that come into play during the design process. Others include:

- **Structural Weight:** Airfoil thickness, wingspan, and aspect ratio have a strong effect on structural weight and cannot be optimized based on aerodynamics alone.

- **Stiffness:** In addition to having the strength required to support the airloads, the wing must be stiff enough to prevent excessive elastic deformations and flutter.

- **Manufacturing costs:** The final product must be affordable and easy to maintain and repair. This usually rules out the use of labor-intensive construction methods and expensive materials such as titanium and exotic aluminum alloys. Carbon fiber has become more affordable in recent years and has found widespread application in high performance sailplanes.

- **Cockpit layout and visibility:** Sailplane performance ultimately depends on pilot performance and a comfortable cockpit is essential. Pilot comfort requires a sufficiently large cockpit, even at the cost of increased drag.

- **Flying qualities:** Similarly, aerodynamic performance cannot take precedence over good handling qualities.

- **Ground handling:** Assembly and disassembly must not leave pilot and crew exhausted. This sets a practical limit on the weight of the individual wing sections. Large wings may require a three- or four-piece design in order to fit in reasonably-sized trailers and reduce the strain on the ground crew.

Clearly, a successful design involves a careful balance of conflicting design requirements. This chapter discusses the considerations affecting the optimization of the individual design parameters (see also [77,113]). For more information on the general topic of aircraft design see D. Stinton [25] and E. Torenbeek [26].

Wing Design

Setting the Aspect Ratio

Relation to other parameters

Aspect ratio is defined in terms of wing area and span. Thus, changes in aspect ratio may result from:

- changes in span, with the chord held fixed
- changes in chord, with the span held fixed
- changes in span and chord, with the area held fixed (Fig. 96).

In the first case, increasing the aspect ratio also increases the wing area, making the sailplane larger, heavier, and more expensive. Fuselage drag remains essentially unchanged, so that its relative importance in the overall

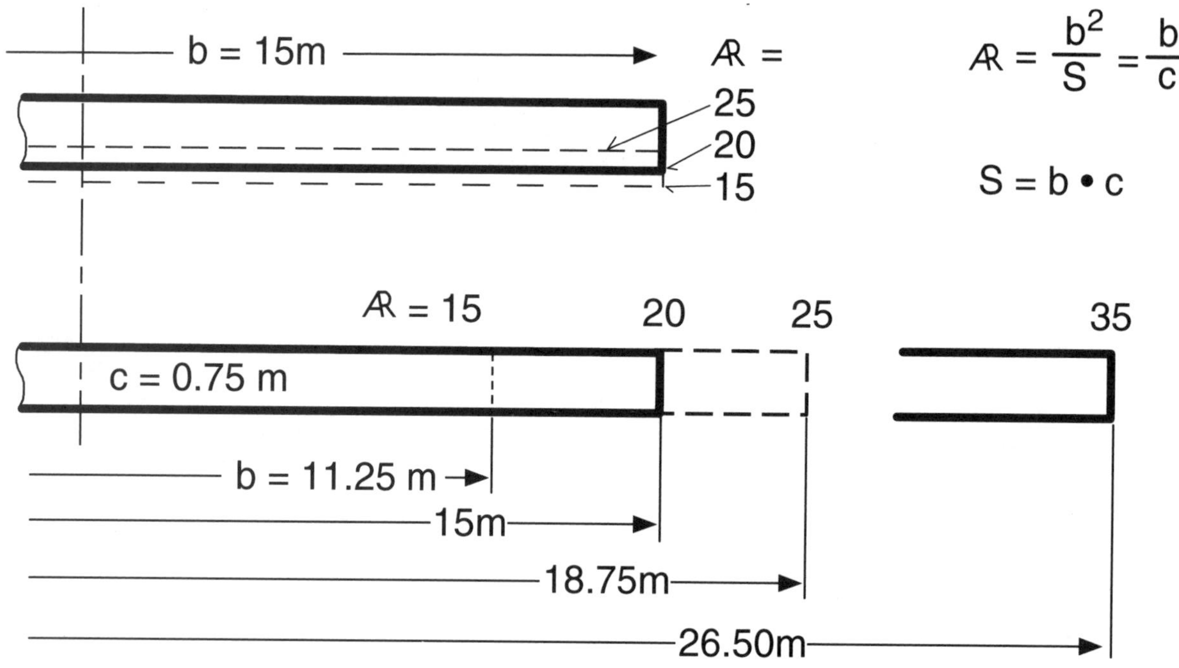

Fig. 96: Aspect ratio variation with rectangular planform wing:
- span held constant; chord varies
- chord held constant; span varies

drag breakdown is reduced. Stability considerations, on the other hand, dictate that the empennage be enlarged to accommodate the larger wing. With the chord fixed, profile Reynolds numbers at a given airspeed remain independent of aspect ratio (Fig. 97).

In the second case, an increase in aspect ratio is achieved by reducing the chord, leading to reduced Reynolds numbers and increased sectional profile drag coefficients. As a result of the reduced wing area, the fuselage contributes a greater fraction of the total drag.

Finally, in the constant wing area case, the relationship between the fuselage and total drag remains practically unchanged, although a small effect due to Reynolds number variations remains.

The second case is of particular interest because it applies to the span-limited FAI Classes (Standard, FAI 15m and 18m). Table 5 shows the effects of varying the aspect ratio on wing area and Reynolds number for a rectangular wing of fixed span.

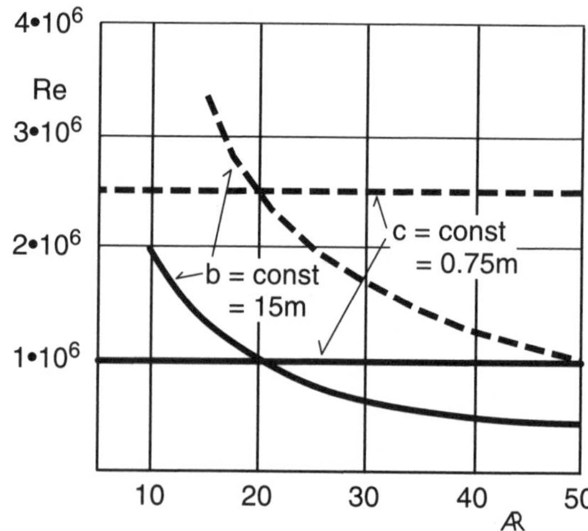

Fig. 97: Effect of aspect ratio on Reynolds number for rectangular wing.
Baseline wing: b = 15m, c = 0.75m, Æ = 20.
- - - cruise, V = 50m/s = 180 km/h
—— slow flight, V = 20m/s = 72 km/h

Table 5: (a) Wing geometric parameters with span held fixed.

AR	b [m]	c [m]	S [m²]	Re_C	Re_G
10	15	1.50	22.50	$2.00 \cdot 10^6$	$5.00 \cdot 10^6$
15	15	1.00	15.00	$1.33 \cdot 10^6$	$3.33 \cdot 10^6$
20	15	0.75	11.25	$1.00 \cdot 10^6$	$2.50 \cdot 10^6$
22.5	15	0.67	10.00	$0.89 \cdot 10^6$	$2.23 \cdot 10^6$
25	15	0.60	9.00	$0.80 \cdot 10^6$	$2.00 \cdot 10^6$
30	15	0.50	7.50	$0.67 \cdot 10^6$	$1.67 \cdot 10^6$
35	15	0.43	6.45	$0.57 \cdot 10^6$	$1.43 \cdot 10^6$
40	15	0.38	5.70	$0.51 \cdot 10^6$	$1.27 \cdot 10^6$

Climb Reynolds number Re_C based on V=72 km/h = 20 m/s.
Glide Reynolds number Re_G based on V=180 km/h = 50 m/s.

(b) Wing geometric parameters for constant chord, c=0.75m, $Re_C = 1 \cdot 10^6$ and $Re_G = 2.5 \cdot 10^6$.

Æ	10	15	20	25	30	35	40
b [m]	7.50	11.25	15.00	18.75	22.75	26.50	30.00
S [m²]	5.63	8.44	11.25	14.06	17.06	19.88	22.50

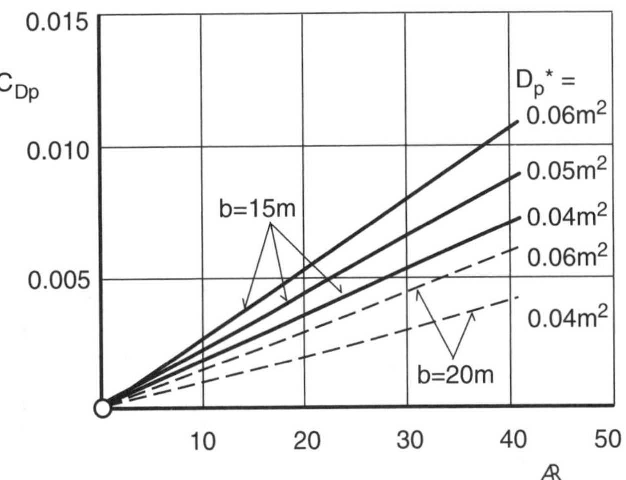

Fig. 99: Influence of aspect ratio on parasite drag coefficient parasite drag C_{D_p} for b = 15 and 20m.
$D_p^\star$ = equivalent flat plate area.

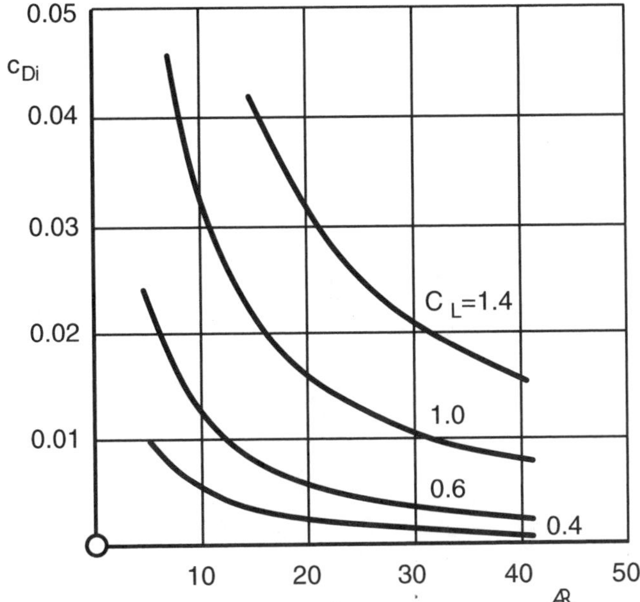

Fig. 98: Induced drag coefficient vs. aspect ratio for k = 1 and various values of C_L.

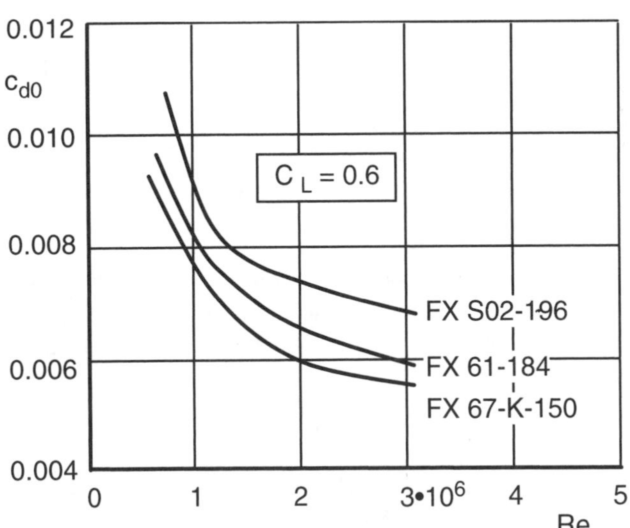

Fig. 100: Profile drag c_{d_0} as a function of Reynolds number for three typical sailplane airfoils for C_L = 0.6, from [168].

Fig. 101: Drag components and total drag as a function of aspect ratio.

$C_{D_i} + C_{D_0}$	wing only
$C_{D_i} + C_{D_0} + C_{D_p}$	complete aircraft
Example:	$C_L = 0.6$
	$b = 15\text{m}$
	$D_p^\star = 0.050\text{m}^2$
	FX S 02-196 Airfoil

AR', AR'' = aspect ratios for minimum overall drag.

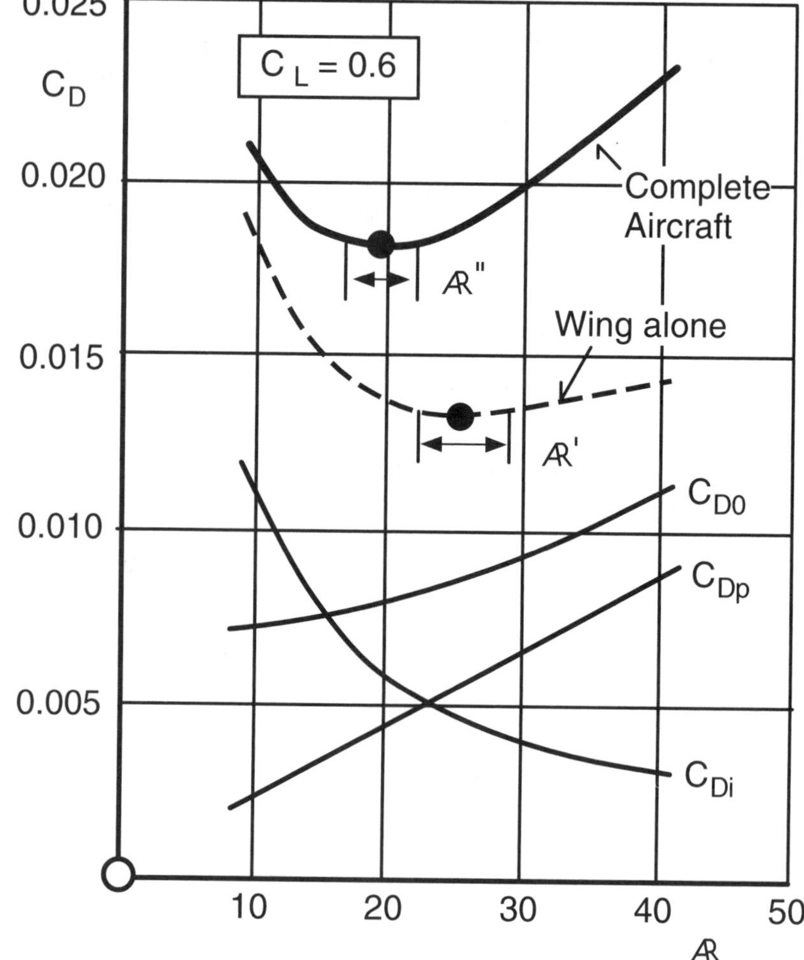

Effect on drag

As will now be discussed in some detail, aspect ratio affects the coefficients of induced drag, profile drag, and fuselage drag. The coefficient of induced drag is calculated using Eq. 47:

$$C_{D_i} = k\frac{{C_L}^2}{\pi AR} \tag{92}$$

with the factor k accounting for a non-elliptic lift distribution. Figure 98 shows the relationship between aspect ratio and induced drag, assuming an ideal lift distribution (elliptical, k = 1). The favorable effects of aspect ratio are especially apparent at high lift coefficients.

Aspect ratio effects on the parasite drag coefficient C_{D_p} are easily calculated by assuming that the total parasite drag D_P of the fuselage, empennage, and various antennas, instrumentation probes etc. remains unchanged with changes in wing area:

$$D_p = C_{D_p} qS \tag{93}$$

$$C_{D_p} = \frac{D_p}{qS} = \frac{D_p}{qS}\frac{b^2}{b^2} = \frac{D_p}{qb^2}AR \tag{94}$$

Defining an *equivalent flat plate area* $D_p^\star = D_p/q$, this becomes

$$C_{D_p} = \frac{D_p^\star}{b^2}AR \tag{95}$$

Equation 95 shows that the parasite drag coefficient of a wing of fixed span and equivalent flat plate area increases linearly with aspect ratio. This is shown for a typical case

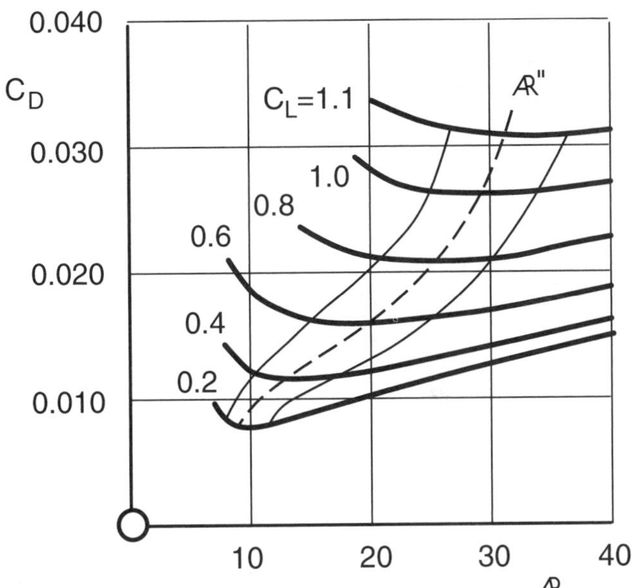

Fig. 102: Effect of lift coefficient and aspect ratio on total drag.

Example: b=15m
$D_p^{\star}$=0.050m²
W/S=30 daN/m²
FX 62-K-131 Airfoil
A" = Aspect ratio for minimum total drag

in Fig. 99. To some extent, this is an artifact of the normalization process - in physical units, the parasite drag is independent of aspect ratio. As will be discussed, the concept of an equivalent flat plate area is especially useful when calculating drag polars.

In the constant-span case, aspect ratio also affects profile drag because of Reynolds number variations (Fig. 97). A numerical estimate of this effect requires detailed aerodynamic data from a profile catalog and/or airfoil analysis software. Figure 100 illustrates the dependence of profile drag on Reynolds number for three typical sailplane airfoils operating at c_l = 0.6. The trends at other lift coefficients are quite similar. This topic will be discussed in more detail in the section on airfoil selection.

Plotting the individual drag components C_{D_i}, C_{D_p}, and C_{D_0} as a function of aspect ratio shows that the total drag coefficient may be minimized by proper selection of aspect ratio (Fig. 101). Even if only the wing (induced and profile drag) is taken into account, a shallow minimum occurring at relatively high aspect ratio is apparent. Introducing the parasite drag reduces the optimum aspect ratio considerably. The greater the coefficient of parasite drag, the more pronounced the effect. The minimum remains rather shallow, so that for practical purposes a certain range of aspect ratios may be considered optimal.

Because of the strong effect of lift on induced drag (Fig. 98), the aspect ratio for minimum drag coefficient varies considerably with lift coefficient. At high lift coefficients, the induced drag dominates, and the minimum drag coefficient occurs at relatively high aspect ratios. At lower lift coefficients, the profile drag becomes more important, and the optimization favors lower aspect ratios. Figure 102 illustrates the relationship between design lift coefficient and optimum aspect ratio. Even allowing for the relatively shallow nature of the C_D vs. A curves near their respective minima, the selection of an optimum aspect ratio for all flight conditions remains a difficult problem. Basing the selection on a representative lift coefficient C_L = 0.7 yields an aspect ratio that is too high for high speed flight and too low for thermaling; nevertheless, this appears to be a reasonable compromise for the wing loading in the example in the figure (30 daN/m²). Ultimately, however, the aspect ratio must be chosen with regard to its effect on average cross-country speed. This will be discussed in a following section.

Influence of design parameters on optimum aspect ratio

Figure 103 presents the aspect ratio for minimum C_D as a function of lift coefficient C_L for various wing spans with the optimum aspect ratios for C_L = 0.7 highlighted. Not surprisingly, the optimum aspect ratio increases with wingspan. These results correspond to W/S = 30 daN/m². Higher wing loadings are generally flown at higher lift coefficients, leading to an increase in the optimum aspect ratios. Conversely, reduced wing loading tends to favor lower aspect ratios. Figure 103 shows this variation in optimum aspect ratio with additional constant-C_L lines corresponding to 20 and 40 daN/m². The results are generalized by stating that, all other factors being equal, the sailplane with the higher wing loading should also have the higher aspect ratio.

As shown in Fig. 104, the equivalent flat plate area also affects the aspect ratio optimization. The lower the parasite drag, that is, the better the aerodynamic design of the fuselage and empennage, the greater the optimum aspect

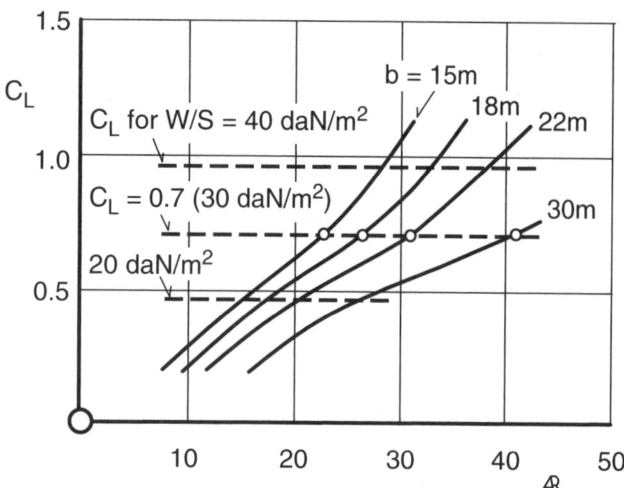

Fig. 103: Effect of span and wing loading on aspect ratio for minimum drag.

Example: $D_p^{\star}=0.050\text{m}^2$
FX 62-K-131 Airfoil
Design $C_L=0.7$ for W/S=30daN/m²

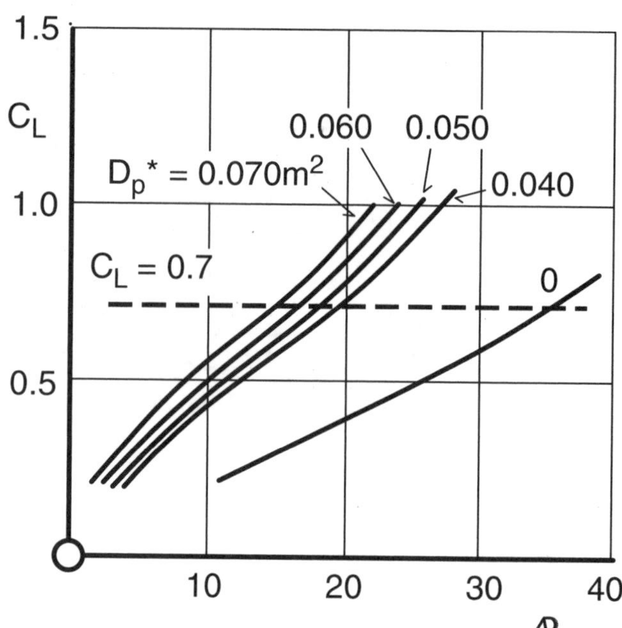

Fig. 104: Effect of parasite drag on aspect ratio for minimum drag.

b=15m
W/S=30 daN/m²
FX 62-K-131 Airfoil

ratio.

In contrast to the parameters discussed so far, variations in the wing planform parameters have no significant influence on the aspect ratio optimization. An aspect ratio chosen for a rectangular wing will also be appropriate for a moderately tapered or double-tapered wing. Airfoil selection also has relatively little influence, provided that the airfoils being compared show similar profile drag trends with Reynolds number.

Figure 105 shows maximum glide ratio as a function of wing span, assuming optimum aspect ratio. Best glide angles for modern sailplanes of various wingspans are currently:

World Class	13.4m	32
Standard Class	15m	42
15m Racing Class	15m	45
18m Class	18m	50
Open Class	> 22m	60

The beneficial effects of wing span are readily apparent.

Aspect ratio and structural weight

Modern materials have largely eliminated the structural problems associated with high aspect ratios. Consequently, an increase in aspect ratio is not always associated with increased structural weight, as was the case with wood sailplanes. To the contrary, with the span held fixed, the reduced wing area associated with increased aspect ratio may even lead to decreased structural weight.

Figure 106 shows the wing weights of some typical production fiberglass sailplanes as a function of aspect ratio. With the span held constant, a pronounced decrease in wing weight with increased aspect ratio is evident. Upon normalizing the wing mass to the wing area, the data show that Standard Class sailplanes have a wing mass of 11 to 13 kg per square meter of total wing area, regardless of aspect ratio. In other words, the wing weight may for practical purposes be considered proportional to the wing area. Wing weight is also influenced by the airfoil thickness, wing stiffness required, and other design and manufacturing details. Carbon fiber, which now finds widespread application in modern sailplanes, allows wings to be built even stiffer and lighter than suggested by Fig. 106. Recent aircraft such as the Discus, ASW-24, LS-7, and DG-400

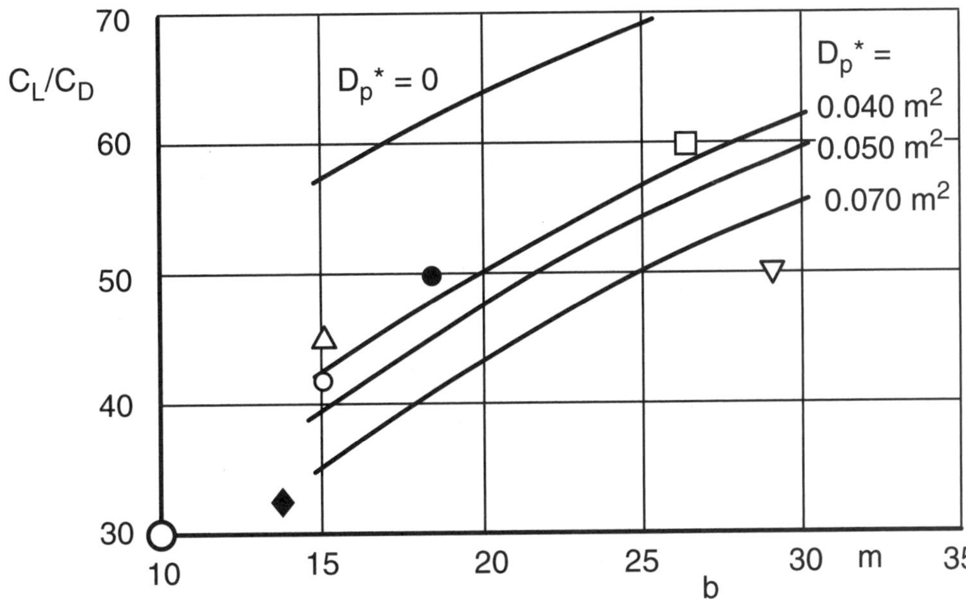

Fig. 105: Best glide ratio as a function of span b and parasite drag $D_p^\star$, assuming optimum aspect ratio and FX 62-K-131 airfoil.

Typical data for:
- ♦ World Class
- ○ Standard Class
- △ 15m Class
- • 18m class
- □ Open Class
- ▽ SB 10

nevertheless exhibit approximately the same wing weight as older fiberglass sailplanes because the trend towards higher maximum airspeeds and increased water ballast has led to increased structural strength and stiffness requirements. Also, since manufacturers now often plan from the start to develop motorglider versions of their sailplanes, wings may be stronger than required for the initial, pure sailplane versions.

The relative lack of empirical data precludes useful generalizations of this sort for sailplanes with large wingspans. Nevertheless, wing weights per unit area for large-span sailplanes tend to be considerably higher than those for 15m span sailplanes. With careful design and construction, the empty weights of one-off sailplanes can be much lower than those of production aircraft. This was the case, for example, with the SB-8 and fs-25 (although the SB-8 wing was built with relatively low stiffness). For further information concerning sailplane weight estimation see W. Stender [108].

Optimum aspect ratio

Up to this point, the discussion has been limited to the optimization of aspect ratio solely with respect to the drag coefficient and structural weight. As indicated earlier, it is the effect on cross-country speed that is important in the final analysis. Both wing loading and choice of thermal model strongly influence the results. Figure 107 shows average cross-country speed as a function of aspect ratio for two thermal models and wing loadings of 20, 30, and 40 daN/m². In all cases the span was fixed at 15m, and the equivalent flat plate area at $D_p^\star = 0.050\text{m}^2$. All cases assume the same airfoil. As the figure shows, very high aspect ratios make sense only for high wing loadings. Light wing loadings, on the other hand, are best combined with moderate aspect ratios.

For a typical, moderate wing loading of 30 daN/m² and a span of 15m, good results are obtained with aspect ratios between 20 and 25. Most modern Standard Class sailplanes lie in this range.

Extending these results to larger wingspans, one finds that certain combinations of span and aspect ratio seem to provide a good compromise. Fig. 108 shows the range of favorable design solutions as a region bounded by the curves $b/\mathcal{R}$ = 15m/18 = 0.83m and $b/\mathcal{R}$ = 15m/23 = 0.65m. Since $b/\mathcal{R}$, the ratio of span to aspect ratio, is identical to the average wing chord, the results may be summarized as follows:

For sailplanes with wing loadings of around 30–40 daN/m², the aspect ratio is reasonably well optimized by

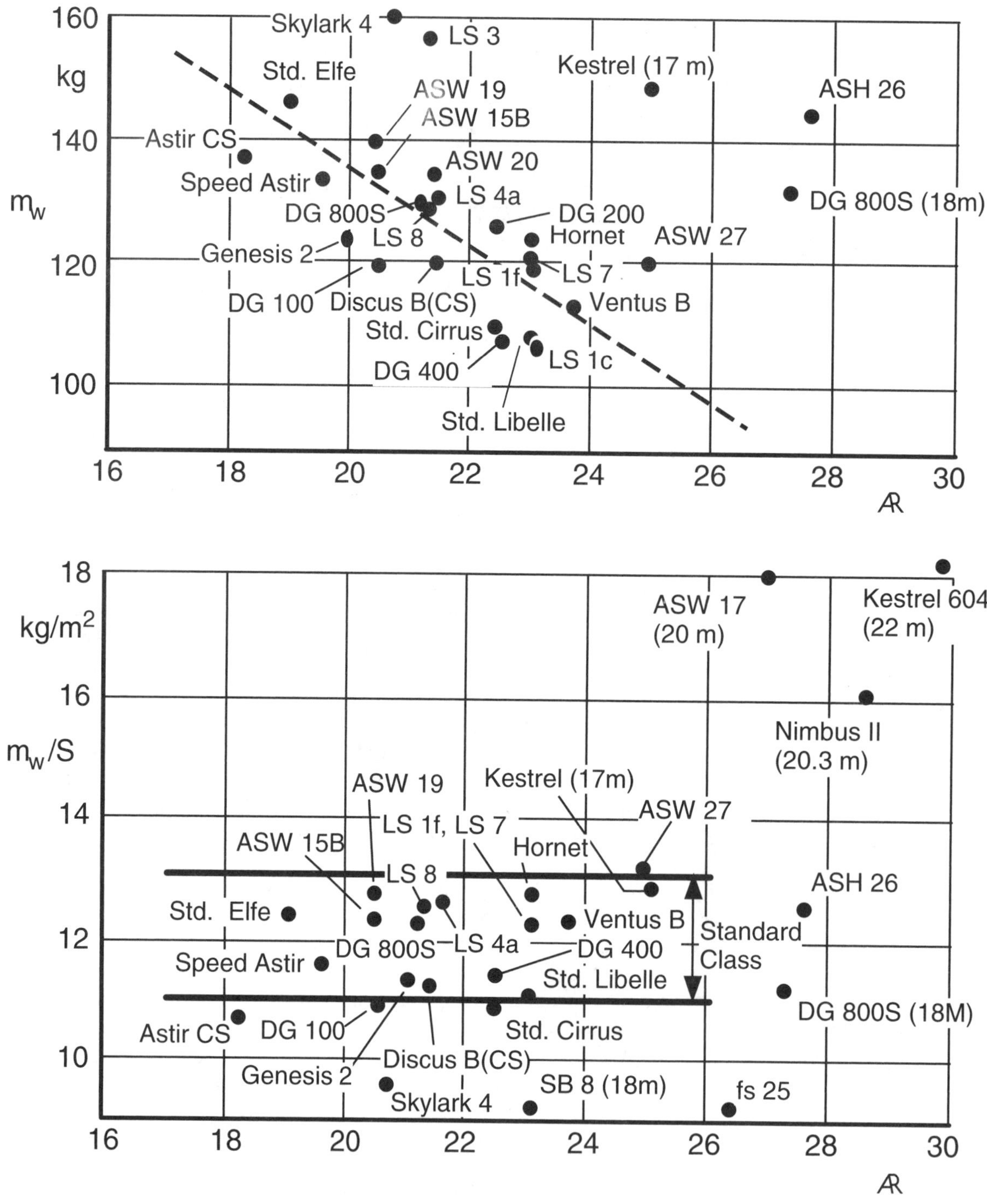

Fig. 106: Wing mass and wing mass per unit area of various sailplanes.

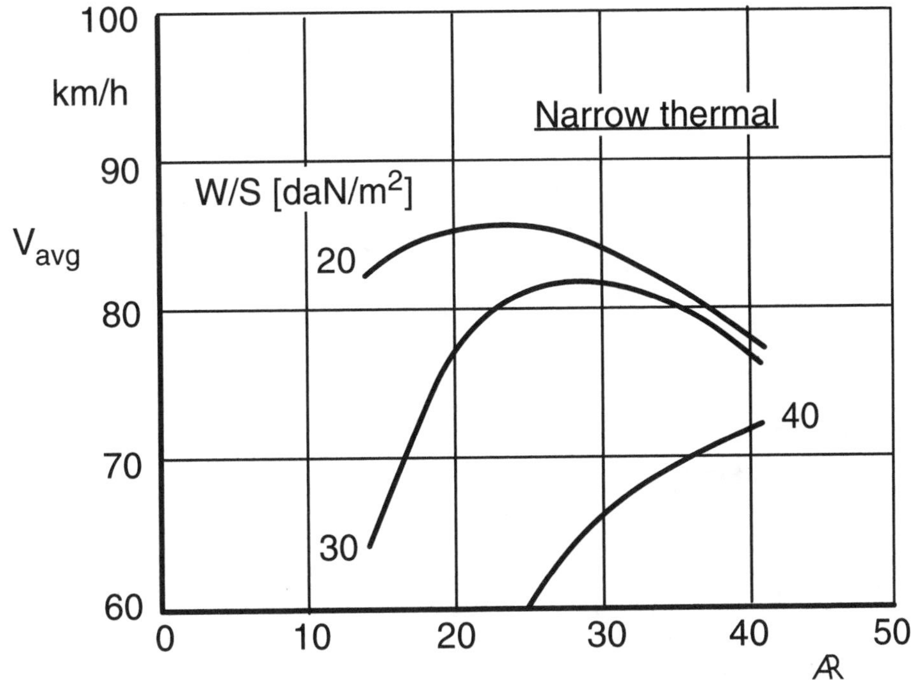

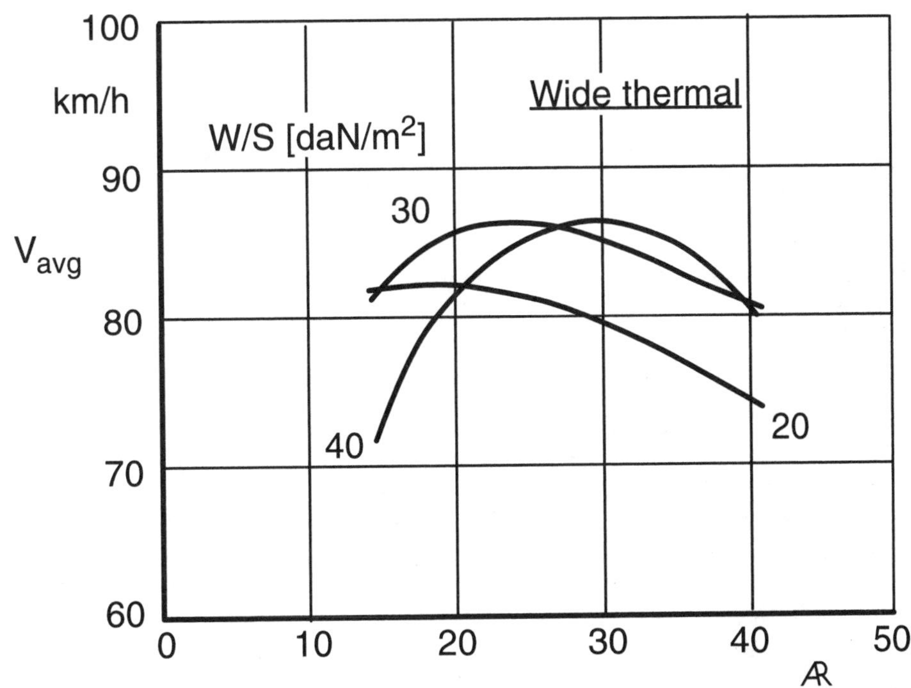

Fig. 107: Effect of aspect ratio on average cross-country speed for various wing loadings and two thermal types.
FX 62-K-131 airfoil
b=15m

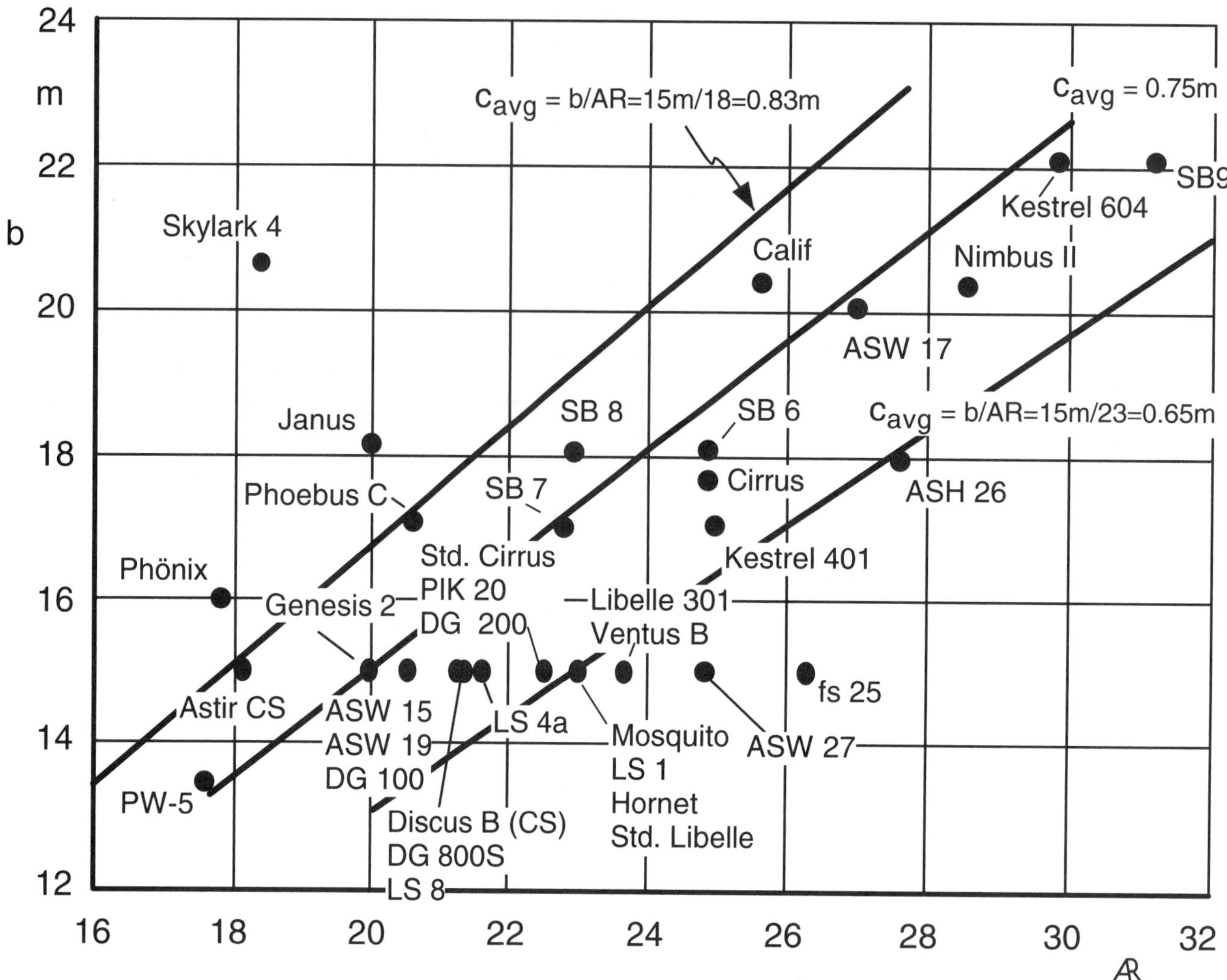

Fig. 108: Favorable combinations of aspect ratio and wingspan, with design data for some well-known designs.

setting the mean wing chord to

$$c_{avg} = 0.70 \pm 0.10\text{m} \qquad (96)$$

Most sailplanes flying today lie in this region of the b vs. $\mathcal{R}$ chart. An overall trend towards higher aspect ratios (and, therefore, smaller wing chords) is evident, encouraged by the tendency towards higher wing loadings and wider use of carbon fiber. Another consideration is the fact that optimizing the aspect ratio for best glide ratio leads to aspect ratios that are higher than desirable from the point of view of cross-country performance (Fig. 109). High glide ratios can be important, for example when executing a final glide late in the day after the lift has died, or when crossing a large area of no lift. These scenarios have not been incorporated in the cross-country model used here. The results in Fig. 109 include Reynolds number effects, hence the improvement in best glide angle as the wing loading is increased.

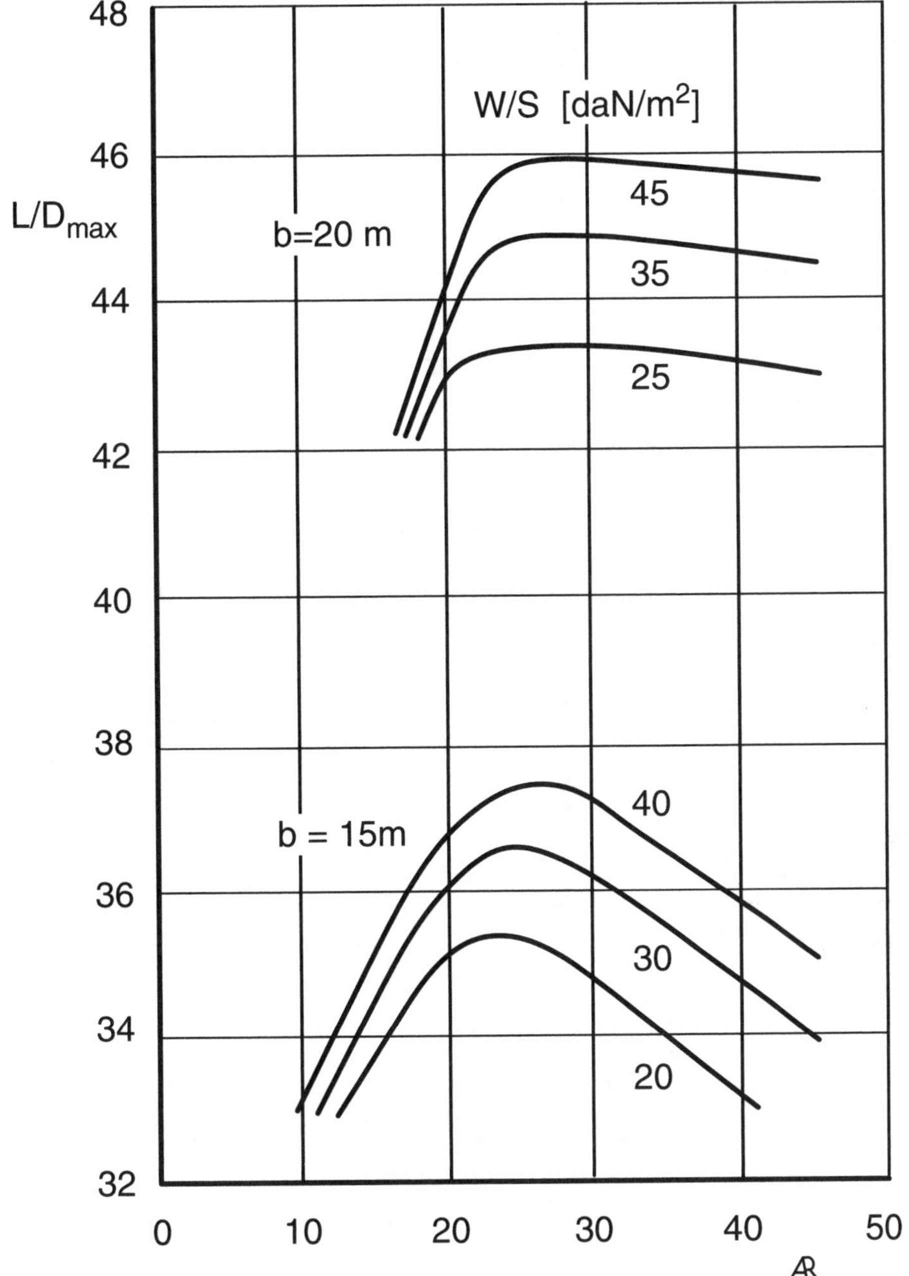

Fig. 109: Best glide ratio as a function of aspect ratio and span.

- Open Class: b=20m FX 67-K-170/150
- Standard Class: b=15m FX 61-184

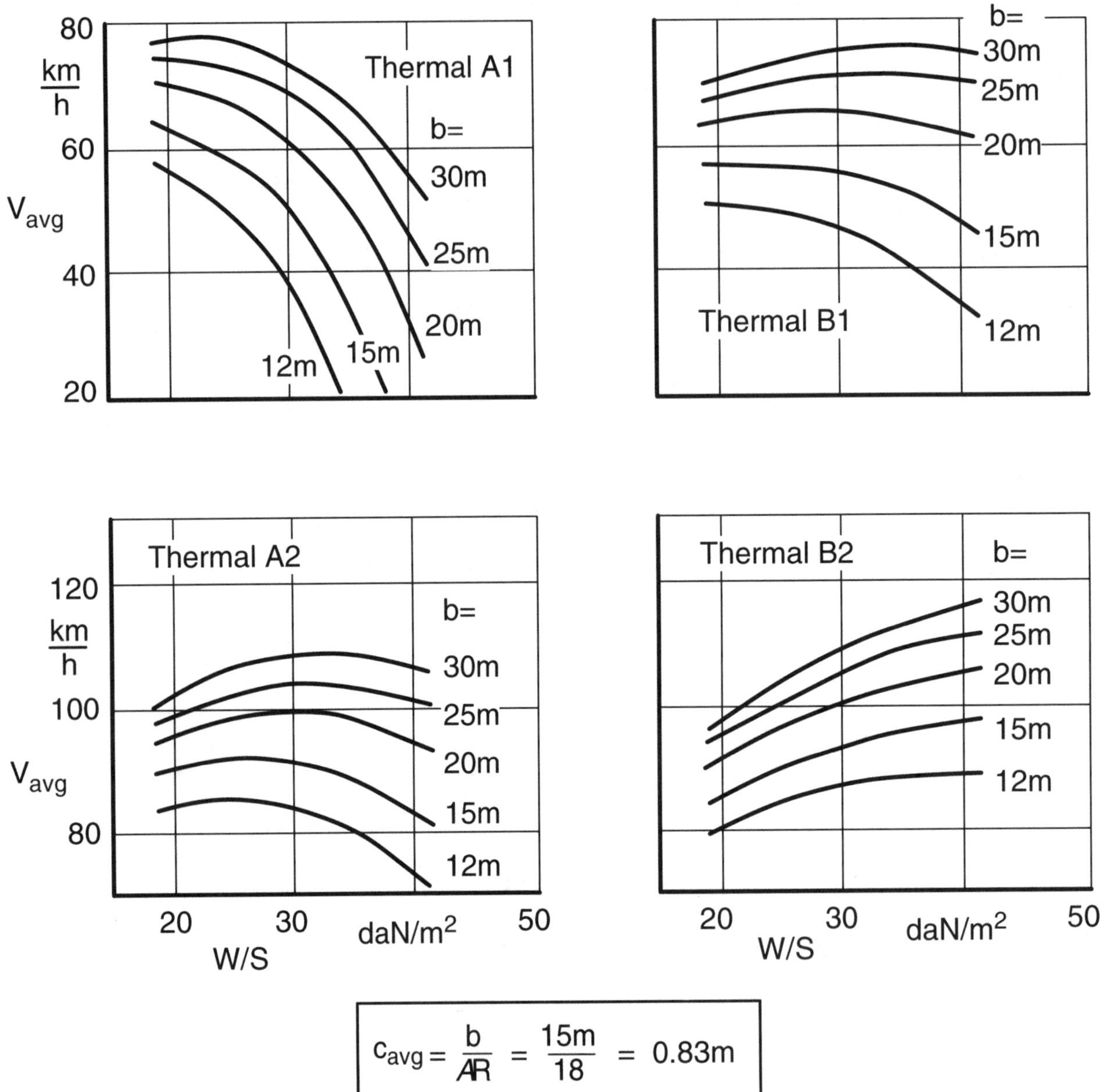

$$c_{avg} = \frac{b}{AR} = \frac{15m}{18} = 0.83m$$

Fig. 110: Effect of span, aspect ratio, and wing loading on average cross-country speed for sailplane with:

- **double-taper wing**
- **FX 62-K-131 airfoil (root), FX 60-126 (tip)**
- **equivalent flat plate area $D_p^{\star} = 0.050m^2$**
- **Horstmann weather model**

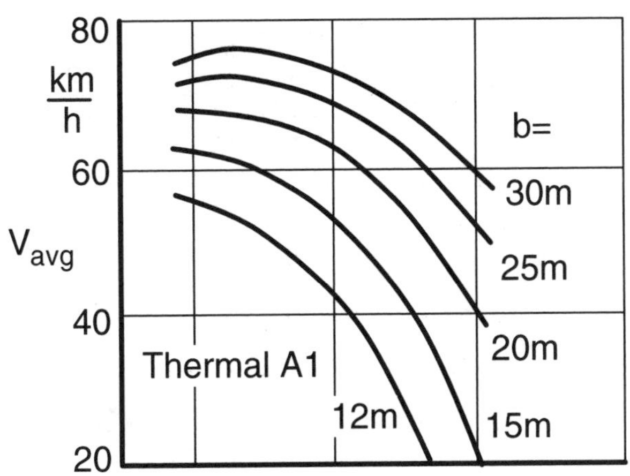

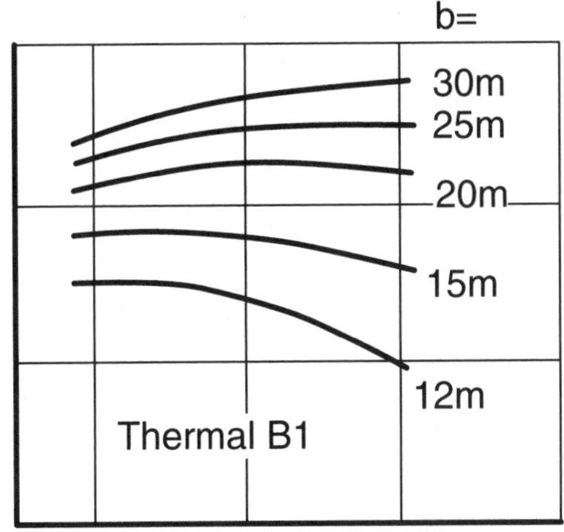

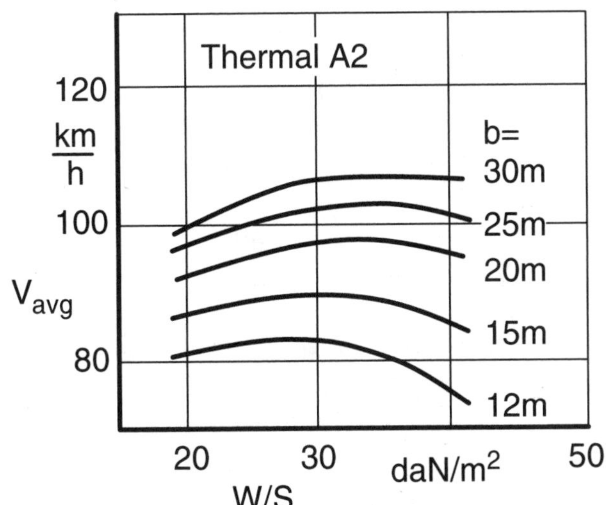

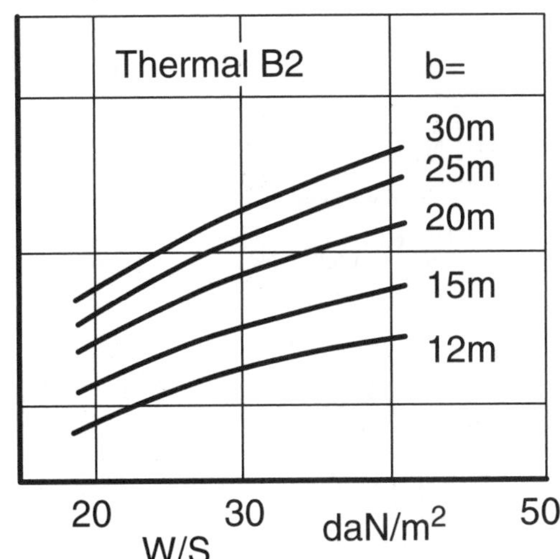

$$c_{avg} = \frac{b}{AR} = \frac{15m}{23} = 0.65m$$

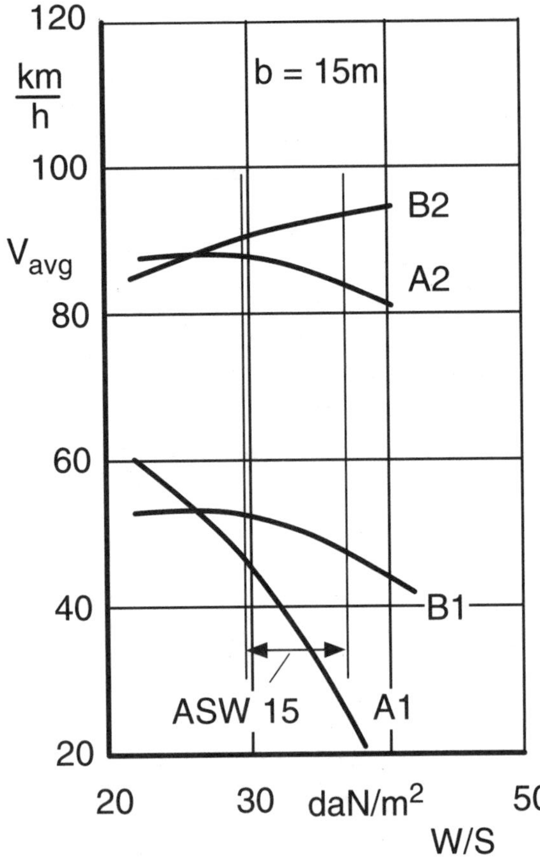

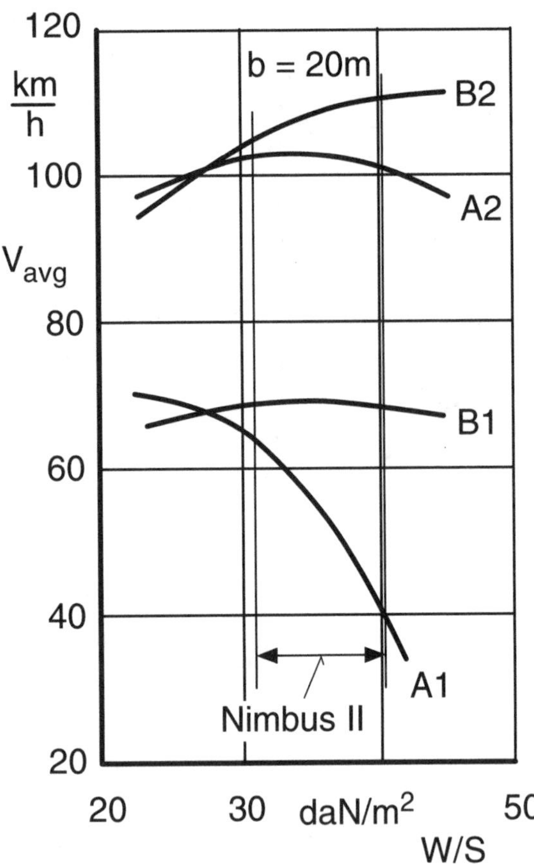

Fig. 111: Average cross-country speed as a function of wing loading and thermal model for representative sailplanes with ASW 15 and Nimbus II wings.

Wing Loading

Importance of thermal model

The optimum wing loading is a function of the prevailing meteorological conditions. Figure 110 shows cross-country speed vs. wing loading and span for the four Horstmann thermal models, assuming a generic double-tapered wing and two values of the mean wing chord c_{avg}. The optimum wing loading varies considerably with the choice of thermal model. While the wide/weak and narrow/strong thermals (B1 and A2), favor a wing loading between 25 and 35 daN/m^2, the B2 (wide/strong) requires a very high wing loading (over 40 daN/m^2) and the A1 (narrow/weak) thermal an extremely low wing loading (under 20 daN/m^2).

The difficulty of selecting the right wing loading is underscored in Fig. 111, which presents average cross-country speed as a function of wing loading for the two specific cases (the ASW-15 and Nimbus II).

Compared with meteorological assumptions, wingspan and aspect ratio have relatively little effect on the choice of wing loading (Fig. 110). The reasonably consistent effects of these design parameters - namely, that higher wing spans and aspect ratios favor higher wing loadings - make them relatively easy to account for during the design process. The influence of aspect ratio and wing loading on cross-country speed is well illustrated in Fig. 112, which shows the effects of deviating from the optimum combination. If the "-2%" regions from such figures are combined in a single chart (Fig. 113), it becomes evident that, while

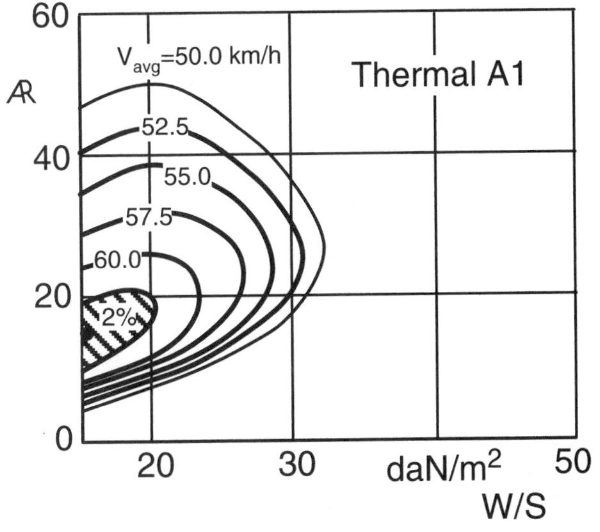

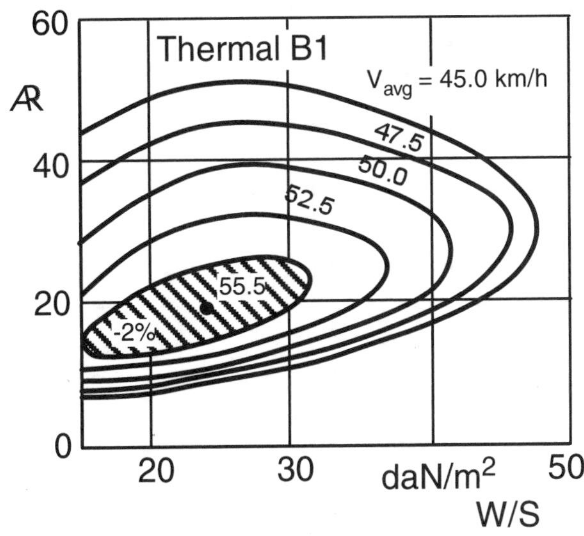

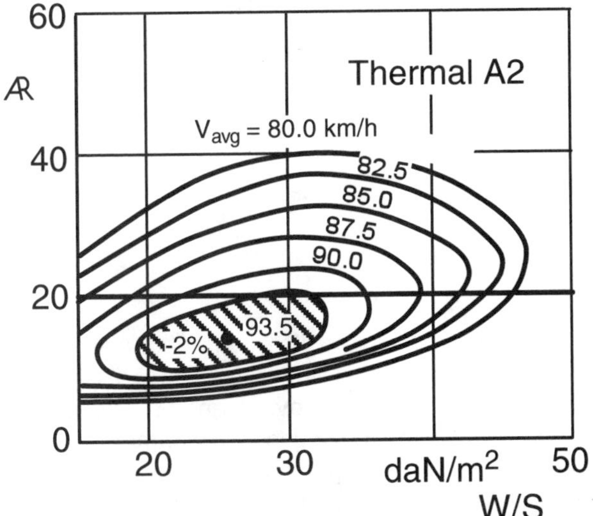

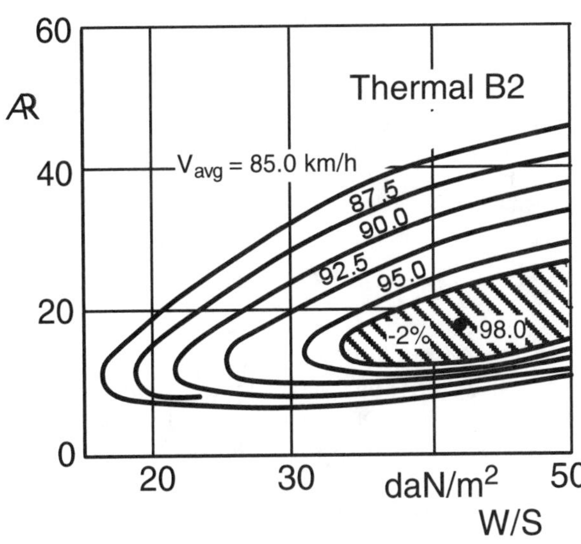

Fig. 112: Average cross-country speed as a function of aspect ratio, wing loading, and thermal model for a sailplane with double-taper wing, 15m span, and FX 61-184 airfoil for various thermal models, from [55].

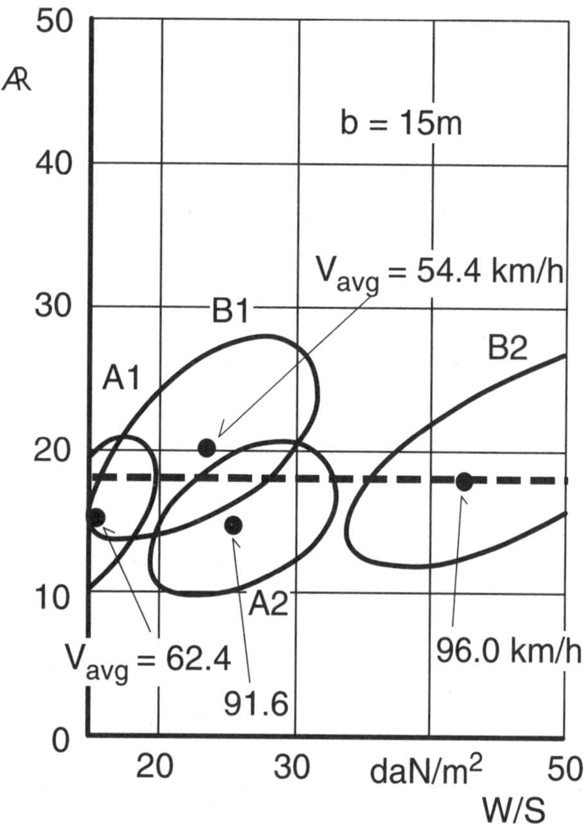

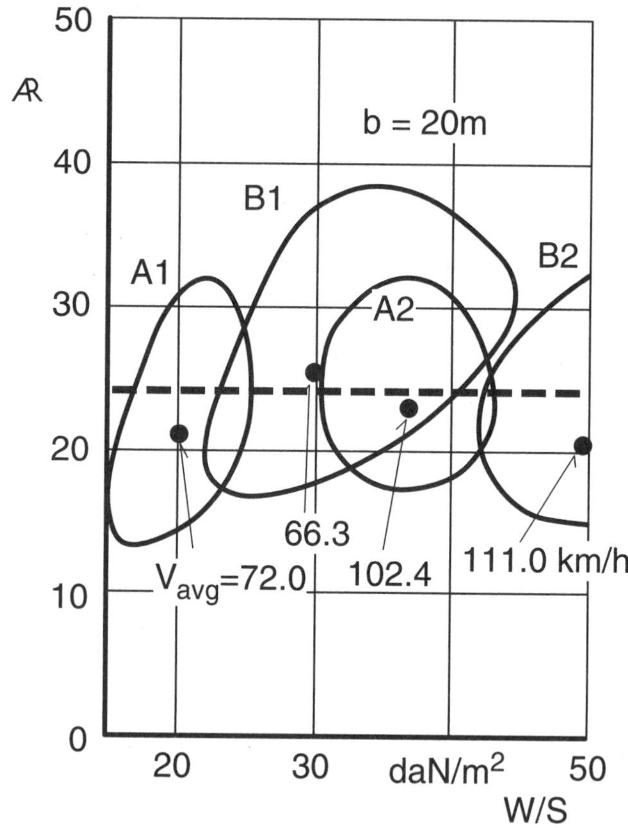

Fig. 113: Combinations of wing loading and aspect ratio yielding near-optimum average cross-country speeds. Regions shown yield speeds within 2% of maximum. Calculations based on various lift distributions and two examples:

Standard Class: b=15m
FX 61-184 airfoil
Open Class: b=20m
FX 67-K-170/150

– – – – – Aspect ratio for highest average cross-country speed.

the aspect ratio may be selected to provide good performance in all weather conditions, the optimum wing loading varies considerably. Obviously, it would be useful to vary the sailplane's wing loading according to the actual weather conditions.

Water ballast

Wing loading may in fact be varied using either fixed ballast, for example, lead bars mounted in the wing (*e.g.* the SB-8), or water ballast carried in tanks or bags in the wings. The main advantage of water ballast over fixed ballast is, of course, that it can be disposed of in flight. This is especially important at the end of a long flight late in the day, when the thermals tend to weaken. Disadvantages of water ballast include the possibility of freezing in cold weather or at high altitudes, and the need to provide tanks or bags in the wings. Careful design is required here, since a ruptured bag or tank can pose a serious safety problem.

For most cross-country flights in typical central European weather conditions, there is usually little to be gained by flying with too much water (that is, at very high wing loadings). On the other hand, it is highly advantageous to carry water ballast in strong conditions and, usually, in contests. In contests, thermaling is often done in large gag-

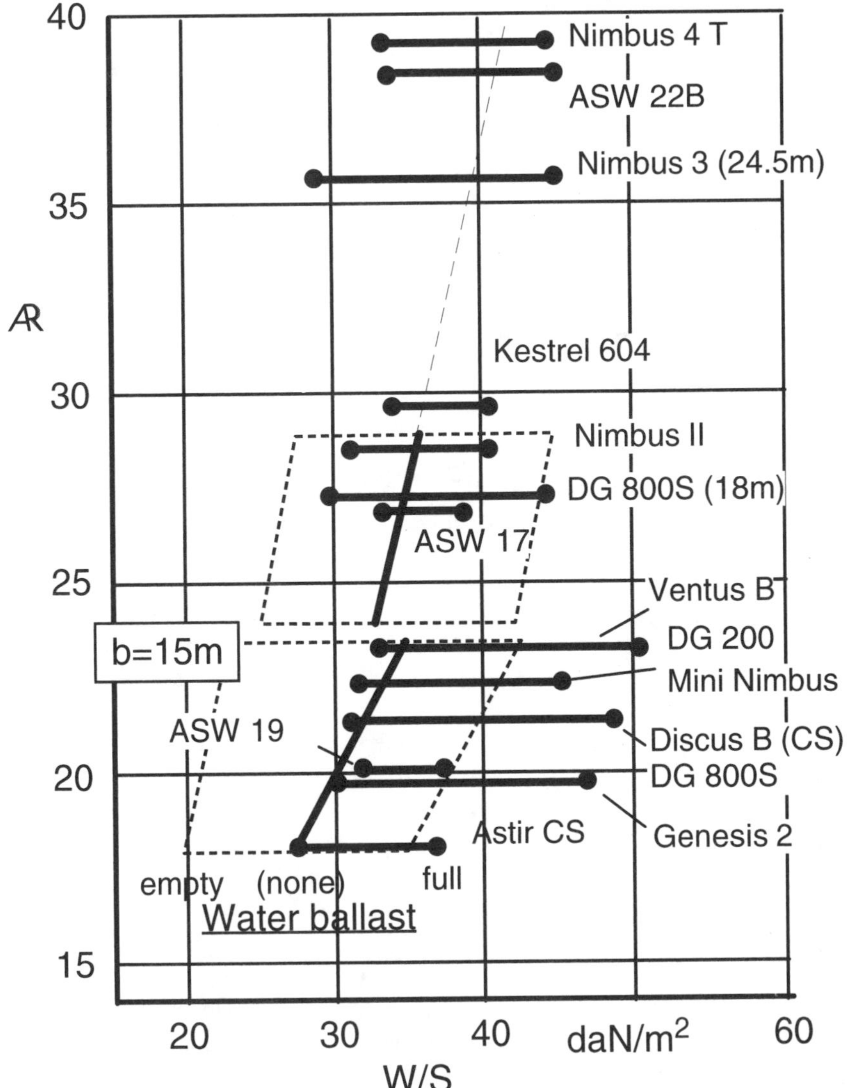

Fig. 114: Wing loading and aspect ratios appropriate for sailplanes with and without water ballast.

gles, making it difficult to take advantage of the improved climb performance that comes with light wing loading. Furthermore, a high wing loading is often required to keep up with other sailplanes between thermals. The water can always be dumped later in the flight if conditions warrant. Needless to say, the greater the wing loading range provided by the water ballast, the easier it is to adapt to widely varying weather conditions. Note also that the ability to dump water permits reasonable landing approach speeds, regardless of the sailplane's takeoff weight.

Optimizing the wing loading

How, then, to choose the proper wing loading? If one opts for no water ballast (as required, for example, in the World Class), choosing the wing loading equates to defining the weather conditions in which the sailplane will best perform. Wing loadings in excess of 30 daN/m^2 degrade weak weather performance and lead to undesirably fast approach speeds. Use of an airfoil with good climb performance (*e.g.* FX 66-S-196, FX 67-K-150/170) allows the wing loading to be increased by a few daN/m^2 over what

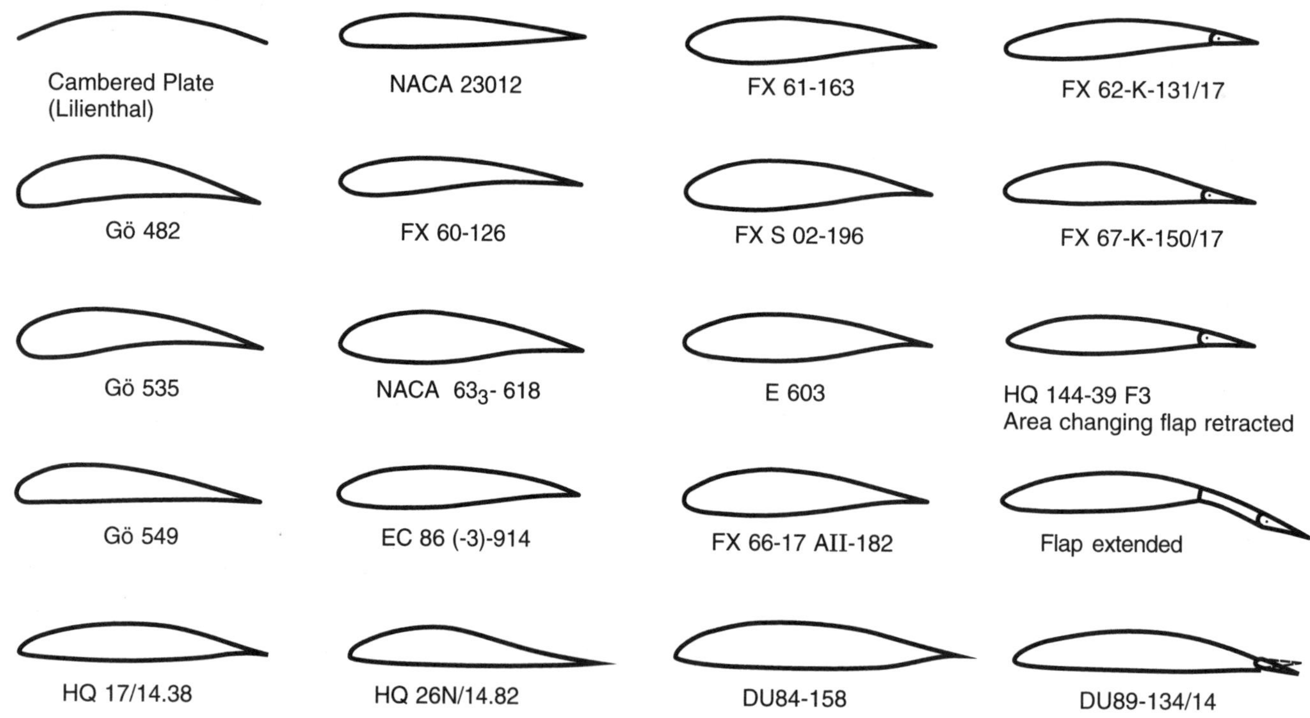

Fig. 115: Some common sailplane airfoils.

might be appropriate for an airfoil optimized for interthermal glide (*e.g.* FX 62-K-131). High aspect ratio wings also favor higher wing loadings.

Except where prohibited by class rules, most modern high performance sailplanes are delivered with provisions for water ballast. The zero-ballast wing loading should be held as low as possible to allow for good weak-weather performance, and the water capacity should be as large as possible to allow the wing loading to be increased in strong weather conditions.

Based on these considerations, it is possible to define a range of combinations of aspect ratio and wing loading representing a reasonable compromise for cross-country performance in varying weather conditions (Fig. 114). Current sailplanes tend to have wing loadings higher than the optimum range indicated in the figure. Despite the increasingly common use of carbon fiber, the trend towards higher water ballast loads and increased maximum design speeds has led to increased requirements for wing strength and stiffness and, in turn, higher structural weights and wing loadings.

Airfoil Selection

Background

Profile drag typically accounts for about 50% of the total drag in high speed flight and 25% while thermaling. Because of this relatively high drag contribution, proper airfoil selection is of critical importance.

During the course of sailplane development, airfoils have undergone considerable change (see Fig. 115 and Table 6). Following Lilienthal's recognition of the advantages of cambered flat plates, the next major step was the use of thicker airfoils, allowing load-carrying spars and the elimination of external bracing. These included the Joukowsky airfoils (Gö 441 and others) and subsequent improvements in the Göttingen series (Gö 535 and 549) as well as airfoils from the NACA 4- and 5-digit series (NACA 4412 and 23012).

It was only in the 1950's that laminar airfoils began to find widespread application in sailplanes. Most of these early laminar airfoils came from the NACA 6-series. Subsequently, in the early 1960's, improved laminar airfoils

Table 6: Commonly used sailplane airfoils. See also the tabulated data in the Appendix.

Airfoil family	Airfoil	Application	Used since	Thickness (t/c)
Plate	Cambered plate	Lilienthal glider	1890	0.01
Joukowsky	Gö 482	Vampyr	1922	0.17
Göttingen Series	Gö 535	Konsul, Kranich II, Grunau Baby	1925	0.164
	Gö 549	Weihe, Kranich III, Ka 7, ASK 13	1930	0.138
NACA 4- and 5-digit series	NACA 23012 mean line Gö 600 thickness form	D-30	1930	0.12
	NACA 4412	Outboard wing (Sagitta)	1930	0.12
	NACA 43012	SGS 1-26 (1954); SGS 2-33 (1966)	1954	0.12
NACA 6-Series	65_2-714	HKS I	1953	0.14
	63_3-618	Ka 6, SB 5, Foka, B 4	1955	0.18
	65_2-1116	HKS III	1955	0.16
	65_2-515	Zefir	1960	0.15
Fixed Geometry Airfoils:				
Eppler	EC 86(-3)-914	Phoenix	1957	0.14
	STE 871-514	SB 6	1960	0.14
	E 403	Phoebus A-C	1964	0.15
	E 603	Astir, Twin Astir	1974	0.19
	E 583	Twin III Acro	1986	0.165
Wortmann	FX 61-163	ASW 15, Std. Elfe S4	1961	0.163
	FX 61-184	D-38, DG 100	1961	0.184
	FX 66-S-196	Cirrus, fs 25	1966	0.196
	FX 66-S-196V1	LS 1c, LS 1f	1966	0.196
	FX S02-196	Std. Cirrus	1966	0.196
Horstmann and Quast	HQ 14/18.43	SB 12	1980	0.184
	HQ 21/17.15	Falcon	1980	0.172
	HQ 21/II	DG 300	1983	0.172
Boermans	DU 84-158	ASW 24	1987	0.158
	DU 99-147	ASW 28	1999	0.147
Somers and Maughmer	SM701	World Class	1991	0.159
Flapped Airfoils (camber changing)				
Eppler	E 662	Speed Astir	1977	0.15
Wortmann	FX 62-K-131	SB 8, SB 9, SB 10, D-36, ASW 12, ASW 17, ASW 20	1962	0.131
	FX 62-K-153	SB 8, SB 9, SB 10, FK 3	1962	0.153
	FX 67-K-170/150	Nimbus II, Kestrel, Janus, PIK 20, SZD Jantar, DG 400, LS 3, B 12	1967	0.17/0.15
	FX 73-K-170	fs 29, DG 500	1973	0.17
	FX 81-K-130	LS 6	1983	0.13
Horstmann and Quast	HQ 17/14.38	ASW 22,ASH 25 (root)	1981	0.144
	HQ 35	DG 600	1987	0.122
Horstmann, Quast, Rohardt	HQR 1,2,3,4,5	eta	1997	
Boermans	DU 84-132V3	ASW 22, ASH 25 (tip)	1986	0.132
	DU 89-138/14	DG 800	1993	0.138
	DU 89-134/14	ASH 26E, ASW 27	1993	0.134
Flapped Airfoils (area changing)	FX 67-VC-170/36	Sigma, AN66C, Mü 27	1970	0.17
	HQ 144-39 F3	SB 11	1978	0.144

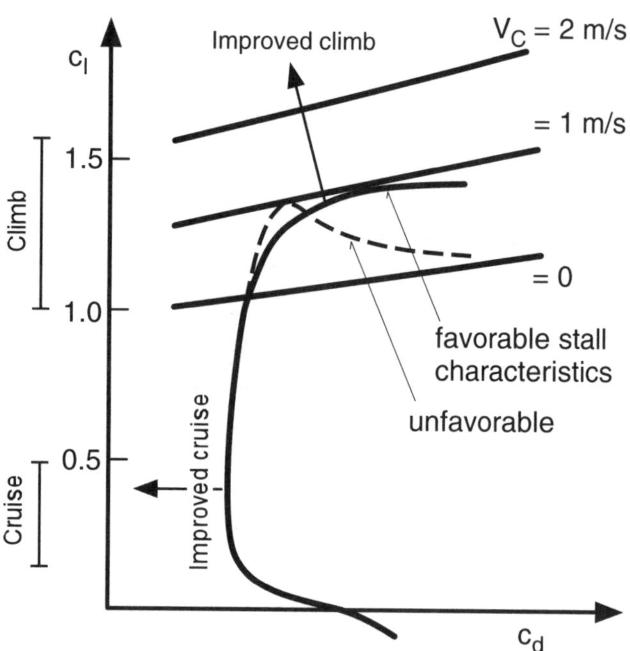

Fig. 116: Desirable aerodynamic characteristics for sailplane airfoils.

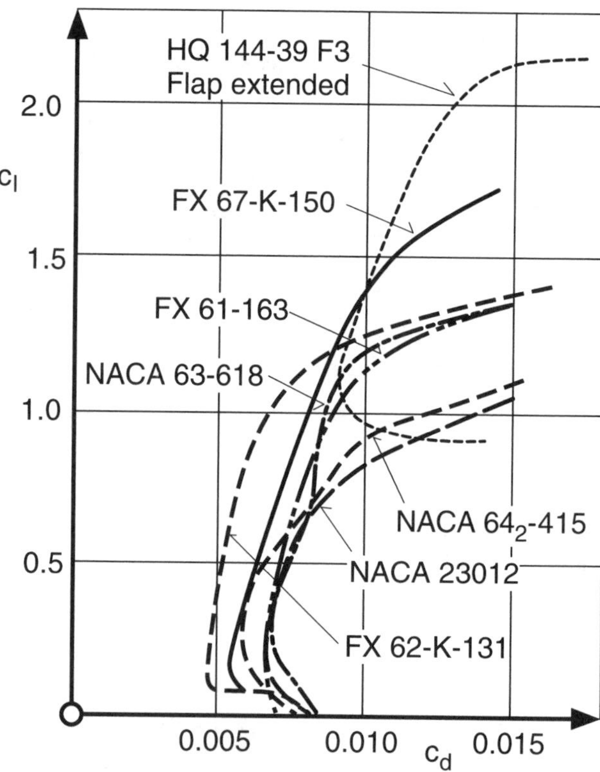

Fig. 117: Progress in airfoil design. Airfoil polars at full-scale Reynolds numbers, based on c=0.75m and W/S=30 daN/m^2.

developed by R. Eppler and F. X. Wortmann gradually became the standard for sailplane design. Together with the manufacturing precision and good surface quality offered by fiberglass construction, these airfoils led sailplane design into a new era and are largely responsible for the improvements in performance occurring during this period.

Since the 1970's further developments in sailplane airfoils have been made by K. H. Horstmann and A. Quast [182, 184, 193] at the DFVLR, L. M. M. Boermans [170–172] at the Delft University of Technology, and D. M. Somers and M. D. Maughmer [195] in the United States.

In addition to fixed-geometry airfoils, flapped airfoils have played an increasingly significant role. Following the introduction of the FAI 15m Racing Class in the mid-1970's, application of these flaps was no longer restricted to large Open Class sailplanes. Recent advances in airfoil design include area-varying flaps that allow the wing's surface area to be varied in flight.

Considerations for airfoil selection

Airfoil selection is based on a number of design considerations. To a certain extent, the requirements conflict and are difficult to resolve. The airfoil should:

- exhibit low drag in high speed flight (*i.e.* at low lift coefficients),
- have low drag at high lift coefficients for good thermaling performance,
- provide a high maximum lift coefficient for low landing speeds,
- contribute to gentle stall characteristics,
- exhibit low sensitivity to insect contamination, and
- be as thick as possible, to allow for large water ballast capacity, deep spars, and high torsional stiffness.

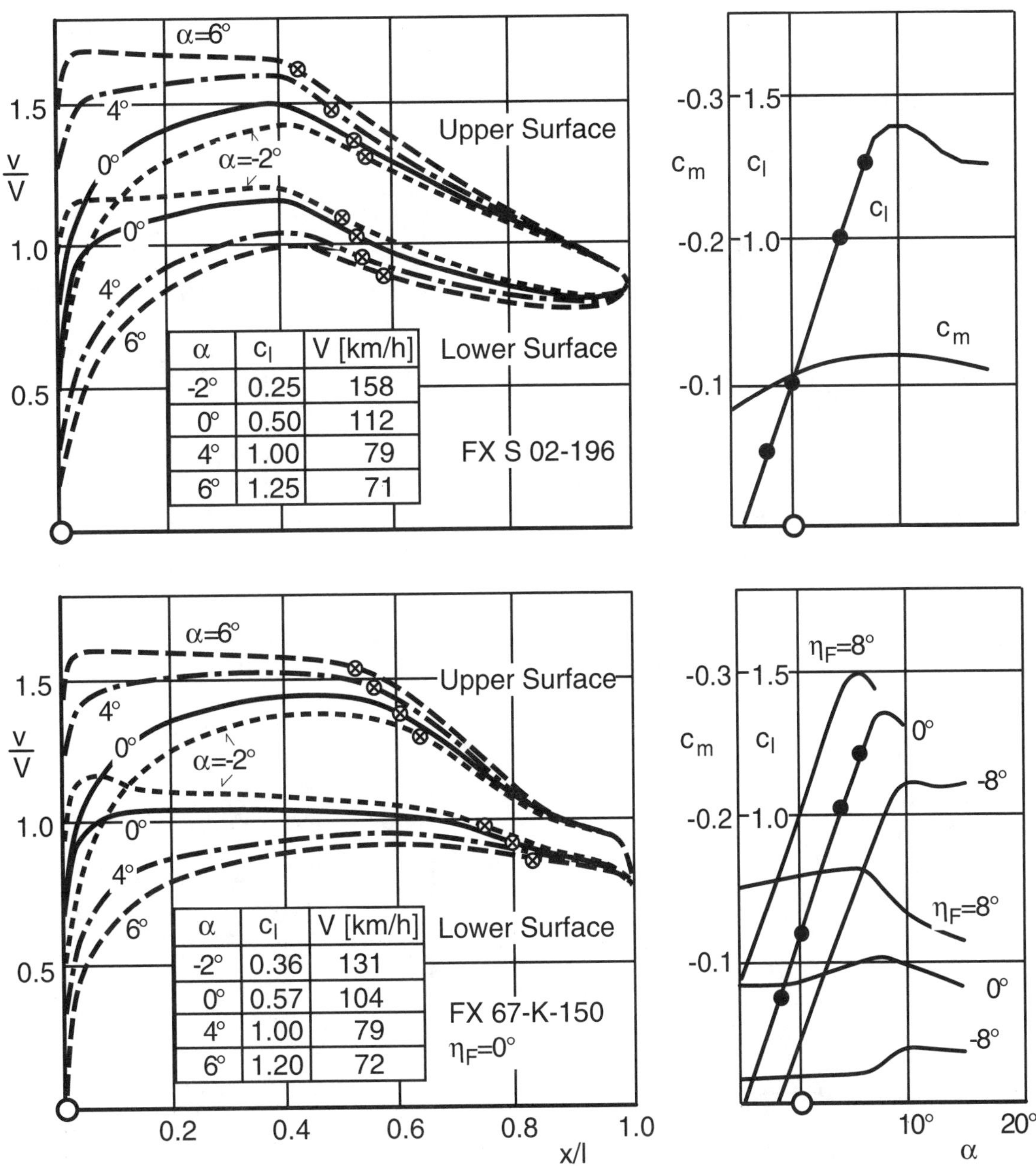

Fig. 118: Velocity distributions and lift and moment curves for two airfoils [168]. Airspeeds based on W/S=30daN/m^2.

Upper figure: FX S02-196 (fixed geometry)
Lower figure: FX 67-K-150 (camber-changing flaps)
⊗ Transition point for Re=1.5 · 10^6
• Lift coefficients at which velocity distributions are shown

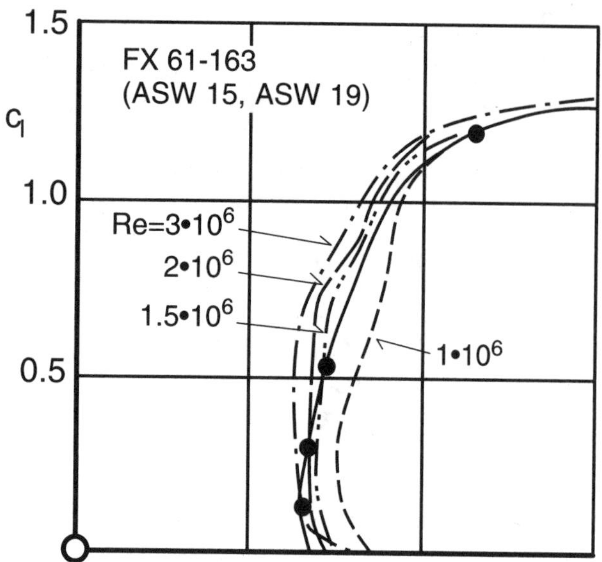
1.5
1.0
0.5
c_l
FX 61-163
(ASW 15, ASW 19)
Re=3•10^6
2•10^6
1.5•10^6
1•10^6

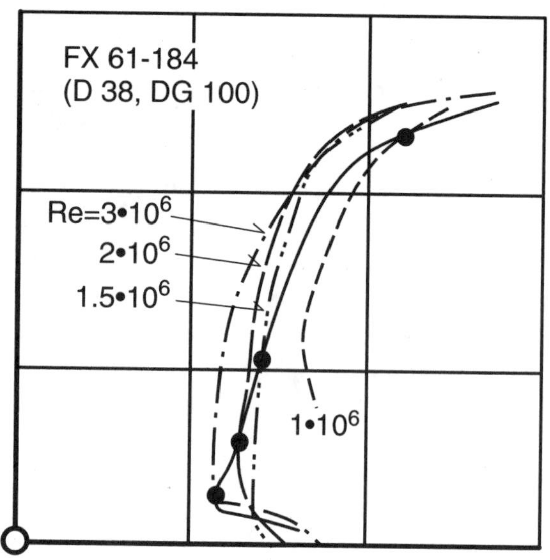
FX 61-184
(D 38, DG 100)
Re=3•10^6
2•10^6
1.5•10^6
1•10^6

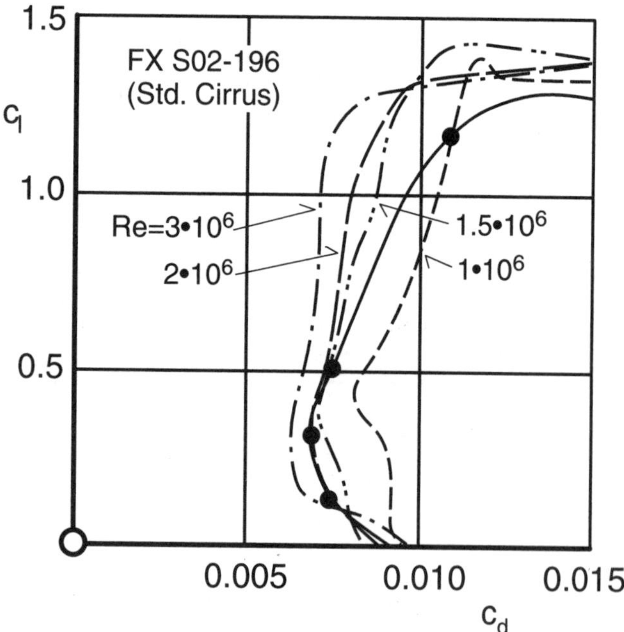
1.5
1.0
0.5
c_l
FX S02-196
(Std. Cirrus)
Re=3•10^6
2•10^6
1.5•10^6
1•10^6
0.005
0.010
0.015
c_d

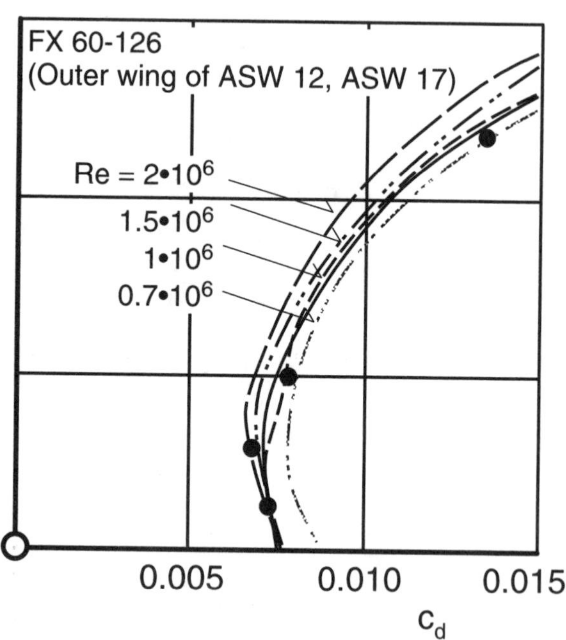
FX 60-126
(Outer wing of ASW 12, ASW 17)
Re = 2•10^6
1.5•10^6
1•10^6
0.7•10^6
0.005
0.010
0.015
c_d

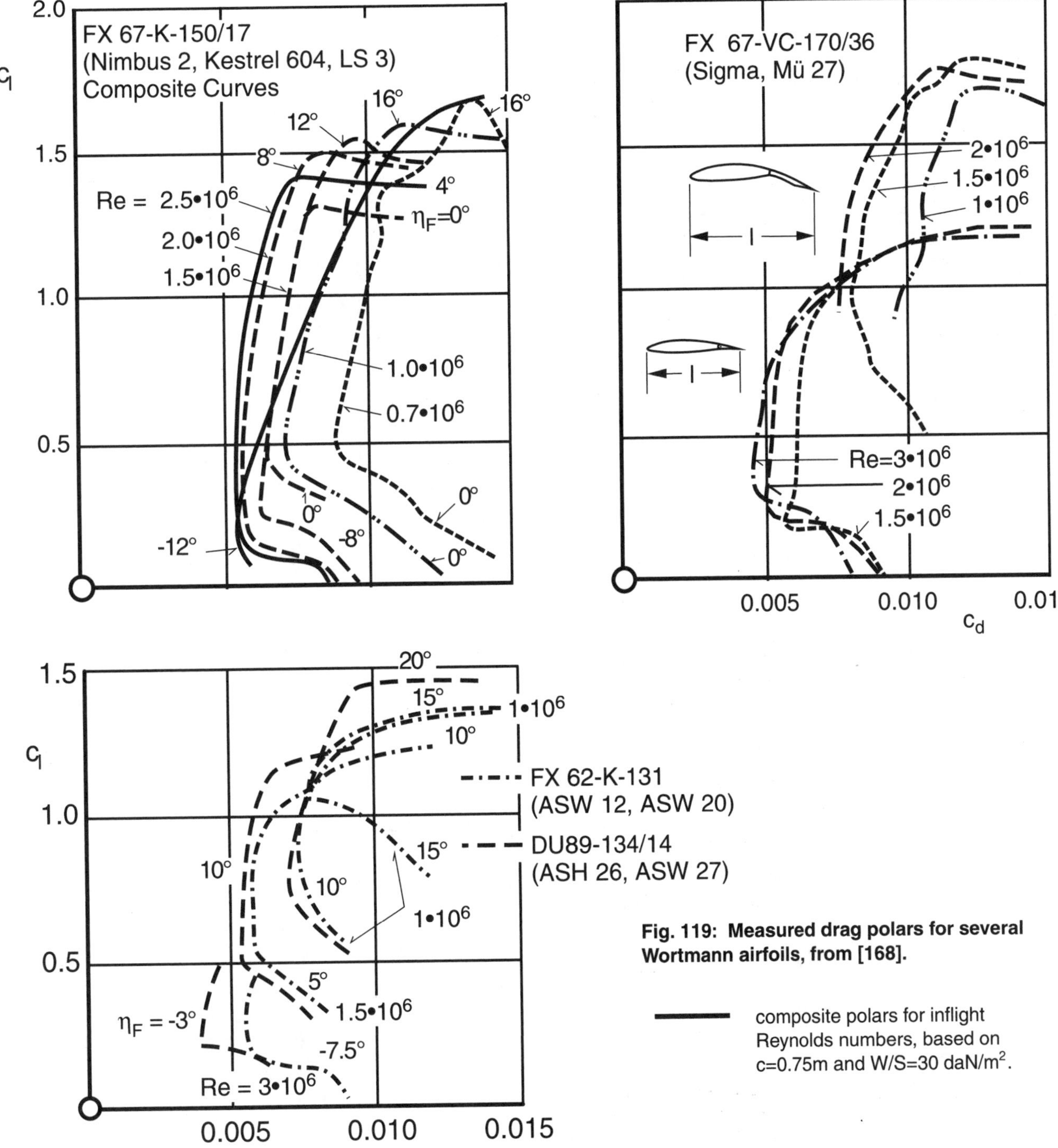

Fig. 119: Measured drag polars for several Wortmann airfoils, from [168].

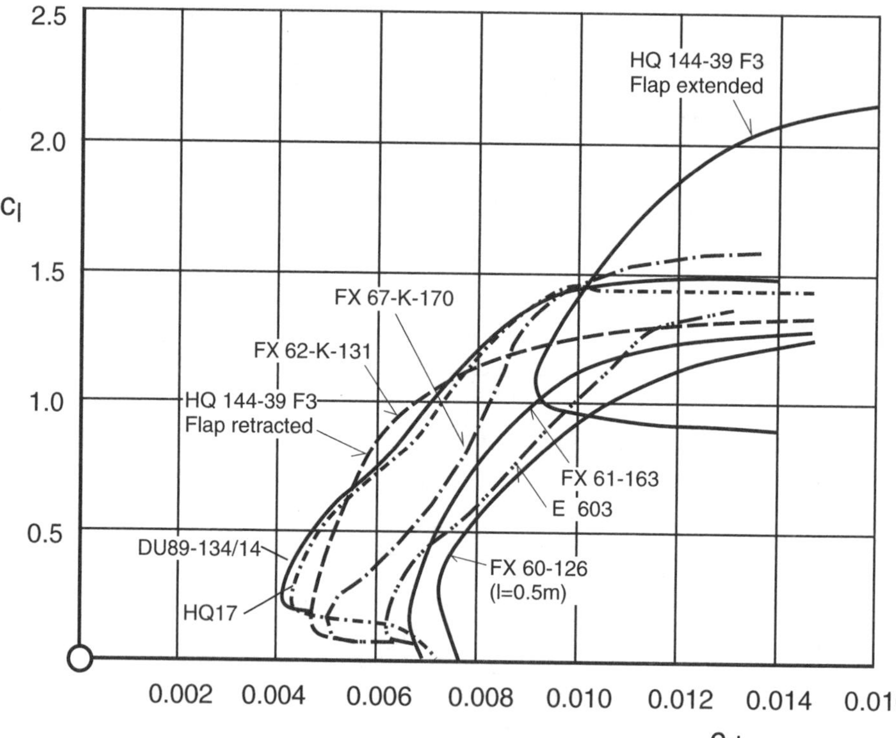

Fig. 120: Comparison of composite polars for various airfoils at flight Reynolds numbers. Reynolds numbers based on c=0.75m and W/S=30daN/m^2.

Figure 116 provides a general picture of the aerodynamic requirements. The figure presents the range of lift and drag coefficients together with constant-climb lines similar to those in Fig. 90. The arrows signify the direction of improvement in the polar. In climb, the polar should be as parallel as possible to the constant climb lines indicated in the figure in order to reduce the sensitivity of climb performance to airspeed. A sharp drop-off in lift coefficient beyond $c_{l_{max}}$ must be avoided in order to provide acceptable stalling characteristics.

The requirement for low drag in both high speed and thermaling flight is difficult to satisfy with fixed-geometry airfoils. A comparison of various airfoils (Fig. 117) shows that it is possible for an airfoil to be optimized for high speed, achieving exceptionally low drag at low lift coefficients, while failing to provide adequate low speed performance. An acceptable compromise requires a wide laminar bucket, even though this comes at the price of reduced high speed performance.

Airfoils with camber changing flaps have the ability to shift their laminar buckets in flight, combining good high speed and low speed performance in a single airfoil. Area-changing flaps (discussed later) are even more effective in this respect, at the cost, however, of increased mechanical complexity.

The Stuttgart Profile Catalog

Geometric and aerodynamic data for many of the most commonly used sailplane airfoils are available in a series of publications by R. Eppler [174, 175, 178, 179] and F. X. Wortmann and D. Althaus [196, 198–202]. An especially useful collection of airfoil data has been assembled by D. Althaus and F. X. Wortmann as the "Stuttgart Profile Catalog I" [168] and its successor, [167], summarizing data for all the Wortmann airfoils as well as a number of others. Included are data such as airfoil coordinates, theoretical velocity distributions, and extensive experimental results from the Stuttgart laminar flow wind tunnel. This valuable reference belongs in every sailplane designer's library. Other useful sources of airfoil data include works by I. H. Abbott and A. E. von Doenhoff [1], M. S. Selig,

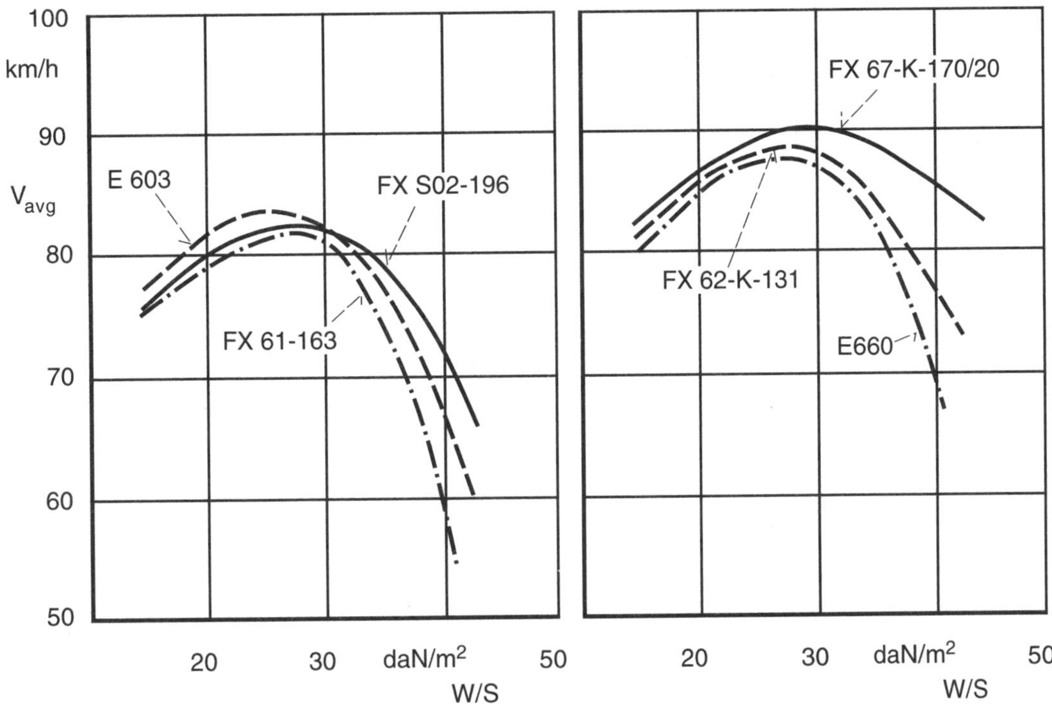

Fig. 121: Average cross-country speed for various fixed geometry and flapped airfoils for Æ=20, C_{D_p} = 0.0035, b=15m, and Quast weather model (Fig. 95).

J. F. Donovan, and D. B. Fraser [194], D. Althaus [164], R. Eppler [180], and L. M. M. Boermans [170].

Typical results from the Stuttgart Catalog I are presented in Figs. 118-119. Figure 118 presents the theoretical velocity distributions and corresponding lift and moment curves for the FX S02-196 (fixed geometry) and FX 67-K-150 (flapped) airfoils. The figures show boundary-layer transition points for Re = $1.5 \cdot 10^6$. In the case of the fixed geometry airfoil, laminar flow extends over both upper and lower surface to over 50% of the chord. On the flapped airfoil, laminar flow extends even further, to 0.60c on the upper surface and 0.80c on the lower surface. The lift and moment curves show the influence of flap deflection on the zero lift moment and angle of attack.

Drag data for some typical airfoils are reproduced in Fig. 119. The Stuttgart Profile Catalog presents drag measurements taken at various Reynolds numbers. In an actual sailplane, the Reynolds number varies with velocity, and, in turn, on the lift coefficient and wing loading. For evaluating the airfoil's effect on overall performance, an effective drag polar can be constructed based on the actual Re vs. C_L variation. This has been done in Fig. 119 assuming typical values c = 0.75m and W/S = 30 daN/m^2. With increased wing loading and chord, the Reynolds number increases and the effective polar shifts to the left - that is, the drag coefficient is reduced. It is observed that with some airfoils, for example the FX S02-196, the exceptionally low drag coefficients at high lift coefficient and Reynolds number cannot be taken advantage of in the effective polars. These airfoils have low drag at high lift coefficients thanks to an extensive region of laminar flow over the upper surface, up to the maximum lift coefficient. In case of turbulent flow (bugs, rain), however, these airfoils suffer from premature separation at relatively low lift coefficients [171].

That flapped airfoils offer considerably improved performance over their fixed geometry counterparts is readily apparent. The advantages of variable geometry are even more pronounced with area-changing flaps.

Comparing airfoils

A direct comparison of the effective polars of various airfoils (Fig. 120) underscores the advantages of camber-changing and area-changing flaps. Thicker airfoils (FX 67–K-170, FX S02-196) tend to be superior in low speed flight, while thinner airfoils (FX 62-K-131, FX 61-163) provide better performance at high speeds. Practical experience has

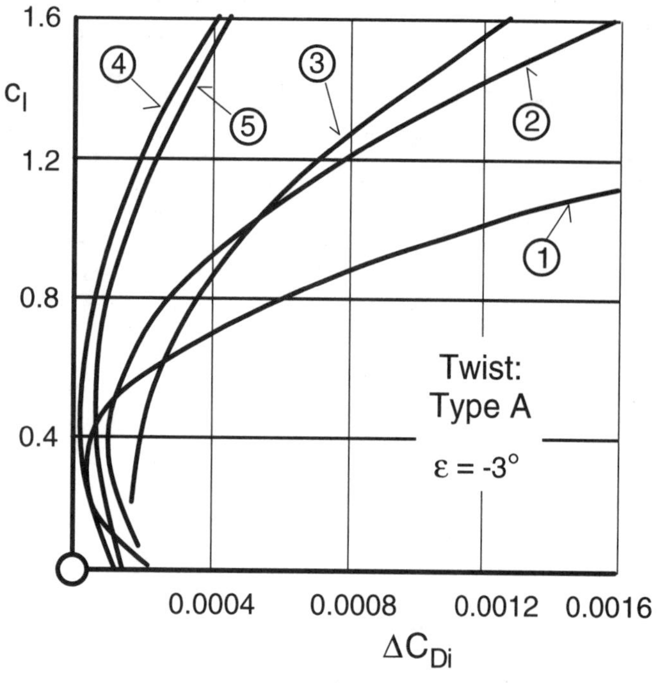

1.6
c_l
1.2
0.8
0.4
④
⑤
③
②
①
Twist:
Type A
ε = -3°
0.0004
0.0008
0.0012
0.0016
ΔC_{Di}

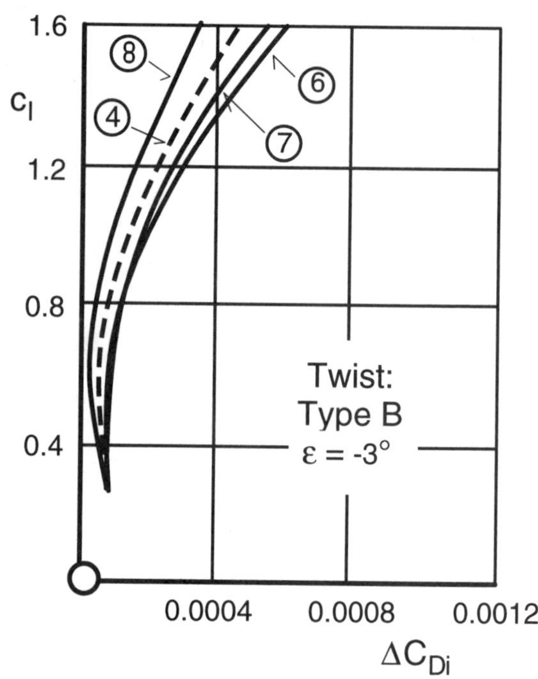

1.6
c_l
1.2
0.8
0.4
⑧
④
⑥
⑦
Twist:
Type B
ε = -3°
0.0004
0.0008
0.0012
ΔC_{Di}

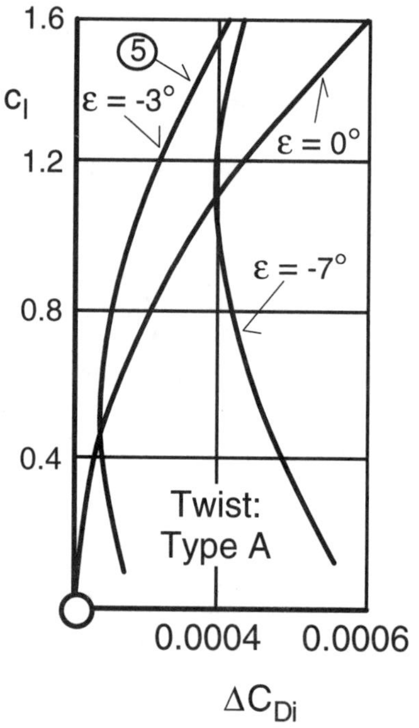

1.6
c_l
1.2
0.8
0.4
⑤
ε = -3°
ε = 0°
ε = -7°
Twist:
Type A
0.0004
0.0006
ΔC_{Di}

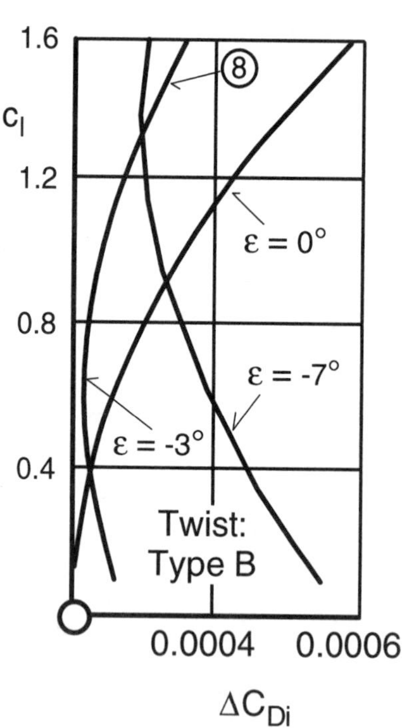

1.6
c_l
1.2
0.8
0.4
⑧
ε = 0°
ε = -7°
ε = -3°
Twist:
Type B
0.0004
0.0006
ΔC_{Di}

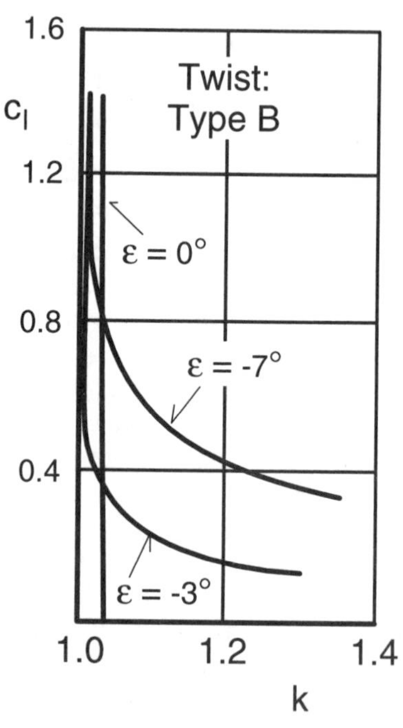

1.6
c_l
1.2
0.8
0.4
Twist:
Type B
ε = 0°
ε = -7°
ε = -3°
1.0
1.2
1.4
k

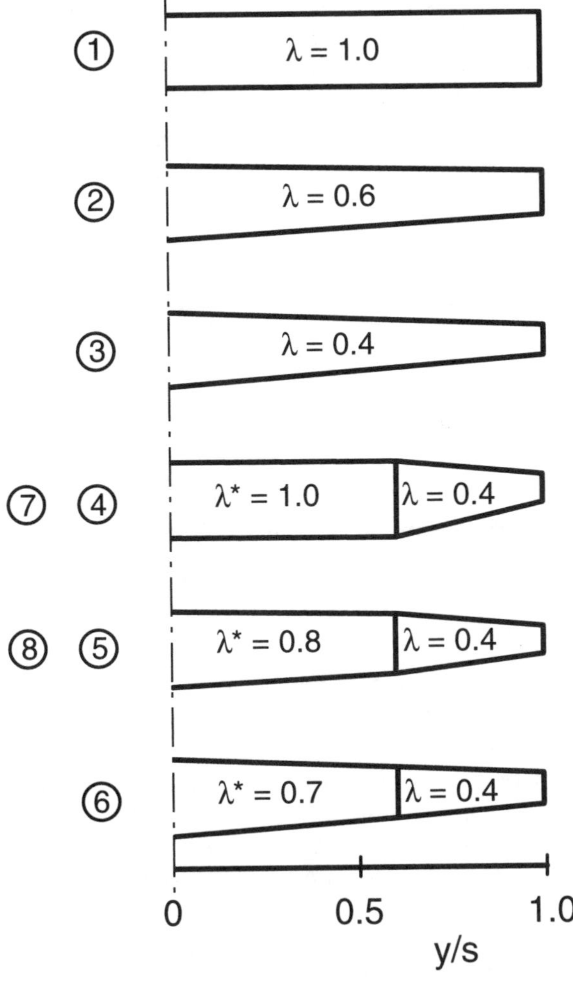

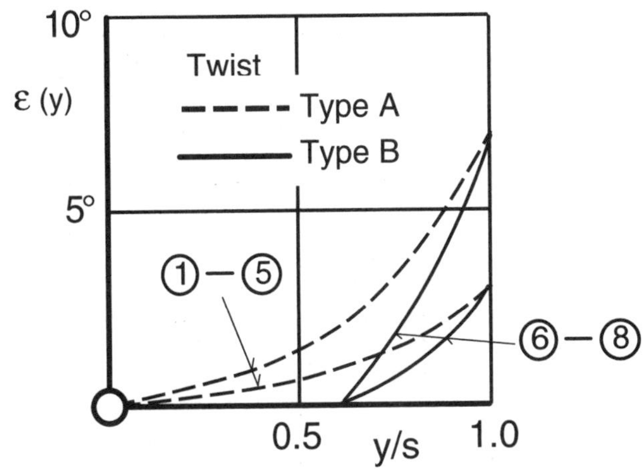

Fig. 122: Effect of wing planform and twist on induced drag, based on Æ= 25 (see also facing page).
ΔC_{D_i} = induced drag relative to minimum (elliptical lift distribution)

shown that the relative performance benefits of thick and thin airfoils balance out, provided the wing loading can be adjusted accordingly. However, the selection of airfoil thickness involves more than just performance considerations. In addition to permitting a lighter wing structure, thicker wings provide more room for dive brakes, control linkage, and water ballast. On the other hand, thicker airfoils seem to be more sensitive to insect contamination, a serious problem in some regions at certain times of the year. The introduction and widespread use of stronger and stiffer materials has made thinner airfoils more practical from a structural point of view - for example the HQ 17 and DU89-134 (see Table 6), both approximately 14% thick .

The net effect of airfoil selection on the average cross-country speed is shown in Fig. 121, which compares some well-known fixed-geometry and flapped airfoils as a function of wing loading. The airfoil data are from the Stuttgart Profile Catalog I.

The question of selecting an appropriate airfoil for the empennage and the aileron region is discussed in more detail in a following section.

Wing Planform and Twist

Design considerations

As discussed in the first chapter, wing planform, structural twist, and aerodynamic twist combine to determine the spanwise lift distribution. The lift distribution in turn de-

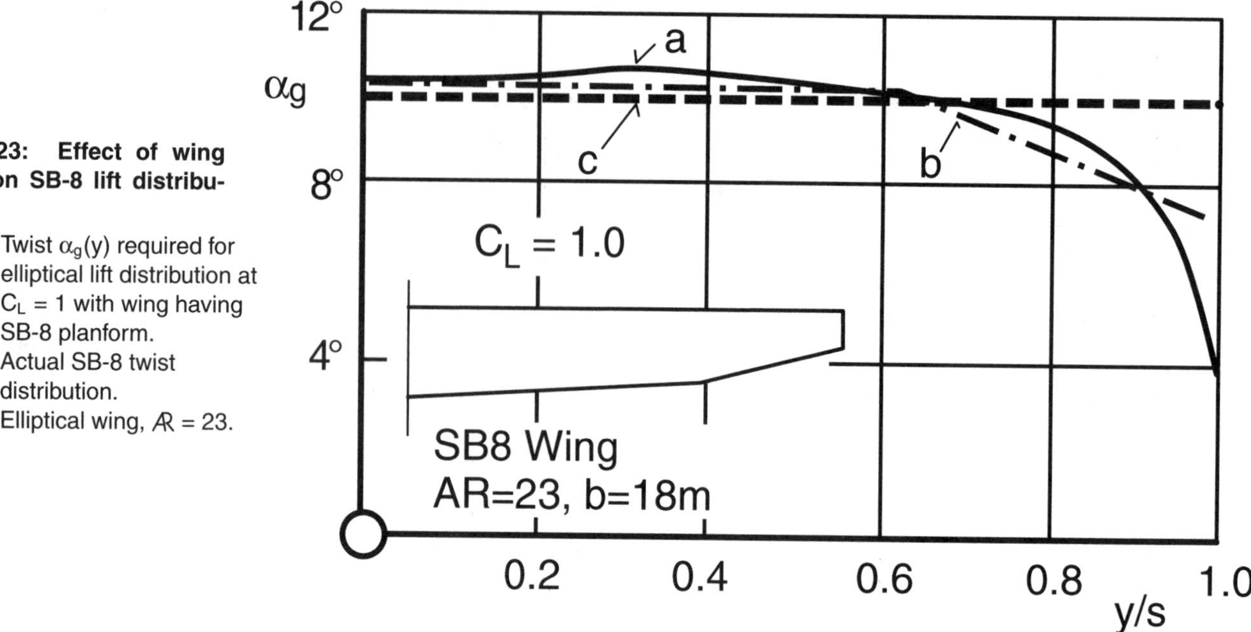

Fig. 123: Effect of wing twist on SB-8 lift distribution.

(a) Twist $\alpha_g(y)$ required for elliptical lift distribution at $C_L = 1$ with wing having SB-8 planform.
(b) Actual SB-8 twist distribution.
(c) Elliptical wing, $\mathcal{R} = 23$.

termines the induced drag factor (k) and has a significant effect on stall behavior.

An untwisted, elliptical wing provides an elliptical circulation distribution at all lift coefficients, thus minimizing induced drag at all airspeeds. The surfaces of elliptical wings, however, form compound curves, making them difficult to manufacture to adequate tolerances. This, along with unfavorable stalling characteristics, eliminates elliptical wings as an option in most cases.

It is considerably easier to manufacture aerodynamic surfaces formed by ruled surfaces (surfaces defined in terms of straight lines), and wing planforms for nearly all modern sailplanes are synthesized from rectangular and trapezoidal sections. A combination of several trapezoidal sections together with an appropriate twist distribution can produce a planform that performs nearly as well as an elliptical wing. The operating conditions for a low induced drag factor k may, however, be limited to a relatively small range of lift coefficients.

Influence on induced drag

Figure 122 presents the induced drag for a number of typical planforms and twist distributions relative to the ideal (elliptical-wing) values. A double tapered wing with -3° twist in the outer section seems to offer the best compromise. These results correspond to $\mathcal{R} = 25$ but vary little with aspect ratio.

For a given planform, the twist required for an elliptical lift distribution at a particular lift coefficient may be obtained using the Multhopp method. Figure 123, for example, shows the twist required for the SB-8 operating at $C_L = 1$. The double-tapered SB-8 wing comes very close to this twist distribution. In order to better approximate an elliptical planform, some recent designs have featured triple tapered wings (Discus, ASH 25, Nimbus 4, Grob Twin II).

Stall characteristics

Sailplane wings must be designed for good stalling characteristics right from the start. With powered aircraft, unacceptable stalling behavior can often be corrected late in the development process with simple means such as leading-edge modifications to the airfoil and flow tripping devices. These can severely degrade the performance of laminar airfoils and are thus unsuitable for sailplane use.

In order to ensure forgiving stall characteristics, the wing should be designed so that flow separation occurs first on the inboard sections of the wing. This prevents premature loss of aileron control, and reduces the tendency of the

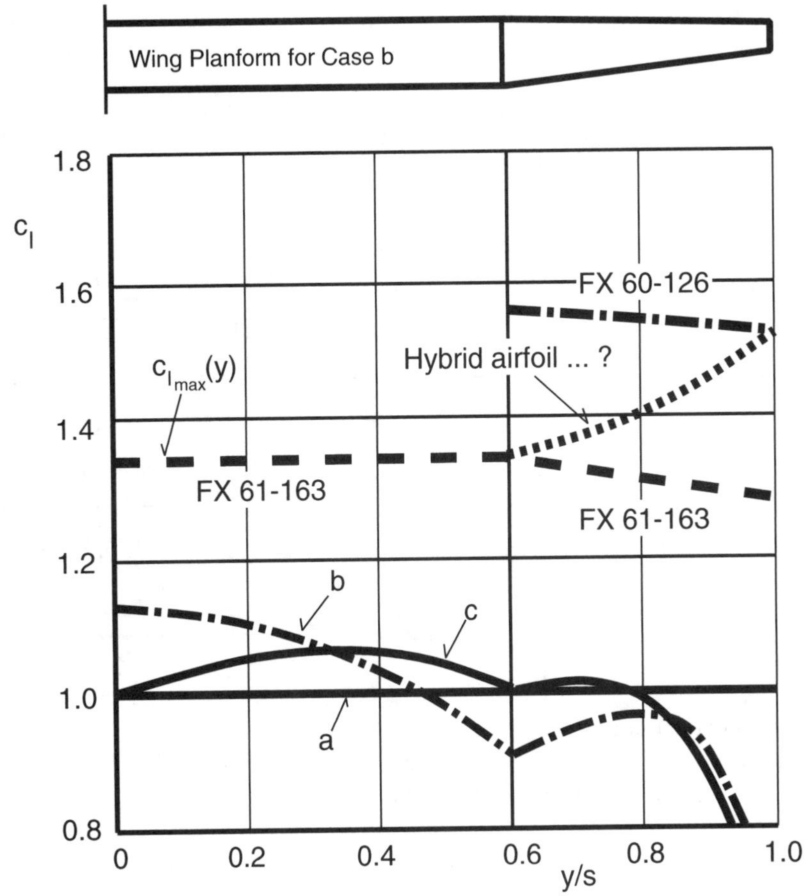

Fig. 124: Spanwise distribution of lift coefficient for three wings having elliptical lift distribution and operating at $C_L = 1$.

(a) Elliptical wing
(b) Rectangular/tapered
(c) Double-taper wing

– – – – Maximum lift coefficient, including Reynolds number effects.

aircraft to fall off on one wing and enter a spin. The lift distribution is thus tailored so that the maximum lift coefficient is exceeded first on the inboard section of the wing. Due to reduced chord and Reynolds numbers, the maximum lift coefficient tends to drop off near the tip (Fig. 124). A typical wingtip Reynolds number corresponding to slow flight at 70km/h and a local wing chord of c = 0.40m amounts to around $0.5 \cdot 10^6$. Little data for such low Reynolds numbers exist, and the designer must resort to extrapolation of data measured at higher Reynolds numbers. For example, data for $Re=10^6$ and $0.7 \cdot 10^6$ are often available, in which case extrapolating to $Re=0.5 \cdot 10^6$ is quite reasonable (Fig. 125).

Some improvement in stall characteristics is possible through the selection of the wingtip airfoil. This, however, leads to a hybrid airfoil in the transition region between the inboard and outboard wing section (Fig. 124). Although little experimental data are available for these hybrid airfoils, practical experience suggests that they do not degrade the stalling characteristics to any great extent. As shown by L. M. M. Boermans and B. Oolbekkink [72], considerable room for improvement remains in the aerodynamic design of the outer wing region.

The three wings in Fig. 124 are twisted to provide an elliptical lift distribution. The c_l-distribution for the rectangular-tapered wing yields the best stalling behavior since the highest lift coefficients are found right at the wing root. With the elliptical wing, $c_{l_{max}}$ is reached over the entire wing at once and the stall characteristics will likely be problematic. Although the double tapered wing also appears somewhat critical, good behavior may be obtained through proper airfoil tailoring. In this respect, the airfoils - especially in the outer wing - should be selected for gentle trailing-edge stall behavior. Airfoils exhibiting sudden leading-edge stall are to be avoided.

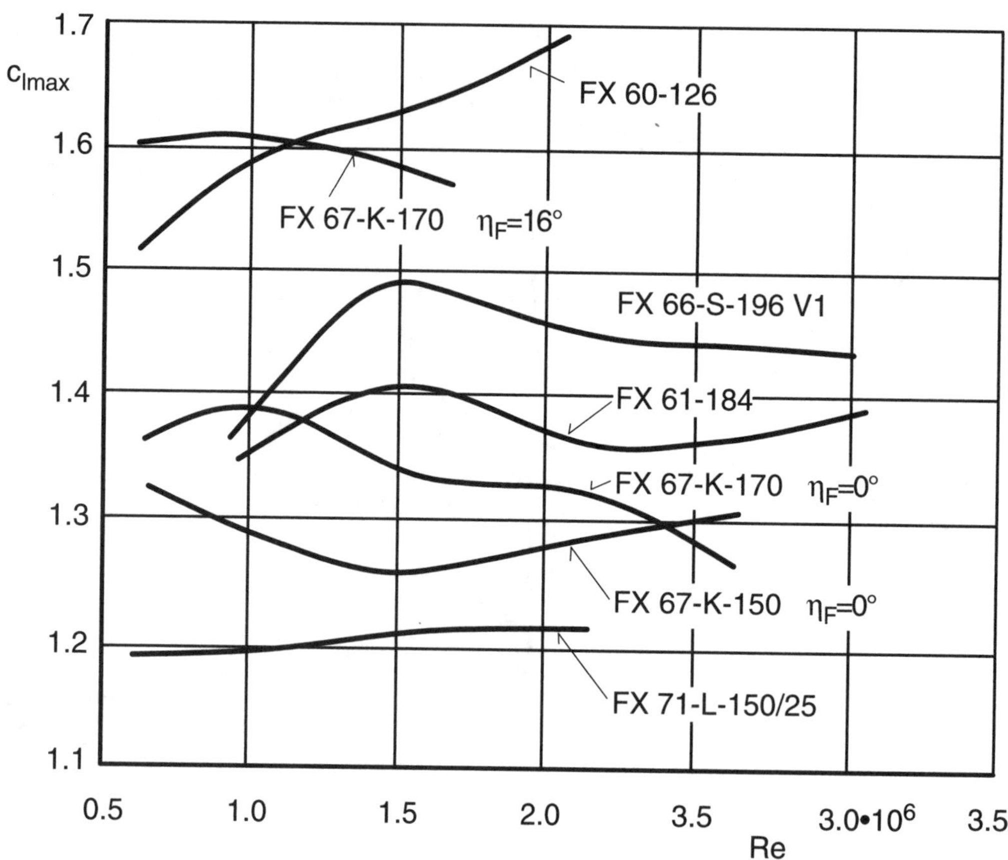

Fig. 125: Maximum lift coefficient vs. Reynolds number for various airfoils, from [168].

Flap and aileron deflections

When deflected, partial-span flaps have an effect similar to that of introducing an additional spanwise twist distribution. A poorly designed flap system can lead to considerable increases in induced drag (Fig. 126). For multi-segment flaps and flaps coupled with ailerons, it is well worth the effort to optimize the flap deflection schedule using, for example, the Multhopp method. Studies of this sort have shown that best results are obtained with a partial span flap coupled with symmetrical aileron deflection (droop). Full-span flaperons and uncoupled partial span flaps appear less efficient. See also W. Feifel [78] for optimization of the flap/aileron system to minimize induced drag during turn entries and exits.

The Multhopp analysis can also be used to verify that the local wing sections are operating in the laminar bucket throughout the required airspeed range. A poorly designed flap or improperly scheduled aileron droop can shift portions of the wing out of the laminar bucket, with significant increases in drag.

Flaps place additional requirements on wing torsional stiffness. The aerodynamic pitching moments associated with the flap deflection can induce torsional deflections that distort the lift distribution and reduce the aileron effectiveness. Systematic flight tests by G. Stich [162] have shown that aeroelastic deflections of this sort cannot be neglected, especially at high airspeeds.

Finally, the flap actuation linkage must be stiff enough to prevent reductions in flap deflection due to aerodynamic loads. There have been cases where compliance in the flap linkage has, unknown to the pilot, resulted in unintended and improper flap settings.

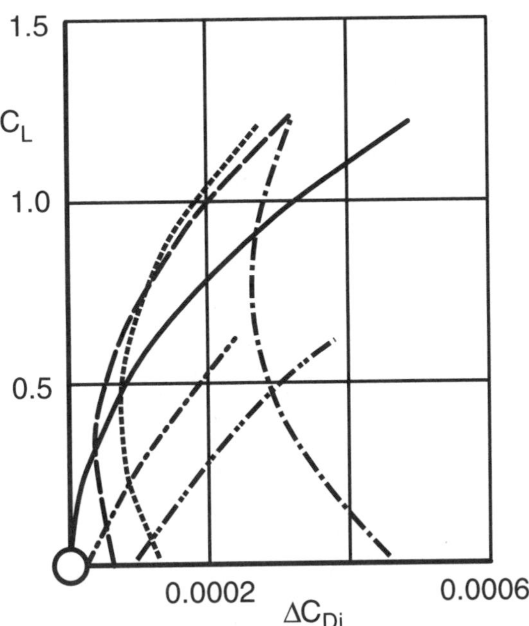

Fig. 126: Induced drag of flapped wing with various camber flap settings η_K and aileron deflections η_A.

η_F	η_A
-7°	-5.25°
-4°	-3°
0°	0°
4°	3°
6.5°	4°
11°	8.2°

Optimum planform and twist

Both theoretical investigations and practical experience suggest that a double tapered wing having a taper ratio of 0.4:0.8:1 and a taper break at y/s = 0.6 yields especially good results (planform 8 in Fig. 122) [115]. Tapered and rectangular/tapered wings provide nearly the same performance and are often selected for ease of manufacture.

For flapped wings, the induced drag can be kept to its theoretical minimum over a wide range of C_L by combining an appropriate twist distribution for the zero-flap configuration with proper scheduling of the flap/aileron deflections.

Although, at one time, highly tapered wings ($\mathcal{R} \leq 0.3$) were common for structural reasons - the "Weihe", and "Kranich III" being typical examples - they are seldom employed in modern sailplanes. Highly tapered wings require considerable twist (up to -8°) to provide satisfactory stall characteristics.

Winglets and Unconventional Planforms

Despite high aspect ratios and carefully optimized wing planforms, induced drag remains a significant source of drag, amounting to around 50% of the total drag while thermaling, and about 20% in high speed flight. In the Open Class, efforts to reduce induced drag have led to wing spans exceeding 25m.

However, when span is limited by class rules, longer wings are no longer an option. It may nevertheless be possible to reduce the induced drag through optimization of the wingtip geometry. Over the years, numerous attempts have been made to reduce induced drag with wingtip modifications, *e.g.* the tip fairings of the Kranich III. For further discussion of wingtip geometry see, for example, S. F. Hoerner [11] and O. Nicks [124].

One approach employs *winglets*, small aerodynamic surfaces extending upwards from the wingtip, designed to lift inwards. According to the simplest theory, this allows some of the wing vorticity to continue into the winglet where it is trailed away from the plane of the wing. Recall from the first chapter that Prandtl's lifting-line theory assumes that all vorticity is trailed in the plane of the wing. According to the Biot-Savart law, the velocity induced by a vortex filament decreases as the distance from the filament increases. Thus, by trailing some of the vorticity away from the plane of the wing, a properly designed winglet can reduce the downwash at the wing and with it the induced drag factor k (Eq. 47) to a value below 1. A more detailed analysis shows that the winglet also inhibits the development of the strong tip vortex that "rolls up" just downstream of the wingtip [117, 123].

Balanced against the reduced induced drag is the profile drag of the winglet itself. This leads to a fundamental tradeoff in winglet design: winglets optimized for minimum induced drag tend to be fairly large, incurring profile drag penalties and a net performance penalty in high-speed flight.

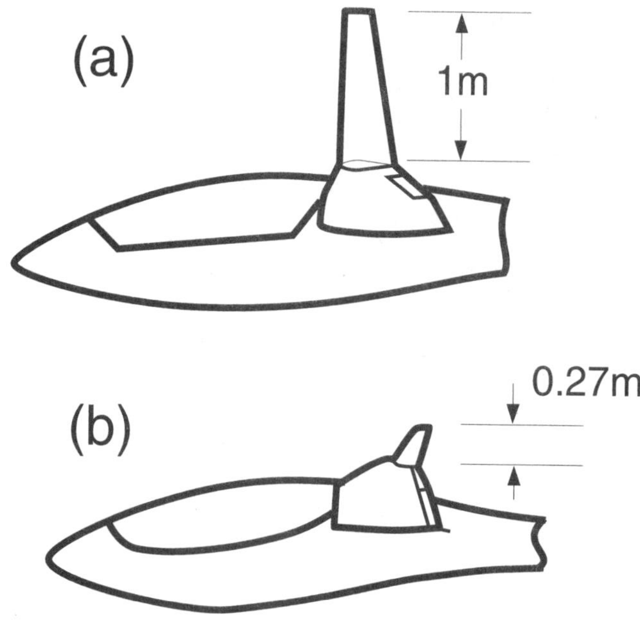

Fig. 127: Winglet configurations for two sailplanes with b = 15m

(a) ASW-19, Akaflieg Braunschweig, 1983, from [118]
(b) ASW-27, factory winglets, 1997

Modern interest in winglets for drag reduction began in the mid-1970's. See, for example, a study by R. T. Whitcomb [129]. Serious attempts to design sailplane winglets began in the early 1980's. An early theoretical and flight test investigation is documented by U. Dressler [118]. The first sailplane winglets tended to be optimized to minimize induced drag and were thus fairly large. The winglet tested in [118], for example, was 1m high (Fig. 127). The additional mass located away from the wing elastic axis has a significant effect on the wing torsional frequency, requiring additional wing torsional stiffness to ensure aeroelastic stability. Thus, in addition to the costs involved in manufacturing the winglet, the winglet could in some cases require expensive modifications to the wing itself. This led to an opinion that winglets were not in the spirit of the span-limited class rules because — it was argued — winglets were more expensive and provided less of a performance benefit than an equivalent increase in wingspan (see [118] and G. Waibel [127]).

Subsequently, it has been shown that good results may be obtained with relatively small winglets. In contrast to early winglets, which were essentially upward wing extensions, recent winglet designs are optimized to diffuse the vortex rollup at the wingtip, thus reducing its strength. There is also evidence that the velocity field induced by winglets can improve airfoil aerodynamics in the vicinity of the wingtip by prolonging laminar flow and delaying separation [128]. Winglets are now featured on several production sailplanes and are often retrofitted to older designs.

For further information on winglets, the reader is referred to D. J. Marsden [121], P. C. Masak [122], R. Eppler [119] and M. D. Maughmer and P. J. Kunz [123]. The latter reference presents a detailed winglet analysis capable of predicting the tip vortex roll-up and comparison with flight test data. See also Crosby *et al* [117] for numerical predictions and flight test results for a full scale winglet.

In addition to winglets, two other approaches to minimizing induced drag are worthy of mention.

As with winglets, *polyhedral*, a variation of the dihedral angle at several stations along the wingspan, provides a non-planar geometry offering the possibility of reducing induced drag below the minimum value predicted by basic Prandtl theory. A study by C. D. Cone [116, 120] has shown that the optimum wing curvature is elliptical. A recent sailplane with polyhedral is the Discus 2 (Fig. 128).

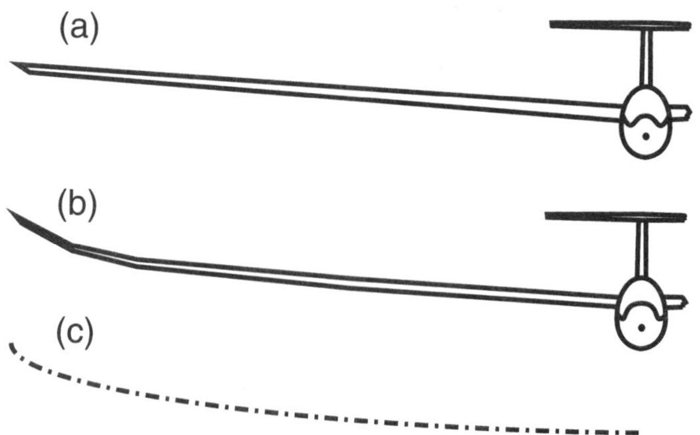

Fig. 128: Polyhedral.

(a) Discus (1984)
(b) Discus 2 (1998)
(c) semi-ellipse

Beginning in the early 1980's, a number of new sailplanes have appeared with unconventional wing planforms featuring straight or nearly-straight trailing edges, with wing taper achieved by sweeping the leading edges. These planforms had been implemented earlier in powered aircraft, for example, the Dornier TNT technology demonstrator (1979) and Do-228 commuter aircraft (1981) [34]. An early application to sailplanes came in 1982 with a modified ASW-12 by W. Schuemann [125]. Similar planforms have appeared on a number of production sailplanes including the Discus (1983), S-10 (1986), SZD-55 (1988), Duo-Discus (1993), and Ventus 2 (1994) (see Fig. 129).

Here as well the advantage appears to result from a reduction in induced drag. Crescent-shaped wings have been shown, at least computationally, to offer a small induced drag advantage over elliptical wings (see S. C. Smith and I. Kroo [126]). However, as with winglets, the complex interactions between the planform and behavior of the boundary layer have yet to be thoroughly researched.

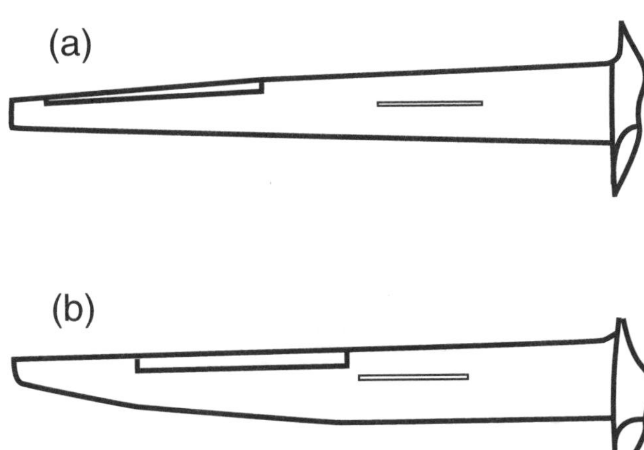

Fig. 129: Planform with straight trailing edge. Planforms of two Standard Class sailplanes.

(a) Std. Cirrus (1969) S=10.04m^2.
(b) Discus (1984) S=10.58m^2.

Variable Geometry

Camber changing and area changing flaps, telescoping wings

The conflicting aerodynamic requirements for high speed and thermaling flight have prompted exploration of methods for varying the wing geometry and wing loading in flight.

Camber changing flaps are themselves a simple form of variable geometry (Fig. 130). These flaps typically have a flap/chord ratio of around 17%. Care must be taken to keep the hinge gap as small as possible in order to minimize its effect on the boundary layer. Hinge gaps must also be well sealed to prevent air flow through the wing surfaces. One approach to the hinge gap problem extends a continuous skin over the wing upper surface, flap, and aileron, with elastic skin sections covering the hinge gaps. Flaps of this sort have appeared on several one-off sailplanes (*e.g.* the HKS I, HKS III, SB 9 and Phoebus B3), as well as a production aircraft, the "Speed Astir".

Dive brakes are usually mounted as far aft as possible on the wing in order to minimize their impact on the laminar flow when retracted. This has led to an interesting solution in which the dive brakes and camber changing flaps are combined in a single element, an approach that has been successfully implemented in production aircraft such as the Mini-Nimbus, Mosquito, and early versions of the Ventus.

While camber changing flaps affect only the airfoil geometry, area-changing flaps and the telescoping wing change the wing loading as well. By modifying the wing area, aircraft can be thermaled at low wing loading and flown between thermals at a high wing loading.

The telescoping wing features a close-fitting outer wing panel supported by and extending over the inner panel. By sliding the outer panel outboard over the inner panel (Fig. 131) the wing area and aspect ratio are increased, while the chord and taper remain constant.

The term "area changing flap" refers to a flap that extends aft from the wing trailing edge. These are not to be confused with Fowler flaps, which feature a sizeable slot between flap and wing. With area-changing flaps, the wingspan remains constant, while the chord and airfoil geometry change. The aspect ratio is affected as well, albeit in the opposite sense from telescoping wing. That is, the aspect ratio is reduced when the flap is deployed.

Airfoil sections with area-changing flaps have been developed by F. X. Wortmann [199], and K. H. Horstmann and

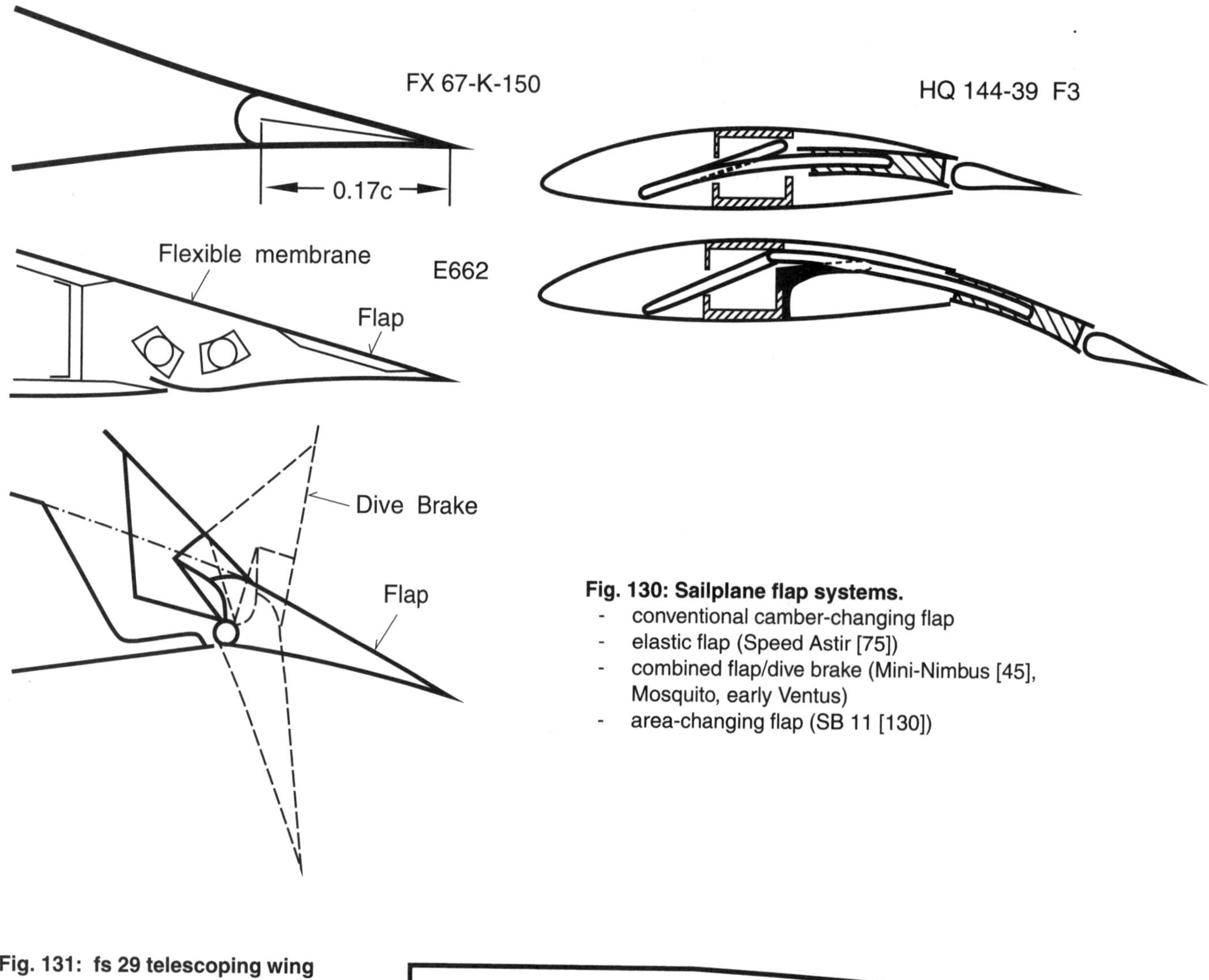

Fig. 130: Sailplane flap systems.
- conventional camber-changing flap
- elastic flap (Speed Astir [75])
- combined flap/dive brake (Mini-Nimbus [45], Mosquito, early Ventus)
- area-changing flap (SB 11 [130])

Fig. 131: fs 29 telescoping wing

13.30 m

19.00 m

A. Quast [182]. Slotted flaps for sailplane application have been investigated by D. G. Marsden and his colleagues at the University of Alberta, Canada [186, 187].

Each of these variable geometry systems offers a number of qualitative advantages and disadvantages.

Telescoping wing: advantages

- aspect ratio varies in the desired manner, *i.e.* it increases in the low-speed configuration, and decreases when the wing is retracted for high-speed
- large variations in wing area in excess of 50% are possible

Disadvantages

- variable geometry airfoils cannot be used
- water ballast capacity is limited

Area-changing flaps: advantages

- airfoil geometry can be adjusted in flight
- good water ballast capacity
- with wingspan of 15m, the aircraft can be flown in the FAI 15m class
- additional camber changing flaps may be installed

Disadvantages

- changes in wing area are relatively small at around 25–36%
- aspect ratio is highest in high speed flight, and lowest while thermaling
- difficult fuselage-wing interference drag problem

A comparison of various flap systems for a generic 15m sailplane (Fig. 132) shows that the advantages of area-changing flaps over camber-changing flaps (and, in turn the advantages of camber-changing flaps over unflapped airfoils) become more pronounced as the wing loading is increased. The greatest improvements are seen with the weak/narrow thermal models [139]. In practical terms, area-changing flaps allow cross-country flights with full water ballast in relatively poor conditions. With wide, strong thermals and moderate wing loadings, camber-changing flaps provide little advantage, and the area-changing flaps almost none at all. Since area-changing flaps reduce only the thermaling airspeed (not the actual sink speed), their benefits are fully realized only in weather conditions with narrow thermals. Exploiting the ability to circle tightly at low airspeed does, however, require a certain degree of pilot skill.

Figure 133 combines results for the four thermal models using Quast's composite cross-country weather model [60]. Considerable variation in the optimum wing loading is observed. For the unflapped wing, 24–29 daN/m^2 yields the best results. Adding camber-changing flaps shifts the optimum to 26–32 daN/m^2, and with area-changing flaps, wing loadings of 34–43 daN/m^2 are preferred. Overall, introducing camber-changing flaps to an unflapped wing increases the average cross-country speed by around 7.5%, and the area-changing flap improves performance by about 6% beyond that. Similar results are obtained for wingspans of 18 and 21m.

Figure 134 shows the average cross-country speed and best glide ratio as a function of span for each of these configurations. It is assumed that the wing loading and aspect ratio are always optimum for the given flap configuration and wingspan. In terms of performance, adding a camber-changing flap to an unflapped wing is roughly equivalent to increasing the wingspan from 15 to 19m (Fig. 134). Replacing the camber changing flap with an area changing flap has a similar effect.

This observation must be tempered by the fact that best glide ratios tend to improve with wingspan. Clearly there are situations where a high glide ratio provides the decisive advantage; such scenarios are not reflected in the mathematical cross-country model used here (see also F. Thomas and R. Eppler [139]).

The comparison in Fig. 135 suggests that area-changing flaps enjoy a slight advantage over the telescoping wing. The two configurations, however, represent fundamentally different design philosophies, so it is difficult to establish an appropriate basis for comparison. Naturally, if the span is fixed by class rules, the area changing flap is superior. However, comparisons based on equal wing area (flap deployed and wing extended, respectively), equal takeoff weight, or manufacturing cost might lead to entirely different conclusions.

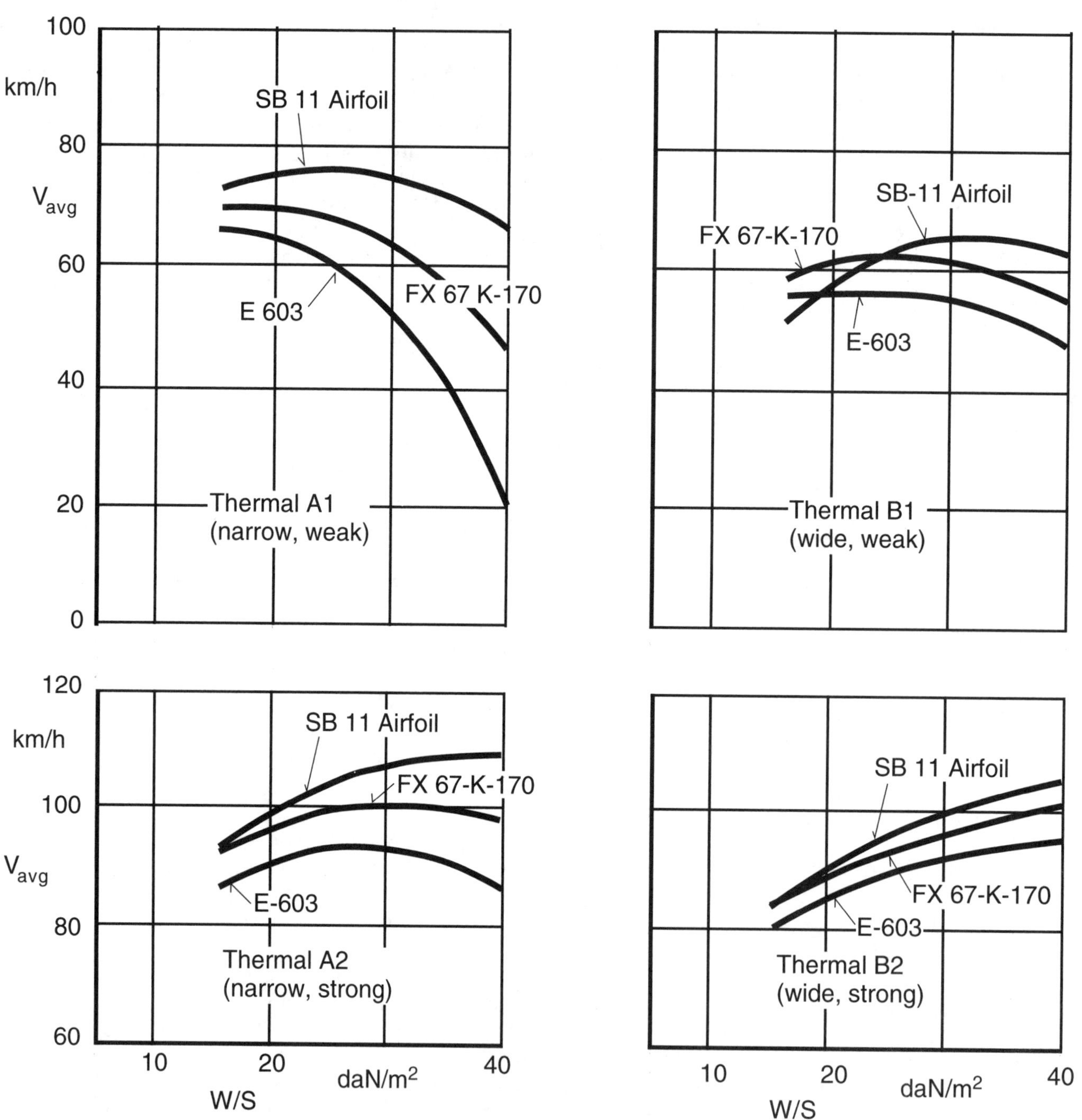

Fig. 132: Comparison of average cross-country speed with fixed geometry airfoils, camber-changing flaps, and area-changing flaps. Results based on Horstmann model (Fig. 87) and b=15m, $A\!\!\!/R$=20, and C_{D_p}=0.00035.

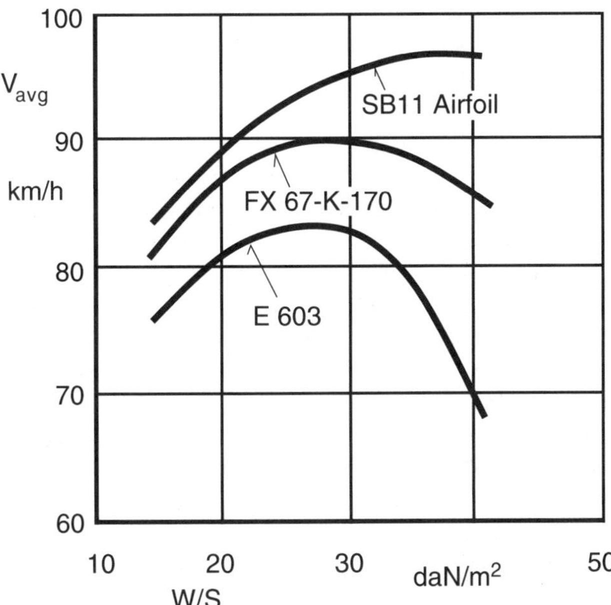

Fig. 133: Average cross-country speed for a wings with fixed geometry airfoil, camber-changing flaps, and area-changing flaps, based on Quast mixed weather model (Fig. 95).
b=15m, Æ=20, and C_{D_p}=0.0035.

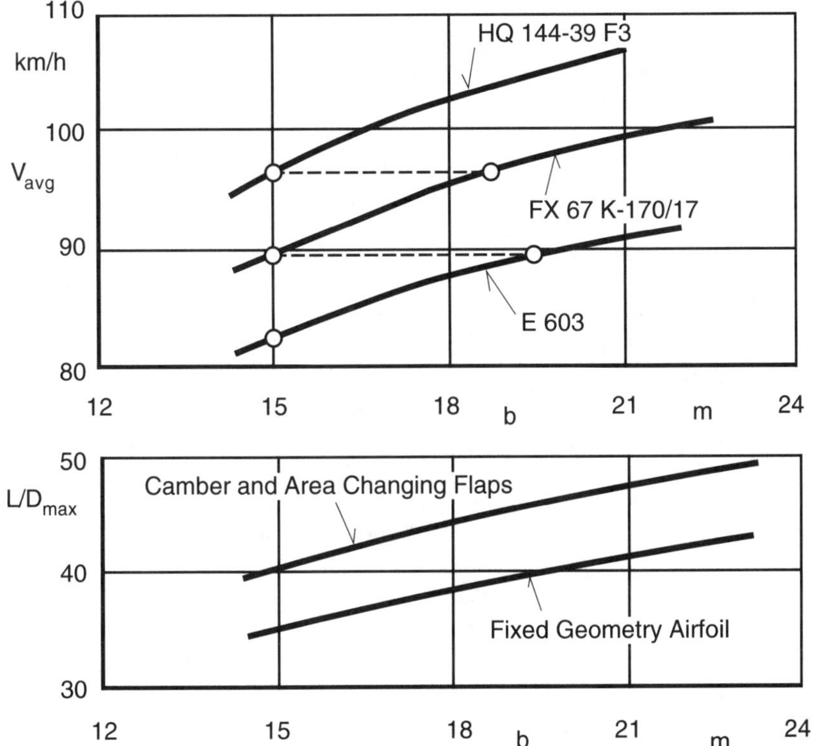

Fig. 134: Average cross-country speed and best glide ratio for various airfoils and wingspans, in each case assuming optimum wing loading and aspect ratio.

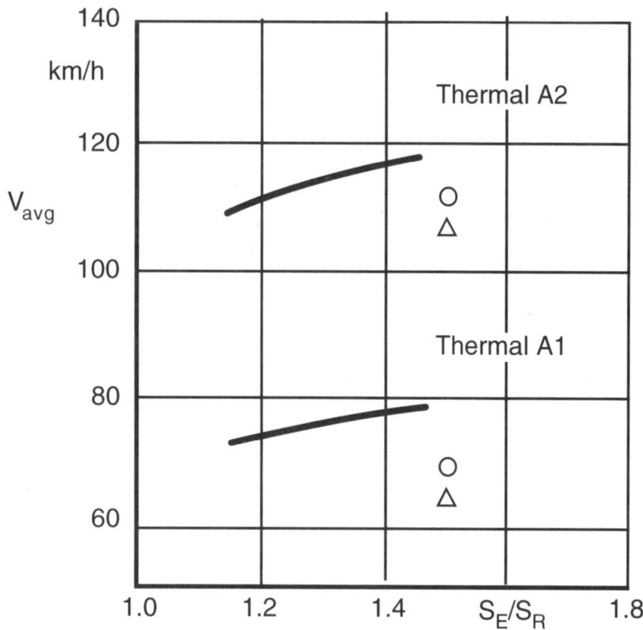

Fig. 135: Comparison of telescoping wing and area changing flaps (typical results).

S_E wing area with flaps or wing extended
S_R wing area with flaps or wing retracted
○ telescoping wing with camber changing flaps
△ telescoping wing with fixed geometry airfoil
▬ area changing flap

The relative merits of these two variable geometry concepts were debated at Idaflieg meets throughout the 1970's. Members of the Akaflieg Stuttgart were proponents of the telescoping wing, while the Akaflieg Braunschweig advocated area-changing flaps. Eventually, the two Akafliegs each built a sailplane in their preferred configuration. Both faced challenging design problems that had never before been tackled. Previous experiments with area-changing flaps had not proven particularly successful, and there never had been a telescoping wing aircraft of any sort.

Both Akafliegs succeeded in building and flying their aircraft. Akaflieg Stuttgart first flew the fs 29 on June 15, 1975, and the Akaflieg Braunschweig's sailplane, the SB 11, flew on May 14, 1978.

The fs 29

The fs 29 is the first and, to date, only successful telescoping wing aircraft in the world. Despite the obvious technical challenges, the Stuttgart Akafliegers were able to take this impressive aircraft from drawing board to first flight in an astonishingly short period of time. Since then, many years of flight experience with this aircraft have firmly established the viability of the telescoping wing concept.

Preliminary design studies predicted a slight performance advantage for the area-changing flap. The Akafliegers were nevertheless attracted by the comparative mechanical simplicity of the telescoping wing as well as its potential for reduced structural weight. Another factor was the relative lack of success of earlier experiments involving area-changing flaps (Sigma [133, 137], AN 66 [136]). Overall, this approach appears to offer the greatest performance improvement relative to the design and construction effort.

Detailed accounts of the design of the fs 29 have appeared elsewhere [31, 131, 132] and need not be reviewed here. A three-view drawing of this remarkable aircraft is in Fig. 136; additional data are found in Appendix 1.

Despite the overall success of the project, the configuration is complex to build and the actuation system required an unacceptable pilot workload. Consequently, no attempts have been made to develop the concept for series production. The fs 29 was nevertheless an ambitious experiment, earning an important place in soaring history.

The SB 11

The Akaflieg Braunschweig's variable-geometry project began with a series of preliminary studies [112] and an analysis of the difficulties encountered in earlier experiments in area-changing flaps. Three crucial design requirements were identified:

- flap extension and retraction must be quick and easy to prevent pilot fatigue during long flights,
- with the flaps retracted, performance must be comparable to that of a sailplane with camber-changing flaps, and
- sufficient water ballast is required to provide good performance in a wide variety of weather conditions.

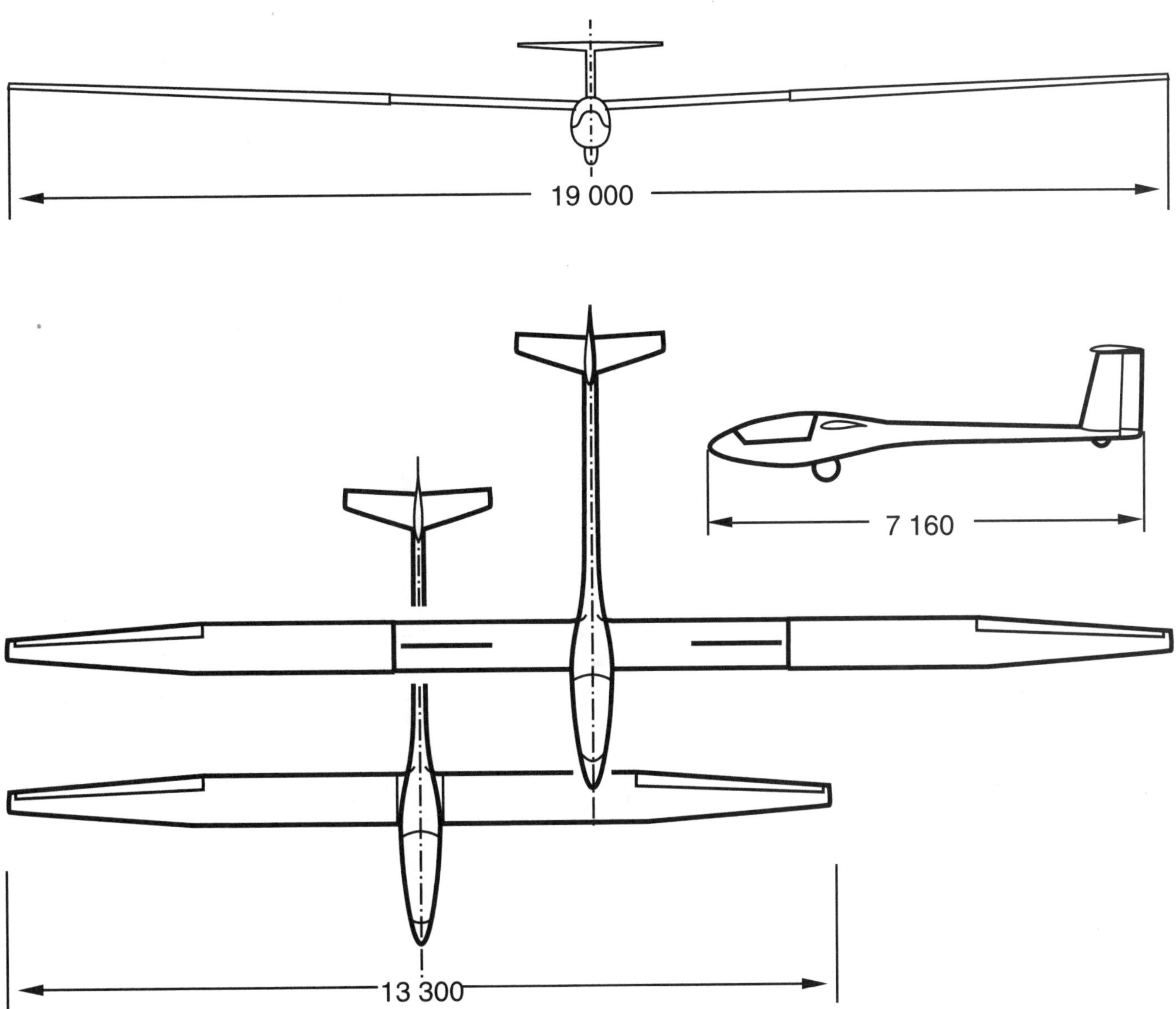

Fig. 136: The fs 29 (Akaflieg Stuttgart, 1975).

The greatest single technical challenge proved to be the mechanical design of the flap/wing fit. While aerodynamic considerations demand a snug fit between flap and wing, care must be taken to avoid excessive mechanical friction and high actuation loads. Elastic flap seals were rejected since, if made soft enough to prevent friction, they tend to flutter (see also K. H. Horstmann and A. Quast [182]). Wing bending presented another problem. If the wing is too soft, the bending deflections can cause binding of the flap, hindering extension and retraction.

The wing was built with carbon fiber to ensure adequate bending and torsional stiffness without excessive structural

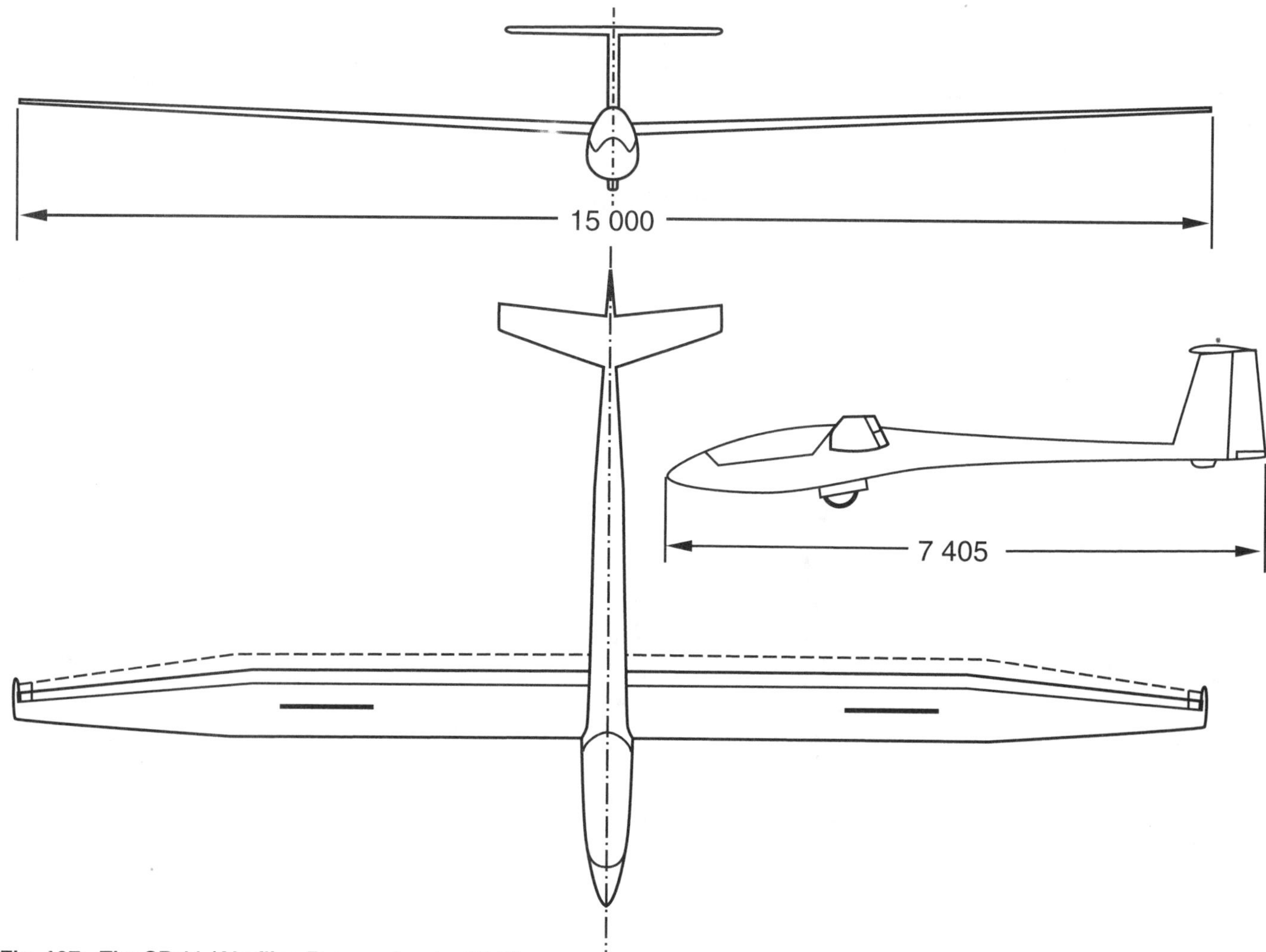

Fig. 137: The SB 11 (Akaflieg Braunschweig, 1978).

weight. Mechanical friction was held to a minimum by fitting the wing with a rigid trailing edge and tapering the flap so that it contacted the wing inner skins only in the first and last few millimeters of travel (Fig. 130).

Previous variable geometry aircraft (both area-changing flap projects and the Stuttgart telescoping wing) were designed to change their wing areas by around 36 to 50%. For the SB 11, however, a relatively conservative flap depth was chosen providing only a 25% variation. This allowed the wing to be built with an extremely stiff torsion box extending to 55% chord, providing ample room for water ballast. This also allowed the aft portion of the flap to be built as a conventional camber-changing flap (or aileron). The ability to operate as a conventional flapped sailplane while cruising or searching for thermals proved to be a significant advantage.

The hinged portion of the flap was sized at 21% of the wing chord (17%, with flap extended). The large aileron depth with flaps retracted provided unusually good maneuverability. The roll time for a +/- 45° roll reversal at 1.4 V_s was measured at around 2.8 seconds. With flap extended the roll rate is less impressive (4.5s) but nevertheless adequate.

Fig. 138: Students of the Akaflieg Braunschweig advocated area-changing flaps over the telescoping wing. By varying the wing area, the aircraft could be adapted inflight for climb or cruise. The SB-11 first flew in 1978 following several years of preliminary research. In the hands of a capable pilot, the aircraft was an excellent performer, as demonstrated by H. Reichmann, who in 1978 flew the SB-11 to win his third World Championship. Photographs at left show the area-changing flap in its retracted and extended positions.

The airfoil/flap configuration was based on a 14.4% thick variant of the Wortmann FX 62-K-131 profile. Airfoil aerodynamics were evaluated inflight at full-scale Reynolds numbers by mounting a 1.5m wing section on a Kranich III sailplane (this method is described in the following chapter). A series of modifications were made during these tests, with the final airfoil being designated the HQ 144-39 F3.

With water ballast the wing loading could be varied from 26/33 daN/m^2 (flaps out/in) to 36/45 daN/m^2.

Figure 137 shows the aircraft in three-view (see also Fig. 138). Major components were built in the molds for the ASW 19 (fuselage) and Janus (empennage), so that with the flaps retracted the aircraft looks remarkably similar to other 15m sailplanes.

Drag and airspeed polars are presented in Figs. 139 and 140 respectively. Basic design data are in Appendix 1, and more detailed technical information is found in [130, 134].

Shortly after its first flight in the summer of 1978, the SB 11 was flown by Helmut Reichmann in the World Soaring Championships in Châteauroux, France, placing first in the FAI 15m Racing Class. This success was without doubt due largely to the well-known talents of the pilot, but nevertheless confirmed the basic feasibility of the configuration.

Unfortunately, the SB 11's subsequent contest record did not live up to this spectacular initial success. This has been attributed to having designed the sailplane with too low a wing loading. The basic design philosophy was to provide an aircraft that performed as well as other 15m sailplanes in cruise while providing superior climb performance. In practice, however, the superior climb performance cannot be fully exploited when circling in crowded gaggles and/or weak thermals. In addition, modern contest practice emphasizes dolphin-style flying rather than circling, reducing the importance of thermaling performance and favoring higher wing loadings. Nevertheless, it is felt that this design concept still has a future.

Other sailplanes with area changing flaps include the "Delphin", by F. Mahrer, the Mü 27, the D 40 (Akaflieg Darmstadt), the fs 32 "Aguila" from the Akaflieg Stuttgart [32, 138], and D. G. Marsden's Minisigma [135].

Fig. 139: Calculated drag polar for SB 11 with flaps retracted and extended. Coefficients normalized to wing area with flap retracted.

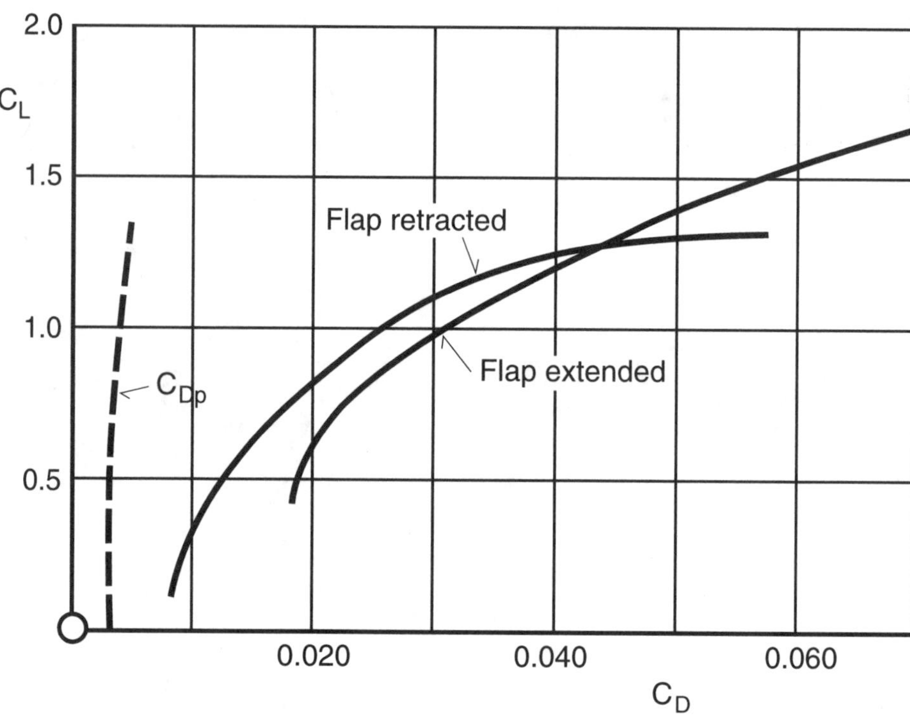

Fig. 140: Calculated airspeed polars for SB 11 without water ballast, with flaps retracted and extended.

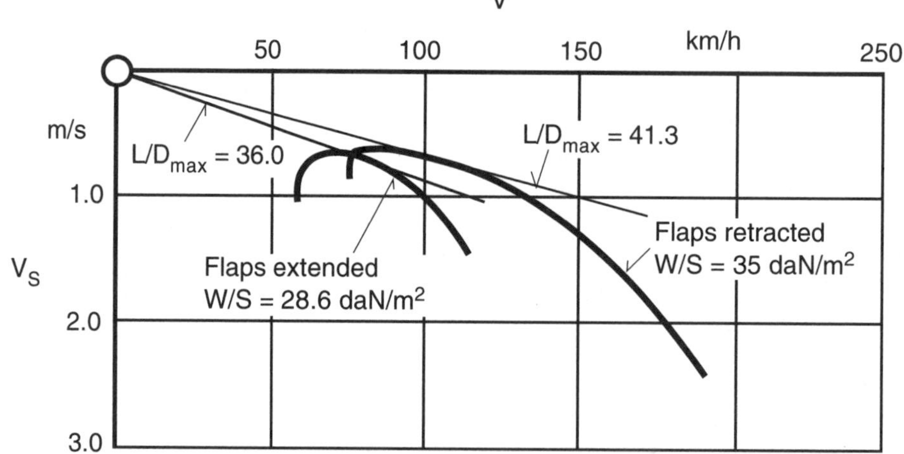

Flying Wings

One obvious approach to reducing drag and structural weight is simply to omit the empennage and aft fuselage. Such flying wing aircraft derive their longitudinal stability entirely from the wing. For this reason the wing can no longer be optimized for minimum drag, but must be carefully tailored to meet stability and handling qualities requirements without incurring excessive drag penalties.

As will be discussed in the section on the horizontal stabilizer (page 130), an aircraft in level flight is longitudinally stable only if its zero-lift moment is positive and the pitching moment gradient is negative. While the pitching moment gradient is mainly a function of the CG position, the trim condition is determined primarily by wing and airfoil ge-

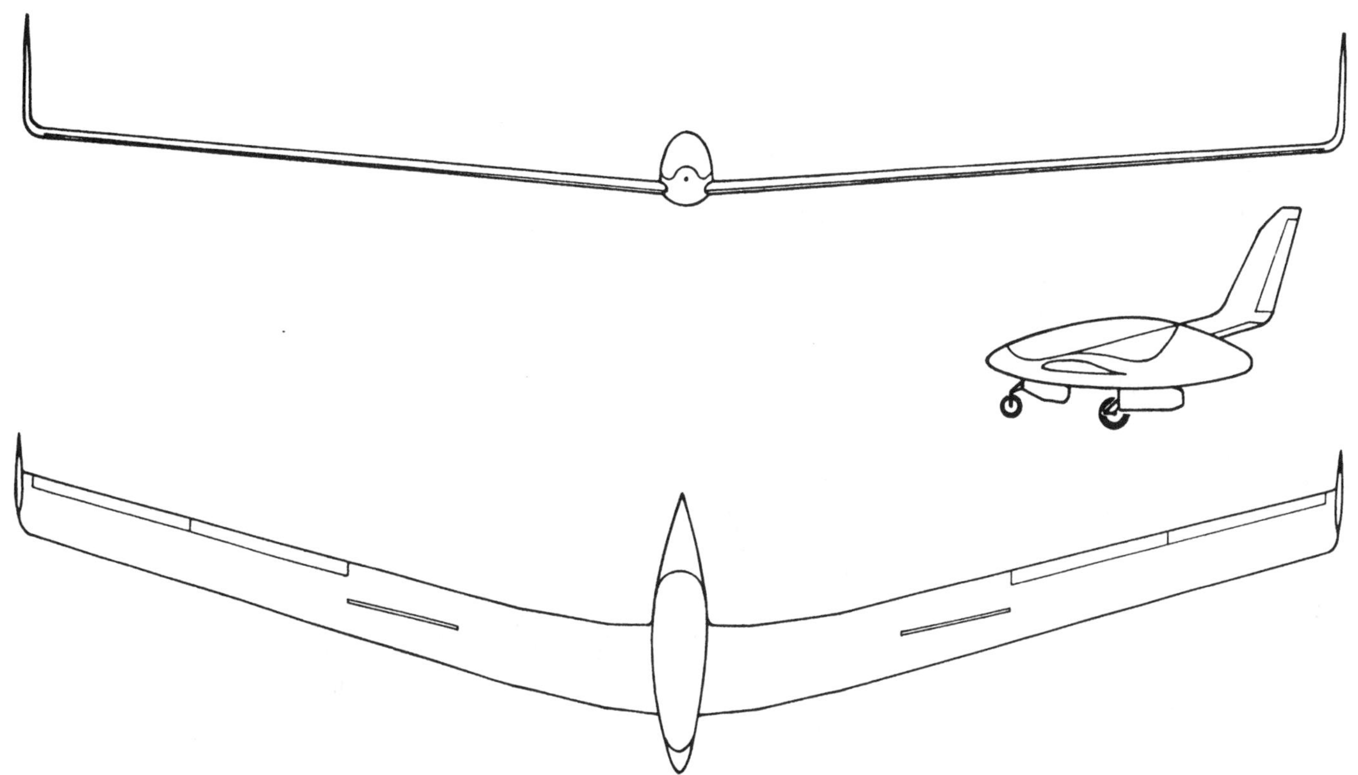

Fig. 141: The SB 13 (Akaflieg Braunschweig, 1988).

ometry. With no horizontal stabilizer, a positive zero lift moment requires either a reflexed airfoil (having reverse camber near the trailing edge) or a swept wing with appropriate twist distribution. These approaches can be combined. Both, however, run contrary to the goal of low drag, especially since they make it difficult to take full advantage of laminar airfoils.

For this reason, most flying wing sailplanes date back to the 1940's and 50's, before the advent of laminar airfoils. The swept-wing Horten designs [82,141,142] were some of the highest performing sailplanes of their day. The Fauvel AV-36 [20] was an unswept design that found its way into series production. Flying wing sailplanes have also been built in Poland [146] and the United States [143,144].

Subsequent advances in airfoil design methodology have made it possible to design laminar airfoils with almost no pitching moment, and competitive flying wing sailplanes are once again a possibility. A high performance flying wing sailplane is nevertheless an ambitious undertaking, as the overall body of design experience pertaining to flying wings is relatively small. With the success of the SB 10 and SB 11 behind them, the Akaflieg Braunschweig felt up to the challenge and commenced development of the SB 13 (Fig. 141).

The SB 13

Early in the design of the SB 13 [140,145] it was decided to limit the span to 15m in order to permit flying in the Standard Class. Its 15° wing sweep allows winglets to double as vertical stabilizers and provides more pitch damping than available with unswept designs. The nearly constant chord is a result of tailoring the wing planform to the twist distribution and control surface deflections for minimum induced drag. The wing features *elevons*, control surfaces combining the functions of elevator and aileron. Rudders mounted on the winglets deflect differentially, with the rudder on the inside wing producing additional induced drag and, with it, a favorable yaw moment. To keep the wing twist to a minimum, great care was taken to design a laminar airfoil with low pitching moment [193]. Special attention was given to the portions of the wing that carried the control surfaces in order to provide acceptable control force gradients. The combination of sweep and large aspect ratio generally leads to a tendency for the flow to separate first over the outboard wing. This is mitigated by tailoring the airfoil and wing planform. Preliminary tests of a 1/5 scale radio controlled model revealed a strong tendency to flutter. Considerable effort was required to modify the design to provide adequate aeroelastic stability.

Following many years of design and construction, the first flight took place in 1988. Although the initial flight tests revealed very good performance, the handling qualities were problematic. Numerous modifications were required to bring about the necessary improvements.

Longitudinal stability proved to be very sensitive to the CG position, *i.e.* the static margin. Static margins ranging from 5.5% to 15% were tested. The inherently low pitch damping, low pitch moment of inertia, and the short offset between nose and main gear led to a tendency to enter short period pitch oscillations, especially during ground roll. Typically, these were aggravated by the pilot's efforts to control them. Pilot induced oscillations ("PIO") of this sort result from pilot inputs that are shifted in phase just enough to cause energy to be added to the system - that is, negative damping. At the forward CG position, a pronounced short-period mode oscillation of 1–2 Hz lasting for about one period was often observed following gusts. The frequency of this transient response is too high for the pilot to control. On the other hand, at aft CG the stall and spin characteristics proved somewhat critical. Modifications to the control system rigging and installation of a boundary-layer fence finally led to acceptable handling qualities. Although the sailplane climbed well in thermals, the maneuverability was relatively poor (5 sec for $\pm 45°$ roll reversals at $1.4V_S$=90km/h).

In the meantime, contest experience as well as routine daily operation has shown that the SB 13's performance is on par with that of modern Standard Class sailplanes, albeit with higher pilot workload.

One unusual feature is the specially developed emergency rescue system. A parachute mounted in the aft fuselage behind the pilot may be deployed in an emergency, bringing the entire aircraft safely to the ground.

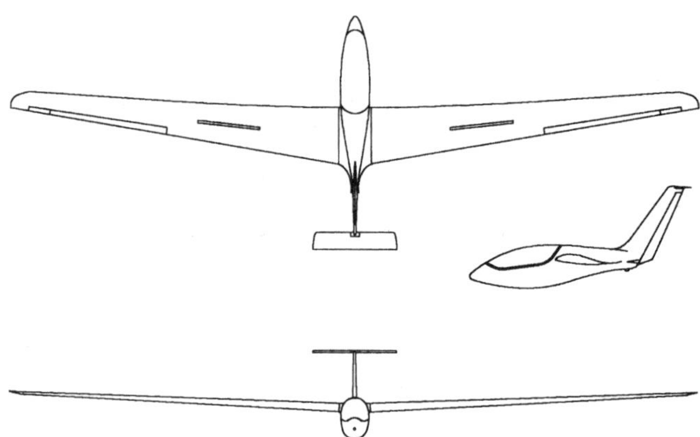

Fig. 142: The Genesis 2

All in all, the design, construction, and flight testing of this modern high performance flying wing has proved to be quite a challenge. Although its flying qualities leave something to be desired, it has been successfully flown by a large number of pilots. That the project was completed despite the numerous difficulties and design challenges is a tribute to the perseverance and ingenuity of the Akafliegers involved.

Genesis

A more recent flying wing, the Genesis, by Jim Marske and John Roncz [5, 143, 144], has been flying in the Standard Class since 1994 (Fig. 142) and is currently in series production. In lieu of wing-mounted control surfaces, a small horizontal stabilizer is provided to trim the aircraft and generate longitudinal control inputs. The horizontal stabilizer contributes relatively little to the longitudinal static stability (see Figs. 179 and 180). As with the eta (discussed in a following section), a turbulent flow airfoil section is used near the wing root, transitioning to a laminar section approximately 0.5 meter outboard of the root.

The World Class

During the mid 1980's, as part of a general effort on the behalf of the FAI to reduce the cost of sport aviation equipment, the FAI's International Gliding Commission (IGC) initiated discussion of a new one-design glider class intended

One-design Classes

Fig. 143: The first one-design class to enjoy widespread success was the Schweizer SGS 1-26, introduced in 1954. An inexpensive, easy-to-fly aircraft, the 1-26's rugged construction made it suitable for low-time students and club use. Early models featured a steel-tube and fabric fuselage and all-metal wings with some fabric covering. The "E" model (shown) has an all-metal monocoque fuselage. The sailplane was also sold in kit form. Altogether, around 700 1-26's were built. National 1-26 competitions have been held annually in the United States since 1965.

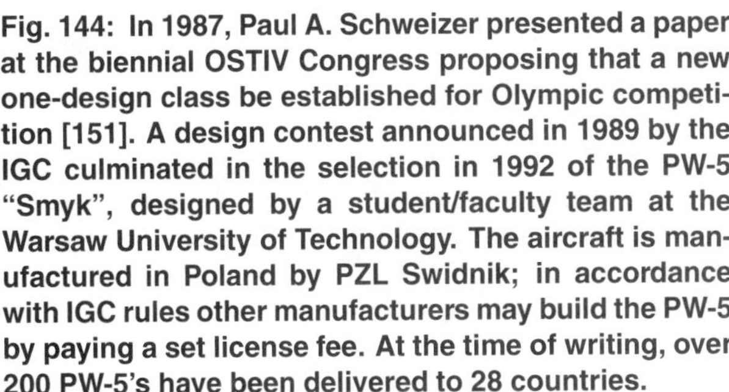

Fig. 144: In 1987, Paul A. Schweizer presented a paper at the biennial OSTIV Congress proposing that a new one-design class be established for Olympic competition [151]. A design contest announced in 1989 by the IGC culminated in the selection in 1992 of the PW-5 "Smyk", designed by a student/faculty team at the Warsaw University of Technology. The aircraft is manufactured in Poland by PZL Swidnik; in accordance with IGC rules other manufacturers may build the PW-5 by paying a set license fee. At the time of writing, over 200 PW-5's have been delivered to 28 countries.

to enable more pilots with limited financial resources - especially young people and pilots in developing countries - to compete effectively in FAI sanctioned events.

The one-design concept had been attempted previously in the late 1930's, with a design competition for a sailplane to be flown in the 1940 Olympics in Finland. In early 1939, the Olympia "Meise" was selected from five prototypes. Although the design itself proved to be popular, the war prevented its development as a one-design class.

Another one-design class based on the Schweizer SGS 1-26 series has been quite successful in the United States with regular organized competition (Fig. 143). While still popular, the aircraft has been out of production for over a decade and, as a 1954 design, offers considerably less performance than more modern sailplanes.

The inspiration for the modern one-design initiative came from a paper presented at the 1987 OSTIV Congress by P. A. Schweizer [151]. In November, 1987, the IGC announced a design contest for the new "World Class" sailplane and approved the technical specifications [148] and detailed rules defining the selection process [147].

The IGC's World Class effort was led primarily by P. Morelli. Following a preliminary screening of over 40 entries, nine designs were selected for the final phase. Of these, 6 prototypes were tested by the IGC in October, 1992 at Oerlinghausen, Germany. Subsequently, in early 1993 the IGC announced the selection of the PW-5 "Smyk" (Figs. 145,144), designed at the Warsaw University of Technology [150, 152].

The PW-5 is currently produced in Poland by PZL-Swidnik. In addition, a number of other companies around the world are preparing to produce the aircraft under the license agreement mandated by the design competition rules. The aircraft features fiberglass construction, a rel-

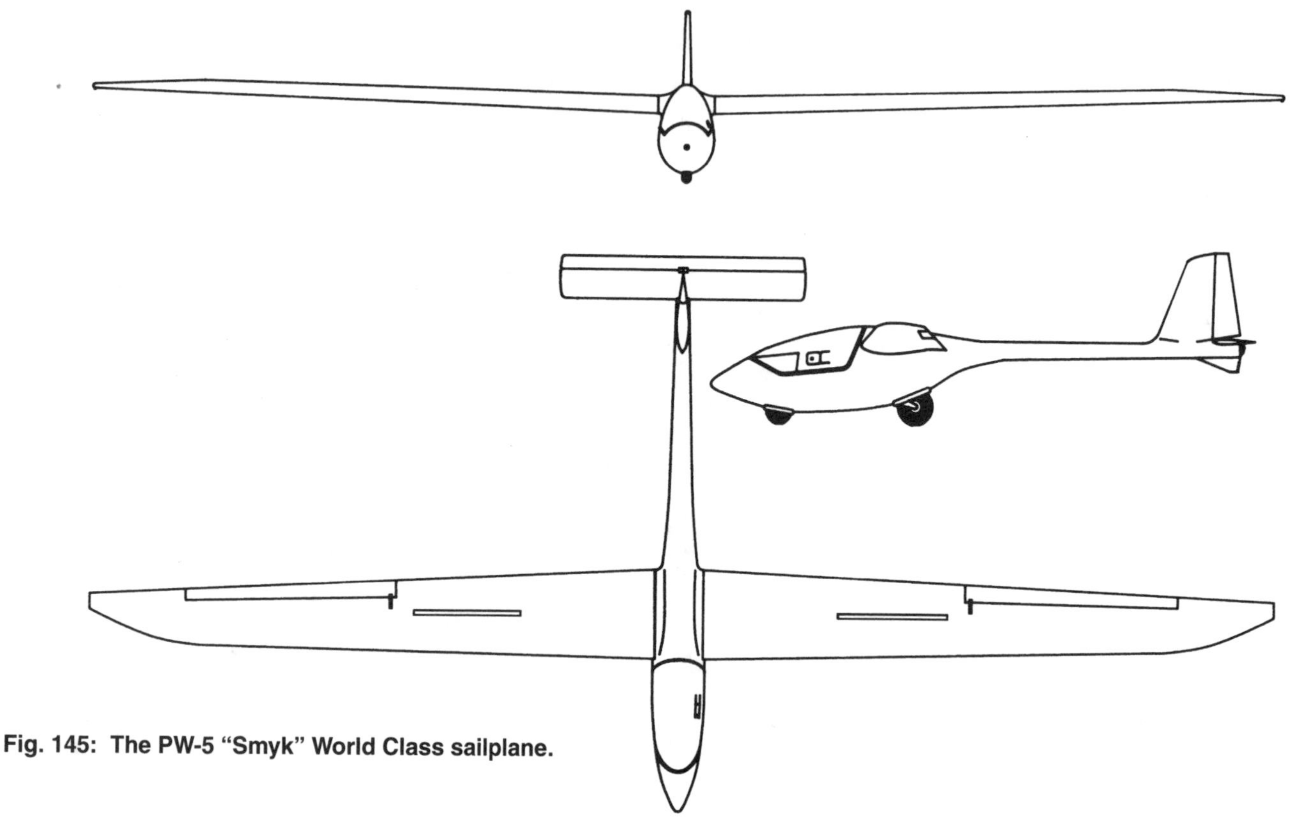

Fig. 145: The PW-5 "Smyk" World Class sailplane.

atively small wing of 13.4m span, and a wing loading of approximately 30 daN/m^2. Per IGC requirements, the wing is unflapped, the landing gear is fixed, and no water ballast system is permitted. The best glide ratio is estimated at approximately 32. See [149] for a detailed flight test evaluation.

The "eta"

The World Class sailplane provides a good illustration of design compromise - the aircraft is configured and sized for maximum simplicity and low cost, at the expense of some performance. On the other end of the design spectrum is the recent "eta" project [93], intended to produce a sailplane of maximum performance, with no constraints placed on size or expense (Fig. 146).

Chief designer is R. Kickert, previously involved in the SB 13 project and other high-performance sailplane designs such as modifications to the ASW-22 and ASH-25. The aircraft is currently under construction by W. Binder and H. J. Streifeneder. Some components are taken from other designs, for example the forward fuselage and cockpit controls from the ASH-25.

For maximum performance, the wingspan has been set at 30.9 m, making the eta one of the largest sailplanes ever built. The aspect ratio is just over 50:1, also unusually high. The aircraft is equipped with a retractable engine, and as a powered sailplane is limited by JAR-22 [49] to a maximum takeoff mass of 850 kg, or 833 daN gross weight. At this gross weight, the wing loading comes to approximately 50 daN/m^2.

The advantages of such a large wing and high aspect ratio are seen in the study presented in Figs. 103 and 105. In Fig. 103, the aspect ratio for minimum drag at low airspeed increases with wingspan and wing loading. It is evident that extrapolating the b = 30m results to W/S = 40daN/m^2

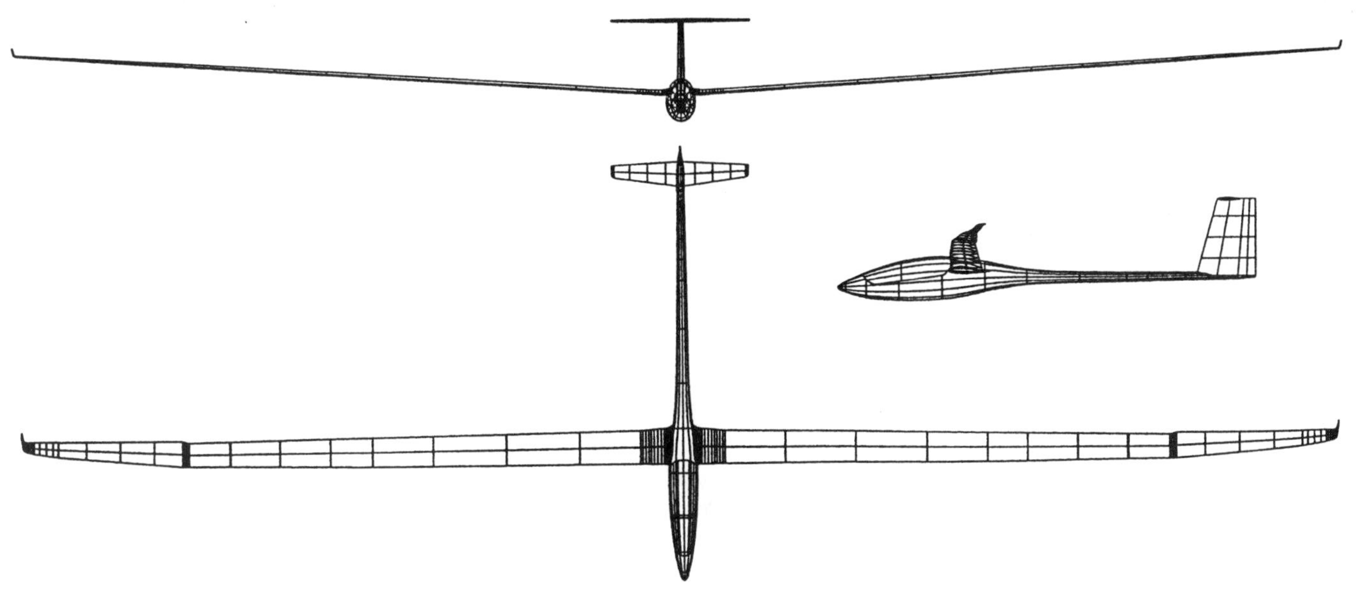

Fig. 146: The "eta"

will yield an optimum aspect ratio of around $\mathcal{R} \approx 50 - 60$, and the eta's design value of $\mathcal{R} = 51.3$ falls neatly in this range.

In Fig. 105, given the airfoil and fuselage drag, the maximum glide ratio increases with increasing wingspan (assuming the aspect ratio is varied appropriately). The trade-off seems to favor the largest possible span; b = 30m is perhaps a practical limit from a ground handling point of view.

The wing is a conventional fixed-area design with camber-changing flap. An effort has been made to make use of the latest developments in airfoil design methodology as employed in recent 15m and Standard Class sailplanes. The wing and empennage profiles were developed by C. H. Rohardt together with K. H. Horstmann and A. Quast, based on the HQ-17 (ASW-22, ASH-25, ASW-20C) airfoil. Wind-tunnel tests of the two-dimensional profile suggest a reduction in the minimum drag coefficient of up to 10%, together with good low speed characteristics. The wing root features a relatively thick profile designed for the turbulent flow conditions typical of the wing/fuselage junction area. The control system employs full span flaperons. A small improvement in rudder authority during turn entries is anticipated due to vortices trailing downstream from the flaperon roots, passing close by the vertical stabilizer.

The eta features a conventional stabilizer and elevator. Longitudinal trim is achieved by adjusting the incidence of the fixed portion of the stabilizer - an arrangement rarely employed in sailplanes. This feature is important due to the large changes in angle of attack induced at the stabilizer during turns (*i.e.* the product of the pitch rate $\Omega \sin \varphi$ and the stabilizer arm). For a large aircraft such as the eta this effect can be significant (see G. Stich [109, 110]).

The structural design of such a large, high aspect ratio wing is particularly challenging. For high strength and stiffness, the design uses the latest carbon fiber pre-pregs. Wing spars are cured in an autoclave under high pressure and temperature, and high-modulus fibers are used in the wing skin to increase torsional stiffness.

At the time of writing, the design has been frozen and construction has begun. First flight is expected in 1999.

Fuselage and Wing-Fuselage Junction

Cockpit and Tail Boom

Function of fuselage

The fuselage has two basic tasks:

- carry the pilot, and
- form structural connection between wing and empennage.

To some extent, the cockpit and aft fuselage may be thought of as separate components. While the forward fuselage is sized to provide room for the pilot, the tail boom need only satisfy strength and stiffness requirements, without regard to its internal volume (except for the minimal space required by control cables and pushrods). This leads naturally to the tapered fuselage typical of most modern sailplanes.

Seating position and visibility

Since fuselage drag typically accounts for 10–15% of the sailplane's total drag, a clean aerodynamic form is essential. Here, seating position is important because it directly influences the fuselage cross sectional area. The three basic seating positions are upright, semi-reclined, and fully reclined (Fig. 147). The selection involves a compromise between aerodynamics, pilot comfort and visibility. Extreme solutions in which cockpit room and visibility are sacrificed for the sake of aerodynamics have proven to be counterproductive, especially for long flights where pilot fatigue is an important factor. The prone pilot position, commonly associated with the Horten flying wings [141], has been completely abandoned. A semi-reclined position is the most popular compromise, providing good visibility and cockpit room with an acceptably small cross sectional area. Modern sailplane fuselages are around 0.6m wide and 0.8m deep in the cockpit area.

When designing a multiplace sailplane, there is a further question of the seating arrangement. The two basic configurations, side-by-side and tandem (forward/aft), have each been employed in numerous sailplanes. The traditional tandem arrangement allows a narrow fuselage and places both pilots along the longitudinal axis. On the other hand, side-by-side seating ("Gövier", Caproni "Calif", Darmstadt D-41, RHJ-8, and others) allows for better communication between the pilots, valuable for both training and cross-country flying. Other points in favor of side-by-side seating are the more compact fuselage and the possibility of providing semi-reclined seating without excessive fuselage length. A compromise solution, staggered seating, has also been employed (ES 52 "Kookabura", M-200, H 121 "Globetrotter").

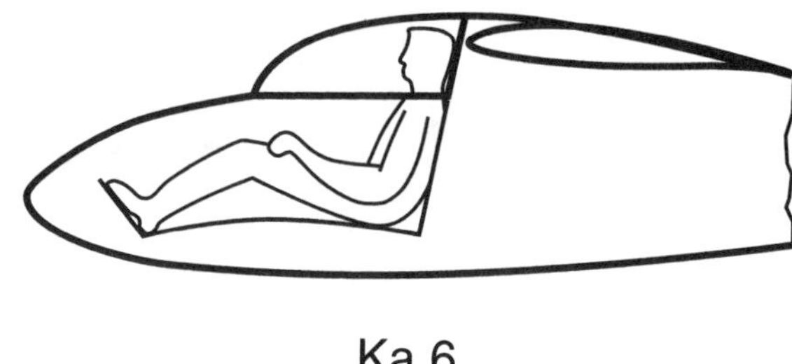

Ka 6

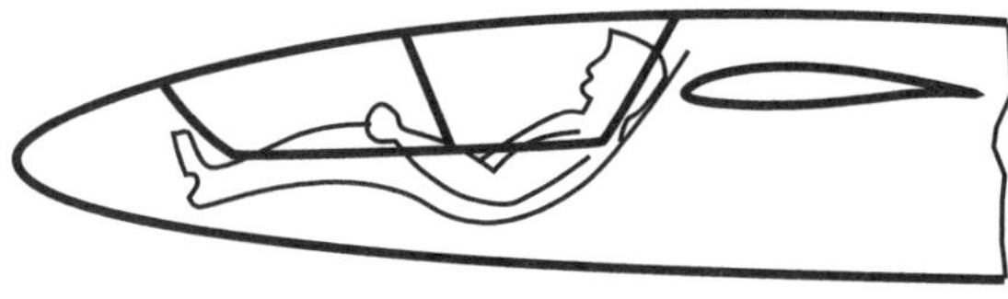

SB 7

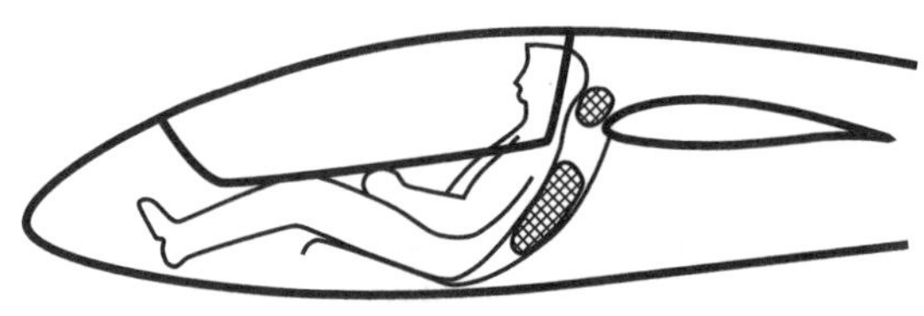

Nimbus II

Fig. 147: Seating positions: upright, reclined, and semi-reclined.

Whatever the seating arrangement, the pilots must be properly placed relative to the aircraft's center of gravity. It should be possible to fly the aircraft dual or solo without

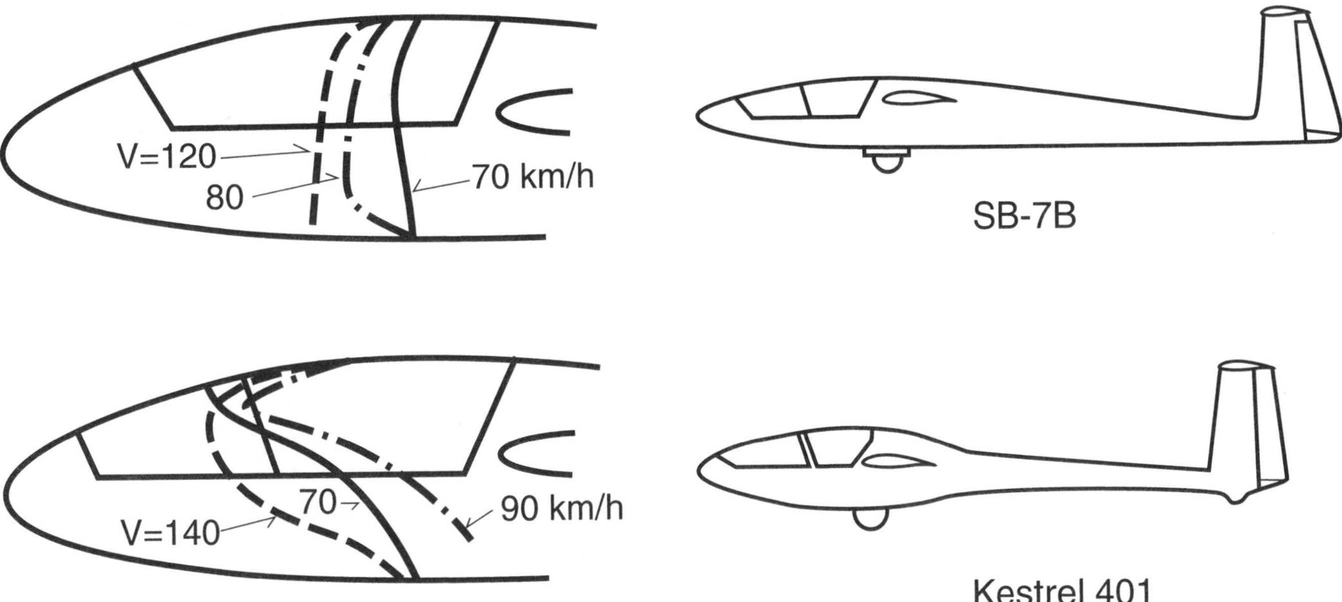

Fig. 148: Position of boundary-layer transition line at several airspeeds, based on Idaflieg measurements [222].

(a) one-piece canopy
(b) split canopy

Fig. 149: Untapered and Tapered fuselages.

removable trim weights. With a tandem seating arrangement, this requirement places the aft seat near the center of gravity, with the front seat always occupied. Often, the wing is swept forward by a few degrees so that it joins the fuselage aft of the CG, improving the rear pilot's visibility (Blanik, T 53, Ka 7, ASK 13, Janus). Forward sweep also allows the wing spar to be placed behind the cockpit.

Fuselage drag and boundary-layer development

Care must be taken to prevent flow disturbances caused by externally mounted equipment. The landing gear should, if possible, be retractable and the antennas mounted inside the fuselage. Pitot, static, and total energy probes as well as ventilation inlets should be designed for low drag and positioned away from the forward fuselage area (unless they can be placed directly on the stagnation point).

The canopy design may have a measurable effect on the fuselage aerodynamics. Flight tests by Idaflieg [222] have shown that single piece canopies offer a small aerodynamic advantage over segmented canopies (Fig. 148). With a properly contoured forward fuselage and a well-sealed canopy, the boundary-layer transition line can be shifted aft to around the middle of the canopy and near the landing gear doors. A small flow disturbance around the canopy edges is inevitable, even on the most carefully built aircraft. With a single piece canopy, the forward canopy edge is located well forward on the fuselage, where the boundary layer is less likely to be affected. However, if the canopy is improperly fitted or sealed, this advantage is lost since the boundary layer will be tripped immediately at the canopy forward edge. Other points in favor of the single piece canopy are an uninterrupted field of view, easier access to the instrument panel, and easier emergency egress. Segmented canopies on the other hand, being smaller and lighter, are less likely to be damaged during ground handling.

The fuselage is usually tapered aft of the boundary-layer transition line to minimize wetted area and skin friction (Fig. 149). Proper fuselage tapering requires that careful consideration be given to fuselage-wing interference effects.

Fig. 150: Fuselage-wing interference:

- Symmetrical fuselage in free flow
- Velocity field induced by wing in plane of symmetry
- Symmetrical fuselage in presence of wing
- Fuselage drooped to match flow field of wing

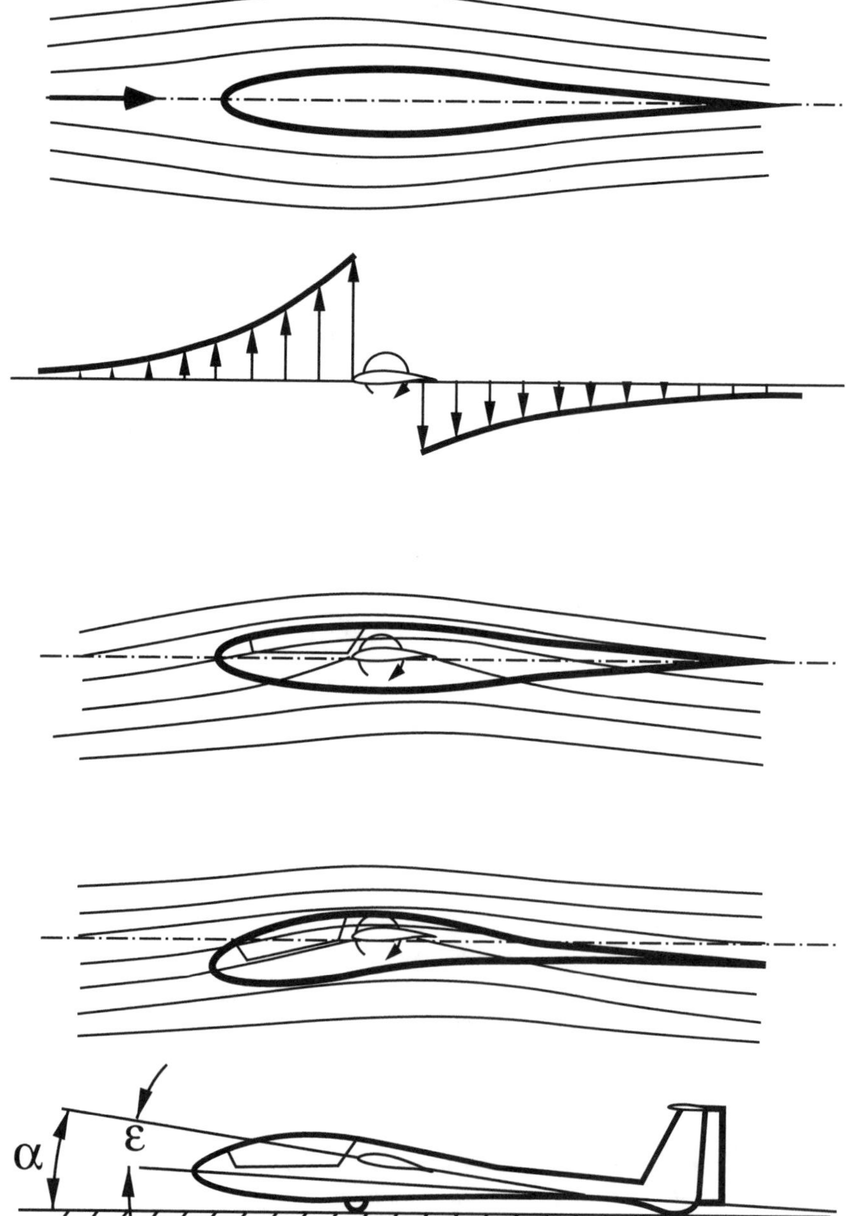

Fig. 151: Effect of landing gear on angle of incidence:

- Fixed landing gear requiring high angle of incidence
- Retractable landing gear with increased height allowing small angle of incidence

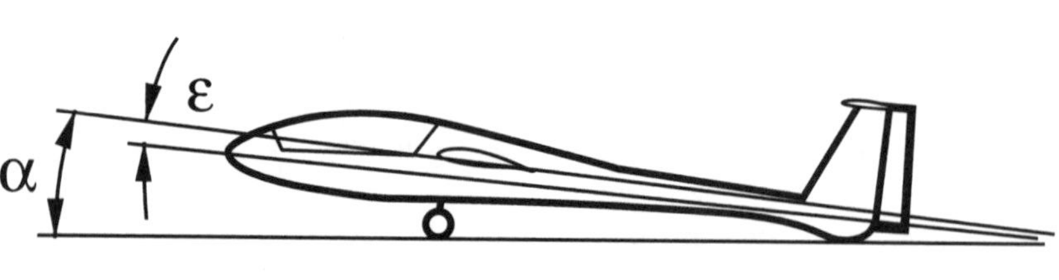

Wing-Fuselage Interference

Flow field induced by wing

As noted in an earlier chapter, fuselage aerodynamics are strongly influenced by the flow field induced by the wing. The aft fuselage and empennage are subject to the wing's downwash, and the forward fuselage to an induced upwash (Fig. 150). In order to keep the flow in line with the fuselage centerline, sailplane fuselages are usually built with a slight nose-down droop. The proper droop varies according to flight condition, with more droop being required at low speeds. However, the fuselage is usually optimized for high airspeeds as its drag contribution is more significant in this flight regime. A cambered fuselage line also improves pilot visibility, especially during approach and landing.

Angle of incidence

The *angle of incidence* is the angle between fuselage reference axis and wing root chord line. Although it is best to keep this angle small in order to minimize wing-fuselage interference effects, it must still be large enough to allow the sailplane to take off and land in two-point attitude (main and tail wheel on ground). Setting the wing at too low an angle of attack with respect to the ground can result in an unacceptably high liftoff airspeed with a correspondingly long ground roll. Furthermore, landings will require higher approach speeds to prevent touching down on the tail skid while the main gear is still high in the air.

A small angle of incidence is therefore only permissible with a landing gear (Fig. 151) tall enough to provide the required angle of attack on the ground. This is why a sailplane with fixed landing gear requires a higher angle of incidence than one with retractable gear.

Camber-changing flaps have a marked effect on the variation of pitch attitude with airspeed. This is illustrated by comparing the unflapped ASW 19 (Fig. 152) with the otherwise identical flapped sailplane ASW 20 (Fig. 153). In both aircraft the angle of incidence is identical at 5.25°. While the unflapped aircraft undergoes a pitch change of 12° from slow flight (C_L=1.4, corresponding to V = 73 km/h EAS at W/S = 35 daN/m^2) to high speed flight (C_L=0.2, or 192 km/h), the flapped ship experiences only a 5° variation. The unflapped version would therefore benefit from a taller landing gear. Camber changing flaps also improve visibility during takeoff and landing.

Wing-fuselage junction

Almost all aircraft exhibit flow separation over portions of the upper or lower wing surface near the fuselage, with corresponding drag penalties. This is due mainly to the superposition of the adverse pressure gradient caused by fuselage taper over the adverse gradient present on the aft airfoil section. It is therefore important to ensure that these pressure gradients are moderate in all flight conditions.

The wing upper surface is more sensitive in this respect than the lower surface due to considerably stronger pressure gradients. This is especially true in slow (high C_L) flight. One good solution is the shoulder wing arrangement with a continuous upper surface. This arrangement reduces the problem to that of designing the lower surface for high speed flight. Despite this aerodynamic advantage and the side benefit of the increased ground clearance, the mid-wing configuration is preferred for its relative ease of manufacture - the wing carry-through structure is easier to design and more room is available behind and above the pilot seat for control linkage and equipment.

What recommendations can be made concerning the design of the wing-fuselage junction? The most important rule is to separate the adverse pressure gradients associated with wing and fuselage. This means that the fuselage taper must occur either ahead of the point of maximum thickness of the wing root airfoil, or aft of the wing's trailing edge. Both are difficult to accomplish. If the fuselage taper occurs aft of the wing trailing edge, the wing should be set as high as possible on the fuselage and the taper limited to the fuselage lower surface (Fig. 154). That is, near the wing, the fuselage should taper only in depth, not width. This is especially important for flapped aircraft. It is also essential to ensure that the flow remains attached on the wing lower surface in high speed flight at negative flap settings. The wing and fuselage should be faired with a relatively narrow radius near the wing leading edge. At the trailing edge, a broader fairing is appropriate as it helps reduce the magnitude of the adverse pressure gradients in that region. A trailing edge fairing may however create difficulties when flaps, (especially area changing flaps) are employed (Fig. 155).

Even with proper design, adverse pressure gradients are inevitable in the area of the wing-fuselage junction. To reduce separation tendencies in this region, the wing root should feature an airfoil designed for a primarily turbulent boundary layer. A smooth spanwise transition to a laminar

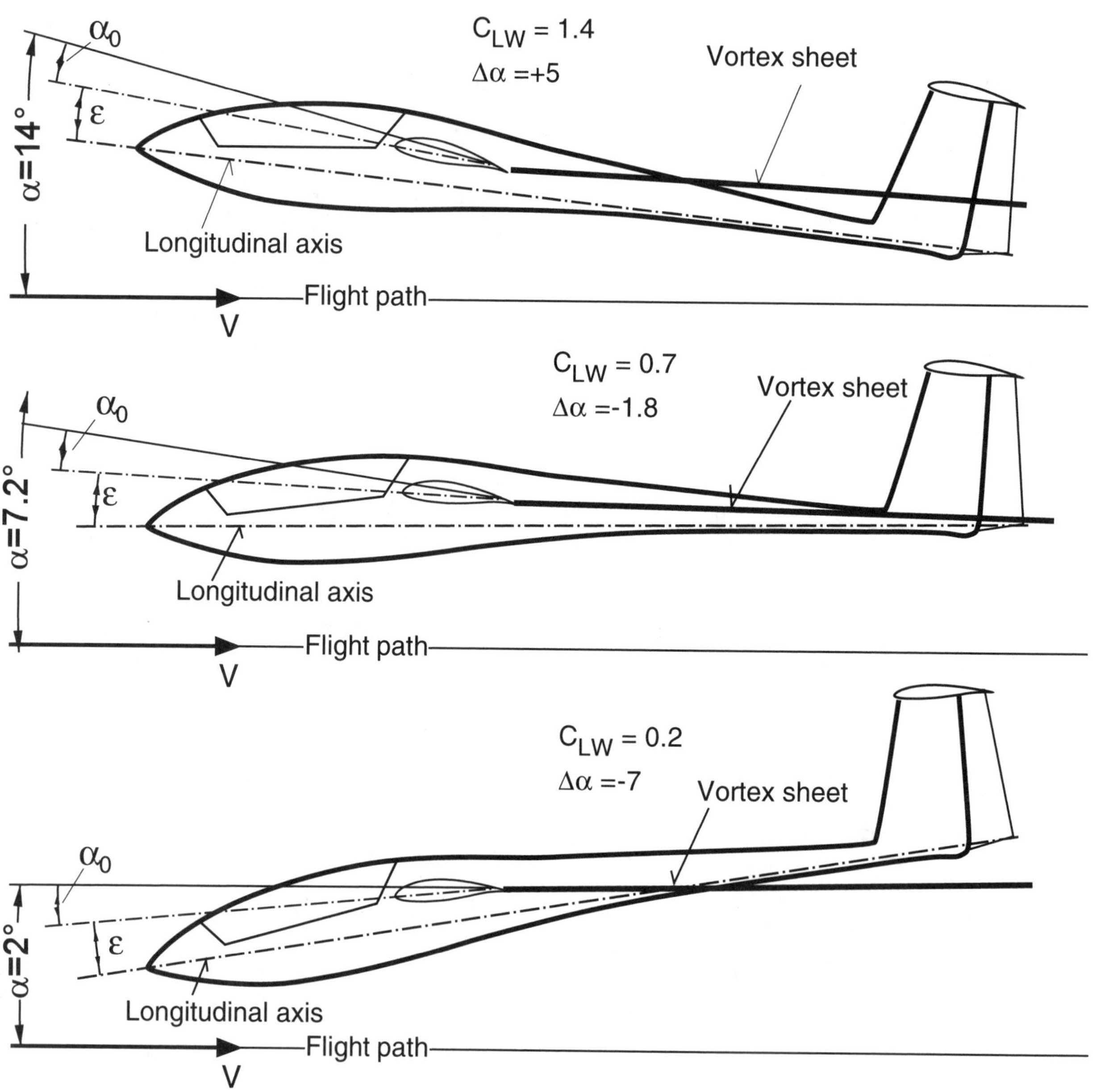

Fig. 152: Variation of body angles in trimmed level flight and position of trailing vortex sheet for sailplane with fixed geometry airfoil (ASW 19).

FX 61-163 airfoil, $\varepsilon = 5.2°$, $\alpha_0 = -3.8°$

$\Delta\alpha$ = angle between flight path and fuselage reference axis = $\alpha + \alpha_0 - \varepsilon$

Over the range $0.2 \leq C_{L_W} \leq 1.4$ the body angle varies by 12°.

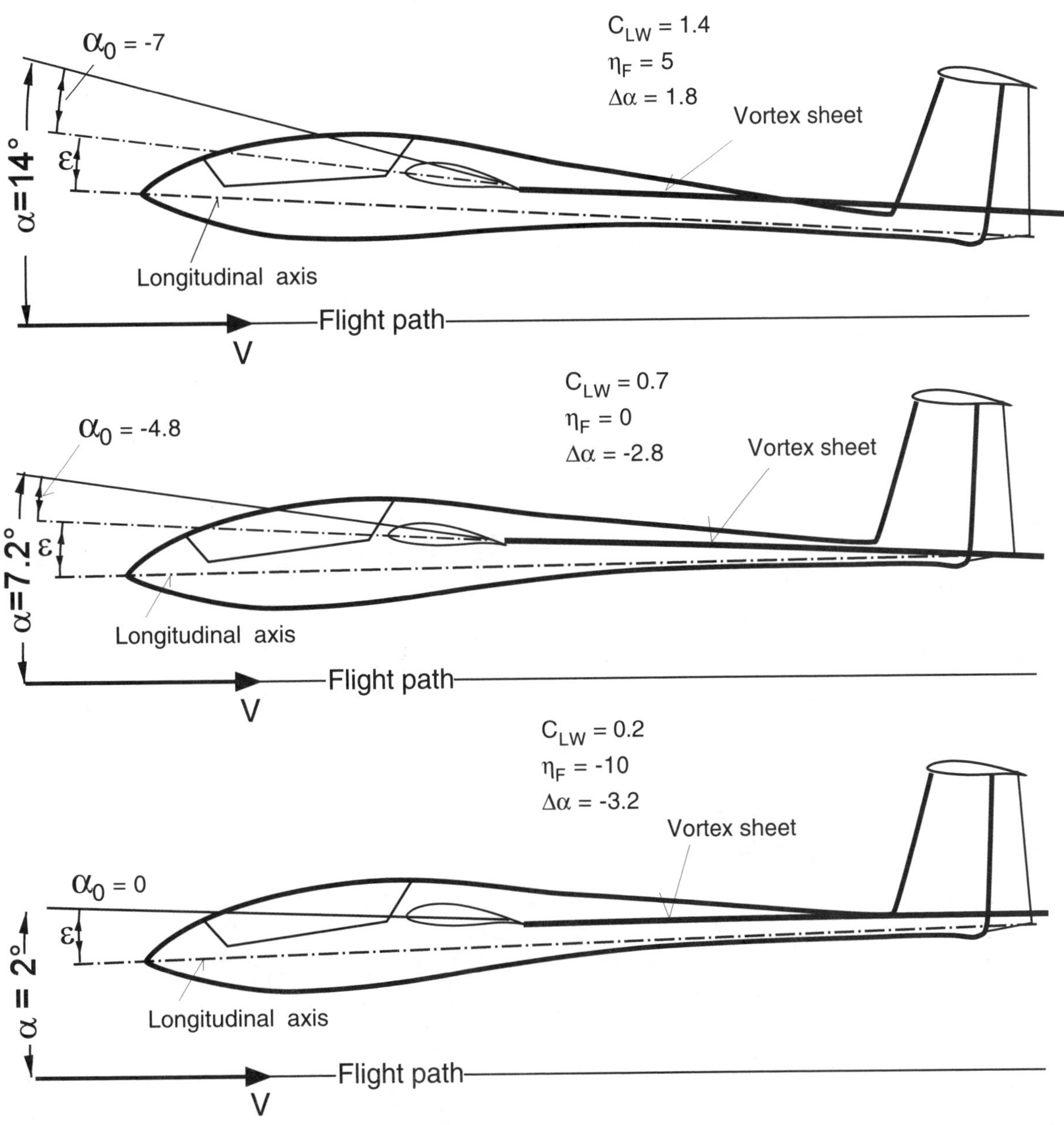

Fig. 153: Variation of body angles in trimmed level flight and position of trailing vortex sheet for sailplane with camber changing flaps (ASW 20).

FX 62-K-131 airfoil, $\varepsilon = 5.2°$

$\Delta\alpha$ = angle between flight path and fuselage reference axis = $\alpha + \alpha_0 - \varepsilon$

Over the range $0.2 \leq C_{L_W} \leq 1.4$ the body angle varies by 5°.

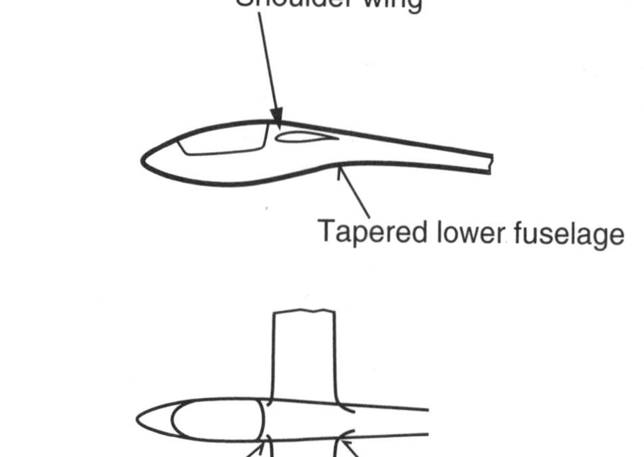

Fig. 154: Wing-fuselage junction for minimum interference drag.

airfoil should take place within a short distance (roughly a quarter of the wing root chord) of the wing root. This approach has been taken (for example) with the “eta” to help reduce the interference drag.

At Braunschweig, efforts to improve wing-fuselage aerodynamics have included wind-tunnel tests of various fuselages by R. Radespiel [102] and flight tests of numerous wing-fuselage combinations by B. Junker (unpublished; however see R. Johnson [210] for an account of an inflight tufting study). Systematic studies to improve wing-fuselage aerodynamics have also been conducted by L. M. M. Boermans and colleagues at the Delft University of Technology [71, 73, 74] and M. D. Maughmer *et al* at Pennsylvania State University [94]. See also D. Althaus [70] and J. Ostrowski *et al* [98].

The extent of separation provides only a rough indication of the interference drag. Another approach is to take the polar as measured inflight and subtract the calculated drag components of fuselage, wing, and empennage. The difference yields the interference drag (Fig. 156). Typical results are shown in Fig. 157. The drawback to this approach is that the measurement errors in the aircraft's total drag are large compared to the interference drag, so that the results are not particularly accurate.

Empennage and Controls

Control System Elements on Wing

Sailplane stability and control is provided by horizontal and vertical stabilizers, elevator, rudder, flaps, ailerons, and dive brakes. In a few cases drogue chutes have been used as well.

Fig. 155: Wing-fuselage junction with fixed-geometry airfoil (left, DG 100) and camber-changing flap (right, DG 200).

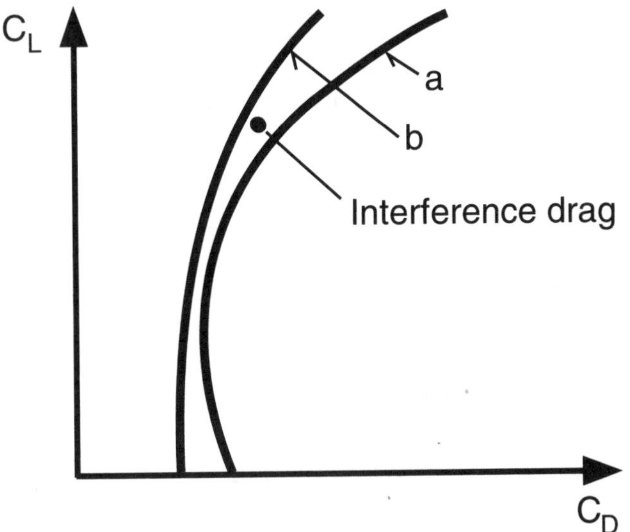

Fig. 156: Estimation of interference drag based on calculated polar and flight test measurements.

a	Polar measured in flight
b	Calculated polar
a-b	Estimated interference drag

Ailerons

Ailerons are mounted on the wings and sized to provide the roll maneuverability prescribed by the certification regulations. These require that the time (in seconds) for roll reversals of $\pm 45°$ at $1.4V_s$ does not exceed one third the wingspan (in meters). For Standard and FAI 15m Racing Class sailplanes this amounts to exactly 5 seconds.

Ailerons are located at the wing trailing edge where the boundary layer is thickest. Since the dynamic pressure within the boundary layer is smaller than its free stream value, aileron effectiveness is improved by keeping the boundary layer as thin as possible. Very thick airfoils are thus unsuitable for use in the aileron region. Laminar airfoils feature relatively thin boundary layers and this, combined with the trend towards thinner wings, has led to modern sailplanes with relatively small ailerons. While ailerons of 20–25% wing chord extending spanwise from y/s=0.6–0.95 were typical of the first generation of laminar wing sailplanes (Fig. 158), modern practice favors longer ailerons of smaller chord (around 15%). It is essential to blend the aileron cleanly into the airfoil and to seal the hinge gap to prevent flow from the wing lower surface to upper surface. Ailerons usually terminate inboard of the wingtip

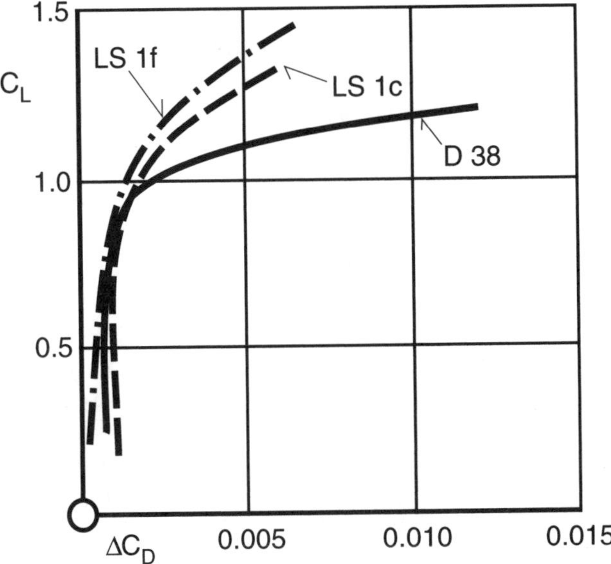

Fig. 157: Typical results for interference drag estimated from flight test results (Fig. 156).

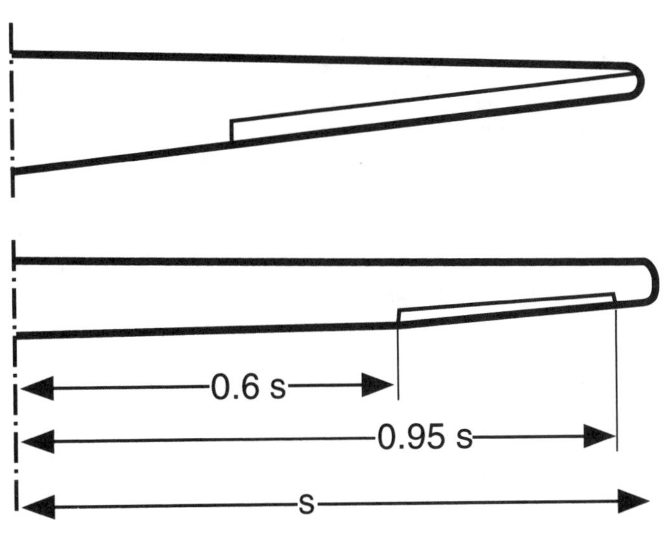

Fig. 158: Typical aileron configurations:

- Typical early sailplane (Weihe 50)
- Modern configuration (Standard Cirrus)

Fig. 159: Aileron-induced asymmetric flutter.

in order to prevent damage during landing.

Asymmetric aileron deflection leads to an asymmetric lift distribution, and with it an asymmetric distribution of induced drag. In a turn entry, the wing with the downward aileron deflection has a higher induced drag, producing an adverse yaw moment acting against the direction of the turn. Coordinated flight requires that this adverse yaw be compensated through rudder inputs. Often, the aileron control linkage is designed to provide differential aileron deflections, with the upward aileron moving 2:1 to 3:1 compared to the downward. This reduces the adverse yaw, allows good aileron effectiveness with minimum increase in profile drag, and reduces lateral stick forces.

The relatively small chord of modern ailerons helps reduce aerodynamic hinge moments. Lateral stick forces can thus be kept acceptably low without having to resort to aerodynamic balancing and its associated drag penalty. On the other hand, mass balancing is often required to reduce the risk of asymmetric flutter, especially when the wings are soft in torsion or bending, or when masses are installed well off the fuselage axis (*i.e.* T-tails - see Fig. 159).

With camber-changing flaps, it is essential to couple the ailerons so to droop or rise symmetrically with the flaps. Here the compromise is between optimum lift distribution and good maneuverability, since sufficient aileron travel beyond the symmetrical (coupled) deflection must be available to ensure adequate low speed roll control. The Multhopp method may be used to calculate the lift distribution with combined flap and aileron deflections and provide estimates of the roll rate, roll damping, and adverse yaw (see also W. Feifel [78] for a discussion of optimization of aileron/flap coupling).

Dive brakes

Dive brakes control the glide angle during landing and limit the maximum airspeed in dives. According to JAR-22 [49] the dive brakes must provide a glide angle no shallower than 7:1 in approach at $1.3V_{S_0}$ and limit the airspeed to no greater than V_{NE} in a 45°dive. Early OSTIV airworthiness regulations required the dive brakes to be velocity limiting in a vertical dive, but this requirement was relaxed as wing loadings increased.

Dive brakes are invariably mounted on the wings. Various types of brakes are popular, but they all feature flat surfaces extending from the wings, aligned normal to the air flow (Fig. 160). Typically they are 2 × 1.5m long in the spanwise direction, about 10–20cm wide, and positioned mid-span on the wing to avoid aerodynamic interference with the empennage or ailerons.

The chordwise placement of the dive brakes is determined by several factors. Even if great care is taken to ensure a good fit when the dive brakes are retracted, a small flow disturbance is usually present where the dive brake caps fit into the wing surface. The risk of boundary layer transition at this location is minimized by placing the dive brakes well aft on the airfoil, where the boundary layer thickness is large compared to the flow disturbance. With the dive brakes located at around 60% wing chord, it is possible to maintain laminar flow even downstream of the retracted dive brakes. Placing the dive brakes further aft is impractical because the shallow depth of the wing near the trailing edge leaves insufficient room for brakes of reasonable size. In addition, the brakes lose aerodynamic effectiveness when placed too far aft. For maximum effectiveness, the dive brake linkage should be designed to allow a gap of a few centimeters between the brakes and the wing surface when the brakes are fully deployed. Dive brakes are usually placed only on the upper wing surface, especially in the more modern aircraft. Upper surface dive brakes, especially the simple hinged-panel type that swing up and forward, are sometimes referred to as "spoilers". Lower surface dive brakes can cause ground clearance problems, particularly with mid-wing designs. Also, with upper/lower surface dive brakes the dive brake caps must mate perfectly with the wing in order to prevent air flow from the lower to upper surface. Single upper-surface dive brakes tend to be more effective than an upper/lower surface pair of equivalent size because of the higher air velocities present on the upper surface.

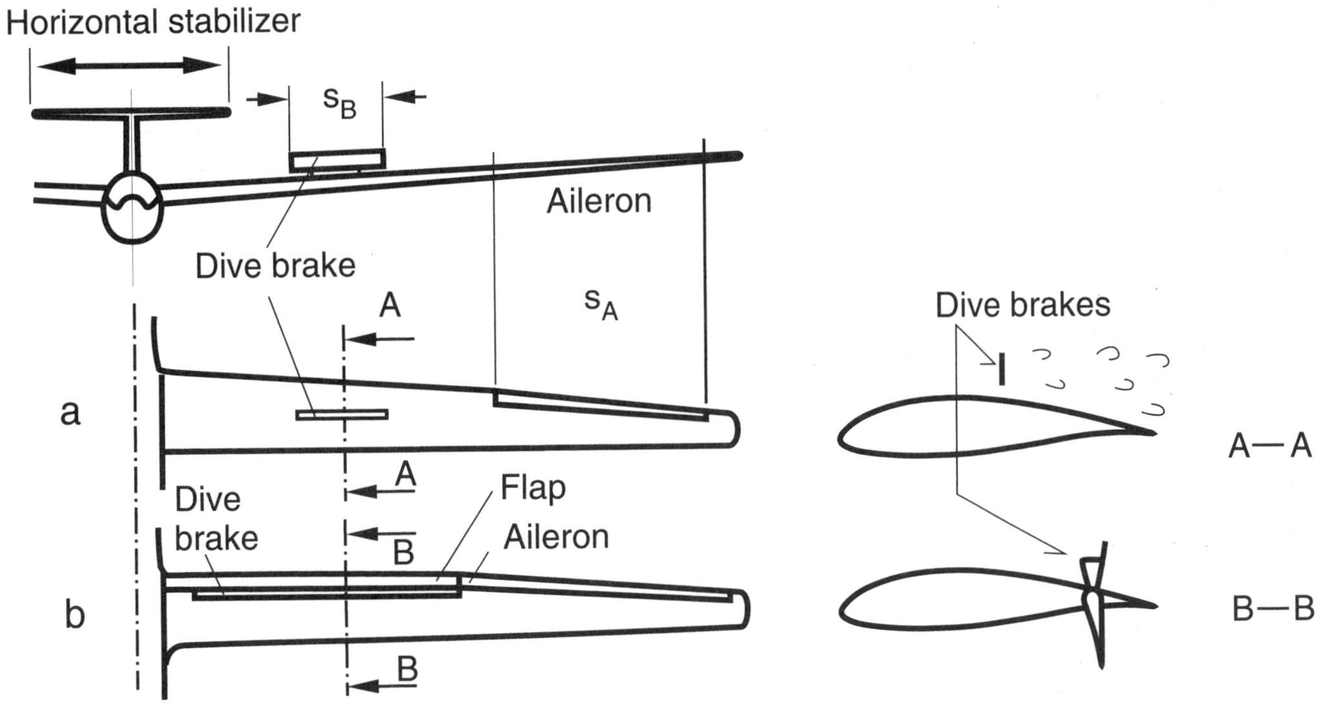

Fig. 160: **Dive brake systems.**

(a) Conventional Schempp-Hirth dive brakes (*e.g.* Standard Cirrus)
(b) Combined flap-brake system (*e.g.* Mini-Nimbus, early Ventus)

With flapped sailplanes there is the possibility of a combined trailing-edge flap/brake, as shown in Figs. 130, 160, and 225. The poor dive brake effectiveness at the trailing-edge location is compensated with a larger span, usually extending from the fuselage to the inboard end of the ailerons. This arrangement presents the least likelihood of disturbing the laminar flow over the wing surface. Typical examples are the Mosquito and early production versions of the Ventus (Figs. 160, 225).

Many flapped sailplane designs dispense with dive brakes altogether, relying on large flap deflections (up to 90°) to provide the required drag. Examples are the early PIK-20 models and a number of American designs (BG-12, Schreder HP series, Schweizer 1-35, Concept 70, Laister Nugget, and Zuni). This arrangement allows for excellent glide path control and visibility during approach. The choice of high-deflection flaps or dive brakes is somewhat subjective - while flaps enjoy a certain popularity, many pilots express a clear preference for dive brakes.

Occasionally designers opt for a drogue chute in lieu of or in addition to dive brakes. While forgoing the dive brakes eliminates a number of aerodynamic, structural, and mechanical complications, drogue chutes are not nearly as reliable as dive brake systems and are impossible to modulate in flight. Also, because of structural limitations they are useful only over a limited airspeed range. Since precise glide path control is so essential during off-field landings, dive brakes are always preferred, and few sailplanes have relied exclusively on drogue chutes (HKS-I, HKS-III, Zefir, ASW-12). On the other hand, it is sometimes advantageous to provide a drogue chute as a supplement to dive brakes.

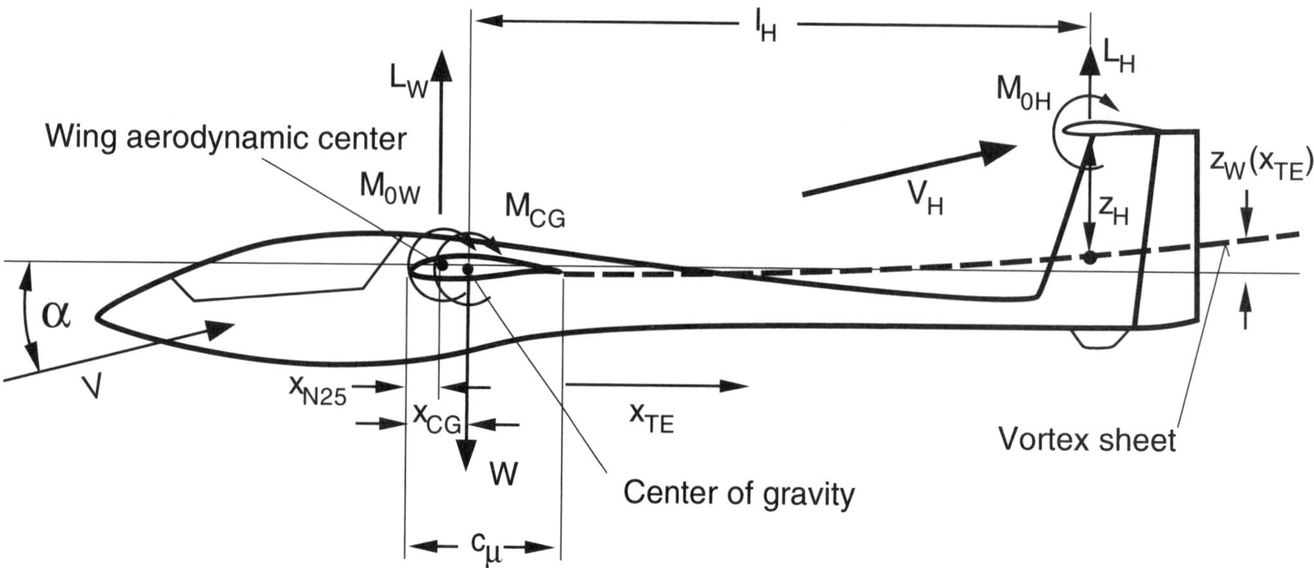

Fig. 161: Force and moment definitions for longitudinal stability analysis.

Horizontal Stabilizer and Elevator

Longitudinal stability and trim

The horizontal stabilizer has the task of maintaining the longitudinal stability and pitching moment equilibrium (longitudinal trim) in all steady and transient flight conditions.

An aircraft is in moment equilibrium when the sum of all moments about any arbitrary reference point is zero (Fig. 161). Writing the aerodynamic forces and moments with respect to the center of gravity,

$$M_{CG} = L_W(x_{CG} - x_{AC}) + M_{0_W} - l_H L_H = 0 \qquad (97)$$

Here, the longitudinal stations x_{CG} and x_N are measured from the leading edge of the mean aerodynamic chord. If the horizontal stabilizer is cambered or the elevator is deflected, the equation must be modified to reflect the zero lift moment M_{0_H} of the horizontal stabilizer. An exact calculation would also take into account a similar contribution from fuselage. Both of these factors are ignored in the present discussion.

This relationship is written in nondimensional form by normalizing to the dynamic pressure q, the wing area S, and the mean aerodynamic chord, c_μ:

$$C_{M_{CG}} = C_{L_W}\frac{x_{CG} - x_{AC}}{c_\mu} + C_{M_{0W}} - C_{L_H}\frac{l_H S_H q_H}{c_\mu S q} = 0 \qquad (98)$$

C_{L_W} is the lift coefficient of the wing, approximately equal to the lift coefficient C_L for the entire aircraft. $C_{M_{0W}}$ is the zero lift moment coefficient of the wing alone, S_H is the horizontal stabilizer surface area, q_H the dynamic pressure at the empennage, l_H the moment arm between the aerodynamic center of the horizontal stabilizer and the center of gravity, and x_{AC} is the location of the aerodynamic center of the isolated wing. Usually, $x_{AC} \approx 0.25c_\mu$. The ratio $\eta_t = q_H/q$ is the *tail efficiency*, usually just slightly less than unity due to energy losses in the airflow due to the wing and fuselage.

For longitudinal stability, the quantity of interest is the moment gradient, obtained by differentiating the equilibrium equation (Eq. 98). Here it is assumed that $C_{L_W} = C_L$.

$$\begin{aligned}\frac{dC_{M_{CG}}}{dC_L} &= \frac{dC_{M_{CG}}}{dC_{L_W}} \\ &= \frac{x_{CG}}{c_\mu} - 0.25 \\ &\quad - \frac{dC_{L_H}}{d\alpha_H}\frac{d\alpha_H}{d\alpha}\frac{d\alpha}{dC_{L_W}}\frac{l_H S_H q_H}{c_\mu S q}\end{aligned} \qquad (99)$$

For convenience we introduce the *horizontal tail volume* [1]:

$$V_H = \frac{dC_{L_H}}{d\alpha_H} l_H S_H \qquad (100)$$

[1]Some texts define a nondimensional *tail volume coefficient*, $(l_H S_H)/(Sc_\mu)$ - that is, without the lift-curve slope term.

Fig. 162: Angle definitions for horizontal stabilizer:

α	wing angle of attack
ε_H	stabilizer incidence angle
α_w	induced angle of attack due to wing downwash
α_H	stabilizer angle of attack
δ_e	elevator deflection

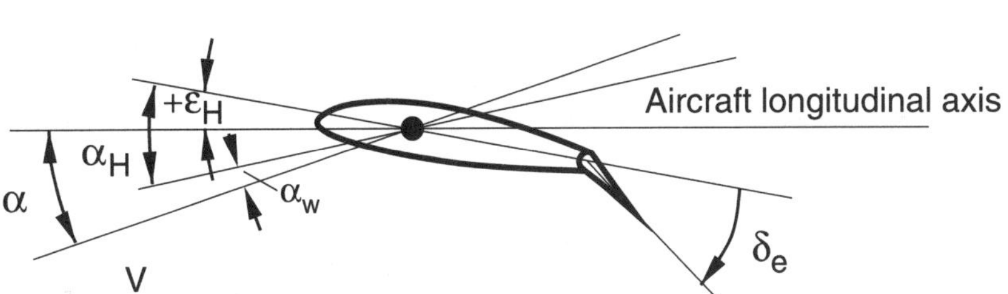

and the *wing reference volume:*

$$V_W = \frac{dC_{L_W}}{d\alpha} c_\mu S \tag{101}$$

If one furthermore assumes that the horizontal stabilizer is located sufficiently far from the wing trailing vortex sheet, that is, $\eta_t = 1$, then the moment equilibrium equation becomes:

$$\frac{dC_{M_{CG}}}{dC_L} = -\frac{d\alpha_H}{d\alpha}\frac{V_H}{V_W} + \frac{x_{CG}}{c_\mu} - 0.25 \tag{102}$$

The horizontal stabilizer operates in the induced velocity field of the wing and its angle of attack is decreased by the downwash angle α_w. Also, the wing and horizontal stabilizer are usually built with different angles of incidence with respect to the fuselage reference axis. The angle between the fixed portion of the horizontal stabilizer and the fuselage reference axis is the *stabilizer incidence angle*, ε_H (Fig. 162):

$$\alpha_H = \alpha + \varepsilon_H - \alpha_w \tag{103}$$

α_w, the induced downwash angle, is in turn a function of the wing angle of attack. Differentiating Eq. 103 with respect to the angle of attack α leads to:

$$\frac{d\alpha_H}{d\alpha} = 1 - \frac{d\alpha_w}{d\alpha} \tag{104}$$

Values of $d\alpha_H/d\alpha$ for conventional empennage configurations range from 0.75 to 0.9. For canard configurations (empennage ahead of the wing), $d\alpha_H/d\alpha$ may exceed unity.

The moment gradient then becomes:

$$\frac{dC_{M_{CG}}}{dC_L} = -\left(1 - \frac{d\alpha_w}{d\alpha}\right)\frac{V_H}{V_W} + \frac{x_{CG}}{c_\mu} - 0.25 \tag{105}$$

In the first chapter it was shown that the moment gradient is a measure of the degree of stability, and may in turn be expressed in terms of the longitudinal offset between the center of gravity and neutral point for the complete aircraft:

$$\frac{dC_{M_{CG}}}{dC_L} = \frac{x_{CG} - x_N}{c_\mu} \tag{106}$$

Defining the *effective tail volume*

$$\left(\frac{V_H}{V_W}\right)^{\star} = \left(1 - \frac{d\alpha_w}{d\alpha}\right)\frac{V_H}{V_W} \tag{107}$$

and introducing these expressions into Eq. 105 leads to:

$$\left(\frac{V_H}{V_W}\right)^{\star} = -\frac{x_{CG} - x_N}{c_\mu} + \frac{x_{CG}}{c_\mu} - 0.25 \tag{108}$$

This result provides the horizontal stabilizer volume required for a specified stability margin as a function of center of gravity location.

The horizontal stabilizer lift required to maintain pitching moment equilibrium results from the moment equilibrium equation (Eq. 98):

$$C_{L_H}\frac{dC_{L_W}/d\alpha}{dC_{L_H}/d\alpha_H}\frac{V_H}{V_W} = C_L\left[\frac{x_{CG}}{c_\mu} - 0.25\right] + C_{M_{OW}} \tag{109}$$

As will be discussed, the lift curve slopes $dC_{L_W}/d\alpha$ and $dC_{L_H}/d\alpha_H$ are calculated based on the aspect ratios of the empennage and wing, respectively.

Further information pertaining to longitudinal static stability and horizontal stabilizer design are provided by F. G. Irving [13,83–85] and P. Morelli [95]. See also M. Abzug and E. E. Larrabee [2] for a general discussion of aircraft stability and control, as well as C. D. Perkins and R. E. Hage [21].

Empennage contribution to longitudinal stability

Before determining the horizontal stabilizer volume and lift coefficient required for trimmed flight, the basic function of

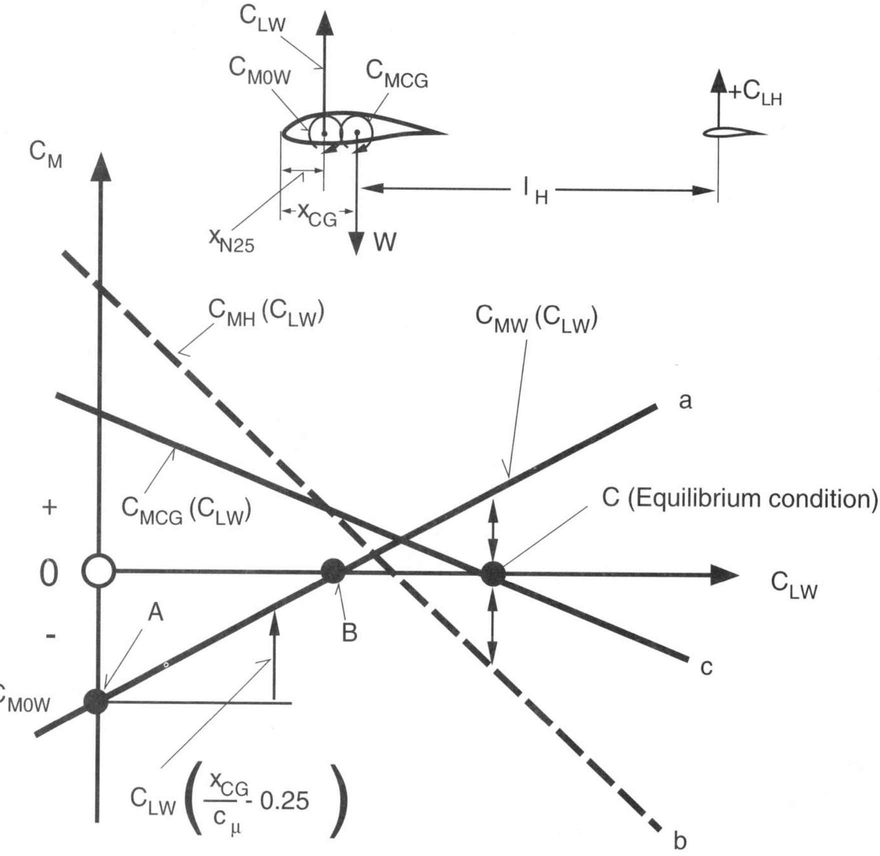

Fig. 163: Horizontal stabilizer contribution to longitudinal stability.
(a) Isolated wing (unstable)
(b) Stabilizer contribution (stabilizing)
(c) Complete aircraft (stable)

the horizontal stabilizer (Fig. 163) should be considered.

Let us first consider the wing alone. If the lift is zero, the only pitching moment is the zero lift moment $C_{M_{0W}}$ (Point A in Fig. 163). For an airfoil with positive camber this is always negative (*i.e.* nose-down). Using the center of gravity as a reference point for the forces and moments, and assuming that it lies in the typical range $0.25 \leq x_{CG}/c_\mu \leq 0.50$, then increasing the angle of attack increases the lift, producing a positive (nose up) moment equal to $C_{L_W}(x_{CG}/c_\mu - 0.25)$. Since this is opposite in sign to the zero lift moment, at a certain wing lift coefficient the moments balance out, allowing moment equilibrium to be achieved without any load from the horizontal stabilizer (Point B in Fig. 163). The condition is unstable, however, since the wing by itself has a positive gradient of moment with respect to lift coefficient.

For stability, the positive slope of the moment curve $C_{M_W}(C_{L_W})$ must be balanced by a correspondingly strong negative moment gradient $C_{M_H}(C_{M_W})$ superimposed over the wing basic moment curve. The resulting moment curve for the entire aircraft $C_{M_{CG}}(C_{L_W})$ must have a negative gradient (line "c" in Fig. 163). The gradient of the horizontal stabilizer curve is primarily a function of the stabilizer volume, but also depends on the tail efficiency η_t, the stabilizer lift curve slope, downwash effects, and the location of center of gravity. Stability throughout the center of gravity range requires a certain minimum value of the horizontal stabilizer volume.

Longitudinal trim in unaccelerated flight

Apart from satisfying the stability requirements, the empennage must provide the moments necessary to trim the aircraft. Here, both the horizontal stabilizer volume and lift coefficient C_{L_H} of the horizontal stabilizer play a role, along with the sailplane angle of attack, induced downwash, stabilizer incidence, and elevator deflection. Horizontal stabilizers fall in one of three categories (Fig. 164):

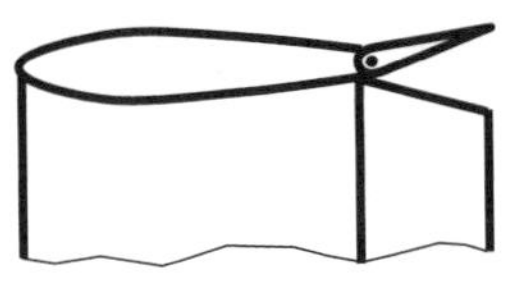
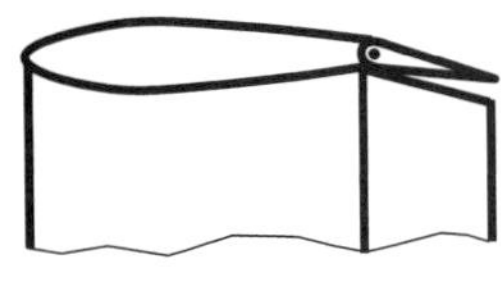
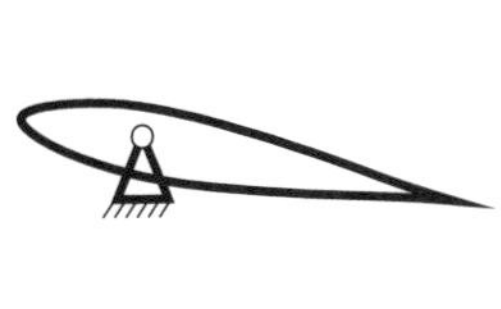
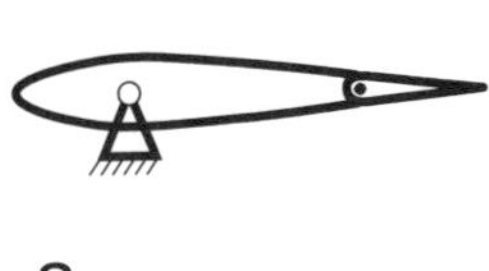
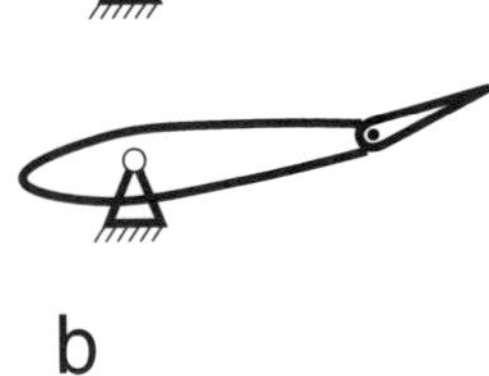

Fig. 164: Conventional stabilizer/elevator, all-flying tail, and all-flying tail with servo-tab.

a Neutral position
b Aft stick
c Forward stick

- conventional stabilizer/elevator combination
- all-flying tail
- all-flying tail with servo-tab

The conventional stabilizer/elevator configuration comprises a fixed portion rigidly attached to the fuselage with a moving elevator of about 20–30% chord, controlled from the cockpit with the control stick. Unlike some powered aircraft, in sailplanes the fixed portion of the horizontal stabilizer is usually not adjustable in flight for trim purposes. An exception here is the eta (see page 119).

The all-flying tail is a single aerodynamic surface, hinged to allow its angle of incidence to be controlled.

Sometimes all-flying tails are fitted with servo-tabs on their trailing edges. These resemble trim tabs, but unlike simple trim tabs are provided with a linkage causing them to move along with the stabilizer. Servo-tabs are usually sized to 5–20% of the stabilizer chord.

The advantages and disadvantages of these configurations are discussed below.

Steady control inputs do not affect the gradient of the pitching moment generated by the stabilizer, but merely shift the stabilizer moment curves in parallel. Fig. 165 presents the stabilizer moment curves for four different control positions. For each of these cases there is a single trim condition in which the horizontal stabilizer's pitching moment is exactly equal and opposite to the wing's pitching moment. With the wing operating at low lift coefficients the stabilizer must generate a downward load; for high lift coefficients a positive (upward) lift is required.

It is interesting to note that the horizontal stabilizer lift varies in an aerodynamically unfavorable sense, that is, in the direction of the flap deflection. In other words, the required lift becomes increasingly positive (upward) as the elevator is deflected trailing-edge up. For a conventional stabilizer/elevator combination, this phenomenon can severely limit the stabilizer's maximum lift coefficient. The all-flying stabilizer eliminates this difficulty, as shown in Fig. 166. The figure compares the all-flying and conventional stabilizers for the same four trim conditions presented in Fig. 165. Note that the stabilizer angle of attack α_H is always modified relative to the aircraft's angle of attack α by the downwash angle α_w and the angle of incidence ε_H. The all-flying tail with servo-tab provides somewhat of a compromise between the two configurations shown in the figure.

Maneuvers

Maneuvers are important as well. By definition, maneuvers involve transient conditions arising when changing from one trim condition to another, for example pullups and turn entries and exits. Sailplane structures are designed for the loads encountered in specific maneuvers defined in the airworthiness regulations (Fig. 167). For the symmetrical pullup and pushover cases at high airspeed, not only must the structure be designed for the anticipated loads, elevator authority must be sufficient to actually perform these maneuvers. In general, however, the regulations do not establish requirements for control authority in pitching maneuvers.

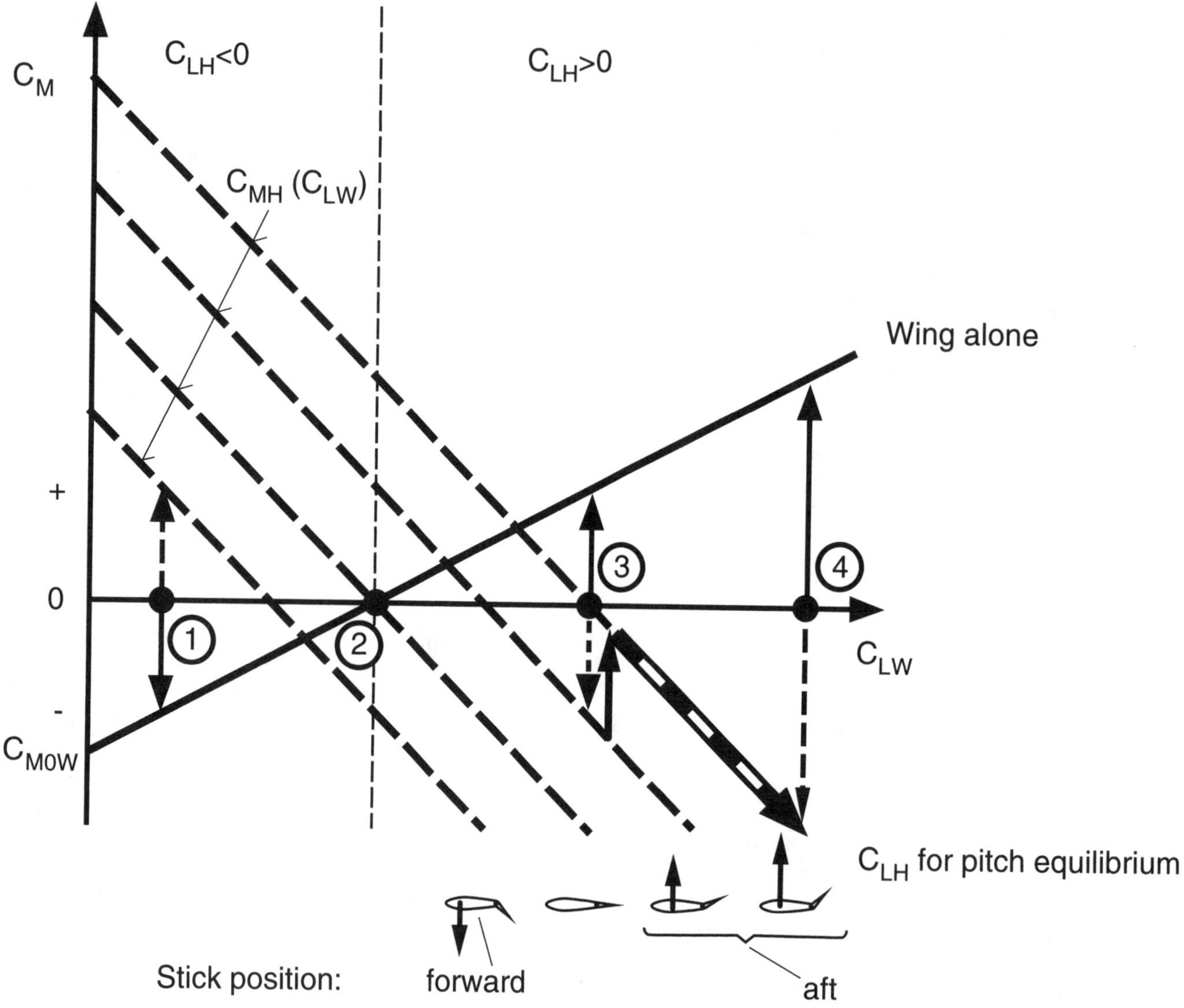

Fig. 165: Moment curves and equilibrium condition for four elevator positions.

As an example of a transient maneuver, consider the transition from high-speed flight to slow flight using the example in Fig. 165. Starting point for the maneuver is condition (3). To maneuver from this condition to condition (4), the pilot applies back pressure on the control stick, bringing the horizontal stabilizer into the position indicated in condition (4). As a result, the stabilizer lift is changed in the downward direction and the aircraft begins to pitch up about its center of gravity. Consequently, the wing angle of attack and the stabilizer angle of attack both increase, so that in both cases additional lift develops. The incremental moments so developed act on the wing in a destabilizing (nose-up) direction and on the stabilizer in a stabilizing (nose down) direction. Since the horizontal stabilizer exhibits a steeper moment gradient, the moment difference gradually diminishes until equilibrium is once again established in condition (4). Since the wing is operating at an increased lift coefficient, the lift exceeds the aircraft's weight,

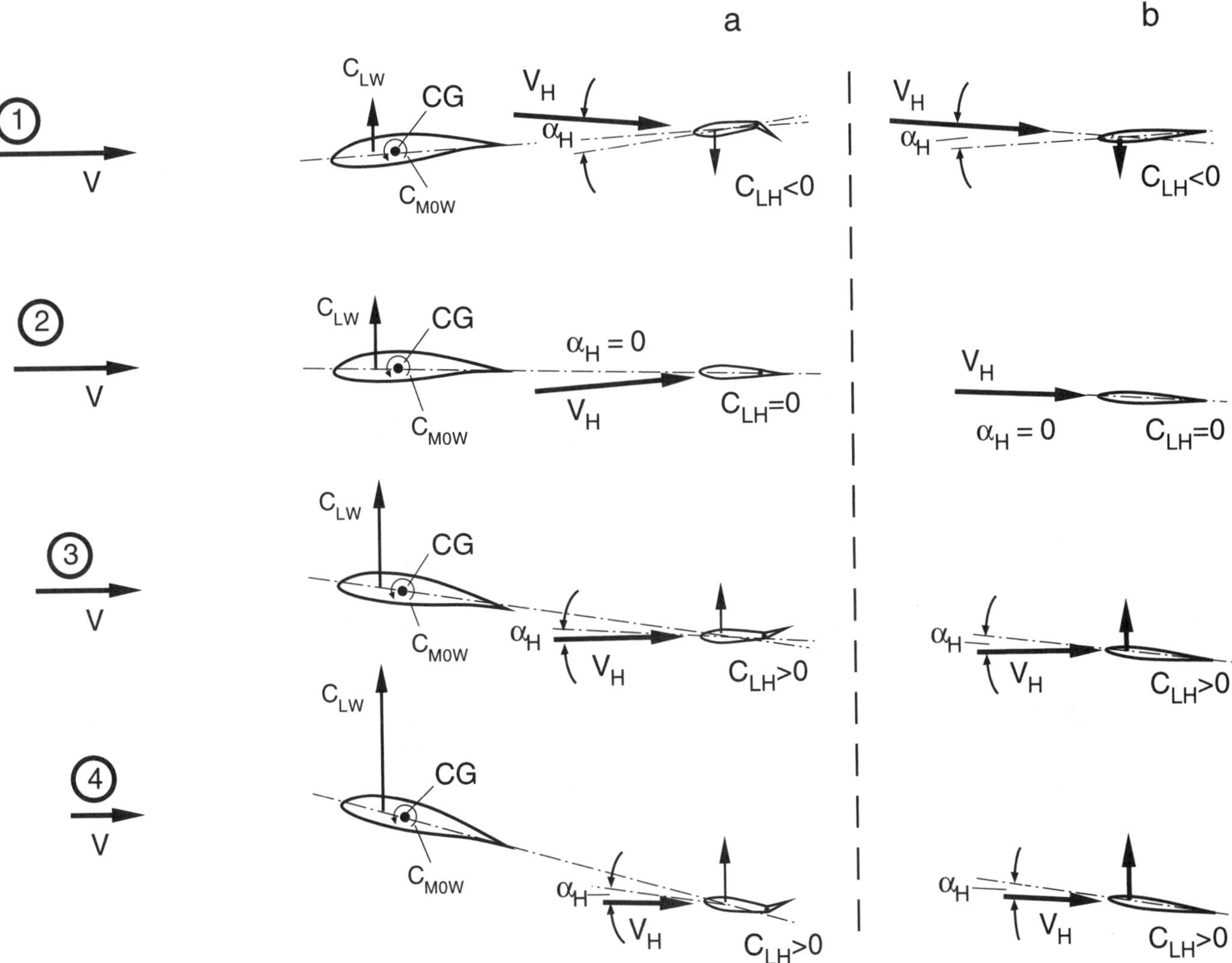

Fig. 166: Flow conditions and lift coefficient at horizontal stabilizer for the four equilibrium conditions in Fig. 165.

(a) conventional stabilizer
(b) all-flying tail

changing the flight path angle, and the sailplane begins to climb. The energy for the climb comes from the kinetic energy - that is, airspeed is traded for altitude. As the airspeed bleeds off, the wing lift gradually diminishes until a new equilibrium condition is established with lift and weight equal. The sailplane is now in trimmed flight at a lower airspeed (higher lift coefficient).

In reality, the maneuver is not initiated with a step elevator input as in the above narrative. Rather, the pilot applies the elevator smoothly, initially more than required, gradually relaxing the control input as the new trim condition is approached. A sudden elevator input with no subsequent modulation would result in the sailplane overshooting its new trim airspeed with the subsequent phugoid gradually damping out and converging on the new trim condition.

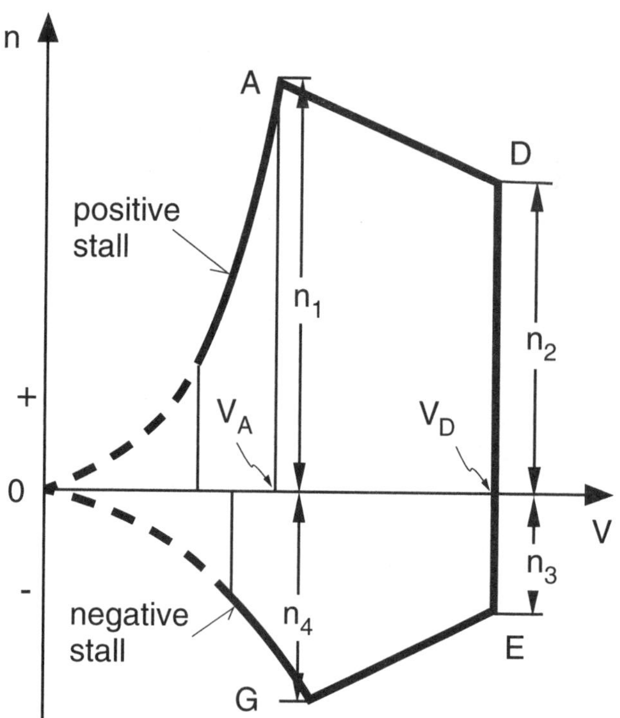

Fig. 167: Maneuvering envelope (V-n diagram) from JAR-22 [49].

	Utility	Acrobatic
n_1	+5.3	+7.0
n_2	+4.0	+7.0
n_3	−1.5	−5.0
n_4	−2.65	−5.0

Winch launch

Unique to sailplanes is the winch launch. Winch launching places special demands on the horizontal stabilizer (Fig. 168). Primarily, the stabilizer must be able to counteract the nose-up moment generated at liftoff by the cable tension. There are, however, a variety of opinions concerning the appropriate load assumptions. In the final stages of the tow, it must be possible to trim the aircraft at maximum towing speed with full aft stick and a cable angle of 75°. In both cases the stabilizer maximum lift coefficient plays a critical role. Since the stabilizer lift acts here in a favorable direction relative to the elevator deflections, this is a case where the conventional stab/elevator has an advantage over the all-flying tail. For further discussion of winch launching the reader is referred to [76, 80, 81, 91].

Stabilizer Volume

Determining the horizontal stabilizer volume

As is the case with most design tasks, establishing the proper horizontal stabilizer volume is an iterative process. While various approaches may be taken, the following discussion uses a simplified method to illustrate the basic considerations involved.

First, the desired center of gravity range and minimum stability margin is established. These parameters lead to the reduced stabilizer volume per Eq. 108. For example, if the aft center of gravity limit is set at $x_{CG}/c_\mu = 0.5$ and the minimum stability margin at $(x_{CG} - x_N)/c_\mu = -0.05$, the required reduced stabilizer volume is $(V_H/V_W)^\star = 0.3$ (Fig. 169). With this reduced stabilizer volume, the stability margin will suffice throughout the center of gravity range. The actual horizontal stabilizer volume is derived from the reduced stabilizer volume using Eq. 107. For this example we assume a tail efficiency $\eta_t = 1$ and $d\alpha_w/d\alpha = 0$.

Next, it must be verified that this stabilizer volume provides the required longitudinal control power to trim the aircraft in all flight conditions. Here the critical cases are maximum wing lift (both positive and negative) with the center of gravity at its aft limit. Figure 170 presents the

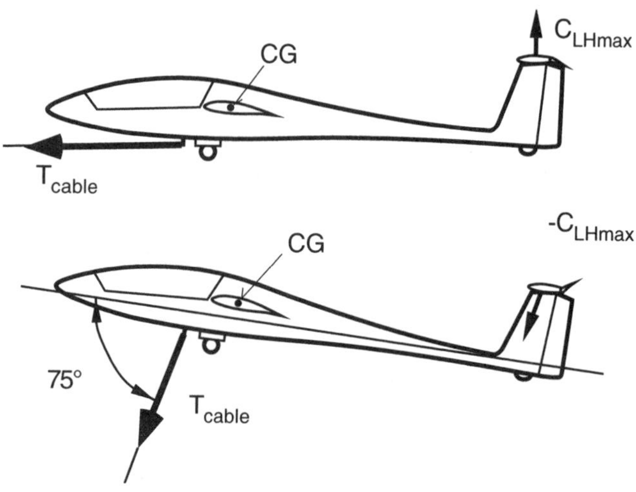

Fig. 168: Stabilizer loads during winch launch.

- initial acceleration
- at top of launch

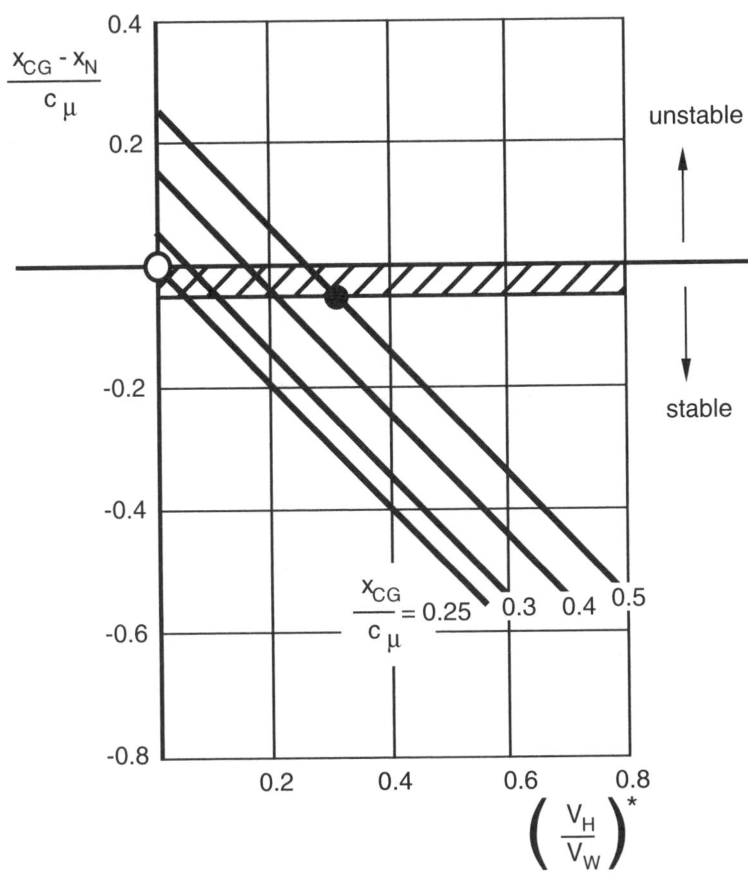

Fig. 169: Reduced horizontal stabilizer volume as a function of stability margin and CG location. Example: for a minimum stability margin $(x_{CG} - x_N)/c_\mu = -0.05$, the minimum required horizontal stabilizer volume at aft CG $x_{CG}/c_\mu = 0.5$ is $(V_H/V_W)^* = 0.3$

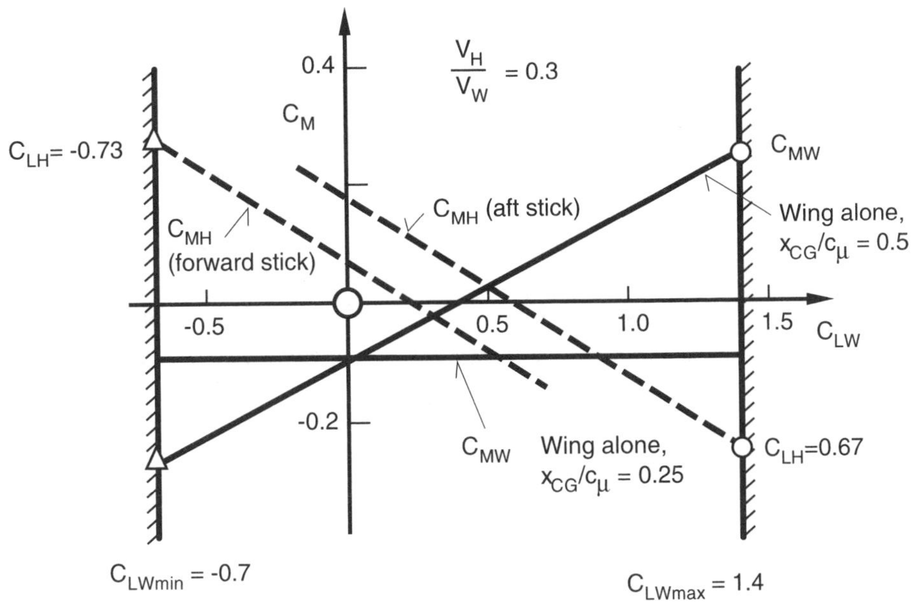

Fig. 170: Equilibrium conditions for maximum and minimum wing lift coefficients for sailplane with cambered profile ($C_{M_{0W}} = -0.10$) and stabilizer volume $(V_H/V_W) = 0.3$.

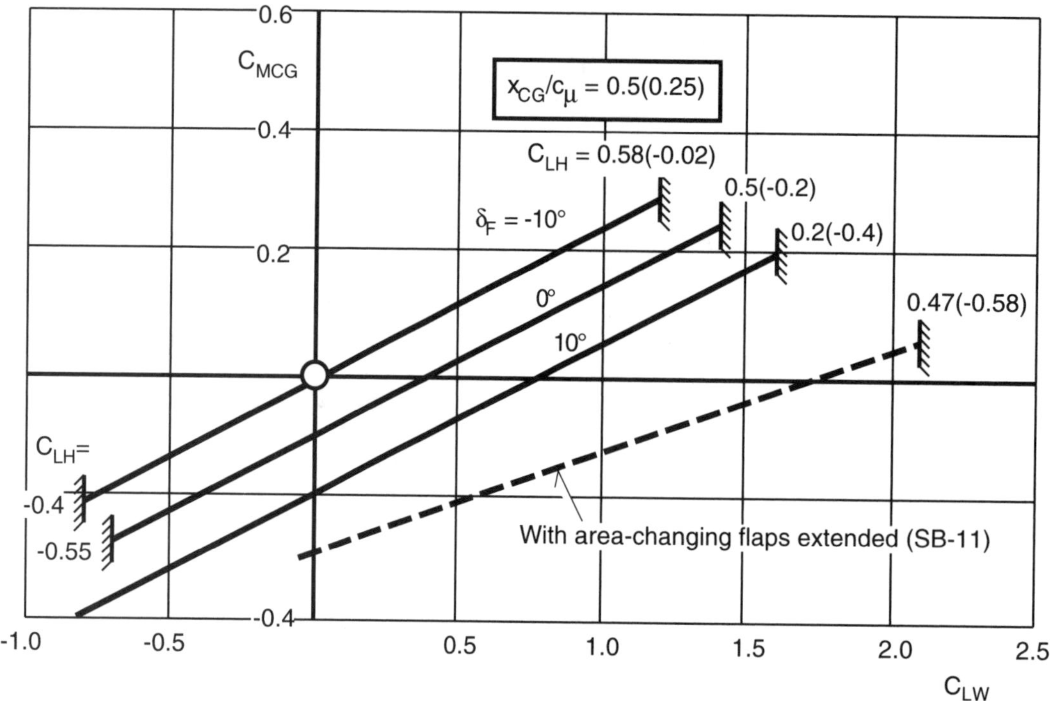

Fig. 171: Pitching moment curves for wing with various flap deflections.
Stabilizer lift coefficient required for CG location $x_{CG}/c_\mu = 0.5$ and 0.25 and stabilizer volume $(V_H/V_W) = 0.4$.

Fig. 172: Required maximum stabilizer lift coefficient as a function of stabilizer volume.

(a) $x_{CG}/c_\mu = 0.5$
(b) $x_{CG}/c_\mu = 0.25$

////// limit of laminar operating region for all-flying tail (FX 71 L-150 airfoil)

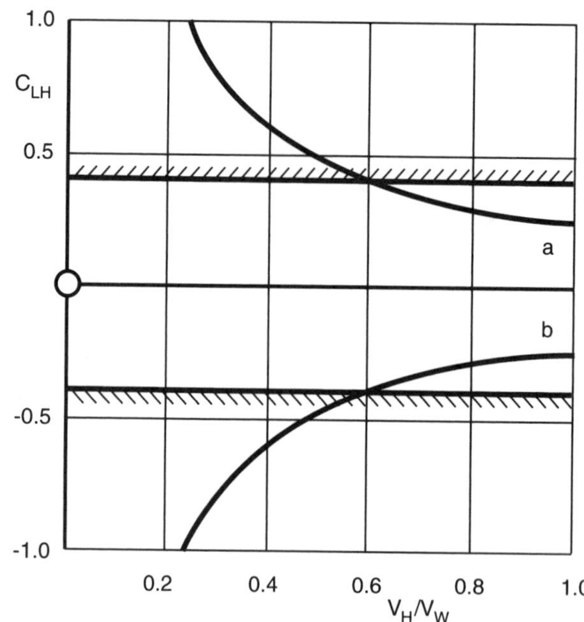

example of a wing with a cambered airfoil ($C_{M_{0W}}$=-0.10), aft center of gravity location and a horizontal stabilizer volume of (V_H/V_W) = 0.3. The stabilizer lift coefficients are calculated using Eq. 109. Based on Fig. 54, and assuming $\mathcal{R}$ = 22 and $\mathcal{R}_H$ = 7, the lift curve slope ratio was set at $(dC_{L_W}/d\alpha)/(dC_{L_H}/d\alpha_H) = 5.8/4.7 \approx 1.25$. For the trim condition at maximum or minimum lift, a stabilizer C_{L_H}-range of $-0.73 \leq C_{L_H} \leq +0.67$ is required.

If the wing has a cambered airfoil, camber-changing flaps, or even area-changing flaps, each flap position has a different range of maximum and minimum wing lift coefficients and the empennage must be designed for all possible flight conditions. Figure 171 shows the required stabilizer lift coefficients assuming a stabilizer volume of 0.4. If these cannot be achieved with the given stabilizer, the stabilizer volume must be increased accordingly. The relationship between stabilizer volume and stabilizer lift coefficient is shown in a further example in Fig. 172.

Airfoils for horizontal stabilizer

Since the available C_{L_H}-range is of particular importance when determining the required stabilizer volume, the aerodynamic characteristics of the stabilizer airfoil must be taken into account. Usually, since the stabilizer needs to produce similar amounts of lift in both directions, symmetric airfoils are employed. Camber is used only occasionally to provide the required stick force gradients with all-flying tails.

While it was at one time common to use symmetric airfoils from the NACA 63- and 64-series, most modern sailplanes use airfoils taken from the Stuttgart Profile Catalog [168] or developed at the Delft University of Technology [170].

Typical of these airfoils is the FX 71-L-150 with an elevator depth of 20%, 25%, or 30% (see also [201]). Figure 173 shows drag polars and C_{L_H} vs. α_H curves for this airfoil with various flap deflections. If the airfoil is used in an all-flying tail, the curves for $\delta_e = 0$ apply. Unfortunately, the most interesting case, maximum lift coefficient with negative flap settings, remains to be tested. The data were measured at $Re = 1.0 \cdot 10^6$. This relatively low Reynolds number is appropriate for the horizontal stabilizer, as it has a much smaller chord than the wing.

The drag polars in Fig. 173 show a pronounced laminar bucket with the drag increasing rapidly to either side of the bucket. For this reason it is important to ensure that the horizontal tail volume is sufficient to allow all steady flight conditions to be trimmed out with stabilizer lift coefficients C_{L_H} lying in the airfoil's laminar bucket. This also provides a considerable C_{L_H} reserve, reducing the possibility of the stabilizer stalling, for example during a gust encounter.

Another well-known horizontal stabilizer airfoil is the DU86-137/25, designed by L. M. M. Boermans and F. Bennis [170]. This airfoil was especially designed for forced boundary-layer transition using zig-zag turbulator tape. Wind-tunnel measurements down to $Re = 0.5 \cdot 10^6$ show a drag reduction of approximately 10% relative to the FX 71-L-150 airfoil discussed above, with only a 5% reduction in $c_{l_{max}}$.

As previously mentioned (page 65), a turning sailplane undergoes a steady pitching motion due to its bank angle and turn rate, providing an additional upward contribution to the flow at the stabilizer. This can increase the stabilizer angle of attack by about 2–4°, depending on airspeed, stabilizer moment arm, turn radius, and bank angle. The pilot compensates for this with additional aft stick inputs. This is of little concern if an all-flying stabilizer is used; however, for conventional stabilizer/elevator combinations, it increases the difficulty of keeping the airfoil within its laminar operating range (see G. Stich [109]).

Conventional stabilizer vs. all-flying tail

Figure 174 compares the laminar operating range of a conventional stabilizer/elevator combination with that of an all-flying tail. The all-flying tail remains in laminar flow over a range of approximately $-0.4 \leq C_{L_H} \leq +0.4$. The conventional stabilizer, being essentially a flapped airfoil, has a larger laminar operating range. In practice however this proves to be of limited advantage, since the elevator (*i.e.* flap) deflection changes with C_{L_H} in a manner opposite to that required for laminar flow.

The figure shows the required stabilizer lift coefficients as a function of wing lift coefficient C_{L_W} for various horizontal tail volumes, The data correspond to an unflapped wing with $-0.8 \leq C_{L_W} \leq 1.4$, $\alpha_{0_W} = -0.5°$, $dC_L/d\alpha = 5.73$ (*i.e.* $\Delta C_L = 0.1$ per degree), $\mathcal{R}$ = 22, and an aft center of gravity $x_{CG}/c_\mu = 0.5$. For the conventional stabilizer/elevator combination, a stabilizer incidence of $\varepsilon_H = -4°$ was assumed. The stabilizer is completely unloaded (C_{L_H}=0) at a wing lift coefficient $C_{L_W} = 0.4$. It is evident that the smaller the stabilizer volume, the higher the required stabilizer lift

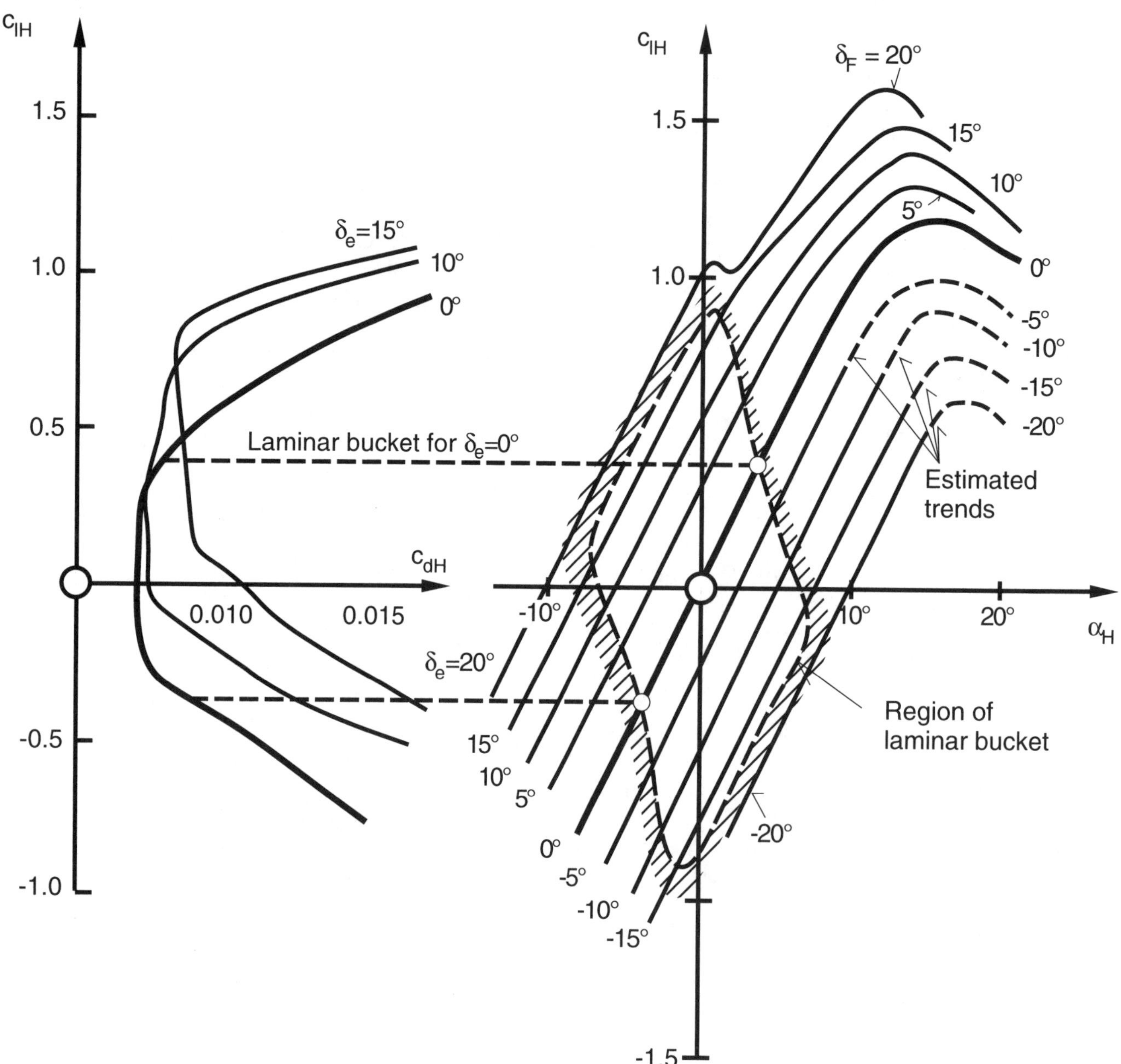

Fig. 173: Drag polars and laminar operating region for stabilizer airfoil FX 71-L 150/26 at Re = 1 · 10^6 and various elevator deflections δ_e.

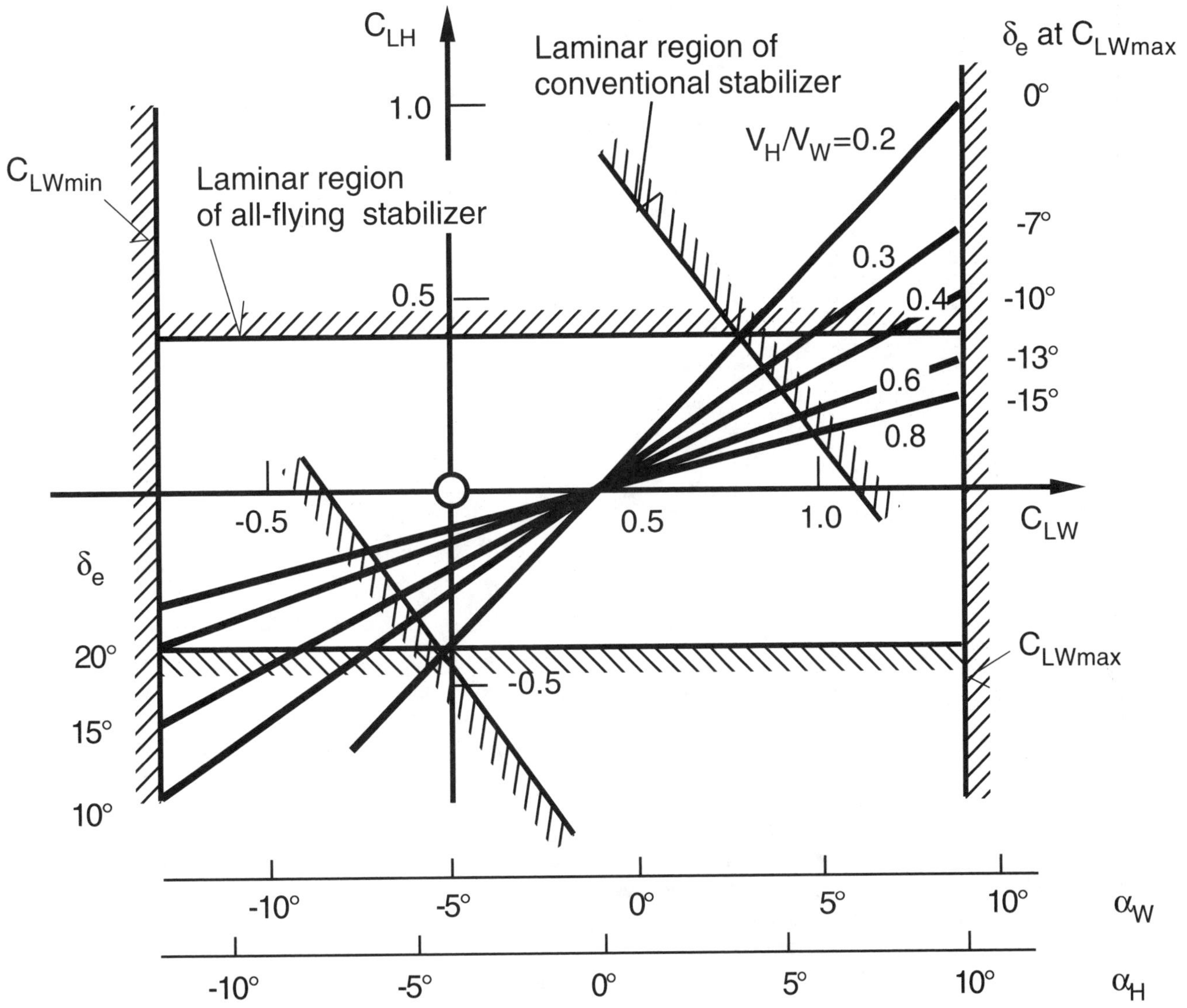

Fig. 174: Stabilizer volume required to trim aircraft at aft CG (x_{CG}/c_μ= 0.5) throughout entire wing operating C_L-range. Fixed geometry airfoil is assumed, with $C_{L_{max}}$ = 1.4, $C_{L_{min}}$ = −0.8 and $dC_L/d\alpha$ = 5.73. Limits of laminar operating regions are shown for both conventional and all-flying stabilizer. Conventional stabilizer assumes $\alpha_{0_W} - \alpha_{0_H} = \Delta\varepsilon = -4°$ and lift curve slope $dC_{L_H}/d\alpha_H$ = 5.73. All values have been rounded.

coefficients.

Since the all-flying tail can adapt itself to the local flow conditions at the empennage, generating the required lift coefficients presents no problem. In this example, with a stabilizer volume of V_H/V_W = 0.5 or greater it is possible to keep the stabilizer operating in its laminar bucket throughout the entire range of positive wing coefficients.

With the conventional stabilizer/elevator, however, the situation is a bit more difficult. Since the incidence of the fixed portion of the stabilizer cannot be adjusted in flight,

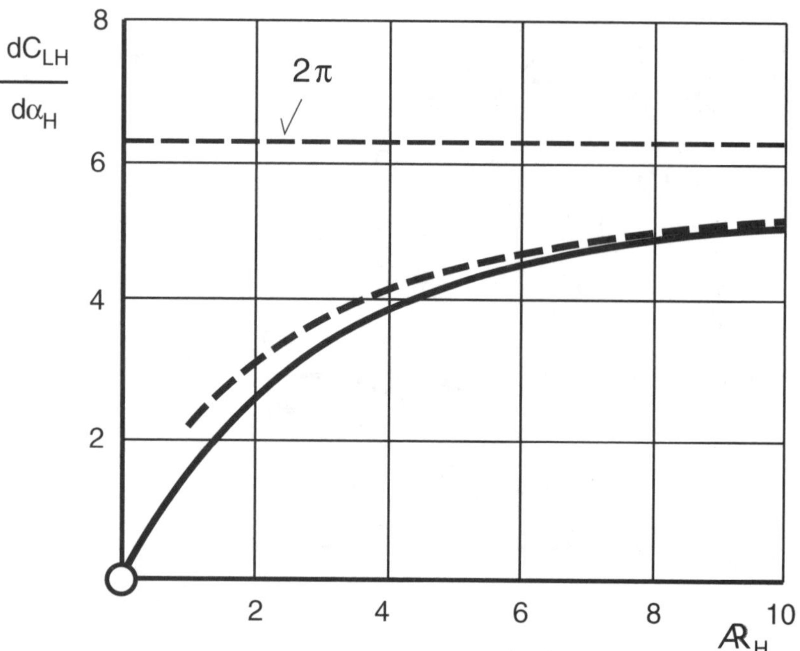

Fig. 175: Lift curve slope vs. aspect ratio for low aspect ratio wings (Eq. 110).

– – – Prandtl theory, valid only for Æ > 5

the required angle of attack is affected by the angle of attack of the wing, the downwash angle and the stabilizer incidence angle and lift curve slope. Assuming for the sake of simplicity that the stabilizer lift curve slope is identical to that of the wing and ignoring as well the induced downwash α_W, we obtain the stabilizer angle of attack α_H and elevator deflection δ_e shown in Fig. 174. In this case (extreme for the sake of illustration), positive stabilizer lift must be produced with negative flap deflections. This is an aerodynamically unfavorable situation, since both the available C_{L_H} range and laminar operating range are considerably limited. The range of wing lift coefficients for which the stabilizer remains within its laminar bucket narrows as the stabilizer volume is reduced. If the stabilizer volume is reduced too far, the available control power may not suffice to trim the aircraft at maximum lift coefficient.

An even more serious situation develops with flapped sailplanes since the zero-lift moment $C_{M_{0W}}$ and zero-lift angle of attack α_{0_W} vary considerably with flap deflection. In this case the stabilizer lift coefficients remain in their usual range, so that an all-flying tail can provide equilibrium without trouble. However, the difficulties described above for the conventional stabilizer/elevator combination become even more severe.

On the other hand, as previously discussed, the conventional stabilizer has an advantage over the all-flying tail during winch launch. In both cases, the control deflections are in an aerodynamically favorable direction, so that the conventional tail can generate a higher maximum lift coefficient, requiring a smaller tail volume to trim the aircraft. Also, as will be discussed, it is easier to provide appropriate stick force gradients (*i.e.* dynamic stability) with a conventional stabilizer than with an all-flying tail.

Tail efficiency and downwash effects

A more precise determination of the stabilizer volume requires a closer look at the stabilizer lift curve slope, downwash effects, and tail efficiency.

Since the horizontal stabilizer (and, for that matter, the vertical stabilizer) has a comparatively low aspect ratio, its lift curve slope can no longer be calculated using the Prandtl lifting line theory result in Eq. 50. Instead, a result from an extended lifting line theory is employed:

$$\frac{dC_L}{d\alpha} = \frac{2\pi Æ}{2 + \sqrt{Æ^2 + 4}} \qquad (110)$$

(see Fig. 175). In place of 2π one may use a measured or calculated lift curve slope for the selected airfoil.

The following relationship from Schlichting [23, 24] may be used to calculate the position of the vortex sheet as it convects downstream from the wing:

$$\frac{z_w}{\alpha} = \left(1 - \frac{d\alpha_w}{d\alpha}\right)\frac{x}{s} \tag{111}$$

The angle of attack α is measured in radians from the zero lift angle of the wing and the coordinate x is the distance aft from the wing trailing edge. The position of the vortex sheet is shown in Figure 176 for a typical Standard Class sailplane.

If the horizontal stabilizer lies in or near the vortex sheet, energy losses reduce the dynamic pressure q_H at the empennage compared with the free stream value q. This effect is quantified as the tail efficiency, $\eta_t = q_H/q$.

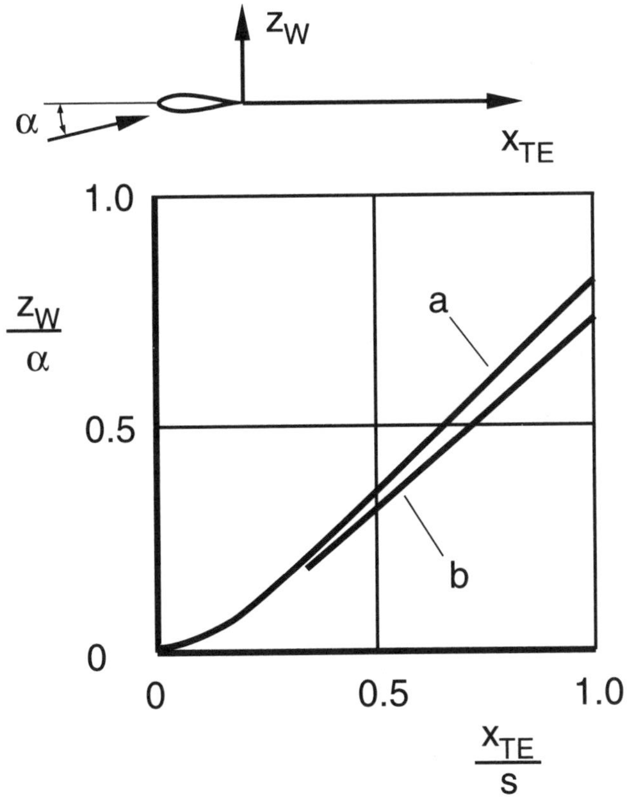

Fig. 176: Position of trailing vortex sheet aft of wing (see also Fig. 161).

(a) with fuselage influence
(b) neglecting fuselage

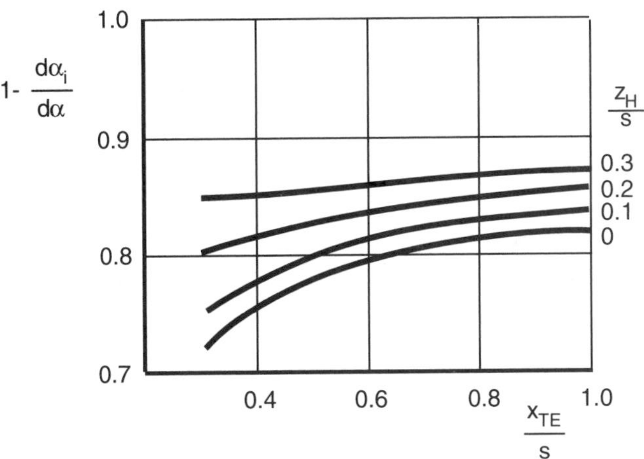

Fig. 177: Effect of stabilizer position on horizontal stabilizer effectiveness (see also Fig. 161).
Mean values for typical horizontal stabilizer spans.

The downwash factor $(1 - d\alpha_w/d\alpha)$ is a function of stabilizer location and distance from the wing's vortex sheet. For the usual empennage arrangements, it is always less than unity, converging on unity as the stabilizer is moved further and further aft of the wing. Values for a typical Standard Class sailplane are shown in Fig. 177 as a function of the stabilizer position. The values vary depending on whether the downwash is measured in the aircraft's plane of symmetry or taken as an average value over the stabilizer span. A more sophisticated analysis would also account for fuselage effects on the wing vortex sheet.

Vertical stabilizer volume

The vertical stabilizer provides directional stability and contributes to lateral stability. With rudder deflection, it provides the yaw moments for turn entries and steady turns. In all flight conditions, the rudder provides a means of controlling the sideslip angle, making coordinated flight possible.

While the required horizontal stabilizer volume may be calculated based on a number of specific operational requirements, when establishing the vertical stabilizer area one must rely mainly on experience.

A vertical stabilizer volume is defined analogous to the

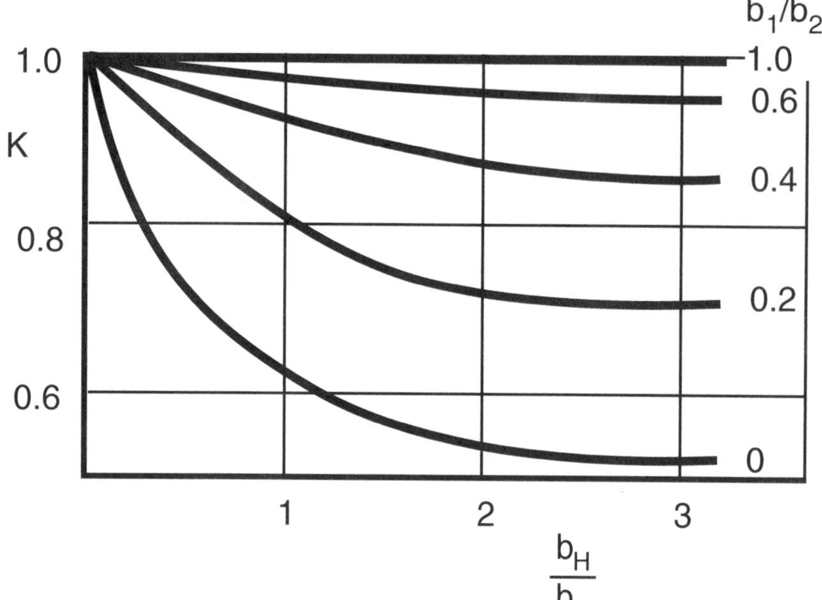

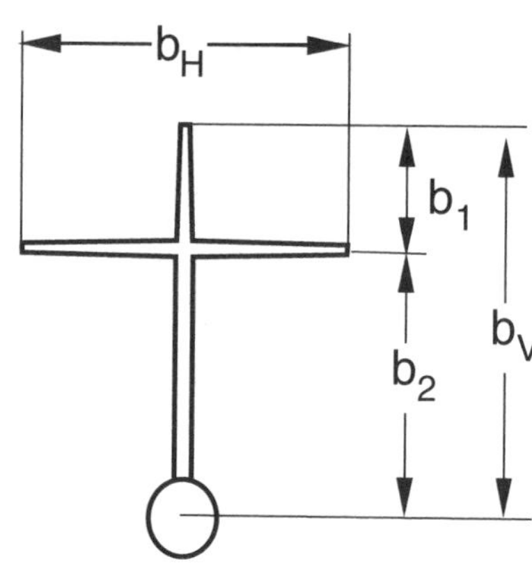

Fig. 178: Increase in effective aspect ratio due to endplate effect, per J. Rotta (see also [24]).

$$AR_{eff} = AR_{geom}/K$$

horizontal stabilizer volume[2]:

$$\frac{V_V}{Sb} = \frac{S_V}{S}\frac{l_V}{b}\frac{dC_{L_V}}{d\beta} \qquad (112)$$

Here, normalization is based on the product of wing area and wing span. l_V is the distance from the aerodynamic center of the vertical stabilizer to the center of gravity, C_{L_V} is the vertical stabilizer lift coefficient, and β is the sailplane slip angle. The low aspect ratio relationship in Eq. 110 can be used to calculate the vertical stabilizer lift curve slope.

Due to the endplate effect of the vertical stabilizer (especially in the case of T-tails), the vertical stabilizer has an effective aspect ratio somewhat larger than its geometric aspect ratio. This effect is shown for various empennage arrangements in Fig. 178.

Figure 179 provides vertical and horizontal stabilizer volumes of a number of well-known sailplanes. For the most part the values lie in the following ranges:

- Horizontal stabilizer: $0.35 \leq V_H/V_W \leq 0.55$
- Vertical stabilizer: $0.045 \leq V_V/Sb \leq 0.075$

[2]As with the tail volume coefficient, some texts define this parameter without the lift-curve slope term - see footnote page 130.

Tail moment arm

A given horizontal or vertical stabilizer volume is achieved by appropriate combination of empennage size and moment arm. The moment arm is optimized for drag minimization on one hand and structural weight of the aft fuselage and empennage on the other.

A longer empennage arm provides more aerodynamic damping in pitch and yaw, which, among other things, improves the stability of the spiral dive mode. On the other hand, longer moment arms require increased stiffness to ensure aeroelastic stability.

Although the optimal moment arms for vertical and horizontal stabilizer differ (the vertical stabilizer favoring a slightly longer arm), conventional empennage arrangements place both at the same station. Moment arms of

$$5 \leq l_H/c_\mu \leq 6.5$$

are well suited for the horizontal stabilizer from both a weight and drag point of view. For the vertical stabilizer, values towards the upper end of this range are preferred.

Designers are strongly advised not to extend the moment arm by sweeping the tail surfaces. The decrease in lift curve slope (proportional to the cosine of the sweep angle) by itself more than offsets the gain due to the longer arm. Furthermore, sweeping the tail surfaces may lead to

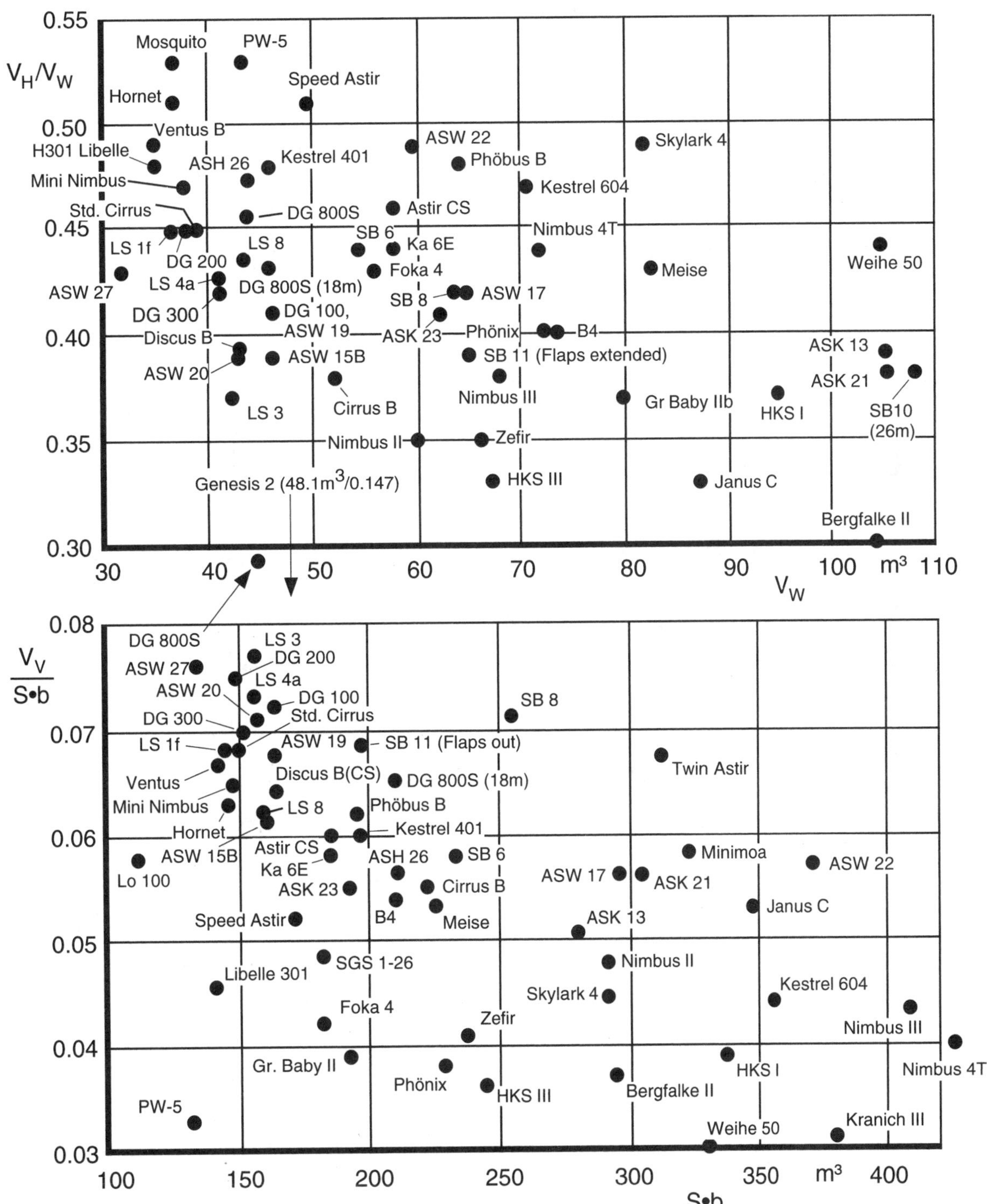

Fig. 179: Horizontal and vertical stabilizer volumes of various sailplanes.

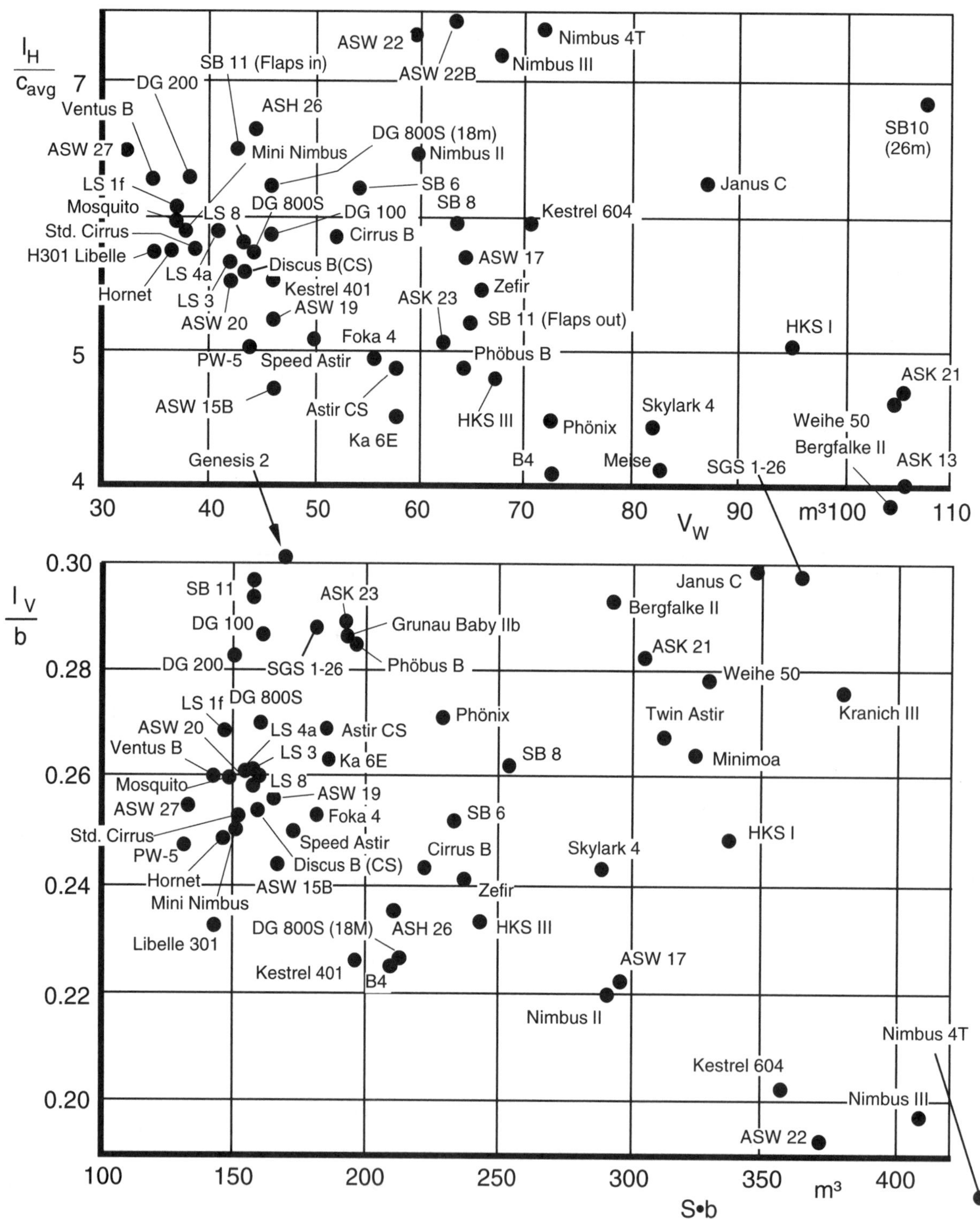

Fig. 180: Horizontal and vertical stabilizer moment arms of various sailplanes.

Fig. 181: Empennage arrangements: Conventional, cruciform, T-tail, and V-tail.

premature boundary-layer transition.

Moment arms for a number of sailplanes are shown in Fig. 180. An interesting study treating the selection of the empennage design parameters was published in the early 1950's by W. Stender [107]. See also E. E. Larrabee [91].

For the sake of simplicity, in the following discussion and in the data tables in Appendix 1, the average wing chord c_{avg} is used in place of the mean aerodynamic chord c_μ. The difference is small for the typical tapered and double tapered wing planforms. For an elliptical wing, $c_\mu = 1.08 c_{avg}$.

Stabilizer Planform and Empennage Arrangement

Planform

As with the wing, the primary empennage planform parameters are aspect ratio, sweep, and taper. Early sailplane designers generally favored rounded empennage planforms, especially for the vertical stabilizer. Planforms of this type minimize induced drag by providing a nearly-elliptical lift distribution. Modern sailplanes almost always feature trapezoidal planforms because they are simpler to manufacture and have proven acceptable from an aerodynamic point of view.

The optimum aspect ratio for each of the tail surfaces is a function of the profile drag of the selected airfoil, the induced drag, weight considerations, and effects on lift curve slope. Various studies have shown that horizontal stabilizer aspect ratios in the range of

$$5 \leq A\!\!\!R_H \leq 8$$

yield good results. Higher aspect ratios are appropriate for heavily loaded stabilizers, for example in the case of sailplanes having high stability margins.

Aspect ratios for sailplane vertical stabilizers lie mainly in the range

$$1.5 \leq A\!\!\!R_V \leq 2.0$$

This range lies well below typical horizontal stabilizer aspect ratios for the following reasons:

- In level flight the vertical stabilizer generates no lift, and therefore no induced drag.
- A small aspect ratio allows the vertical stabilizer to operate at very high yaw angles without stalling.
- With T-tails, the effective aspect ratio is significantly higher.
- Total structural weight is reduced considerably, especially with T-tails.

However, since the lift curve slope $dC_{L_V}/d\beta$ decreases with aspect ratio, the aspect ratio should not be made too small.

As previously mentioned, sweeping the tail surfaces, where not otherwise necessary from an aeroelastic standpoint, is not recommended.

The induced drag of the individual tail surfaces is minimized with a taper ratio of approximately 0.4. This value should, however, be considered an absolute minimum. Increasing the taper ratio (*i.e.* reducing the taper) brings only a small penalty compared to the optimum. Note that empennage chords are typically small, so that Reynolds number effects must be considered when optimizing stabilizer planform parameters.

Empennage arrangement

The basic empennage arrangements are (Fig. 181):

- conventional

- cruciform tail
- T-tail
- V-tail

The conventional configuration, in which the horizontal and vertical tail surfaces are mounted separately on the fuselage, is seldom found in modern sailplanes due to the poor ground clearance provided by the relatively thin aft fuselages. The cruciform tail alleviates this difficulty somewhat but brings with it increased interference drag due to the four corners created by the intersection of the horizontal and vertical stabilizers.

By comparison, the T-tail offers:

- reduced interference drag,
- improved ground clearance,
- greater clearance from wing wake,
- good spin characteristics, and
- improved vertical stabilizer effectiveness due to end plate effect.

As a disadvantage, the T-tail places the horizontal stabilizer mass well away from the fuselage axis. Aeroelastic considerations necessitate increased fuselage and vertical stabilizer stiffness and with it an increase in structural weight (see Fig. 159). The offset stabilizer mass can also lead to fuselage damage if the tail skid contacts an obstacle during ground loops (Fig. 182). For this reason, if a T-tail is used, the weight on the tail should be kept relatively low via suitable location of the main landing gear. To minimize any tendency to flutter, the horizontal stabilizer should be located ahead of the vertical stabilizer elastic axis. Overall, the many advantages of the T-tail have led to it becoming the standard for modern high performance sailplanes.

Care must be taken to design the junction between the tail surfaces so that the horizontal stabilizer requires no cutout for the vertical stabilizer. Cutouts are difficult to seal and the probability of significant air flow through the resulting gap is high (Fig. 183). Gap effects can be reduced somewhat by fitting a fairing to the horizontal stabilizer, extending into the vertical stabilizer. Gaps in the vertical stabilizer are less critical since it normally operates at zero lift coefficient with pressures equal on both surfaces.

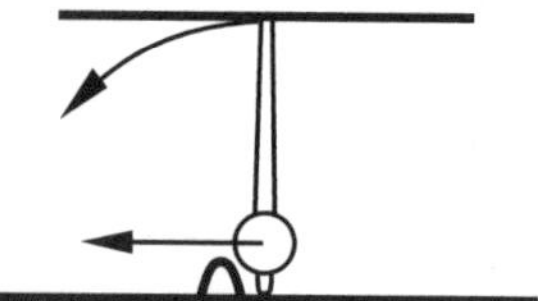

Fig. 182: Torsional load in tail boom resulting from tail skid ground contact during ground loop or touchdown with lateral drift.

One special form of empennage, the V-tail, differs from the other configurations by combining the longitudinal and lateral stability and control functions in a single set of control surfaces.

Advantages of the V-tail are:

- reduced interference drag,
- reduced drag due to profile drag,
- lower weight,
- adequate ground clearance, and
- very low height when disassembled (minimum trailer height).

There are, however, several disadvantages. The mixing linkage required to combine the pitch and yaw inputs is difficult to build without at least a small degree of kinematic coupling between the two axes. Also, maximum control deflections are reduced when both controls are applied simultaneously. This can be a problem when recovering from a spin, when combinations of full forward stick and full opposite rudder may be required. Another spin-related danger is the possibility of one of the control surfaces "shadowing" the other, rendering it aerodynamically ineffective. Finally, since the empennage loads are projected onto the vertical or horizontal aircraft axis, the loads generated must be larger, leading to increased induced drag.

Although seldom seen in modern designs, V-tails have over the years been employed in a number of successful high-performance sailplanes (HKS III, SHK, SB 5, Salto, Schreder HP series).

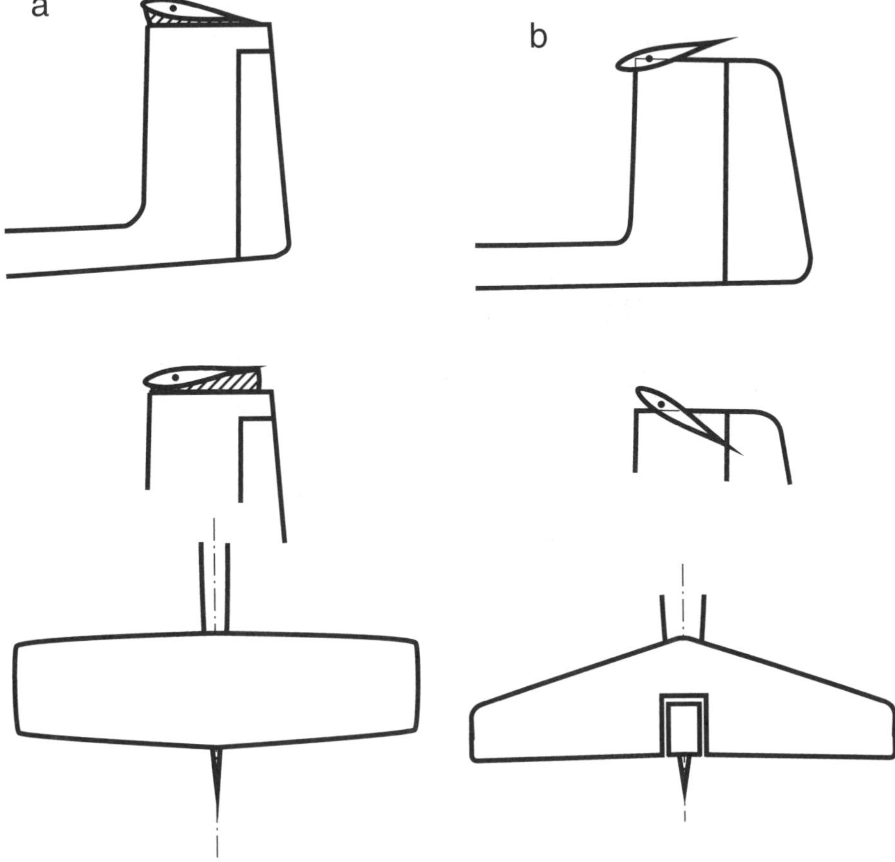

Fig. 183: Integration of horizontal and vertical stabilizer.

(a) Favorable arrangement - flow across surfaces minimized with sliding fairings within upper vertical stabilizer.

(b) Undesirable configuration with gaps in horizontal stabilizer.

Stick-Force Gradient with All-Flying Tails

The airworthiness regulations list specific requirements pertaining to longitudinal stick force characteristics. Among these is a requirement that, starting from trimmed level flight at a constant airspeed, establishing level flight at a new airspeed must require a stick force in the direction of the airspeed change. In other words, if the stick is released, the aircraft must tend to return to its original trim condition.

In the case of all-flying tails, the stick force gradient is very much a function of the relative positions of the hinge axis and the stabilizer aerodynamic center.

Consider first the case where the stabilizer is hinged at its aerodynamic center and features a symmetric airfoil (Fig. 184). The lift is applied directly at the stabilizer hinge, so that no loads are transmitted to the stick. In all flight conditions, the stick force is zero and the required stick force characteristics must be provided artificially by a mechanical spring. If a spring is employed, the stick force is proportional to stick position, but not to airspeed, leading to unnatural stick force characteristics and a very low gradient at high speeds (Fig. 185).

Preloading the spring has the effect of shifting the stick force curve. This can be used to select the airspeed at which the stick force is zero, providing a means for longitudinal trim. Trimming out the stick forces is then accomplished by moving a trim lever to adjust the spring preload. As will be discussed, longitudinal trim can also be effected with a trim tab. Trim systems that allow the angle of incidence of the fixed portion of the stabilizer to be adjusted inflight, while often seen in powered aircraft, are rarely used in sailplanes due to the difficulties involved in implementing a low drag design (see however the “eta”, page 119).

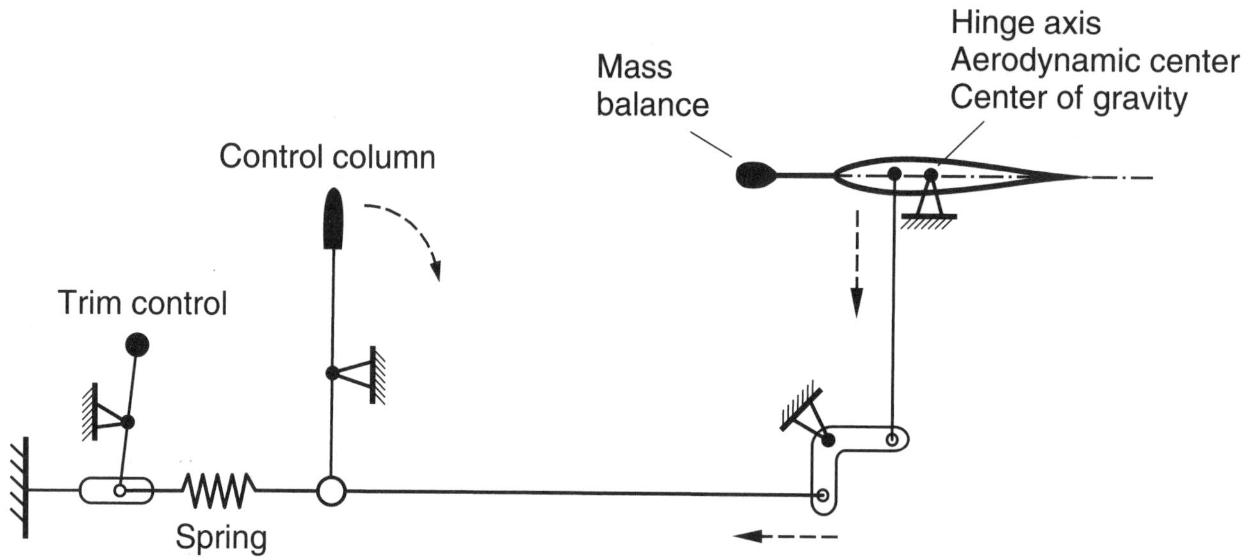

Fig. 184: All-flying tail hinged at aerodynamic center, with symmetrical airfoil, mass balance and spring trim mechanism.

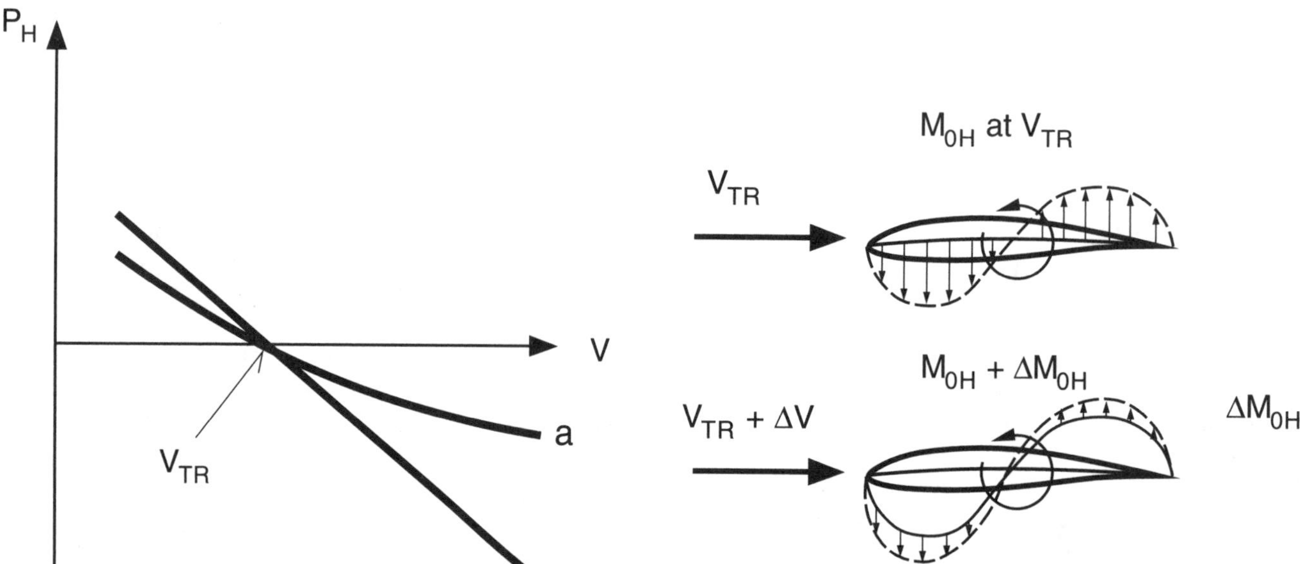

Fig. 185: Stick force trends with airspeed, $P_H(V)$. V_{TR} = trim airspeed.

(a) with spring trim
(b) with servo-tab

Fig. 186: Improvement of stick force gradients with cambered stabilizer airfoil. Camber produces pitching moment proportional to dynamic pressure.

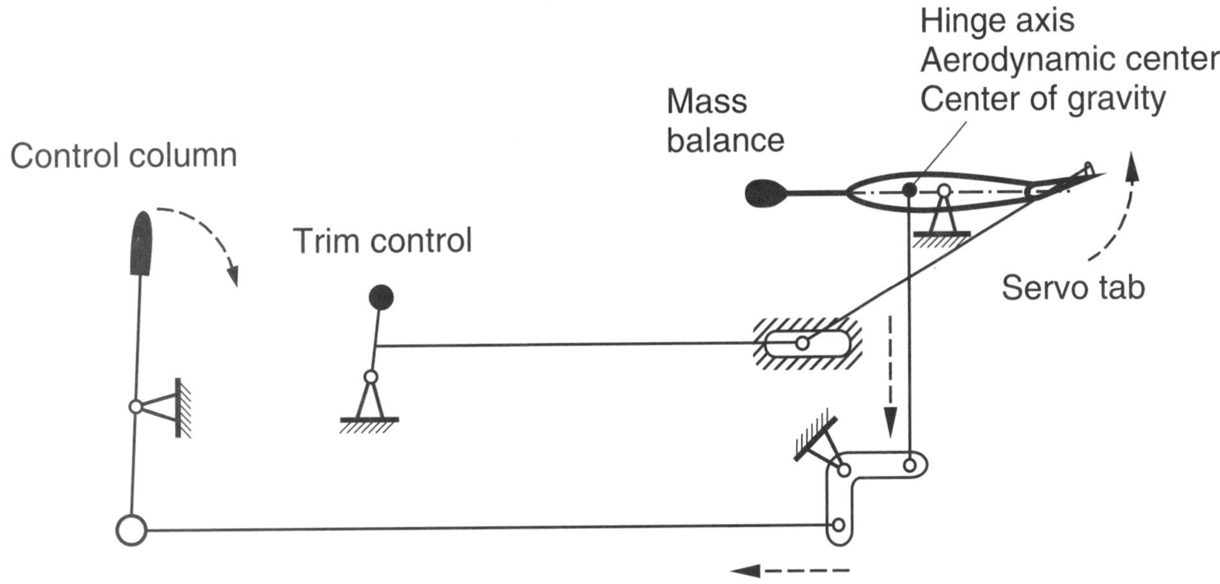

Fig. 187: All-flying tail with servo-tab and mass balance, hinged at aerodynamic center.

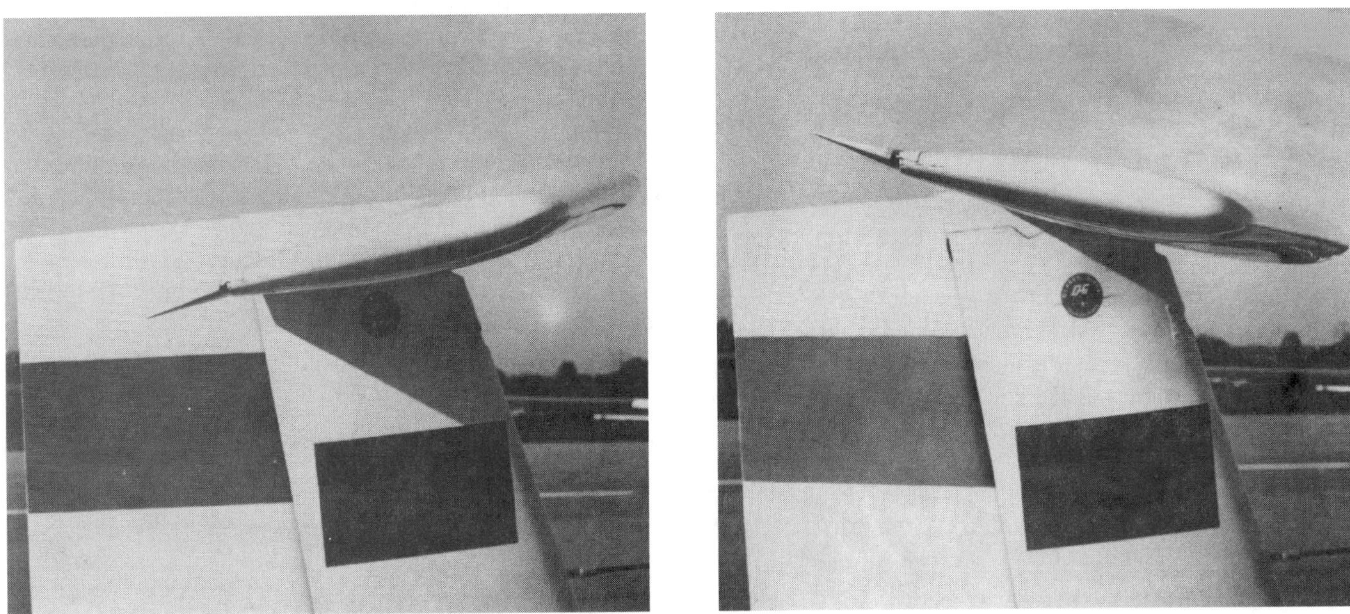

Fig. 188: DG-100 horizontal stabilizer with servo-tab. Left, forward stick; right, aft stick.

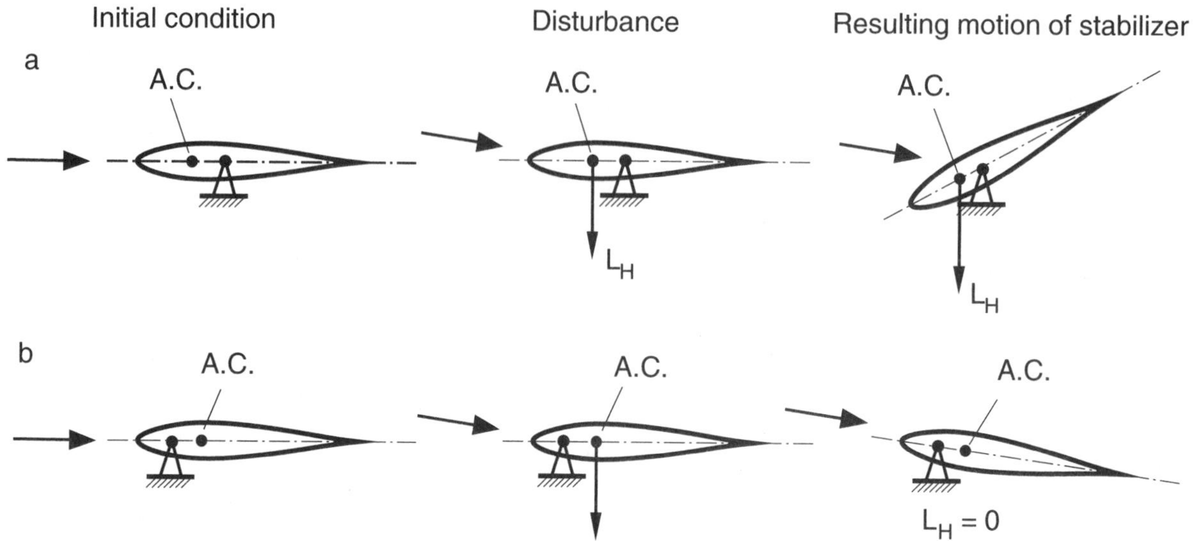

Fig. 189: Reaction of all-flying tail without spring following a disturbance (stick free).

(a) Aerodynamic center ahead of hinge axis
(b) Aerodynamic center aft of hinge axis

Stick force characteristics of all-flying tails can be improved by:

- cambering the horizontal stabilizer airfoil,
- providing a servo-tab (Flettner tab), or
- hinging the surface behind its aerodynamic center.

Positive camber in the stabilizer airfoil generates a leading-edge down aerodynamic moment proportional to the dynamic pressure (Fig. 186). With increasing airspeed, this leads to the development of the control forces indicated by the arrows in Fig. 184. The stick force is thus approximately proportional to the dynamic pressure.

Stick force characteristics can be tailored with a servo-tab mounted on the stabilizer trailing edge (Figs. 187,188). Servo-tabs (also known as Flettner tabs) have long been used on powered aircraft to reduce excessive stick forces. To accomplish this, the servo-tab must move in a direction opposite to that of the control surfaces, generating aerodynamic hinge moments that tend to increase the control surface deflection.

Exactly the opposite effect is needed in sailplanes, especially at high speeds where the stick force gradients diminish. Here, the servo-tab linkage must cause it to move in the same direction as the control surface, so that the resulting moment is opposite in sense to the control surface deflection[3]. This generates a resistive force on the control stick proportional to dynamic pressure (Figs. 187,188). The force gradient can be fine-tuned by adjusting the kinematics of the servo-tab linkage. Trim control is effected by biasing the servo-tab deflection, making it possible to trim away the longitudinal stick forces at any airspeed. For this reason the servo-tab is sometimes referred to as a trim tab, although the latter term is usually reserved for the simpler type of tab that is controlled directly by the pilot. The favorable effect of the servo-tab on the stick force characteristics is evident in Fig. 185. Disadvantages are increased complexity and manufacturing cost.

A third method of improving stick-force gradients consists of adjusting the offset between hinge axis and aerodynamic center of the stabilizer. This, however, must be done with great caution. Figure 189 shows the reaction of an all-flying tail following a disturbance. The figure assumes that the control stick is released with zero friction in the control system. If the hinge axis is aft of the stabilizer aerodynamic center, the stabilizer will, following the slightest disturbance, rotate immediately to its stop. On the other hand, with

[3]Servo-tabs of this kind are sometimes called "anti-servo tabs."

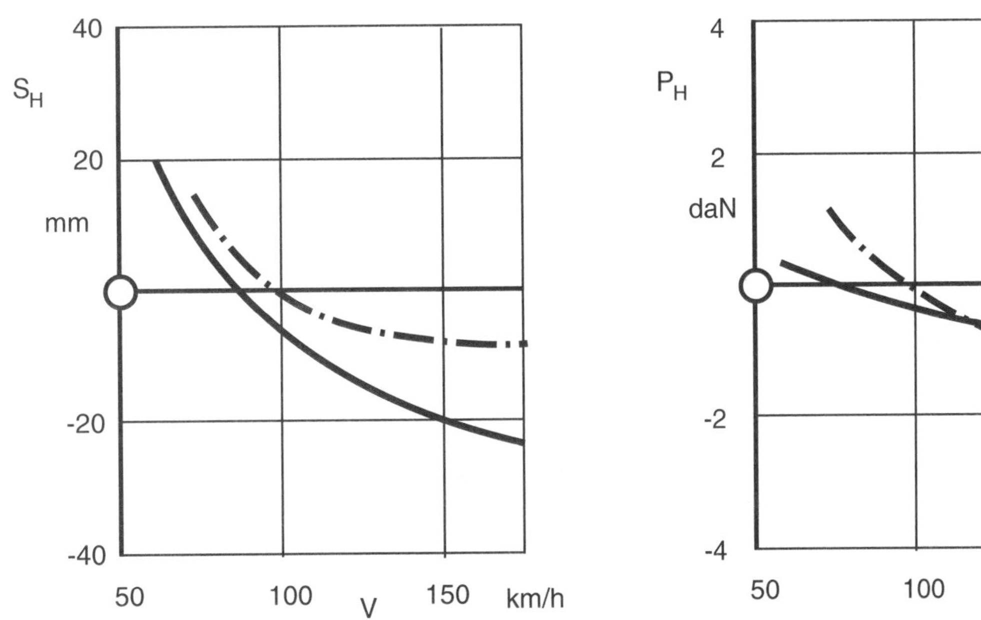

Fig. 190: Typical stick position (S_H) and stick force (P_H) trends from flight test measurements.
CG and trim setting held fixed.

——— All-flying tail with spring trim and positive camber
— · — · All-flying tail with servo-tab

the stabilizer hinged ahead of its aerodynamic center, the control surface will float to align itself with the local direction of flow, providing no contribution to the longitudinal stability. Both stick free cases are therefore unstable. Stability can only be provided with a hinge spring.

In any event, with the hinge ahead of the aerodynamic center, the stick force gradients are in the wrong direction, so this configuration need not be considered further.

With the hinge aft of the aerodynamic center, however, the restoring forces are in the desired direction. This is apparent in the equilibrium conditions in Fig. 166. As the airspeed is decreased (case 1 $\rightarrow$ case 4), the increased lift on the horizontal stabilizer, applied ahead of the hinge axis, tends to push the control stick forward. That is, increased aft pressure is required to trim lower airspeeds. However, if the stick is released, the control surface does not float to an intermediate position (as it would in the case of a conventional stabilizer/elevator), but rotates immediately to its full leading-edge-up position. Similarly, if the stick is released from a flight condition where forward pressure is required, the stabilizer will rotate to its full leading-edge-down stop, producing a severe pitch-up. This can be critical from a structural point of view, especially at high airspeeds. One must take care not to confuse the effects of control system friction with actual stability. An instability masked by control system friction can emerge following lubrication during routine maintenance, with serious consequences. For these reasons, an all-flying tail may only be hinged behind its aerodynamic center if it is also provided with a sufficiently strong hinge spring.

Methods for improving the stick force characteristics can be combined, for example positive camber with hinging the stabilizer behind its aerodynamic center. However, these approaches must be combined with care. It is strongly recommended that new designs draw on the wealth of accumulated design experience, with variations in camber, servo-tab gearing, and hinge-aerodynamic center offset introduced gradually in small steps. As mentioned, when doing so it is also important to ensure that the control system friction does not mask the actual stick force characteristics. The surest approach is a servo-tab of adequate size. Typical measured stick force curves are shown in Fig. 190.

In addition to the steady flight stability requirements, an adequate stick force gradient is required in maneuvers. Elevator control forces during turns or maneuvers must be such that an increase in load factor requires an increase in control force. The minimum value of this force for a stabilized turn with 45° bank at $1.4V_{s_1}$ is 0.5 daN [49]. Control forces in maneuvers can also be tuned with elevator mass distribution or bobweights in the control system.

The position of the stabilizer center of gravity relative to the hinge axis is important for other reasons as well. To prevent unintended control inputs during gust encounters, the center of gravity must be placed as close as possible to the hinge axis. This is achieved either by mounting a balance mass ahead of the leading edge of the stabilizer on a short boom, or by sweeping the stabilizer slightly and tapering it with $\lambda_H \approx 0.4$ to 0.6. The pushrod also contributes to the mass balance. Improper mass balancing can also lead to poor longitudinal dynamic stability, with a tendency towards pilot induced oscillations in pitch.

Evaluation of Performance and Flying Qualities

Theoretical Methods

Drag Polars

An accurate drag polar is the starting point for all sailplane performance calculations. Three basic methods are used to determine the drag polar:

- theoretical calculation
- wind-tunnel measurement
- flight test

These methods vary in accuracy and effort required.

The simplest approach, theoretical calculation, can be used even during the preliminary design phase. However, most of the existing literature in this area (for example Fiecke [79] and Hoerner [10]) is directed towards the calculation of the performance of powered aircraft and thus lacks data for Reynolds numbers typical of modern sailplanes.

Performance prediction methods are generally based on separate analyses of the individual aerodynamic components. Drag contributions from the wing, fuselage, empennage, and so forth are summed with an allowance for interference drag. Since individual aircraft components have different reference areas, drag coefficients of the individual components must be normalized to the wing reference area before they are summed to yield the drag coefficient for the complete aircraft. The polar is obtained by repeating this calculation over the entire range of lift coefficients (*i.e.* airspeed), whereby the effects of Reynolds number variations must also be taken into account.

It is convenient to divide the total drag into individual components:

- Induced drag of wing, assuming an ideal (elliptical) lift distribution
- Induced drag increment due to a non-ideal lift distribution
- Profile drag including flow disturbances on wing surface (spoiler caps; control surface hinge gaps, etc.)
- Idealized fuselage, including surface quality and extent of laminar flow
- Surface imperfections and externally mounted equipment such as antennas, total energy probe, and canopy seal
- Wing-fuselage interference drag
- Horizontal stabilizer drag, including profile drag and induced drag due to stabilizer lift
- Vertical stabilizer drag and empennage interference drag
- miscellaneous

These drag contributions may be determined as follows.

Induced drag for a wing with ideal lift distribution is calculated as outlined in the first chapter (Eq. 46). The drag penalty due to non-ideal lift distribution may be calculated using the Multhopp method (see Redeker [103]).

Aerodynamic data for many commonly used airfoils are found in the Stuttgart Profile Catalog [168], as well as more recent works by R. Eppler [180] and D. Althaus [167]. Usually the profile and chord (*i.e.* Reynolds number) vary along the wing span, so that it is useful to divide the wing into a number of sections, each with uniform airfoil properties. Drag due to the aileron control linkage, dive brake caps,

Fig. 191: **Calculated drag polars.**

- Ka 6
- Phoenix
- SB 8
- D 36
- SB 10 (26 m)

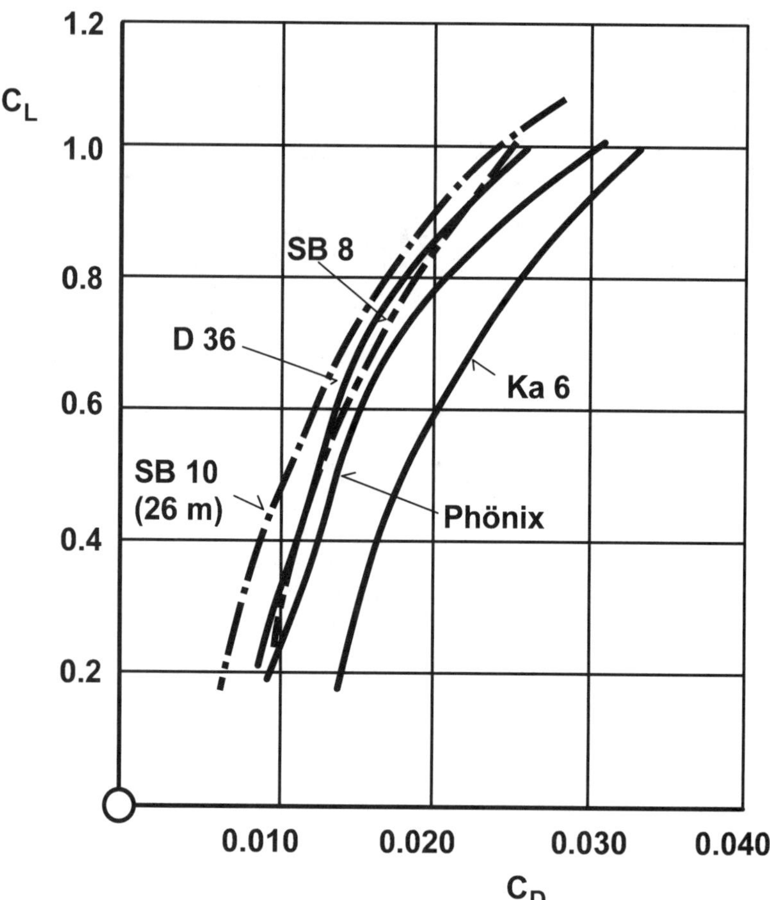

and aileron hinge gaps is also included in the wing profile drag contribution.

Fuselage drag is determined initially for an idealized fuselage having the same cross-sectional area distribution as the actual fuselage. This method is based on estimated boundary-layer transition lines such as those presented in Fig. 148 (see also [71]). Added to this are the parasite drag contributions due to landing gear (or, in the case of retractable landing gear, imperfections in the landing gear door seals), ventilation, antennas, Pitot and total energy probes, etc.

Interference drag does not lend itself to simple closed form solutions and is thus the most difficult of the drag components to determine. Here one must rely on empirical flight test data.

Horizontal and vertical stabilizer drag contributions are calculated as for the wing. Here again the interference drag must be estimated based on flight test data.

Additional useful information concerning drag estimation is found in [10,21].

Typical Drag Polars

Figure 191 presents representative drag polars calculated for several sailplanes. The airspeed polars corresponding to a given gross weight are determined using:

$$V = \frac{1}{\sqrt{C_L}}\sqrt{\frac{2}{\rho}\frac{W}{S}} \qquad (113)$$

$$V_s = \frac{C_D}{C_L^{3/2}}\sqrt{\frac{2}{\rho}\frac{W}{S}} \qquad (114)$$

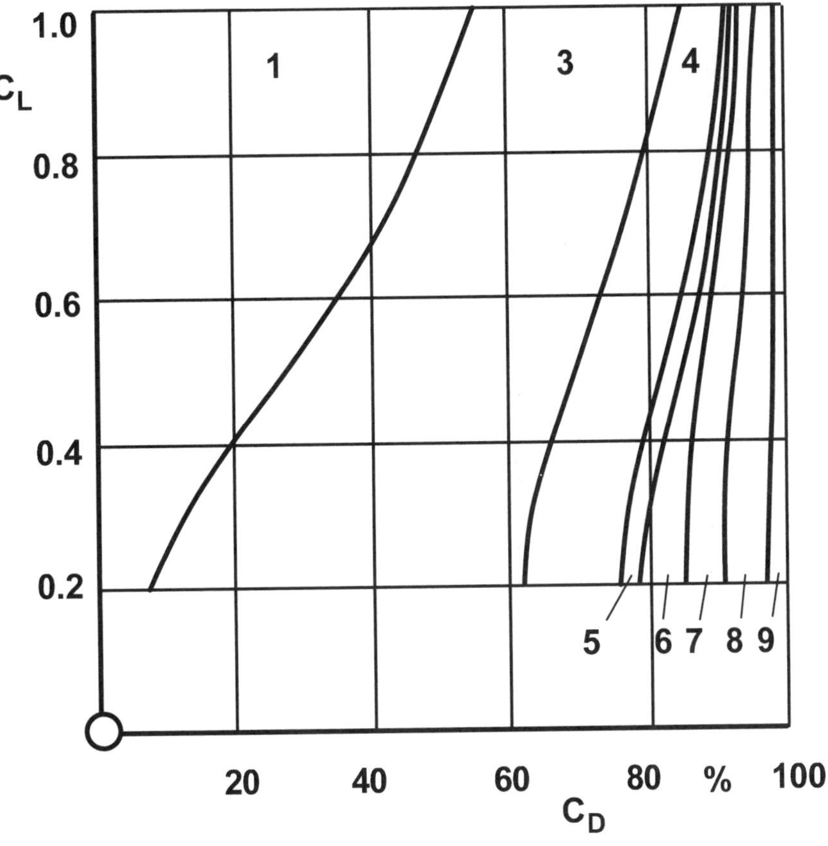

Fig. 192: Typical sailplane drag breakdown (SB 8).

1) Induced drag (elliptical lift distribution)
2) Additional induced drag (here negligible and not shown)
3) Profile drag
4) Fuselage
5) Parasite drag
6) Interference
7) Horizontal stabilizer
8) Vertical stabilizer
9) Miscellaneous

It is also interesting to compare the relative magnitudes of the individual drag contributions at different airspeeds. Figure 192 shows the drag breakdown for the SB-8. Considerable airspeed variation is observed. At low airspeed (high C_L), the induced drag contributes over 50% of the total drag. This decreases to only around 10% of the total at high speed. The profile drag amounts to 50% at high speed, and contributes strongly to the total even at low airspeeds.

Experimental Methods

Wind-tunnel testing

It is usually difficult or impossible to obtain sufficiently accurate drag data using theoretical methods. Therefore, the designer must rely ultimately on experimental measurements from wind-tunnel or flight tests.

Sailplane airfoils typically operate at Reynolds numbers at which the boundary-layer transition characteristics are highly sensitive to factors such as airfoil geometry, surface quality, and free stream turbulence. Wind-tunnel testing requires careful attention to these factors. First, the Reynolds number of the wind tunnel must match the full-scale inflight Reynolds number. The model must duplicate the airfoil geometry as accurately as possible. This becomes increasingly difficult as the size of the test sections is reduced. Finally, since free-stream turbulence in the wind tunnel can have a significant effect on boundary-layer behavior, useful results are obtained only in special low-turbulence wind tunnels. To date, the majority of wind-tunnel investigations for sailplane airfoils have been made by F. X. Wortmann and D. Althaus at the Stuttgart Laminar Wind Tunnel [203] and L. M. M. Boermans at the Delft University of Technology. A highly useful collection of wind-tunnel data is found in the Stuttgart Profile Catalog [167, 168]. See also

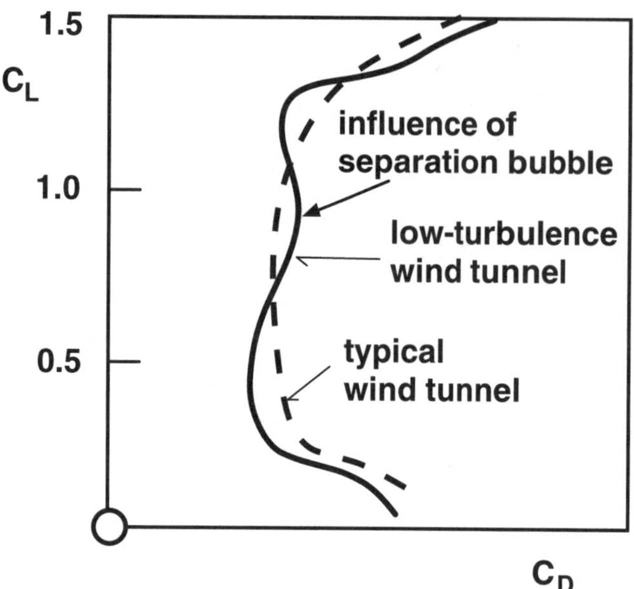

Fig. 193: Airfoil performance data measured for airfoil with laminar bubble in a low-turbulence wind tunnel compared with results obtained in conventional wind tunnel.

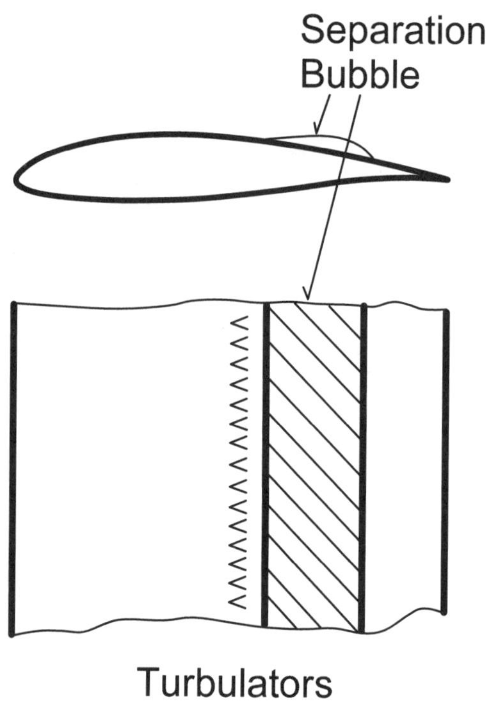

Fig. 194: Application of turbulators for inhibiting formation of laminar bubble.

D. Althaus [164] and M. Selig *et al* [194] for wind-tunnel data applicable to airfoils operating at very low Reynolds numbers.

Airfoils have also been tested in wind tunnels with relatively high turbulence levels [227]. The difficulty here is that the drag may appear too low at high coefficients of lift. In flight, or in a low-turbulence wind tunnel, boundary-layer transition may be accompanied by a laminar bubble, with associated drag increase. Freestream turbulence in a general-purpose wind tunnel can trigger boundary-layer transition, inhibiting formation of the laminar bubble (see also Fig. 24). Figure 193 compares drag data for a generic airfoil measured in wind tunnels of different flow quality. It is possible to prevent the formation of a laminar bubble by bonding "turbulators" such as small pieces of bent wire, "zig-zag", "bump", or "dimple" tape, or installing pneumatic turbulators directly ahead of the transition point (Fig. 194). Another approach is to cement a thin layer of abrasive powder to the airfoil surface [1].

Certain details, such as the drag produced by deployed dive brakes, are largely independent of Reynolds number and do not require a low-turbulence wind tunnel.

Wind-tunnel measurements on complete models of sailplanes are rarely performed and of relatively little value since, once a model has been scaled to fit in a wind-tunnel test section, the Reynolds number is inevitably too low.

Flight Test

The sailplane as wind tunnel

Reliable airfoil data may also be obtained in flight by mounting a wing section on a sailplane, as shown in Figs. 195 and 196. The section can be of full scale chordwise and constructed in the same manner as the wing of the actual aircraft. By operating the sailplane at appropriately chosen airspeeds and varying the angle of attack of the test section, high quality experimental data may be obtained at full-scale Reynolds numbers over a wide range of operating conditions. The only correction required is a small adjustment to account for flow distortion due to the wing upwash. The pressure distribution over the airfoil test section is obtained via a row of pressure taps drilled along the axis of

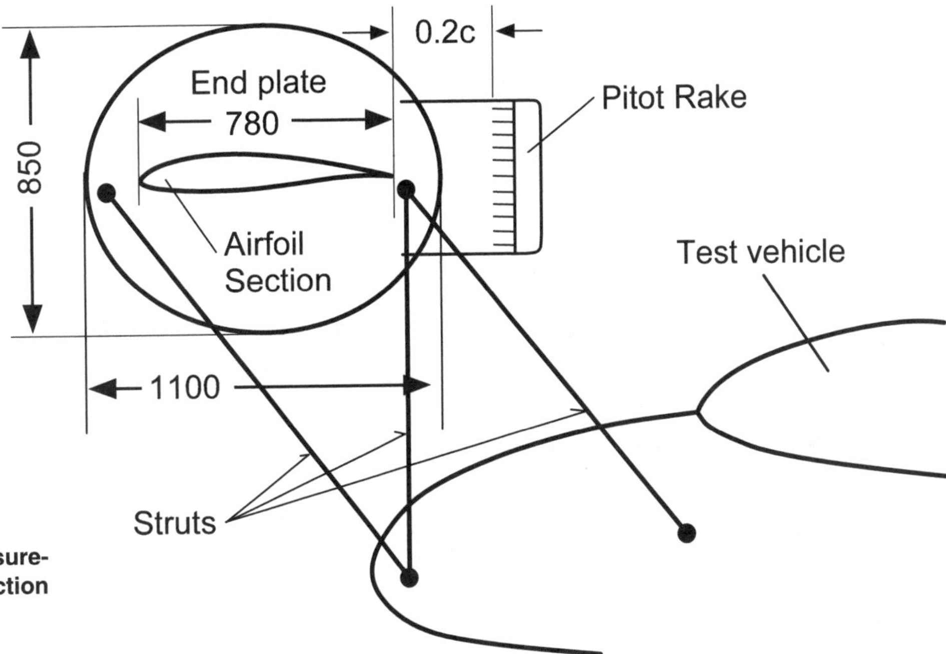

Fig. 195: Apparatus for inflight measurement of two-dimensional airfoil section at full-scale Reynolds numbers.
Test section has span of 1.5 m.

Fig. 196: In the early 1970's, the Akaflieg Braunschweig, together with the DLR, began to conduct airfoil measurements in free flight using a specially modified "Kranich III". This was subsequently replaced with a two-place Janus, pictured here with K. H. Horstmann at the controls. The main-wheel/nose-wheel landing gear arrangement shown here has become common in aircraft designed for club and training use.

symmetry. Numerical integration of the pressure distribution provides the airfoil lift and pitching moment. The drag is obtained using a Pitot rake. These methods may also be employed to measure the sectional aerodynamic loads on the wing itself (Figs. 201, 200).

The boundary-layer transition point can be determined using a stethoscope fitted at the end with a thin metal tube. When the open end of the metal tube is drawn along the surface of the airfoil from leading to trailing edge, a noticeable change in the sound will occur at the transition point. A far superior method employs infrared imaging techniques to map the boundary-layer transition zone in great detail. There is usually a small temperature difference between the surface of a body and the surrounding air and the resulting heat transfer varies according to the characteristics of the boundary layer. Modern infrared cameras are capable of imaging the resulting differences in infrared radiation at the appropriate wavelength. See also A. Quast [220].

Areas of separated flow are identified using tufts attached to the surface of the aircraft. This method is especially useful for observing the areas of flow separation over the wing when operating at high lift coefficient. Tufting is also used to evaluate the flow in the area of the wing-fuselage junction (Figs. 197, 198; see also [210]).

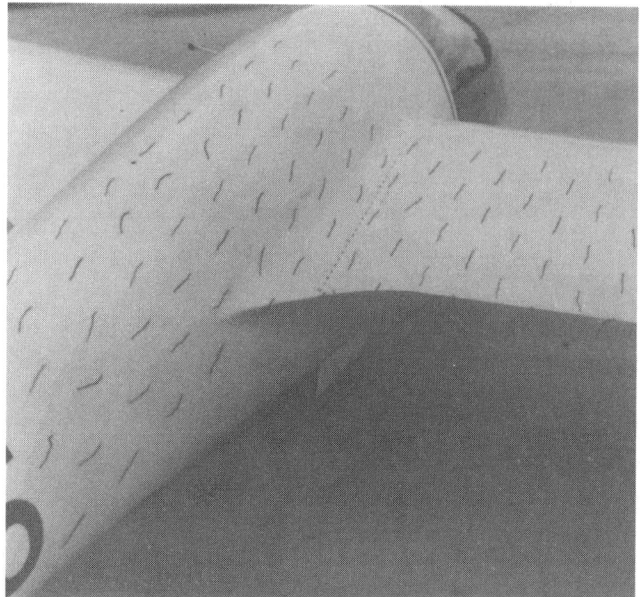

Fig. 197: Tufting study to detect separation in the wing-fuselage junction region. Short tufts of yarn are bonded to the wing and fuselage upper surfaces (left) and filmed with a camera mounted to the tail boom (right) at various operating conditions. Tufting studies often provide clues to improving the flow around the wing-fuselage junction.

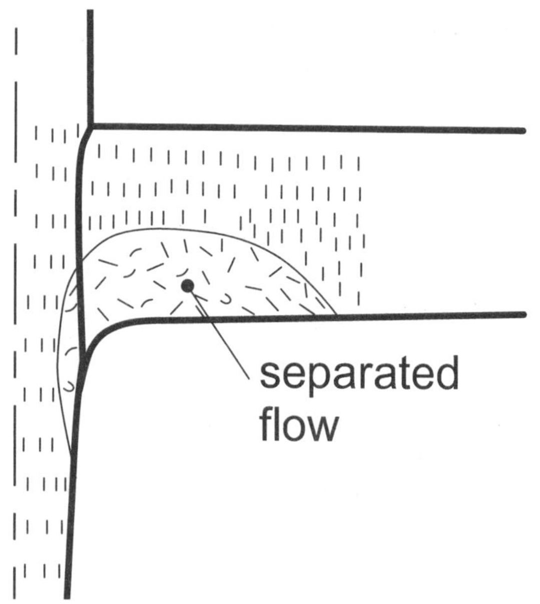

Fig. 198: Tufting applied to wing and fuselage to determine areas of flow separation.

Sailplane flight testing

A significant part of the effort required to certify a new sailplane design — for example, compliance with the structural requirements — may be completed using analytic methods. Compliance with other regulatory requirements, in particular those pertaining to operating characteristics, can be demonstrated only by flight test.

Certification flight testing requires instrumentation of suitable precision. Air data measurements (static and dynamic pressure) demand particular attention. It is almost always necessary to calibrate the air data system using a "static bomb" towed from the aircraft (Fig. 200). Static calibration flights of this kind are discussed by H. J. Merklein [217] (see also Fig. 202). Other specialized equipment includes hand-held spring scales for measuring control forces, a measuring tape affixed to the instrument panel with suction cups for measuring the stick positions, and a test rig for the tow release. A suitably marked clear plastic template (the "phi-psi-theta") suffices to measure the aircraft attitude (see Fig. 199).

Before testing begins, the sailplane is carefully weighed

Cockpit Flight Test Instrumentation

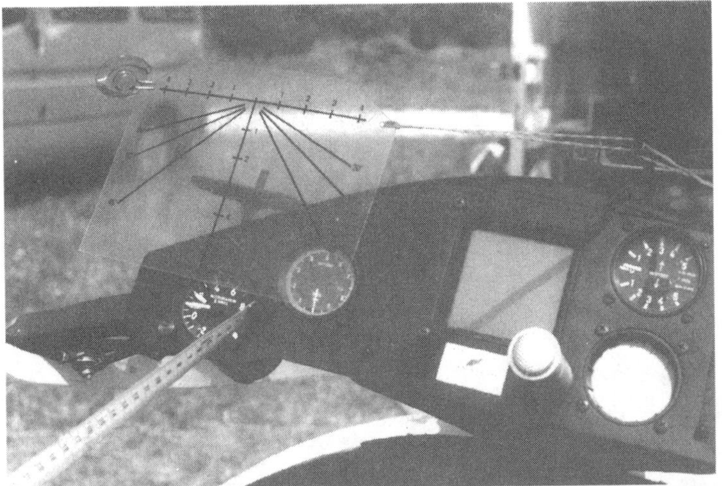

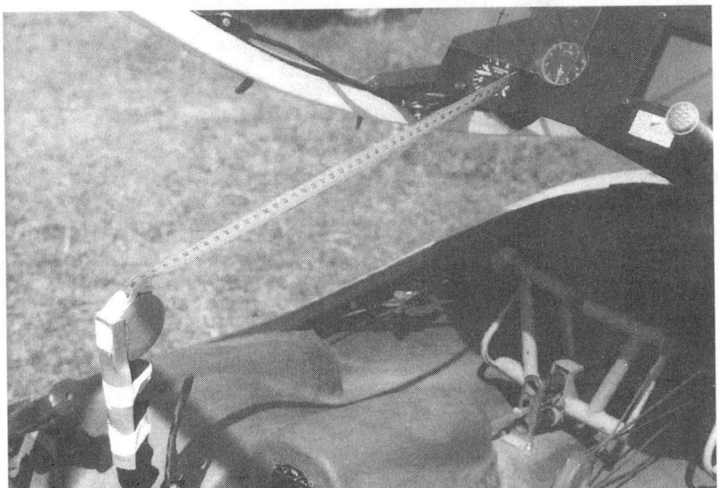

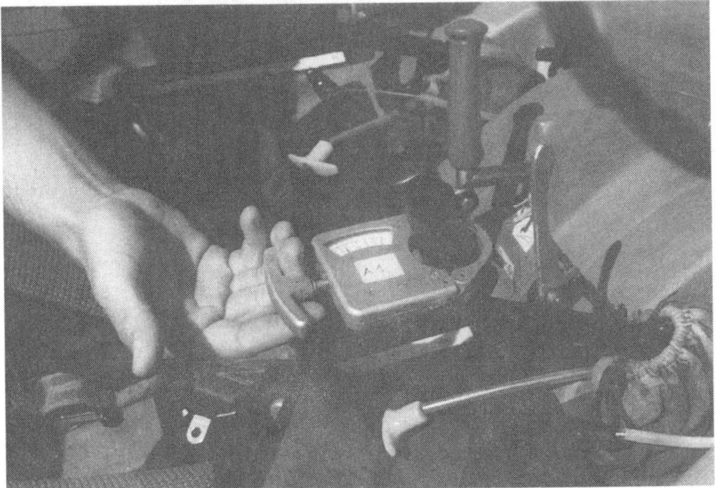

Fig. 199: The measurements required for the flying qualities evaluation (certification tests and/or "Zacher" program) can be made with relatively simple instrumentation. Top, the "phi-psi-theta", a clear plastic template marked to help pilot determine the aircraft attitude. The horizontal scale allows estimation of sideslip angles. The aircraft is first trimmed in coordinated flight with the template centered on an external landmark. Sideslip is introduced until the landmark lines up with the appropriate value on the sideslip scale. Center, a tape measure taped to the stick for measurement of longitudinal stick position. The free end of the tape is hooked to a knob on the instrument panel. Suction cups are also used. Bottom: a simple spring scale for measuring control forces. Cockpit shown is that of the D-41, a side-by-side multiplace from the Akaflieg Darmstadt.

Fig. 200: Experimental setup for inflight measurement of airfoil drag. Left, a Pitot rake is mounted to the wing to measure dynamic pressure within the wing wake. The rake comprises a number of small Pitot tubes distributed in the spanwise direction and is driven with an electric motor to traverse the wake vertically. Right, a trailing "static bomb", deployed in flight to provide an accurate source of ambient static pressure.

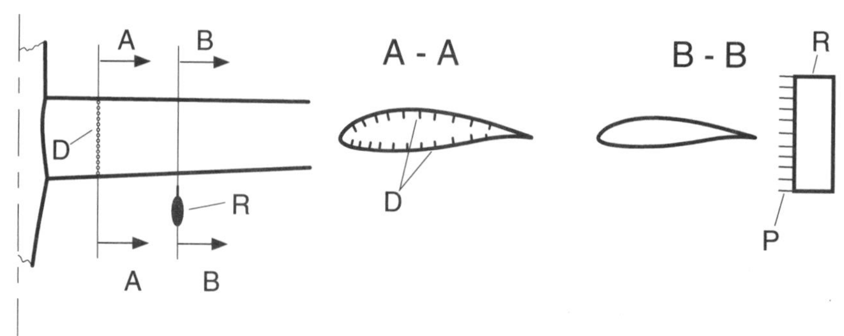

Fig. 201: Measurement of pressure distribution and profile drag on wing in flight.

D Pressure taps
R Pitot rake
P Pitot probes

and its center of gravity determined. Flight tests must be conducted over the entire center of gravity range, including the critical case of the center of gravity 10mm or 1% of the mean chord aft of the rear limit. The aft CG flights are often conducted with disposable ballast (water or sand) installed near the tail of the aircraft, so that in an emergency (for example, an uncontrollable spin) the ballast can be released, shifting the center of gravity forward. Anti-spin chutes (tail-mounted drogue chutes) are often installed as well (Fig. 207). For all test flying, the pilot is equipped with a parachute and must be well versed in the bailout procedure. Some critical tests (such as flutter testing) are performed at relatively high altitudes (2000m or higher) to allow margin for recovery or bailout in the event of emergency.

The most important tests required for type certification are outlined as follows. More detailed information is found

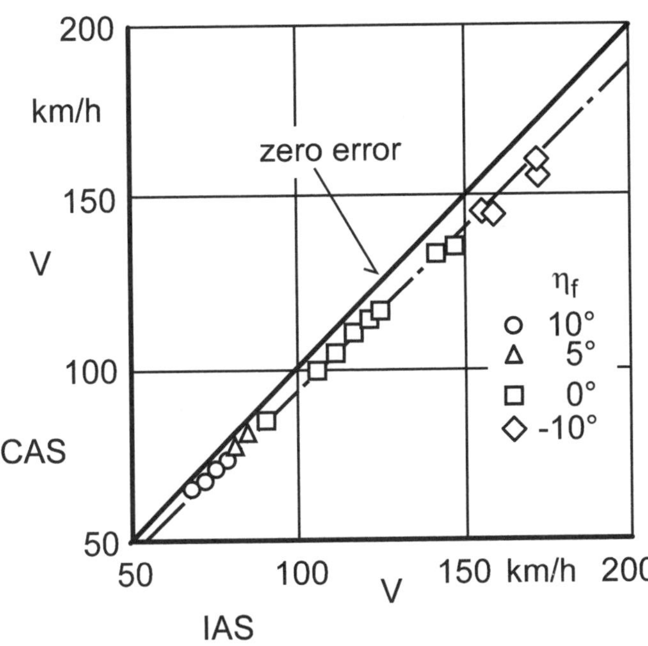

Fig. 202: Sample airspeed system calibration data. Based on flight tests with static bomb.

IAS Indicated Airspeed
CAS Calibrated Airspeed

in JAR-22 [49].

A number of these tests are performed on the ground, including measurements of control system stiffness and friction, control cable tension, and maximum control deflections. The tow release must function flawlessly under all foreseeable combinations of tow rope tension and angle. Figure 203 shows typical force/deflection measurements for elevator and ailerons. The hysteresis in the control force curve provides a measure of the control system friction.

The regulations require demonstration of aero tows and winch launches at all allowable combinations of center of gravity and airspeed. Takeoffs with a crosswind component of 15 km/h or 20% of stall speed must be demonstrated as well. The same applies to approaches and landings, whereby certain requirements pertaining to dive brake and retractable landing gear operation must also be satisfied. The dive brakes, for example, must provide a glide angle of 7:1 or steeper at $1.3V_{S_0}$.

Other flight characteristics to be investigated include controllability, trim effectiveness, stability, stall characteristics, spin behavior, and high speed handling. Special tests are conducted to verify that the aircraft is free from flutter and buffeting. It must also be shown that the following control forces are not exceeded:

	transient	steady state
pitch	20 daN	2.0 daN
roll	10 daN	1.5 daN
yaw	40 daN	10.0 daN
dive brakes tow release flaps landing gear	20 daN	

The elevator control force must exhibit a positive gradient with load factor for both pullups and turns. That is, increasing the load factor must require an increase in the control force. The stick force in a 45° turn entered from trimmed level flight at $1.4V_{S_1}$ must increase by no less than 0.5daN. Further requirements limit the force required to control the aircraft in extreme out-of-trim conditions.

The regulations pertaining to longitudinal static stability require the elevator control force to become increasingly forward (nose down) as the airspeed increases. Although it is also desirable for the stick position to move forward with increasing airspeed, a negative gradient is acceptable if the stick force gradient is adequate and no difficulties in control are observed. Longitudinal stability is demonstrated by trimming the sailplane at selected airspeeds between V_{S_1} and V_{NE}, applying control pressure to vary the airspeed by approximately 20%, and smoothly releasing the control pressure. The sailplane must return to within 15% or 15 km/h of its original trimmed speed. This test is conducted both in cruise and approach configurations.

Regarding longitudinal dynamic stability, JAR-22 requires all short period oscillations to be heavily damped, whether with controls free or controls fixed.

Of particular importance are the stall tests. These are conducted at an appropriate altitude, since in some cases large altitude losses may occur. Stall tests are initiated from level flight by reducing the airspeed gradually at a rate of 2 km/h per second until the aircraft pitches nose-down, drops a wing, or until the elevator reaches its aft stop. The aircraft must be controllable in roll and yaw without control reversal down to the airspeed where the stall begins. It must be possible, with normal use of the controls, to recover without

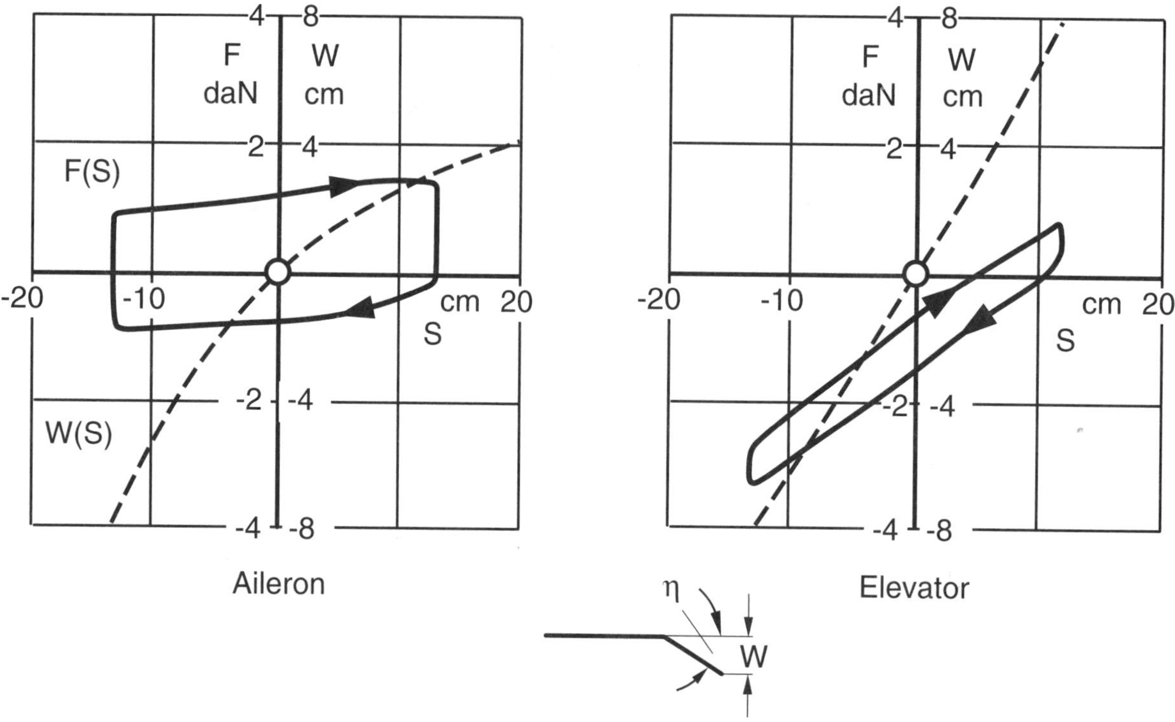

Fig. 203: Control system force-displacement measurements obtained in ground test [224].

exceeding a roll angle of 30°. There must be no uncontrollable tendency to enter a spin. Stalling characteristics must not be excessively sensitive to sideslip. This requirement may be satisfied by demonstrating no appreciable change up to 5° of sideslip. The altitude loss during recovery must be determined.

A steep nose-up stall test must also be performed with the sailplane in a typical winch launching configuration. From level flight at $1.2V_{S_1}$, the stick is rapidly pulled aft until a pitch attitude of 30° is reached. The resulting stall must not be so severe as to make a prompt recovery difficult.

The most critical of the level flight stall tests are repeated from a coordinated 45° banked turn. Uncontrollable rolling or spinning tendencies must not be encountered.

Whether turning or in level flight, the sailplane must provide a clear and distinct stall warning, either through its inherent aerodynamics (buffeting, vibration in controls or empennage) or through a special device. The warning must be audible or tactile — that is, a visual stall warning device is by itself not acceptable. A stall warning is not required if the sailplane exhibits sufficiently docile stalling characteristics. Specifically, it must be possible to control the sailplane in roll using ailerons alone, and there must be no significant tendency to drop a wing when both ailerons and rudder are held neutral.

Spin tests are required for all configurations, including the entire center of gravity range and asymmetric water ballast (unless the design of the ballast system makes this condition unlikely). Following a spin of at least five turns, the sailplane must be able to recover within one turn following application of anti-spin control. The altitude required for the recovery is also to be determined. Under any circumstances it must be impossible to enter an uncontrollable spin, even with intentional misuse of the controls. If the spin tends to degenerate into a spiral dive, it must be possible to recover within airspeed and load factor limitations without use of the dive brakes.

The dive brakes must be sufficiently powerful to prevent the sailplane from exceeding V_{NE} in a dive of 45° (sailplanes certified for aerobatics or cloud flying) or 30° (all others). It must be possible to operate the dive brakes safely at any airspeed up to $1.05V_{NE}$.

Freedom from flutter in all configurations and at all airspeeds up to V_D must be demonstrated by both analysis and flight test. During the flight test, systematic attempts must be made to induce flutter up to V_{DF}, the maximum flight test demonstration speed ($V_{NE} \leq 0.90V_{DF}$). In many of the structural design loading conditions specified by the JAR, the design airspeeds, including V_D, are defined as equivalent airspeeds. However, in the case of flutter, the complexity of the problem makes it impossible to relate flutter characteristics to either a fixed equivalent or true airspeed. The question of how to extend the flutter flight test results to higher altitudes than actually tested has been discussed by W. Stender *et al* [160, 161]. See also [153, 211] for footage of a sailplane flutter flight test.

Performance measurement

Although it is now possible to predict sailplane performance to a fair degree of accuracy, a reliable assessment is possible only through inflight measurements of the actual aircraft. Wind-tunnel measurements of sailplane performance are generally of little use due to the difficulty in matching the full-scale Reynolds numbers.

Currently, two basic techniques are commonly used:

- timed descents, and
- side-by-side comparison flights,

The timed descent method requires several high altitude tows in the smoothest possible meteorological conditions. Since large scale vertical motion of the atmosphere cannot be measured directly, the results may be of only limited accuracy. Comparison flight testing, however, requires fewer flights and yields more accurate results. It has the disadvantage, however, of requiring a well calibrated aircraft of known performance.

In practice, these considerations have led to the measurement of a few individual sailplanes through timed descents and the use of these aircraft as calibrated references for comparison flight testing. Since sailplanes change with time, for example the quality of their surface finish, the sailplane must be recalibrated from time to time using the timed descent method. Performance is affected by weight and balance, so that care must be taken to ensure that the calibrated sailplane always operates at the same gross weight and center of gravity. Furthermore, an accurate calibration of the airspeed system is of utmost importance. Static errors are determined in flight using towed static probes [217] (Fig. 200). Other than errors in the measurement systems, the greatest source of error is the atmosphere itself (see also [216]). Although every attempt is made to conduct the tests in smooth atmospheric conditions, it is difficult to exclude the possibility of large-scale settling or rising of the airmass in which the test is conducted. These errors are minimized by conducting the tests at or perhaps even before sunrise at the greatest possible altitude (3000 to 4000m initial altitude). In the case of timed descents, steady glides at constant airspeed are flown for 2–5 minutes and the altitude loss determined from the altimeter. Every effort must be made to avoid unnecessary control inputs or sideslip. By observing the variometer, the pilot can often get a rough indication as to whether the measurements are being affected by vertical motion of the airmass.

The entire airspeed range is investigated at a number of discrete airspeeds. Due to the inevitable scatter in the data, each test must be repeated several times (usually at least five). The polar is determined by fitting a curve to the experimental data. Evaluation of the results and reduction to sea level is discussed by H. J. Merklein [216]. See also [210, 225].

In comparison flight testing, the reference and test sailplanes fly in formation adjacent to one another at constant airspeed. At the beginning and end of each test point, the two sailplanes are photographed from a powered airplane flying off to the side of the formation (Fig. 204). The airplane is positioned vertically so that the horizon appears in the photograph between the two sailplanes. The formation is held as steady as possible to minimize relative motion of the three aircraft. Parallax errors are minimized by having the two sailplanes fly as close as possible laterally and slightly staggered in the direction of flight, so that the nose of the trailing sailplane is positioned around 2m behind the tail of the leading sailplane. The results may be distorted by the fact that the trailing sailplane is operating in the downwash of the sailplane in front of it (see D. Hummel [207, 208]). For this reason an excessively tight formation is undesirable. Each measurement run lasts from two to five minutes. The change in the relative altitude between the two sailplanes together with the elapsed time leads directly to the relative sink speed. This procedure is repeated for a series of airspeeds. The re-

Fig. 204: Comparison performance testing at the annual Idaflieg summer meet. Each year a number of Akafliegs meet in Aalen, Germany to evaluate performance and flying qualities of new aircraft. Testing is conducted with the cooperation and supervision of the DLR. The photo shows a comparison flight between the calibrated aircraft (the DLR-owned "Holy Cirrus" — since replaced by a DG 300) and an ASW 20. The tow plane in the foreground serves as chase aircraft for taking the photos used to evaluate the relative sink rates of the two sailplanes.

sults are reduced to sea level to provide the airspeed polar of the aircraft being tested.

Recently, a satellite navigation system has been developed to measure the relative positions of the test and reference aircraft. This approach reduces workload and cost by eliminating the need for a photographer and chase aircraft (see A. Lipp [215]).

A large number of sailplanes have been tested using these methods. In particular, the numerous tests performed by H. Zacher, H. J. Merklein, H. Laurson, and G. Stich [212–214, 216, 218, 221, 225, 226, 229, 232–234] conducted in cooperation with Idaflieg and the DLR (formerly, the DFVLR) provide a good overview of the performance of modern sailplanes. Timed descent tests have also been conducted in the United States by R. Johnson [210] and P. F. Bikle [205].

The appropriate presentation of the performance data depends on their intended use. A pilot flying a contest or a cross-country flight uses the information to select the appropriate speed to fly, for general flight planning, and as an aid to making inflight tactical decisions. In this case, the airspeed polar is of the greatest interest. The designer, on the other hand, is also interested in an engineering assessment of the sailplane's aerodynamic characteristics, and here the drag polar is more appropriate. Neglecting the effects of the relatively small Reynolds number variations, every sailplane has a single drag polar, regardless of wing loading. The airspeed polar, however, varies with the wing loading and can be calculated from the drag polar. In order to provide a uniform basis for comparison, the Idaflieg airspeed polars are always presented for a wing loading based on empty mass plus 90 kg (180 kg for multiplace sailplanes). A selection of flight test results from the various publications cited above is presented in Fig. 205. Strictly speaking, these data apply only to the aircraft measured, and not necessarily to all other aircraft of the same type. Variations in surface quality, profile accuracy, insect contamination, and center of gravity may lead to differences in performance among individual examples of a given design. Figure 206 presents the results in a nondimensional form, allowing quick calculation of the airspeed polar for a

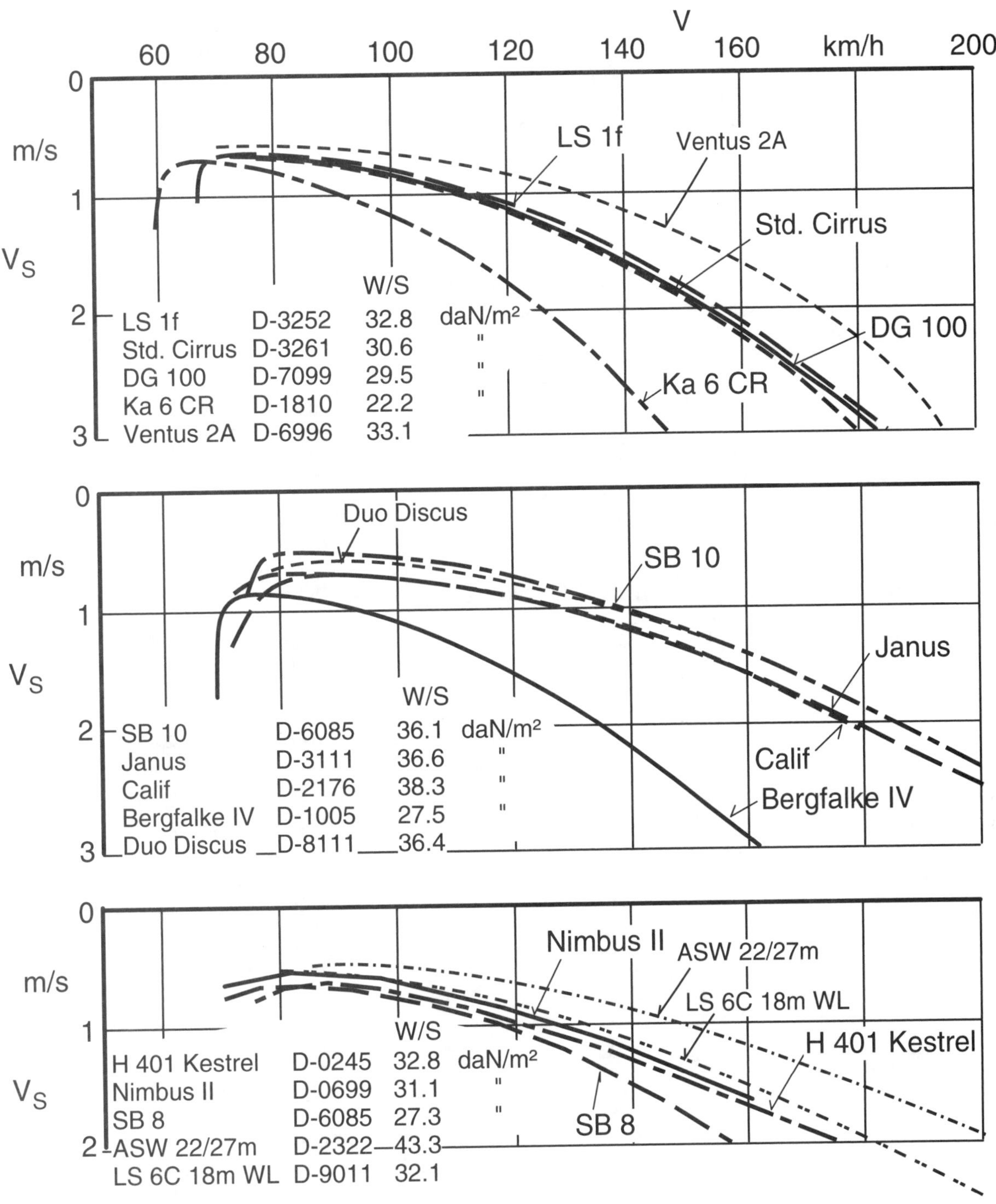

Fig. 205: Airspeed polars measured in flight for representative Standard Class, Multiplace, and Open Class sailplanes [213, 214].

Aircraft	Reg. No.	W/S [daN/m²]	max L/D	$V_{S_{min}}$… [m/s]	…at [km/h]	V_S at: 100 km/h [m/s]	150	180
Cirrus	D-0471	29.0	39.0	0.60	80	0.74	1.88	3.13
Nimbus II	D-2111	30.2	47.5	0.49	75	0.60	1.33	2.17
Kestrel 401	D-0475	32.8	42.0	0.59	84	0.65	1.35	2.12
D 36 V1	D-4685	29.3	44.0	0.53	82	0.65	1.47	(2.40)
ASW 17	D-1110	33.0	49.0	0.55	85	0.58	1.19	1.88
SB 8 V2	D-6085	27.7	40.0	0.62	86	0.70	1.67	(2.77)
Phoebus C	D-0559	25.6	39.0	0.63	83	0.73	1.76	
fs 29	D-2929	35-50	44.0	0.56	81	0.63	1.26	1.80
ASW 22 (27m)	D-2322	33.4	57.0	0.40	77	0.51	1.20	1.86
ASW 22 (25m)	D-2255	32.5	57.0	0.40	77	0.52	1.25	1.90
Nimbus 3 (24m)	D-5896	29.5	58.0	0.42	75	0.52	1.28	1.94
Std. Cirrus	D-3261	30.6	37.0	0.63	78	0.76	1.81	2.79
ASW 15	D-0510	27.7	36.5	0.63	77	0.80	1.93	
LS 1c	D-0558	29.5	36.0	0.63	78	0.80	2.02	
LS 1f	D-3252	32.8	37.0	0.62	73	0.76	1.72	2.74
DG 100	D-7099	29.5	37.0	0.60	75	0.78	1.88	(2.95)
Elfe S 4	D-6301	28.4	34.5	0.69	78	0.82	1.75	2.70
fs 25	D-8141	28.5	38.5	0.60	79	0.79	2.12	
D 38	D-0938	27.3	37.0	0.62	78	0.78	1.82	2.97
Discus A	D-6111	29.7	42.0	0.59	82	0.65	1.50	2.77
ASW 24	D-1124	33.0	43.0	0.57	84	0.65	1.40	2.20
LS 4	D-2628	31.6	40.0	0.61	82	0.68	1.50	2.62
LS 7	D-5774	33.3	42.0	0.63	89	0.66	1.35	2.45
DG 300	D-1300	33.2	41.0	0.60	83	0.68	1.53	2.70
Discus WL	D-4045	31.8	42.0	0.58	80	0.66	1.37	2.50
Libelle 301	D-9412	29.8	40.5	0.59	82	0.70	1.60	
LS 3 a	D-3917	32.6	41.0	0.62	83	0.68	1.48	2.22
Mosquito	D-0471	34.0	41.0	0.61	83	0.68	1.40	2.20
Mini-Nimbus	D-4986	34.2	41.0	0.61	85	0.67	1.41	2.26
DG 200	D-6781	34.4	41.0	0.62	86	0.69	1.45	2.18
ASW 20	D-7474	32.2	41.5	0.62	84	0.68	1.41	2.20
Ventus CT	D-KITL	39.1	42.0	0.67	82	0.68	1.20	2.00
Ventus B	D-4060	34.3	42.0	0.59	80	0.64	1.34	2.05
ASW 20C	D-4859	34.3	42.0	0.60	80	0.67	1.34	1.95
LS 6	D-0322	33.2	42.0	0.59	82	0.66	1.30	1.90
DG 600	D-1666	32.5	42.0	0.59	85	0.65	1.36	2.00
ASW 27	D-8115	36.3	45.6	0.56	75	0.61	1.28	1.95
LS 8WL	D-1871	33.0	42.5	0.59	82	0.65	1.32	2.40
Ventus 2A	D-6996	33.1	44.5	0.55	75	0.61	1.35	2.20
ASH 26 (18m)	D-2603	34.2	46.3	0.52	75	0.62	1.16	1.88
LS 6c (18m)	D-9011	32.1	46.2	0.52	75	0.61	1.24	2.00
SB 10 (26 m)	D-6085	36.1	48.5	0.53	85	0.57	1.19	1.83
Calif	D-2176	38.3	38.0	0.69	80	0.74	1.28	1.99
Janus	D-3111	36.6	38.5	0.73	92	0.75	1.33	1.97
Twin Astir	D-4857	33.4	36.3	0.74	92	0.77	1.54	2.32
G-103C Twin III	D-4279	32.4	37.0	0.64	82	0.76	1.83	3.05
ASH 25	D-1025	40.7	57.0	0.46	82	0.52	1.12	1.68
Nimbus 3DT	D-KEXX	42.8	57.0	0.49	87	0.50	1.02	1.55
G 103 II	D-4279	32.4	37.0	0.64	82	0.76	1.83	3.05
Duo-Discus	D-8111	36.4	45.0	0.59	85	0.61	1.17	1.82

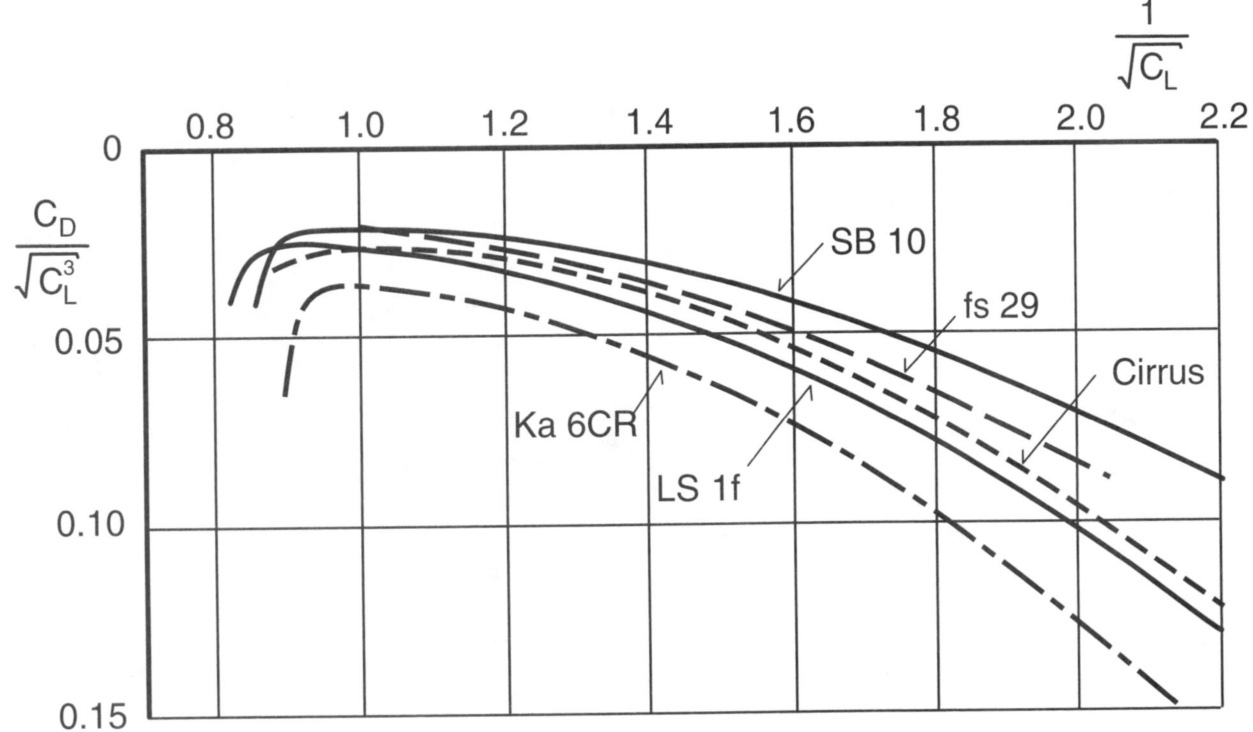

Fig. 206: Drag polars based on flight test results for SB 10, Cirrus, fs 29, LS 1f, and Ka-6.

given wing loading.

Additional flight test results are summarized in Table 7; see also [189, 228].

Flying qualities

A fatigued pilot cannot make full use of the sailplane's capabilities. Good flying qualities are essential if the pilot is to perform well during long flights. While it is relatively easy to rate performance using numerical data such as polars, establishing objective criteria for the evaluation of sailplane flying qualities is considerably more difficult. H. Zacher has made a great contribution to the soaring community by developing a comprehensive set of handling qualities criteria based on his many years of experience flight testing sailplanes [231]. These criteria have to a large extent been adopted in the certification regulations. Numerous flying qualities evaluations are found in works by H. Zacher, H. Laurson, and G. Stich [209, 212, 213, 221, 225, 226, 229–231, 233], based primarily on results obtained at the annual Idaflieg "Sommertreffen" flight test workshops (see [219, 223] for descriptions of the Idaflieg summer meets). The Zacher program is reproduced in full in Appendix 2. Bennett [204] examined the flying qualities of several sailplanes using the Cooper-Harper rating system [206]. Additional qualitative evaluations have been provided by P. Bikle [205], G. Moffat [18], and R. Johnson [210].

The most important questions to be answered in flight test fall in the following categories:

Table 7: Selected results from comparison flight tests conducted by Idaflieg and the DLR from 1968-98.
The results apply to the specific aircraft listed by registration number and are not necessarily valid for other aircraft of the same type. The data were assembled from various sources [213, 214, 225, 229]. Multiplace sailplanes were tested with pilot and passenger.

- Cockpit layout, visibility, and ergonomics
- Takeoff and tow
- Slow flight and stalling behavior
- Level flight and trim
- Control harmony (aileron and rudder)
- Control forces, displacement, effectiveness, harmony
- Longitudinal stability
- Directional stability
- Dihedral effect
- Glide path control (dive brakes, flaps)
- Landing
- Thermaling

Cockpit layout includes such items as pilot comfort, control arrangement, instrumentation, visibility, and ventilation.

The takeoff and tow evaluation considers the distance required to liftoff, the airspeed and pitch angle at liftoff, and control effectiveness during the takeoff run. The control loads are assessed in aero tow. For winch tow, any pitch-up tendency is identified and the back-pressure tow hook release is evaluated. Any unusual operating characteristics are identified and noted.

The stall behavior is evaluated at a safe altitude, first by a series of stalls from level, zero-slip flight. These are entered with a deceleration of 1 to 2 km/h per second. The wings are held level with the rudder, and, if required, the ailerons. The behavior is categorized as follows:

- the sailplane settles at a steady airspeed and rate of sink. This is considered especially docile behavior.
- the sailplane pitches nose down in a pronounced manner, during which both rudder and ailerons remain effective. This also qualifies as docile behavior.
- uncontrollable pitch and roll motions develop due to asymmetrical flow separation over the wing, leading to sudden dropping of a wing, possibly with subsequent spin. Such behavior is rated as unacceptable.

Fig. 207: Temporary spin chute installation on fs 33. The teardrop container holding the chute is released from the cockpit by a cable. When deployed in an uncontrollable spin, the chute facilitates recovery by reducing the rate of rotation, pitching the aircraft nose down, and limiting speed buildup during recovery from the subsequent dive. The chute is removed following the spin tests.

Stall tests are repeated from 10° slips, in 30° banked turns, and with flaps and dive brakes extended. The tendency to enter accelerated stalls is investigated by pulling back rapidly on the stick. Before conducting any stall tests, it is extremely important to verify the weight and balance, since an extreme aft center of gravity can lead to an uncontrollable spin. A spin chute is strongly recommended (Fig. 207).

The level flight evaluation is conducted at 1.4 times the stall speed. If equipped with a trim system, the stick force is trimmed out, whereby the control system friction may be evaluated.

Control forces and deflections are measured using (for example) hand-held spring scales and tape measures (Fig. 199). Good control harmony (the relative control pressures and deflections in the three axes) is of primary importance. Here, however, the rating relies primarily on the pilot's subjective evaluation. Particular attention is paid to adverse yaw and ease of coordination. The following tests are flown at 1.4 times the stall speed:

- Aileron effectiveness: The sailplane is placed in level flight with the rudder held fixed. Full aileron is applied over a period of 0.5 to 1 second. The time to reach

30° of bank and the resulting slip angle are measured.

- Yaw-roll coupling: evaluated indirectly by measuring the time required to level the wings from a 30°turn using full rudder input and with stick fixed.

- Roll rate: From a 45° turn, the aircraft is rolled into a 45° turn in the opposite direction. The time required to reverse the turn provides a measure of the maneuverability and is noted on the form. The maneuver is performed with rudder as required (or available) to keep the yaw string centered.

- Control effectiveness while slipping: With the rudder deflected to its stop, an attempt is made to maintain straight flight using the ailerons alone. The resulting slip and bank angles are estimated, as well as the control forces and deflections. Particular attention is paid to the possibility of rudder pedal force reversal (rudder lock).

- Rudder effectiveness with respect to adverse yaw: Repeated roll reversals of ±30° bank are performed using full aileron. Rudder is applied as required to maintain coordinated flight. If the rudder available is insufficient to keep the yaw string centered, the maneuver is repeated with reduced aileron input.

The longitudinal stability evaluation considers stick-fixed and stick-free static stability as well as longitudinal dynamic stability.

- Stick-fixed stability is evaluated starting at level flight at 1.4 times the stall speed. The test pilot verifies that the changes in stick position required to trim to a new airspeed occur in the proper direction. That is, an increase in trim airspeed should require a more forward stick position, and vice versa. The CG location can significantly affect this result.

- The stick-free case is evaluated by measuring the stick forces required to trim at various airspeeds. Here also the result is strongly dependent on CG location.

- Longitudinal dynamic stability is investigated starting from trimmed level flight. Without changing the trim setting, the airspeed is varied by 15 km/h and the stick released. The maximum and minimum airspeeds encountered during the subsequent oscillations are noted — these data are used to estimate the damping of the transient motion. In addition, a stopwatch is used to measure the period of the motion (typically around 15 sec.). Excessive control system friction or binding can distort the results. During this test it is important to ensure that the sailplane remains in coordinated level flight.

The directional stability investigation begins from a steady slip with about 1/3 rudder. All controls are released, and the resulting motion is observed, during which the airspeed is held as constant as possible using gentle elevator inputs. The aircraft may return to slip-free flight in a well-damped, aperiodic fashion, with damped yaw oscillations, or it may be directionally unstable. Spiral dive tendencies are evaluated as well.

Dive brakes are evaluated by observing the sink rate with dive brakes applied. The forces required to deploy the brakes are noted, as well as the transient reaction (pitch up or down) of the aircraft following deployment, changes in longitudinal trim and buffeting characteristics.

Landing characteristics of interest include visibility in final approach and flare, effectiveness of dive brakes and slip for glide path control, touchdown and rollout, landing gear stiffness and stroke, braking distance, and touchdown attitude (in particular, the preferred touchdown method — two-point, tail first, etc.).

Finally, an overall subjective impression is recorded. This provides the pilot the opportunity to note particularly good or bad qualities.

The flight test form developed by H. Zacher [231] is provided in Appendix 2, together with an example of a completed form. Control force measurements have been presented earlier in Fig. 190.

Trends in Sailplane Development

Class Definitions

As a consequence of the various optimization considerations discussed in the preceding chapters, sailplane designs have converged on a common set of basic design characteristics, such as relatively high aspect ratios and tapered wing planforms. Nevertheless, considerable room remains for the designer to provide the aircraft with a unique character.

For example, in some cases a relatively thick airfoil, optimized for climb, together with a high wing loading, can provide as good a result as a relatively thin airfoil and reduced wing loading. Additional design decisions concern the layout of the wing-fuselage junction, where the basic shoulder-wing or mid-wing configurations may be combined with various fuselage forms and wing root fairings. The control system, empennage, flaps, and dive brakes also provide a room for the designer's individual tastes. Although the wing planform is, of necessity, nearly elliptical, there is room to choose between a single, double, or multiple-taper planform, a straight or a canted leading or trailing edge, and various wing tip designs, including winglets.

On the other hand, aircraft that depart significantly from the conventional configuration, for example canards or flying-wings, will probably remain relatively rare. The experience base for these unusual configurations is comparatively small, and their development effort can be quite high, as illustrated by the case of the SB-13.

Certain design constraints and limitations are established by the class definitions. These are primarily intended to limit development and manufacturing costs, and, in turn, the cost of the finished sailplane. Class definitions also serve as a means for allowing competition among pilots flying sailplanes of similar capabilities.

Currently, the following classes are defined:

- Open Class
- 18m Class
- FAI 15m Racing Class
- Standard Class
- Club Class (in USA, Sports Class)
- World Class
- 1-26 (non-FAI; primarily USA)
- Multiplace

The Open Class is entirely free of design restrictions other than those imposed by airworthiness regulations. FAI 15m class sailplanes are limited only by a 15m wingspan restriction. Additional requirements placed on the Standard Class include the prohibition of camber-changing flaps (even if locked and sealed in a fixed position), a minimum size for the main wheel, and the provision of dive brakes.

From a design point of view, the Club Class is also an unrestricted class. Although water ballast may not be used, a water ballast system may be installed on the aircraft. In order to allow participation of older sailplanes that are no longer competitive in other FAI competition classes, the Club Class specifies a handicapping factor to be applied in contests. A list of handicapping factors is currently maintained by the German Aero Club [54]. In England, the British Gliding Association (BGA) maintains its own handicapping list [52,66,67] and in the United States this class is administered under similar rules as the Sports Class [64].

The 18m and World Class are presently in their early stages. The 18m Class is intended to fill the gap that has developed between the 15m Class and the Open Class as the latter has evolved towards expensive sailplanes with wingspans exceeding 25m. That this class fills an important niche is demonstrated by the proliferation of sailplanes featuring interchangeable wingtips that allow the span to be extended from 15 to 16.5 or 18 m. Sailplanes such as the SB-14, ASH 26E, DG800S, and Ventus 2 are likely to become quite popular in this class.

Another interesting new class is the "World Class", discussed in an earlier chapter. However, as the World Class design has already been chosen, from the designer's point of view it is interesting only as a case study.

The Open Class remains an interesting proving ground for new design concepts. Aerodynamic configurations in this class are limited only by the designer's creativity and imagination. The most recent attempt to expand the sailplane design envelope is the "eta", discussed earlier. With a span of 30.9m and an aspect ratio of 51.3, this sailplane is expected to achieve a glide ratio in excess of 60:1.

It should be kept in mind that the class definitions evolve with time. For example, as originally introduced in the late 1950's, the Standard Class prohibited retractable landing gear and water ballast, both of which were allowed by the end of the 1960's.

Evolution of the Sailplane

One hundred years have passed since Otto Lilienthal's first gliding flights, and just over 75 years since the actual beginning of sailplane development at the Wasserkuppe in 1920. That the sport of soaring has made enormous progress during this time is evident when one compares the Lilienthal's first flights of only 100 m with the current list of world records, including a distance flight of over 2000 km, an absolute altitude of nearly 15,000 m, and speed records exceeding 200 km/h.

This development is interesting to trace. A recent book by G. Brinkmann and H. Zacher [32] provides an excellent account of the technical development of the sailplane from Lilienthal to the present and contains what is perhaps the most extensive collection of technical data presently available. The history of sailplane development is also discussed in books by G. Brütting [33], P. F. Selinger [35, 45, 141], and D. Geistmann [36, 37]. P. Riedel, a well known soaring pilot, has written a first-hand account of the first two decades of sailplane development that is also worth reading [38–40]. For a comprehensive history of soaring in the United States, see P. A. Schweizer [43] and W. Schweizer [44].

Since ample literature on the topic already exists, what follows is limited to a short overview of the history of sailplane development. Only the most important milestones in the long path from the early wood and fabric sailplanes to modern high performance carbon fiber aircraft will be discussed. Basic design data and three-view drawings of typical sailplanes representing the various phases of development are provided in Appendix 1.

Wooden Sailplanes

The first sailplane that could no longer be categorized simply as a "glider" was built in 1922 by Akaflieg Hannover. This aircraft, the "Vampyr", flew the world's first multi-hour flights in ridge lift at the Wasserkuppe and exhibited many of the design features characteristic of modern sailplanes, such as an enclosed fuselage and cockpit and a high aspect ratio wing of sufficient thickness to allow a load-carrying spar and torsion-box (Fig. 208). In the following 20 years, sailplanes evolved steadily, with performance improving thanks to unbraced wings and clean design. Wing loadings steadily increased as interest shifted from endurance flying on ridges to cross-country flying using thermals. Significant sailplanes from this period include the Konsul, Fafnir, Austria, Grunau Baby, Rhönadler, Minimoa (Fig. 209), Windspiel, Olympia Meise, Weihe, and D-30 (Fig. 210).

During this time, an interesting branch of development arose with the flying wing designs of the Horten brothers [82, 141, 142]. Although these aircraft were among the highest performing sailplanes of their day, the configuration gradually lost its competitive edge when it began to appear that longitudinal stability and trim considerations would preclude the use of the new laminar airfoils then being introduced. Recently, renewed interest in flying wings has developed, for example with the SB-13 of Akaflieg Braunschweig [140, 145] and the Genesis [144], both of which have demonstrated the potential as well as the limitations of this configuration.

In Germany, postwar sailplane development resumed in the early 1950's. Up to that time, the standard for performance had been established by the "Weihe" and a few similar designs. Until the mid 1950's, soaring competitions

Sailplanes of the pre-war era

Fig. 208: The "Vampyr", designed and built by students of the Akaflieg Hannover. Flown in ridge lift at the Wasserkuppe, this became the first sailplane to complete multi-hour flights. The design, due largely to G. Madelung, is characterized by a number of — for that era — revolutionary design features. Some of these, for example the high-aspect ratio wing with single embedded spar and D-tube leading edge, and low-drag enclosed fuselage, remain basic design features of sailplanes to this day. Far advanced over the primary gliders of its day, the "Vampyr" was the first aircraft that could actually be termed a "sailplane".

Fig. 209: The "Minimoa", by Wolf Hirth, a well-known high-performance sailplane of the 1930's. Numerous cross-country flights were made with this machine. This was the first production high-performance sailplane to be built in numbers greater than 100. The distinctive gull-wing, developed by F. Wenk, provided the aircraft with excellent lateral stability, making it suitable for cloud-flying. A. Lippisch had earlier employed a gull-wing for aerodynamic reasons in the "Fafnir".

Fig. 210: With the D-30, students of Akaflieg Darmstadt reached the limits of performance possible with the technology then available. Featuring new airfoils and construction techniques, a 20.10 m wingspan, and an aspect ratio of 33.6, the sailplane achieved a glide ratio of 38 and a minimum sink speed of 0.55 m/s.

Wooden Sailplanes of the Post-War Era

Fig. 211: Following the war, sailplane development continued on the path set by wooden pre-war designs such as the "Weihe". The Ka-6, designed by R. Kaiser, first flew in 1955 and won the OSTIV prize for the best Standard Class Design at the 1958 World Championships. Ka-6's were in production at Schleicher for nearly 15 years, with a total of over 1300 produced in various models. Heinz Huth won in Standard Class at the 1960 and 1963 Worlds and became German National Champion six times, all in a Ka-6.

Fig. 212: Characteristic of the Munich School was wooden wing/steel tube fuselage construction. This robust construction was also favored by Egon Scheibe, a graduate of the Akaflieg Munich. The 17m Zugvogel III enjoyed considerable competition success during the 1950's and 60's. Steel tube fuselages became especially popular in two-seaters as their ruggedness proved valuable in training operations.

Fig. 213: The HKS III is a one-off sailplane from the design team of Haase, Kensche, and Schmetz. With features such as a laminar airfoil, exceptional surface quality, carefully hinged and blended ailerons and flaps, drogue chute, and water ballast, this sailplane represented the culmination of wooden sailplane development. E. G. Haase demonstrated the sailplane's excellent performance with a decisive win in the 1958 World Championships in Poland. The HKS III was later flown for many years by Akaflieg Braunschweig.

were dominated by these aircraft, with the "Weihe" winning the World Championships in 1948 and 1950. Some new multiplace sailplanes appeared during these postwar years, including the "Kranich III", the "Bergfalke", and the Schweizer 2-22. In the United States, numerous surplus military training gliders such as Schweizer TG-2's and TG-3's, Pratt-Read G1's and Laister-Kauffmann LK-10's entered civilian service (the LK-10 had actually been a prewar civilian design). Other than steel tube fuselages, these aircraft offered little in the way of technological innovation (see Fig. 212).

A decisive improvement came with the introduction of laminar airfoils. The sensitivity these airfoils exhibit to surface quality and profile accuracy presented a significant challenge to manufacturers who, at the time, were primarily using wooden construction (although one of the first sailplanes to employ a laminar flow airfoil, the Ross RJ-5 [20], did feature a metal wing). Careful attention to design details led to the success of the HKS I and III, which set new standards for sailplane performance (Fig. 213). This was amply demonstrated when the designer, E. G. Haase, won the 1958 World Championships in the HKS III by a decisive margin. Despite this success, the HKS aircraft did not mark the beginning of a new era in design, but rather the high point and conclusion of the development of the wooden sailplane. The advent of fiberglass allowed manufacturers to achieve the performance of the HKS aircraft with considerably less manufacturing effort. However, before fiberglass finally revolutionized sailplane design and manufacture, another significant wooden design appeared. This aircraft, the Ka-6 was designed at about the time the Standard Class was formed and enjoyed worldwide popularity (Fig. 211). Built in great numbers, this was the most successful and frequently flown wooden sailplane of the 1960's. Other wood-era designs worthy of mention include the SB-5, Standard Austria, SHK, Foka, Zefir, K-8, and ASK-13.

Metal Sailplanes

Compared with wood and fiberglass, metal construction has enjoyed only limited popularity with sailplane designers. As with wood, the primary difficulty lies in the effort required to manufacture aircraft with adequate tolerances and surface quality. Good results may often be obtained by applying a thin layer of filler to the wings and sanding to match a set of airfoil templates. This procedure, however, requires considerable effort and the resulting wing surface finish may require frequent maintenance.

Nevertheless, several significant all-metal designs have appeared over the years. The Ross RJ-5, mentioned above, won the United States National Championships four times during 1950–54 and in 1951 set a world distance record that stood for 13 years; the Sisu 1A, featuring slotted flaps and winner of U.S. Nationals three times in the 1960's; a series of successful designs from R. Schreder including the Open Class HP-14 and 15m Class HP-18; and the well-known Schweizer series, including the SGS 2-32, one of the highest performance multiplace sailplanes of its time [42], and the FAI 15m Class SGS 1-35. Bonded metal wings appeared in 1970 with the 15m Class Laister Nugget.

Although metal construction has been most popular in the United States, several successful metal designs have originated in Europe, including the aerobatic Pilatus B-4 and multiplace sailplanes such as the Blanik L-13, its successor, the L-23, and the Caproni A-21 "Calif".

Fiberglass Sailplanes

The Phoenix

That laminar airfoils such as the NACA 6-series offered considerable performance improvements was demonstrated in the early 1950's by the HKS I and the RJ-5 (see also A. Raspet [189]). It proved difficult, however, to manufacture wooden or metal sailplanes with the surface quality and airfoil accuracy necessary to take full advantage of these improvements.

It remained for R. Eppler and H. Nägele [97,190] to combine the aerodynamic potential of the laminar airfoil with newly developed fiberglass technology. This step marked the beginning of a new era of sailplane design, revolutionized soaring worldwide, and opened the door to what was then unimaginable performance. Their design, the "Phoenix", first flew on November 27, 1957 and featured a laminar airfoil specially developed by Eppler for sailplane application (Fig. 214). Eight examples were built, a few of which are still flying. The Phoenix provided the first practical experience in the design and construction of fiberglass sailplanes.

The First Fiberglass Sailplanes of the Akafliegs

Fig. 214: Akaflieg Stuttgart's Phoenix marked the beginning of a new era. For the first time a sailplane was built entirely of fiberglass, allowing the aerodynamic surfaces to be formed to high precision, with a surface quality surpassing all earlier designs. R. Eppler and H. Nägele, the "fathers" of the Phoenix, are credited with bringing sailplane design into the fiberglass era. New laminar airfoils, developed by Eppler specially for the Phoenix, helped contribute to the Phoenix's becoming the first sailplane with a drag coefficient of less than 0.0100 [190]. This photograph shows the sailplane as originally designed with a conventional stabilizer. This was subsequently replaced with a T-tail.

Fig. 215: Fiberglass presented the Akafliegs with both opportunity and challenge. In Braunschweig, Darmstadt, and Stuttgart, revolutionary new designs were developed that influenced production sailplanes for years to come. Braunschweig's first fiberglass design was the SB 6. Björn Stender, who played an important role in the project, developed the SB 6 further as the BS 1. In 1963 Stender lost his life during a flight test of the prototype BS 1, before he could realize his goal of putting the sailplane into series production [92].

Fig. 216: Encouraged by the success of the SB 6, the Braunschweig students embarked on their next project, the SB 7, with great enthusiasm. The airfoil, however, exhibited overly sensitive stalling characteristics, which, together with the then-unfamiliar fully-reclined seating position, made the aircraft unsuitable for all but the most experienced pilots. Several years later, the SB 7 was rebuilt with the wingspan increased from 15 to 17 m. These modifications improved the handling characteristics, making it a popular aircraft among the Akafliegers. The photograph shows the SB 7 in its original configuration.

Fig. 217: In the meantime, the Darmstadt students succeeded in creating an exceptionally capable Open-Class sailplane, the D 36. The D 36 was successful right from the start, with G. Waibel flying it to become German National Champion in 1964. The aircraft created a sensation at 1965 World Championships in England, where R. Spänig flew it to second place. The D 36 was designed and built primarily by G. Waibel, W. Lemke, and K. Holighaus, all of whom went on to become influential sailplane designers, and H. Friess, who later joined the German LBA as lead engineer responsible for sailplane certification matters. The ASW 12 and its successor, the ASW 17, are direct descendents of the D 36.

Fig. 218: Following the somewhat extreme design of the SB 7, the SB 8 was intended to be easy to fly with good visibility, combining good performance with low wing loading. The project was successful in all respects. Flying qualities and performance were so impressive that after a short time a second SB 8 was built, albeit with a stiffer, heavier wing (the relatively soft wing of the original SB 8 made the aircraft prone to flutter — see [153, 211]). The wings were later provided with 22m wingtip extensions (later shortened to 21m). This version, pictured here, was designated the SB 9. Today the SB 9 wings serve as outer wing panels for the SB 10.

Fig. 219: The Akaflieg Stuttgart's Standard Class fs 25 dates to the same period as the SB 8 and SB 9. This graceful sailplane featured an extremely high aspect ratio, tapered fuselage, and trailing-edge dive brakes. The sailplane was considered quite pleasant to fly provided the pilot was not too tall for the relatively small cockpit.

Fig. 220: The SB 10, an aircraft of extremes. With a 29m wingspan, an aspect ratio of 36.7, and good fuselage aerodynamics, it became the first sailplane to achieve a glide ratio of 50:1. This high aspect ratio was possible only with the use of carbon fiber in the spar and torsion box in each of the 4 m long inner wing sections. The aircraft is flown primarily as a 26 m multiplace by removing the outer wingtip extensions. The photo shows the 29m version.

Fig. 221: The SB 10 in a pullup. The difference in stiffness between the carbon fiber inner wing and the glass fiber outer wing is apparent — the outer wing shows considerable bending, while the inner wing exhibits practically none.

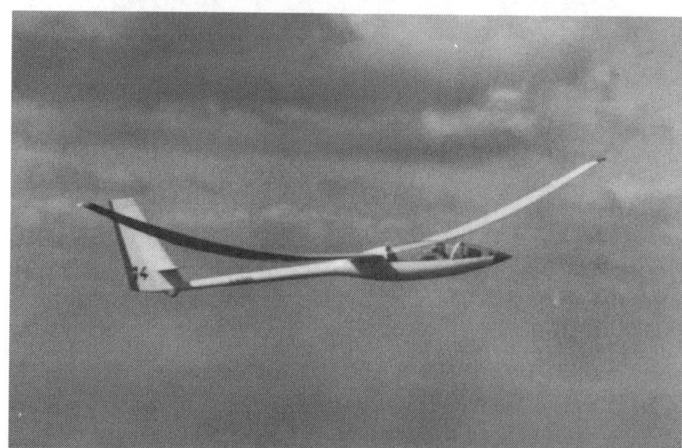

Sailplanes of the Akafliegs

The Akafliegs found considerable inspiration in the possibilities offered by fiberglass construction. In particular, the Akafliegs in Braunschweig [27], Darmstadt [28,29,46], and Stuttgart [31] (where the Phoenix was originally developed) produced entire series of successful fiberglass sailplanes, from which a number of production aircraft were derived. See also [41] and [32].

In 1961, a few years after the first flight of the Phoenix, came the SB-6 of Akaflieg Braunschweig (Fig. 215) and its successor, the BS-1, designed by Björn Stender [92]. Following the somewhat temperamental SB-7 (Fig. 216), the students at Braunschweig developed the pleasant-flying SB-8 and its 22m version, the SB-9 (Fig. 218). The introduction of carbon fiber made it possible to build the next sailplane, the SB 10, with a wingspan of 29 m and aspect ratio of 37 (Figs. 220, 221). This was the first sailplane to achieve a 50:1 glide ratio. The SB-11, built entirely from carbon fiber, was the first sailplane to successfully demonstrate the use of area-changing flaps. The SB-12 was a fairly conventional sailplane used to demonstrate the effectiveness of pneumatic turbulators in inhibiting laminar separation bubbles. The SB-13, a swept flying wing, was a daring step into relatively unexplored territory. Despite various technical problems that were solved only with considerable difficulty, the aircraft proved to be quite a capable performer. Currently, Akaflieg Braunschweig is developing the SB-14, a modern successor to the SB-8, intended to demonstrate that an 18m sailplane provides a good compromise between high performance and low development and construction costs.

In Darmstadt, the Akaflieg gained its first fiberglass experience with various versions of the 12.65m D-34, before advancing to the well-known D-36 in 1964 (Fig. 217). This graceful sailplane demonstrated its capabilities by winning the German Nationals and placing 2nd in the 1965 World Championships. Two derivatives of this aircraft, the ASW-12 and ASW-17, entered series production and were extremely successful. A number of spectacular flights were made with these sailplanes, including a straight-line world distance record by Hans-Werner Grosse, who in 1972 flew nearly 1500 km from the Baltic Sea to the Atlantic. The Darmstadt group also developed the Standard Class D-38 (which found its way into production as the DG-100) and, more recently, the D-41, a side-by-side multiplace.

Following the Phoenix, Akaflieg Stuttgart built several fiberglass sailplanes including the fs-23 "Hidalgo", a lightweight 13m design first flown in 1966, and the fs-25, a Standard Class sailplane with graceful lines offering excellent performance and handling (Fig. 219). The fs-25 made its first flight in 1968 and the following year was flown to 4th place in the German Nationals by Helmut Reichmann. 1975 saw the first flight of the fs-29, a telescoping wing sailplane offering a 50% increase in wing span (discussed in a previous chapter).

Further variations on the variable-geometry theme were developed by Akaflieg Munich with the Mü 27 [30,32], Akaflieg Darmstadt with the D 40 [32], and the fs-32 from Akaflieg Stuttgart [32,138].

Production fiberglass sailplanes

It was not until 1964, that is, seven years following the first flight of the Phoenix, that the first commercially produced fiberglass sailplanes became available. These were the Glasflügel "Libelle" and the Boelkow "Phoebus" (Figs. 222, 223).

The series of 17–18m Open Class sailplanes that followed dispelled all doubt as to their superiority over wooden designs. This group included the ASW 12 (1966), Cirrus (1967), Phoebus C (1967), and Kestrel (1968) (Fig. 226).

Following this, during 1967–69, a number of fiberglass Standard Class sailplanes appeared in rapid succession, completely displacing wooden designs from the market. The LS 1 (Fig. 224), Standard Libelle, ASW 15, and Standard Cirrus were all produced in great numbers. Variations and successors included the Salto (1970), LS 1f (1974), DG 100 (1974), Astir (1974), ASW 19 (1975), Hornet (1974), LS 4 (1980), DG 300 (1983), Discus (1984), ASW 24 (1987), LS 7 (1988), and Discus 2b (1998).

The FAI 15m Class, formed in the early 1970's, required only relatively small design changes over the Standard Class (Fig. 225). A number of flapped sailplanes appeared starting around this time, including the PIK-20, LS 3, Mosquito, Mini-Nimbus, DG 200, and ASW 20 (all 1976/77), Speed Astir (1978), Ventus (1980), DG 400 (1981), LS 6 (1983), DG 600 (1987), and DG 800S (1993), Ventus 2b (1994), LS 8 (1994), and ASW 27 (1995). Most of these aircraft were later offered with wingtip extensions allowing them to be flown with wingspans of 17 to 18m. Winglets of various kinds were also made available, making it possible to extend the effective span of 15m sailplanes without violating the class wingspan limit.

Open Class sailplanes have evolved steadily towards larger and larger wingspans. Following the first wave of 17–18m fiberglass sailplanes mentioned above came the 22m Nimbus I (1969), the 22m Kestrel 604 (1970), the 20.3m Nimbus II (Fig. 227) and the 20m ASW 17 (Fig. 228; both 1971). These were followed by the 24.5m Nimbus 3 (1981), the ASW 22 in various versions with wingspans ranging from 22 to 25 m, and the Nimbus 4 with 26.5 m (1991). The relatively recent high performance multiplace sailplanes ASH 25 (25m) and Nimbus 3D (24.6m, both 1986) belong more to the Open Class than to the multiplace class. Other modern multiplace sailplanes produced in series include the DG 500 (1989) and the Duo-Discus (1993). During the late 1970's, even the more basic two-place sailplanes intended for training and club use began to evolve from traditional wood-wing/steel tube fuselage construction to fiberglass designs. This new generation of trainers included the Janus (1974) and the Twin Astir (1976), each built in several versions, and the ASK 21 (1979).

In addition to these traditional sailplane categories, the popularity of wingtip extensions for 15m sailplanes has led to the formation of the new 18m Class. Several new designs have appeared, optimized from the start for an 18m wingspan. These include the SB 14, DG 800 (1991), ASH 26E (1993), and the LS 9 (1995). Some of these sailplanes are expected to have maximum glide ratios in excess of 50:1.

Although the majority of fiberglass sailplanes have been developed and produced in Germany, a number of excellent designs have appeared in other countries as well. The

Early Fiberglass Standard Class Sailplanes

Fig. 222: Among the first to experiment with fiberglass construction techniques were Eugen and Ursula Hänle. The Hütter H-30, a 1962 design, can be regarded as the predecessor of the "Libelle" (Glasflügel H 301). The Libelle, with its distinct canopy shape (seen later in the Salto) was, with the Phoebus, among the first fiberglass sailplanes to enter production. Built in great numbers, the sailplane became popular worldwide. The H 301 was one of the first 15m sailplanes to feature camber-changing flaps and as such can be considered a predecessor to the 15m Racing Class. Camber-changing flaps were omitted in the Standard Class H 201 Libelle, but the aircraft was otherwise similar to the H 301 pictured here.

Fig. 223: After 8 examples of the "Phoenix" had been built, its successor, the Bölkow "Phoebus" went into production with a total of 253 built in a number of variants. The Standard Class "Phoebus A" shown in the photograph exhibited the high wing chord characteristic of Eppler designs and, accordingly, a relatively low aspect ratio, high wing area, and high Reynolds number.

Fig. 224: A number of well-known fiberglass Standard Class sailplanes appeared towards the end of the 1960's. These aircraft — the LS-1, ASW 15, Standard Cirrus, and the Standard Libelle — completely displaced wooden designs in soaring competition. The DG 100 and "Astir", which appeared shortly thereafter, and follow-on designs such as the LS-1f, "Cirrus 75", ASW 19, and "Hornet" were no less successful. The LS 1 pictured here was representative of this generation of Standard Class sailplanes.

FAI 15m Racing Class

Fig. 225: The FAI 15m Racing Class was formed in the early 1970's to accommodate the flapped 15m sailplanes then becoming popular. The examples shown here illustrate the three basic types of flap systems in common use. Upper left, the "Mini-Nimbus" and "Mosquito", with integrated flap/dive brake. The upper surface panels remain flush with the wing for typical cruise and thermaling flap settings, extending when the flap is placed in a landing setting. Lower left, the ASW 20, with camber-changing flap in landing setting and conventional upper-surface dive brakes. Below, the Grob "Speed Astir" with "elastic flap" providing a continuous, gap-free upper surface along the length of the flap. Bottom right: cross section of the Speed Astir wing showing the elastic flap mechanism.

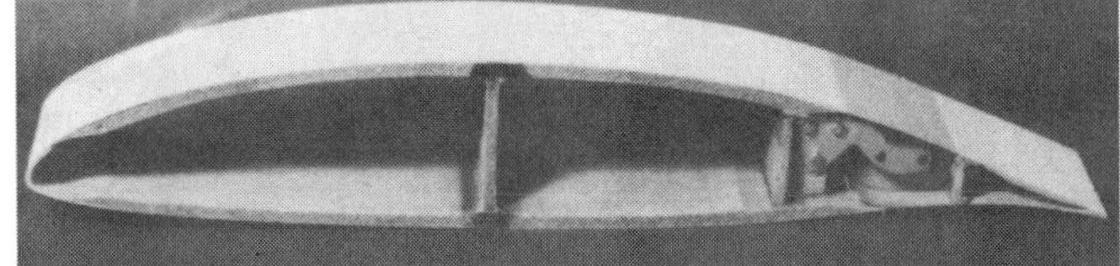

The Open Class

Fig. 226: One of the first production Open Class sailplanes to be built in fiberglass, the Kestrel 17 (Glasflügel H 401) was much admired by pilots for its handling and performance. It was soon displaced by longer-span sailplanes such as the Nimbus and ASW-17. A 19m version, the Kestrel 19, was built in Great Britain by Slingsby; a further variant, the 22m H 604, placed second in the 1974 World Championships. The tapered fuselage characteristic of the Kestrel series is clearly visible in the photo.

Fig. 227: With numerous contest wins, including three World Championships, the "Nimbus II" is one of the most successful Open Class sailplanes ever built. K. Holighaus — the aircraft's designer, builder, and pilot — flew the first 1000 km triangle in Germany in a Nimbus IIC on May 7, 1979.

Fig. 228: Successor to the ASW-12, the ASW-17 was the Nimbus II's primary competition, winning the World Championships twice. The design is perhaps best known for a number of spectacular world record flights, including a 1635 km goal-and-return flight by K. Striedeck. The photo shows H.-W. Grosse flying a 19m "clipped wing" version of the aircraft.

Swiss "Diamant" and "Elfe", the "PIK-20" from Finland, and the Polish "Jantar", are all well-known, successful aircraft. In the United States, the Zimmerman "Concept 70" and Applebay "Zuni", both FAI 15m class sailplanes produced in limited numbers during the 1970's, continue to enjoy a certain popularity.

Overall, the push toward ever higher performance has led to designs that are increasingly expensive to develop and manufacture. In many parts of the world, the high cost of new sailplanes has hindered the development and popularity of soaring as a sport. The recent "World Class" is an attempt to address this problem. At the time of writing, the PW-5, the World Class sailplane, has been granted a type certificate and has entered production.

Outlook

Modern sailplanes have already reached a high level of perfection. At this stage, significant improvements are possible only with considerable effort in research and development. Nevertheless, a number of potential areas of improvement remain.

The optimum wingspan will remain an open question because the tradeoff between cost and performance depends on a wide range of factors. There will always be a limited number of pilots seeking the ultimate sailplane no matter what the cost. Most pilots and clubs, however, need to set their sights on lower-cost aircraft. Under present conditions — actually, for the last two decades — the optimum compromise seems to lie around 18m. This is supported by the fact that many 15m sailplanes have been extended to 18m span. Beyond 18m, the cost and the ground handling problems rise rapidly. On the other end, reducing span below 15m leads to a rather steep loss in performance without much cost savings.

In the area of airfoil development, the two most difficult technical challenges (and sources of headaches for the aerodynamicist) remain the prevention of laminar bubbles and the minimization of the effects of insect contamination. No less problematic is the task of reducing the wing-fuselage interference drag, especially when flaps are employed. Interference drag in the empennage area remains a significant problem as well.

Many new structural concepts are worthy of consideration. The advent of carbon fiber opened up a number of possibilities for stiff, lightweight structures. As it continues to drop in price, one may expect to see carbon fiber in more and more sailplane designs. Nevertheless, considerable research is devoted worldwide towards the development of new materials, and it is always possible that a new material with even better design properties will become available.

The combination of lightweight structures and the trend towards increased water ballast capacity makes possible large variations in wing loading. Low wing loadings allow for good climb performance, reduced touchdown speeds, and, thanks to reduced moments of inertia, better maneuverability. Reducing the wing weight also eases the task of assembly and disassembly. Finally, carbon fiber may allow the development of unusual configurations not easily realized with other materials.

There is also room for improvement in design details such as the cockpit layout (seating arrangement, instrument panel, and controls — see [111]). Indeed, many modern sailplanes appear to offer less than ideal solutions to this problem. Crashworthiness [104,105] and pilot restraint systems [100,106] present another area for improvement.

Improvements in manufacturing technology to reduce production costs are always a possibility.

Recent years have seen a veritable explosion in the growth of the microelectronics industry. Sophisticated electronic devices are now available combining GPS navigation, inflight task selection and evaluation, interthermal speed direction, and final glide calculations. It is likely that sailplane instrumentation will continue to improve at a rapid rate.

Although sailplane performance seems to be approaching a plateau of sorts, and significant improvements appear unlikely, there will always be creative engineers who succeed in applying their ingenuity to develop breakthroughs in sailplane design. Boundary-layer control with solar-powered air pumps or wind turbines has been proposed, as have unconventional configurations that eliminate wing-fuselage interference drag.

The boundary-layer control concept leads to the more philosophical question as to what extent solar power may be used in a sailplanes. Is it still a sailplane, if the exhaust of a solar powered BLC pump is used as thrust? Should storage of excess solar power be allowed to help to bridge thermal free areas? There may be different answers for contest and fun flying.

Regarding unconventional configurations, it appears at

present that the standard canard configuration is undesirable for sailplane applications due to canard wake impingement on the wing. Perhaps providing horizontal stabilizers on the ends of winglets, together with a relatively small, lightly loaded all-flying stabilizer at the sailplane nose, would greatly reduce this flow disturbance. Such a solution, if proved effective, would drastically change the outward appearance of future sailplanes. A further improvement could be realized by relocating the dive brakes inboard towards the fuselage, perhaps even mounting them on the fuselage itself, as there is no danger of interference with the empennage.

These examples show that the possibilities for progress in sailplane design have by no means been exhausted. Future sailplane designers will continue to face a wide variety of challenging problems.

Bibliography

General texts and references

[1] Abbott, I. H. and von Doenhoff, A. E. *Theory of Wing Sections*. Dover, New York, 1959. See also Abbott, von Doenhoff, and Stivers, "Summary of Airfoil Data", NACA Report 824, 1945.

[2] Abzug, M. J. and Larrabee, E. E. *Airplane Stability and Control: A History of the Technologies that Made Aviation Possible*. Cambridge University Press, Cambridge, 1997.

[3] Anderson, J. D. *Fundamentals of Aerodynamics*. McGraw-Hill, New York, 1984.

[4] Anderson, J. D. *Introduction to Flight*. McGraw-Hill, New York, 1978.

[5] Carswell, D. et al. 1997 Sailplane Directory. *Soaring*, 61(7), July 1997.

[6] Flugmechanik: Begriffe, Benennungen, Zeichen, Grundlagen. Technical Report DIN LN9300, DIN, December 1970.

[7] Etkin, B. and Reid, L. D. *Dynamics of Flight: Stability and Control*. Wiley, New York, 1995.

[8] Federal Aviation Administration. *Aeronautical Information Manual*. U.S. Government Printing Office, Washington, DC, October 1996. Section 7-3.

[9] Hafer, X. and Sachs, G. *Flugmechanik. Moderne Flugzeugentwurfs- und Steuerungskonzepte*. Springer, Berlin, 3rd edition, 1993.

[10] Hoerner, S. F. *Fluid-Dynamic Drag*. Published by author, Brick Town, NJ, 2nd edition, 1965.

[11] Hoerner, S. F. *Fluid Dynamic Lift*. Liselotte Hoerner, Brick Town, NJ, 1975.

[12] International Civil Aviation Organization (ICAO). Manual of the ICAO Standard Atmosphere (extended to 32 kilometres), 1964.

[13] Irving, F. G. *An Introduction to the Longitudinal Static Stability of Low Speed Aircraft*. Franklin Book Co., London, 1966.

[14] Jones, R. T. *Wing Theory*. Princeton University Press, Princeton, New Jersey, 1990.

[15] Kuethe, A. M. and Chow, C.-Y. *Foundations of Aerodynamics*. Wiley, New York, 1976.

[16] McCormick, B. W. *Aerodynamics, Aeronautics, and Flight Mechanics*. McGraw-Hill, New York, 1979.

[17] Minzner, R. A., Champion, K. S. W., and Pond, H. L. The ARDC Model Atmosphere, 1959. Technical Report TR-59-267, Air Force Cambridge Research Center, U.S. Air Force, Bedford, Mass., 1959.

[18] Moffat Jr., G. B. *Winning on the Wind*. The Soaring Press, Los Altos, California, 1974.

[19] Ojha, S. K. *Flight Performance of Aircraft*. American Institute of Aeronautics and Astronautics, Washington, DC, 1995.

[20] Organisation Scientifique et Technique Internationale du Vol à Voile. *The World's Sailplanes*, volume I and II. OSTIV and Swiss Aero-Revue, Zürich, 2nd edition, 1962/63.

[21] Perkins, C. D. and Hage, R. E. *Airplane Performance Stability and Control*. Wiley, New York, 1949.

[22] Schlichting, H. *Boundary Layer Theory*. McGraw-Hill, New York, 1979.

[23] Schlichting, H. and Truckenbrodt, E. *Aerodynamik des Flugzeuges*, volume I and II. Springer, Berlin, 2nd edition, 1967.

[24] Schlichting, H. and Truckenbrodt, E. *Aerodynamics of the Airplane*. McGraw-Hill, New York, 1979.

[25] Stinton, D. *The Design of the Aeroplane*. Granada, London, 1983.

[26] Torenbeek, E. *Synthesis of Subsonic Airplane Design*. Kluwer, Delft, 1982.

History

[27] Akaflieg Braunschweig. 75 Jahre Akademische Fliegergruppe Braunschweig, 1997.

[28] Akaflieg Darmstadt. 50 Jahre Akaflieg Darmstadt, 1970.

[29] Akaflieg Darmstadt. Studenten Forschen, Bauen, Fliegen, 1990.

[30] Akaflieg München. *50 Jahre Akademische Fliegergruppe München*. Luftfahrt-Verlag Walter Zuerl, Steinebach-Wörthsee, Germany, 1974.

[31] Akaflieg Stuttgart. 1926-1976, 50 Jahre Akaflieg Stuttgart, 1976.

[32] Brinkmann, G. and Zacher, H. *Die Evolution der Segelflugzeuge*. Bernard & Graefe, Bonn, 1992. Vol. 19 of the series, "Die deutsche Luftfahrt: Buchreihe über die Entwicklungsgeschichte der deutschen Luftfahrttechnik," edited by T. Benecke.

[33] Brütting, G. *Die berühmtesten Segelflugzeuge*. Motorbuch Verlag, Stuttgart, 7th edition, 1991.

[34] Dornier - Eine Dokumentation zur Geschichte des Hauses Dornier. Friedrichshafen, Germany, 1983.

[35] Ferrière, P. and Selinger, P. F. *Rhönsegler. Alexander Schleichers Segelflugzeuge und Motorsegler 1951-1987.* Motorbuch Verlag, Stuttgart, 1988.

[36] Geistmann, D. *Die Entwicklung der Kunststoffsegelflugzeuge.* Motorbuch Verlag, Stuttgart, 2nd edition, 1980.

[37] Geistmann, D. *Die Segelflugzeuge in Deutschland. Ein Typenbuch.* Motorbuch Verlag, Stuttgart, 2nd edition, 1994.

[38] Riedel, P. *Start in den Wind. Erlebte Rhöngeschichte 1911-1926.* Motorbuch Verlag, Stuttgart, 1977. Series edited by J. von Kalckreuth.

[39] Riedel, P. *Vom Hangwind zur Thermik. Erlebte Rhöngeschichte 1927-1932.* Motorbuch Verlag, Stuttgart, 1984. Series edited by J. von Kalckreuth.

[40] Riedel, P. *Über sonnige Weiten. Erlebte Rhöngeschichte 1933-1939.* Motorbuch Verlag, Stuttgart, 1985. Series edited by J. von Kalckreuth.

[41] Schneider, R. *75 Jahre Idaflieg.* Verlag Wehle, Witterschlick/Bonn, 1997.

[42] Schweizer, E. Development and Design History of the SGS 2-32 Sailplane. OSTIV Publication VIII. Presented at the X OSTIV Congress, South Cerney, England, 1965.

[43] Schweizer, P. A. *Wings Like Eagles.* Smithsonian Institution Press, Washington, DC, 1988.

[44] Schweizer, W. *Soaring with the Schweizers.* Rivilo Books, 1991.

[45] Selinger, P. F. *Segelflugzeuge. Vom Wolf zum Discus. Flugzeugbau bei Schempp-Hirth und Wolf Hirth 1935-1985.* Motorbuch Verlag, Stuttgart, 3rd edition, 1989.

[46] Zacher, H. *Studenten Forschen, Bauen, und Fliegen. 60 Jahre Akademische Fliegergruppe Darmstadt e.V.* Akaflieg Darmstadt, Darmstadt, Germany, 1981.

Certification regulations

[47] Federal Aviation Administration. *Basic Glider Criteria Handbook.* United States Government Printing Office, Washington, DC, 1962.

[48] Federal Aviation Administration. Advisory Circular AC 21.17-2A: Type Certification - Fixed Wing Gliders (Sailplanes) Including Self-Launching (Powered) Gliders. US Department of Transportation, Federal Aviation Administration, Aircraft Certification Service, February 1993.

[49] Joint Aviation Authorities Committee. JAR-22, Sailplanes and Powered Sailplanes. Change 5, 28 October 1995. Civil Aviation Authority, Printing and Publication Services, Greville House, 37 Gratton Rd., Cheltenham, Glos GL50 2BN, United Kingdom.

[50] Luftfahrt Bundesamt. Lufttüchtigkeitsforderungen für Segelflugzeuge und Motorsegler. (1. DV LuftBau O - JAR-22 Change 5), Juli 1998.

[51] OSTIV. OSTIV Airworthiness Standards for Sailplanes, October 1986. Amendments 1 (Sept. 1991), 2 (June 1992), and 3 (June 1994).

Cross-country theory and weather models

[52] Bridge, J. Current Glider Handicaps. *Sailplane and Gliding,* IL(5):287, October/November 1998.

[53] Carmichael, B. H. What Price Performance. *Soaring,* 18, May/June 1954.

[54] Deutscher Aero Club, e.V. Deutsche Meisterschaft im Streckensegelflug, DMSt Wettbewerbsordnung. Published by the German Aero Club, Feb. 1998. Part D, Index List of Sailplane Types. Subject to periodic revision.

[55] Horstmann, K. H. Neue Modellaufwindverteilungen und ihr Einfluß auf die Auslegung von Segelflugzeugen. OSTIV Publication XIV. Presented at the XV OSTIV Congress, Räyskälä, Finland, 1976.

[56] Irving, F. *The Paths of Soaring Flight.* Imperial College Press, London, 1999.

[57] Konovalov, D. A. On the Structure of Thermals. OSTIV Publication XI. Presented at the XII OSTIV Congress, Alpine, Texas USA, 1970.

[58] MacCready, P. Die Beste Streckenfluggeschwindigkeit für Segelflugzeuge. *Schweizer Aero Revue,* 24:441–443, Zürich, 1949.

[59] Nickel, K. Die günstigste Geschwindigkeit des Streckensegelfluges. *Schweizer Aero-Revue,* 24:223–225,352–353, Zürich, 1949. See also Thermik 2, pages 168-173, 1949.

[60] Quast, A. Mittlere Reisegeschwindigkeit vermessener Segelflugzeuge unter gleichzeitiger Berücksichtigung von vier Modellaufwindverteilungen. *Aerokurier,* pages 137–140, 1978.

[61] Reichmann, H. *Streckensegelflug.* Motorbuch Verlag, Stuttgart, 1975. Appeared in English as "Cross-Country Soaring", Knauff and Grove, Julian PA, USA, 1994.

[62] Reichmann, H. *Zum Problem der Fahrtoptimierung im Streckensegelflug.* PhD thesis, Universität Karlsruhe, 1976.

[63] Schänzer, G. Dynamic Energy Transfer between Wind and Aircraft. In *Proceedings of the 13th Congress of the ICAS,* pages 615–621, Seattle, USA, 1982. Paper 82-3.4.1.

[64] Soaring Society of America. 1998 Sailplane Handicaps. Published by the Soaring Society of America, 1998. Subject to periodic revision.

[65] Späte, W. Beste Reisegeschwindigkeit beim Segelflug. In *Handbuch des Segelfliegens,* pages 283–288. Wolf Hirth, Stuttgart, 6th edition, 1952. See also Weltluftfahrt, Vol 1, Heft 11/12, 1950.

[66] Strachan, I. A New Look at Glider Handicapping. *Sailplane and Gliding,* pages 459–461, December 1967.

[67] Strachan, I. Calculation of Glider Competition Speeds. *Sailplane and Gliding,* pages 266–271, Dec./Jan. 1974/75.

[68] Weinholtz, F. *Grundtheorie des modernen Streckensegelflugs.* Luftfahrt- und Luftsportverlag, Bochum, 1967.

[69] Welch, A., Welch, L., and Irving, F. *New Soaring Pilot.* John Murray, London, 3rd edition, 1977.

General design topics

[70] Althaus, D. Wind Tunnel Measurements on Bodies and Wing-Body Combinations. In *Motorless Flight Research*, pages 159–178, November 1973. NASA CR-2315.

[71] Boermans, L. M. M., Nicolosi, F., and Kubrynski, K. Aerodynamic Design of High-Performance Sailplane Wing-Fuselage Combinations. In *Proceedings of the 21st Congress of the ICAS*, Melbourne, Australia, 1998. Paper 98-2.9.2.

[72] Boermans, L. M. M. and Oolbekkink, B. Wind tunnel Tests on an Outer Wing Segment of the ASW 19X Sailplane. OSTIV Publication XVII. Presented at the XVIII OSTIV Congress, Hobbs, New Mexico, USA, 1983.

[73] Boermans, L. M. M. and Terleth, D. C. Wind Tunnel Tests of Eight Sailplane Wing-Fuselage Combinations. *Technical Soaring*, 8(3):70–85, February 1984. See also OSTIV Publication XVII. Presented at the XVIII OSTIV Congress, Hobbs, New Mexico, 1983.

[74] Boermans, L. M. M. and Waibel, G. Aerodynamic Design of the Standard Class Sailplane ASW 24. *Technical Soaring*, 13(3):72–83, July 1989. Presented at the XX OSTIV Congress, Benalla, Australia, 1987. See also "Aerodynamic and Structural Design of the Standard Class ASW 24,", in Proceedings of the 16th Congress of the ICAS, pages 969-978, Jerusalem, Israel, 1988. Paper 88-2.7.2.

[75] Bretting, E. B. Elastic Flap: Prinzip der reinen Profilwölbung. *Aerokurier*, pages 250–251, 1978.

[76] Byrne, J. V. Towards Optimization of Ground-Powered Glider Launch. OSTIV Publication VIII. Presented at the X OSTIV Congress, South Cerney, England, 1965.

[77] Eppler, R. Die Auslegung von Segelflugzeugen. OSTIV Publication IV. Presented at the VI OSTIV Congress, St. Yan, France, 1956.

[78] Feifel, W. M. Combination of Aileron and Flap Deflection for Minimum Induced Drag Roll Control. *Technical Soaring*, 5(4), June 1980. See also OSTIV Publication XV. Presented at the XVI OSTIV Congress, Châteauroux, France, 1978.

[79] Fiecke, D. Die Bestimmung der Flugzeugpolaren für Entwurfszwecke. Technical Report 15, Deutsche Versuchsanstalt für Luftfahrt, 1956.

[80] Gibson, J. Understanding the Winch Launch. *Sailplane and Gliding*, pages 28–31, February/March 1987.

[81] Goulthorpe, P. Flight on the Winch. *Sailplane and Gliding*, pages 140–143, June/July 1996.

[82] Györgyfalvy, D. Performance Analysis of the Horten IV Flying Wing. OSTIV Publication VI. Presented at the VIII OSTIV Congress, Cologne, Germany, 1960.

[83] Irving, F. G. All Moving Tailplanes. OSTIV Publication VII. Presented at the IX OSTIV Congress, Junin, Argentina, 1963.

[84] Irving, F. G. The Optimum Size of Horizontal Tail for a Glider. OSTIV Publication VII. Presented at the IX OSTIV Congress, Junin, Argentina, 1963.

[85] Irving, F. G. The Stick Force/Speed Characteristics of Various Types of Tails and Elevator Trimmers. OSTIV Publication X. Presented at the XI OSTIV Congress, Leszno, Poland, 1968.

[86] Irving, F. Centre of Gravity Position and Performance. *Sailplane and Gliding*, pages 222–223, October/November 1981. See also [87].

[87] Irving, F. The Optimum Centre of Gravity Position for Minimum Overall Energy Loss. OSTIV Publication XVI. Presented at the XVII OSTIV Congress, Paderborn, Germany, 1981.

[88] Kroo, I. Trim Drag, Tail Sizing, and Soaring Performance. *Technical Soaring*, 8(4), July 1984.

[89] Laitone, E. V. Tail Load Calculations for Light Airplanes. *Journal of Aircraft*, 31(2), 1994.

[90] Larrabee, E. E. Lateral Control and Sailplane Design Considerations to Optimize Altitude Gain While Thermalling. In *Proceedings of the AIAA/MIT/SSA 2nd International Symposium on the Technology and Science of Low Speed and Motorless Flight*, Cambridge, Mass., September 1974. AIAA/MIT/SSA.

[91] Larrabee, E. E. The Aerodynamic Design of Sailplane Tail Assemblies. *Technical Soaring*, 5(1):21–28, May 1978.

[92] Lasch, H. The Story of the BS-1. *Sailplane and Gliding*, 17(6):452–455, December/January 1966-67.

[93] Marzinzik, G. Aufbruch in eine neue Dimension? Das eta-Projekt. *Aerokurier*, pages 110–114, January 1998.

[94] Maughmer, M. D., Hallman, D., Ruszkowski, R., Chappel, G., and Waitz, I. Experimental Investigation of Wing/Fuselage Integration Geometries. *Journal of Aircraft*, 26(8), August 1989.

[95] Morelli, P. *Static Stability and Control of Sailplanes.* Organisation Scientifique et Technique Internationale du Vol à Voile (OSTIV), Voorburg, Netherlands, May 1976.

[96] Multhopp, H. Die Berechnung der Auftriebsverteilung von Tragflügeln. *Luftf. Forschung*, 15, 1938.

[97] Nägele, H. and Eppler, R. Kunststoffsegelflugzeug Fs 24 Phönix. OSTIV Publication IV. Presented at the VI OSTIV Congress, St. Yan, France, 1956.

[98] Ostrowski, J., Litwinczyk, M., and Turkowski, L. Flow Phenomena along Fuselage and Wing-Fuselage Systems of Gliders. Technical Report TM 75401, NASA, Dec. 1980. Translated from *Archiwum Budowy Maszyn*, Vol. 25, No. 1, 1978, pp 1-13.

[99] Pfenninger, W. Untersuchungen über Reibungsverminderungen an Tragflügeln, insbesondere mit Hilfe von Grenzschichtabsaugung. Mitteilungen aus dem Institut für Aerodynamik der ETH Zürich, No. 13, Zürich, 1946.

[100] Pusch, D. and Sperber, M. Investigation of Glider Safety Belt Behavior under Accident Conditions. *Technical Soaring*, 15(3):68–74, July 1991. Presented at the XXI OSTIV Congress, Wiener-Neustadt, Austria, 1989.

[101] Quast, A. and Thomas, F. Einfluss der Flügelauslegung auf die Flugleistungen von Segelflugzeugen. *Z. Flugwiss. (ZFW)*, 15:386–392, 1967. See also Aerokurier, 1978, pages 846-849.

[102] Radespiel, R. Wind Tunnel Investigations of Glider Fuselages with Different Waistings and Wing Arrangements. Technical Report TM 77014, NASA, Jan. 1983. Translated from *Akademische Fliegergruppe Braunschweig*, Germany, 1981.

[103] Redeker, G. Auslegung von ungepfeilten Tragflügeln großen Seitenverhältnisses mit Wölbklappen für zwei Entwurfspunkte. Forschungsbericht 75-34, DLR, 1975. OCLC Nr. 20843147. Available in English as The Design of Unswept Large Aspect Ratio Wings with Flaps for Two Flight Conditions", ESA TT 224, NASA Report (STAR Catalog) Nr. N76-20128, European Space Agency, Paris, 1976.

[104] Segal, D. A. M. Aircraft (Full-Size Glider) Crash-worthiness Impact Test. *Technical Soaring*, 14(2):40–45, April 1990. Presented at the XXI OSTIV Congress, Wiener-Neustadt, Austria, 1989.

[105] Segal, T. Crashworthiness Test. *Sailplane and Gliding*, pages 130–131, June/July 1989.

[106] Sperber, M. Restraint System in Gliders Under Biomechanical Aspect. *Technical Soaring*, 19(2):52–57, April 1995. Presented at the XXIII OSTIV Congress, Borlänge, Sweden, 1993.

[107] Stender, W. Entwurfsgrundlagen für den Segelflug. *Weltluftfahrt*, 1951.

[108] Stender, W. *Sailplane Weight Estimation*. OSTIV, Elstree-Wassenaar, Netherlands, 1969.

[109] Stich, G. Das gedämpfte Höhenleitwerk im Kreisflug. OSTIV Publication XVI. Presented at the XVII OSTIV Congress, Paderborn, Germany, 1981.

[110] Stich, G. Effect of the Fixed Horizontal Tail on Flight Characteristics in Circling. *Technical Soaring*, 8(1), April 1983. See also [109].

[111] Strunk, E. Gestaltung eines Segelflugzeug-Cockpits nach arbeitswissenschaflichen Gesichtspunkten. *Aerokurier*, pages 651–652, 1978.

[112] Thomas, F. and Wieland, U. Leistungsvergleich von Segelflugzeugen mit im Fluge veränderlicher Flächenbelastung. OSTIV Publication XII. Presented at the XIII OSTIV Congress, Vrsac, Yugoslavia, 1972.

[113] Thomas, F. Der Einfluß der aerodynamischen Entwurfsgrößen auf die Leistungen von Segelflugzeugen. *Aerokurier*, pages 846–849, 1971.

[114] Vernon, C. Trim Drag. *Technical Soaring*, 16(1):17–25, January 1992. Presented at the XXII OSTIV Congress, Uvalde, Texas, 1991.

[115] Wortmann, F. X. Widerstandsverminderung bei Segelflugzeugen. OSTIV Publication VIII. Presented at the X OSTIV Congress, South Cerney, England, 1965.

Winglets, unconventional planforms

[116] Cone Jr., C. D. The Theory of Induced Lift and Minimum Induced Drag of Nonplanar Lifting Systems. Technical Report TR 139, NASA, Feb. 1962.

[117] Crosby, C. P., Ashman, P., and Terblanche, H. Full Scale Pressure Measurements on a Winglet Fitted to an ASW 20. *Technical Soaring*, 20(3):74–77, July 1996. Presented at the XXIV OSTIV Congress, Omarama, New Zealand, 1995.

[118] Dressler, U. Aerodynamic Design of Winglets for a Standard-Class Glider. *Technical Soaring*, 8(4):118–126, July 1984. See also OSTIV Publication XVII. Presented at the XVIII OSTIV Congress, Hobbs, 1983.

[119] Eppler, R. Induced Drag and Winglets. *Technical Soaring*, 20(2):89–96, July 1996. Presented at the XXIV OSTIV Congress, Omarama, New Zealand, 1995. Also appeared in Aerospace Science and Technology (AST), 1(1):3-15, January, 1997.

[120] Jones, R. T. Minimizing Induced Drag. *Soaring*, 43(10):26–29, October 1979.

[121] Marsden, D. J. Winglets for Sailplanes. *Technical Soaring*, 15(4):119–124, October 1991. Presented at the XX OSTIV Congress in Benalla, Australia, 1987.

[122] Masak, P. C. Design of Winglets for Sailplanes. *Soaring*, 57(6):21–27, June 1993.

[123] Maughmer, M. D. and Kunz, P. J. Sailplane Winglet Design. *Technical Soaring*, 22(4):116–123, October 1998. Presented at the XXV OSTIV Congress, St. Auban, France, 1997.

[124] Nicks, O. W. Experimental Comparison of Two Wing Tips. *Technical Soaring*, 14(3):81–88, July 1990. Presented at the XXI OSTIV Congress in Wiener-Neustadt, Austria, 1989.

[125] Schuemann, W. A New Wing Planform with Improved Low-Speed Performance. *Soaring*, pages 16–26, February 1983.

[126] Smith, S. C. and Kroo, I. Computation of Induced Drag for Elliptical and Crescent-Shaped Wings. *Journal of Aircraft*, 30(4):446–452, July-Aug. 1993.

[127] Waibel, G. Nonsense of Winglets. *Technical Soaring*, 12(4):123, October 1988. Presented at the XX OSTIV Congress, Benalla, Australia, 1987.

[128] Waibel, G. The Case for Winglets. *Sailplane and Gliding*, pages 140–141, June/July 1993.

[129] Whitcomb, R. T. A Design Approach and Selected Wind-Tunnel Results at High Subsonic Speed for Wing-Tip Mounted Winglets. Technical Report TN D-8260, NASA, July 1976.

Variable geometry

[130] Akaflieg Braunschweig. Die SB 11, Auslegung, Konstruktion und Bau. In *Die Akademische Fliegergruppe Braunschweig 1973-1978*, pages 14–27. Akaflieg Braunschweig, 1979.

[131] Akaflieg Stuttgart. fs 29, erster Leistungssegler der Welt mit Teleskopflügeln. *Aerokurier*, pages 592–764, 1975.

[132] Akaflieg Stuttgart. The fs-29, a Telescoping-Wing Sailplane. *Soaring*, 40(1):21–27, January 1976.

[133] Goodhart, N. Project Sigma. *Sailplane and Gliding*, 20(2):134–137, 1969.

[134] Hansen, M. Design and Contruction of the SB-11. OSTIV Publication XV. Presented at the XVI OSTIV Congress, Châteauroux, France, 1978.

[135] Marsden, D. J. Variable Geometry Sailplane Minisigma. *Technical Soaring*, 17(2):56–63, April 1993. Presented at the XXII OSTIV Congress in Uvalde, Texas, USA, 1991.

[136] Sailplane and Gliding Editorial Staff. AN-66C - The Swiss Sigma. *Sailplane and Gliding*, 22(3):205, June/July 1971.

[137] Sailplane and Gliding Editorial Staff. Sigma - the Sailplane of Tomorrow? *Sailplane and Gliding*, 22(3):192–201, June/July 1971.

[138] Schuon, F. FS 32 - A New Glider Project with Retractable External Airfoil Flap. *Technical Soaring*, 13(4):112–115, October 1989. Presented at the XX OSTIV Congress in Benalla, Australia, 1987.

[139] Thomas, F. and Eppler, R. Aufwand and Nutzen von Klappen bei Segelflugzeugen. *Aerokurier*, pages 448–451, 1979.

Flying wings

[140] Akaflieg Braunschweig. Die Entwicklung der SB 13. In *66 Jahre Akademische Fliegergruppe Braunschweig 1922-1988*, pages 5–34. Akaflieg Braunschweig, Braunschweig, Germany, 1989.

[141] Horten, R. and Selinger, P. F. *Nurflügel. Die Geschichte der Horten-Flugzeuge 1933-1960*. H. Weishaupt, Graz, 1985.

[142] Nickel, K. and Wohlfahrt, M. *Schwanzlose Flugzeuge*. Birkhäuser, Basel, 1990. Flugtechnische Reihe, Band 3. Available in English as *Tailless Aircraft in Theory and Practice*, American Institute for Aeronautics and Astronautics, Washington, DC, 1994.

[143] Redsell, M. Group Genesis. *Soaring*, pages 23–26, January 1995.

[144] Redsell, M. Jim Marske and his Flying Wings. *Soaring*, pages 14–18, February 1997.

[145] Sandmann, T. Nicht ohne Allüren: SB 13. Erfahrungen mit dem Nurflügel in Flugbetrieb und Wettbewerb. *Aerokurier*, pages 40–43, 1994.

[146] Zientek, A. Polish Flying Experience with Tailless Gliders. *Technical Soaring*, 16(2):48–56, April 1992. Presented at the XXI OSTIV Congress, Wiener-Neustadt, Austria, 1989.

The World Class

[147] International Gliding Commission. Rules for the Selection and Production of the World Class Glider. Fédération Aéronautique Internationale (FAI), October 1989.

[148] International Gliding Commission. Technical Specifications for the "World Class" Glider. Fédération Aéronautique Internationale (FAI), October 1989.

[149] Johnson, R. H. A Flight Test Evaluation of the PW-5 World Class Sailplane. *Soaring*, pages 19–25, April 1997.

[150] Morelli, P. World Class: Present Status and Expected Future Developments. *Soaring*, 57(12):20–24, December 1993.

[151] Schweizer, P. A. An International One-Design Class and the Olympics. *Technical Soaring*, 13(2):42–44, April 1989. Presented at the XX OSTIV Congress, Benalla, Australia, 1987.

[152] World Class Winner Announced. Soaring Magazine, June 1993. Report of announcement by International Gliding Commission of Fédération Aéronautique Internationale (FAI).

Aeroelasticity

[153] Akaflieg Braunschweig. Durch Querruder beeinflußtes Biegeflattern eines Segelflugzeugs. Film presented at the XIII OSTIV Congress, Vrsac, Yugoslavia, 1972. Some footage incorporated in [211].

[154] Berns, H.-J. Aeroelastic Problems of a Swept-Back Tailless. OSTIV Publication XVIII. Presented at the XIX OSTIV Congress, Rieti, Italy, 1985.

[155] Bisplinghoff, R. L., Ashley, H., and Halfman, R. L. *Aeroelasticity*. Addison-Wesley, Cambridge, Mass., 1955. Republished 1996, Dover Publications, Mineola, New York.

[156] Chajec, W. C. Critical Flutter Speed of Sailplanes Calculated for High Altitude - Examples of Computation. *Technical Soaring*, 18(3):69–72, July 1994. Presented at the XXIII OSTIV Congress, Borlänge, Sweden, 1993.

[157] Försching, H. W. *Grundlagen der Aeroelastik*. Springer, Berlin, 1974.

[158] Kießling, F. On Simplified Analytical Flutter Clearance Procedures for Light Aircraft. *Technical Soaring*, 15(3):83–91, July 1991.

[159] Labuc, T. and Skrzydiewski, S. The Effect of Wing Twist Distortion on Glider Static Longitudinal Stability with Stick Fixed. OSTIV Publication IX. Presented at the X OSTIV Congress, South Cerney, England, 1965.

[160] Stender, W. and Kießling, F. Aeroelastic Flutter Prevention in Gliders and Small Aircraft. Technical Report 91-03, DLR, Köln, 1991.

[161] Stender, W., Kiessling, F., and Kuettner, J. P. Possibilities of High Altitude Flutter During Wave Flights. *Technical Soaring*, 18(4):114–119, October 1994. Presented at the XXIII OSTIV Congress, Borlänge, Sweden (1993).

[162] Stich, G. Einfluss der im Flugversuch vermessenen Tragflächendeformationen auf die Flugleistungen eines Kunststoffsegelflugzeuges. OSTIV Publication XII. Presented at the XIII OSTIV Congress, Vršac, Yugoslavia, 1972.

Airfoils

[163] Althaus, D. Windkanalmessungen an Profilen mit Klappen bei mittleren Reynoldszahlen. OSTIV Publication XI. Presented at the XII OSTIV Congress, Alpine, Texas USA, 1970.

[164] Althaus, D. *Profilpolaren für den Modellflug*. Neckar-Verlag, Villingen, Germany, 1980.

[165] Althaus, D. Influencing Transition on Airfoils. OSTIV Publication XVI. Presented at the XVII OSTIV Congress, Paderborn, Germany, 1981.

[166] Althaus, D. Performance Improvement on Tailplanes by Turbulators. *Technical Soaring*, 15(4):125–128, October 1991.

[167] Althaus, D. *Niedergeschwindigkeitsprofile.* Vieweg-Verlag, Braunschweig/Wiesbaden, 1996.

[168] Althaus, D. and Wortmann, F. X. Stuttgarter Profilkatalog 1: Meßergebnisse aus dem Laminarwindkanal des Instituts für Aerodynamik und Gasdynamik der Universität Stuttgart. Braunschweig, 1981.

[169] Althaus, D. and Wurz, W. Windtunnel Tests of the SM 701 Airfoil and the UAG 88-143/20 Airfoil. *Technical Soaring*, 17(1):21–32, January 1993.

[170] Boermans, L. M. M. and Bennis, F. Design and Windtunnel Tests of an Airfoil for the Horizontal Tailplane of a Standard Class Sailplane. *Technical Soaring*, 16(2):35–40, April 1992. Presented at the XXII OSTIV Congress, Uvalde, Texas, 1991.

[171] Boermans, L. M. M. and Selen, H. J. W. On the Design of Some Airfoils for Sailplane Application. OSTIV Publication XVI. Presented at the XVII OSTIV Congress, Paderborn, Germany, 1981.

[172] Boermans, L. M. M. and van Garrel, A. Design and Wind Tunnel Test Results of a Flapped Laminar Flow Airfoil for High Performance Sailplane Application. In *Proceedings of the 19th Congress of the ICAS*, pages 1241–1247, Anaheim, California, 1994. Paper 94-5.4.3.

[173] Drela, M. XFOIL: An Analysis and Design System for Low Reynolds Number Airfoils. In *Low Reynolds Number Aerodynamics.* Springer, Jun 1989. Lecture Notes in Engineering, No. 54.

[174] Eppler, R. Laminarprofile für Segelflugzeuge. OSTIV Publication III. Presented at the V OSTIV Congress, Buxton, England, 1954.

[175] Eppler, R. Vergleich theoretischer und experimenteller Profilwiderstände. OSTIV Publication VII. Presented at the IX OSTIV Congress, Junin, Argentina, 1963.

[176] Eppler, R. An Empirical Criterion for Laminar-to-Turbulent Boundary-Layer Transition. *Technical Soaring*, 23(2):34–42, April 1999. Presented at the XXV OSTIV Congress, Saint Auban, France, 1997.

[177] Eppler, R. and Somers, D. M. A Computer Program for the Design and Analysis of Low-Speed Airfoils. TM 80210, NASA, 1980. Supplement appeared as NASA TM 81862, 1980. Updated version of program is available from Universität Stuttgart, Inst. A für Mechanik, Pfaffenwaldring 9, Stuttgart, Germany.

[178] Eppler, R. Direkte Berechnung von Tragflügelprofilen aus der Druckverteilung. *Ing. Archiv*, 25:32–57, 1957. Available in English as NASA TT T-15,417, 1974.

[179] Eppler, R. Ergebnisse gemeinsamer Anwendung von Grenzschicht und Profiltheorie. *Z. Flugwiss.*, 8:247–260, 1960.

[180] Eppler, R. *Airfoil Design and Data.* Springer, Berlin, 1990.

[181] Gooden, J. H. M. Experimental low-speed aerodynamic characteristics of the Wortmann FX 66-S196 V1 airfoil. OSTIV Publication XV. Presented at the XVI OSTIV Congress, Châteauroux, France, 1978.

[182] Horstmann, K. H. and Quast, A. Tragflügelprofilentwurf für das Weltmeisterschaftssegelflugzeug SB 11. Technical Report 28, DFVLR, 1979.

[183] Horstmann, K. H. and Quast, A. Profilwiderstandsverringerung durch Ausblasen. OSTIV Publication XVI. Presented at the XVII OSTIV Congress, Paderborn, Germany, 1981.

[184] Horstmann, K. H. and Quast, A. Widerstandsverminderung durch Blasturbulatoren. Technical Report FB 81-33, DFVLR, Köln, 1981.

[185] Horstmann, K. H., Quast, A., and Boermans, L. M. M. Pneumatic Turbulators - a Device for Drag Reduction of Reynolds Numbers below 5×10^5. Technical Report CP-365, AGARD, 1984. Paper 20.

[186] Marsden, D. G. Wind Tunnel Tests of the UAG 92 170/SF Slotted Flapped Wing Section. *Technical Soaring*, 18(1):21–26, January 1994. Presented at the XXIII OSTIV Congress, Borlänge, Sweden, 1993.

[187] Marsden, D. G. and Toogood, R. W. Wind tunnel Tests of a Slotted Flapped Wing Section for Variable Geometry Sailplanes. *Technical Soaring*, 12(1):4–9, January 1988.

[188] Nicks, O., Steen, G., Heffner, M., and Bauer, D. Wind Tunnel Investigation and Analysis of the SM701 Airfoil. *Technical Soaring*, 16(4):109–115, October 1992. Presented at the XXII OSTIV Congress in Uvalde, Texas USA, 1991.

[189] Raspet, A. Leistungssteigerung von Segelflugzeugen durch Berücksichtigung der Grenzschichtforschung. In *Handbuch des Segelfliegens*, pages 125–145. Wolf Hirth, Stuttgart, 6th edition, 1952.

[190] Raspet, A. and Györgyfalvy, D. Boundary Layer Studies on the Phoenix Sailplane. OSTIV Publication VI. Presented at the VIII OSTIV Congress, Cologne, Germany, 1960.

[191] Riegels, F. W. Aerodynamische Profile. München, 1958.

[192] Schmitz, F. W. Aerodynamics of the Model Airplane - Part 1. Airfoil Measurements. Technical Report RSIC-721, Redstone Scientific Information Center, Research and Development Directorate, U.S. Army Missile Command, Redstone Arsenal, Alabama, November 1967. English translation; German original dated 1942. OCLC 4891518. NTIS Accession Nr. N70-39001.

[193] Schürmeyer, C. and Horstmann, K. H. Development of Airfoil Sections for the Sweptback Tailless Sailplane SB 13. OSTIV Publication XVIII. Presented at the XIX OSTIV Congress, Rieti, Italy, 1985.

[194] Selig, M. S., Donovan, J. F., and Fraser, D. B. *Airfoils at Low Speeds.* H. A. Stokely, Viginia Beach, Virginia, USA, 1989.

[195] Somers, D. M. and Maughmer, M. D. The SM701 Airfoil, an Airfoil for the World Class Sailplanes. *Technical Soaring*, 16(3):70–77, July 1992. Presented at the XXII OSTIV Congress in Uvalde, Texas USA, 1991.

[196] Wortmann, F. X. Einige Laminarprofile für Segelflugzeuge. OSTIV Publication VII. Presented at the IX OSTIV Congress, Junin, Argentina, 1963.

[197] Wortmann, F. X. Über eine Möglichkeit zur Vermeidung von Insektenrauhigkeiten. OSTIV Publication VII. Presented at the IX OSTIV Congress, Junin, Argentina, 1963.

[198] Wortmann, F. X. Zur Optimierung von Klappenprofilen. OSTIV Publication X. Presented at the XI OSTIV Congress, Leszno, Poland, 1968.

[199] Wortmann, F. X. Airfoils for the Variable Geometry Concept. OSTIV Publication XI. Presented at the XII OSTIV Congress, Alpine, Texas USA, 1970.

[200] Wortmann, F. X. Windkanalmessungen an Profilen mit Klappen bei mittleren Reynoldszahlen. OSTIV Publication XI. Presented at the XII OSTIV Congress, Alpine, Texas USA, 1970.

[201] Wortmann, F. X. Symmetrical Airfoils Optimised for Small Flap Deflection. OSTIV Publication XII. Presented at the XIII OSTIV Congress, Vrsac, Yugoslavia, 1972.

[202] Wortmann, F. X. and Althaus, D. Messungen an drei Flügelprofilen des Segelflugzeuges Ka-6. OSTIV Publication VI. Presented at the VIII OSTIV Congress, Cologne, Germany, 1960.

[203] Wortmann, F. X. and Althaus, D. Der Laminarwindkanal des Instituts für Aero- und Gasdynamik an der Technischen Hochschule Stuttgart. *Z. Flugwiss.*, 12:129–134, 1964.

Flight test methodology and results

[204] Bennett, G., Enevoldson, E., and Gera, J. Pilot Evaluation of Sailplane Handling Qualities. *Technical Soaring*, 5(4):3–14, June 1980. See also OSTIV Publication XV. Presented at the XVI OSTIV Congress, Châteauroux, France, 1978. See also NASA CR-2960, May, 1978.

[205] Bikle, P. F. Sailplane Performance Measured in Flight. OSTIV Publication XI. Presented at the XII OSTIV Congress, Alpine, Texas, USA, 1970.

[206] Cooper, G. E. and Harper, R. P. The Use of Pilot Rating in the Evaluation of Aircraft Handling Qualities. Technical Report TN D-5153, NASA, Washington, DC, April 1969.

[207] Hummel, D. Die Leistungsersparnis in Flugformationen von Vögeln mit Unterschieden in Größe, Form und Gewicht. *J. f. Ornithol.*, 119:52–73, 1978.

[208] Hummel, D. Recent aerodynamic contributions to problems of bird flight. In *Proceedings of the 11th Congress of the ICAS, Lisbon, Portugal*, pages 115–129, 1978. Paper A 1.05.

[209] Idaflieg. 25. Idaflieg-Vergleichsfliegen. Published by the Interessengemeinschaft Deutscher Akademischer Fliegergruppen, 1976.

[210] Johnson, R. H. *The Johnson Flight Tests.* Soaring Society of America, 1979. Collection of reprints of articles appearing in Soaring Magazine.

[211] Jöst, C. Grenzschicht - Segelflug im Dienst der Wissenschaft. Film. Video Film & Video Produktion Charlie Jöst, Ladenburgerstr. 10, D-69198 Schriesheim, Germany.

[212] Laurson, H. and Zacher, H. Fluguntersuchungen mit den Segelflugzeugen D 36, BS 1 und ASW 12. OSTIV Publication X. Presented at the XI OSTIV Congress, Leszno, Poland, 1968.

[213] Laurson, H. and Zacher, H. Flugmessungen mit 25 Segelflugzeugen (Flugleistungen und Flugeigenschaften). OSTIV Publication XII. Presented at the XIII OSTIV Congress, Vrsac, Yugoslavia, 1972.

[214] Laurson, H. and Zacher, H. Flugmessungen an 35 Segelflugzeugen und Motorseglern. *Aerokurier*, 21:114, 1977. See also OSTIV Publication XIII. Presented at the XIV OSTIV Congress in Waikerie, Australia, 1974.

[215] Lipp, A. Use of Satellite Navigation for Sailplane Performance Measurements. *Technical Soaring*, 22(1):17–23, January 1998. Presented at the XXV OSTIV Congress, St. Auban, France, 1997.

[216] Merklein, H. J. Bestimmung aerodynamischer Beiwerte durch Flugmessungen an 12 Segelflugzeugen mit Brems- und Landeklappen. Technical Report 63, Flugwissenschaftliche Forschungsanstalt, München, Germany, 1963.

[217] Merklein, H. J. Schleppsondeneichflüge mit 12 Segelflugzeugen. Technical Report 60, Flugwissenschaftliche Forschungsanstalt, München, Germany, 1963.

[218] Merklein, H. J. and Zacher, H. Flight Performance Measurements on Twelve Sailplanes. *Deutscher Aerokurier*, 1963-64. 1963(12) and 1964(1). Presented at the IX OSTIV Congress in Junin, Argentina, 1963. See also OSTIV Publication VII.

[219] Milgram, J. Flight Testing Sailplanes at the 1998 Idaflieg Summer Meet. *Soaring*, 63(4):36–39, April 1999.

[220] Quast, A. Detection of Transition by Infrared Image Techniques. *Technical Soaring*, 13(3):96–101, July 1989. Presented at the XX OSTIV Congress in Benalla, Australia.

[221] Rade, M., Weishaupt, P., and Zacher, H. Flugeigenschaftsprüfung von 7 doppelsitzigen Segelflugzeugen im OSTIV Kurs Varese, 1963. Technical Report 62, Flugwissenschaftliche Forschungsanstalt, München, 1963.

[222] Schott, E. Untersuchungen von Rumpf-Flügel-Übergängen an vier Segelflugzeugen im Flugversuch während des 20. Idaflieg-Vergleichsfliegens 1971 in Aalen-Elchingen. Technical Report, Idaflieg, 1972.

[223] Scott, J. Sailplanes on the Test Track. *Soaring*, 47(4):16–19, April 1983.

[224] Stich, G. Mustererprobungsflüge der FK 3. Technical Report IB 151-773/56, DFVLR, Braunschweig, 1973.

[225] Stich, G. Flugmessungen an einigen modernen Segelflugzeugen. *Aero-Revue*, pages 714–719, 1978. See also OSTIV Publication XV. Presented at the XVI OSTIV Congress, Châteauroux, France, 1978.

[226] Stich, G., Eberius, O., and v. Werne, D. Standard-Klasse auf dem Prüfstand. *Aerokurier*, 34(1):76–81, 1990.

[227] Thomas, F. and Laude, J. Vergleichsmessungen an Laminarflügeln mit starrer und flexibler Wölbklappe. OSTIV Publication X. Presented at the XI OSTIV Congress, Leszno, Poland, 1968.

[228] van Oosterom, T. Performance testing of sailplanes. OSTIV Publication III. Presented at the V OSTIV Congress, Buxton, England, 1954.

[229] Wieland, P., Stich, G., Schmerwitz, D., and Laurson, H. Doppelsitzer auf dem Prüfstand. *Aerokurier*, 33(4):84–91, 1989.

[230] Zacher, H. Vorschläge zur zahlenmäßigen Erfassung von Flugeigenschaften (Flugeigenschaftsrichtwerte). OSTIV Publication III. Presented at the V OSTIV Congress, Buxton, England, 1954.

[231] Zacher, H. Flugeigenschaftsuntersuchungen an 14 Segelflugzeugen. Technical Report 40, Flugwissenschaftliche Forschungsanstalt, München, Germany, 1960.

[232] Zacher, H. Ergebnisse neuerer Messungen mit Segelflugzeugen. OSTIV Publication VII. Presented at the IX OSTIV Congress, Junin, Argentina, 1963.

[233] Zacher, H. Flugmessungen mit Segelflugzeugen von 12 bis 13 m Spannweite. OSTIV Publication IX. Presented at the X OSTIV Congress, South Cerney, England, 1965.

[234] Zacher, H. Flugmessungen mit Standard-Segelflugzeugen. OSTIV Publication IX. Presented at the X OSTIV Congress, South Cerney, England, 1965.

[235] Zacher, H. Messungen zum Einfluß der Insektenrauhigkeit auf die Flugleistungen. *Aerokurier*, pages 131–133, 1978.

Appendix 1: Sailplane Design Data and Drawings

Before undertaking the design of a new sailplane, the designer needs to develop a basic familiarity with existing designs. This appendix provides design data for a large number of well-known sailplanes. In most cases, three-view drawings are provided as well. The data were assembled from sources such as brochures, OSTIV's "The World's Sailplanes" [20], articles in various periodicals, and, wherever possible, directly from the manufacturer. The three-view drawings vary in scale and quality, and data derived from them (empennage areas, moment arms, etc.) may not be as reliable as those provided by the manufacturer. Some data, especially the weights, may vary considerably among individual examples of the same design or may depend on the age of the aircraft or on specific version (as with, for example, the HKS-III or SB 7). Hence, the tabulated data and drawings should be used for reference only. The goal here is not to provide precise engineering data for particular aircraft, but rather, to present a broad statistical overview of the primary design parameters as well as basic configuration information for the individual types.

The following apply to the individual data in the tables (see also the Nomenclature List on page 261 and Figs. 34, 160, and 181).

(1) First flight of basic design
(5) Fuselage and vertical stabilizer mass = (2)-90kg-(4)-(6)
(6) Includes V-tail mass
(10) = $(9)^2/(11)$
(12) based on empty mass + 90kg (2)
(13) based on maximum mass (3)
(14) = (11)/(9)
(16) spanwise location of wing taper breakpoint, normalized to wing half-span
(17) chord at wing taper breakpoint, normalized to wing root chord, $\lambda_k = c_k/c_r$
(18) wing tip chord, normalized to root chord, $\lambda = c_t/c_r$

(23) Empennage type: (see Fig. 181)
N = Conventional
C = Cruciform
T = T-tail
V = V-tail
H = double-fin

(24,25,26) For V-tail, the horizontal projection
(29,38) The moment arms l_H and l_V are referred to the c/4 points of the mean aerodynamic chords of the wing and stabilizer
(31) The lift curve slope is based on Eq. 110:

$$\frac{dC_L}{d\alpha} = \frac{2\pi \mathcal{R}}{2 + \sqrt{\mathcal{R}^2 + 4}}$$

The effects of wing sweep are not considered.
(33) For V-tail, the vertical projection
(34) For H- and V-tail, the vertical projection of **one** surface
(40) Lift curve slope is based on Eq. 110. Sweep neglected. For T-tails, the aerodynamic effects of the horizontal stabilizer are accounted for by assuming $\mathcal{R}_{eff} = 1.5\mathcal{R}_V$ with $\mathcal{R}_V$ from column (35). For conventional tails $\mathcal{R}_{eff} = 1.0\mathcal{R}_V$ and for V-tails $\mathcal{R}_{eff} = 0.75\mathcal{R}_V$. For V- and H-tails, the volume is multiplied by an additional factor of 2 in order to reflect both surfaces.
(42) u,l - Schempp-Hirth style dive brakes on upper (lower) wing surface.
F - high deflection trailing edge flaps
SF - split flap
TE - trailing edge flap/brake combination
chute - deployable drogue chute
(43) s_B = spanwise length of dive brakes (Fig. 160). For drogue chutes, the diameter of the chute.
(44) referenced to local wing chord

The following are gratefully acknowledged for their assistance in assembling the data in this section: Akaflieg Braunschweig • Akaflieg Darmstadt • Akaflieg Hannover • Akaflieg München • Akaflieg Stuttgart • Blanik America • DG Flugzeugbau • Grob Luft- und Raumfahrt • Idaflieg • Dr. Reiner Kickert • Jim Marske • John Monnett • Gary Osoba • OSTIV • Rolladen-Schneider Flugzeugbau • Russia Sailplanes • Schempp-Hirth Flugzeugbau • A. Schleicher Segelflugzeugbau • Schweizer Aircraft Corp. • Soaring Society of America • Stemme GmbH Co. KG • Gerd Stich • SZD Sailplanes • George Applebay • ... and many others.

Wooden sailplanes

	①	②	③	④	⑤	⑥	⑦	⑧	⑨	⑩	⑪	⑫	⑬	⑭	⑮	⑯	⑰	⑱	⑲	⑳
	first flight	mass, empty + 90kg	mass, Max. takeoff	mass, wing, m_W	mass, fuse. + vert. stab.	mass, horizontal stab.	water ballast	fuselage length	wingspan, b	aspect ratio, $\mathcal{R}$	wing area S	wing loading, min.	wing loading, max.	average chord $c_m = S/b$	root chord c_r	taper change point y_k/s	inner taper λ_k	taper ratio λ	twist	Airfoil root/tip
	(year)	[kg]	[kg]	[kg]	[kg]	[kg]	[kg]	[m]	[m]	[-]	[m²]	[daN/m²]	[daN/m²]	[m]	[m]	[-]	[-]	[-]	[°]	
Vampyr	1921	210	210				-	5.00	12.60	9.9	16.00	12.9	12.9	1.27	1.35	0.54	1.00	0.56		Gö 482
Fafnir	1930	290	315				-	7.76	19.00	19.4	18.60	15.3	16.6	0.98		-	-	0.27		Gö 652 / Gö 535
Grunau Baby IIb	1933	239	250	85	57	7	-	6.05	13.60	13.0	14.20	16.5	17.3	1.04	1.18	0.53	1.00	0.42	-9.5	Gö 535 / sym
Minimoa	1935	340	350	145	95	10	-	7.00	17.00	15.2	19.00	17.5	18.1	1.12	1.30	0.58	1.00	0.58	-2.0	Gö 681 / Gö 693 / sym
Weihe 50	1938	335	335	140	93	12	-	8.14	18.00	17.7	18.34	17.9	17.9	1.02	1.56	-	-	0.28	-6.5	Gö 549 / M 12
RJ-5	1950	385	385				-		16.80	24.3	11.60	32.5	32.5	0.69	1.00	-	-	0.30		NACA 63(2)-615
HKS I	1953	540	588	250	183	17	-	8.30	19.00	20.3	17.79	29.8	32.4	0.94	1.27	-	-	0.47	0.0	NACA 65_{215}-714
HKS III	1955	389	410	173	109	17	75	7.16	17.20	20.8	14.23	26.8	28.3	0.83	1.23	-	-	0.44	0.0	NACA 65_{215}-1116
Breguet 901	1956	340	430				-	7.28	17.30	20.0	15.00	22.2	28.1	0.87	1.30	-	-	0.35		NACA 63 Series
Briegleb BG 12	1956	338	340	133	104	11	-	5.87	15.24	18.0	12.91	25.7	25.8	0.85	1.14	-	-	0.27	1.0	NACA 4415 / 4406
Zugvogel III	1957	335	365	150	88	7	-	7.10	17.00	20.1	14.37	22.9	24.9	0.85	1.16	0.52	0.78	0.33	0.0	NACA 63_{215}-616 / 614
Zefir	1958	385	415	185	103	7	-	7.07	17.00	20.6	14.00	27.0	29.1	0.82	0.96	0.56	1.00	0.36	0.0	NACA 65_2-515 mod
Skylark 4	1961	346	373	160	85	11	-	7.60	18.20	20.6	16.10	21.1	22.7	0.88	1.07	0.32	1.00	0.50	-2.0	NACA 63_3-620 / NACA 6415
SHK	1965	352	370	164	87	11	-	6.30	17.00	19.7	14.65	23.6	24.8	0.86	1.20	-	-	0.43	0.0	E 266
Woodstock	1978	201	204	61	50[1]		-	5.90	11.90	14.6	9.73	20.3	20.6	0.82	1.07	-	-	0.43		Culver 18% / 13%

[1] includes stab

Wood (cont'd)

	Aileron		Emp.	Horizontal Stabilizer									Vertical Stabilizer									Dive Brakes		
	(21)	(22)	(23)	(24)	(25)	(26)	(27)	(28)	(29)	(30)	(31)	(32)	(33)	(34)	(35)	(36)	(37)	(38)	(39)	(40)	(41)	(42)	(43)	(44)
	aileron span	mean aileron chord	arrangement	span	area	aspect ratio	mean chord	elevator chord	moment arm	$l_H S_H$	horiz. stab. volume $(dC_L/d\alpha)_H l_H S_H$	airfoil	height	area	aspect ratio	mean chord	mean rudder chord	moment arm	$l_V S_V$	vert. stab. volume $(dC_L/d\beta)_V l_V S_V$	airfoil	arrangement	span	location on airfoil
	[-]	[m]		[m]	[m²]	[-]	[m]	[-]	[m]	[m³]	[m³]		[m]	[m²]	[-]	[m]	[-]	[m]	[m³]	[m³]			[m]	[-]
Vampyr	0.32	0.46	N	2.50	1.88	3.32	0.75	1.00	3.40	6.39	22.71		0.90	1.28	0.63	1.42	0.38	2.50	3.20	3.11	symm.			
Fafnir	0.60		N	3.50									1.66											
Grunau Baby IIb	0.52	0.32	N	2.90	2.32	3.63	0.80	0.47	3.45	8.00	29.69	symm.	1.20	0.81	1.78	0.68	0.91	3.90	3.16	7.55	symm.	u,l	0.72	0.37
Minimoa	0.58	0.40	N	3.00	1.98	4.55	0.66	0.41	4.13	8.18	33.53	symm.	1.42	1.20	1.68	0.85	1.00	4.50	5.40	12.36	symm.			
Weihe 50	0.64	0.33	N	3.50	2.25	5.44	0.64	0.55	4.70	10.58	46.38	Gö 409	1.15	1.27	1.04	1.10	0.69	5.00	6.35	9.76	symm.	u,l	0.89	0.70
RJ-5	0.30		N	2.20	2.60	1.86	1.18	0.40	3.50	9.10	22.49		1.60	1.70	1.51	1.06		4.00	6.80	14.29		l	0.26	
HKS I	elastic		V	2.90	1.97	4.27	0.68	0.44	4.88	9.61	38.41	NACA 65-014	1.13	0.83	1.54	0.73	0.44	4.72	3.92	13.18	symm. 14%	chute	1.30	
HKS III	elastic		V	2.45	1.39	4.32	0.57	0.44	4.00	5.56	22.32	NACA 64-012	1.03	0.59	1.80	0.57	0.44	4.00	2.36	9.06	symm. 12%	chute	1.30	
Breguet 901			N	3.00	2.07	4.35	0.69		4.21	8.71	35.08		1.00	1.20	0.83	1.20	0.60	4.20	5.04	6.33				
Briegleb BG 12	0.56	0.10	N	2.41	1.57	3.70	0.65		3.44	5.40	20.23	symm.	1.00	0.84	1.19	0.84		4.00	3.36	5.81	symm.	f	2.00	0.18
Zugvogel III	0.32	0.23	N	2.60	1.81	3.73	0.70	0.46	4.28	7.75	29.15	NACA 63-012	1.50	1.37	1.64	0.91	0.59	4.66	6.38	14.36	NACA 63-012	u,l	1.11	0.51
Zefir	0.42	0.17	N	2.40	1.28	4.50	0.53	0.44	4.45	5.70	23.26	NACA 65-012	1.34	0.99	1.81	0.74	0.44	4.10	4.06	9.84	NACA 65-012	chute		
Skylark 4	0.56		N	3.26	2.56	4.15	0.79	0.33	3.94	10.09	39.81	NACA 0009	1.41	1.76	1.13	1.25	0.47	4.40	7.74	12.79	symm.	u,l		
SHK	0.38	0.18	V	2.73	1.94	3.84	0.71	1.00	3.73	7.24	27.59	NACA 64-012	1.32	0.94	1.85	0.71	1.00	3.73	3.51	13.81	NACA 64-012	u,l	1.79	0.68
Woodstock	0.38	0.20	N	2.25	1.10	4.60	0.49	0.48	3.20	3.52	14.50		1.20	0.80	1.80	0.67		3.40	2.72	6.56		u,l	1.10	0.60

	① first flight	② mass, empty + 90kg	③ mass, Max. takeoff	④ mass, wing, m_W	⑤ mass, fuse. + vert. stab.	⑥ mass, horizontal stab.	⑦ water ballast	⑧ fuselage length	⑨ wingspan, b	⑩ aspect ratio, Æ	⑪ wing area S	⑫ wing loading, min.	⑬ wing loading, max.	⑭ average chord c_m = S/b	⑮ root chord c_r	⑯ taper change point y_k/s	⑰ inner taper λ_k	⑱ taper ratio λ	⑲ twist	⑳ Airfoil root/tip
	(year)	[kg]	[kg]	[kg]	[kg]	[kg]	[kg]	[m]	[m]	[-]	[m^2]	[daN/m^2]	[daN/m^2]	[m]	[m]	[-]	[-]	[-]	[°]	
Wooden sailplanes, 15m																				
Meise	1939	250	255	82	71	7	-	7.27	15.00	15.0	15.00	16.3	16.7	1.00	1.45	-	-	0.38	0.0	Gö 549 / Gö 676
Ka 6E	1955	281	300	116	69	6	-	6.70	15.00	18.1	12.40	22.2	23.7	0.83	1.17	0.61	0.68	0.32	-2.0	NACA 63_3-618m / 614/Jouk. 12%
SZD-22 Mucha Standard	1958	309	383	112	96	11	-	7.00	14.98	17.6	12.75	23.8	29.5	0.85	1.45	-	-	0.30	0.0	
K 8b	1958	281	310	110	74	7	-	7.00	15.00	15.9	14.15	19.5	21.5	0.94	1.30	0.60	0.74	0.38	-4.0	Gö 533(16.7%) / Gö 532
Standard Austria	1958	298	323	122	78	8	-	6.20	15.00	16.7	13.50	21.6	23.5	0.90	1.20	-	-	0.50	-1.5	NACA 65_2-416 [1]
SB 5 B	1959	293	300	122	69	12	-	6.50	15.00	17.3	13.00	22.1	22.6	0.87	1.00	0.54	1.00	0.56	0.0	NACA 63_3-618
M-100S	1960	308	315	124	87	7	-	6.36	15.00	17.2	13.10	23.1	23.6	0.87	1.30	-	-	0.35	-2.5	NACA 63_3-618 / 15 mod
Sagitta	1960	307	320	132	76	9	-	6.47	15.00	18.8	12.00	25.1	26.2	0.80	1.20	-	-	0.42	-1.0	NACA 63-618 / 4412
Foka 4	1960	335	385	130	107	8	-	7.00	15.00	18.5	12.16	27.0	31.1	0.81	1.22	-	-	0.31	0.0	NACA 63_3-618 / 4415
PIK-16C Vasama	1961	281	300	115	70	6	-	5.97	15.00	19.2	11.70	23.6	25.1	0.78	1.08	0.62	0.69	0.37	0.0	FX 05-188(14%) / NACA 63_2-615
Standard Elfe	1965	334	350	147	89	8	-	7.30	15.00	19.0	11.86	27.6	28.9	0.79	0.90	0.57	1.00	0.41	0.0	FX 61-163 / FX 60-126
Aerobatic, all types (cont'd)																				
Lo 100	1952	258	265	80	80	8	-	6.15	10.00	9.2	10.90	23.2	23.8	1.09	1.30	0.30	1.00	0.43	-3.0	Clark Y
B 4	1966	314	350	121	93	10	-	6.57	15.00	16.1	14.00	22.0	24.5	0.93	1.07	0.59	1.00	0.40	0.0	NACA 64-618
Salto	1970	259	270	86	75	8	-	5.90	13.60	21.5	8.60	29.5	30.8	0.63	0.86	-	-	0.42	-2.0	FX 66-17 A 182
Mü 28 (14m)	1983	417	436	185	129	13	-	6.75	14.00	13.5	14.56	28.1	29.4	1.04	1.43	-	-	0.42	0.0	FX 71-L-150/20
Mü 28 (12m)	1983	410	425	178	129	13	-	6.75	12.00	10.9	13.20	30.5	31.6	1.10	1.43	-	-	0.51	0.0	FX 71-L-150/20
SZD 59 Acro (13.2m)		355	380				-	6.85	13.20	17.8	9.80	35.5	38.0	0.74						NN 8

[1] SH-1 featured Eppler E266

	Aileron		Emp.	Horizontal Stabilizer									Vertical Stabilizer									Dive Brakes		
	(21)	(22)	(23)	(24)	(25)	(26)	(27)	(28)	(29)	(30)	(31)	(32)	(33)	(34)	(35)	(36)	(37)	(38)	(39)	(40)	(41)	(42)	(43)	(44)
	aileron span	mean aileron chord	arrangement	span	area	aspect ratio	mean chord	elevator chord	moment arm	$l_H S_H$	horiz. stab. volume $(dC_L/d\alpha)_H l_H S_H$	airfoil	height	area	aspect ratio	mean chord	mean rudder chord	moment arm	$l_V S_V$	vert. stab. volume $(dC_L/d\beta)_V l_V S_V$	airfoil	arrangement	span	location on airfoil
	[-]	[m]		[m]	[m²]	[-]	[m]	[-]	[m]	[m³]	[m³]		[m]	[m²]	[-]	[m]	[-]	[m]	[m³]	[m³]			[m]	[-]
Wood, 15m (cont'd)																								
Meise	0.30	0.20	N	2.90	2.35	3.58	0.81	0.40	4.13	9.71	35.78	symm.	1.40	1.07	1.83	0.76	0.67	4.53	4.85	11.84	symm.	u,l	0.88	0.40
Ka 6E	0.29	0.20	N	2.80	1.61	4.87	0.58	1.00	3.75	6.04	25.43	symm. 12%	1.43	1.15	1.78	0.80	0.55	3.95	4.54	10.85	symm. 12%	u,l	1.01	0.44
SZD-22 Mucha Standard	0.42	0.20	N	3.15	1.88	5.28	0.60	0.42	3.90	7.33	31.81	NACA 0012	1.50	1.20	1.88	0.80	0.64	3.80	4.56	11.33	NACA 0012	u,l	2.00	0.36
K 8b	0.32	0.23	N	2.80	1.95	4.02	0.70	0.49	3.82	7.45	28.99	symm. 12%	1.50	1.40	1.61	0.93	0.54	4.18	5.85	12.94	symm. 12%	u,l	1.01	0.44
Standard Austria	0.28	0.20	V	2.60	2.00	3.38	0.77	1.00	3.80	7.60	27.23	NACA 64-012	1.30	1.00	1.69	0.77	1.00	3.80	3.80	13.86		u,l	1.76	0.67
SB 5 B	0.36	0.25	V	2.80	1.70	4.61	0.61	0.41	3.96	6.73	27.76	NACA 64-009	0.98	0.60	1.60	0.61	0.41	3.96	2.38	8.27		u,l	0.98	0.48
M-100S	0.35	0.20	N	3.00	1.60	5.62	0.53	0.50	3.52	5.63	24.98	NACA 64-010	1.60	0.98	2.61	0.61	0.54	3.86	3.78	11.74	NACA 64-010	u,l		0.42
Sagitta	0.40	0.16	N	3.00	1.35	6.67	0.45	0.45	3.48	4.70	21.96	symm. 14%	1.13	1.60	0.80	1.42	0.21	3.45	5.52	6.66	symm. 10%	u,l	1.03	0.45
Foka 4	0.40	0.15	N	2.70	1.40	5.21	0.52	0.40	4.00	5.60	24.18	NACA 63-012/9	1.20	0.98	1.47	0.82	0.45	3.80	3.72	7.67	NACA 63-012/9	u,l	1.06	0.67
PIK-16C Vasama	0.32	0.20	C	2.20	1.27	3.81	0.58	0.50	3.65	4.64	17.61		1.35	1.10	1.66	0.81	0.50	3.80	4.18	9.47		u,l	0.95	0.65
Standard Elfe	0.32	0.18	N	2.90	1.45	5.80	0.50	1.00	4.27	6.19	27.74	NACA 65-012	1.43	1.05	1.95	0.73	0.40	4.33	4.55	11.61		u,l	1.11	0.58
Aerobatic, all types (cont'd)																								
Lo 100	0.56	0.24	C	2.70	1.00	7.29	0.37	0.42	3.24	3.24	15.52	Gö mod	1.10	0.78	1.55	0.71	0.63	3.74	2.92	6.28	Gö mod	TE	2.30	0.50
B 4	0.37	0.19	T	3.08	1.71	5.55	0.56	0.33	3.83	6.55	28.91	NACA 0009	1.32	1.22	1.43	0.92	0.34	3.38	4.12	11.26	NACA 64-012A	u,l	1.31	0.62
Salto	0.43	0.10	V	2.14	1.09	4.20	0.51	0.38	3.61	3.93	15.61		0.91	0.46	1.80	0.51	0.38	3.61	1.66	6.38		TE	1.30	0.71
Mü 28 (14m)	0.71	0.21	C	3.00	1.83	4.92	0.61	0.25	3.51	6.42	27.16	FX 71-L-150/25	1.40	1.22	1.61	0.87	0.54	3.57	4.36	9.63	FX 71-L-150	u	1.40	0.50
Mü 28 (12m)	0.70	0.22	C	3.00	1.83	4.92	0.61	0.25	3.51	6.42	27.16	FX 71-L-150/25	1.40	1.22	1.61	0.87	0.54	3.57	4.36	9.63	FX 71-L-150	u	1.40	0.50
SZD 59 Acro (13.2m)			C																			u,l		

	1	2	3	4	5	6	7	8	9	10	11	12	13	14	15	16	17	18	19	20
	first flight	mass, empty + 90kg	mass, Max. takeoff	mass, wing, m_W	mass, fuse. + vert. stab.	mass, horizontal stab.	water ballast	fuselage length	wingspan, b	aspect ratio, $\mathcal{R}$	wing area S	wing loading, min.	wing loading, max.	average chord $c_m = S/b$	root chord c_r	taper change point y_k/s	inner taper λ_k	taper ratio λ	twist	Airfoil root/tip
	(year)	[kg]	[kg]	[kg]	[kg]	[kg]	[kg]	[m]	[m]	[-]	[m²]	[daN/m²]	[daN/m²]	[m]	[m]	[-]	[-]	[-]	[°]	
Metal sailplanes																				
SGU 1-19	1944	235	250				-	6.60	11.20	7.9	15.80	14.6	15.5	1.41	1.45			1.00		NACA 43012A
SGU 1-20	1946	265	285				-	6.60	13.10	10.2	16.90	15.4	16.5	1.29	1.45	0.53	1.00	0.63		NACA 43012A
SGS 1-21	1947	304	450	152	57	6	118	6.72	15.50	15.7	15.30	19.5	28.8	0.99	1.37	-	-	0.45	-2.0	NACA 23012 / 23009
SGS 1-26	1954	252	260	105	54	3	-	6.57	12.16	9.9	14.87	16.6	17.1	1.22	1.61	0.40	1.00	0.53	-2.5	NACA 43012A
HP-8	1958	381	386	159	100		-	6.36	15.65	23.9	10.25	36.5	36.9	0.65	0.76		1.00	0.50	0.0	NACA 65_3 618
FK 3	1968	364	400	152	113	9	50	7.22	17.40	21.9	13.80	25.9	28.4	0.79	0.87	-	-	0.34	0.0	FX 62-K-153
Monnett Monerai	1979	190	204				-	6.00	10.97	16.6	7.25	25.7	27.6	0.66		-	-	1.00	-	FX 61-192 (mod)
SGS 1-36		305	322				-	6.20	14.00	15.0	13.10	22.8	24.1	0.94	1.25	-	-	0.48	-0.9	FX 61-163 / 60-126
Metal, 15m																				
SGS 1-23H-15	1959	340	340	127	81	7	-	6.23	14.98	15.2	14.81	22.5	22.5	0.99	1.22		1.00	0.37	-2.5	NACA 43012A / 23009
SGS 1-34	1969	339	363				-	7.80	15.00	16.0	14.03	23.7	25.4	0.94	1.30	-	-	0.46		FX 61-163 / 60-126
SGS 1-35	1973	290	422				122	5.79	15.00	23.3	9.64	29.5	42.9	0.64	0.90	-	-	0.40		FX 67-K-170 / 150
Laister Nugget	1971	300	408	95	98[1]		84	6.10	15.00	22.2	10.12	29.1	39.5	0.67	0.95	-	-	0.42		Wortmann
HP-18	1975	303	417	123	90[2]		91	7.16	15.00	21.1	10.66	27.9	38.4	0.71	0.90	-	-	0.50	0.0	FX 67-K-150
Flying wing, all types																				
AV 361 (AV 36 Mk II)	1951 (AV 36) 1960 (AV 361)	210	225	-	-	-	-	2.48	12.78	11.2	14.60	14.1	15.1	1.14	1.60	0.24	1.00	0.25	0.0	F_2 17%
Pioneer II-D	1973	233	257	91	52	0	-	3.80	14.00	14.8	13.20	17.3	19.1	0.94	1.52			0.27	0.0	NACA 33012R/33010R
SB 13	1988	348	427				135	3.02	15.00	19.4	11.60	29.4	36.1	0.77	0.95	0.10 0.25	0.96 0.86	0.29	0.0	HQ 34/HQ 36 K
Genesis 2	1994	328	525	123	111	4	182	4.80	15.00	20.0	11.24	28.6	45.8	0.75	1.18			0.30	-3.0	R74S

[1] includes stab
[2] includes stab

	Aileron		Emp.	Horizontal Stabilizer									Vertical Stabilizer									Dive Brakes		
	21	22	23	24	25	26	27	28	29	30	31	32	33	34	35	36	37	38	39	40	41	42	43	44
	aileron span	mean aileron chord	arrangement	span	area	aspect ratio	mean chord	elevator chord	moment arm	l_HS_H	horiz. stab. volume $(dC_L/d\alpha)_H l_H S_H$	airfoil	height	area	aspect ratio	mean chord	mean rudder chord	moment arm	l_VS_V	vert. stab. volume $(dC_L/d\beta)_V l_V S_V$	airfoil	arrangement	span	location on airfoil
	[-]	[m]		[m]	[m²]	[-]	[m]	[-]	[m]	[m³]	[m³]		[m]	[m²]	[-]	[m]	[-]	[m]	[m³]	[m³]			[m]	[-]
Metal (cont'd)																								
SGU 1-19	0.27	0.43	N	2.36	1.91	2.92	0.81	0.45	4.00	7.64	25.29		1.50	1.21	1.86	0.81	0.54	3.60	4.36	10.76		-		
SGU 1-20	0.52	0.32	N	2.36	1.91	2.92	0.81	0.45	3.75	7.16	23.71		1.50	1.21	1.86	0.81	0.54	3.60	4.36	10.76		u	0.40	
SGS 1-21	0.53	0.24	N	2.60	1.62	4.17	0.62	0.45	3.70	5.99	23.71	S.A.C.	1.50	1.10	2.05	0.73	0.61	3.95	4.35	11.49	S.A.C.	u,l		
FK 3	0.32	0.14	C	2.80	1.28	6.12	0.46	0.45	3.95	5.06	23.05	NACA 64-012/9	1.68	1.35	2.09	0.80	0.51	4.20	5.67	15.22	NACA 64-012	u,l	1.50	0.45
SGS 1-26	0.38		N	2.29	1.72	3.05	0.75	0.50	3.97	6.83	23.17	symm.	1.35	1.21	1.51	0.90		3.50	4.23	8.90	symm.			
HP-8	0.38	0.11	V	2.42	1.24	4.72	0.51	0.38	3.61	4.48	18.63	NACA 65 009	2.40	1.04	5.54	0.43	0.26	3.61	3.75	29.65	NACA65 009	u,l,f		
Monnett Monerai	0.33	0.10	V	1.05	0.42	2.62	0.40	1.00	3.75	1.57	4.90		0.75	0.38	1.50	0.50	1.00	3.70	1.39	4.57		f	3.35	
SGS 1-36	0.36	0.20	T	2.10	1.26	3.50	0.60	0.42	3.70	4.66	17.00		1.10	0.83	1.46	0.75		3.50	2.90	8.04		u,l		
Metal, 15m (cont'd)																								
SGS 1-23H-15	0.49	0.23	N	2.13	1.41	3.22	0.66	0.44	3.79	5.34	18.66		1.37	1.21	1.55	0.88	0.54	3.44	4.16	8.95		u,l	1.15	
SGS 1-34	0.33	0.20	N	2.65	1.34	5.24	0.51		4.70	6.30	27.25		1.30	1.00	1.69	0.77		4.50	4.50	10.35	1.0	u,l	1.20	
SGS 1-35	0.44	0.08	T	2.05	1.01	4.16	0.49	0.43	3.70	3.74	14.77		1.02	0.78	1.33	0.76	0.50	3.40	2.65	6.90		F	3.70	0.80
Laister Nugget	0.37	0.10	T	2.30	1.00	5.29	0.43	0.43	4.00	4.00	17.37		1.20	0.90	1.60	0.75	0.50	3.70	3.33	9.80		F	4.10	0.85
HP-18	0.28	0.10	V	2.00	1.30	3.08	0.65	0.45	4.20	5.46	18.62		1.00	0.65	1.54	0.65	0.45	4.20	2.73	9.19		F	4.70	0.80
Flying wing, all types (cont'd)																								
AV 361 (AV 36 Mk II)	0.47	0.19	H										1.35	1.14	1.60	0.84	0.40	1.50	1.71	7.53	symm. 8%			
Pioneer II-D			C																					
SB 13	0.47	0.19	H										1.25	0.68	2.31	0.54	0.26	1.45	0.98	5.63	FX 71-L-150/30 mod	u	1.28	0.50
Genesis 2		0/19	T	1.83	0.64	5.23	0.35	1.00	2.57	1.64	7.11	RH-3	1.46	0.80	2.66	0.55		1.80	1.44	5.59	RF-3	u	2.20	

Multiplace, all types, pre-1980

	①	②	③	④	⑤	⑥	⑦	⑧	⑨	⑩	⑪	⑫	⑬	⑭	⑮	⑯	⑰	⑱	⑲	⑳
	first flight	mass, empty + 90kg	mass, Max. takeoff	mass, wing, m_W	mass, fuse. + vert. stab.	mass, horizontal stab.	water ballast	fuselage length	wingspan, b	aspect ratio, Æ	wing area S	wing loading, min.	wing loading, max.	average chord $c_m = S/b$	root chord c_r	taper change point y_k/s	inner taper λ_k	taper ratio λ	twist	Airfoil root/tip
	(year)	[kg]	[kg]	[kg]	[kg]	[kg]	[kg]	[m]	[m]	[-]	[m²]	[daN/m²]	[daN/m²]	[m]	[m]	[-]	[-]	[-]	[°]	
Kranich II	1935	380	465	163	117	10	-	7.70	18.00	14.3	22.70	16.4	20.1	1.26	1.60	0.33	1.00	0.38		Gö 535
Goevier	1938	325	410	122	102	11	-	6.24	14.84	11.6	19.00	16.8	21.2	1.28	1.45	0.37	1.00	0.39	0.0	Joukowsky
LK 10	1942	305	397	100	103	12	-	6.50	15.24	15.3	15.20	19.7	25.6	1.00	1.43	-	-	0.39	-4.0	NACA 4418/4409
SGU 2-22	1945	295	380				-	7.70	13.10	8.8	19.50	14.8	19.1	1.49	1.53	-	-	1.00	-3.0	NACA 43012 A
Kranich III	1951	410	520	204	105	11	-	9.10	18.10	15.6	21.06	19.1	24.2	1.16	1.75	-	-	0.33	-8.0	Gö 549
Bocian	1952	423	510	166	155	12	-	8.00	18.11	16.4	20.00	20.7	25.0	1.10	1.60	-	-	0.33	-2.0	NACA 43018 A/012 A
Bergfalke II/55	1955	349	440	152	97	10	-	7.88	16.60	15.6	17.70	19.3	24.4	1.07	1.51	-	-	0.40	0.0	Mü 14.5
Blanik L-13 (metal)	1956	382	500	172	106	14	-	8.40	16.20	13.7	19.15	19.6	25.6	1.18	1.67	-	-	0.42	-3.0	NACA 63_2-615 A
Ka 7	1957	382	480	162	120	10	-	8.15	16.00	14.6	17.50	21.4	26.9	1.09	1.50	-	-	0.41	-3.0	Gö 533m/532
SGS 2-32 (metal)	1962	408	490	168			-	8.15	17.40	18.1	16.70	24.0	28.8	0.96	1.45	-	-	0.33	-2.0	NACA 63_3-618 / 43012A
T 49 Capstan	1961	439	567	164	162	19	-	7.72	16.78	13.8	20.43	21.1	27.2	1.22	1.68	-	-	0.69	-3.0	NACA 63_3-620 / 6412
SGS 2-33A (metal)	1966	362	472				-	7.85	15.54	11.8	20.39	17.4	22.7	1.31	1.55	0.44	1.00	0.50		NACA 43012A
ASK 13	1966	408	480	161	147	10	-	8.18	16.00	14.6	17.50	22.9	26.9	1.09	1.50	-	-	0.41	-5.0	Gö 535/549 / Gö 541
A-21 Calif (metal)	1970	532	644	257	169	16	-	7.74	20.38	25.7	16.19	32.2	39.0	0.79	0.90	0.63	1.00	0.36	0.0	FX 67-K-170 / FX 60-126
SB 10 (26m)	1972	708	889	397	211	10	100	10.36	26.00	31.0	21.80	31.9	40.0	0.84	0.97	0.34 0.82	1.00 0.80	0.46	-1.5	FX 62-K-153/131 / FX 60-126
SB 10 (29m)[1]	1972	647	897	419	127	11	100	10.36	29.00	36.7	22.90	27.7	38.4	0.79	0.97	0.30 0.67	1.00 0.80	0.30	-1.5	FX 62-K-153/131 / FX 60-126
LSD-Ornith	1972	377	450				-	7.50	18.00	26.1	12.40	29.8	35.6	0.69	0.96	-	-			FX 66-S-196 mod
Twin Astir	1976	495	650	194	196	15	100	8.10	17.50	17.1	17.90	27.1	35.6	1.02	1.30	0.58	0.78	0.51	0.0	E 603
Globetrotter	1977	490	600				-	7.66	17.00	18.4	15.72	30.6	37.4	0.92	1.30	-	-		0.0	E 603
B 12	1977	528	620	225	204	9	-	8.73	18.20	20.0	16.60	31.2	36.6	0.91	1.20	0.59	0.77	0.22	0.0	FX 67-K-170/150
Scheibe SFH 34	1978	380	490				-	7.50	15.80	16.9	14.80	25.2	32.5	0.94		-	-	0.40		FX 61-184 / FX 60-126
ASK 21	1979	457	600	202	150	15	-	8.35	17.00	16.1	17.95	25.0	32.8	1.06	1.50	0.61	0.67	0.35	-1.5	FX S02-196 / FX 60-126
Janus C	1979	464	700	210	157	7	240	8.62	20.00	23.0	17.40	26.2	39.5	0.87	1.18	0.54	0.80	0.30	0.0	FX 67-K-170/150

[1] flown solo only

	Aileron		Emp.	Horizontal Stabilizer									Vertical Stabilizer									Dive Brakes		
	(21)	(22)	(23)	(24)	(25)	(26)	(27)	(28)	(29)	(30)	(31)	(32)	(33)	(34)	(35)	(36)	(37)	(38)	(39)	(40)	(41)	(42)	(43)	(44)
	aileron span	mean aileron chord	arrangement	span	area	aspect ratio	mean chord	elevator chord	moment arm	$l_H S_H$	horiz. stab. volume $(dC_L/d\alpha)_H l_H S_H$	airfoil	height	area	aspect ratio	mean chord	mean rudder chord	moment arm	$l_V S_V$	vert. stab. volume $(dC_L/d\beta)_V l_V S_V$	airfoil	arrangement	span	location on airfoil
	[-]	[m]		[m]	[m²]	[-]	[m]	[-]	[m]	[m³]	[m³]		[m]	[m²]	[-]	[m]	[-]	[m]	[m³]	[m³]			[m]	[-]
Multiplace, all types, pre-1980 (cont'd)																								
Kranich II	0.69	0.40	N	3.00	2.20	4.09	0.73	0.45	4.35	9.57	37.53	symm.	1.58	1.36	1.84	0.86	0.73	4.78	6.50	15.90		u,l	1.67	0.40
Goevier	0.61	0.34	N	3.18	2.64	3.83	0.83	0.42	4.26	11.25	42.82	symm.	1.74	1.72	1.76	0.99	0.64	4.64	7.98	18.92	symm.	u,l	0.90	0.40
LK 10	0.54	0.24	N	2.79	1.98	3.93	0.71	0.67	3.46	6.85	26.40	NACA 0009	1.37	1.23	1.53	0.90	0.62	3.86	4.75	10.08	NACA 0009	u,l	1.21	0.46
SGU 2-22	0.27	0.87	N	2.36	1.91	2.92	0.81	0.45	5.00	9.55	31.61		1.80	1.21	2.68	0.67	0.54	4.50	5.45	17.15		u		
Kranich III	0.46	0.37	N	3.50	2.32	5.28	0.66	0.41	4.70	10.90	47.31		1.26	1.68	0.95	1.33	0.82	5.00	8.40	11.84		u,l	1.21	0.46
Bocian	0.48	0.34	N	3.85	2.80	5.29	0.73	0.45	4.35	12.18	52.90	NACA 0010/12	1.63	1.51	1.76	0.93	0.60	4.85	7.32	17.36	NACA 0011/12	u,l	1.18	0.44
Bergfalke II/55	0.46	0.26	N	2.80	2.00	3.92	0.71	0.46	4.11	8.22	31.63		1.27	1.09	1.48	0.86	0.77	4.87	5.31	11.00		u,l	1.10	0.55
Blanik L-13 (metal)	0.42	0.34	N	3.45	2.66	4.47	0.77	0.42	4.76	12.66	51.58	symm.	1.53	1.61	1.45	1.05	0.56	4.74	7.63	15.59		u,l		
Ka 7	0.37	0.27	N	3.00	2.25	4.00	0.75	0.42	4.43	9.97	38.71	symm. 12%	1.45	1.21	1.74	0.83	0.58	4.95	5.99	14.06	symm. 12%	u,l	1.47	0.38
T 49 Capstan	0.44	0.29	N	3.81	3.51	4.14	0.92	0.35	4.97	17.44	68.75	NACA 66_1-012	1.42	1.61	1.25	1.13	0.35	4.97	8.00	14.44	NACA 64-009	u,l	0.17	0.40
SGS 2-32 (metal)	0.38	0.21	N	2.44	1.73	3.44	0.71	1.00	5.10	8.82	31.90		1.62	1.27	2.07	0.78	0.43	4.20	5.33	14.20	NACA 0009	u,l	1.39	0.80
SGS 2-33A (metal)	0.44	0.25	N	2.30	1.70	3.11	0.74	0.47	4.90	8.33	28.58		1.50	1.35	1.67	0.90		4.50	6.08	13.82		u,l		
ASK 13	0.37	0.27	N	3.00	2.25	4.00	0.75	0.42	4.40	9.90	38.44	symm. 12%	1.45	1.21	1.74	0.83	0.57	5.05	6.11	14.35	symm. 12%	u,l	1.47	0.38
A-21 Calif (metal)	0.28	0.18	T	3.15	1.70	5.84	0.54	0.20	5.08	8.64	38.77	NACA 64-012A/008A	1.95	1.34	2.84	0.69	0.47	4.92	6.59	26.30	NACA 65-012A/	TE	3.50	0.80
SB 10 (26m)	0.64	0.16	C	3.30	1.47	7.41	0.45	0.41	5.74	8.44	40.60	NACA 63-006A	2.40	2.61	2.21	1.09	0.49	6.14	16.03	44.64	NACA 65-012A/009A	u,l,TE	1.20	0.53
SB 10 (29m)[1]	0.68	0.16	C	3.30	1.47	7.41	0.45	0.41	5.74	8.44	40.60	NACA 63-006A	2.40	2.61	2.21	1.09	0.49	6.14	16.03	44.64	NACA 64-012A/009A	TE,u,l	4.03/1.2	0.8/0.53
LSD-Ornith			T	2.30				1.00					1.30	1.20	1.41	0.92								
Twin Astir	0.36	0.18	T	3.30	2.05	5.31	0.62	0.27	4.81	9.86	42.88	E 528	1.60	1.43	1.79	0.89	0.38	4.68	6.69	21.11	E 608	u	1.40	0.48
Globetrotter			T	2.75	1.47	5.14	0.53						1.20	1.00	1.44	0.83						u		
B 12	0.37	0.15	T	3.10	1.45	6.63	0.47	0.30	5.13	7.44	34.72	FX 71-L-150/30	1.40	1.39	1.41	0.99	0.30	4.95	6.88	18.62	FX 71-L-150/30	u	1.21	0.57
Scheibe SFH 34			T					0.25				FX 71-L-150	1.45				0.40				FX 71-L-150	u	1.40	0.55
ASK 21	0.33	0.20	T	3.10	1.92	5.01	0.62	0.30	4.93	9.47	40.28	FX 71-L-150/30	1.36	1.33	1.39	0.98	0.30	4.80	6.38	17.11	FX 71-L-150/30	u	1.38	0.41
Janus C	0.43	0.14	T	2.50	1.25	5.00	0.50	0.31	5.41	6.76	28.77	FX 71-L-150	1.27	1.17	1.38	0.92	0.38	5.96	6.97	18.58	NACA 64-013/012	u,chute	1.2/1.3	0.57

[1] flown solo only

Multiplace, all types, post-1980

	①	②	③	④	⑤	⑥	⑦	⑧	⑨	⑩	⑪	⑫	⑬	⑭	⑮	⑯	⑰	⑱	⑲	⑳
	first flight	mass, empty + 90kg	mass, Max. takeoff	mass, wing, m_W	mass, fuse. + vert. stab.	mass, horizontal stab.	water ballast	fuselage length	wingspan, b	aspect ratio, $\mathcal{R}$	wing area S	wing loading, min.	wing loading, max.	average chord c_m = S/b	root chord c_r	taper change point y_k/s	inner taper λ_k	taper ratio λ	twist	Airfoil root/tip
	(year)	[kg]	[kg]	[kg]	[kg]	[kg]	[kg]	[m]	[m]	[-]	[m^2]	[daN/m^2]	[daN/m^2]	[m]	[m]	[-]	[-]	[-]	[°]	
Twin III Acro	1986	470	600	182	185	13	-	8.20	18.00	18.5	17.52	26.3	33.6	0.97	1.30	0.50 0.83	0.81 0.56	0.29	0.0	E 583
ASH 25	1986	558	750	290	170	8	180	9.00	25.00	38.3	16.31	33.6	45.1	0.65	0.83	0.30 0.66	0.94 0.73	0.44	0.0	HQ 17/14,38 / DU 84-132 V3
Nimbus 3D-T	1986	627	800	305	225	7	280	8.87	25.00	37.0	16.90	36.4	46.4	0.68	0.91	0.32 0.58 0.72 0.95	0.87 0.77 0.66 0.32	0.17	0.0	XX 79/18N2 / ZZ 135/20
Stemme S-10	1986	735	850				-	8.42	23.00	28.3	18.70	38.5	44.6	0.81	1.00	0.43 0.72	0.90 0.70	0.30		HQ41/14.35
DG 500 M	1987	650	825	240	306	14	100	8.65	22.00	26.5	18.29	34.9	44.2	0.83	1.16	0.52	0.79	0.25	0.0	FX 73-K-170/17
DG 500 S	1989	538	750	240	194	14	160	8.65	22.00	26.5	18.29	28.8	40.2	0.83	1.16	0.52	0.79	0.25	0.0	FX 73-K-170/17
DG 500 Trainer	1989	478	615	180	194	14	-	8.65	18.00	19.5	16.65	28.2	36.2	0.92	1.16	0.64	0.79	0.45	0.0	FX 73-K-170/17
B 13	1991	680	820	340	241	9	-	8.42	23.20	28.4	18.95	35.2	42.4	0.82	1.04	0.43 0.72	0.89 0.74	0.22	0.0	HQ 41/14,35
Janus Ce	1992	507	700	210	200	7	240	8.87	20.00	23.1	17.30	28.7	39.7	0.86	1.20	0.54	0.76	0.29	0.0	FX 67-K-170/150
Duo-Discus	1993	498	700	200	200	8	180	8.87	20.00	24.4	16.40	29.8	41.9	0.82	1.03	0.45 0.81 0.91	0.93 0.62 0.46	0.24	0.0	HX 83
L-23 Super Blanik (metal)	1988	400	510	156	132		-	8.50	16.20	13.7	19.15	20.5	26.1	1.18	1.65			0.45		NACA 63_2A615/612
Blanik L-13AC (metal)		395	500				-	8.40	14.10	11.4	17.40	22.3	28.2	1.23						
D-41	1993	493	650	192	202	9	150	8.55	20.00	28.6	14.00	34.5	45.5	0.70	0.96	-	0.69	0.27	0.0	as LS 6; root mod
Eta		710	850	370	242	8	110	9.75	30.90	51.3	18.61	37.4	44.8	0.60	0.87				0.0	HQR 3 / HQR 1 / HQR 2

Multiplace, all types, post-1980 (cont'd)

	Aileron		Emp.	Horizontal Stabilizer									Vertical Stabilizer									Dive Brakes		
	21	22	23	24	25	26	27	28	29	30	31	32	33	34	35	36	37	38	39	40	41	42	43	44
	aileron span	mean aileron chord	arrangement	span	area	aspect ratio	mean chord	elevator chord	moment arm	$l_H S_H$	horiz. stab. volume $(dC_L/d\alpha)_H l_H S_H$	airfoil	height	area	aspect ratio	mean chord	mean rudder chord	moment arm	$l_V S_V$	vert. stab. volume $(dC_L/d\beta)_V l_V S_V$	airfoil	arrangement	span	location on airfoil
	[-]	[m]		[m]	[m²]	[-]	[m]	[-]	[m]	[m³]	[m³]		[m]	[m²]	[-]	[m]	[-]	[m]	[m³]	[m³]			[m]	[-]
Twin III Acro	0.44	0.16	T	3.39	2.18	5.27	0.64	0.28	4.66	10.16	44.05	E 528 mod	1.30	1.37	1.23	1.05	0.37	4.49	6.15	15.14	E 608	u	1.70	0.50
ASH 25	0.32	0.09	T	3.13	1.27	7.71	0.41	0.30	5.30	6.73	32.73	FX 71-L-150/30 (12%)	1.54	1.71	1.39	1.11	0.30	5.16	8.82	23.61	FX 71-L-150/30 (12%)	u	1.20	0.53
Nimbus 3D-T	0.61	0.11	T	2.50	1.25	5.00	0.50	0.30	5.30	6.62	28.18	FX 71-L-150/30	1.43	1.48	1.38	1.03	0.30	5.05	7.47	19.94	FX 71-L-150/30	o	1.37	0.56
Stemme S-10	0.47	0.18	T	3.50	1.75	7.00	0.50		5.00	8.75	41.47		1.52	1.36	1.70	0.89	0.34	5.00	6.80	20.78		u	1.40	0.40
DG 500 M	0.45	0.13	T	3.17	1.90	5.29	0.60	0.31	5.04	9.58	41.57	D 38-137 000	1.64	1.49	1.81	0.91	0.35	5.01	7.46	23.67	FX 71-L-150/35	u	1.50	0.59
DG 500 S	0.45	0.13	T	3.17	1.90	5.29	0.60	0.31	5.04	9.58	41.57	D 38-137 000	1.64	1.49	1.81	0.91	0.35	5.01	7.46	23.67	FX 71-L-150/35	u	1.50	0.59
DG 500 Trainer	0.40	0.15	T	3.17	1.90	5.29	0.60	0.31	5.03	9.56	41.49	D 38-137 000	1.64	1.49	1.81	0.91	0.35	4.99	7.44	23.57	FX 71-L-150/35	u	1.50	0.59
B 13	0.37	0.15	T	3.10	1.45	6.63	0.47	0.30	5.13	7.44	34.72	FX 71-L-150/30	1.40	1.39	1.41	0.99	0.30	4.95	6.88	18.62	FX 71-L-150/30	u	1.21	0.57
Janus Ce	0.45	0.14	T	2.50	1.25	5.00	0.50	0.31	5.40	6.75	28.71	FX 71-L-150/30	1.43	1.48	1.38	1.03	0.30	5.10	7.55	20.14	FX 71-L-150/30	u	1.30	0.49
Duo-Discus	0.45	0.13	T	3.10	1.36	7.07	0.44	0.30	5.16	7.02	33.35	FX 71-L-150/30	1.43	1.48	1.38	1.03	0.30	5.00	7.40	19.75	FX 71-L-150/30	u	1.43	0.62
L-23 Super Blanik (metal)	0.39	0.37	T	3.40	2.69	4.30	0.79		4.95	13.32	53.34											u,l	1.50	0.50
Blanik L-13AC (metal)																								
D-41	0.68	0.11	T	3.13	1.27	7.71	0.41	0.30	5.67	7.20	35.01	FX 71-L-150/30 (12%)	1.54	1.71	1.39	1.11	0.30	5.26	8.99	24.06	FX 71-L-150/30 (12%)	u	1.41	0.50
Eta	0.97		T	3.22	1.31	7.91	0.41		6.23	8.16	39.93	HQR 5	1.75	2.01	1.52	1.15		6.06	12.18	34.73	HQR 4	u	1.95	0.61

	①	②	③	④	⑤	⑥	⑦	⑧	⑨	⑩	⑪	⑫	⑬	⑭	⑮	⑯	⑰	⑱	⑲	⑳
	first flight	mass, empty + 90kg	mass, Max. takeoff	mass, wing, m_W	mass, fuse. + vert. stab.	mass, horizontal stab.	water ballast	fuselage length	wingspan, b	aspect ratio, Æ	wing area S	wing loading, min.	wing loading, max.	average chord $c_m = S/b$	root chord c_r	taper change point y_k/s	inner taper λ_k	taper ratio λ	twist	Airfoil root/tip
	(year)	[kg]	[kg]	[kg]	[kg]	[kg]	[kg]	[m]	[m]	[-]	[m²]	[daN/m²]	[daN/m²]	[m]	[m]	[-]	[-]	[-]	[°]	
Standard Class, composite construction, pre-1980																				
Phoebus B1	1964	314	350	130	85	9	-	6.98	15.00	17.2	13.11	23.5	26.2	0.87	1.21	-	-	0.37	-2.0	E 403
fs 23 "Hidalgo"	1966	192	190	54	43	4	-	5.00	13.00	24.1	7.00	27.0	26.6	0.54	0.72	0.71	0.64	0.33		FX 61-184/168/147 / FX 60-126
LS 1c	1967	293	312	107	91	5	-	7.20	15.00	23.1	9.74	29.5	31.4	0.65	0.85	0.60	0.78	0.38	-2.0	FX 66 S 196 mod
Std. Libelle	1967	289	350	108	84	7	50	6.20	15.00	23.0	9.80	28.9	35.0	0.65	0.88	0.58	0.74	0.40	-2.5	FX 66-17A II 182
fs 25	1968	238	250	78	66	4	-	6.48	15.00	26.3	8.54	27.3	28.7	0.57	0.76	0.74	0.67	0.32	0.0	FX S 196/184/168/147 / FX 60-126
ASW 15B	1968	324	408	135	90	9	82	6.48	15.00	20.5	11.00	28.9	36.4	0.73	0.91	0.59	0.85	0.42	-2.0	FX 61-163 / FX 60-126
Standard Cirrus	1969	302	390	110	95	7	60	6.35	15.00	22.4	10.04	29.5	38.1	0.67	0.92	0.60	0.70	0.38	-0.8	FX S-02-196/66-17AII182
D 38	1972	306	360	118	91	7	40	6.92	15.00	20.5	11.00	27.3	32.1	0.73	0.94	0.60	0.80	0.40	-2.6	FX 61-184 / FX 60-126
Std. Jantar	1973	340	440	136	106	8	100	7.11	15.00	21.1	10.66	31.3	40.5	0.71	0.95	-	-	0.47	-3.0	NN 8
LS 1f	1974	317	390	119	102	6	90	6.70	15.00	23.1	9.75	31.9	39.2	0.65	0.84	0.60	0.80	0.38	-2.0	FX 66-S-196 V1
DG 100	1974	316	418	120	98	8	100	7.00	15.00	20.5	11.00	28.2	37.3	0.73	0.94	0.60	0.80	0.40	-1.8	FX 61-184 / FX 60-126
Astir CS	1974	342	450	138	105	9	100	6.47	15.00	18.1	12.40	27.0	35.6	0.83	1.00	0.60	0.85	0.45	0.0	E 603
Club Libelle	1974	290	330	110	83		-	6.40	15.00	23.0	9.80	29.0	33.0	0.65	0.85			0.41		
Hornet	1974	334	420	124	112	8	100	6.40	15.00	23.0	9.80	33.4	42.0	0.65	0.88	0.58	0.74	0.40	-2.5	FX 66-17 A II 182
ASW 19	1975	344	408	140	104	10	120	6.80	15.00	20.5	11.00	30.7	36.4	0.73	0.91	0.59	0.85	0.42	-2.0	FX 61-163 / FX 60-126

	Aileron		Emp.	Horizontal Stabilizer									Vertical Stabilizer									Dive Brakes		
	(21)	(22)	(23)	(24)	(25)	(26)	(27)	(28)	(29)	(30)	(31)	(32)	(33)	(34)	(35)	(36)	(37)	(38)	(39)	(40)	(41)	(42)	(43)	(44)
	aileron span	mean aileron chord	arrangement	span	area	aspect ratio	mean chord	elevator chord	moment arm	$l_H S_H$	horiz. stab. volume $(dC_L/d\alpha)_H l_H S_H$	airfoil	height	area	aspect ratio	mean chord	mean rudder chord	moment arm	$l_V S_V$	vert. stab. volume $(dC_L/d\beta)_V l_V S_V$	airfoil	arrangement	span	location on airfoil
	[-]	[m]		[m]	[m²]	[-]	[m]	[-]	[m]	[m³]	[m³]		[m]	[m²]	[-]	[m]	[-]	[m]	[m³]	[m³]			[m]	[-]
Standard Class, composite construction, pre-1980 (cont'd)																								
Phoebus B1	0.32	0.17	T	3.20	1.56	6.56	0.49	1.00	4.24	6.61	30.78	E 484	1.20	1.16	1.24	0.97	0.49	4.28	4.96	12.27		u,l	1.51	0.72
fs 23 "Hidalgo"	0.27	0.11	V	1.96	1.48	2.60	0.76	0.50	3.10	4.59	14.18	NACA 64_1-012	0.95	0.74	1.22	0.78	0.50	3.10	2.29	6.28	NACA 64_1-012	chute	0.60	
LS 1c	0.35	0.14	T	2.30	0.84	6.30	0.37	1.00	4.05	3.40	15.64		1.30	1.00	1.69	0.77	0.35	4.10	4.10	12.49		u	0.93	0.49
Std. Libelle	0.39	0.10	C	2.50	1.16	5.39	0.46	0.21	3.65	4.23	18.50	NACA-012	1.19	0.78	1.82	0.66	0.40	3.59	2.80	6.79	NACA 64-009	u,l	1.20	0.66
fs 25	0.36	0.11	T	2.00	0.72	5.56	0.36	1.00	4.05	2.92	12.88	FX 66-0120	1.20	0.72	2.00	0.60	0.40	4.05	2.92	9.81	FX 66-0160/0180	TE	1.20	0.67
ASW 15B	0.33	0.17	C	2.62	1.15	5.97	0.44	1.00	3.45	3.97	17.94	cambered	1.48	1.13	1.94	0.76	0.47	3.66	4.14	10.53	NACA 63-012A	u,l	1.00	0.45
Standard Cirrus	0.33	0.12	T	2.40	1.02	5.65	0.43	1.00	3.85	3.93	17.44	NACA 65-012	1.20	0.95	1.52	0.79	0.35	3.79	3.60	10.23	NACA 63-013A/012A	u	1.20	0.42
D 38	0.35	0.17	T	2.30	1.00	5.29	0.43	1.00	4.27	4.27	18.54	D 38 137 000	1.25	0.79	1.98	0.63	0.40	4.29	3.39	11.33	NACA 64-012	u	1.35	0.38
Std. Jantar	0.32	0.11	T	2.60	1.35	5.01	0.52	0.29	3.92	5.29	22.52		1.35	1.10	1.66	0.81	0.42	3.98	4.38	13.17		u,l	1.33	0.52
LS 1f	0.35	0.14	T	2.20	0.98	4.94	0.45	0.25	3.95	3.87	16.39	FX 71-L-150/25	1.15	0.90	1.47	0.78	0.35	3.99	3.59	9.99		u	1.35	0.49
DG 100	0.35	0.17	T	2.30	1.00	5.29	0.43	1.00	4.29	4.29	18.63	D 38 137 000	1.24	0.92	1.67	0.74	0.50	4.29	3.95	11.94	NACA 64-012	u	1.34	0.55
Astir CS	0.33	0.18	T	2.80	1.50	5.23	0.54	0.25	4.05	6.07	26.26	E 528	1.22	0.96	1.55	0.79	0.30	4.04	3.88	11.18	FX 71-L-150/30	u	1.21	0.43
Club Libelle	0.39		T	2.50	1.13	5.53	0.45	0.28	3.70	4.18	18.44		1.10	0.83	1.46	0.75	0.30	3.70	3.07	8.50		f		
Hornet	0.39	0.10	T	2.50	1.15	5.43	0.46	0.25	3.74	4.30	18.85	FX 71-L-150/25	1.15	0.89	1.49	0.77	0.30	3.73	3.32	9.31	FX 71-L-150/30	TE	3.72	0.85
ASW 19	0.33	0.15	T	2.50	1.10	5.68	0.44	0.30	3.82	4.20	18.70	FX 71-L-150/30 (12%)	1.25	1.00	1.56	0.80	0.30	3.84	3.84	11.13	FX 71-L-150/30 (13.5%)	u	1.20	0.45

	①	②	③	④	⑤	⑥	⑦	⑧	⑨	⑩	⑪	⑫	⑬	⑭	⑮	⑯	⑰	⑱	⑲	⑳
	first flight	mass, empty + 90kg	mass, Max. takeoff	mass, wing, m_W	mass, fuse. + vert. stab.	mass, horizontal stab.	water ballast	fuselage length	wingspan, b	aspect ratio, $\mathcal{R}$	wing area S	wing loading, min.	wing loading, max.	average chord $c_m = S/b$	root chord c_r	taper change point y_k/s	inner taper λ_k	taper ratio λ	twist	Airfoil root/tip
	(year)	[kg]	[kg]	[kg]	[kg]	[kg]	[kg]	[m]	[m]	[-]	[m²]	[daN/m²]	[daN/m²]	[m]	[m]	[-]	[-]	[-]	[°]	
Standard Class, composite construction, post-1980																				
LS 4a	1980	336	525	130	110	6	170	6.78	15.00	21.7	10.35	31.8	49.7	0.69	0.90	0.60	0.80	0.40	-2.0	FX 79-162 / FX 79-133
SB 12	1980	307	450	117	93	7	100	6.40	15.00	22.5	10.02	30.0	44.0	0.67	0.90	0.58	0.72	0.43	-1.7	HQ 14/18,43 / HQ 15/18,72
Falcon	1981	344	450	137	110	7	130	6.80	15.00	21.1	10.66	31.6	41.4	0.71	0.83	0.40 0.84	1.00 0.69	0.37	0.0	HQ 21/17,5
DG 300	1983	335	525	125	113	7	190	6.80	15.00	21.8	10.30	31.9	50.0	0.69	0.85	0.30 0.73	1.00 0.69	0.38	0.0	HQ 21/II
ASK 23	1983	323	380	130	91	12	-	7.05	15.00	17.4	12.90	24.6	28.9	0.86	1.10	0.60	0.78	0.45	-1.5	FX 61-168 / FX 60-126
Discus B(CS)	1984	336	525	120	120	6	184	6.56	15.00	21.3	10.58	31.1	48.7	0.71	0.88	0.45 0.81	0.93 0.60	0.26	0.0	HX 83
ASW 24	1987	317	500	114	106	7	170	6.55	15.00	22.5	10.00	31.1	49.0	0.67	0.87	0.61	0.81	0.31	-1.0	DU 84-158
LS 7	1988	322	486	120	105	7	150	6.66	15.00	23.0	9.80	32.2	48.6	0.65	0.85	0.60	0.78	0.38	0.0	
AK-5	1990	368	485	133	138	7	120	6.80	15.00	21.1	10.66	33.9	44.6	0.71	0.83	0.37	0.36		0.0	HQ 21/17,5
AFH 24	1991	335	465	125			127	6.58	15.00	21.9	10.27	32.0	44.4	0.68	0.85	0.30 0.73	1.00 0.69	0.38	0.0	HQ 21/ II
Discus 2b	1998	335	525	128	110	7	200	6.81	15.00	22.1	10.16	32.3	50.7	0.68	0.85	0.45 0.81 0.91	0.90 0.63 0.50	0.27	0.0	HQ
World Class Entrants																				
PW-5 Smyk	1992	280	300				-	6.22	13.44	17.8	10.16	27.0	29.0	0.76	1.00	0.81	0.61	0.20		
L33 Solo	1992	300	340	110	96	8	-	8.50	14.12	18.1	11.00	26.7	30.3	0.78	0.95	0.53	1.00	0.40		FX 60-17A11-182, FX 60-126
Russia AC-4A	1993	231	274				-	5.24	12.60	20.6	7.70	29.4	34.9	0.61						FX 60-157

	Aileron		Emp.	Horizontal Stabilizer									Vertical Stabilizer									Dive Brakes		
	(21)	(22)	(23)	(24)	(25)	(26)	(27)	(28)	(29)	(30)	(31)	(32)	(33)	(34)	(35)	(36)	(37)	(38)	(39)	(40)	(41)	(42)	(43)	(44)
	aileron span	mean aileron chord	arrangement	span	area	aspect ratio	mean chord	elevator chord	moment arm	$l_H S_H$	horiz. stab. volume $(dC_L/d\alpha)_H l_H S_H$	airfoil	height	area	aspect ratio	mean chord	mean rudder chord	moment arm	$l_V S_V$	vert. stab. volume $(dC_L/d\beta)_V l_V S_V$	airfoil	arrangement	span	location on airfoil
	[-]	[m]		[m]	[m²]	[-]	[m]	[-]	[m]	[m³]	[m³]		[m]	[m²]	[-]	[m]	[-]	[m]	[m³]	[m³]			[m]	[-]
Standard Class, composite construction, post-1980 (cont'd)																								
LS 4a	0.40	0.15	T	2.50	1.00	6.25	0.40	0.30	4.10	4.10	18.80	FX 71-L-150/30	1.26	1.01	1.57	0.80	0.30	3.90	3.94	11.46	FX 71-L-150/30	u	1.50	0.45
SB 12	0.39	0.10	T	2.50	1.15	5.43	0.46	0.25	3.74	4.30	18.85	FX 71-L-150/25	1.15	0.89	1.49	0.77	0.30	3.73	3.32	9.31	FX 71-L-150/30	TE	3.72	0.85
Falcon	0.44	0.14	T	2.50	1.16	5.39	0.46	0.25	4.38	5.08	22.20	FX 71-L-150/25	1.15	0.94	1.41	0.82	0.33	4.20	3.95	10.67	FX 71-L-150/30	u	1.30	0.53
DG 300	0.40	0.13	T	2.29	0.95	5.52	0.41	0.27	4.05	3.85	16.95	D 38 137 000	1.21	0.88	1.66	0.73	0.45	4.06	3.57	10.78	NACA 64-012	u	1.46	0.53
ASK 23	0.33	0.18	T	2.60	1.38	4.90	0.53	0.30	4.35	6.00	25.34	FX 71-L-150/30 (12%)	1.05	0.95	1.16	0.90	0.30	4.31	4.09	9.63	FX 71-L-150/30 (14%)	u	1.23	0.43
Discus B(CS)	0.35	0.14	T	2.30	0.97	5.45	0.42	0.29	3.94	3.82	16.77	FX 71-L-150/30 mod	1.12	0.93	1.35	0.83	0.35	3.80	3.53	9.27	NACA 64-012	u	1.28	0.62
ASW 24	0.40	0.08	T	2.55	0.90	7.22	0.35	0.25	3.86	3.47	16.61	DU 86-137/25	1.20	0.95	1.52	0.79	0.30	3.83	3.64	10.34	DU 86-137/20	u	1.15	0.55
LS 7	0.50	0.11	T	2.50	1.04	6.01	0.42		4.00	4.16	18.85		1.25	1.00	1.56	0.80	0.24	4.00	4.00	11.59		u	1.40	0.54
AK-5	0.44	0.22	T	2.50	0.95	6.58	0.38	0.26	4.12	3.91	18.23	FX 71-L-150/25	1.25	1.00	1.56	0.80	0.30	3.99	3.99	11.56	OK-1-130/30	u	1.46	
AFH 24	0.40	0.13	T	2.55	0.92	7.07	0.36	0.24	4.19	3.85	18.32		1.20	0.84	1.71	0.70	0.31	4.07	3.42	10.51	FX 71-L-150/20	u	1.46	0.53
Discus 2b	0.45	0.12	T	2.30	0.96	5.51	0.42	0.25	4.13	3.96	17.46	DU 92-131/25	1.16	0.99	1.36	0.85	0.29	3.97	3.93	10.37	DU 86-131/30	u	1.29	0.55
World Class Entrants (cont'd)																								
PW-5 Smyk	0.36	0.18	N	2.75	1.38	5.48	0.50	0.30	3.80	5.24	23.05		0.95	0.67	1.35	0.71	0.32	3.35	2.24	4.31		u	1.20	0.50
L33 Solo	0.36	0.13	T	0.39	1.31	0.12	3.36	0.35	3.85	5.04	0.92		1.18	1.09	1.28	0.92	0.32	3.85	4.20	10.59		u	1.40	0.58
Russia AC-4A			T																					

	①	②	③	④	⑤	⑥	⑦	⑧	⑨	⑩	⑪	⑫	⑬	⑭	⑮	⑯	⑰	⑱	⑲	⑳
	first flight	mass, empty + 90kg	mass, Max. takeoff	mass, wing, m_W	mass, fuse. + vert. stab.	mass, horizontal stab.	water ballast	fuselage length	wingspan, b	aspect ratio, Æ	wing area S	wing loading, min.	wing loading, max.	average chord c_m = S/b	root chord c_r	taper change point y_k/s	inner taper λ_k	taper ratio λ	twist	Airfoil root/tip
	(year)	[kg]	[kg]	[kg]	[kg]	[kg]	[kg]	[m]	[m]	[-]	[m²]	[daN/m²]	[daN/m²]	[m]	[m]	[-]	[-]	[-]	[°]	
FAI 15M Class, composite construction																				
Libelle H 301	1964	275	300	105	75	5	-	6.18	15.00	23.7	9.50	28.4	31.0	0.63	0.94	-	-	0.35	0.0	Hütter
Concept 70	1970	340	397				91	5.10	15.00	19.4	11.60	28.7	33.6	0.77	0.95	0.52	1.00	0.53		Eppler (mod) 14%
PIK 20D	1973	338	450	140	102	6	140	6.45	15.00	22.5	10.00	33.1	44.1	0.67	0.90	0.60	0.72	0.40		FX 67-K-170/150
Zuni II	1976	340	544				-	6.63	15.00	22.3	10.10	33.0	52.8	0.67	0.83	0.59	0.86	0.43	-1.3	FX 67-K-170 / 150mod
LS 3	1976	370	472	158	115	7	150	6.86	15.00	21.4	10.50	34.6	44.1	0.70	0.97	-	-	0.47	0.0	FX 67-K-170 / 150 m
Mosquito	1976	332	450	134	102	6	125	6.40	15.00	23.0	9.80	33.2	45.0	0.65	0.84	0.47	0.83	0.48	0.0	FX 67-K-150
Mini-Nimbus	1976	326	450	130	99	7	140	6.41	15.00	22.7	9.90	32.3	44.6	0.66	0.87	0.47	0.79	0.48	0.0	FX 67-K-150
DG 200	1976	331	450	126	108	7	110	7.00	15.00	22.5	10.00	32.5	44.1	0.67	0.84	0.68	0.78	0.40	0.0	FX 67-K-170 m
Slingsby T-65 Vega	1977	324	440				109	6.72	15.00	22.4	10.05	31.6	42.9	0.67	0.85	0.61	0.82	0.46		
ASW 20	1977	335	454	134	102	9	120	6.82	15.00	21.4	10.50	31.3	42.4	0.70	0.70	0.63	0.77	0.43	-2.5	FX 62-K-131(14.4)/60-126
Speed Astir	1978	354	515	134	119	11	140	6.68	15.00	19.6	11.47	30.3	44.0	0.76	1.03	-	-	0.49	0.0	E662
Ventus B	1980	318	525	116	106	6	168	6.58	15.00	23.7	9.51	32.8	54.1	0.63	0.80	0.49 0.65	0.89 0.75	0.34	0.0	XX 79/18 N2/ZZ135/20
DG 400	1981	406	480	114	196	6	90	7.00	15.00	22.5	10.00	39.8	47.1	0.67	0.86	0.60	0.80	0.40	0.0	FX 67-K-170/17
LS 6	1983	342	525	135	110	7	170	6.78	15.00	21.4	10.53	31.9	48.9	0.70	0.90	0.60	0.80	0.40	0.0	FX 81-K-130/17 / 148/17
DG 600	1987	351	525	130	125	6	190	6.83	15.00	20.5	10.95	31.4	47.0	0.73	0.93	0.60	0.81	0.41	0.0	HQ 35 / HQ 37
DG 600 M	1987	401	525	130	175	6	190	6.83	15.00	20.5	10.95	35.9	47.0	0.73	0.93	0.60	0.81	0.41	0.0	HQ 35 /HQ 37
DG 800 S	1993	351	525	130	125	6	180	6.83	15.00	21.1	10.68	32.2	48.2	0.71	0.89	0.60	0.80	0.50	0.0	DU 89-138/14
DG 800 M	1993	416	525	130	190	6	100	7.03	15.00	21.1	10.68	38.2	48.2	0.71	0.89	0.60	0.80	0.50	0.0	DU 89-138/14
Ventus 2b	1994	323	525	116	110	7	200	6.58	15.00	23.2	9.70	32.7	53.1	0.65	0.81	0.42 0.76 0.88	0.83 0.73 0.57	0.33	0.0	XX 79/18 N2 / ZZ135/20
LS 8	1994	342	525	130	115	7	185	6.78	15.00	21.4	10.50	31.9	49.0	0.70	0.90	0.60	0.80	0.40	0.0	FX 81-K-130 / 148/17
ASW 27	1995	325	500	120	109	6	180	6.50	15.00	25.0	9.00	35.4	54.5	0.60	0.77	0.63	0.81	0.30	0.0	DU 89-134/14
SZD-56-1 Diana	1991	272	410				-	6.88	15.00	27.6	8.16	32.7	49.3	0.54	0.75	0.20 0.60	1.00 0.81	0.40		NN27-13 (13%)

FAI 15M Class, composite construction (cont'd)

	Aileron		Emp.	Horizontal Stabilizer									Vertical Stabilizer									Dive Brakes		
	21	22	23	24	25	26	27	28	29	30	31	32	33	34	35	36	37	38	39	40	41	42	43	44
	aileron span	mean aileron chord	arrangement	span	area	aspect ratio	mean chord	elevator chord	moment arm	$l_H S_H$	horiz. stab. volume $(dC_L/d\alpha)_H l_H S_H$	airfoil	height	area	aspect ratio	mean chord	mean rudder chord	moment arm	$l_V S_V$	vert. stab. volume $(dC_L/d\beta)_V l_V S_V$	airfoil	arrangement	span	location on airfoil
	[-]	[m]		[m]	[m²]	[-]	[m]	[-]	[m]	[m³]	[m³]		[m]	[m²]	[-]	[m]	[-]	[m]	[m³]	[m³]			[m]	[-]
Libelle H 301	0.44	0.12	N	2.50	1.00	6.25	0.40	0.25	3.62	3.62	16.60		1.19	0.78	1.82	0.66	0.40	3.50	2.73	6.62	NACA 64-009	u/l	1.20	0.64
Concept 70	0.33	0.20	C	2.90	1.40	6.01	0.48	1.00	4.10	5.74	26.00		1.45	1.00	2.10	0.69	0.38	4.40	4.40	11.86		f		
PIK 20D	0.94	0.13	T	2.00	1.00	4.00	0.50	0.23	3.66	3.66	14.21	FX 71-L-150/25	1.20	0.93	1.55	0.78	0.31	3.60	3.35	9.65	FX 71-L-150/30	u	1.20	0.60
Zuni II	0.41	0.10	T	2.43	0.90	6.56	0.37	1.00	3.70	3.33	15.50	NACA 64-012	1.20	0.90	1.60	0.75	0.45	3.60	3.24	9.53				
LS 3	0.95	0.16	T	2.20	0.89	5.44	0.40	0.25	3.95	3.52	15.41		1.32	1.00	1.74	0.76	0.35	3.90	3.90	12.10		u	1.38	0.44
Mosquito	0.45	0.11	T	2.50	1.15	5.43	0.46	0.25	3.88	4.46	19.56	FX 71-L-150/25	1.40	0.90	2.18	0.64	0.30	3.90	3.51	12.36	FX 71-L-150/30	TE	3.20	0.87
Mini-Nimbus	0.45	0.11	T	2.40	1.02	5.65	0.43	1.00	3.91	3.99	17.71	NACA 65-012	1.15	0.95	1.39	0.83	0.30	3.76	3.57	9.58	NACA 64-013A/012A	TE	3.20	0.78
DG 200	0.40	0.09	T	2.24	0.95	5.28	0.42	0.27	4.23	4.02	17.44	D 38 137 000	1.21	0.88	1.66	0.73	0.50	4.24	3.73	11.26	NACA 64-012	u	1.46	0.50
Slingsby T-65 Vega	0.38	0.08	T	2.57	1.09	6.06	0.42	0.24	4.00	4.36	19.81	FX 71_L-150/30	1.35	1.22	1.49	0.90	0.25	3.90	4.76	13.39	FX 71_L-150/30	TE	4.10	
ASW 20	0.36	0.09	T	2.20	1.00	4.84	0.45	0.32	3.89	3.89	16.35	FX 71-L-150/25	1.25	1.00	1.56	0.80	0.30	3.88	3.88	11.25	FX 71-L-150/30(13.5)	u	1.40	0.58
Speed Astir	0.47	0.13	T	3.00	1.44	6.25	0.48	0.28	3.87	5.57	25.56	E 650	1.09	0.98	1.21	0.90	0.30	3.75	3.67	8.93	E 651	u	1.50	0.50
Ventus B	0.56	0.10	T	2.30	0.97	5.45	0.42	0.28	3.98	3.86	16.94	FX 71-L-150/25	1.12	0.93	1.35	0.83	0.35	3.90	3.63	9.52	NACA 64-012	TE	2.90	0.82
DG 400	0.40	0.09	T	2.24	0.95	5.28	0.42	0.27	4.23	4.02	17.44	D 38 137 000	1.21	0.88	1.66	0.73	0.45	4.24	3.73	11.26	NACA 64-012	u	1.46	0.59
LS 6	0.88	0.12	T	2.50	1.00	6.25	0.40	0.20	4.10	4.10	18.80	FX 81-K-131/20/90/20	1.14	0.91	1.43	0.80	0.30	3.90	3.55	9.69	FX 81-K-132/30	u	1.50	0.50
DG 600	0.92	0.97	T	2.34	1.06	5.17	0.45	0.30	4.09	4.34	18.66	FX 71-L-150/30	1.27	0.97	1.66	0.76	0.35	4.07	3.95	11.90	FX 71-L-150/35	u	1.46	0.60
DG 600 M	0.92	0.97	T	2.34	1.06	5.17	0.45	0.30	4.09	4.34	18.66	FX 71-L-150/30	1.27	0.97	1.66	0.76	0.35	4.07	3.95	11.90	FX 71-L-150/35	u	1.46	0.60
DG 800 S	0.91	0.10	T	2.52	1.07	5.93	0.42	0.25	4.10	4.39	19.80	D 38 138 000	1.27	0.97	1.66	0.76	0.35	4.05	3.93	11.85	FX 71-L-150/35	u	1.46	0.60
DG 800 M	0.91	0.10	T	2.52	1.07	5.93	0.42	0.25	4.30	4.60	20.76	D 38 138 000	1.25	0.95	1.64	0.76	0.35	4.25	4.04	12.09	FX 71-L-150/35	u	1.46	0.60
Ventus 2b	0.95	0.10	T	2.30	0.97	5.45	0.42	0.28	4.08	3.96	17.37	FX 71-L-150/30	1.14	0.95	1.37	0.83	0.34	4.12	3.91	10.37	NACA 64-012	u	1.29	0.53
LS 8	0.50	0.11	T	2.50	1.00	6.25	0.40	0.20	4.10	4.10	18.80	FX 81-K-131/90/20	1.14	0.91	1.43	0.80	0.30	3.90	3.55	9.69	FX 81-K-132/30	u	1.50	0.50
ASW 27	0.46	0.07	T	2.30	0.72	7.35	0.31	0.25	3.90	2.81	13.48	DU 92-131/25	1.20	0.95	1.52	0.79	0.30	3.82	3.63	10.31	DU 86-131/30	u	1.20	0.57
SZD-56-1 Diana	0.40	0.07	T	2.60	1.82	3.71	0.70	0.13	4.60	8.37	31.42		1.00	1.00	1.00	1.00	0.27	4.30	4.30	9.01		u	0.75	0.50

	①	②	③	④	⑤	⑥	⑦	⑧	⑨	⑩	⑪	⑫	⑬	⑭	⑮	⑯	⑰	⑱	⑲	⑳
	first flight	mass, empty + 90kg	mass, Max. takeoff	mass, wing, m_W	mass, fuse. + vert. stab.	mass, horizontal stab.	water ballast	fuselage length	wingspan, b	aspect ratio, Æ	wing area S	wing loading, min.	wing loading, max.	average chord $c_m = S/b$	root chord c_r	taper change point y_k/s	inner taper λ_k	taper ratio λ	twist	Airfoil root/tip
	(year)	[kg]	[kg]	[kg]	[kg]	[kg]	[kg]	[m]	[m]	[-]	[m^2]	[daN/m^2]	[daN/m^2]	[m]	[m]	[-]	[-]	[-]	[°]	
Open Class, composite construction (b ≤ 18m)																				
Phoenix T	1957	269	300	96	75	8	-	6.90	16.00	17.8	14.36	18.4	20.5	0.90	1.25	-	-	0.42	-2.0	EC 86 (-3)-914
SB 6	1961	360	350	145	119	6	-	7.50	18.00	24.9	13.00	27.2	26.4	0.72	0.90	0.66	0.76	0.53	0.0	STE 871-514
SB 7 B	1962	390	390	181	112	7	-	7.08	17.00	22.8	12.66	30.2	30.2	0.74	0.92	0.41	1.00	0.36		FX 61-163 oben/E 306 unten
BS 1	1962	425	500	192	134	9	-	7.58	18.00	22.8	14.20	29.4	34.5	0.79	0.99	0.56	0.85	0.41	0.0	E 348 K
D 36	1964	375	401	166	110	9	-	7.35	17.80	24.8	12.80	28.7	30.7	0.72	0.95	0.60	0.77	0.36	-3.0	FX 62-K-131 / FX 60-126
ASW 12	1965	409	430	194	117	8	-	7.35	18.30	25.8	13.00	30.9	32.4	0.71	0.96	0.59	0.81	0.34	-3.0	FX 62-K-131m / FX 60-126
Cirrus B	1967	366	400	165	104	7	100	7.20	17.70	24.9	12.60	28.5	31.1	0.71	0.87	0.58	0.88	0.40	-2.0	FX 66-196 / FX 60-161
Phoebus C	1967	360	459	176	85	9	-	6.98	17.00	20.6	14.06	25.1	32.0	0.83	1.21	-	-	0.31		E 403
SB 8	1967	301	334	129	76	6	-	7.70	18.00	23.0	14.10	20.9	23.2	0.78	0.97	0.62	0.80	0.46	-3.0	FX 62-K-153/131 / FX 60-126
Diamant 18	1967	385	440	182	105	8	-	7.72	18.00	22.7	14.28	26.4	30.2	0.79	0.93	0.56	1.00	0.39		FX 62-K-153m
Kestrel 401	1968	362	400	149	115	8	50	6.72	17.00	25.0	11.58	30.7	33.9	0.68	0.91	0.59	-	0.45	0.0	FX 67-K-170/17 / 150 /17
ASW 20 CL	1984	343	380	142	102	9	120	6.82	16.60	25.0	11.01	30.6	33.8	0.66	0.90	0.33	0.57	0.39	0.0	FX 62-K-131m / FX 60-126
Ventus C(l)	1985	336	500	125	115	6	170	6.60	17.60	30.5	10.14	32.5	48.4	0.58					0.0	
LS 6c	1990	359	525	140	122	7	155	6.82	17.50	27.1	11.30	31.2	45.6	0.65	0.90	0.51	0.80	0.25	0.0	FX 81-K-130/17 / 148/17
LS 6C-18	1992	347	525	135	115	7	150	6.78	18.00	28.4	11.40	29.9	45.2	0.63	0.90	0.50	0.80	0.25	0.0	FX 81-K-130/17 / 148/17
ASH 26	1993	370	525	145	128	7	175	7.05	18.00	27.7	11.68	31.1	44.1	0.65	0.84	0.62	0.81	0.39	0.0	DU 89-134/14
ASH 26E	1993	430	525	145	188	7	116	7.05	18.00	27.7	11.69	36.1	44.0	0.65	0.84	0.62	0.81	0.39	0.0	DU 89-134/14
LS 9	1995	462	525	145	220	7	-		18.00	28.4	11.40	39.7	45.2	0.63	0.90	0.50	0.80	0.25	0.0	FX 81-K-130/17 / 148/17
LS 8-18	1997	347	525	135	115	7	180	6.78	18.00	28.4	11.40	29.9	45.2	0.63	0.90	0.50	0.80	0.25	0.0	FX 81-K-130/17 / 148/17
SB 14		344	470	146	101	7	100	6.95	18.00	29.9	10.84	31.1	42.5	0.60	0.74	0.46 0.81	0.93 0.72	0.40	0.0	CA 2-134/15 V2

Open Class, composite construction ($b \leq 18m$) (cont'd)

	Aileron		Emp.	Horizontal Stabilizer									Vertical Stabilizer									Dive Brakes		
	(21)	(22)	(23)	(24)	(25)	(26)	(27)	(28)	(29)	(30)	(31)	(32)	(33)	(34)	(35)	(36)	(37)	(38)	(39)	(40)	(41)	(42)	(43)	(44)
	aileron span	mean aileron chord	arrangement	span	area	aspect ratio	mean chord	elevator chord	moment arm	$l_H S_H$	horiz. stab. volume $(dC_L/d\alpha)_H l_H S_H$	airfoil	height	area	aspect ratio	mean chord	mean rudder chord	moment arm	$l_V S_V$	vert. stab. volume $(dC_L/d\beta)_V l_V S_V$	airfoil	arrangement	span	location on airfoil
	[-]	[m]		[m]	[m²]	[-]	[m]	[-]	[m]	[m³]	[m³]		[m]	[m²]	[-]	[m]	[-]	[m]	[m³]	[m³]			[m]	[-]
Phoenix T	0.29	0.12	T	3.20	1.55	6.61	0.48	0.35	4.04	6.26	29.20	NACA 65-009	0.95	1.21	0.75	1.27	0.58	4.33	5.24	8.58		SF	2.20	0.66
SB 6	0.28	0.13	C	2.60	1.20	5.63	0.46	1.00	4.47	5.36	23.80	EA8(-1)-009	1.50	1.27	1.77	0.85	0.40	4.51	5.73	13.65	EA6(-1)-012	chute	1.30	-
SB 7 B	0.35	0.12	T	2.50	1.05	5.95	0.42	1.00	4.10	4.30	19.45	NACA 63-010A	1.35	1.00	1.82	0.74	0.37	4.12	4.12	13.14	NACA 66-012	u,l	1.55	0.62
BS 1	0.39	0.14	T	3.00	1.33	6.77	0.44	1.00	4.53	6.02	28.29	cambered	1.35	1.33	1.37	0.99	0.40	4.66	6.20	16.44		u,l	1.20	0.65
D 36	0.38	0.14	T	2.30	1.00	5.29	0.43	0.21	3.89	3.89	16.89	NACA 0008/6	1.57	1.27	1.94	0.81	0.52	4.02	5.11	16.88		u,l	1.50	0.55
ASW 12	0.37	0.15	T	2.50	1.00	6.25	0.40	0.35	4.17	4.17	19.13	NACA 64-010	1.50	1.20	1.88	0.80	0.50	4.30	5.16	16.73	NACA 62-015A (m)	chute	1.80	-
Cirrus B	0.37	0.15	C	2.50	1.05	5.95	0.42	0.28	4.16	4.37	19.73	NACA 65-010A	1.48	1.15	1.90	0.78	0.45	4.30	4.94	12.43	NACA 63-009A/12A	u,l	0.93	0.47
Phoebus C	0.32	0.16	T	3.20	1.56	6.56	0.49	1.00	4.24	6.61	30.78	E 484	1.20	1.16	1.24	0.97	0.49	4.28	4.96	12.27		u,l	1.51	0.72
SB 8	0.34	0.15	T	2.70	1.30	5.61	0.48	0.30	4.65	6.05	26.78	NACA 0006	1.45	1.30	1.62	0.90	0.35	4.72	6.14	18.18	NACA 63-010	u,l	1.20	0.53
Diamant 18	0.41	0.16	T	2.80	1.19	6.59	0.42	1.00	4.67	5.56	25.89		1.32	1.01	1.73	0.77	0.59	4.63	4.68	14.43		u,l	1.10	0.48
Kestrel 401	0.39	0.09	T	2.85	1.28	6.35	0.45	0.19	3.76	4.81	22.18	FX LV 152/25	1.30	1.00	1.69	0.77	0.35	3.85	3.85	11.73		u,l	1.20	0.61
ASW 20 CL	0.36	0.09	T	2.20	1.00	4.84	0.45	0.32	3.89	3.89	16.35	FX 71-L-150/25	1.25	1.00	1.56	0.80	0.30	3.88	3.88	11.25	FX 71-L-150/25	u	1.40	0.58
Ventus C(l)	1.00		T	2.40	0.97	5.94	0.40	0.25	3.91	3.79	17.12	FX 71-L-150/25	1.20	0.93	1.55	0.78	0.35	3.80	3.53	10.18	FX 71-L-150/25	u	1.28	0.58
LS 6c	0.89	0.12	T	2.50	1.04	6.01	0.42	0.20	4.18	4.35	19.70		1.25	1.00	1.56	0.80	0.24	4.00	4.00	11.59		u	1.40	0.54
LS 6C-18	0.82	0.11	T	2.50	1.00	6.25	0.40	0.20	4.10	4.10	18.80	FX 81-K-131/90	1.14	0.91	1.43	0.80	0.30	3.90	3.55	9.69	FX 81-K-132	u	1.50	0.50
ASH 26	0.43	0.07	T	2.85	0.99	8.20	0.35	0.25	4.33	4.29	21.16	DU 92-131/25	1.23	0.98	1.54	0.80	0.30	4.25	4.17	11.98	DU 89-130/30	u	1.40	0.50
ASH 26E	0.43	0.07	T	2.85	0.99	8.20	0.35	0.25	4.33	4.29	21.16	DU 92-131/25	1.23	0.98	1.54	0.80	0.30	4.25	4.17	11.98	DU 89-130/30	u	1.40	0.50
LS 9	0.82	0.11	T	2.50	1.00	6.25	0.40	0.20	4.10	4.10	18.80	FX 81-K-131/90	1.26	1.01	1.57	0.80	0.30	3.90	3.94	11.46	FX 71-L-150/25	u	1.50	0.50
LS 8-18	0.54	0.11	T	2.50	1.00	6.25	0.40	0.20	4.10	4.10	18.80	FX 81-K-131/90	1.14	0.91	1.43	0.80	0.30	3.90	3.55	9.69	FX 81-K-132	u	1.50	0.50
SB 14	0.41	0.08	T	2.85	0.99	8.20	0.35	0.25	4.33	4.29	21.16	DU 92-131/25	1.23	0.98	1.54	0.80	0.30	4.25	4.17	11.98	DU 89-130/30	u	1.44	0.54

	① first flight	② mass, empty + 90kg	③ mass, Max. takeoff	④ mass, wing, m_W	⑤ mass, fuse. + vert. stab.	⑥ mass, horizontal stab.	⑦ water ballast	⑧ fuselage length	⑨ wingspan, b	⑩ aspect ratio, Æ	⑪ wing area S	⑫ wing loading, min.	⑬ wing loading, max.	⑭ average chord c_m = S/b	⑮ root chord c_r	⑯ taper change point y_k/s	⑰ inner taper λ_k	⑱ taper ratio λ	⑲ twist	⑳ Airfoil root/tip
	(year)	[kg]	[kg]	[kg]	[kg]	[kg]	[kg]	[m]	[m]	[-]	[m²]	[daN/m²]	[daN/m²]	[m]	[m]	[-]	[-]	[-]	[°]	
Open Class, composite construction (b>18m)																				
SB 9	1969	415	421	218	100	7	100	7.50	22.00	31.3	15.48	26.3	26.7	0.70	0.97	0.51	0.80	0.26	-1.5	FX 62-K-153/131 / FX 60-126
Nimbus I	1969	460	500				-	7.50	22.00	30.6	15.80	28.6	31.0	0.72	1.00	0.60	0.71	0.39		FX67-K-170/150
Nimbus II	1971	446	580	230	120	6	150	7.28	20.30	28.6	14.41	30.4	39.5	0.71	0.96	0.57	0.75	0.36	0.0	FX 67-K-170/17 / 150 /17
Kestrel 604	1970	551	650	294	159	8	100	7.56	22.00	29.8	16.23	33.3	39.3	0.74	0.98	0.68	0.69	0.41		FX 67-K-170/17 / 150 /17
ASW 17	1971	494	610	266	127	11	100	7.55	20.00	27.0	14.84	32.6	40.3	0.74	0.94	0.61	0.80	0.43	0.0	FX 62-K-131m / FX 60-126
Nimbus 3/24.5m	1981	486	750	268	122	6	280	7.63	24.50	35.9	16.70	28.5	44.0	0.68	0.92	0.34 0.58 0.72	0.87 0.77 0.66	0.27	0.0	XX 79/18N2 / ZZ 135/20
ASW 22 (24m)	1981	501	650	265	138	8	185	8.10	24.00	37.2	15.50	31.7	41.1	0.65	0.83	0.32 0.69	0.94 0.74	0.29	0.0	HQ 17/14,38 / FX 60-126/25
ASW 22 B	1986	540	750	304	138	8	235	8.10	25.00	38.3	16.31	32.5	45.1	0.65	0.83	0.30 0.66	0.94 0.74	0.41	0.0	HQ 17/14,38 / DU 84-132V3
ASW 22BL	1992	544	750	308	138	8	205	8.10	26.40	41.8	16.67	32.0	44.1	0.63	0.83	0.29 0.63 0.92	0.94 0.74 0.44	0.25	0.0	HQ 17/14,38 / DU 84-132V3
Nimbus 4 T	1991	608	800	312	198	8	240	7.83	26.40	39.2	17.80	33.5	44.1	0.67	0.91	0.32 0.54 0.72 0.88 0.93	0.87 0.78 0.66 0.47 0.37	0.23	0.0	XX 79mod / ZZ 135mod
Variable geometry, all types																				
BJ 2	1960	390	400	188	91	14	-	7.03	15.24	19.8	11.75	32.6	33.4	0.77	0.84	0.59	1.00	0.61	-1.0	NACA 65-3418 / 2412
Sigma	1971	0	698	396	150	8	-	8.81	21.00		12.20 16.50				0.69	0.24	1.00	0.57		FX 67-VC-170/36
SB 11	1978	360	470	169	95	6	100	7.40	15.00		10.60 13.20				0.80 1.00	0.60	1.00	0.40	0.0	HQ 144-39 F3
Mü 27	1979	796	900	450	244	12	-	10.30	22.00		17.60 23.90				1.03 1.39	0.60	1.00	0.40	0.0	FX 67-VC-170 / 36
D40	1986	374	500	167	110	7	120	6.68	15.00		9.48 11.51				0.88 1.20	0.55 0.40	0.52	0.28 0.21	-2.5	FX 67-V6-170 / FX 60-126
fs-32	1991	345	500	150	100	5	190	6.62	15.00	22.6	9.94	34.0	49.3	0.66	0.84	0.32 0.68	0.90 0.79 0.66	0.47	0.0	FX 81-K-144 / 20
fs 29: 13m (19m)	1975	458	461	241	121	6	-	7.16	13.30 (19.00)		8.67 (12.65)				0.76 (0.73)	0.54 (0.68)	1.00	0.40	-1.5	FX 73-170 / FX 73-K-170/22

	Aileron		Emp.	Horizontal Stabilizer									Vertical Stabilizer									Dive Brakes		
	(21)	(22)	(23)	(24)	(25)	(26)	(27)	(28)	(29)	(30)	(31)	(32)	(33)	(34)	(35)	(36)	(37)	(38)	(39)	(40)	(41)	(42)	(43)	(44)
	aileron span	mean aileron chord	arrangement	span	area	aspect ratio	mean chord	elevator chord	moment arm	$l_H S_H$	horiz. stab. volume $(dC_L/d\alpha)_H l_H S_H$	airfoil	height	area	aspect ratio	mean chord	mean rudder chord	moment arm	$l_V S_V$	vert. stab. volume $(dC_L/d\beta)_V l_V S_V$	airfoil	arrangement	span	location on airfoil
	[-]	[m]		[m]	[m²]	[-]	[m]	[-]	[m]	[m³]	[m³]		[m]	[m²]	[-]	[m]	[-]	[m]	[m³]	[m³]			[m]	[-]
Open Class, composite construction (b>18m) (cont'd)																								
SB 9	0.43	0.15	T	2.70	1.30	5.61	0.48	0.30	4.40	5.72	25.34	NACA 0006	1.40	1.30	1.51	0.93	0.43	4.65	6.05	17.11	NACA 63-010	u,l	1.20	0.53
Nimbus I	0.35	0.15	C	2.59	1.24	5.41	0.48	0.34	4.45	5.52	24.15		1.40	1.19	1.65	0.85	0.50	4.40	5.24	11.80		chute		
Nimbus II	0.38	0.12	T	2.40	1.02	5.65	0.43	1.00	4.60	4.69	20.83	NACA 64-012	1.27	1.24	1.30	0.98	0.38	4.46	5.53	14.14	N.64-012/63-013	o	1.20	0.52
Kestrel 604	0.30	0.09	T	3.55	1.50	8.40	0.42	0.50	4.40	6.60	32.76	FX 71-L-150/25	1.35	1.29	1.41	0.96	0.30	4.45	5.74	15.56	FX 71-L-150/30		1.20	0.78
ASW 17	0.37	0.12	C	2.90	1.43	5.88	0.49	0.30	4.22	6.03	27.15	NACA 64-010A	1.70	1.44	2.01	0.85	0.51	4.43	6.38	16.64	NACA 64-010A/65...	u	1.61	0.53
Nimbus 3/24.5m	0.67	0.11	T	2.50	1.21	5.17	0.48	0.29	4.89	5.92	25.47	FX 71-L-150/30	1.39	1.26	1.53	0.91	0.39	4.83	6.09	17.42	NACA 64-012/13	u	1.29	0.56
ASW 22 (24m)	0.37	0.14	T	3.13	1.27	7.71	0.41	0.30	4.77	6.06	29.45	FX 71-L-150/30(12%)	1.38	1.71	1.11	1.24	0.30	4.61	7.88	17.96	FX 71-L-150/30(12%)	o	1.20	0.52
ASW 22 B	0.67	0.11	T	3.13	1.27	7.71	0.41	0.30	4.77	6.06	29.45	FX 71-L-150/30(12%)	1.38	1.71	1.11	1.24	0.30	4.61	7.88	17.96	FX 71-L-150/30(12%)	u	1.20	0.52
ASW 22BL	0.71	0.09	T	3.13	1.27	7.71	0.41	0.30	4.77	6.06	29.45	FX 71-L-150/30(12%)	1.38	1.71	1.11	1.24	0.30	4.61	7.88	17.96	FX 71-L-150/30(12%)	u	1.20	0.52
Nimbus 4 T	0.62	0.11	T	3.10	1.36	7.07	0.44	0.30	4.90	6.66	31.66	FX 71-L-150/30 mod	1.43	1.48	1.38	1.03	0.30	4.80	7.10	18.96	FX 71-L-150/30	u	1.37	0.56
Variable geometry, all types (cont'd)																								
BJ 2	0.40	0.17	T	3.29	2.06	5.25	0.63	0.37	3.86	7.95	34.44	NACA 64-012	0.91	0.87	0.96	0.95	0.46	3.86	3.36	6.81	NACA 65-012	f[1]		
Sigma	0.76		T	2.61	1.12	6.08	0.43	1.00	5.50	6.16	28.02		1.78	1.42	2.23	0.80	0.50	5.40	7.67	27.34		f		
SB 11	0.41	0.14	T	2.70	1.24	5.88	0.46	1.00	4.55 4.50			FX 3-L-142 (13.2%)	1.27	1.17	1.38	0.92	0.40	4.45 4.40			NACA 64-013A/012A	u	1.20	0.44
Mü 27	0.69	0.07 0.13	T	3.14	1.40	7.04	0.45	0.25	6.38 6.30			FX 71-L-150/25	1.67	1.46	1.91	0.87	0.30	6.29 6.22			FX 71-L-150/30	u	2.60	0.50
D40	0.40	1.16 0.14	T	2.50	1.00	6.25	0.40	0.25	3.95	3.95	18.12		1.32	1.00	1.74	0.76	0.35	3.90	3.90	12.10		u	1.35	0.43
fs-32	0.93	0.20	T	2.40	1.02	5.65	0.43	0.22	3.93	4.01	17.80	KL 120/22	1.20	1.06	1.36	0.88	0.38	3.80	4.03	10.62	NACA 64-012 mod	u	1.23	0.48
fs 29: 13m (19m)	0.46 (0.32)	0.24	T	2.40	1.03	5.59	0.43	1.00	4.64	4.78	21.15	NACA 64-012	1.27	1.24	1.30	0.98	0.38	4.50	5.58	14.27	NACA 64-012/13	u, chute[2]	1.50[3]	0.55

[1]fuselage mounted dive brakes
[2]brakes deployable only with wings extended
[3]chute diameter 1.30m

Three-view drawings

As the drawings in the following sections vary in scale, dimensional data should be taken from the tables in the preceding section.

Wooden Sailplanes

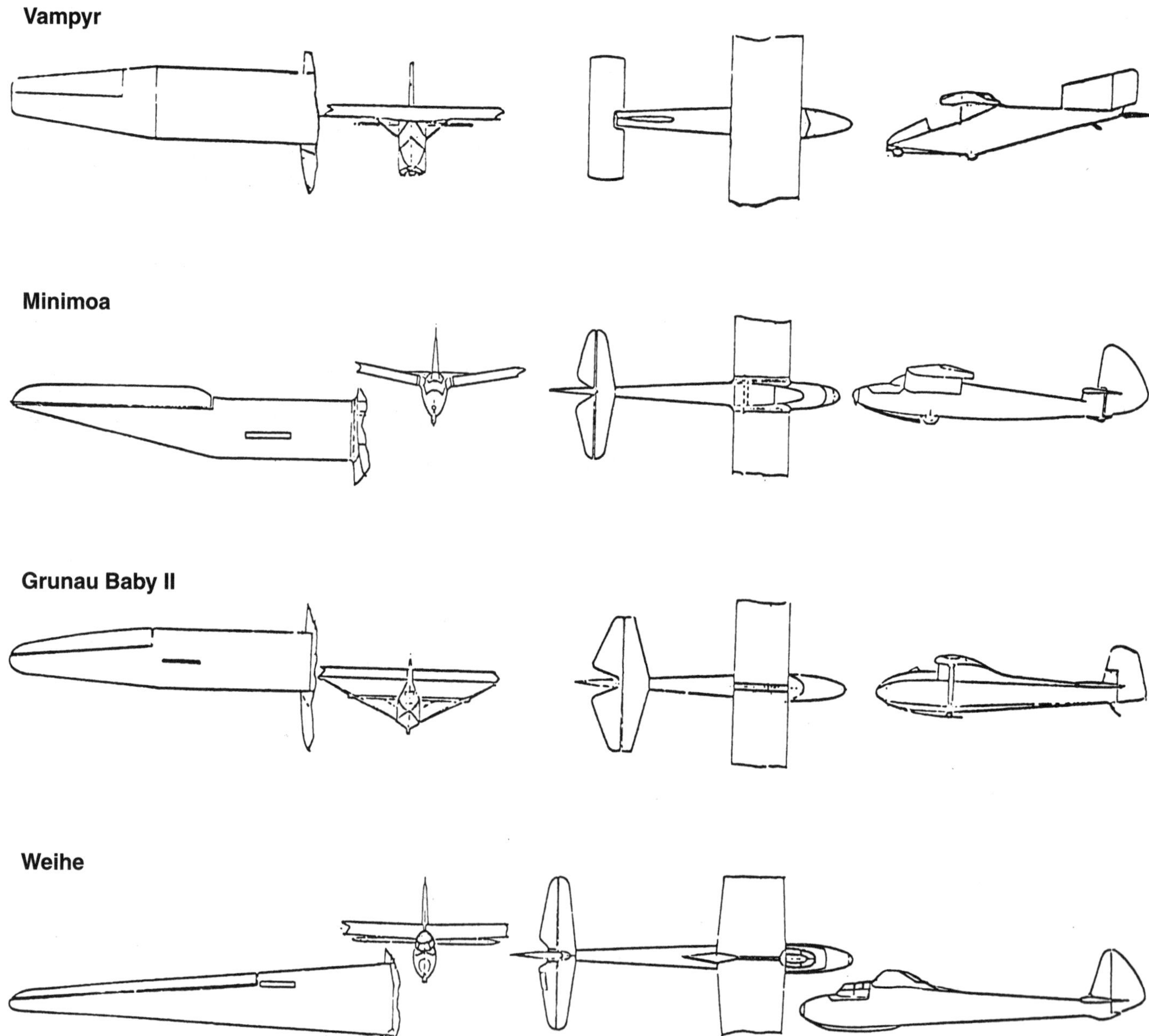

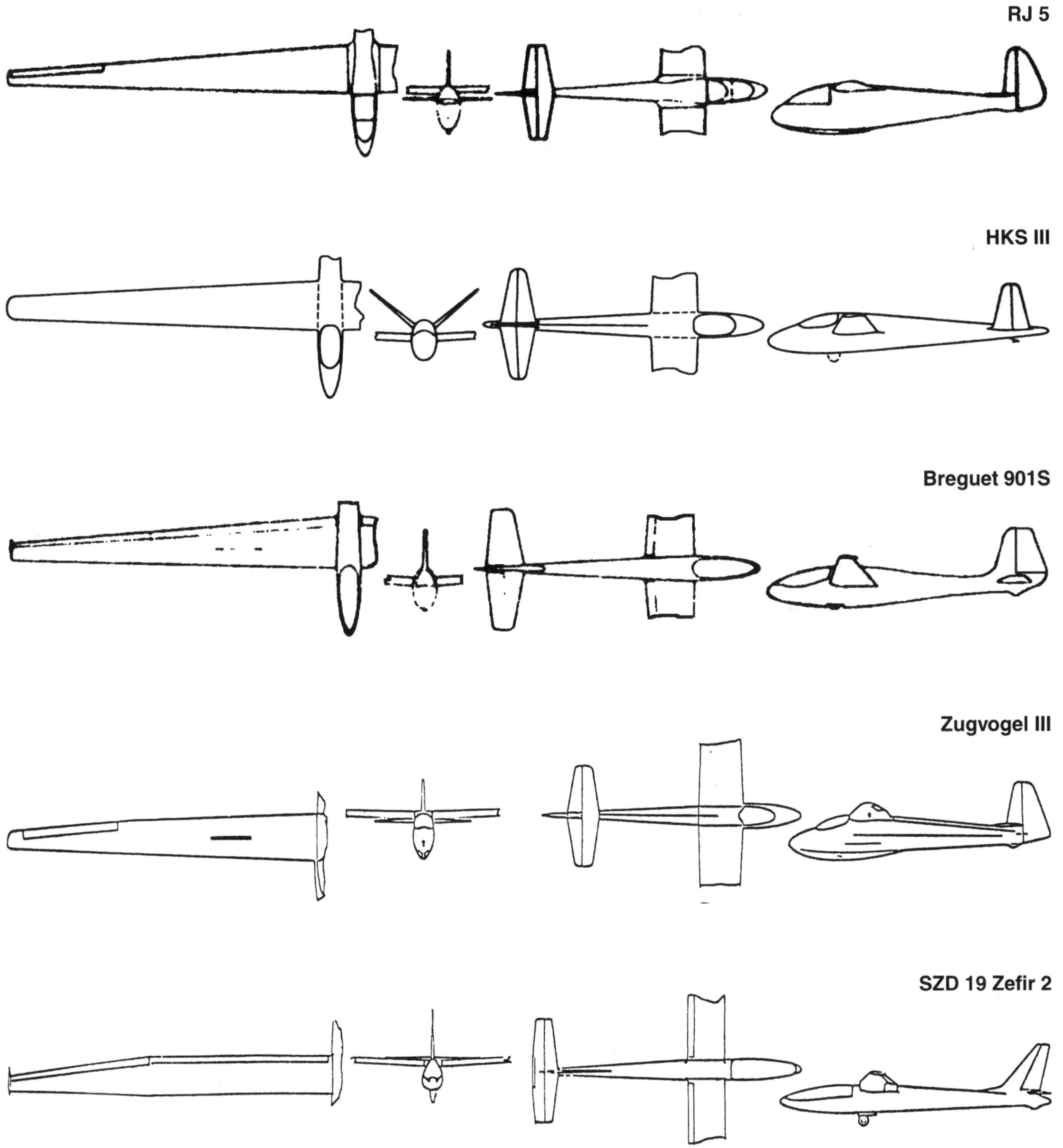
RJ 5
HKS III
Breguet 901S
Zugvogel III
SZD 19 Zefir 2

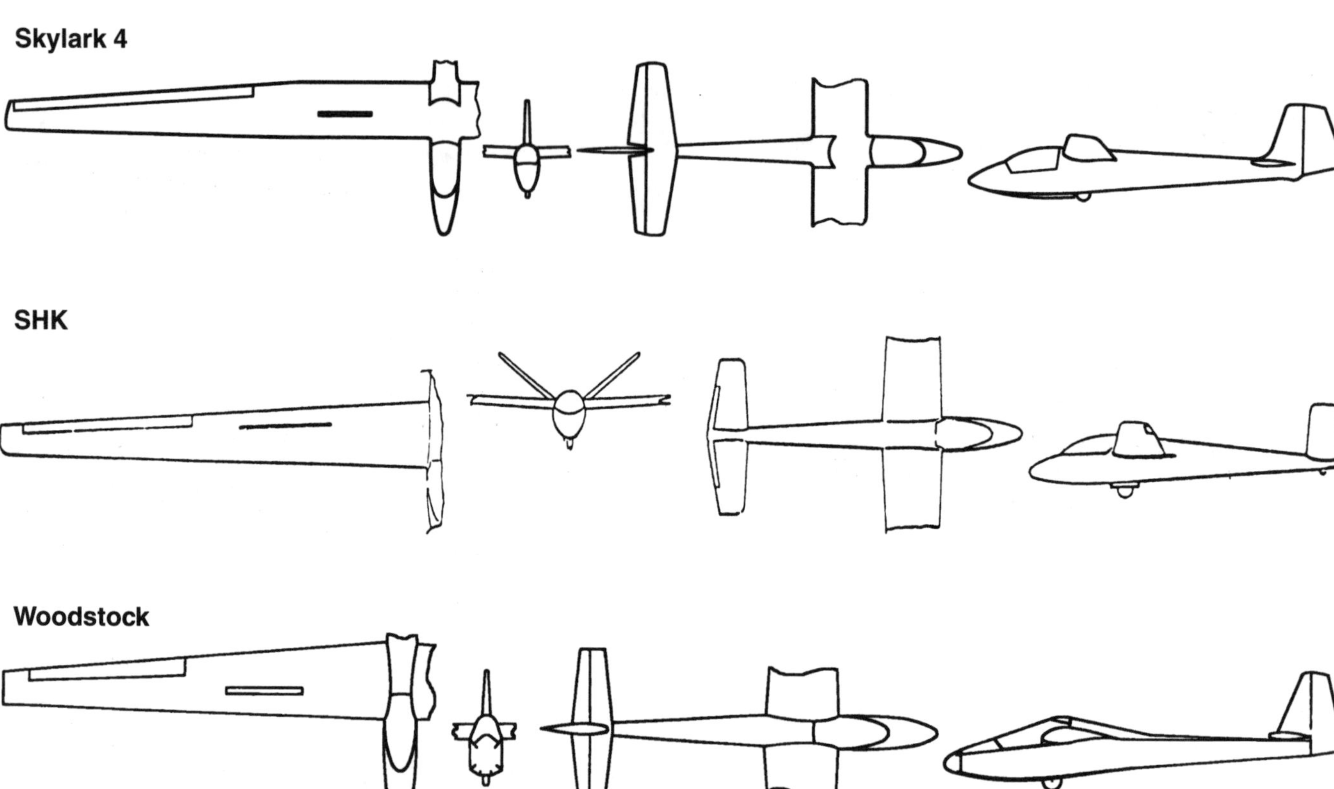

Wood, 15m

Olympia Meise

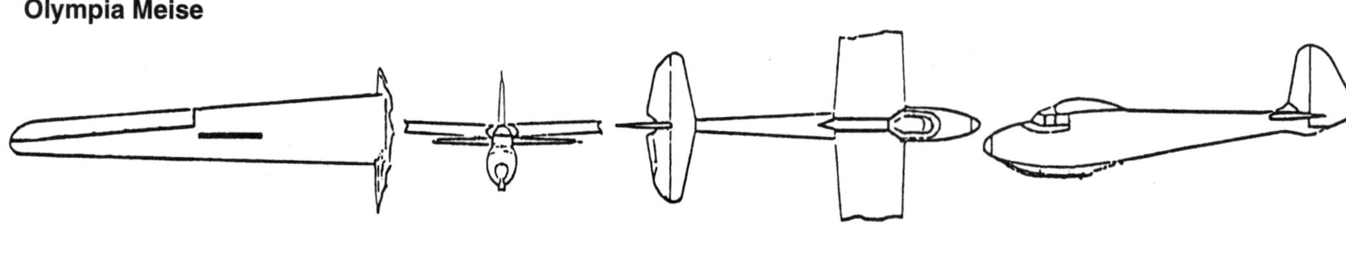

Ka 6E

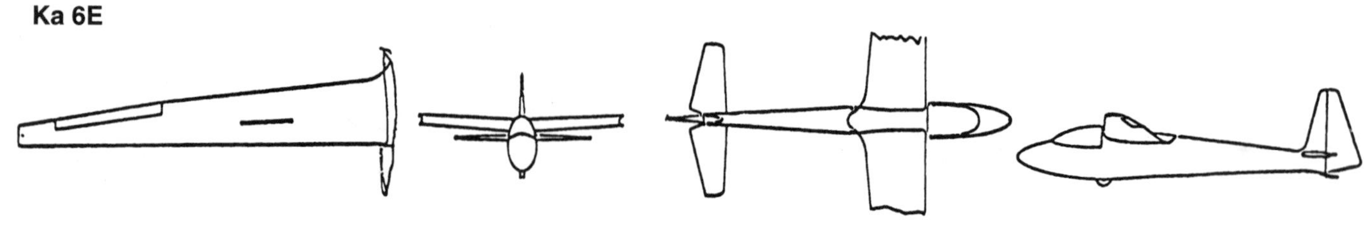

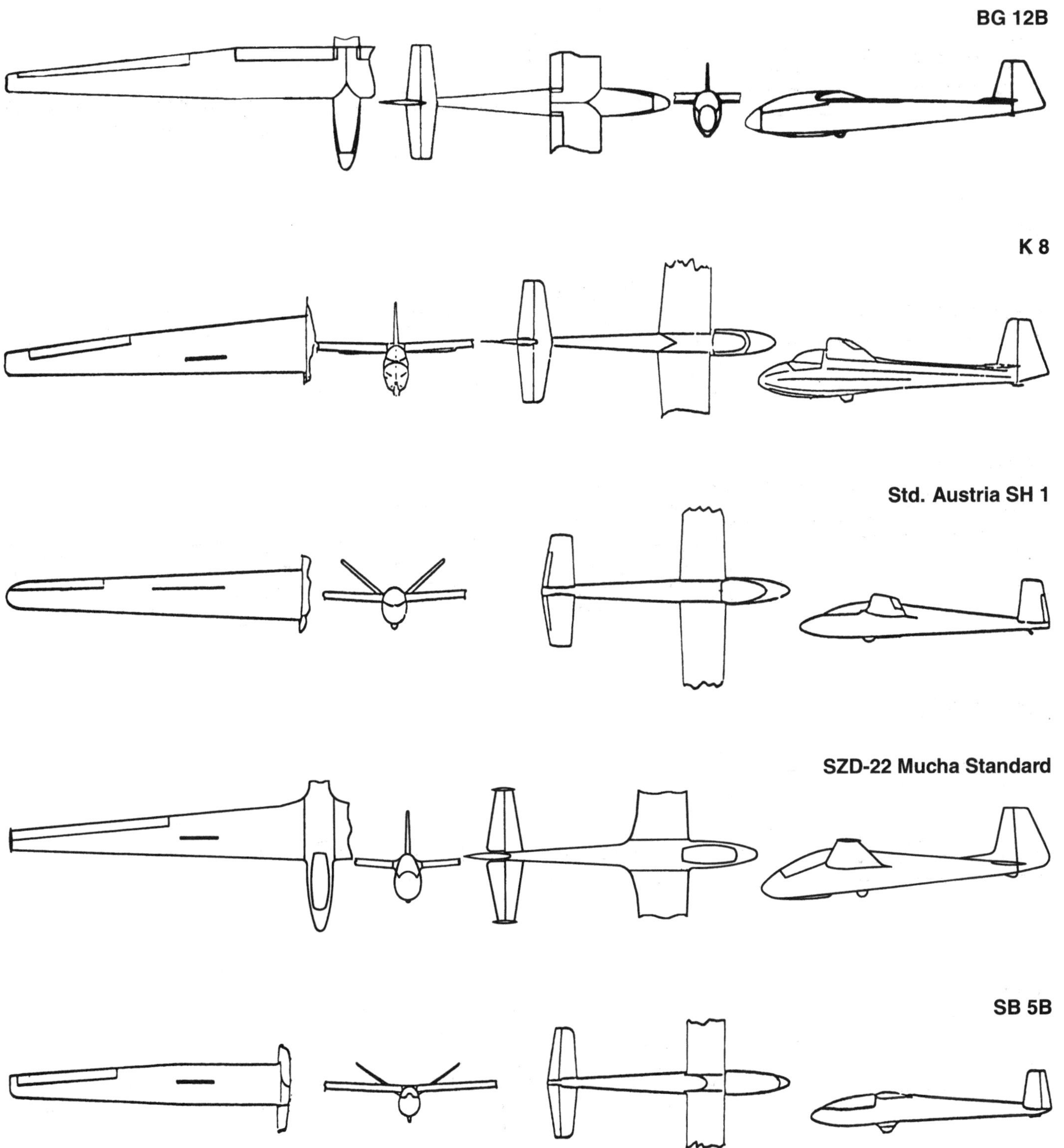
BG 12B
K 8
Std. Austria SH 1
SZD-22 Mucha Standard
SB 5B

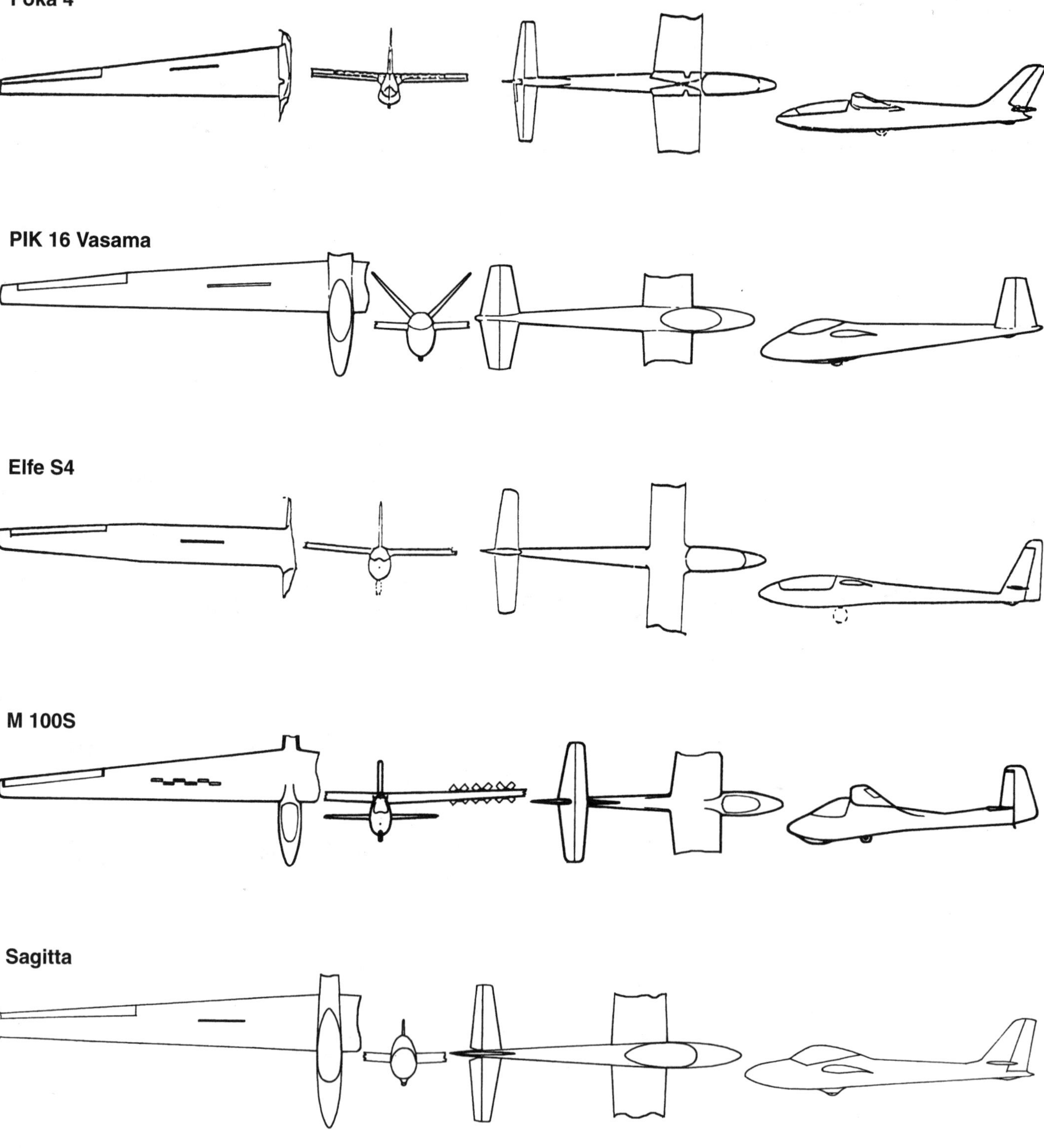
Foka 4
PIK 16 Vasama
Elfe S4
M 100S
Sagitta

Metal Sailplanes

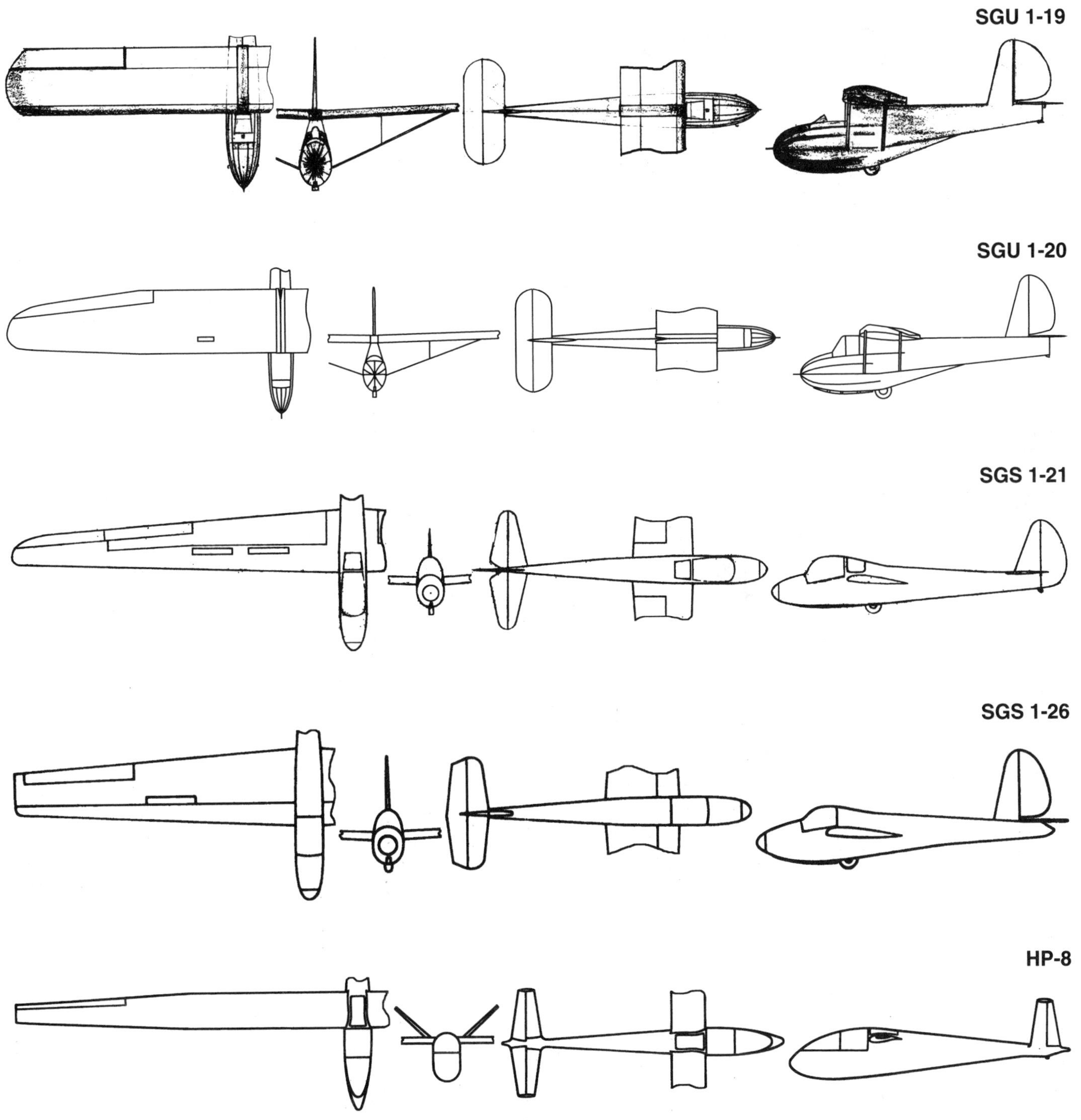

Monerai

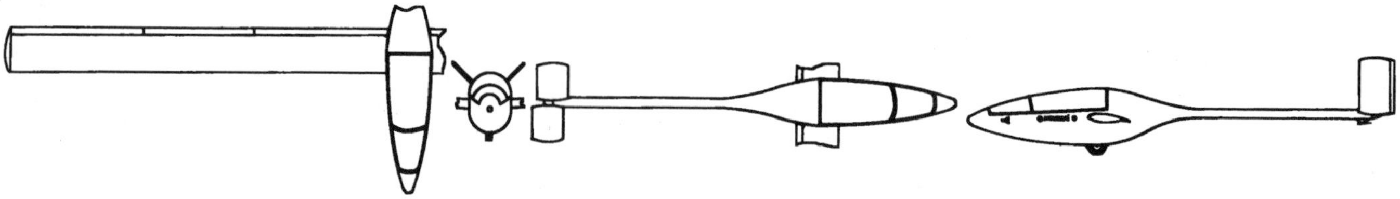

SGS 1-36

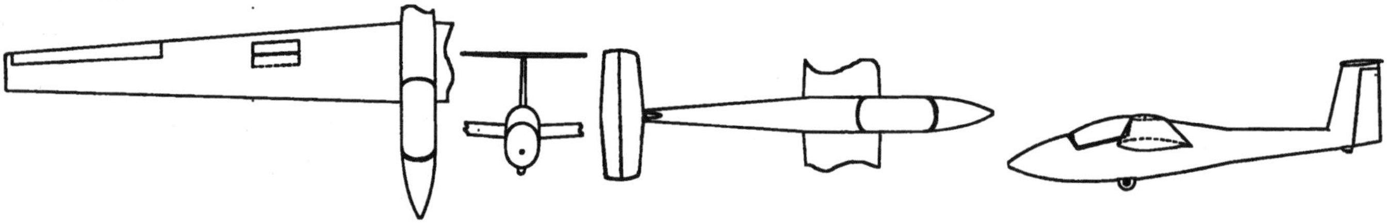

Metal, 15m

SGS 1-23H-15

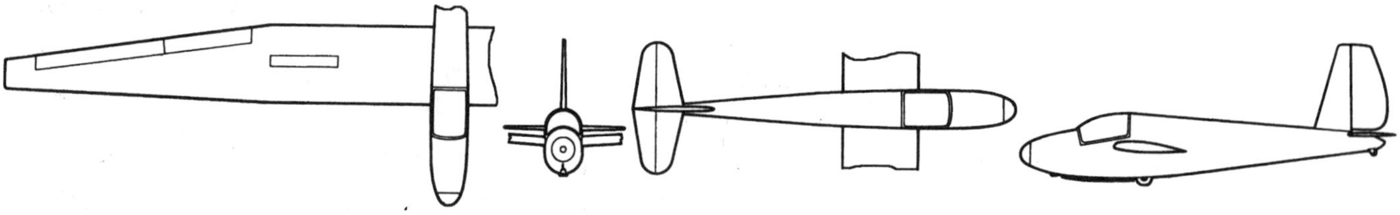

SGS 1-34

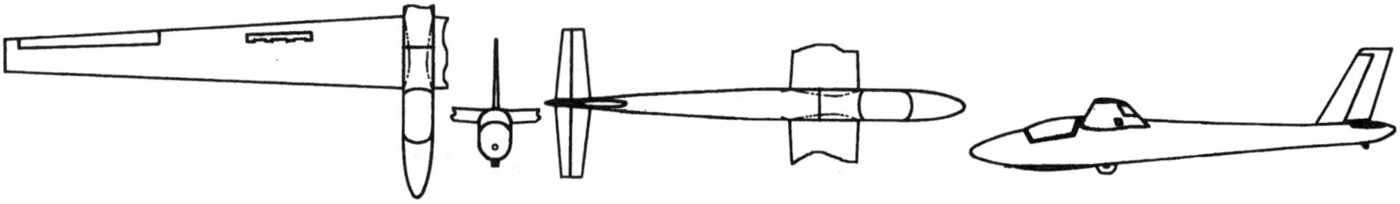

SGS 1-35

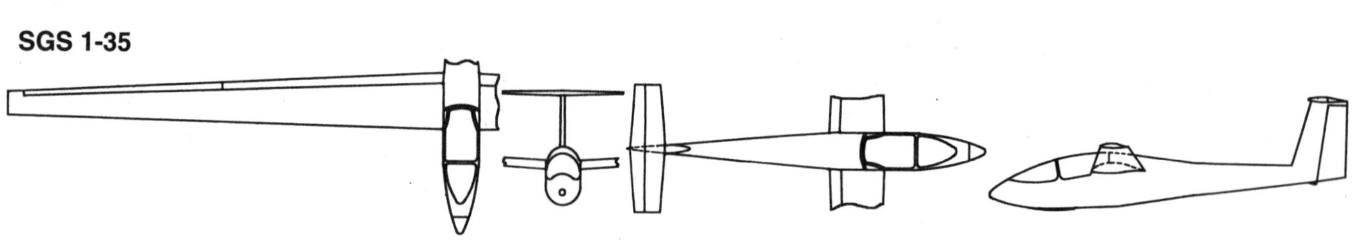

Laister Nugget

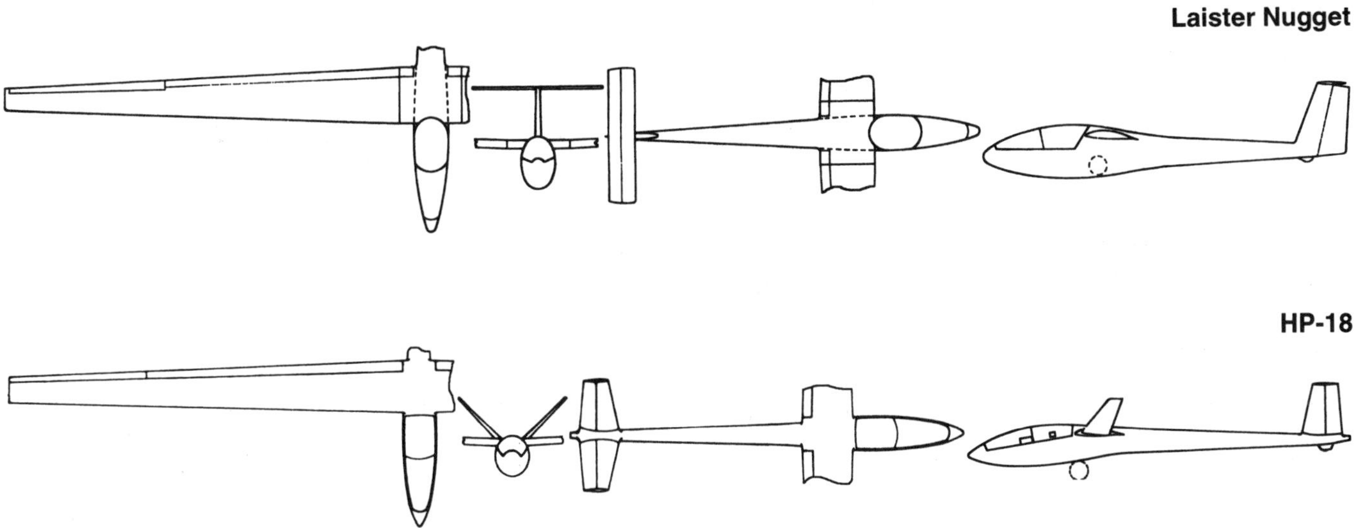

HP-18

Flying Wings

SB 13: see page 115

Genesis 2: see page 116

AV 361 (AV 36 MK II)

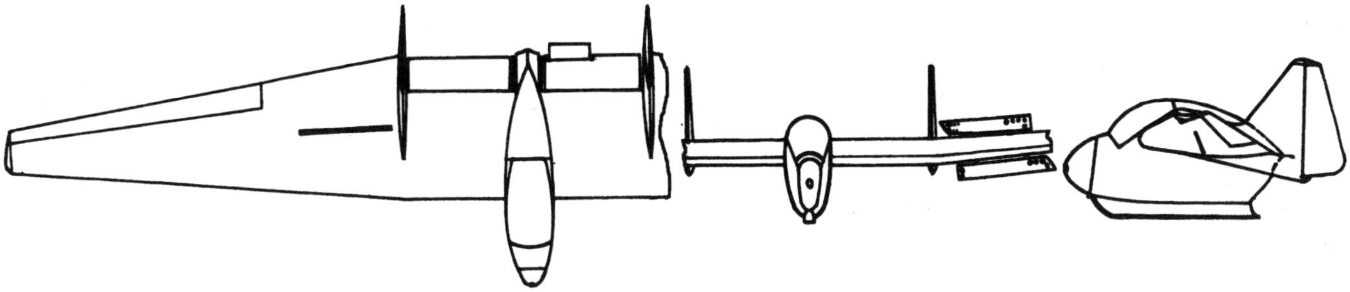

Pioneer II

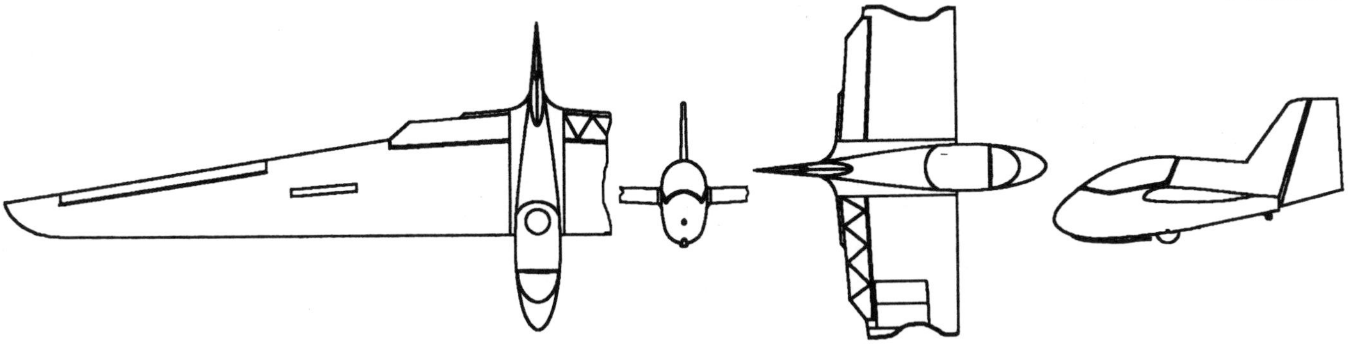

Aerobatic

Lo 100

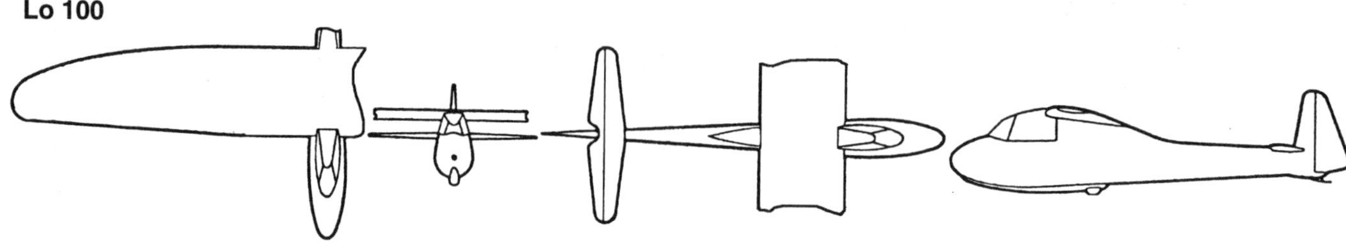

Mü 28

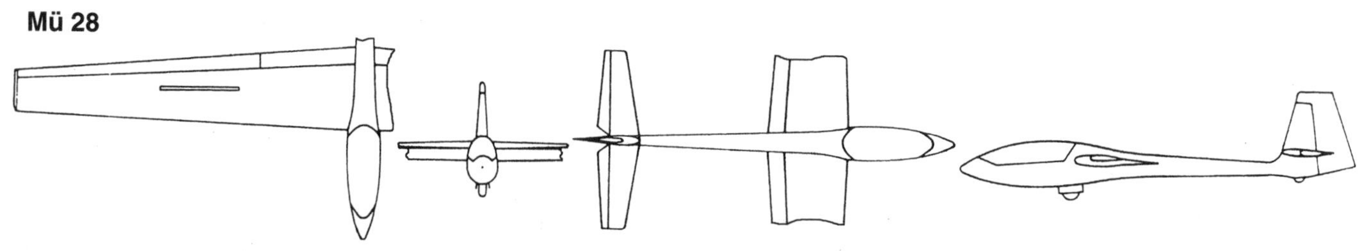

SZD 59 Acro

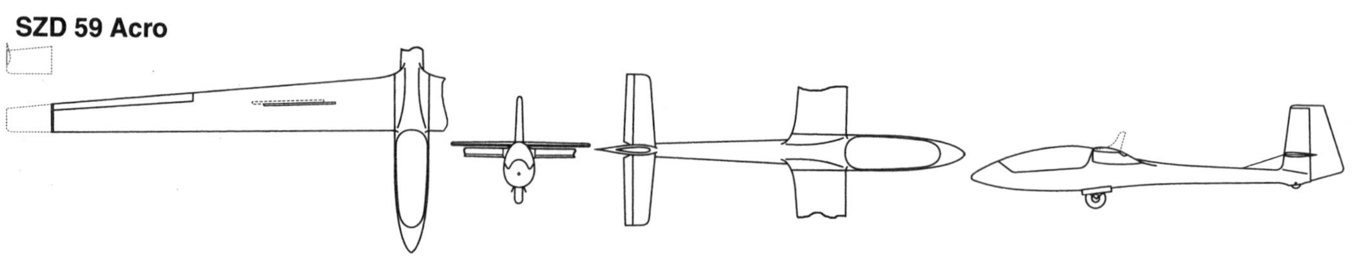

Variable Geometry

fs 29: see page 111

SB 11 (see also page 112)

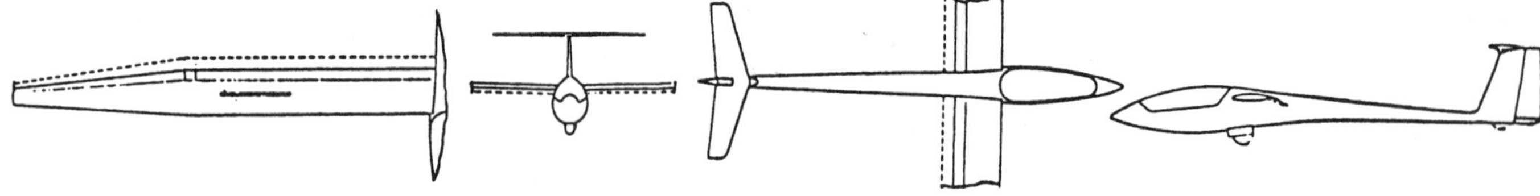

BJ2 Assegai

Sigma

fs 32 "Aguila"

Open Class (b $\leq$ 18m)

Phoenix T

SB 6

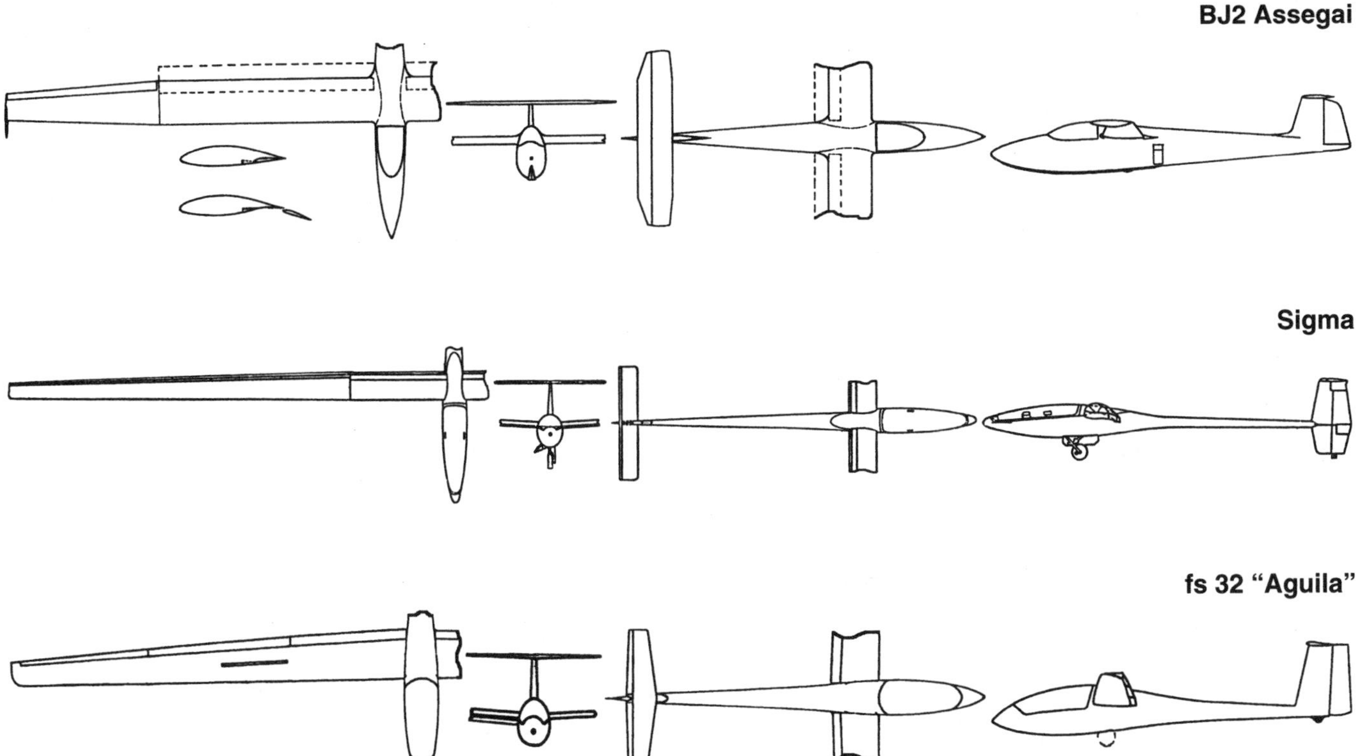

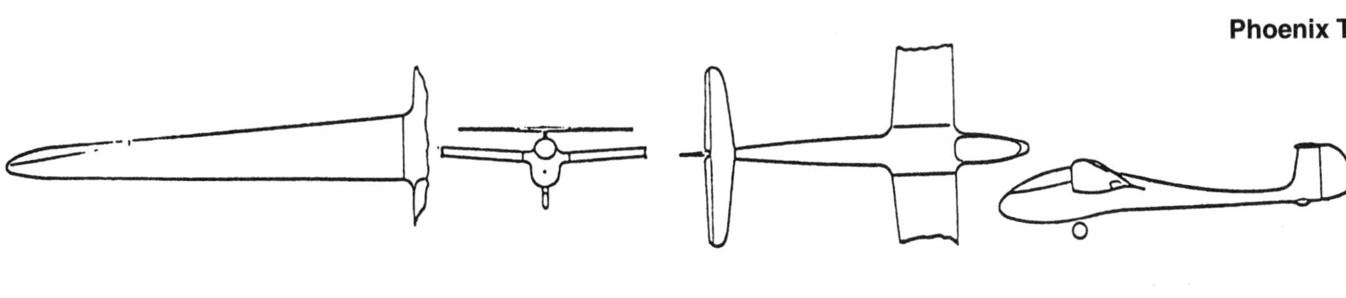

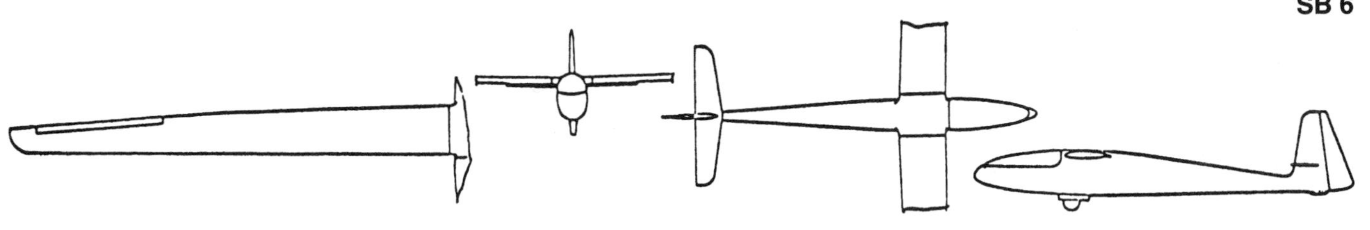

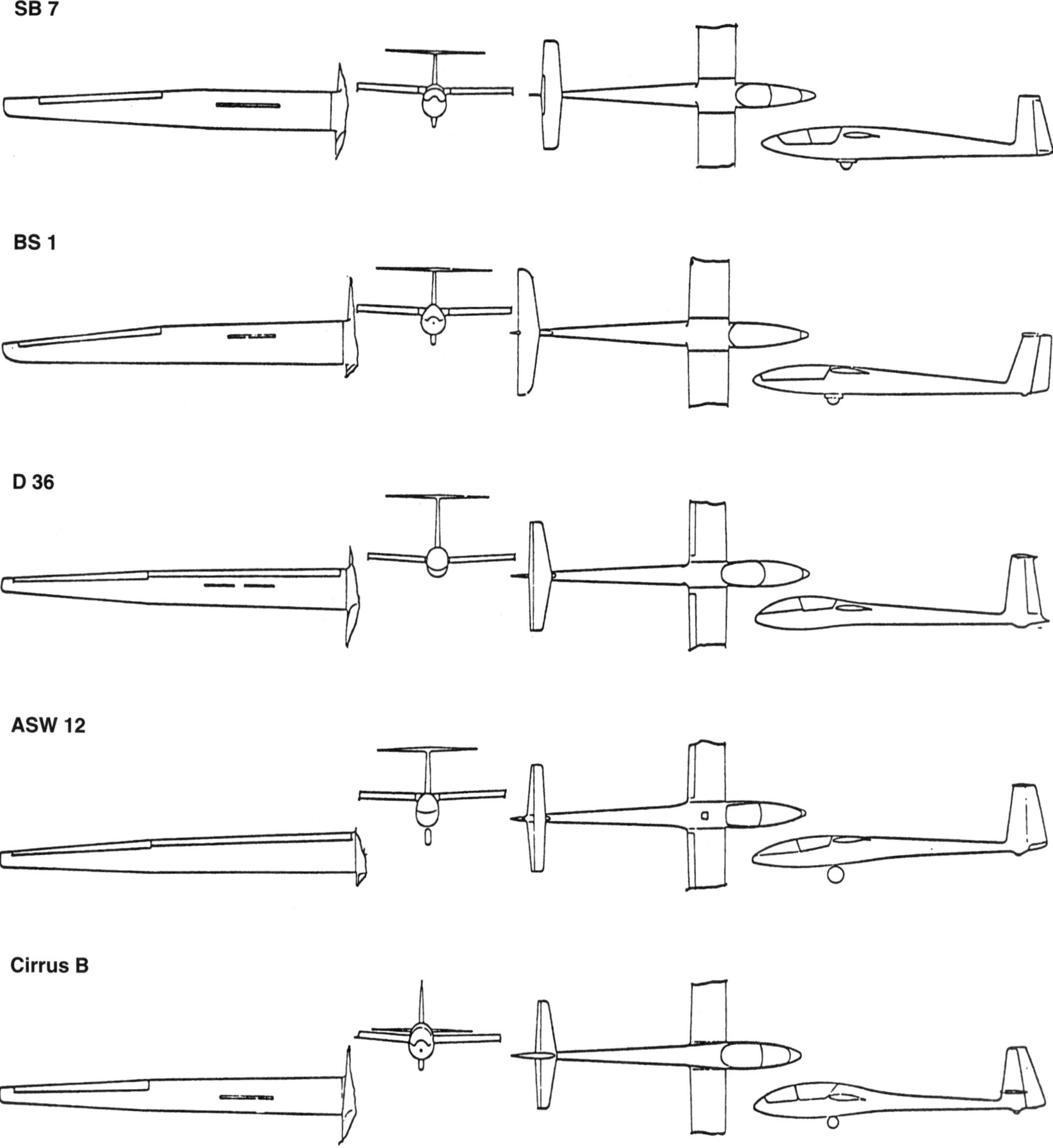
SB 7
BS 1
D 36
ASW 12
Cirrus B

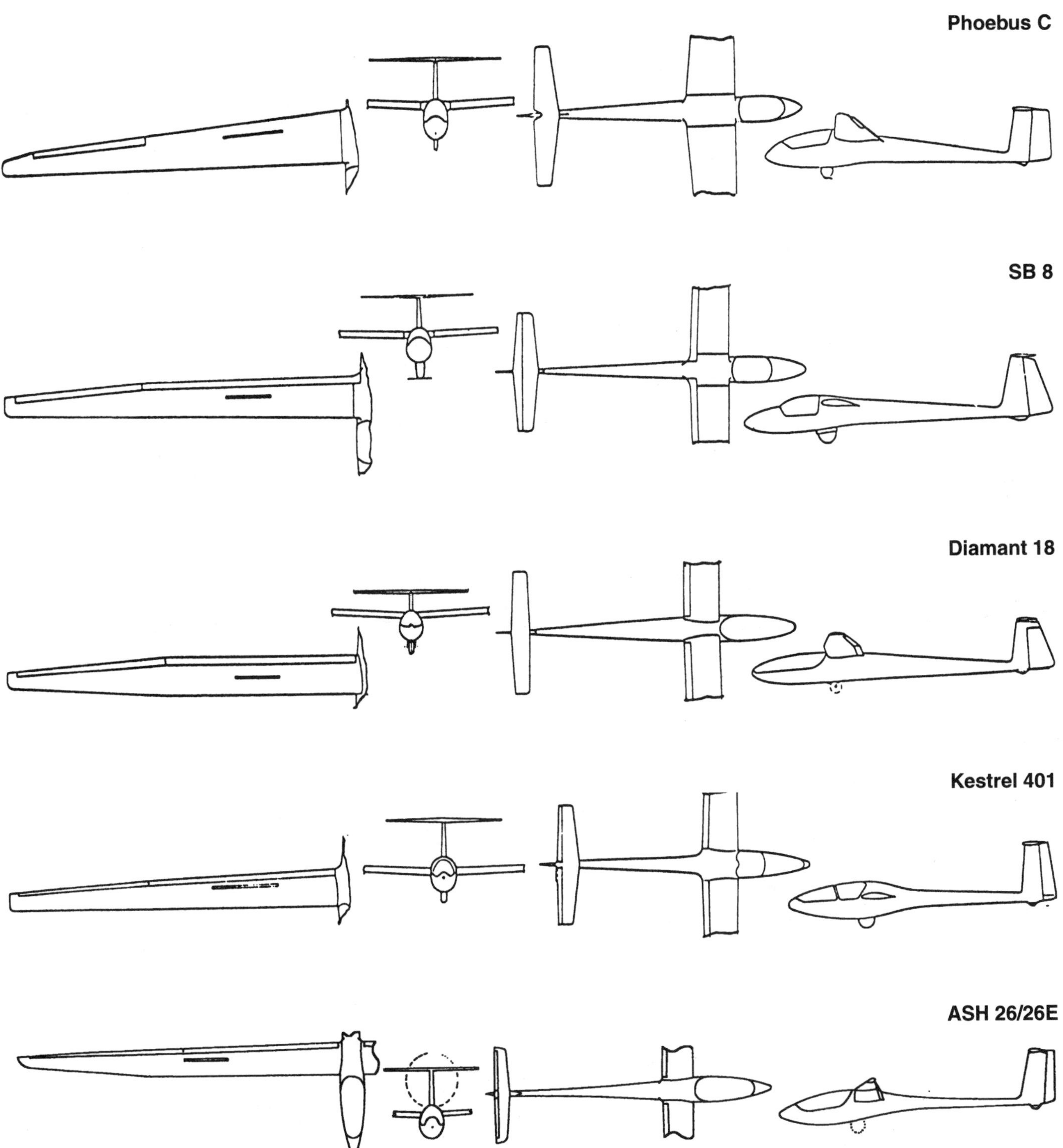
Phoebus C
SB 8
Diamant 18
Kestrel 401
ASH 26/26E

SB 14

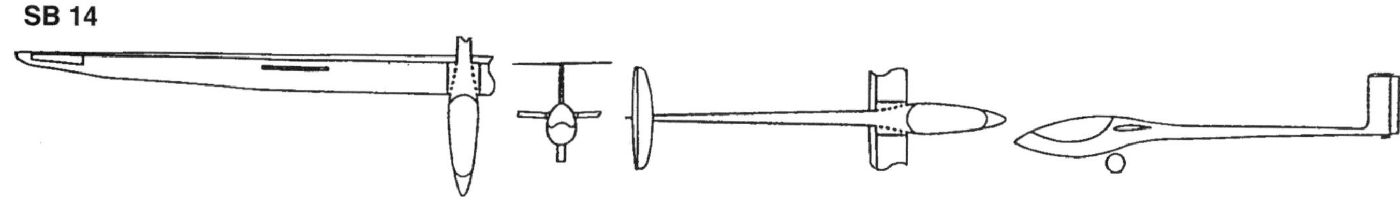

Open Class (b > 18m)

eta: see page 119

SB 9

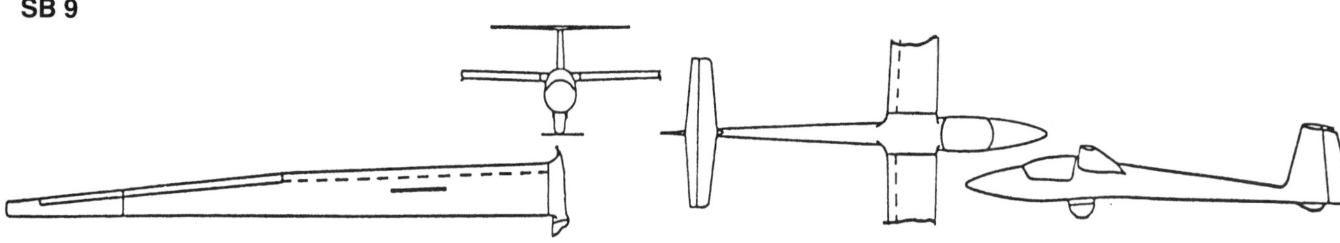

Nimbus I

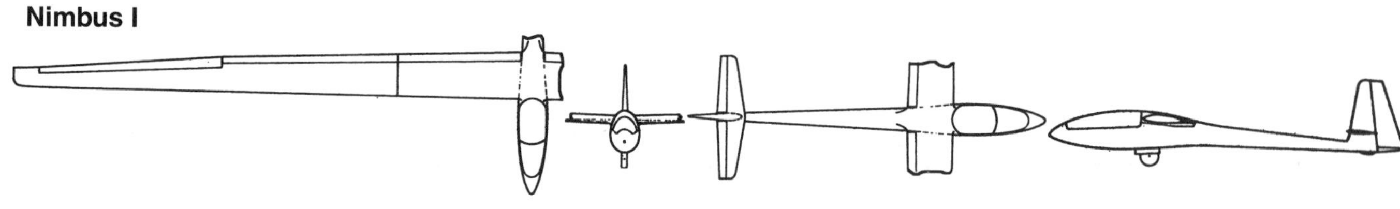

Nimbus II

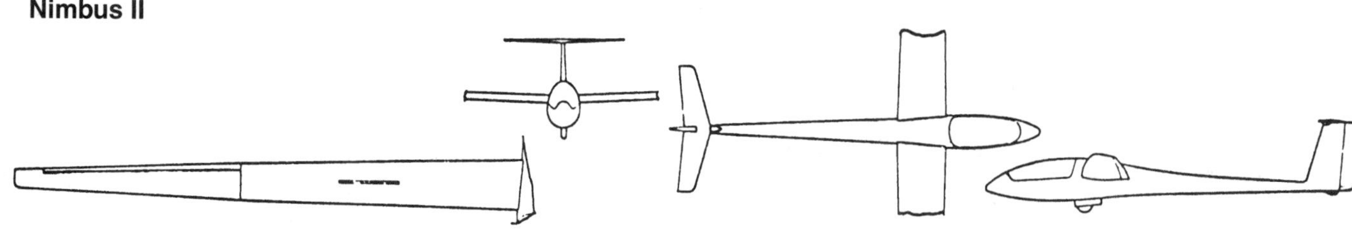

Kestrel 604

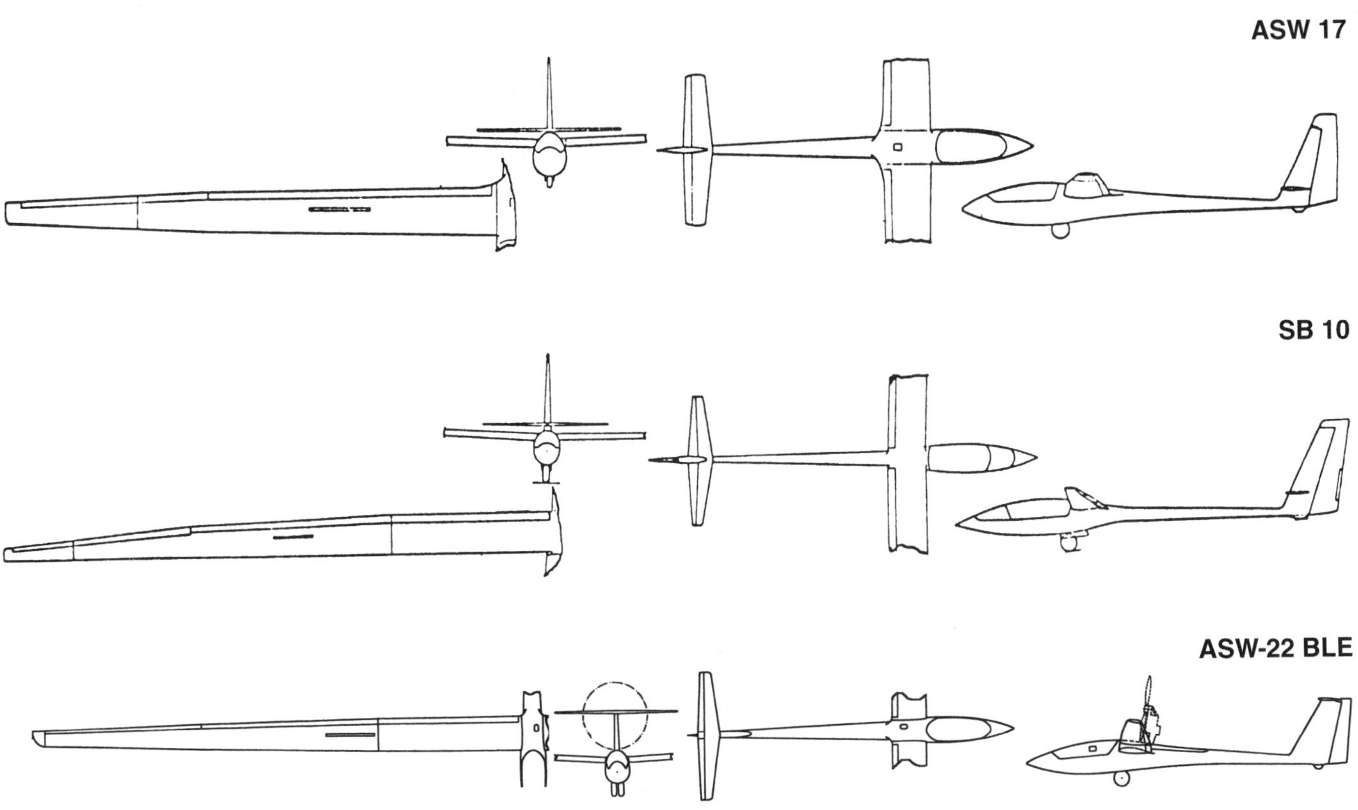

Multiplace (pre-1980)

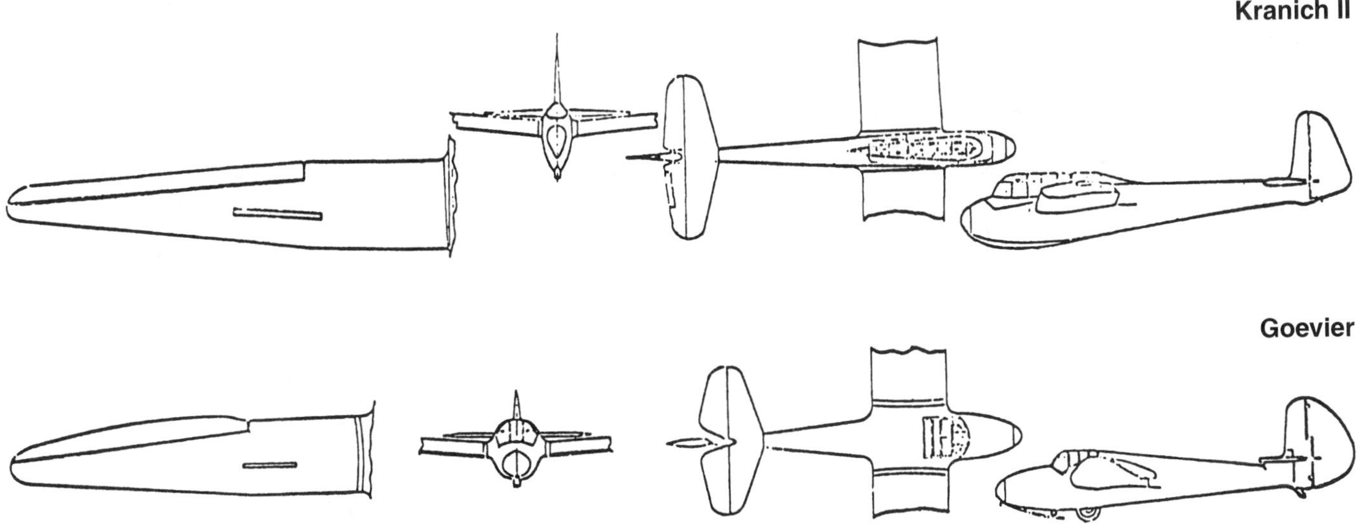

LK 10

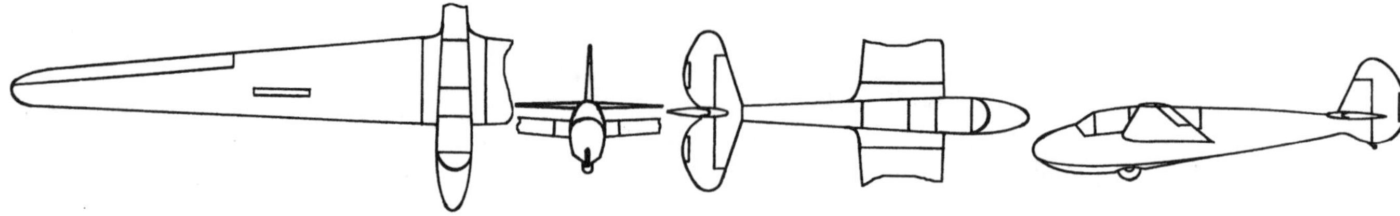

SGU 2-22E

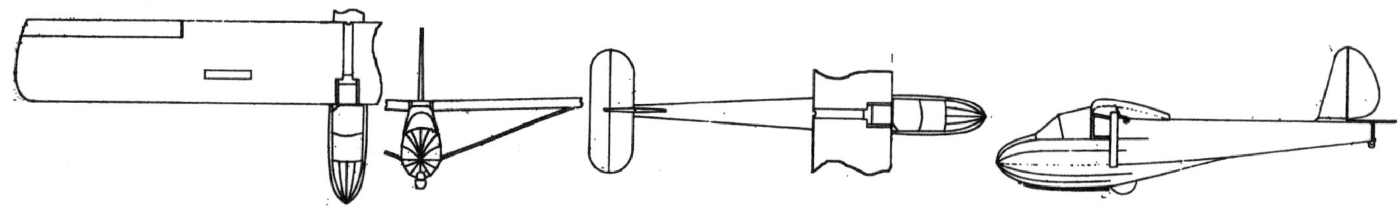

Kranich III

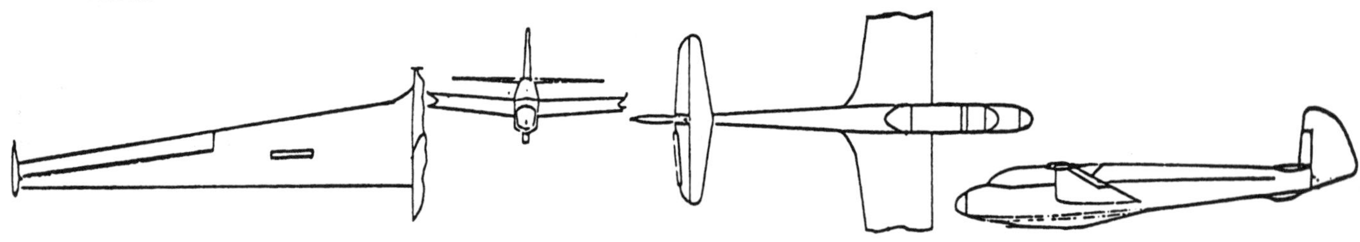

Bocian

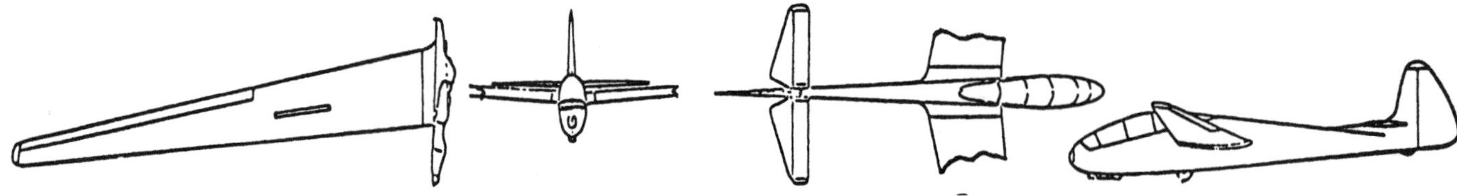

Bergfalke II/55

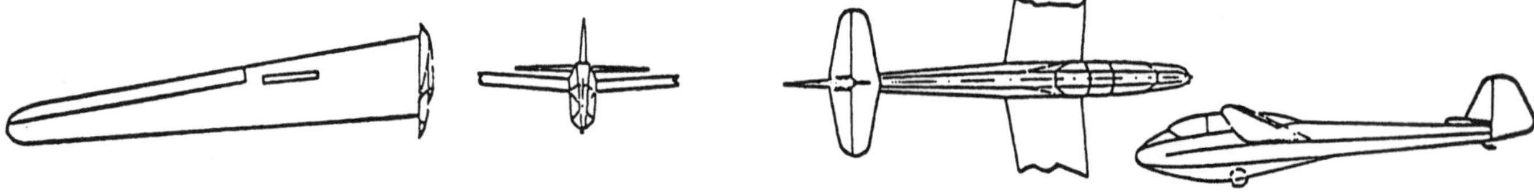

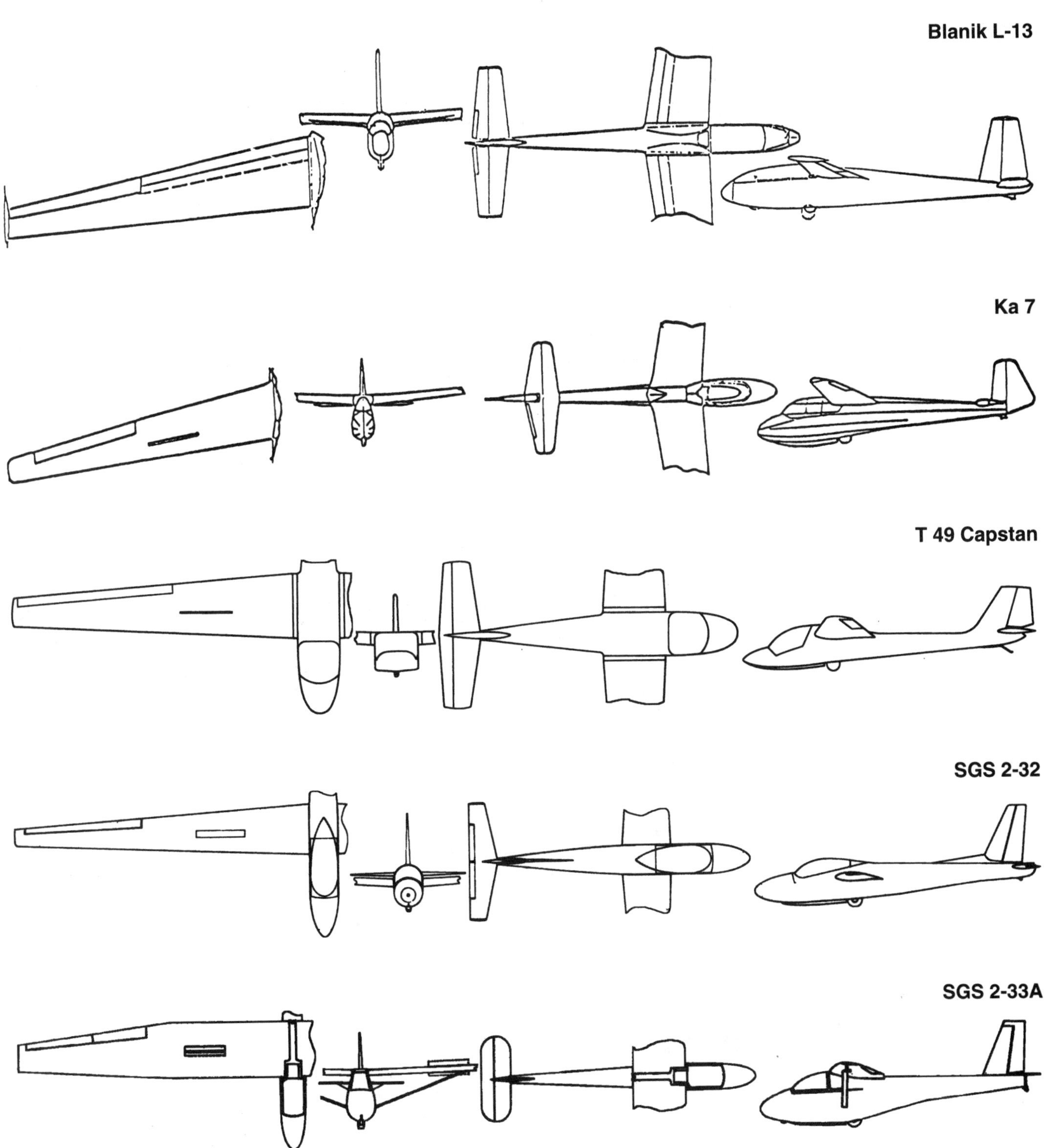
Blanik L-13
Ka 7
T 49 Capstan
SGS 2-32
SGS 2-33A

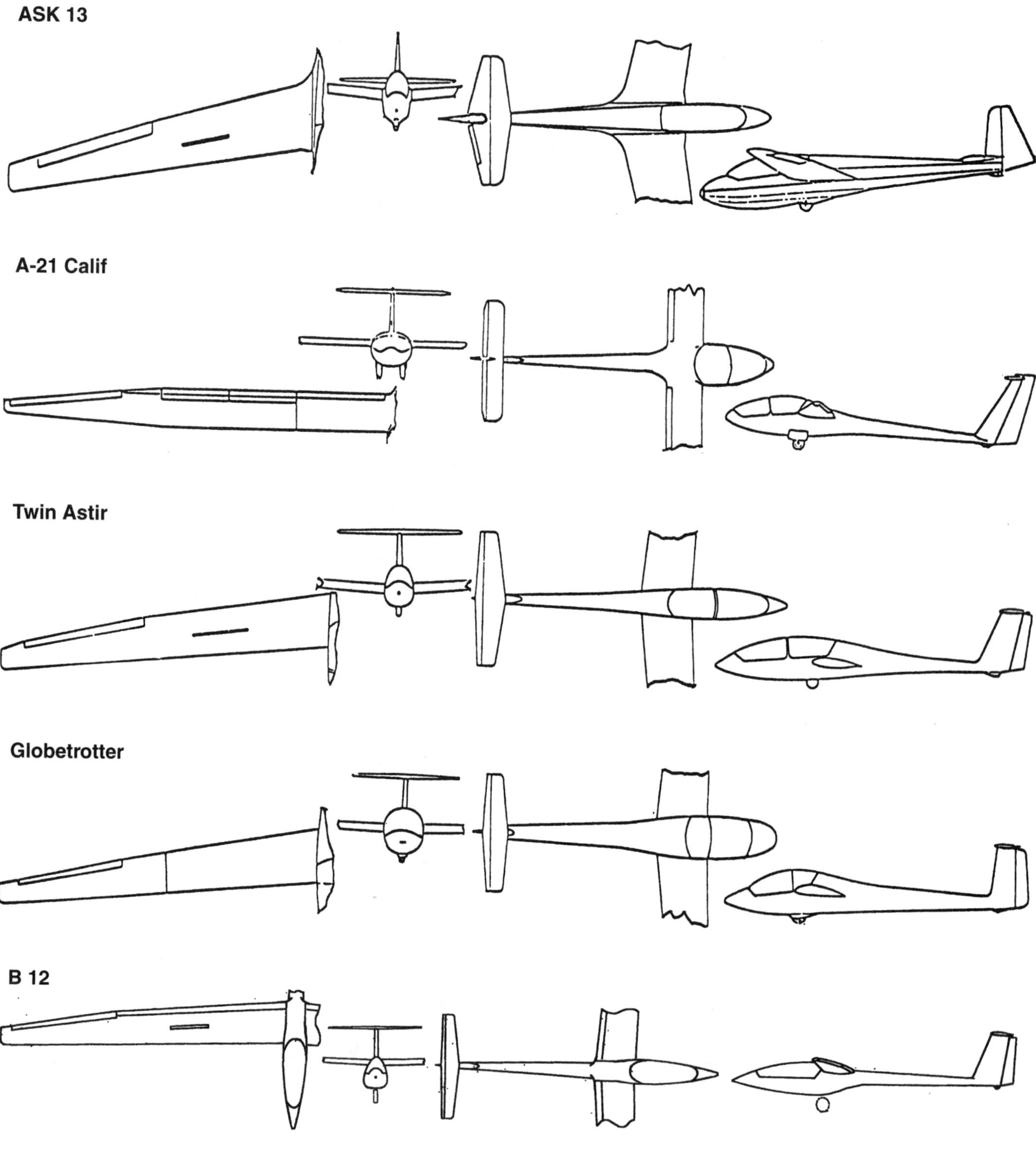
ASK 13
A-21 Calif
Twin Astir
Globetrotter
B 12

SFH 34

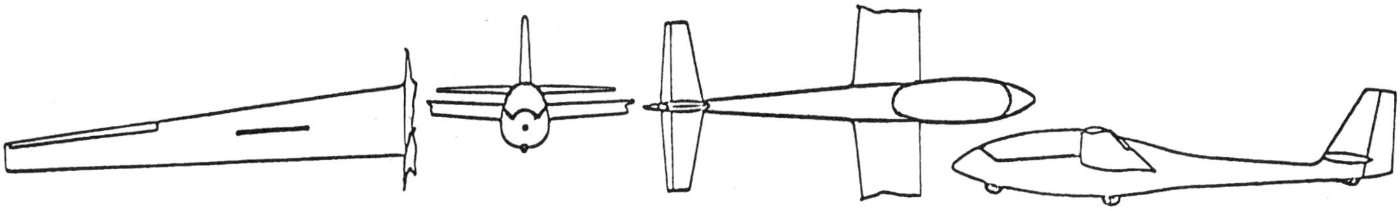

Janus

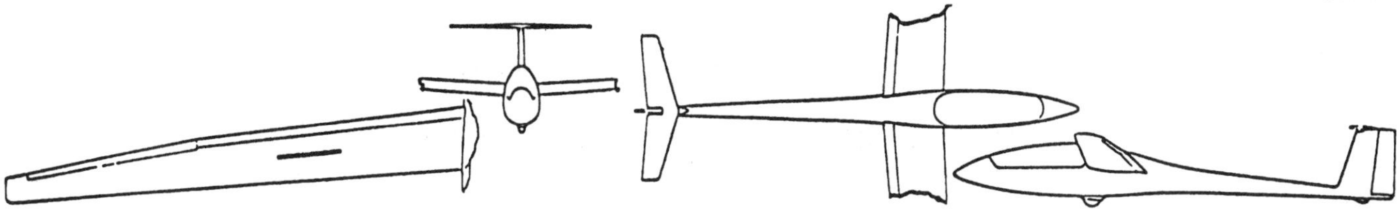

SZD 50-3 Puchacz

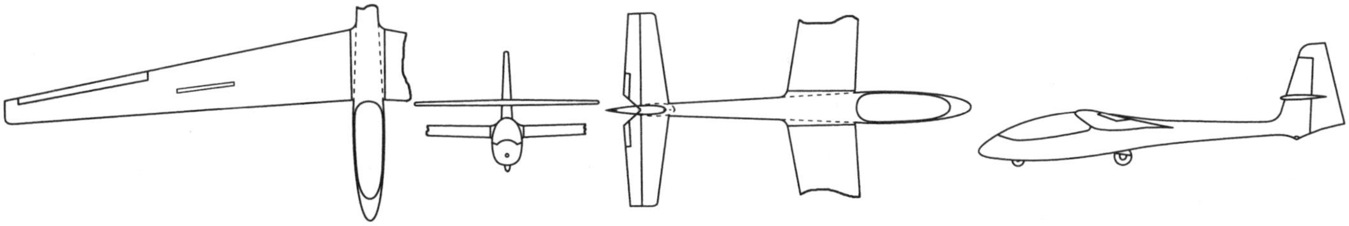

ASK 21

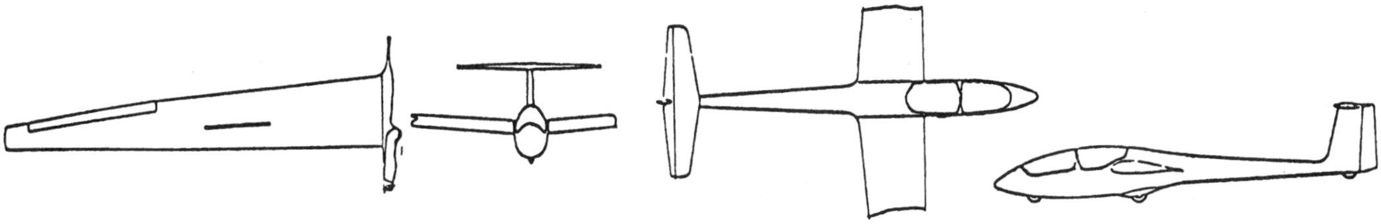

Multiplace (post-1980)

G103 Twin III

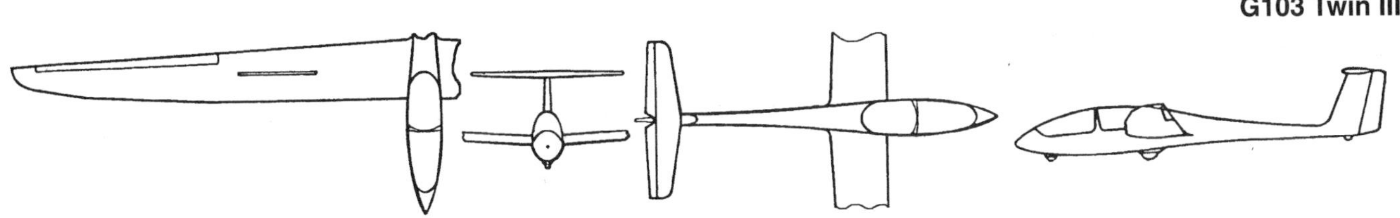

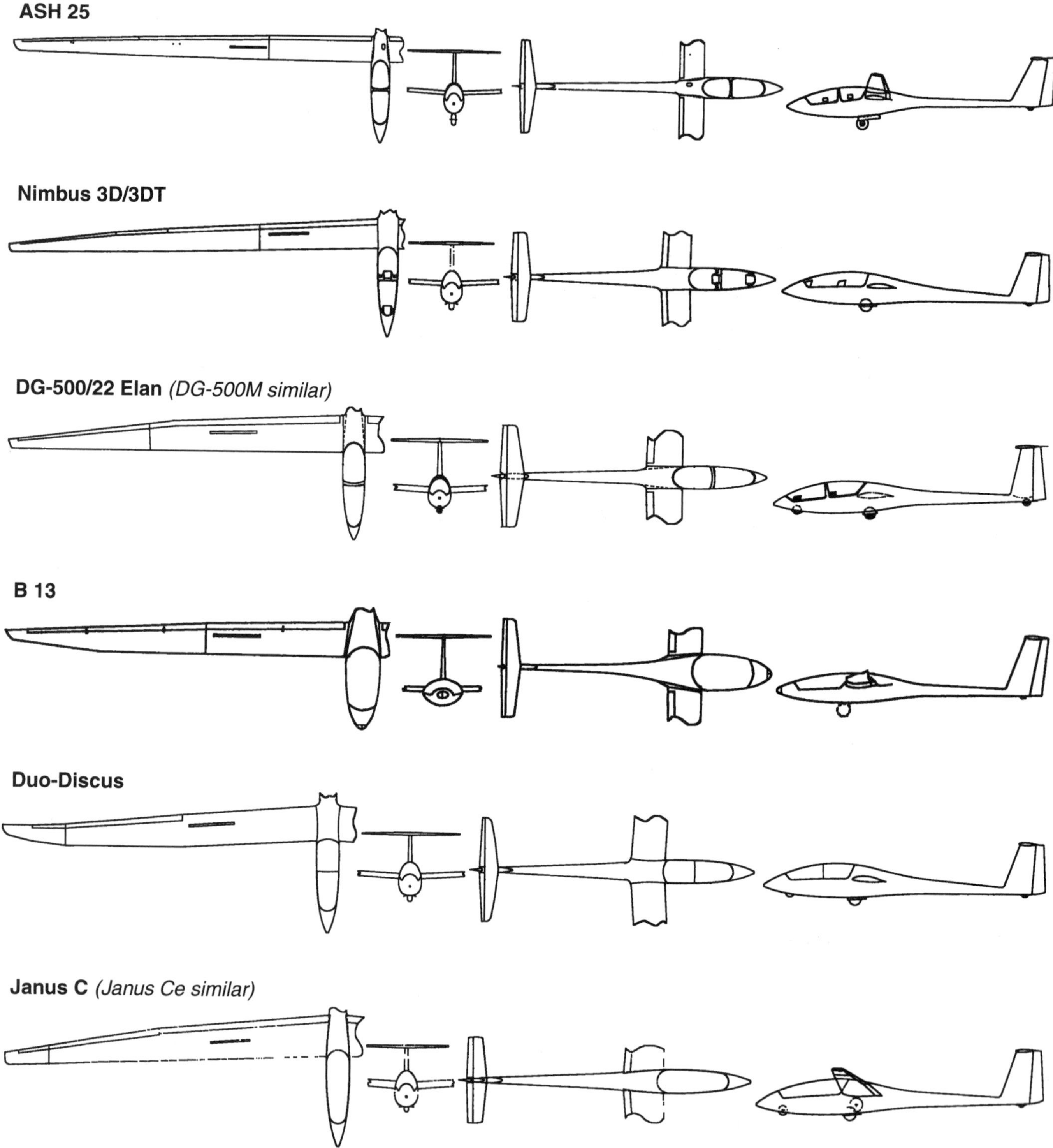

ASH 25
Nimbus 3D/3DT
DG-500/22 Elan *(DG-500M similar)*
B 13
Duo-Discus
Janus C *(Janus Ce similar)*

Stemme S-10

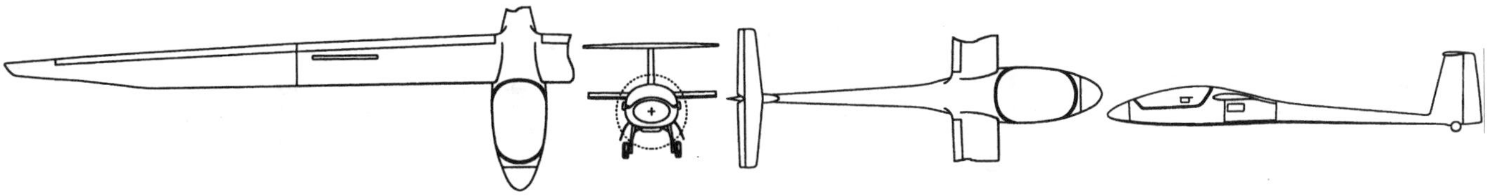

D-41

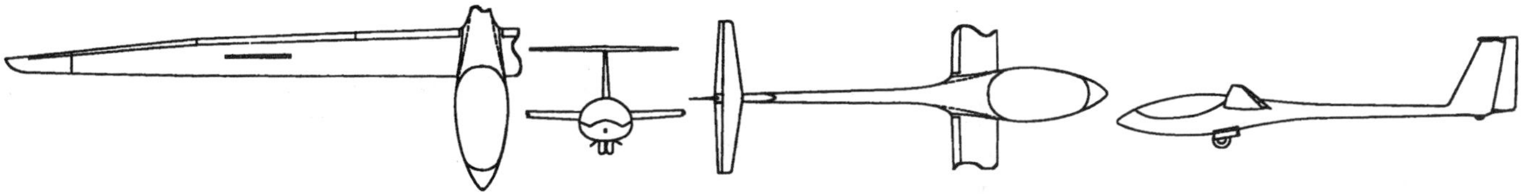

L-23 Super Blanik

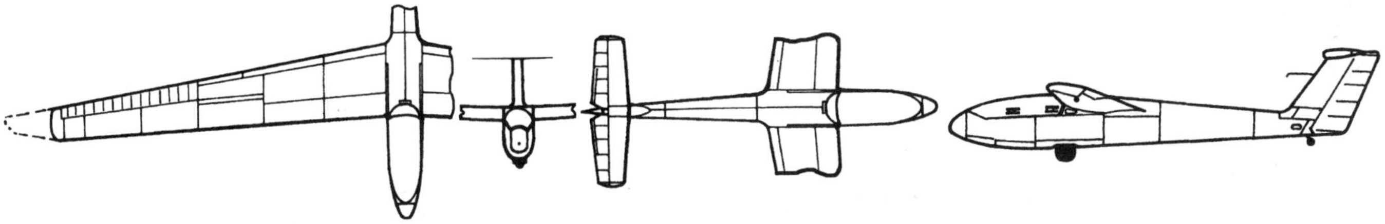

Blanik L-13AC

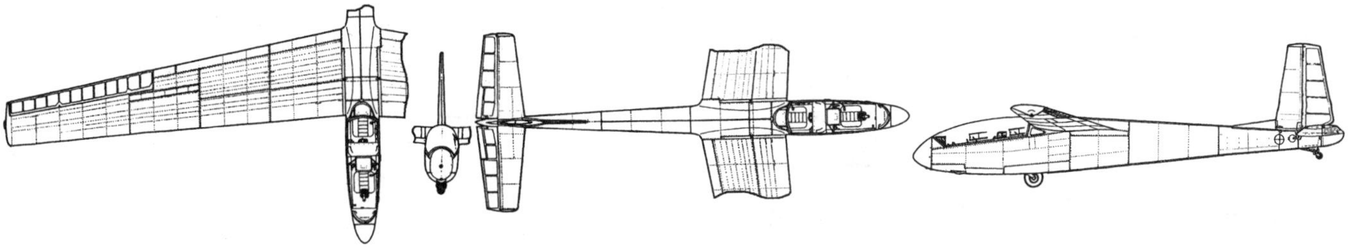

Standard Class (includes all with b $\leq$15m)

Phoebus B1

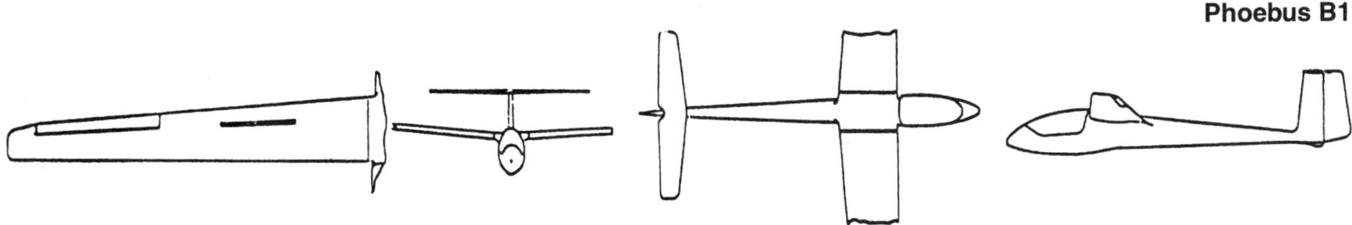

fs 23 "Hidalgo"

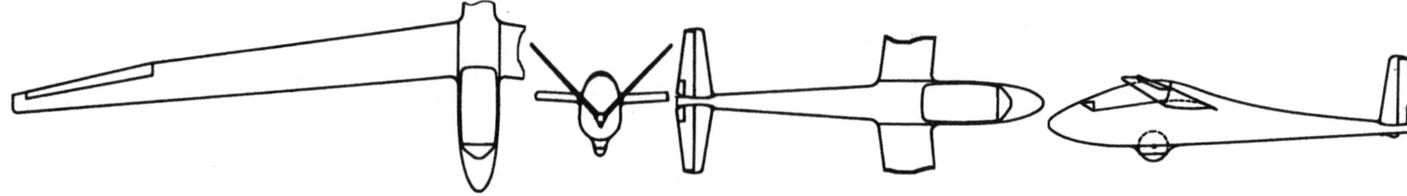

LS 1C

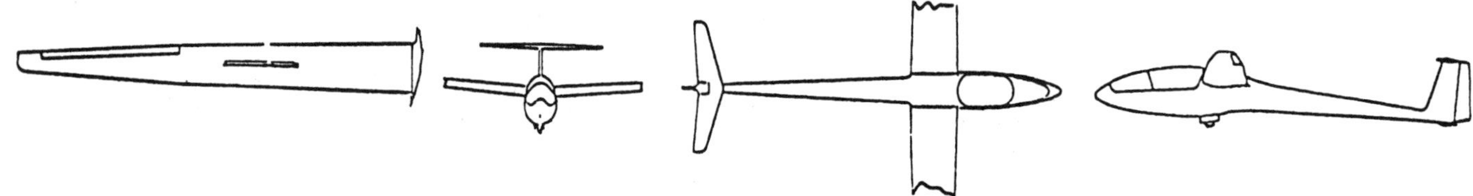

Std. Libelle H201

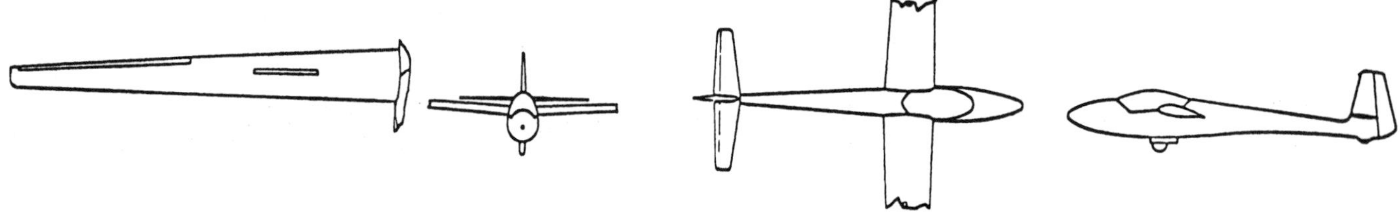

fs 25

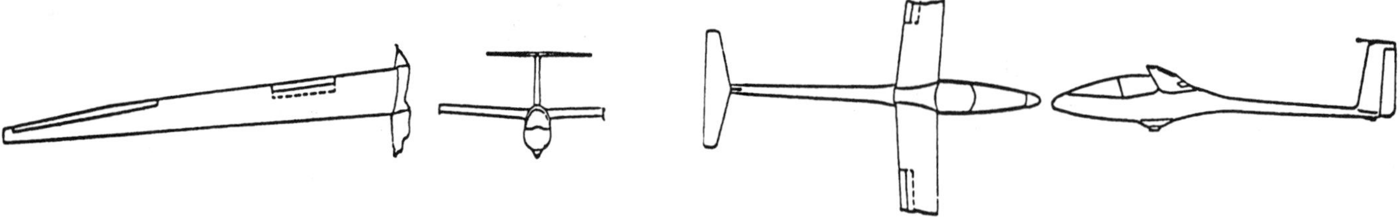

ASW 15

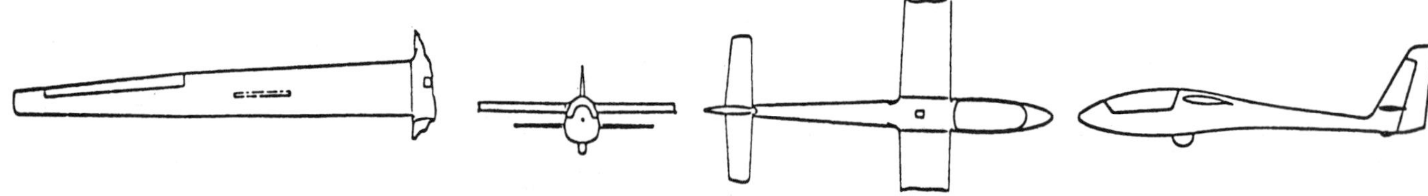

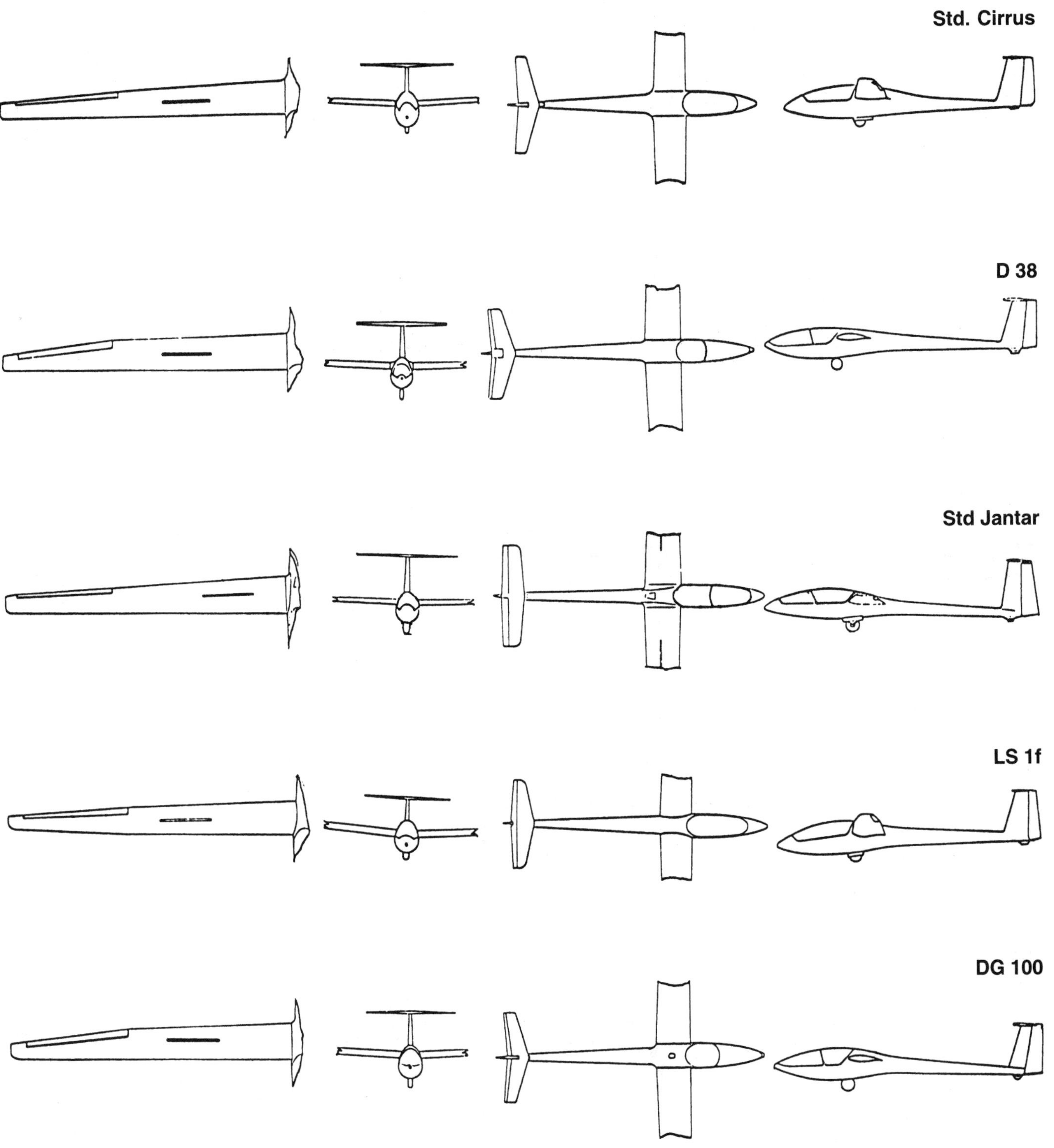
Std. Cirrus
D 38
Std Jantar
LS 1f
DG 100

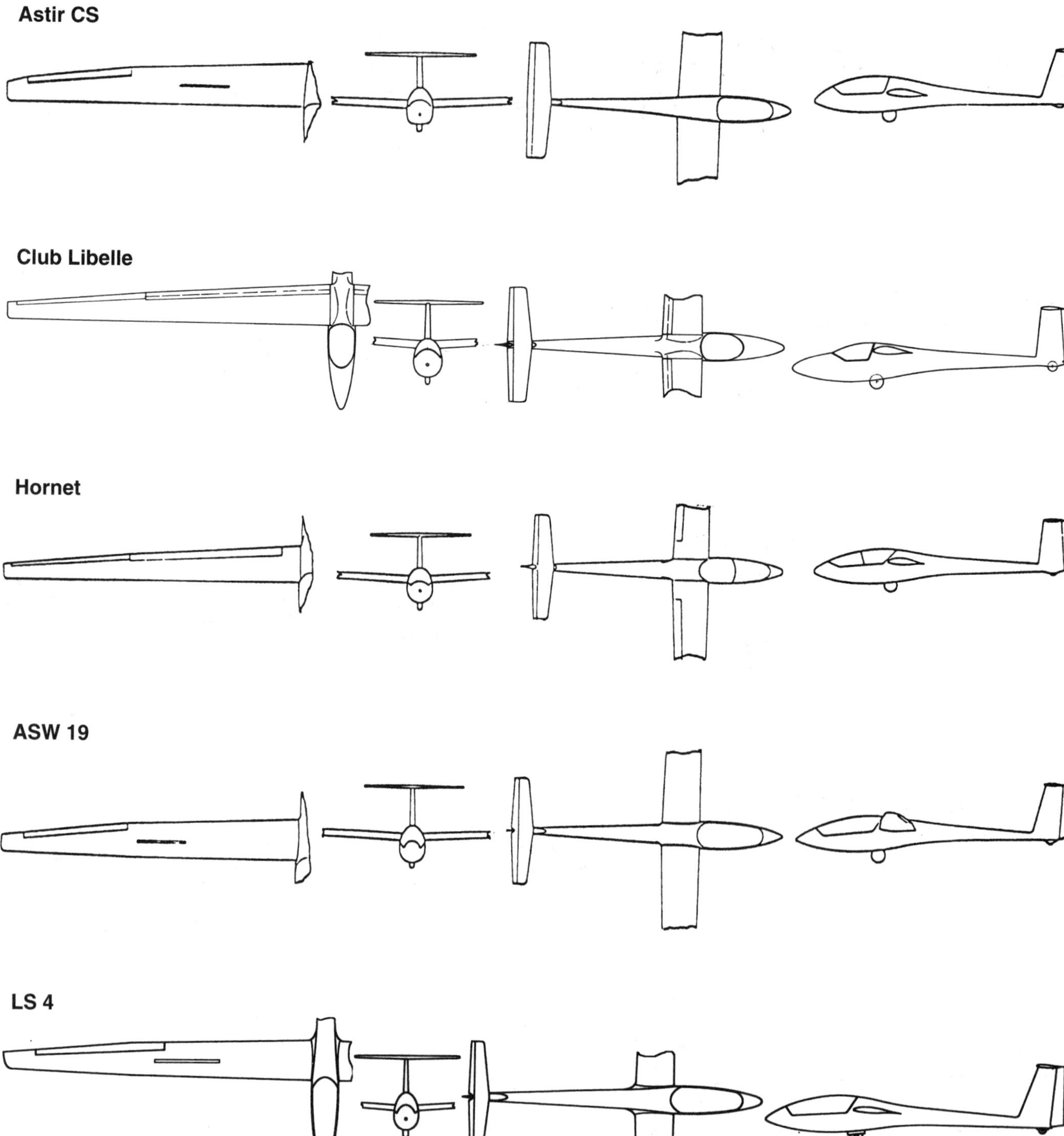
Astir CS
Club Libelle
Hornet
ASW 19
LS 4

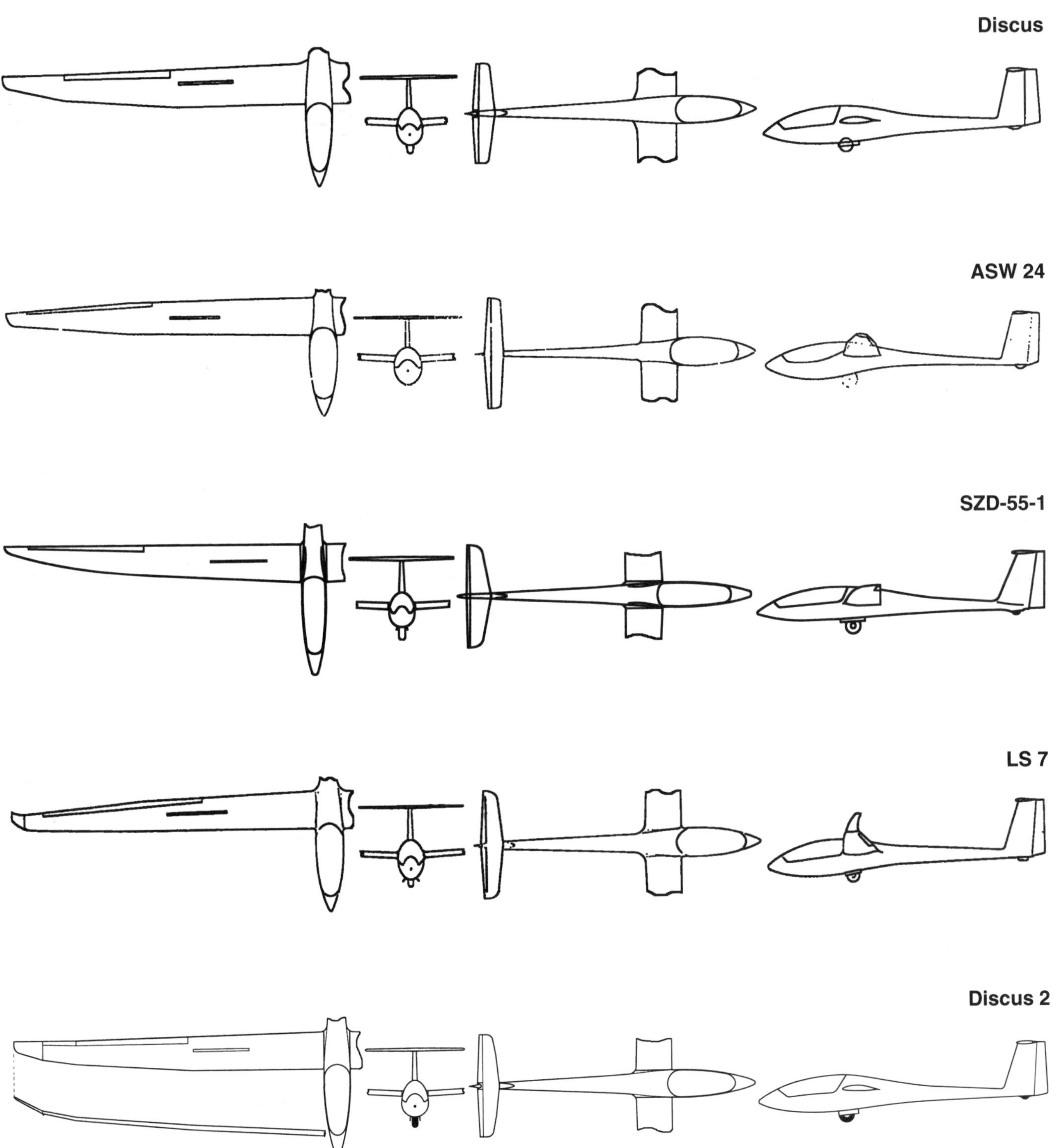
Discus
ASW 24
SZD-55-1
LS 7
Discus 2

LS 8

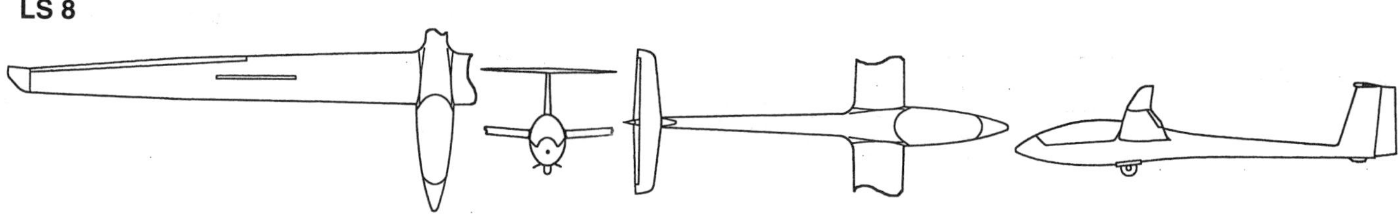

World Class Entrants

PW-5 *(see also page 118)*

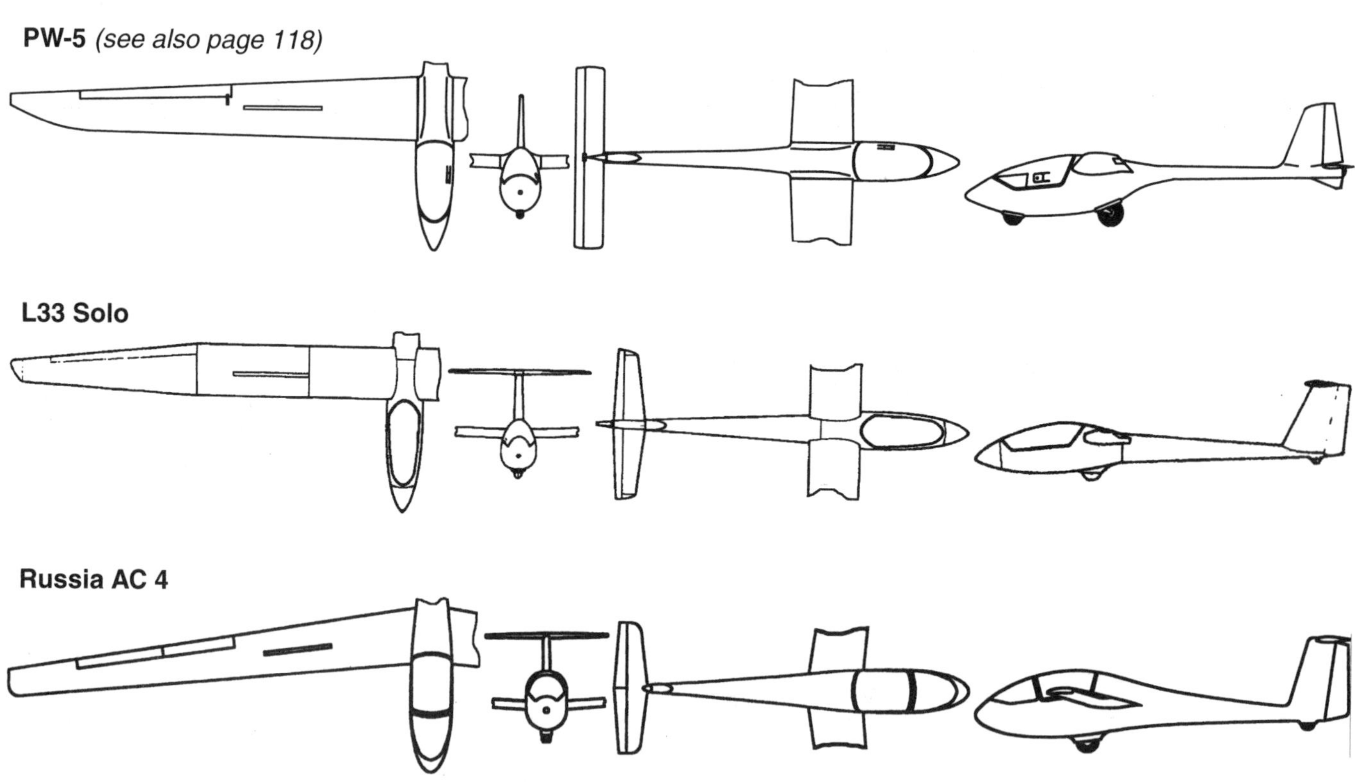

L33 Solo

Russia AC 4

FAI 15m Racing Class

Libelle H 301

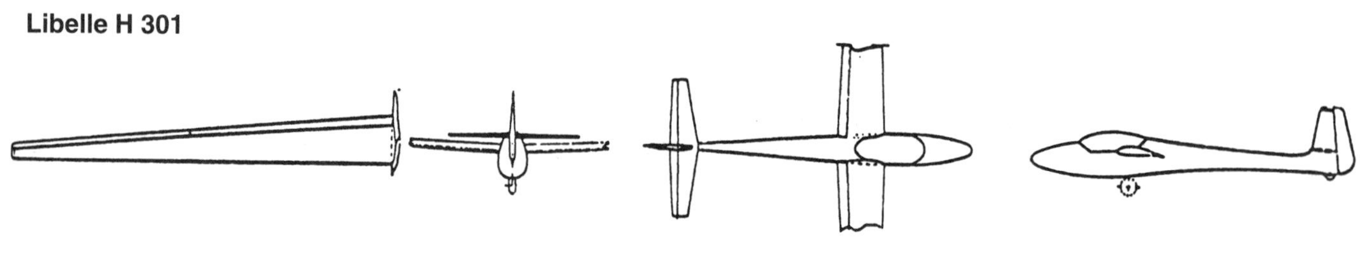

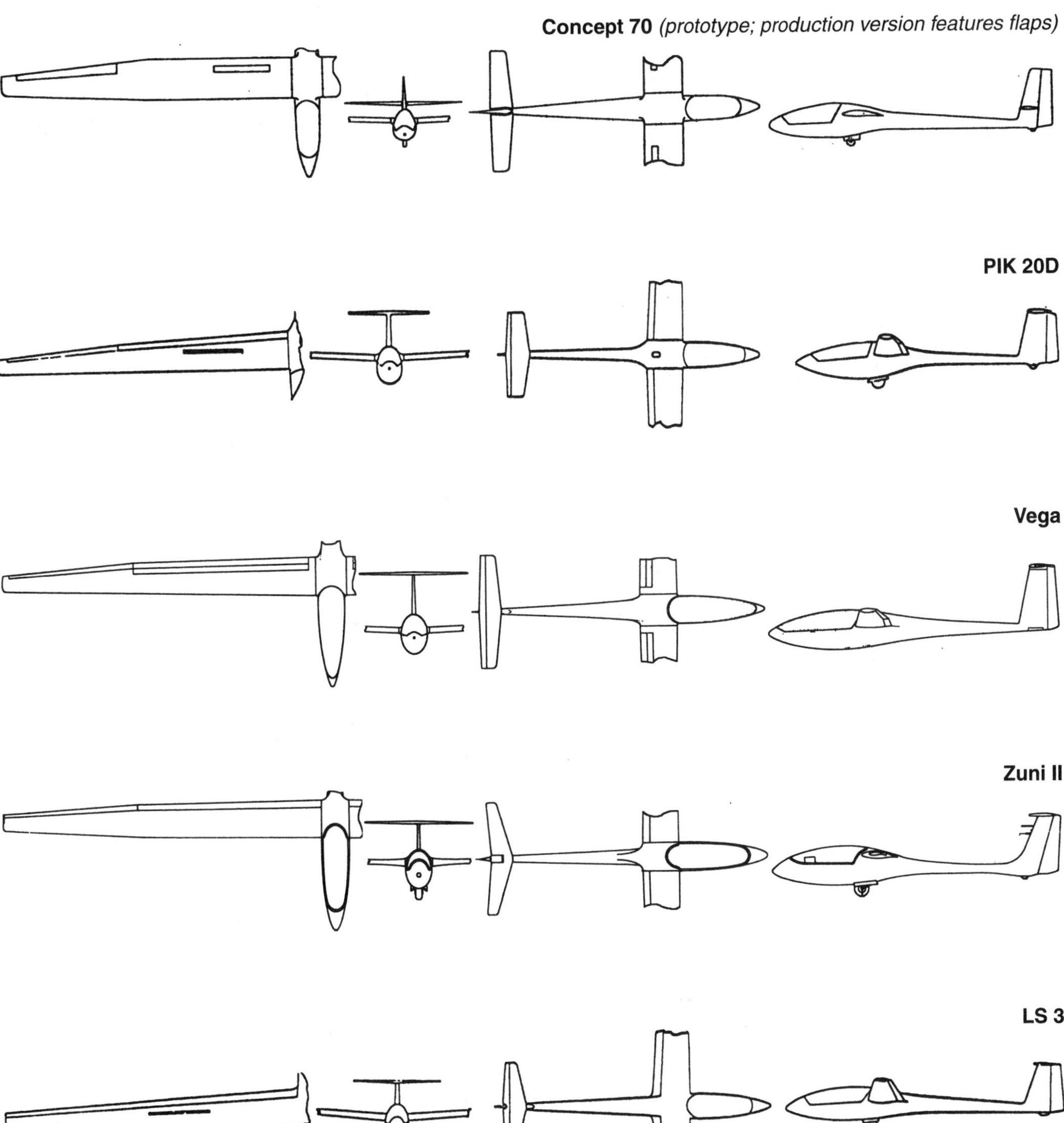
Concept 70 *(prototype; production version features flaps)*
PIK 20D
Vega
Zuni II
LS 3

Mosquito

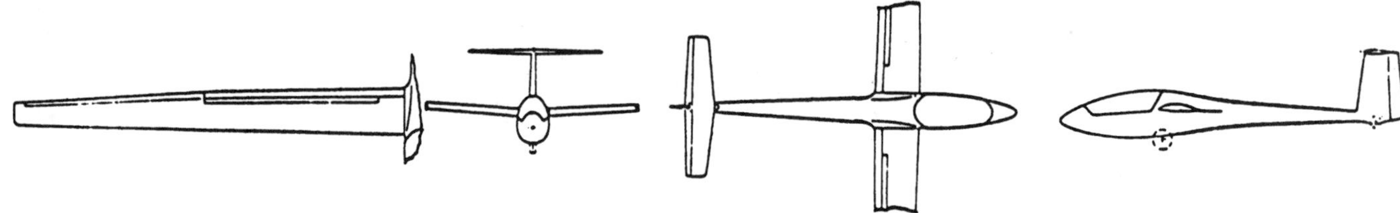

Mini-Nimbus

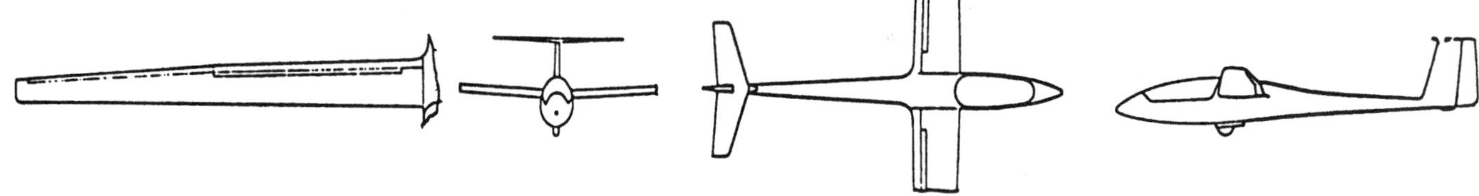

DG 200

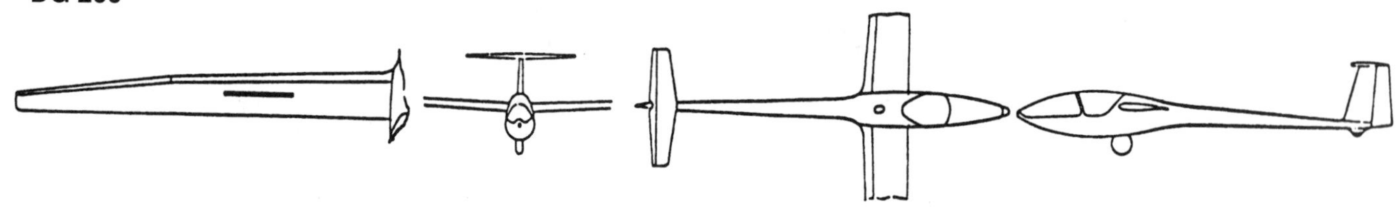

ASW 20

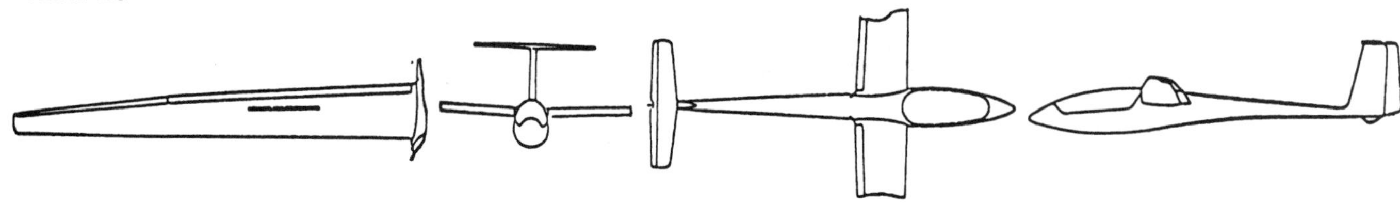

Speed Astir

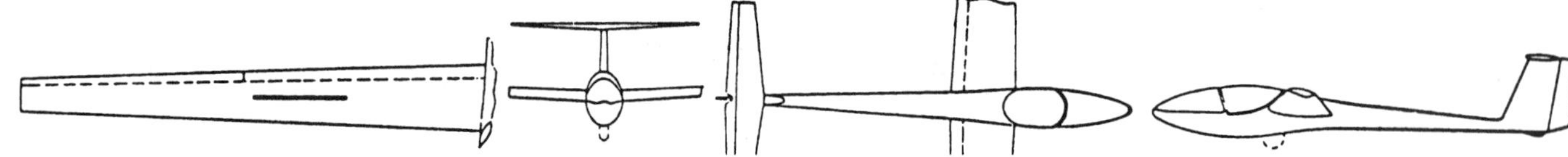

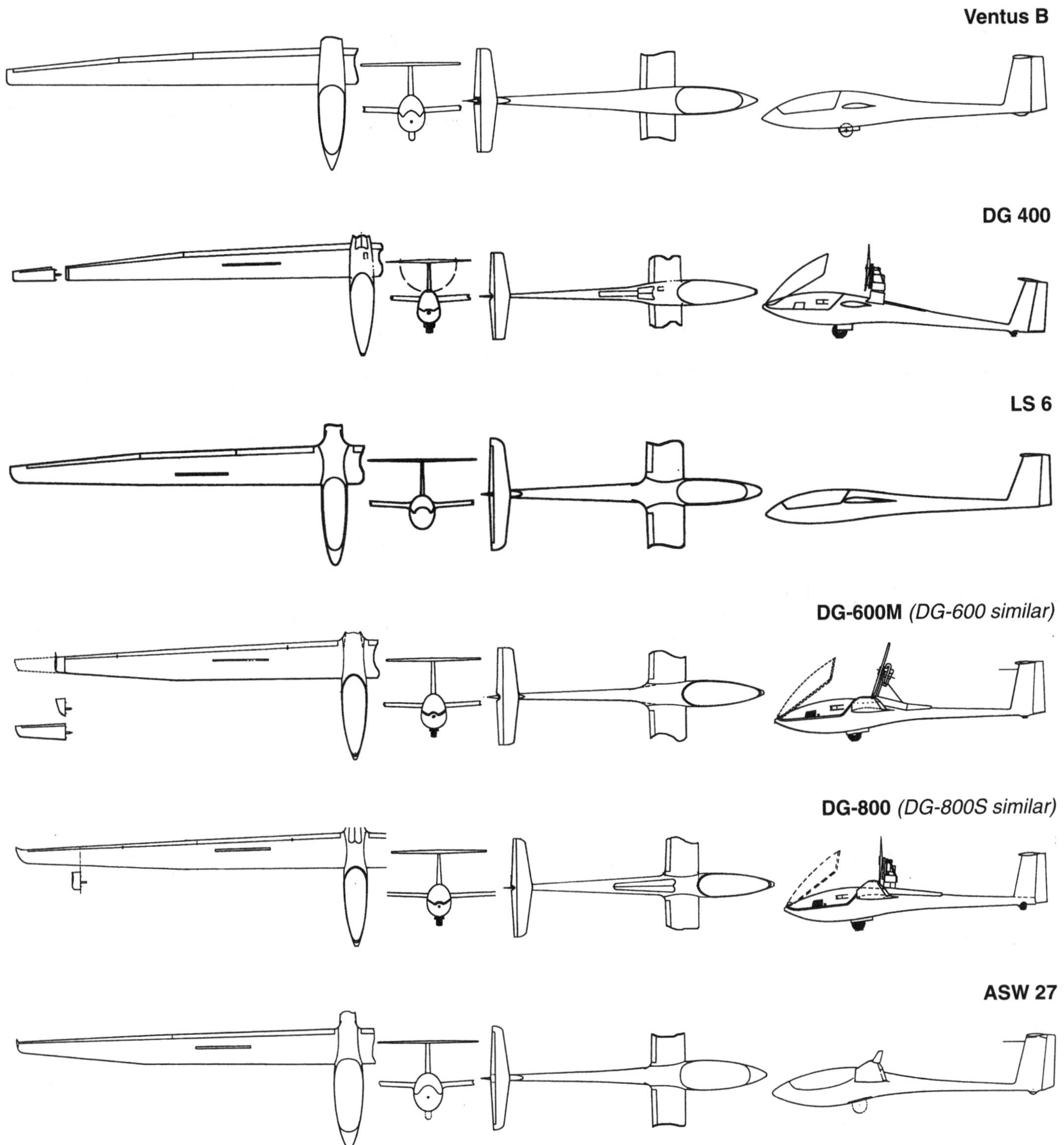
Ventus B
DG 400
LS 6
DG-600M *(DG-600 similar)*
DG-800 *(DG-800S similar)*
ASW 27

Ventus 2

SZD-56-1 Diana

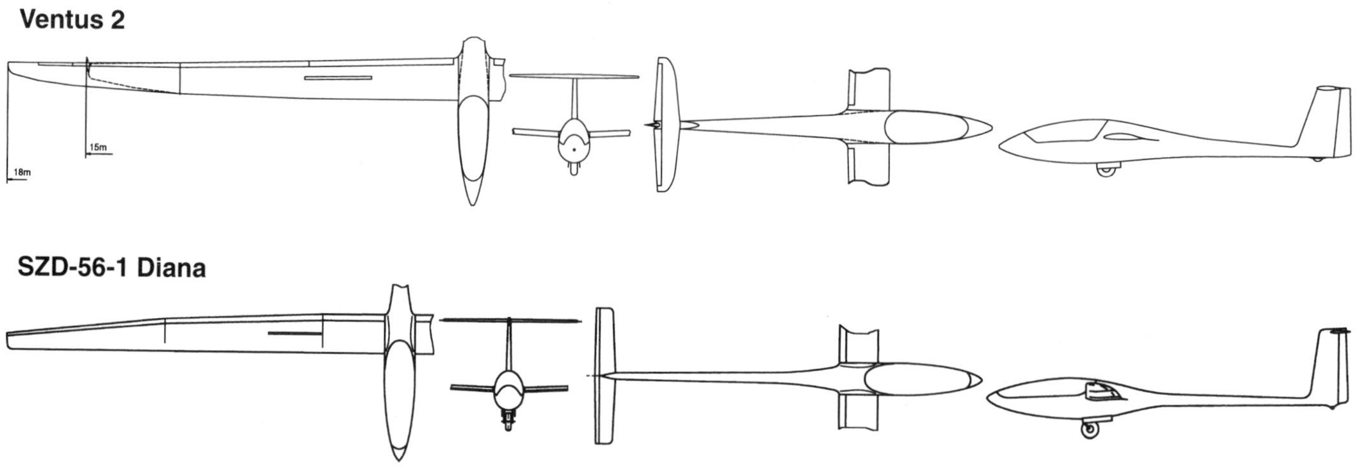

Appendix 2: Flying Qualities Flight Test Protocol

The flight test program found in the following pages has its origins in flight test work conducted by Hans Zacher. It remains in current use by Idaflieg and several sailplane manufacturers.

The form and its instructions are presented in its original German courtesy of the DLR Braunschweig. A summary in English may be found on page 253. A selection of representative results may be found beginning on page 256.

Erläuterungen zum Flugeigenschaftsprogramm

Die Programmpunkte 3 bis einschließlich 10 sind möglichst in turbulenzarmer Luft, d.h. ohne THermikeinfluß, zu erfliegen.

Vom Flugzeugbetreuer sind neben den Segelflugzeugdaten (**Rüstgewicht**, **Baujahr**, und **max. Zuladung**, der **Rüstgewichtschwerpunkt**, (z.B. leicht kopflastig, mittel- oder schwanzlastig), die Art und der Meßbereich des **Variometers**, nach dem hauptsächlich geflogen wird (z.B. Dose, Stauscheibe, Bohli, Badin oder elektrisch) und die Art der "**Total Energie Kompensation**", TEK, (z.B. Druckdose, Venturirohr, Rohr, Bohli oder VW5KB, dazu mit (+) die Über- und mit (-) die Unterkompensation) anzugeben.

Um den Einfluß der verschiedenen Pilotengewichte (Zuladung) auf die statische Stabilität besser erfassen zu können, sollte der Flugzeugführer neben den Daten wie Gesamt**segelflugzeit**, Flugzeit auf dem zu untersuchenden **Muster**, **Anzahl der geflogenen Segelflugzeugmuster**, zurückgelegte **Überland-km**, besonders genau sein **Gewicht** und das des mitgeführten Fallschirmes und Ballastes (z.B. 70 + 8 + 20 [kg]) angeben. (Es muß aber kontrolliert werden, ob der Fallschirm mit zum **Rüstgewicht** des Segelflugzeuges gezählt worden ist).

1. **Führerraum** Die Führerraumgestaltung, Anordnung und Betätigung der Bedienelemente sollte subjektiv beurteilt und wie folgt bewertet werden:

   sehr gut^{+} (entspricht nachahmenswert), sehr gut, gut, befriedigend, ausreichend und mangelhaft. Bei Bewertungen, die schlechter als befriedigend ausfallen, sollten die Gründe, die zu diesem Urteil führten, angegeben werden.

2. **Start an der Winde und im Flugzeugschlepp** Hier wird das Verhalten des Segelflugzeuges beim Start und im Schlepp beschrieben, z.B. Ausbrech-, Aufbäumneigung usw.

3. **Trimmbereich** Es werden die Gleichgewichtsgeschwindigkeiten "$V_A$min" bei 100% schwanzlastiger und "$V_A$max" bei 100% kopflastiger Trimmung erflogen. Bei kopflastiger Trimmung muß der Versuch bei Überschreiten des grünen Geschwindigkeitsbereiches abgebrochen werden. Es wird dann z.B. $V_A$max > 150 km/h aufgeschrieben. Bei Wölbklappenflugzeugen wird der Trimmbereich mit der Neutralklappenstellung erflogen.

4. **Langsamflug und Abkippverhalten** Jeder Überziehversuch ist mit weniger als 2 km/h Fahrtminderung pro Sekunde durchzuführen, dabei sind Schwingungen um die Querachse vorsichtig auszusteuern. Im Falle des **Geradeausfluges** soll das Flugzeug mit Seitensteuer und Quersteuer ohne Querneigung und Schieben geradeaus gehalten werden. Bei **10° Schieben** nach links wird das Seitensteuer nach rechts ausgetreten und beim **10° Schieben** nach rechts umgekehrt verfahren. Die Querneigung ist durch Querruderausschläge klein zu halten.

   Bei den **30°-Kurven** ist der Faden solange wie möglich in der Mitte zu halten. "$V_A$über" wird erreicht, wenn z.B. "Leitwerksschütteln" (Schtt), "Unruhe" im Steuer (USt), "Weichwerden" der Querruder (Wch) zu vernehmen ist. Fahrtgeräuscherhöhungen müssen nicht unbedingt "$V_A$über", sondern können auch "Abreißerscheinungen am Rumpfmittelteil" (AbRu) anzeigen.

   "$V_A$min" und/oder "V_ASfl" sind erreicht, wenn das Flugzeug in den "Sackflug" (Sfl) oder kurz bevor es auf den "Kopf" (Kpf) geht oder über den z.B. "linken Flügel" (liFl) abkippt. Bewegungen um die Querachse werden mit "Nicken" (Nik) und gleichzeitig um die Hochachse mit "Taumeln" (Tau) bezeichnet. Während "$V_A$min" die geringst mögliche erfliegbare Fahrtanzeige bezeichnet, die in den meisten Fällen mit der

1973 f / 2.1999

Flugzeugmuster ....; Kennz. ....; Datum ....

Rüstm. ....kg; max. Flugm. ....kg; Schwerp.-Lage ....

Baujahr .... Variom. .... TEK-Art .... BK-Art ....

Flugzeugf. .... Masse ....+.........+.........kg; Größe .... m

Segelflugzeit ....h; auf d. Muster ....h; Anzahl d. Segelflugzeugmuster ....

Überland-km .... Fluggast .... Masse ....+.........kg; Größe .... m

1) Führerraum: *(Gestaltung, Anordnung, Betätigung usw.)*

Ein-u.Ausstieg ....

Notausstieg ....

Sitz ....

Sicht ....

Lüftung ....

Handsteuer ....

Fußsteuer ....

Bremsklappenhebel ....

Wölbklappenhebel ....

Trimmhebel ....

Fahrwerkshebel ....

Ausklinkvorrichtung ....

Instrumente ....

2) Start: an der Winde ....

im Flugzeugschlepp ....

3) Trimmbereich: $V_A$min ....km/h; V_A max .... km/h

4) Langsambereich: u. Überziehverhalten *(Überziehen mit weniger als 2 km/h/s)*

	V_A über li	V_A über re	V_A min li	V_A min re	V_A Sfl li	V_A Sfl re	Warn- u. Überziehverhalten
a) WK-Neutralst. .... °							
geradeaus							
10° schiebend							
30° Kurve							
b) WK-Kreisflugst. .... °							
geradeaus							
10° schiebend							
30° Kurve							
** c) WK-Landest. .... °							
geradeaus							
10° schiebend							
30° Kurve							
gerade, BK+FW aus							

** *gilt auch für Segelflugzeuge ohne auftriebserhöhende Klappen*

Für weitere Untersuchungen bleibt das Flugzeug ausgetrimmt auf die Gleichgewichtsgeschwindigkeit

Vgl $= 1,4 \times V_A$min = ... km/h *bei der* Wölbklappenst...

5) Freier Geradeausflug, alle Steuer lose: Festgestellte Unregelmäßigkeiten..

Reibungsdifferenzgeschwindigkeiten: $-\Delta V =$ ....km/h; $+\Delta V =$ ....km/h

6) Ruderwirkungen:

a) **QR-Giermoment:** *(SSt fest; QSt-Vollausschlag, Schaltzeit ca. $\frac{1}{2}s$)*

Gierwinkel .... °; Rollzeit bis 30°-Querneigungswinkel .... s ....

b) **Schieberollmoment:** *(QSt fest; SSt-Vollausschlag, Schaltzeit ca. $\frac{1}{2}s$)*

Aufrichtzeit aus 30°Kurve..................s ....

c) 45°-Kurvenwechselzeiten

	li	⇒	re	re	⇒	li
Qst- u. SSt-Vollausschlag			s			s
ohne zu schieben			s			s

d) Slip geradeaus *(SSt-Vollausschlag; Anstellwinkel ändern bis Slipwirkung optimal)*

Schiebewinkel .... °; Querneigungswinkel .... °; SSt: 100%; QSt: .... %; HSt: .... %

Bemerkungen ....

7) Steuerabstimmung: *(30°nach li und re um die Längsachse geradeaus rollen)*

SSt: .... → .... %; QSt: .... → .... %; QSt-Kraft: .... %; HSt: .... %

8) Längstabilität: $\eta_K =$ .... °

a) statische

V_A km/h							
SH (HSt) cm							
V_A km/h							
PH (HSt) N							

b) dynamische *(SSt fest; Fahrtminderung um $-\Delta V = 15 km/h$, danach HSt loslassen)*

1. Schwingung: $V_A$min .... km/h; $V_A$max .... km/h; Schwingungsdauer .... s

6. Schwingung: $V_A$min .... km/h; $V_A$max .... km/h; ....

9) Richtungsstabilität: *(QSt+HSt fest; SSt-vollausschlag 1 s halten, dann SSt freigeben)*

Anfangsschiebe- ∢.................. °; Anfangsquerneigungs- ∢.................. °; SSt ausgeweht? ....

Schwingungszahl um d. Hochachse..................; Spiralsturzneigung?..................

10) Bremsklappenwirkung:

BK eingefahren; WS = ... m/s; BK 100%; WS= .... m/s; Ausfahrkraft..................N

Einfahrkraft...............................N; bei voll ausgefahrenen BK, $\Delta V =$ .... km/h

11) Fahrwerk:

Einfahrkraft..................N; Ausfahrkraft..................N; Federung?..................

12) Landung:

Spornlandung?..................; Radbremswirkung?..................; Federung?..................

13) Thermikflugeigenschaften: $\eta_K =$..................

Thermikart?...; Querneigungswinkel - ∢.................. °

Fahrtanzeigen $V_A \pm \Delta V$: .... ± .... km/h; Hst .... %; SSt .... ±%......; QSt .... ± .... %

Handhabung der Trimmung bis 45°-Kurven:...; HSt-Kraft.........N

45°-Kurven $V_A$min..................km/h; 30°-Kurven $V_A$min..................km/h

....

zu 4: Bei Wölbklappenflugzeugen soll vor dem Flug geprüft werden, ob die allgemein gebräuchliche Landeklappenstellung ähnlich der Kreisflugstellung ist (siehe Flughandbuch). Wenn dies der Fall ist, wird Teil b) ausgelassen und Teil c) mit der Kreisflugklappenstellung erflogen. Am Blattrand ist dann Teil b) und c) mit einem Pfeil in Richtung c) zu verbinden.

Bezeichnungen und Symbole:

Abk	Abkippen
AbRu	Abreißerscheinungen am Rumpf
Absti	Abstimmung
BK	Bremsklappen
BR	Radbremse
Fed	Fahrwerksfederung
FStart	Flugzeugschleppstart
FW	Fahrwerk
HR, HSt	Höhenruder, -steuer
iFl	Abkippen über die innere Fläche
Kpf	auf den Kopf gehen
li	links
liFl	Abkippen über die linke Fläche
nFl	Abkippen über die nachgeführte Fläche
Nik	Nickbewegung
QR, QSt	Querruder, -steuer
re	rechts
reFl	Abkippen über die rechte Fläche
Schtt	Leitwerksschütteln
Sfl	Sackflug
SR, SSt	Seitenruder, -steuer
Tau	Taumeln
Tru	Trudeln
USt	Unruhe im Steuer
$V_A$über	angezeigte Überziehgeschwindigkeit
$V_A$max	angezeigte maximale Geschwindigkeit
$V_A$min	angezeigte minimale Geschwindigkeit
V_A	angezeigte Geschwindigkeit
Vgl	Gleichgewichtsgeschwindigkeit
Wch	Weichwerden in der Querrudersteuerung
β	Schiebewinkel
ΔV	Differenzgeschwindigkeit
ϕ	Querneigungswinkel
$\ldots \rightarrow \ldots$	übergang von $V_A$über zu $V_A$min
$\ldots \overset{\rightarrow}{} \ldots$	eindeutige zeitliche Folge

Das Beispiel Schtt, Wch→Sfl, $\overset{\rightarrow}{}$Tau, liFL besagt: "$V_A$über" wird angezeigt durch "Leitwerksschütteln" und gleichzeitigem "Weichwerden in der Quersteuerung". "$V_A$min", "V_ASfl" wird im "Sackflug" erreicht, der aber schwer auszusteuern ist. Das Flugzeug gerät dabei ins "Taumeln" und kippt anschließend über den "linken Flügel" ab.

Vorzeichen für Änderung der Höhen-, Seiten- und Quersteuerwege gegenüber dem Geradeausflug bei "Vgl" sind wie folgt einzusetzten": Höhensteuerwege in Richtung "Ziehen", Quer- und Seitensteuerwege in Kurvenrichtung mit (+) und entgegen mit (-).

Bemerkung:..

....

....

....

....

....

....

....

....

....

....

....

$V_A$min mit Kreisflugklappenstellung .... geradeaus= .... km/h

QR-Giermoment mit Kreisflugklappenstellung: ....

	V_A [km/h]	Gierwinkel [°]	Rollzeit bis 30°Querneigungswinkel [s]
$1,4 \times V_A min$			
$1,3$ " "			
$1,2$ " "			

45°-Kurvenwechhselzeiten mit Kreisflugklappenstellung: ....

	V_A [km/h]	QSt- u. SSt-vollausschlag li re	 re li	ohne Schieben li re	 re li	
$1,4 \times V_A min$						[s]
$1,3$ " "						[s]
$1,2$ " "						[s]

Steuerabstimmung mit Kreisflugklappenstellung: ....

	V_A [km/h]	SSt %	QSt %	QSt-Kraft [N]
$1,4 \times V_A min$				
$1,3$ " "				
$1,2$ " "				

Sackfluggeschwindigkeit "V_ASfl" übereinstimmt, kann bei Flugzeugen mit ausgeprägt gutmütigem Überziehverhalten durch weitere Erhöhung des Anstellwinkels der maximale Auftriebsbeiwert soweit überschritten werden, daß der jetzt wieder kleiner werdende Auftriebsbeiwert durch die Staudruck-(Fahrt-)erhöhung kompensiert wird. "V_ASfl" ergibt dann bei gleichbleibendem Fehler in der Stau-Statikmeßanlage einen größeren Wert als "$V_A$min". Eine ähnliche Fahrtanzeige kann auch auftreten, wenn bei konstantem Auftriebsbeiwert die statischen Druckabnahmestellen mit weiter wachsendem Anstellwinkel kleinere Werte liefern als den des tatsächlichen oder bei höheren Geschwindigkeiten gemessenen statischen Druckes. Die oben in Klammern stehenden Abkürzungen sollen in der Reihenfolge der festgestellten Überzieheigenschaften eingetragen werden. Der Übergang von "$V_A$über" zu "$V_A$min" ist mit einem Pfeil anzuzeigen. Das Beispiel **Schtt, Wch→$\overrightarrow{\textbf{Sfl Tau}}$, liFl** besagt: "$V_A$über" wird angezeigt durch "Leitwerksschütteln" und gleichzeitigem "Weichwerden" der Quersteuerung. "$V_A$min" wird im "Sackflug" erreicht, der aber schwer auszusteuern ist. Das Flugzeug gerät dabei ins "Taumeln" und kippt anschließend über den "linken Flügel" ab. Der Pfeil über Sfl und Tau soll die eindeutig festgestellte zeitliche Folge anzeigen.

Bei Wölbklappenflugzeugen ist vor dem Flug zu prüfen, ob die allgemein gebräuchliche Landeklappenstellung ähnlich der Kreisflugstellung ist (siehe Flughandbuch). Wenn dies der Fall ist, wird (b) ausgelassen und (c) mit der Kreisflugklappenstellung erflogen. Am Blattrand ist dann (b) und (c) mit einem Pfeil in Richtung (c) zu verbinden.

Für die weiteren Untersuchungen von Programmpunkt 5 bis 10 wird das Segelflugzeug, beim Wölbklappenflugzeug vorzugsweise mit der Wölbklappe in Kreisflugstellung, auf die Gleichgewichtsgeschwindigkeit Vgl = 1,4 × $V_A$min ausgetrimmt. Gleichgewichtsgeschwindigkeit und Wölbklappenstellung sind unbedingt aufzuschreiben (bei zu großer Differenz zwischen wahrer und angezeigter Fahrt im Überziehbereich kann auch die Gleichgewichtsgeschwindigkeit vorgegeben werden).

5. **Freier Geradeausflug, alle Steuer los** Nachdem das Flugzeug bei der Gleichgewichtsgeschwindigkeit Vgl im Geradeausflug ausgerichtet ist (Faden in der Mitte), werden Knüppel und Seitensteuer losgelassen. **Auftretende Unregelmäßigkeiten** wie Drehen um Längs- und/oder Hochachse usw. werden notiert.

   Um die Wirksamkeit der Trimmung erfassen zu können, werden die **Reibungsdifferenzgeschwindigkeiten** +ΔV **und** −ΔV gemessen, die den Geschwindigkeitsbereich angeben, in dem bei losgelassenem Knüppel keine Fahrtänderung in Richtung der vorher eingetrimmten Geschwindigkeit, hier "Vgl", erfolgt. −ΔV erhält man, wenn die Gleichgewichtsgeschwindigkeit Vgl um ca. 15 km/h verringert und der Knüppelkraft in Richtung Drücken feinfühlig, am besten mit dem Zeigefinger, und so langsam nachgegeben wird, daß keine Fahrtschwankungen auftreten und der Geschwindigkeitszuwachs nicht mehr als 2 km/h/sec beträgt. Bei einer Geschwindigkeit, die kleiner oder gleich (niemals größer, sonst war "Vgl" nicht richtig eingetrimmt) der eingetrimmten Gleichgewichtsgeschwindigkeit Vgl ist, bleibt der Knüppel stehen. "Vgl" minus der erflogenen Geschwindigkeit ergibt −ΔV. Die Reibungsdifferenzgeschwindigkeit +ΔV wird ähnlich erhalten, wobei man von einer Geschwindigkeit ausgehen sollte, die um 30 km/h über "Vgl" liegt.

6. **Ruderwirkung**

(a) Bei jedem Querruderausschlag entsteht ein mehr oder weniger großes **Giermoment**, das der erwünschten Richtungsänderung und Drehung um die Hochachse entgegenwirkt. Wird z.B. bei "Vgl" und festgehaltenem Seitensteuer zügig (Schaltzeit ≈ 1/2 sec) Querrudervollausschlag nach links gegeben, dreht das Segelflugzeug zunächst um die Hochachse nach rechts, ohne die Flugbahn wesentlich zu ändern. Zwischen Flugbahn und Flugzeuglängsachse liegt der **Gierwinkel**, der mit Hilfe des Phipsithetas geschätzt wird und somit etwas über die relative Größe des Querrudergiermomentes aussagt. Die Zeit von Beginn des Vesuchs bis **30°-Querneigung**, das Querruder bleibt dabei voll ausgeschlagen, wird gestoppt und eingetragen.

(b) Das **Schieberollmoment** wird hier nur durch Zeitmessung erfaßt. Das Quersteuer wird bei "Vgl" in der 30°-Kurve festgehalten und dann zügig Seitenrudervollausschlag entgegen der Kurvenrichtung gegeben und festgehalten, bis sich das Flugzeug über die Horizontallage hinaus um die Längsachse gedreht hat. Die **Aufrichtzeit aus der 30°-Kurve** (von 30° Querneigung bis zur Horizontallage) wird gestoppt und eingetragen. Die Geschwindigkeit ist dabei konstant zu halten. Unregelmäßigkeiten wie z.B. Aufbäumneigung sollen notiert werden.

(c) Die **45°-Kurvenwechselzeiten** werden zunächst mit Quer- und Seitenrudervollausschlag und dann "ohne Schieben" (Faden in der Mitte) erflogen, und zwar je 3 Versuche von links nach rechts und umgekehrt. Auf der Rückseite des Programms ist unter "Bemerkung" genügend Platz, um die Steuerfolge beim 45°-Kurvenwechsel ohne Schieben eintragen zu können, z.B. QSt 100%, SSt 100% → 50%. Dieses Beispiel besagt, daß das Quersteuer dauernd 100%, das Seitensteuer am Anfang 100% und dann 50% ausgeschlagen war.

(d) Nachdem der **Slip** in größer Höhe geübt worden ist, werden die Slipeigenschaften in geringer Höhe gegen oder mit dem Wind und **geradeaus** auf einen markanten Punkt zu erflogen (möglichst im Gegenanflug), dabei entspricht die Anfangsgeschwindigkeit der "Vgl". Dieses Verfahren ist vom Piloten mit geringer Flugerfahrung oder/und bei mehreren Flugzeugen in der Platzrunde besonders vorsichtig durchzuführen. Im Slip wird dann der Anstellwinkel soweit geändert, bis die Slipwirkung optimal erscheint. Der **Schiebewinkel** wird gegenüber dem markanten Punkt am Boden und die **Querneigung** mit Hilfe des Phipsithetas geschätzt. Um genügend Zeit und Höhe für diesen Versuch zur Verfügung zu haben, sollte der Endanflug oder Queranflug (Seitenwind) bei mindestens 200m Höhe begonnen werden. **Quer- und Höhensteuerknüppelwege** sind zu schätzen und einzutragen, und zwar wird der Knüppelweg bei "Drücken" mit (-) und bei "Ziehen" mit (+) gekennzeichnet.

7. **Steuerabstimmung** Das saubere **30°-Rollen** auf einer Linie bei möglichst maximalen Quer- und/oder Seitensteuerausschlägen erlangt man am besten durch langsames Einschwingen der Querneigung von 10 auf 30 Grad. **Quersteuer** und/oder **Seitensteuer** müssen Vollausschlag aufweisen. Die Quer- und Seitensteuerwege werden in % aufgeschrieben. Die **Quersteuerknüppelkraft** wird mit dem Kraftmesser gemessen oder durch Beurteilungen angegeben wie: angenehm, zu groß, gering usw.

8. **Längsstabilität** Bei Wölbklappenflugzeugen sollte die Neutralstellung der Wölbklappe benutzt werden.

(a) Die **statische Längsstabilität** ist durch den Verlauf der Höhensteuerkräfte und -wege über der Fluggeschwindigkeit gekennzeichnet. Kraft- und Wegmessung sollten sich möglichst auf die Mitte des Knüppelhandgriffes beziehen und bei Knüppelwegmessern mit Federaufzug getrennt erfolgen. Im unteren Geschwindigkeitsbereich von "$V_A$min" bis 100 km/h sollte eine Schrittweite von 10 km/h und darüber von 20 km/h bis etwa 160 km/h gewählt werden.

(b) Die Messung der **dynamischen Längsstabilität** kann nur bei ruhiger Luft durchgeführt werden. Nachdem die Gleichgewichtsgeschwindigkeit Vgl um 15 km/h verringert wurde und der neue Flugzustand stationär geworden ist, wird der Steuerknüppel losgelassen. Zur Feststellung der Schwingungsdämpfung werden die **min** und **max V_A-Werte** der ersten und sechsten Schwingung vom Geschwindigkeitsmesser abgelesen und notiert. Die **Schwingungsdauer T** wird am besten von einer "$V_A$min" bis zur nächsten "$V_A$min" gemessen. Bei Pendelhöhenleitwerken muß die Hand in der Nähe des Knüppels verbleiben, da in der Phase auf "$V_A$min" zu ein Umklappen des Höhenleitwerks in Richtung Ziehen und damit ein starkes Aufbäumen erfolgen kann. Nötige Fluglagekorrekturen um die Hochachse sollten vorsichtig mit dem Seitensteuer und um die Längsachse durch leichte und kurze Finger- oder Handkantenschläge gegen den Knüppel in Richtung der gewünschten

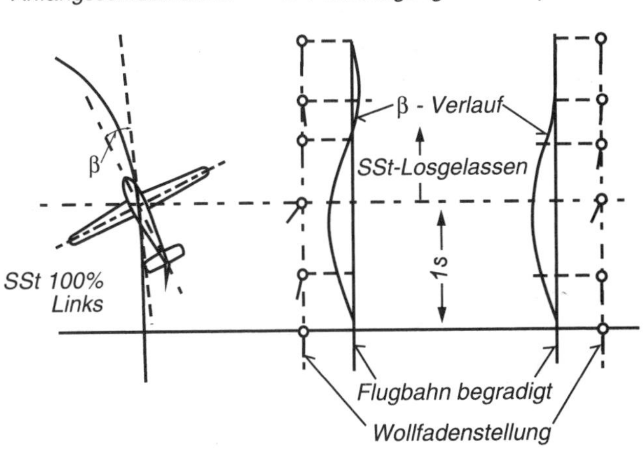

Verbesserung durchgeführt werden. Ein länger andauerndes Führen des Steuerknüppels würde die Messung der dynamischen Längsstabilität verfälschen. Falls bei losgelassenem Höhensteuer Instabilität festgestellt wird, oder der Knüppel aufgrund starker Reibung "stehen" bleibt, ist dieser Versuch mit festem Knüppel durchzuführen.

Dabei wird ähnlich wie bei losgelassenem Steuerknüppel verfahren mit dem einen Unterschied, daß der Steuerknüppel nicht losgelassen, sondern in die der Gleichgewichtsgeschwindigkeit Vgl entsprechenden Stellung zurückgeführt wird (Handwegmesser verwenden).

Die bei der Untersuchung der dynamischen Längsstabilität auftretenden Unregelmäßigkeiten müssen im Protokoll vermerkt werden.

9. **Richtungsstabilität** Der Knüppel wird bei "Vgl" festgehalten und mit dem Seitensteuer eine Sekunde lang Vollausschlag gegeben. Während des z.B. linken Seitensteuervollausschlages dreht das Flugzeug um die Hochachse nach links. Die vorher geradlinige Flugbahn geht nur langsam in einen Kreisbogen nach links über, so daß ein **Anfangsschiebewinkel** zwischen Flugbahn und Flugzeuglängsachse entsteht und nach einer Sekunde aufgrund des Schieberollmomentes die max. **Anfangsquerneigung** erreicht wird (siehe Figur). Nach Loslassen des Seitensteuers schwingt das Flugzeug um die Hochachse zur Flugbahn zurück und bei geringerer Dämpfung sogar über diese hinaus, um sich dann auf die Kreisflugbahn einzupendeln. Wieviele Schwingungen das Flugzeug um die Hochachse durchführt, ist sehr gut am "Faden" festzustellen, der jeglichen Schiebezustand anzeigt.

Die Schwingungszahl um die Hochachse gibt den Grad der Dämpfung an. Die Stärke der **Spiralsturzneigung** kann z.B. mit schwach, stark oder mit der Anzahl der Kreisumdrehungen, die bis 30° Schräglage benötigt wurden, beschrieben werden. Richtungsinstabilität erkennt man am größer werdenen oder gleichbleibenden Schiebewinkel und an dem in Spiralsturzrichtung **ausgewehten Seitensteuer**. Ausgewehtes oder aufgrund großer Reibung feststehendes Seitenruder sollten aber unterschieden werden (Seitensteuerreibung am Boden testen).

10. **Bremsklappenwirkung** Es wird bei "Vgl" und bei Wölbklappenflugzeugen mit Wölbklappe in Neutralstellung geflogen. Der Steuerknüppel wird festgehalten und die Bremsklappe so langsam ausgefahren, daß keine Fahrtschwingungen auftreten können. Je nach Bremsklappenart wird sich bei gleichbleibender Knüppelstellung eine von "Vgl" verschiedene Fluggeschwindigkeit einstellen. Der **Geschwindigkeitsunterschied** ΔV bezogen auf die Gleichgewichtsgeschwindigkeit Vgl wird eingetragen. Nachdem die Gleichgewichtsgeschwindigkeit Vgl bei ausgefahrenen Bremsklappen wieder hergestellt worden ist, wird die Sinkgeschwindigkeit am Variometer abgelesen. Die Sinkgeschwindigkeit bei eingefahrenen Bremsklappen ist schon vorher notiert wordern.

11. **Fahrwerk Ein- und Ausfahrkraft** werden gemessen oder geschätzt, wobei bei einer Schätzung die angewendete Kraft nicht in N, sondern z.B. durch Wertungen wie schwer, leicht usw. angegeben werden sollte. Die Frage nach der **Federung** bezieht sich nur auf das Hauptfahrwerk.

12. **Landung** Hier soll berichtet werden, ob **Spornlandungen** möglich sind, wie die **Radbremse** wirkt und wie der Gesamteindruck der **Federung** ist. Unregelmäßigkeiten wie überlange Gleit- oder Ausrollstrecken oder frühzeitiges Ablegen einer Fläche sind unter "Bemerkungen" zu notieren.

13. **Thermikflug** Die Thermikart wird beschrieben erstens durch Aussagen über den Durchmesser, zweitens über empfundene Turbulenzen oder über Unregelmäßigkeiten in den aufsteigenden Luftmassen. für dei Beschreibung des Thermikquerschnittes sollten die Ausdrücke eng, mittel, weit, unrund und für den Turbulenzgrad bockig, turbulent, unruhig, and ruhig ausreichen. Die **Querneigung** wird mit dem Phipsitheta gemessen. Die mittlere Thermikfluggeschwindigkeit und die Größe der Abweichungen werden notiert.

    Die prozentuale Änderung der Höhen-, Seiten- und Quersteuerwege gegenüber dem Geradeausflug bei "Vgl" und gegebenenfalls die Schwankungen um diese Werte mit $\pm$(%) werden niedergeschrieben. Dabei sind die Höhensteuerwege in Richtung "Ziehen", die Quer- und Seitensteuerwege in Kurvenrichtung mit (+) und entgegen mit (-) zu versehen. Die Handhabung der Trimmung bis zu 45°-Kurven wird beurteilt und die unter Umständen nicht mehr wegtrimmbare **Höhensteuerkraft** gemessen oder geschätzt. Zuletzt werden die $V_A$min **in der 30°- und 45°-Kurve** erflogen. $V_A$min der 30°-Kurve wird in den meisten Fällen von der unter Punkt 4 erflogenen abweichen. Die auffälligsten Eigenarten während des Überziehvorganges sollten ähnlich wie unter Punkt 4 aufgezeichnet werden. Dazu gehören insbesondere ausgeprägt gutmütige Sackflugeigenschaften mit gegenüber $V_A$min erhöhter Sackfluggeschwindigkeit V_ASfl

    Reicht der Platz für die Beschreibung der Flugeigenschaften, Gestaltung des Führerraumes, Anordnung und Betätigung der Bedienelemente nicht aus oder sind Beurteilungen besonders schlecht oder gut ausgefallen, dann sollten weiter ausführende Erläuterungen möglichst unter Benutzung von Symbolen und Abkürkzungen auf der Rückseite des Programmes niedergeschrieben werden.

Bezeichnungen und Symbole:

Abk	Abkippen *dropping a wing*
AbRu	Abreißerscheinungen am Rumpf *fuselage buffeting*
Absti	Abstimmung *(control) harmony*
BK	Bremsklappen *dive brakes*
BR	Radbremse *wheel brake*
Fed	Fahrwerksfederung *landing gear suspension*
FStart	Flugzeugschleppstart *aero tow*
FW	Fahrwerk *landing gear*
HR, HSt	Höhenruder, -steuer *elevator; elevator control*
iFl	Abkippen über die innere Fläche *falling off on the inside wing*
Kpf	auf den Kopf gehen *pitching over*
li	links *left*
liFl	Abkippen über die linke Fläche *falling off the left wing*
nFl	Abkippen über die nachgeführte Fläche *falling off the aft wing (in slip)*
Nik	Nickbewegung *pitch motion*
QR, QSt	Querruder, -steuer *aileron, aileron control*
re	rechts *right*

reFl — Abkippen über die rechte Fläche
falling off the right wing

Schtt — Leitwerksschütteln
empennage shaking

Sfl — Sackflug
"mushing" post-stall flight

SR, SSt — Seitenruder, -steuer
rudder; rudder control

Tau — Taumeln
wing rocking; pitching

Tru — Trudeln
spinning

USt — Unruhe im Steuer
buffeting in controls

$V_A$über — angezeigte Überziehgeschwindigkeit
indicated airspeed at onset of stall

$V_A$max — angezeigte maximale Geschwindigkeit
maximum indicated airspeed during a maneuver

$V_A$min — angezeigte minimale Geschwindigkeit
minimum controllable airspeed; minimum indicated airspeed during a maneuver

V_A — angezeigte Geschwindigkeit
indicated airspeed

Vgl — Gleichgewichtsgeschwindigkeit
nominal airspeed for handling qualities tests, $1.4 \times V_A$min

Wch — Weichwerden in der Querrudersteuerung
"softness" in aileron

β — Schiebewinkel
slip angle

ΔV — Differenzgeschwindigkeit
airspeed offset

φ — Querneigung
bank angle

$.. \rightarrow ..$ — übergang von Vaüber zu $V_A$min
indicates transition from $V_A$über *to* $V_A$min

$.. \overrightarrow{\;} ..$ — eindeutige zeitliche Folge
indicates sequence of events

Summary of Flight Test Procedure

General Items 3 through 10 are to be flown in the smoothest possible conditions. The following data are noted:

Aircraft type, Registration number, Date

Empty weight (equipped), Maximum gross weight CG location

Year of manufacture, Variometer type (vane/electric/etc.), Type of total energy compensation (Diaphragm/Venturi/TE Probe/etc.), Means of glide path control (dive brakes/flaps/chute/etc.)

Pilot, Pilot weight, self + chute + ballast (chute omitted if accounted for empty weight), Pilot height,

Hours in sailplanes, Hours in type, Number of sailplane types flown

Cross-country miles, Passenger, Passenger weight, self + chute, Passenger height

1. **Cockpit** Cockpit layout and operation of controls are rated subjectively as follows: very good+ (exemplary), very good, good, satisfactory, adequate, and deficient. In the latter two cases, the reasons for the rating are noted.

   The following items are considered: Ingress/egress, Emergency egress, Seat, Visibility, Stick, Pedals, Dive brake control, Flap control, Trim, Landing gear, Release, Instrument panel

2. **Takeoff** Takeoff and tow characteristics are noted for winch launch and/or aero tow.

3. **Range of Trimmable Airspeeds** the minimum trim speed (full nose-up trim) and maximum trim speed (full nose-down trim) are determined. During the latter test the sailplane is not to exceed V_{RA} (rough air speed, limit of green arc); rather, the airspeed is entered as (for example) "$V_A$max> 150 km/h". Flapped sailplanes are tested with the flaps neutral.

4. **Slow Flight and stall** Stalls are entered with airspeed reduced no faster than 2 km/h/sec and gentle control inputs to prevent pitch oscillations. For stalls from straight flight, the yaw string should be kept centered and the wings kept as level as possible using the ailerons. "Left" yaw implies right pedal, and vice versa.

   The 30°turns should be flown in a coordinated manner. "$V_A$über" (speed for stall onset) is reached when early stall manifestations are observed, for example shaking of the tail surfaces, control "softness", and/or unsteady control forces. Increased noise may be due to separated flow over the fuselage midsection, and is thus not necessarily an indication of stall onset.

   In this section, "$V_A$min" (minimum airspeed) and/or "V_ASfl" (airspeed in "mushing" flight, or "Sackflug") are airspeeds observed shortly before the nose or a wing drops. Any pitching and yawing motions are noted. $V_A$min, the minimum airspeed observed during the maneuver, usually coincides with V_ASfl. However, in some aircraft with especially good stall characteristics, longitudinal control can be maintained into the stall, with the airspeed increasing slightly to compensate for the reduced lift coefficient due to separation. In this case, V_ASfl will be higher than $V_A$min. An indication of Vasfl > $V_A$min can also result from static system errors. The phemenona (buffeting, etc.) observed during transition from stall onset speed to minimum airspeed are noted in the sequence they appear using the abbreviations listed below.

The following data are recorded: IAS at first stall indication; Minimum IAS observed during maneuver; IAS observed during post-stall controlled flight; warnings and stall characteristics. Each stall series includes straight stalls, both from coordinated flight and from slipping flight with 10°yaw, as well as turn stalls in each direction with 30°bank. For flapped sailplanes, the series is repeated with the flaps neutral, in a climb setting, and the landing setting. If the landing and thermaling settings are similar or identical, series (b) is omitted and series (c) is flown with the thermaling setting.

5. Level flight, controls free For the remaining test points, (items 5–10), the sailplane is trimmed to an equilibrium speed Vgl = 1.4$V_A$min using the value of $V_A$min determined in item 5 above. The actual airspeed and flap setting (preferably, a thermaling setting) is noted.

Starting in trimmed level flight at Vgl and the yaw string centered, the controls are released and any unusual behavior is noted.

The trim hysteresis values $+\Delta V$ and $-\Delta V$ are established by (for example, for $-\Delta V$) reducing the airspeed to approximately 15 km/h below Vgl, then very gently releasing the back pressure, preferably with the index finger, allowing the stick to return to its trim position. Due to control system friction, the stick may not return fully to its original position. $-\Delta V$ is the difference between the new trim speed and the original equilibrium airspeed (by definition, positive). $+\Delta V$ is measured in the same manner, albeit with a 30 km/h increase in airspeed.

6. Control effectiveness

(a) Aileron deflection produces an adverse yaw, which tends to counteract the desired turn direction. If, for example at Vgl, the pedals are held fixed and the aileron deflected rapidly (about 1/2 sec to the stop) to the left, the sailplane yaws initially to the right, without the path of flight being significantly affected.

The slip angle, the angle between the path of flight and the longitudinal axis, may be determined using the "phi-psi-theta", thus providing a measure of the magnitude of the adverse yaw. Full aileron is held until the bank angle reaches 30°. The time required to reach this bank angle is measured with a stopwatch and recorded on the form.

(b) Roll/yaw coupling is evaluated from a 30°turn. With the aileron held fixed, full opposite rudder is applied and held until the aircraft rolls through a wings-level attitude. The time required to level the wings is measured and recorded. The airspeed should be held constant during this maneuver. Unusual characteristics, for example a strong tendency to pitch nose-up, are noted on the form.

(c) 45°-45°turn reversals are performed first with full control deflection (aileron and rudder) and then repeated in a coordinated manner (yaw string centered). Each series includes three reversals each to the right and to the left. The back of the flight test form provides space to describe the control inputs required for the coordinated reversals, for example, "QSt 100%, SSt 100% → 50%". This example indicates that the aileron was fully deflected throughout the maneuver, while the rudder deflection varied from an initial 100% to 50% at the end of the maneuver.

(d) Slips are evaluated at low altitude, in straight flight with or against the wind (against is preferable) towards a prominent landmark. Entry speed is "Vgl". This procedure should be approached with caution, especially if the pilot is inexperienced or if there is other traffic in the landing pattern. Having established the slip, the angle of attack is varied to produce the optimum effect. The slip angle is estimated relative to the landmark using the "phi-psi-theta" template. The bank angle is determined in a similar manner. In order to allow sufficient time for this test, the turn to the crosswind leg or final approach must be made no lower than around 200m altitude. The aileron and pedal positions are estimated and recorded, whereby the sign convention is (-) for forward and (+) for aft stick.

7. Control Harmony Control harmony is evaluated by performing "Dutch rolls", *i.e.* roll reversals of about ±30° with constant heading. To perform this maneuver cleanly, start at level flight and introduce the rolling motion gradually until either the aileron or rudder begins to reaches its stop. The aileron and pedal positions are recorded in terms of %. The lateral stick force is measured using the handheld scale or via subjective evaluations such as pleasant, light, excessive, etc.

8. Longitudinal Stability Aircraft with camber-changing flaps should be evaluated with the flaps in a neutral setting.

(a) Static longitudinal stability is characterized by the stick force and stick position trends with airspeed. Control forces and positions should be referenced to the middle of the hand grip. If the stick force is measured with a spring scale, it should be measured separately from the stick position. In the low airspeed range from "$V_A$min" to 100 km/h, data should be obtained at increments of 10 km/h, and thereafter at increments of 20 km/h until around 160 km/h.

(b) The dynamic longitudinal stability evaluation must be performed in still air. Starting from steady, trimmed level flight at Vgl, the airspeed is decreased around 15 km/h and aircraft allowed to stabilize. The stick is released and the resulting pitch oscillations observed. Damping of the phugoid motion is determined from the amplitude, *i.e.* $V_A$min and $V_A$max, of the first and sixth cycles. The period of oscillation T is best measured from one "$V_A$min" to the next. In the case of all-flying stabilizers, the hand should be kept near the stick as there is the possibility of the stabilizer running hard over without warning to its "aft-stick" stop. The heading should be held constant with the rudder, and the wings held level with aileron inputs. Applying only gentle, "pulsed" inputs with a single finger or the edge of the hand helps reduce the effect of the control inputs on the damping results.

If an instability is observed, or if the stick "hangs up" at some point due to control system friction, the test should be repeated with stick fixed. The stick-fixed procedure is similar to the one described above, except that the stick is held in its initial position, corresponding to level flight at Vgl.

Any unusual behavior observed during the dynamic longitudinal stability test should be noted in the flight test form.

9. **Directional Stability** From trimmed level flight at Vgl, the stick is held fixed and full rudder applied for one second. For example, if left rudder is applied, the aircraft will yaw nose-left. The aircraft slowly begins to turn to the left, giving rise to an initial slip angle between the path of flight and the aircraft's longitudinal axis (see figure). In turn, the slip induces an initial bank angle due to the dihedral effect. Upon releasing the rudder, the nose swings back in the direction of the path of flight and, if the damping is light enough, beyond the original heading, leading to oscillations about the yaw and roll axes. The number and amplitude of the yaw oscillations is readily observed in the yaw string.

The number of yaw oscillations provides a measure of the damping. For example, spiral dive tendencies (if present) can be characterized by the number of oscillations required to reach a 30°bank angle. Yaw oscillations of increasing amplitude indicate directional instability. Rudder control reversal may also occur in the pro-turn direction, whereby a rudder that has traveled hard over to its stop should not be confused with a rudder that sticks due to control system friction. Here, rudder system friction should be evaluated on the ground.

10. **Dive Brakes** With the dive brakes closed, the aircraft is trimmed to level flight at Vgl and camber-changing flaps (if any) in a neutral setting. The rate of descent as indicated by the variometer is noted. The stick is held fixed and the brakes are fully extended, gradually so as not to induce any airspeed/pitch oscillations. The resulting airspeed will differ from the brakes-closed Vgl by an amount that depends on the dive brake design. The difference ΔVgl between Vgl and the brakes-extended airspeed is recorded. Holding the dive brakes open, the airspeed is then returned to the brakes-closed Vgl and the rate of descent indicated by the variometer is noted.

11. **Landing Gear** Retraction and extension forces are measured in N or estimated subjectively as *e.g.* "heavy", "light", etc. The item concerning the suspension refers only to the main landing gear.

12. **Landing** Here it should be noted whether a tail-first landing was possible, how effective the wheel brake is, and a general impression regarding the landing gear stiffness. Unusual characteristics such as tendencies to float in ground effect or drop a wing during the rollout should be recorded.

13. **Thermaling** Thermals flown in during this test should be characterized in terms of diameter and degree of turbulence. Thermal diameter may be described as "narrow", "medium", "wide", and, possibly, "non-circular". Turbulence is described using terms such as "severe", "moderate", "bumpy" and "smooth".

The relative change (in %) in the elevator, rudder, and aileron positions relative to straight and level flight at "Vgl" is recorded. If these values vary during the turn, the variation should be entered as $\pm$%. For this exercise the elevator position is positive aft and the aileron and rudder positions are positive in the pro-turn direction. The ease of trim in turns of up to 45°bank is judged subjectively. If the trim authority is insufficient, the residual longitudinal stick force is measured or estimated. The test concludes with an evaluation of minimum airspeed flight $V_A$min in 30°and 45°turns. $V_A$min observed in these turns is likely to vary from those determined in Item 4 above. The aircraft's behavior during the stall or incipient stall should be noted in the same manner as was done in Item 4. Forgiving stall characteristics with a controllable post-stall "mush" are of particular interest.

The reverse side of the flight test form contains additional space for more detailed descriptions of flight characteristics, cockpit and control layout, general remarks, etc.

See also list of abbreviations, page 252.

Sample Flight Test Reports

This section presents a few representative results from handling qualities flight tests. See also the list of abbreviations on page 252 and the glossary on page 263. Additional reports may be found in [213, 226, 229].

	Flugzeug *Aircraft*	ASW-15 D-0971	Std.-Cirrus D-0883	H-401 D-0832	Nimbus II D-0699
	Anzahl der Programme *number of reports*	14	9	6	6
1.	**Führerraum** *Cockpit*				
	Ein- und Ausstieg *ingress/egress*	gut	gut	gut, aber Beine einfädeln *good, but difficult to get legs in*	gut
	Notausstieg *emergency egress*	gut	gut, aber 2 Verschlüße *good, but 2 latches*	befriedigend, umständlich *satisfactory; awkward*	gut
	Sitz *seat*	gut – befriedigend	gut	gut	gut, aber keine Nackenstütze *good, but no headrest*
	Sicht *visibility*	gut, im F-Schlepp befriedigend *good, satisfactory in aero-tow*	gut	gut	
	Lüftung *ventilation*	gut, aber laut *good, but loud*	gut	befriedigend	gut, aber laut
	Steuerung *controls*	Handsteuer zu weit vorn, sonst gut *stick too far forward, otherwise good*	gut	gut	gut
	Bremsklappenhebel *dive brake handle*	gut, aber dicht an der Bordwand *good, but close to side of cockpit*	gut, Verknieung zu hart *good, excessive locking force*	gut, Verknieung zu groß	gut, aber Verknieung zu stark
	Wölbklappenhebel *flap handle*	-	-	gut	gut, links oben *good, upper left side*
	Trimmhebel *trim control*	gut-befriedigend	gut	gut + befriedigend	befriedigend, große Trimmkräfte *satisfactory, large trim forces*

Flugzeug *Aircraft*	ASW-15 D-0971	Std.-Cirrus D-0883	H-401 D-0832	Nimbus II D-0699
Fahrwerkshebel *landing gear lever*	gut	gut,liegt rechts *good, on right side*	befriedigend	rechts, Verriegelung befriedigend *right side, lock satisfactory*
Ausklinkvorrichtung *release*	gut, aber zwischen den Beinen *good, but between the legs*	befriedigend, Oberschenkel stört *satisfactory, interferes with upper thigh*	gut, aber zwischen den Beinen *good, but between the legs*	Hebel zwischen den Beinen, befriedigend *lever between legs, satisfactory*
Instrumentenanordnung *instrument panel*	übersichtlich *well laid out*	übersichtlich	übersichtlich	übersichtlich
2. Start und F-Schleppflug *takeoff and aero-tow*	bricht im Start nach rechts aus, Schwerpunktkupplung links *veers right on rollout; CG hook on left*	problemlos, Schwerpunktkupplung *no problems, CG hook*	problemlos, Bugkupplung *no problems, nose hook*	angenehm, Schwerpunktkupplung *pleasant, CG hook*
3. Trimmbereich, $V_A min/V_A max$ [km/h] *trimmable airspeed range*	70/130	< 60/ > 150	75/230	< 60/ > 150
4. Langsamflug u. Abkippverhalten *slow flight and stall*				
η_K = [°]* *flap setting*	-	-	+2°	+6°
geradeaus *straight ahead:*	66/63 ($V_A$über/$V_A$min [km/h]) Schtt→Sfl→Tau *buffeting, mushing, pitch and roll oscillations*	62/59 Schtt, Tau→liFl *buffeting, oscillations, falls off to the left*	66/63 Schtt→Sfl, Kpf *buffeting, mushing, nose drops*	59/56 Wch, Schtt→reFl *softness in controls, buffeting, falls off on right wing*
10°schiebend: *10° slip*	67/65 Schtt→Sfl→Tau	62/57 Schtt→nFl	67/64 Schtt→nFl	60/57 Wch, Schtt→nFl
30°schiebend:	71/67 Schtt→Sfl→Tau	68/65 Schtt→iFl	70/67 Schtt→iFl	64/62 Wch→iFl
BK+FW geradeaus:	71/69 Wch,Schtt→Sfl	66/62 Schtt,Tau→iFl	70/66 Schtt→Sfl,Kpf	62/60[1] Wch,Schtt→reFl

	Flugzeug *Aircraft*	ASW-15 D-0971	Std.-Cirrus D-0883	H-401 D-0832	Nimbus II D-0699
5.	**Freier Geradeausflug**** *forward flight*				
	Ausgetrimmt auf V_{TR} [km/h] *trimmed to ...*	87 (84↔91)	83 (76↔85)	93 (91↔98)	84 (83↔85)
	Festgestellte Unregelmäßigkeiten *unusual characteristics*	keine *none*	keine	keine	keine
	Reibungsdifferenz-geschwindigkeit ΔV_A [km/h] *trim hysteresis*	±9(±4 ↔ ±2)	±5(±0 ↔ ±9)	±5(±3 ↔ ±10)	±7(±5 ↔ ±12)
6.	**Ruderwirkungen** *control effectiveness*				
(a)	Querrudergiermoment *adverse yaw*				
	nur mit 100% QSt auf $\varphi = 30°$ $\Delta\psi[°]$ *100% aileron to* $\varphi = 30°$	15/1.8(10 ↔ 20/1 ↔ 2.8)	15/1.9(5 ↔ 30/1.5 ↔ 5)	12/2.2(10 ↔ 20/1.6 ↔ 4)	13/2.4(5 ↔ 20/1.6 ↔ 3.5)
(b)	Schiebe-Rollmoment *roll/yaw coupling*				
	nur mit 100% SSt aus $\varphi = 30°$ Sek. (s) *100% rudder out of* $\varphi = 30°$	3.5(2 ↔ 5)	3.1(1.5 ↔ 4)	4.2(3.5 ↔ 5)	4(3.3 ↔ 5)
(c)	45°-Kurvenwechsel *45° turn reversal*				
	100% SSt u. 100% QSt li→re/re→li [s] *full rudder and aileron*	3.6/3.6(3 ↔ 4.5/3 ↔ 4.5)	3.8/3.9(3.3 ↔ 4.2/3.4 ↔ 4.3)	4.0/4.0(2.5 ↔ 4.5/2.5 ↔ 4.5)	4.9/4.9(4.4 ↔ 5.2/4.1 ↔ 5.5)
	ohne Schieben *yaw string in middle*	4.5/4.5(3 ↔ 6.5/3.2 ↔ 6.5)	4.5/4.5(3.9 ↔ 5.2/3.9 ↔ 5.2)	4.5/4.5(3.5 ↔ 6.0/3.5 ↔ 6.0)	5.6/5.6(5.1 ↔ 6.5/5.1 ↔ 6.5)
(d)	Slip $\psi[°]/\varphi[°]/$ SSt[%]/QSt[%]/HSt[%]	26/12/100/25/+30	30/15/100/35/+35	30/18/100/50/+50	- [2]

	Flugzeug *Aircraft*	ASW-15 D-0971	Std.-Cirrus D-0883	H-401 D-0832	Nimbus II D-0699
7.	**Steuerabstimmung** *control harmony*				
	Rollen ±30° SSt[%]/QSt[%]/QSt-Kraft[daN] *±30° roll reversals*	100/70 / 1↔3.5	100/95 / angenehm *pleasant*	100/100/1.5↔3.6 angenehm	100/100 angenehm
8.	**Längsstabilität** *longitudinal stability*				
(a)	statische Längsstabilität *static*				
(b)	dynamische Stabilität *dynamic*	HSt klappt um (instabil) *elevator runs hard over (unstable)*	HSt klappt um (instabil)	gering stabil *marginally stable*	instabil, aufbäumen *unstable, pitches up*
	Schwingungsdauer [s] *period of phugoid*	16 (12↔20)	15 (13↔16)	21 (18↔24)	20
9.	Richtungsstabilität *directional stability*				
	Anfangsschiebewinkel u. Querneigung $\Delta\psi/\Delta\varphi$ [°] *initial slip angle and bank angle*	22/12 (15↔30 / 10↔20)	17/15 (5↔25 / 5↔30)	25/17 (10↔50 / 5↔25)	7.5/13 (5↔10 / 10↔15)
	Dämpfung um Hochachse *yaw damping*	aperiodisch *aperiodic; overdamped*	aperiodisch	aperiodisch	3/4 Schwingung *overdamped, oscillates 3/4 period*
	Spiralsturzneigung *spiral dive tendency*	geringe *light*	geringe	geringe	deutliche *pronounced*
10.	**Bremsklappenwirkung** *dive brake effectiveness* ΔV_S [m/s]	4(3↔5.2)	3.4(2↔4.0)	2.8(2↔>4)	2.8(2↔3.5)
	Handkräfte, aus/ein [daN] *actuation force, out/in*	angenehm/angenehm (2.5/2)	angenehm/angenehm, Verknieung hart	angenehm/angenehm (4/4)	Verknieung zu stark, sonst angenehm *lock too stiff, otherwise pleasant*
	Geschwindigkeitsänderung *change in airspeed* ΔV_A [km/h]	-7(5↔-20)	+4(0↔+10)	+2(-18↔+15)	+12(+5↔+20)

Flugzeug *Aircraft*	ASW-15 D-0971	Std.-Cirrus D-0883	H-401 D-0832	Nimbus II D-0699
11. Fahrwerk *landing gear*				
Handkräfte, ein/aus *actuation force, in/out* [daN]	angenehm/angenehm	angenehm/angenehm	5/7(3↔6/2↔15) angenehm	groß/angenehm
Federung *suspension*	Schlecht *poor*	ausreichend *adequate*	befriedigend *satisfactory*	schlecht
12. Landung *landing*				
Spornlandung/Bremswirkung *tail-first landing/wheel brake effectiveness*	ja/schlecht	ja/befriedigend	ja/gut	ja/gut
13. Thermikflugeigenschaften *thermaling characteristics*				
η_K [°]*** *flap setting*	-	-	+2°	+6°
φ[°]/V_A-Kreis$\pm\Delta V$ [km/h] *bank angle and airspeed*	43/80 ± 5	43/80 ± 7	40/83 ± 4	40/76 ± 5
HSt[%]/SSt[%]/QSt[%]/-HSt-Kraft [daN] *control positions and long. stick force*	+50/+10/-10/angenehm 1↔2	+12/+6/-12/ angenehm	+6/+5/-15 angenehm 0.5↔3	+8/+5/-30/0.5↔1.2 angenehm
$V_A$min-Kreis für φ = 45°/30° [km/h] *min airspeed in 45°/30° turn*	75/69 (70↔80 / 60↔75)	75/68 (69↔80 / 65↔70)	75/73 (70↔90 / 68↔85)	73/67 (70↔75 / 65↔70)

Notes:

* Bei Wölbklappenflugzeugen wurde die Thermikflugklappenstellung berücksichtigt
camber-changing flaps, if any, in thermal setting

** Die Punkte 5–10 wurden bei Wölbklappenflugzeugen mit der Wölbklappenstellung η_K = 0° erflogen
items 5–10 flown with flaps in neutral setting

*** Gibt die Wölbklappenstellung an, mit der in der Thermik geflogen wurde
flap setting used for thermaling

[1] η_K =WK-St L
flaps in landing setting

[2] Flugbeschränkung nach Reparatur
flight limitation following repair

Nomenclature

Abbreviations

Akaflieg Akademische Fliegergruppe, academically oriented student organization dedicated to the design, construction, and flying of aircraft, especially sailplanes.

DLR Deutsches Zentrum für Luft- und Raumfahrt, German Aerospace Center.

DFVLR Deutsche Forschungs- und Versuchsanstalt für Luft- und Raumfahrt, German Aerospace Research and Test Establishment, since 1989 the DLR.

FAI Fédération Aéronautique Internationale, international air sports federation.

ICAO International Civil Aviation Organization

IGC International Gliding Commission of the FAI (also: CIVV, Commission Internationale de Vol à Voile).

Idaflieg Interessengemeinschaft deutscher akademischer Fliegergruppen, umbrella organization for the German Akafliegs.

JAR Joint Airworthiness Requirements (also: Joint Aviation Requirements)

LBA Luftfahrt-Bundesamt, German federal regulatory agency for aviation matters.

LFSM Lufttüchtigkeitsforderungen für Segelflugzeuge und Motorsegler, German airworthiness requirements for sailplanes and motorgliders, now superceded by JAR-22.

NACA, NASA National Advisory Committee on Aeronautics, and its successor, the National Air and Space Administration.

OSTIV Organisation Scientifique et Technique du Vol à Voile, society for the advancement of scientific and technical aspects of soaring, affiliated with the FAI.

TAS, EAS, CAS, IAS True, equivalent,calibrated, indicated airspeed.

Symbols

A Separation point (Fig. 24)
Ablösepunkt

$\mathcal{R}$ Wing aspect ratio (Eq. 23 and Fig. 96)
Flügelstreckung, Λ

$\mathcal{R}_H$ Horizontal stabilizer aspect ratio
Höhenleitwerksstreckung, Λ_H

$\mathcal{R}_V$ Vertical stabilizer aspect ratio
Seitenleitwerksstreckung, Λ_{SL}

C_{D_0} Drag coefficient at zero lift (Fig. 61)
Widerstandsbeiwert bei Nullauftrieb, C_{W_P}

C_D Drag coefficient
Widerstandsbeiwert, c_W

C_{D_i} Coefficient of induced drag (Eq. 46)
Beiwert des induzierten Widerstands, c_{W_i}

C_{D_p} Parasite drag coefficient
Beiwert des schädlichen Widerstands, c_{W_S}

CF Centrifugal force
Zentrifugalkraft, Z

CG Center of gravity
Schwerpunkt

C_L, C_D, C_M Global coefficients (Eqs. 31-33)
Gesamtbeiwerte, c_A, c_W, c_M

C_L Coefficient of lift
Auftriebsbeiwert, c_A

C_{L_H} Horizontal stabilizer lift coefficient (Fig. 163)
Höhenleitwerksauftriebsbeiwert, C_{AH}

C_{L_V} Lift coefficient of vertical stabilizer
Seitenleitwerksauftriebsbeiwert, $c_{A_{SL}}$

C_{L_W} Coefficient of wing lift (Fig. 163)
Flügelauftriebsbeiwert, C_{AF}

$C_{L_{max}}$ Maximum lift coefficient (global)
Maximaler Auftriebsbeiwert

$C_{L_{min}}$ Minimum lift coefficient (global)
Minimaler Auftriebsbeiwert

C_M, c_m Pitching moment coefficient about c/4 point
Momentenbeiwert bezogen auf den c/4 Punkt, c_M, c_m

C_{M_0}, c_{m_0} Zero lift pitching moment coefficient (Fig. 38)
Nullmomentenbeiwert, c_{M_0}, c_{m_0}

$C_{M_{0W}}$ Zero lift moment coefficient (wing) (Fig. 163)
Flügelnullmomentenbeiwert, C_{M0F}

$C_{M_{AC}}$ Pitching moment about aerodynamic center of three-dimensional wing

C_{M_H} Pitching moment contribution of horizontal stabilizer
Höhenleitwerksmomentenbeiwert, C_{MH}

C_{M_W} Pitching moment contribution of wing
Flügelmomentenbeiwert, C_{MF}

$C_{M_{CG}}$ Pitching moment coefficient about center of gravity (Fig. 163).
Momentenbeiwert bezogen auf den Schwerpunkt, C_{M_S}

$D_p^{\star}$ Equivalent parasite drag area (Eq. 95)
schädliche Widerstandsfläche, $W_s^{\star}$

D_p Parasite Drag (Eq. 93)
Schädlicher Widerstand, W_s

F Resultant force normal to airflow (Fig. 20).
Querkraft, Q

L Lift (Eq. 51, Figs. 20, 36)
Auftrieb, A

L_H Horizontal stabilizer lift (Fig. 161)
Höhenleitwerksauftrieb, A_H

L_W Wing lift (Fig. 161)
Flügelauftrieb, A_F

M_{0_H} Zero lift moment of horizontal stabilizer (Fig. 161)
Nullmoment des Höhenleitwerks, M_{0H}

M_{0_W} Zero lift moment of wing (Fig. 161)
Nullmoment des Flügels, M_{0F}

M_{CG} Pitching moment about center of gravity (Fig. 161)
Nickmoment um den Schwerpunkt, M_S

P_H Longitudinal stick force
Steuerknüppelkraft

Re Reynolds number (Eq. 6).
Reynoldszahl

S Wing area; reference area
Flügelfläche, Bezugsfläche, F

S_E Wing area with area changing flaps or telescoping wing extended
Flügelfläche im ausgefahrenen Zustand, F_L

S_H Longitudinal stick position
Steuerknüppelweg

S_H Horizontal stabilizer area
Höhenleitwerksfläche, F_H

S_R Wing area with area changing flap or telescoping wing retracted
Flügelfläche im eingefahrenen Zustand, F_S

S_V Vertical stabilizer area
Seitenleitwerksfläche, S_{SL}

T Temperature
Temperatur

V Velocity vector
Geschwindigkeitsvektor

V_ASfl Airspeed (IAS) in "mushing" flight
Angezeigte Geschwindigkeit im Sackflug

V_Amax Maximum airspeed (IAS)

V_Amin Minimum airspeed (IAS)

V_D Design maximum speed, JAR-22 [49]
Maximale Geschwindigkeit

V_{DF} Maximum airspeed demonstrated in flight test (JAR 22 [49])
Höchstgeschwindigkeit im Flugversuch

V_H Horizontal stabilizer volume (Eq. 100)
Höhenleitwerksvolumen

V_T Thermal strength (rate of climb of thermal - Fig. 88)
Aufwindgeschwindigkeit, w_A

$V_{TAS}, V_{EAS}, V_{CAS}, V_{IAS}$ True, equivalent, calibrated, indicated airspeed.

V_V Vertical stabilizer volume (Eq. 112)
Seitenleitwerksvolumen, V_{SL}

V_W Wing reference volume (Eqn. 101)
Flügelbezugsvolumen, V_F

V_K Airspeed in turn (Eq. 77)
Fluggeschwindigkeit im Kreisflug

V_c Achieved rate of climb (Figs. 82,88)
Steiggeschwindigkeit, w_{St}

V_g Airspeed in interthermal glide (Fig. 82)
Gleitfluggeschwindigkeit, V_G

$(V_H/V_W)^\star$ Reduced horizontal stabilizer volume (Equation 107)
reduziertes Höhenleitwerksvolumen, $(V_H/V_F)^\star$

V_∞ Freestream velocity
Geschwindigkeit weit entfernt vom Körper

V_{NE} Never exceed (red line) speed, IAS (JAR 22 [49])
Höchstgeschwindigkeit

V_{RA} Rough air speed (JAR 22 [49])

V_{avg} Average cross-country ground speed (Eq. 68).
mittlere Überlandfluggeschwindigkeit, V_R

V_{s_0} Stall speed or minimum controllable airspeed in landing configuration (landing gear, flaps, and dive brakes extended) and maximum gross weight
Überziehgeschwindigkeit im Landezustand

V_s Stall onset speed
Geschwindigkeit mit erster Überziehwarnung, $V_{über}$

V_s Sink rate (Eq. 60, Fig. 82)
Sinkgeschwindigkeit, w_S

V_{s_c} Rate of descent in turn (Eq. 78, Fig. 88).
Sinkgeschwindigkeit im Kreisflug, w_{SK}

W Gross weight (Fig. 161)
Gewicht, G

x_{AC} location of aerodynamic center (three-dimensional wing - Fig. 161)
geometrische Neutralpunktlage, x_{N25}

a Acceleration vector
Beschleunigungsvektor

a Speed of sound
Schallgeschwindigkeit

$\mathbf{a}_{cent}$ Centripetal acceleration

b Wing span
Spannweite

b_H Horizontal stabilizer span
Spannweite des Höhenleitwerks

b_V Height of vertical stabilizer
Seitenleitwerkshöhe, b_{SL}

c Wing chord (Fig. 32)
Profiltiefe, l

c_{d_0} Minimum profile drag coefficient (Fig. 37)
Profilwiderstandsbeiwert bei Nullauftrieb, $c_{w_{p_0}}$

c_d Profile drag coefficient (Fig. 37)
Profilwiderstandsbeiwert, c_{w_p}

c_f local coefficient of friction (see also [22])
örtlicher Reibungsbeiwert

c_k Chord at taper change point (Fig. 34)
Profiltiefe an der Knickstelle, l_K

c_l, c_d, c_m Local (sectional) coefficients (Eqs. 28,29,30)
örtliche Beiwerte, Profilbeiwerte, c_a, c_w, c_m

c_l Local (sectional) lift coefficient
örtliche- bzw. Profilauftriebsbeiwert, c_a

$c_{l_{max}}$ Maximum sectional lift coefficient
Maximaler Profilauftreibsbeiwert

c_μ Mean aerodynamic chord (m.a.c.) (Eq. 41, Fig. 42)
Bezugsflügeltiefe, l_μ

$c_{m_{ac}}$ Pitching moment about aerodynamic center

c_{avg} Average wing chord (Eq. 42)
mittlere Profiltiefe, l_m

c_r root chord (Fig. 34)
Wurzeltiefe, l_W

c_t Tip chord (Fig. 34)
Profiltiefe außen, l_a

e Oswald efficiency factor (Eq. 48)
Faktor des induzierten Widerstands

h Altitude, Table 1
Höhe, H

h_d Density altitude
Dichtehöhe

h_p Pressure altitude
Druckhöhe

k Span efficiency factor (Eq. 47)
Faktor des induzierten Widerstands

k	surface roughness (Eqs. 21, 22; Fig. 29) *Rauhigkeit*
k_{crit}	Critical surface roughness (Eq. 21) *kritische Rauhigkeit,* k_{krit}
k_{perm}	Permissible surface roughness (Eq. 22) *zulässige Rauhigkeit,* k_{zul}
l_H	Horizontal stabilizer moment arm (Fig. 161) *Höhenleitwerkshebelarm,* r_H
l_V	Vertical stabilizer moment arm *Seitenleitwerkshebelarm,* r_{SL}
m.a.c.	Mean aerodynamic chord (c_μ) (Eq. 41, Fig. 42) *Bezugsflügeltiefe,* l_μ
p	pressure; static pressure *Druck; statischer Druck*
p_T	Total pressure *Gesamtdruck,* p_g
p_0, ρ_0, T_0	Sea level standard conditions *Druck, Luftdichte, Temperatur bei Meereshöhe*
q	Dynamic pressure *Staudruck*
q_H	Dynamic pressure at empennage *Staudruck am Höhenleitwerk*
q_∞	Free stream dynamic pressure (Eq. 10) *Staudruck weit entfernt vom Flügel*
s	Wing semi-span (Fig. 34) *Halbspannweite*
t	Airfoil thickness (Fig. 32) *Profildicke,* d
t_c	Time spent in climb *Steigzeit,* t_{St}
t_g	Time spent in glide *Gleitzeit,* t_G
w_i	Induced downwash velocity (Fig. 19) *Induzierte Abwindgeschwindigkeit,* W_i
x	Distance aft of wing trailing edge (Fig. 161) *Koordinate von der Hinterkante aus,* x_{HK}
x_{cp}	location of airfoil center of pressure (Fig. 41) *Druckpunktlage,* x_D
x_N	Neutral point *Neutralpunktlage*
x_{ac}	location of aerodynamic center *Neutralpunktlage (eines Profils),* x_N
x_{CG}	CG location (Figs. 78, 161) *Schwerpunktlage,* x_S
$x_{N_{25}}$	Neutral point (Figs. 42 and 161) *geometrische Neutralpunktlage*
y_k	Taper change point (Fig. 34) *Lage der Knickstelle des Flügels,* y_K
z_u, z_l	Profile coordinates for upper and lower surfaces (Fig. 31) *Koordinaten der Profiloberseite bzw. -unterseite ,* z_o, z_u
z_w	Distance of wing's vortex sheet from fuselage reference axis (Fig. 161) *Abstand der Wirbelschicht von der Flugzeugbezugsachse,* z_W
ΔV_C	Compressibility correction
α_0	Zero lift angle of attack (Figs. 37, 38) *Nullanstellwinkel*
α_{0_H}	Horizontal stabilizer zero lift angle of attack *Nullanstellwinkel des Höhenleitwerks*
α_{0_W}	Zero lift angle of wing *Nullanstellwinkel des Flügels*
α	Angle of attack (Fig. 32) *Anstellwinkel*
α_H	Angle of attack of horizontal stabilizer (Fig. 162) *Anstellwinkel des Höhenleitwerks*
α_e	Effective angle of attack (Eq. 20; Fig. 20) *effektiver Anstellwinkel*
α_g	Geometric angle of attack (Fig. 20) *geometrischer Anstellwinkel*
α_i	Induced angle of attack (Eq. 45; Fig. 20) *Induzierter Anstellwinkel*
α_w	Induced angle of attack at empennage (Fig. 162) *Abwindwinkel*
β	Slip angle (Fig. 66). Positive when yaw string deflects to left *Schiebewinkel*
γ	glide angle (Figs. 66, 82) *Gleitwinkel*
γ	nondimensional circulation ($=\Gamma/bV$) *dimensionslose Zirkulation*
γ	specific heat ratio
ε_H	Stabilizer incidence angle (Fig. 162) *Einstellwinkel des Höhenleitwerks*
φ	Sweep angle (Fig. 34) *Pfeilwinkel*
φ_{LE}	leading edge sweep angle *Pfeilwinkel der Vorderkante,* φ_{VK}
$\varphi_{.25}$	wing quarter-chord sweep angle *Pfeilwinkel der l/4-Linie*
ϕ	Bank angle (Fig. 68). *Querneigungswinkel,* φ
η_A	Aileron deflection *Querruderausschlag,* η_Q
η_F	Flap position *Klappenausschlag,* η_K
δ_e	Elevator deflection (Fig. 66) *Höhenruderausschlag,* η_H
λ	Taper ratio (Eq. 24) *Zuspitzung*
λ_H	Horizontal stabilizer taper ratio
ρ	Air density *Luftdichte*

German-English Glossary

See also the list of abbreviations used in the flight test form (page 252)

CG, center of gravity	*Schwerpunkt*
Dutch roll	*Taumelschwingung*
adverse yaw	*Querruder-Giermoment*
aerobatics	*Kunstflug*
aileron	*Querruder*
airfoil; profile	*Profil*
airspeed indicator	*Fahrtmesser*
airworthiness	*Lufttüchtigkeit*
all-flying tail, all-flying stabilizer	*Pendelruder*
altimeter	*Höhenmesser*
angle of attack	*Anstellwinkel*
area	*Fläche*
area changing flaps	*Flächenklappen*

aspect ratio	*Streckung, Flügelstreckung*
bank angle	*Querneigung*
boundary layer	*Grenzschicht*
camber-changing flap	*Wölbklappe*
canopy, split canopy	*Haube; geteilte Haube*
chord	*Profilsehne, Profiltiefe*
control effectiveness	*Ruderwirksamkeit*
control reversal	*Ruderumkehr*
control surface	*Ruder*
conventional stabilizer/elevator combination	*Gedämpftes Leitwerk ("damped stabilizer")*
cross country flight	*Überlandflug, Streckenflug*
deflection (of a control surface)	*Ausschlag*
density	*Dichte*
dihedral	*V-Stellung*
directional stability	*Richtungsstabilität*
dive brakes	*Bremsklappen; Landeklappen*
drag	*Widerstand*
elevator	*Höhenruder*
elevon	*Flügelklappe, zugleich Querruder und Höhenruder*
empennage	*Leitwerk*
fin; stabilizer	*Flosse, Seitenflosse*
flap	*Klappe*
flaperons	*Flügelklappen, zugleich Querruder und Wölbklappe*
flutter	*Flattern*
flying wing	*Nurflügel*
fuselage	*Rumpf*
glide angle	*Gleitwinkel*
glide ratio	*Gleitzahl*
gust	*Bö*
horizontal stabilizer, horizontal tail	*Höhenleitwerk*
laminar bubble	*Laminarblase*
laminar bucket	*Laminardelle*
landing chute	*Bremsschirm*
landing gear	*Fahrwerk*
lateral (pitch) axis	*Querachse*
leading edge	*Vorderkante*
lift	*Auftrieb; auch: Aufwind, Thermikstärke*
load factor	*Z-Beschleunigung, Lastfaktor*
longitudinal (roll) axis	*Längsachse*
mass balance	*Massenausgleich*
mean aerodynamic chord (m.a.c)	*Mittlere aerodynamische Tiefe*
phugoid	*Phygoide*
pitch; pitching	*Nicken*
pressure	*Druck*
roll; rolling	*Rollen*
root	*Wurzel*
rudder	*Seitenruder*
section	*Profil*
separation	*Strömungsabriß*
servo tab	*Flettner-Klappe*
post-stall settling, "mushing"	*Sackflug*
short-period mode	*schnelle Anstellwinkelschwingung*
slotted flap	*Spaltklappe; Fowlerklappe*
span	*Spannweite*
spoilers	*Bremsklappen, meistens nur auf der Flügeloberfläche*
stall	*Überziehen; Strömungsabriß*
static margin, stability margin	*Stabilitätsmaß*
sweep	*Pfeilung*
taper change point	*Knickstelle der Zuspitzung*
taper	*Zuspitzung, Trapezverhältnis*
tip	*Spitze*
trailing edge	*Hinterkante*
trim	*Trimmung*
trim drag	*Trimwiderstand*
twist	*Verwindung*
velocity	*Geschwindigkeit*
vertical (yaw) axis)	*Gierachse*
vertical stabilizer	*Seitenflosse*
winch	*Winde*
wing(s)	*Flügel, Tragflügel*
yaw; yawing	*Gieren*
zig-zag tape; bump (or dimple) tape	*Zackenbänder; Noppenbänder*

Units of Measure

Length

1 meter [m] = 3.281 feet [ft]
1 kilometer [km] = 3281 ft
= 0.6214 statute miles [sm]
= 0.5400 nautical miles [nm]
1 sm = 5280 ft
1 nm = 6076 ft

m	km	ft	sm	nm	Comment
15		49.2			Standard, 15m Class
18		59.1			18m Class
20		65.6			20m Multiplace Class
30.84		101.2			"eta" wingspan
	50		31.1	27.0	Silver distance
	300		186.4	162.0	Gold distance, Diamond goal
	500		310.7	270.0	Diamond distance

Velocity

1 meter/second [m/s] = 3.6 km/h
= 3.281 feet/sec [ft/s,fps]
= 1.943 nautical miles/hour, knot [kt]
= 196.9 feet/minute [fpm]
= 2.237 statute miles/hour [mph]
1 kt = 76/66 mph
1 kilometer/hour [km/h] = .9113 ft/s
= .6214 mph
= .5396 kt

m/s	km/h	ft/s	fpm	mph	kt	Comment
1.0	3.6	3.3	197		1.9	JAR 22.71(a)
1.2	4.3	3.9	236		2.3	JAR 22.71(b)
4.2	15	13.7		9.3	8.1	Crosswind component, JAR 22.152(b)
7.5	27	24.6	1477		14.6	V_D gust, JAR 22.333
15	54	49.2	2953		29.1	V_B gust, JAR 22.333
55.6	200	182		124	108	Minimum V_D for aerobatic category (JAR 22.335(f))
340.3	1225	1116		762	662	speed of sound, sea level, std. atmosphere

Force, weight

1 deca-newton [daN] = 1.02 kilopond [kp]
= 2.25 slug ft/s^2 (pound) [lb]
1 kp = weight of 1 kg mass at earth's surface.
= 2.205 lb

The following values are based on sea level g = 9.81 m/s^2:

mass [kg]	weight [daN]	weight [lb]	Comment
1	.981	2.25	
55	54.0	124	JAR 22.25
70	68.6	158	JAR 22.23
90	88.3	182	
110	107	248	JAR 22.23,25
180	177	405	JAR 22.25
200	196	450	
500	490	1125	
750	736	1688	JAR 22.1
850	834	1913	JAR 22.1

Mass, density

1 kg = 0.06854 lb ft/s^2 [slug]
1 kg/m^3 = $1.941 \cdot 10^{-3}$ slug/ft^3

1 slug = mass of object weighing 32.17 lb at earth's surface.

The following values are based on sea level g = 9.81 m/s^2:

Density		Specific weight		
kg/m^3	slug/ft^3	daN/m^3	lb/ft^3	Comment
1.225	$2.378 \cdot 10^{-3}$			ρ_0 (sea level)
0.653	$1.267 \cdot 10^{-3}$			ρ 20 000 ft
1000	1.941	980.1	62.44	Water at 4°C
810	1.572	793.9	50.5	Methanol at 0°C

Pressure, wing loading

1 newton/m^2 = 1 Pascal [Pa]
1 bar = 10^5 Pa
1 millibar [mb] = 10^2 Pa
= 1 hectopascal [hPa]
1 atmosphere [atm] = 29.92 inches of mercury [in Hg]
= 760.0 millimeters of mercury [mm Hg]
= 1013 hPa
= 1013 mb
= 14.7 pounds/square inch [psi]
1 daN/m^2 = 10^{-1} hPa
= 1.02 kp/m^2
= 0.209 pound/square foot [lb/ft^2, psf]
= 0.00145 pound/square inch [lb/in^2, psi]

kp/m^2	daN/m^2	psf	hPa	Comment
3	2.9	.62		JAR 22.1
	20	4.18		
	30	6.27		
	40	8.36		
	50	10.5		
	4656	973.0	465.6	20 000 ft
	10 130	2117	1013	sea level

Viscosity

Dynamic viscosity, μ:
1 Pa s = .0209 lb-s/ft^2
= 10 Poise [P]
Kinematic viscosity, $\nu = \mu/\rho$:
1 m^2/s = 10.77 ft^2/s
= 10^4 Stokes [St]

Dynamic		Kinematic		
μ [Pa s]	μ [lb-s/ft^2]	ν [m^2/s]	ν [ft^2/s]	Comment
$1.79 \cdot 10^{-5}$	$3.74 \cdot 10^{-7}$	$1.46 \cdot 10^{-5}$	$1.57 \cdot 10^{-4}$	Sea level
$1.58 \cdot 10^{-5}$	$3.31 \cdot 10^{-7}$	$2.42 \cdot 10^{-5}$	$2.61 \cdot 10^{-4}$	20,000 ft

Reynolds Number = $\rho Vl/\mu = Vl/\nu$

Re ...

per m per m/s	per m per km/h	per ft per ft/s	per ft per kt	Comment
68500	19000	6370	10800	Sea level
41300	11500	3830	6470	20,000 ft

Index

Sailplane Index